MW00438808

From Second Bull Run to Gettysburg

From Second Bull Run to Gettysburg

The Civil War in the East, 1862–63

General Edward J. Stackpole

STACKPOLE BOOKS

Guilford, Connecticut

Published by Stackpole Books

An imprint of The Rowman & Littlefield Publishing Group, Inc.
4501 Forbes Boulevard, Suite 200, Lanham, Maryland 20706
www.rowman.com

Distributed by NATIONAL BOOK NETWORK

800-462-6420

Copyright © 2018 The Rowman & Littlefield Publishing Group, Inc.

All rights reserved. No part of this book may be reproduced in any form or by any electronic or mechanical means, including information storage and retrieval systems, without written permission from the publisher, except by a reviewer who may quote passages in a review.

British Library Cataloguing in Publication Information Available

Library of Congress Cataloging-in-Publication Data Available

ISBN 978-0-8117-3767-8 (paperback)
ISBN 978-0-8117-6787-3 (e-book)

∞™ The paper used in this publication meets the minimum requirements of American National Standard for Information Sciences—Permanence of Paper for Printed Library Materials, ANSI/NISO Z39.48-1992.

Printed in the United States of America

Contents

CHAPTER 1: Union Frustrations 1

CHAPTER 2: Pope versus Jackson. 16

CHAPTER 3: The Battle of Cedar Mountain 31

CHAPTER 4: Lee's Campaign against Pope 44

CHAPTER 5: Second Bull Run I: The Fight Near Groveton 83

CHAPTER 6: Second Bull Run II: The Main Battle Opens 94

CHAPTER 7: Second Bull Run III: The Climax 119

CHAPTER 8: The Battle of Chantilly 139

CHAPTER 9: Lee Invades Maryland 153

CHAPTER 10: The Battle of South Mountain 170

CHAPTER 11: The Harpers Ferry Diversion 188

CHAPTER 12: Antietam I: The Bloodiest Single Day 213

CHAPTER 13: Antietam II: Final Phase 234

CHAPTER 14: Lincoln Tries Another General 262

CHAPTER 15: The Strategy of the Fredericksburg
Campaign 273

CHAPTER 16: Interlude on the Rappahannock. 284

CHAPTER 17: The Curtain Rises at Fredericksburg 297

CHAPTER 18: Across the Rappahannock at Last. 317

CHAPTER 19: Fredericksburg I: Union Failure on the
Southern Flank 327

CHAPTER 20: Fredericksburg II: Slaughter at the Stone Wall . . . 337

CHAPTER 21: Burnside Is Relieved of Command 354

CHAPTER 22: Hooker Plans a Campaign 364

CHAPTER 23: The Strategy of the Chancellorsville
Campaign 369

CHAPTER 24: Chancellorsville I: Jackson's Flank Attack. 430

CHAPTER 25: Chancellorsville II: May 3. 472

CHAPTER 26: Chancellorsville III: Fredericksburg
and Salem Church. 489

CHAPTER 27: Lee Invades Pennsylvania 522

CHAPTER 28: Confederate Strategy in June 1863 545

CONTENTS

CHAPTER 29: Meade Takes Command 550
CHAPTER 30: Gettysburg I: July 1, 1863. 564
CHAPTER 31: Gettysburg II: July 2, 1863 591
CHAPTER 32: Gettysburg III: July 3, 1863. 612

Epilogue 631
Bibliography 637
Index 639

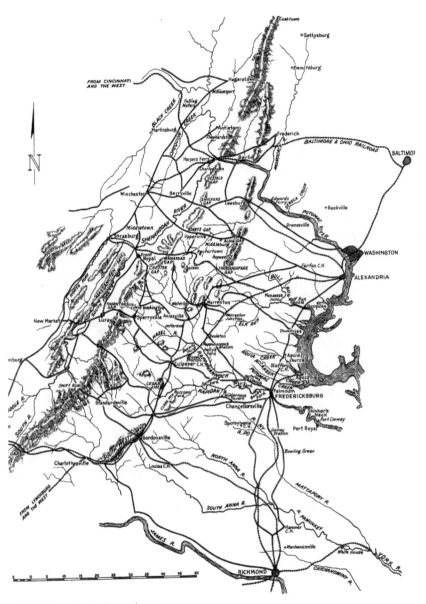

MAP 1 Theater of Operations

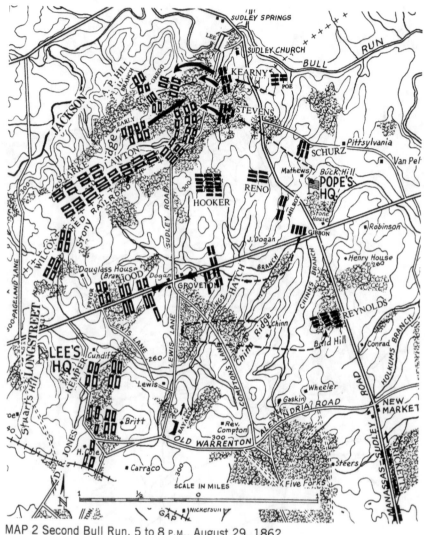

MAP 2 Second Bull Run, 5 to 8 P.M., August 29, 1862

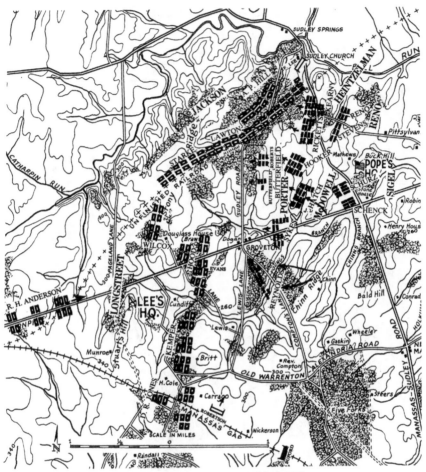

MAP 3 Second Bull Run, Noon to 2 P.M., August 30, 1862

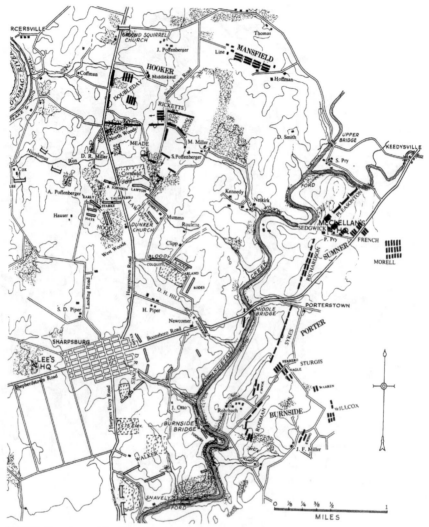

MAP 4 Opening of Antietam, September 17, 1862

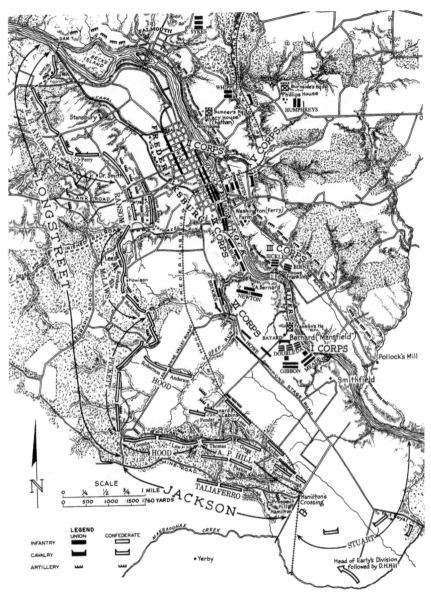

MAP 5 Fredericksburg, Dawn, December 13, 1862

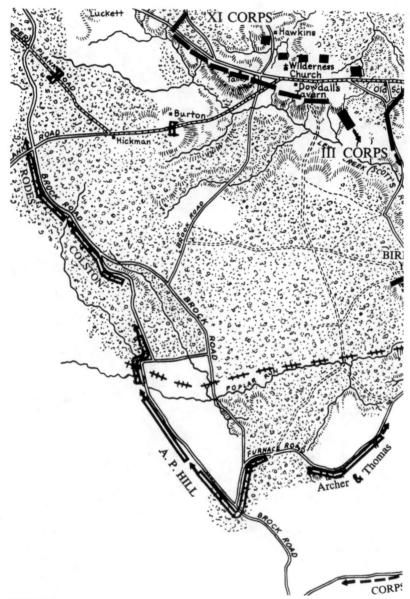

MAP 6 Chancellorsville, 1:30 to 2 P.M., May 2, 1863

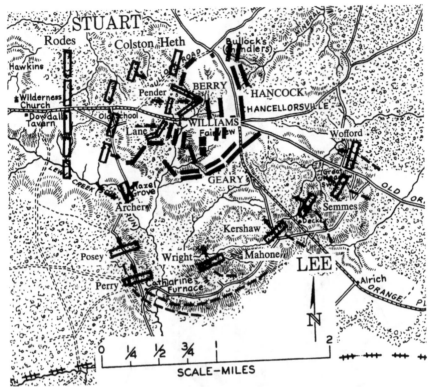

MAP 7 The Fight for Chancellorsville, May 3, 1863

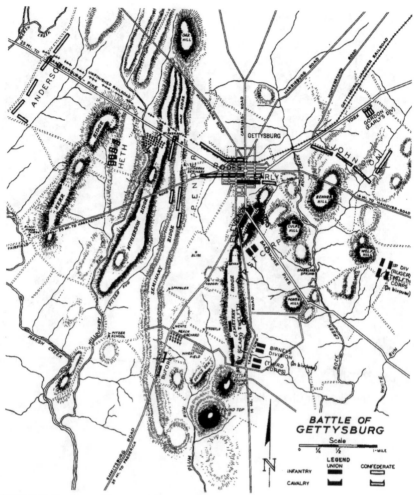

MAP 8 Gettysburg, 6 P.M., July 1, 1863

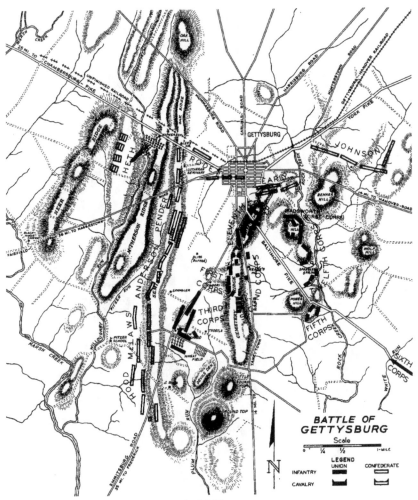

MAP 9 Gettysburg, 3:30 P.M., July 2, 1863

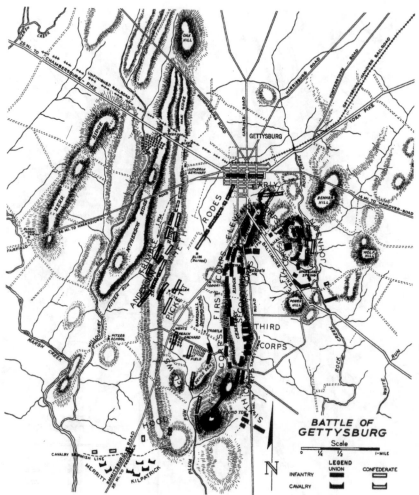

MAP 10 Gettysburg, 3 P.M., July 3, 1863

CHAPTER I

Union Frustrations

"IF GENERAL MCCLELLAN does not want to use the army for some days, I should like to borrow it and see if it cannot be made to do something."

President Abraham Lincoln, Commander-in-Chief of the Armed Forces of the United States, may have made the remark humorously in the latter days of 1861, but the grim implication of his words reflected the growing impatience of the country with the reluctance of the Army's General-in-Chief to make the slightest threatening gesture in the direction of the enemy.

Long on patience and conscious of his own lack of knowledge or experience in the military art, but sensitive to the political realities of the situation, Lincoln studied tactics and strategy diligently during the early winter of 1861-62 in a determined effort to educate himself, insofar as practicable, in the science of war. He pored over all the available books on strategy, conscientiously studied sheafs of reports from the military departments, and conferred for long hours with a variety of generals and admirals. Partly as a result of his rigorous course of self-indoctrination over a period of several months, the President came to the conclusion that McClellan would have to be catapulted into offensive measures by peremptory orders if the North was to get on with the war.

Having reached that decision, on January 27, 1862, Lincoln issued his first General War Order, which directed that all the land and naval forces of the United States engage in "a general movement against the insurgent forces" on February 22 (Washington's birthday). Specifically mentioned as participants in the planned general offensive were the Army of the Potomac, the Army at Fortress Monroe, the Army of Western Virginia, the Army in Kentucky, the Army and flotilla at Cairo, and the naval force in the Gulf of Mexico.

As if that were not sufficient to galvanize supreme Army commander McClellan and the War and Navy Departments into action, Lincoln followed up his initial blast, four days later, with Special War Order No. 1, this one directed specifically to the Army of the Potomac. The order instructed the Commanding General to launch the Army of the Potomac on an expedition "for the immediate object of seizing and occupying Manassas Junction," the movement to commence on or before the 22nd of February.

The President's refreshing initiative aroused new hope in the public mind and appeared to please everybody but Major General George B. McClellan, who took issue with the plan of moving overland through Virginia toward Richmond. He proposed instead a water movement to Urbanna on the Rappahannock by way of Chesapeake Bay and thence overland to the York River, to approach the Confederate Capital from the east. Declining to accept Lincoln's strategic judgment and insisting on his own conception in spite of the unequivocal order already issued, McClellan was finally given his way, doubtless because the President had concluded the general would exert more effort in a project of his own devising.

General Joseph A. Johnston, commanding the Confederate forces in Virginia, had kept the bulk of his troops massed in the vicinity of Manassas, twenty odd miles southwest of Washington, ever since the Union defeat at the first Battle of Bull Run in July 1861. The only other organized Confederate body in the State was Stonewall Jackson's small command in the Shenandoah Valley. McClellan's propensity for vastly overestimating the strength of his enemy was so habitual, however, that he would not accept the fact that he outnumbered the Confederates three to one in the Washington-Manassas area. Lincoln's order to move on Richmond by land through Virginia was militarily sound. Had McClellan obeyed the order it is almost a certainty that Johnston would have had no recourse but to withdraw in the face of the Union army's great preponderance of armed might.

Despite the pressure from Washington, McClellan continued to postpone the movement, while the discontent of the people in the North grew to such an extent as to endanger willing public support of the war effort. Lincoln was acutely aware of the danger, but felt himself to be on the horns of a dilemma which made him hesitate to formally remove McClellan from command lest such action made a bad situation worse. For it was a fact that his little general had performed something of a miracle in welding the raw Union levees into an effectively organized and well-disciplined army, most of whose officers and men believed in and gave to him their undivided loyalty and affection.

In his own good time, then, but not until Lincoln had found it necessary to promulgate two more general orders that put additional burrs under the McClellan saddle, the general condescended to leave the comfortable camps around Washington. The President, his patience exhausted, had found it advisable on March 8, 1862 to issue an order which reduced McClellan from General-in-Chief of the U. S. Army to Commanding General of the Department of the Potomac, a rebuff that reflected in no uncertain terms the waning confidence of the Administration in "Little Mac." A victory of sorts for the radical anti-McClellan element, the action was understandable from the viewpoint of the President. But the effect was militarily a step backward in that the several Union armies in the field would for the next four months be under the direct control of two civilians, the President and the Secretary of War, a condition that left much to be desired.

Finally, however, on March 17 McClellan embarked his army of over 100,000 men for the water trip to the Peninsula. Even then his egomania would not permit him to obey Lincoln's order to leave a more adequate force to protect Washington. As a result, the President took matters into his own hands and pulled one corps (McDowell's) out from under McClellan, holding it for the defense of Washington.

McClellan's preparations to move had taken so long and his counter-intelligence measures were so inadequate that Johnston's Confederate army at Centerville had ample warning of the impending Federal move. While Stonewall Jackson's small force in the Shenandoah Valley made threatening gestures toward Washington, Johnston's army side-slipped to the south to counter McClellan's advance. After a two-day march it took positions at Fredericksburg and Culpeper, putting the Confederates as close to Richmond as was Urbanna. This neat maneuver caused McClellan to revise his plan by changing his concentration point to Fort Monroe, seventy miles from Richmond.

McClellan Fails to Take Richmond

Disembarking his army at Fort Monroe, McClellan moved slowly and ponderously up the Peninsula toward Richmond. The Confederate forces under Johnston opposed him in a series of delaying actions, then withdrew into the outer defenses of Richmond, a series of earthworks. McClellan, adhering to his obsession that the Federals were greatly outnumbered, continued to importune Lincoln for reinforcements. However, the Confederate General Thomas J. (Stonewall) Jackson, with some 10,000 men in the Shenandoah Valley kept the three Union corps in that area at bay and even threatened Washington. Jackson's famous Valley campaign at this time established for all time his reputation as a Great Captain, secured the granary of the Confederacy, as the Shenandoah area was called, and prevented Washington from sending more troops to McClellan.

Meantime, in one of the engagements on the Peninsula, Joe Johnston was wounded and was superseded by General Robert E. Lee. Lee spent the month of May in reorganizing and refitting his army, which he now named the Army of Northern Virginia, and in preparing a counteroffensive against McClellan. This was planned as a battle of annihilation, and to make the blow more effective, Lee brought Jackson secretly from the Valley to strengthen the enveloping force on McClellan's right flank.

At last Lee's preparations were complete. He would attack Major General Fitz John Porter's isolated corps on the north bank of the Chickahominy to cut McClellan's supply line. But Jackson was late in coming up and the Confederates were repulsed at Mechanicsville on June 26, the first of the Seven Days Battles. On June 27, with reinforcements that gave them a two to one advantage over Porter, they tried again and this time were successful at Gaines' Mill, but night came before they could prevent the Federals from escaping across the river.

During the remainder of the campaign, Lee pressed the attack while McClellan was engaged in changing his supply base from White House to Harrison's Landing on the James River. A succession of rearguard actions by the Union forces, as the Union general retired in a southerly direction toward his new base, managed to hold off the Confederates up to the final battle at Malvern Hill. There Lee unwisely attacked a strongly held Union position and was severely repulsed, chiefly through the performance of Brigadier General Henry Hunt's superbly employed Union artillery.

The Peninsular Campaign, launched by the self-assured McClellan to save the Union, as he confided in a letter to his wife, but which failed either to take Richmond or inflict a serious defeat on Robert E. Lee, was the first major campaign of the war in the East. Covering a period of three and one-half months, the campaign ended on July 1 with the Confederate repulse at Malvern Hill; that same night McClellan, with cumulative losses of 16,000 of his 105,000 troops, fell back to Harrison's Landing, where he entrenched. Lee, having lost 20,000 of his 80,000 men, withdrew behind the defense works of Richmond. It was clear that both armies needed rest and time to pull themselves together for further effort.

The year 1862 was now more than half gone. A Union victory seemed far away. With at least twice as many troops as the Confederates could muster in Virginia, the military forces of the North had made a miserable showing in the Shenandoah Valley and accomplished nothing in the vicinity of Richmond. In both areas the outnumbered Confederates had cleverly conducted active defensive campaigns in which the Federal commanders were consistently out-generaled by Jackson and Lee.

A NEW GENERAL-IN-CHIEF

It had become apparent that the combination of Lincoln and Stanton as military commanders by remote control from Washington was a poor substitute for a General-in-Chief, the position held by McClellan until Lincoln relieved him. Perhaps the President had kept the post vacant from March through early July in the hope that McClellan would restore his confidence by taking Richmond, a feat that would undoubtedly have brought about his restoration to supreme command. Unfortunately the Peninsular Campaign proved to be a failure, so Lincoln turned to the Western theater in his search for a key to unlock the secret of how to win battles. The choice fell on the saturnine Halleck.

Major General Henry W. Halleck, whose intellectual qualities exceeded his command ability by a considerable margin, had on March 11, 1862, been elevated to command all the forces in the West, in which theater the North had made notable progress. It was logical that Lincoln should cast his eyes in that direction as he mulled over the problem of finding a general to improve the Union fortunes in the East. The belief was current that Halleck, highly respected by Lincoln's colleagues in Washington, had been responsible for the western successes. The fact that Grant and other generals were really the ones who deserved the battle credit had not as yet filtered down to the man in the street.

Born January 16, 1815, in New York State, Halleck attended Union College and graduated from West Point in 1839, third in his class. A serious student of the military art, his lectures on the science of war, published in 1846 as *Elements of Military Art and Science,* became during the Civil War a manual for officers of the Army and was universally in demand by students of the military profession. After the war with Mexico, in which he served, Halleck played a leading part in drafting a constitution for the new State of California, following which he resigned from the Army, took up the practice of law, and wrote a number of books on mining and international law.

It is easy to see why he gained the sobriquet, "Old Brains," for in addition to his intellectual accomplishments he had acquired large interests and much valuable property as the head of San Francisco's most prominent law firm, served as president of a small railroad, and was in every respect one of the leading citizens of California when Civil War broke out in 1861.

Halleck immediately offered his services to the Union, was appointed a major general in the Regular Army at the behest of General Winfield Scott, and was assigned command of the Department of the Missouri, with headquarters at St. Louis. There was great need for a man of administrative ability to bring efficiency and order to the chaotic situation which existed in that department, and Halleck succeeded admirably. So effective was his work that in March 1862, the Departments of Kansas and Ohio were merged with that of the Missouri, with Halleck promoted to command the entire territory from the Alleghenies to the Rocky Mountains, the whole constituting the Department of the Mississippi.

When Halleck on July 23 was called to Washington his star was in the ascendancy. Under his overall departmental command the Confederates had been driven from Missouri, the northern half of Arkansas, Kentucky, and most of Tennessee, and the Union forces had gained a foothold in Mississippi and Alabama. But when Halleck had doffed his administrative headgear and taken command of troops in the field, the results were less than spectacular, for his abilities as a field general fell considerably short of his accomplishments as a disciplinarian and administrator.

Nevertheless, he had built a solid foundation for getting results, hence his selection to command all the Union armies was a perfectly natural one for the President to make. Interestingly enough the idea didn't appeal to Halleck, who at first declined the honor, and it was only after Lincoln had made it an order that he packed his bags for a reluctant departure from his western post.

Immediately upon assuming command of the armies in July, Halleck's first official action was to visit McClellan at Harrison's Landing. He told the latter that not more than 20,000 reinforcements could be spared for him if he would attack Richmond. McClellan agreed, but after Halleck had returned to Washington McClellan reneged, sending a wire that on reconsideration he felt it could only be done with almost twice that number of additional troops, or 35,000. This old refrain was no surprise to the President, who would have relieved McClellan then and there if Major General Ambrose E. Burnside, to whom the post was offered, had been willing to accept the responsibility. Burnside, however, a good friend and loyal to McClellan, recommended that the latter be retained.

It had become quite clear that the Federal troops in the East, other than the Army of the Potomac, needed two things and needed them desperately: unified command and a commander who could make unification work. Even as Lee was pushing McClellan back from Richmond, the latter had taken time from the operations to write Secretary of War Edwin M. Stanton urging him to combine the troops in the Valley with those in front of Washington, under a single commander. As Commanding General of the Army of the Potomac, the defense of Washington was not

McClellan's concern, but that made little difference to the self-sufficient general. As it happened, Lincoln had independently reached the same conclusion and had already selected the man for the job of heading the new army about to be created.

The solution was to organize a second army by putting together the separate corps of Banks, McDowell, and Fremont, under a new commander. This army would have the same mission as the separate commands of the three corps commanders, viz., to protect Washington, control the Shenandoah Valley, and draw Confederate troops from Richmond. This time, however, a single general would head the heretofore uncoordinated fighting teams, which was a step in the right direction. The wistfully hopeful desk-chair strategists in Washington would thus have to deal only with two generals, McClellan and the new commander of the Army of Virginia, as it was to be called. Two hundred thousand men would be available to overwhelm less than half that number of Confederates.

But there was still a serious defect in the Administration's reasoning. Unity of command had not been achieved. Two armies would take the place of one army and three separate corps, and Halleck may have felt that as Commander-in-Chief the desired integration would be effected in his person. If so, firm action to produce the desired result was not forthcoming.

There was one ray of hope. The war in the east would be pursued with vigor. The summer and fall months were ideal for fighting. Lincoln saw clearly the need for offensive action, even if his field generals did not. He would keep trying to find a leader who would give the North a victory, no matter how great his frustrations. Fortunately the heavily burdened President still maintained his incomparable, dry sense of humor—an asset whose worth to the Union could not be measured in terms of dollars or manpower.

The problem that confronted Halleck, now that he had two armies in Virginia with Lee and Richmond between them, was how best to employ them in combination. Should he revive Lincoln's pincers plan, when both armies could be readied for an offensive campaign, or would it be better to unite them under a single commander? And if so, what then? The difficulty was that Halleck, who had an aversion to politicians, hated the Washington scene and had tried his best to avoid the important assignment of General-in-Chief. He liked to counsel and advise but seemed constitutionally incapable of making decisions in his new role. Really a theorist at heart, still he tried to function as General-in-Chief in fact, until after the failure of the first great eastern campaign under his direction, which culminated in the Battle of Second Manassas. Thereafter he sidestepped command responsibilities, confining himself to acting merely as the President's military adviser.

Halleck's inability to reach a firm decision on how to employ the two separate armies under his command was a keen disappointment to the President, who had plenty of problems of his own without having to solve those of the military as well. It finally became apparent that, if there was to be a solution, Lincoln himself would have to dictate it. Despairing of offensive action by McClellan, and knowing of no other general to whom he could safely entrust the job after Burnside declined to take it, Lincoln reluctantly discarded his nutcracker project, that is, to attack Lee at Richmond from two directions, and directed Halleck to call the Army of the Potomac back north with a view to operations in conjunction with the newly formed second army on the line of the Rappahannock River.

Despite McClellan's strenuous objections, the order stuck. Further operations against Richmond were suspended for the time being. McClellan was directed to withdraw his forces from the Peninsula forthwith. The lessons taught by Jackson's Shenandoah Valley campaign, notably the disastrous results that can stem from divided command when opposed by a resolute enemy, had not been lost on Lincoln. Furthermore, McClellan's reluctance to take any risks, regardless of his preponderance in combat strength, had been proven so repeatedly that it would not do, in Lincoln's judgment, to place supreme reliance on him.

JOHN POPE RIDES IN FROM THE WEST

Major General John Pope of Illinois was the Administration's choice to command the newly designated Army of Virginia. But it was soon to become apparent that the President's military education had not proceeded far enough to master the art of successfully appraising the capabilities of generals with the potential to lead armies to victory.

Lincoln had known both the general and his father before the war. Pope had achieved little success under Halleck in capturing New Madrid and Island No. 10 in the Mississippi earlier in the year. Although conceited and a braggart, he was quick-tempered and liked to fight, a trait so lacking in many of the generals upon whom Lincoln had to rely that it undoubtedly influenced the President's decision. The fact that the corps commanders who would now be subordinate to Pope were all senior to him in rank seemed to upset only one of them, General Fremont, whose prompt resignation could scarcely be construed as a major disaster to Union armies.

Pope was gifted with a vivid imagination, was impatient of contradiction, and almost violently unorthodox in his conception of the military art. This latter trait manifested itself in the views that he freely expressed before committees of Congress and was quick to announce in orders to his new army, to the effect that "the time had come for the adoption of a truly American system of warfare. Such traditions of the past as lines of retreat, bases of supplies, positions, etc., which had bothered all commanders from Agamemnon to Banks, were to be at once discarded." This was but one of the ill-advised, and foolishly conceived pronouncements that the freshman army commander would live to regret, and soon.

Like Joe Hooker, John Pope was a striking figure who made quite an impression in uniform. His large frame and piercing eyes were balanced by a goatee (an early photo of Pope shows him with a fairly full beard. A postwar portrait has him with only a mustache), so that the first reaction of those whom he met was extremely favorable. He also talked a great deal, but when those with whom he conferred in Washington had escaped from his conversational charm, and thought about the matter, they recalled that much of his talk had centered about John Pope.

Pope's assigned mission, somewhat similar to but with more offensive implications than that of the three corps which were now being combined to make up his army, was to cover Washington, exercise control over the Shenandoah Valley, threaten Gordonsville and Charlottesville, and make every effort to draw Confederate troops from Richmond. The ultimate objective, clearly stated in the order, would be to move against Richmond from the west as McClellan attacked from the east.

The Army of Virginia, officially brought into being on June 26, could be a powerful force for the Union when pulled together from its scattered positions and welded into a well-organized fighting team. With all present or accounted for, Pope would be in command of an army about half as large, although not so well blooded, as the Army of the Potomac. As constituted, his army included Fremont's First Corps of 11,500 men now commanded by Major General Franz Sigel; the Second Corps, Major General Nathaniel P. Banks, 8,800 strong; and the Third Corps under Major General Irvin McDowell, strongest of the lot with 18,500 men. These three corps represented Pope's striking force, which together with some 5,000 poorly mounted and imperfectly organized cavalry totaled 43,800. Also assigned to Pope, but not yet organized and consequently unavailable, was a small Reserve Corps under Brigadier General Samuel D. Sturgis, then being formed in the vicinity of Alexandria, in the Washington area.

Sigel reported his corps, newly acquired from Fremont, as being badly disorganized. He and Banks were in the Shenandoah Valley between Winchester and Middletown. McDowell had one division at Manassas Junction and the other at Falmouth, across the Rappahannock from Fredericksburg, the latter designated by the War Department to cover Aquia Creek Landing against a possible enemy incursion from the direction of Richmond.

Unfortunately Pope got off to a bad start in his first General Order to his new troops, when he undiplomatically informed them, with an oratorical flourish, that he was from the west "where we have always seen the backs of our enemies" and where the policy had been to seek out, attack, and defeat the enemy. This was bad psychological medicine to administer to proud troops of whom the worst that could be said was that they had been ineffectively led. Nor did it raise Pope in their estimation when he stated that his headquarters would be in the saddle, an unfortunate remark which naturally invited the enlisted rejoinder that that was where most people placed their hindquarters.

UNION TEAMWORK SADLY LACKING

McClellan's chronic reluctance to fight and his ridiculous habit of always vastly overestimating the strength of his opponents finally caught up with him. Had he been an effective combat leader, the decision to withdraw his large army from its position only a few miles from the enemy's capital, with a secure line of supply and communications, and with another strong Union army on the opposite side of Richmond, would have been an historic blunder of great magnitude. But the blame cannot fairly be placed on Lincoln, who had at long last reached the conclusion that McClellan simply did not have a fighting heart. Still, one cannot understand why the President failed to replace McClellan outright and give the army a decent chance to gain its objective. One reason was of course that good generals were hard to find and even then they seemed unwilling to accept responsibility for high command. It was also a fact that Halleck, going by the book as usual, advised Lincoln to unite the two armies before resuming the offensive, on the premise that otherwise they might be defeated in detail. In so recommending, Halleck ignored the fact that the position of Lee's army between McClellan and Pope placed the Confederates in a vulnerable situation which could have proven fatal had the Union's preponderant strength been utilized to advantage. In any event, the President ordered McClellan's army back to the Washington area and the groundwork was laid for a succession of battles that, coupled with McClellan's failure on the Peninsula, would make 1862 a year of great frustrations for the Union.

When Pope assumed command of the Army of Virginia on June 26, his first task was to improve the organization and supply of the separated corps and effect a concentration. Jackson's Confederates having left the Valley to join Lee for the showdown battles with McClellan, there were no hostile forces of any size in Pope's area. Keeping in mind his threefold mission, Pope ordered Sigel and Banks to move via Luray Gap to the vicinity of Sperryville and ten miles east thereof, respectively, and McDowell was directed to transfer his division at Manassas to Waterloo Bridge on the Rappahannock, leaving his other division at Falmouth.

Pope was concerned when McClellan, following Malvern Hill, withdrew south of Richmond to his new position on the James River. He felt that this was strategically unsound in that this movement away from Washington would make it difficult for McClellan to effect a junction with his own army and would likewise expose both to the danger that

Lee could attack each separately from his central position between them. Pope wrote Halleck urging him to direct McClellan to halt in place, and at the same time sent a letter to McClellan offering to cooperate with him by adapting his own tactical moves to McClellan's plan, whatever it might be. McClellan's reply, full of generalities, avoided suggesting specific ways and means as Pope had requested. This was a short-sighted but typical reaction from the "little Napoleon," who evidently considered Pope an upstart competitor who was not to be given the opportunity to gain distinction if McClellan could help it. Pope at least felt keenly the need for a unified command and showed his willingness to cooperate with McClellan in achieving that result. The latter's indifference, however, convinced Pope that a superior to both was not only militarily desirable but an absolute necessity if the operations of the two armies were to be effectively coordinated.

Halleck's new plan, in July, was for the Army of the Potomac to move down the James to the Chesapeake and up the Potomac to Aquia Landing, from which new base it would be available to cooperate with Pope's army. As usual, McClellan acted with exasperating slowness, so that August was almost half gone before the movement got underway, despite repeated telegrams from Halleck to speed it up.

There was good reason for Halleck's urgency. In order to strengthen the lone division of McDowell's corps at Falmouth and more fully secure the approaches to Washington from Richmond, Halleck had ordered Burnside to embark his corps at Newport News. Burnside responded with gratifying speed and on August 3 his troops debarked at Aquia Creek for the short overland march to a position opposite Fredericksburg. Pope's army, operating from Culpeper, was by that time south of the Rappahannock River threatening Gordonsville.

With strategic foresight, Lee suspected that Washington might recall McClellan from the Peninsula, a development which would be very much to his liking. On July 13 he sent Jackson from Hanover Court House toward Gordonsville to engage Pope with part of the Army of Northern Virginia, but held his main body at Richmond until he could be certain of McClellan's intentions. When McClellan finally started from the Peninsula, Lee on August 13 left Richmond with the rest of his army for

Gordonsville, with the avowed purpose of destroying Pope before the two Union armies could be joined. By that time a preliminary engagement, the Battle of Cedar Mountain, had been fought and Jackson had retired to Gordonsville.

McClellan Wastes Valuable Time

McClellan seemed strangely indifferent to the fate of anyone but McClellan. Willing compliance with orders from Halleck, Stanton, or even Lincoln himself was rarely evidenced in his egotistical code of conduct. Directives from higher authority invariably brought long dissertations of disagreement from the general, whose letters to his wife best reveal his self-centered attitude. Since it was McClellan's opinion that he was destined as the chosen one to save the country, it seemed perfectly clear to him that all else should be subordinated to his own plans and wishes. Much has been written about Longstreet's propensity on occasion for dragging his feet in his uncooperative attitude toward orders from General Lee, but Longstreet ran a poor second to McClellan in that respect.

In spite of positive orders from Halleck, who early in August had received reliable information of Lee's probable intention to destroy Pope's army before moving on Washington; and virtually ignoring the follow-up letters and telegrams with which Halleck sought to galvanize him into action, it was August 14, eleven days after receipt of the initial order, before McClellan commenced to evacuate Harrison's Landing.

George B. McClellan was a great organizer who with even a small amount of humility in his makeup might have proven to be the man of the hour to lead the armies of the North to victory. The great flaw in his character, his egocentricity, dominated his every thought and action, however. There was no room left for those traits which might have made him a great battle leader and subsequently President of the United States—self-discipline, the ability to work in harness with others of equal or greater authority, a willingness to take the calculated risks inherent in warfare, and a readiness to do the best he could with the means available.

McClellan's personality and military deficiencies may fairly be said to have been largely responsible for the series of depressing events which plagued the Lincoln Administration in its conduct of the war in the East during 1862. McClellan had the men, weapons, and equipment with which to wage successful offensives; his strength was twice that of the Confederates; and his officers and soldiers from the division level down were just as good as their opposite numbers in the Confederate Army. But McClellan was pitted against Robert E. Lee and it was that, coupled with his own lesser character and lack of aggressiveness, together with the trial and error floundering of the Washington administration and the lack of unified field command, which came perilously close to losing the war for the Union during the summer of 1862.

There was one other prominent Union general whose fleeting appearance in the eastern theater of operations had much to do with the depressing results for the North during that summer. His name was John Pope. Zooming in from the west, he came, he saw, and almost in the twinkling of an eye was conquered.

Chapter 2

Pope versus Jackson

THE LETTERS and telegrams that passed between Halleck, McClellan, and Pope during the first few weeks of the summer of 1862 are so revealing that one may pause to wonder how the North was able to maintain any sort of a military posture in the face of the crosscurrents that characterized the strategic planning in Washington and at the headquarters of the two armies.

President Lincoln's attempt to achieve unity of command in the military forces was a proper move but made with the wrong men. McClellan was the strongest of the three, Pope the weakest. Halleck had the right idea but lacked the strength of character to make his orders stick, with the inevitable result that military operations suffered from a debilitating climate of disunity, lack of harmony and cooperation, and the resulting low morale among officers and men in the field.

Lincoln and Stanton had passed the ball to Halleck, who for the present at least felt constrained to call the signals, while McClellan, from his self-constructed "Olympian Heights" in the unhealthy Peninsula country, remained steadfast in the obsession that only he could save the country. In his annoyance that Halleck had succeeded him as General-in-Chief, and consistent with the savior role in which in his mind's eye he pictured himself, McClellan objected to every plan that emanated from Washington, no matter from what high source. Arguing endlessly with his superiors in favor of his own strategy, stalling interminably when peremptory and unequivocal orders reached him from an exasperated Halleck, and discouraging Pope's effort toward teamwork between the two armies, it is difficult to conclude otherwise than that McClellan wanted both Halleck and Pope to fail so that he himself could emerge as the sole leader capable of leading the North to victory. In no other way can the following excerpt from a letter to his wife be interpreted, in light of the fact that he was clearly doing everything in his own power to make it certain that Halleck's revised strategy should *not* succeed. Coincident with the final overruling of McClellan's stalling tactics by Halleck, who bluntly informed him by telegraph that "It (the order for withdrawal from the James) will not be rescinded and you will be expected to execute it with all possible promptness," McClellan wrote his wife: "They are committing a fatal error in withdrawing me from here, and the future will show it. I think the result of their machinations will be that Pope will be badly thrashed within ten days, and that they will be very glad to turn over the redemption of their affairs to me." Apparently the thought never crossed the general's little mind that he was pursuing the wrong path that leads to greatness, even though his two-point forecast would in the end prove correct.

Halleck was fully aware of the danger that Lee might attack one or the other of the widely separated Federal armies either before or during McClellan's northward movement. The latter's recalcitrance could prove fatal, so Halleck cautioned Pope not to be precipitous, "but to avoid an advance from the line of the Rappahannock so as to expose yourself to any disaster, unless you can better your line of defense, until we can get more troops upon the Rappahannock."

The application of such a restrictive check rein to the newly appointed, ambitious army commander was disappointing, particularly after Pope's flamboyant early orders to his troops, all breathing the spirit of the offensive and decrying such ordinary precautions as security for the rear areas. Furthermore, Pope believed that Halleck should force McClellan to cooperate by more energetic action rather than to hamstring his own army by requiring him to mark time. There is also some evidence that Pope may have pictured himself at the head of his army, sweeping across country toward Richmond and, brushing aside all opposition, pounding at Lee's back door while the latter kept an eye on McClellan in front.

However, Pope was not completely reckless, only prone to reach hasty decisions without considering all the implications; in the present circumstances he reluctantly allowed himself to be guided by Halleck's injunction to go slow.

A New General Gets Tough

The appointment of General John Pope to command the new Army of Virginia was dated June 26, 1862. For some weeks thereafter his headquarters remained in Washington while he took account of stock, conferred with War Department officials, devised plans, and issued orders to effect the concentration of his several corps and to define organizational procedures and operational policies.

As already noted, his first ill-advised general order to the troops had just the opposite effect from what he had intended. With his foot still in his mouth, during his extended sojourn in the Capital, he caused General Orders Nos. 5, 6, and 7 to be published, dated July 18, setting forth the methods by which he had determined to keep the citizens of occupied Virginia territory under strict control. The series of orders prescribed that the Army of Virginia should live off the country to the maximum extent practicable. Supplies requisitioned for the army would, on presentation of vouchers to be rendered by the requisitioning officer, "be paid for at the conclusion of the war, upon sufficient testimony being furnished that such owners have been loyal citizens of the United States since the dates of the vouchers."

Furthermore, the people of the South would be notified that persons living in the vicinity of Federal camps or bivouacs were to be held responsible for damage done to all railroad tracks, telegraph lines, and roads, and for any attacks upon army trains or stragglers, whether perpetrated by private citizens or guerrillas. Payment for such damage would be exacted by turning out the local populace within five miles of the spot, not only to repair the damage but in addition to pay to the United States in money or property the full amount of the pay and subsistence of the Federal troops required to enforce performance by the citizens of the corrective measures.

Still harsher punishment was promised to any Southerner from whose house a soldier should be fired on. All such houses were to be immediately destroyed and the occupants sent to army headquarters as prisoners. If any person should be caught in the act he was to be shot forthwith, "without awaiting civil process."

There was no doubt that Pope believed strongly in the strictest kind of martial law in occupied territory. Doubtless his intent was to intimidate the Southerners as a preventive measure and to effect economy in his own operations, on the premise that his troops would thus be more secure and would not be diverted from essential military operations by excessive police duties. While his purpose may have been militarily justified, the psychology was defective, for his harsh measures only served to harden the resistance and strengthen the will of Confederate citizens to outsmart the invaders at every opportunity.

The broad latitude granted to a large army on the loose in enemy country, particularly one whose morale and discipline (in many of the units) would rate less than satisfactory on an efficiency report, inevitably resulted in depredations and pillage against innocent Southerners, which shamed the more intelligent and sensitive officers and men of Pope's army.

The effect of Pope's blanket "live off the country" order was to strip handsome plantations and small farms alike of all means of livelihood, reducing the inhabitants to penury and almost complete dependence on the goodwill of the invading army. The heavy weight of Federal license descended indiscriminately on the just and unjust alike.

General Orders No. 11, issued July 23, were equally punitive in directing commanders down to brigades and detached commands "to arrest all disloyal male citizens within their lines or within their reach in rear of their respective stations." Those Southerners who were willing to take the oath of allegiance to the United States would be permitted to remain at home during good behavior; all others would be routed from their homes, conducted south beyond Federal picket lines, and turned loose under penalty of being treated as spies should they later be found within or in rear of the Union lines.

Pope subsequently defended these policies affecting the Southern people by asserting that they were in accord with accepted practice in time of war, adding that they had been publicly and willfully misconstrued as authorizing indiscriminate robbery and plunder. He claimed that they were completely justified by the embarrassment and long delay imposed on Lee's army in its subsequent invasion of Maryland in September 1862, because of the resulting shortages of food and supplies from the country which Pope's army had wrung dry during the campaign.

Concentration of the infantry and artillery of the Army of Virginia in late July and early August was partially screened by cavalry, which at that stage of the war was little more than an aggregation of uniformed men and horses that had not been allowed either to acquire the necessary branch training or to function as organized combat units, trained or untrained. To be a good trooper called for equal efficiency either mounted or dismounted, but the steps necessary to attain the needed state of training were precluded by the wasteful use of the green Union horsemen on inconsequential duties such as orderlies and messengers for infantry corps and division commanders, outposts and patrols, and guards for slow-moving wagon trains. The resulting waste of horseflesh was disgraceful because of the lack of training and foolish dissipation of resources on inappropriate missions, so that reliability could not be placed on the Federal cavalry arm until the facts of cavalry life were finally recognized and applied by General Joe Hooker during the first half of 1863.

In spite of these deficiencies, part of Pope's cavalry, operating under two capable commanders, Brigadier Generals John Buford and George D. Bayard, displayed a bold aggressiveness that surprised the Confederates, unaccustomed as the latter were to any display of ambition or dash by the Union horsemen. Moving many miles in advance of their infantry, the two Federal detachments reconnoitered actively and tirelessly with surprising effectiveness, keeping Pope well informed of the general movements of Jackson's advance elements as they moved west toward Gordonsville.

POPE PUTS OUT INEFFECTUAL FEELERS

Pursuant to that portion of his instructions which called for the protection of Washington while the Army of the Potomac was returning north from the Peninsula, Pope ordered McDowell's division commander at Fredericksburg, Brigadier General Rufus King, early in July to dispatch part of his cavalry to impair and, to the extent practicable, destroy communications along the line of the Virginia Central Railroad between Richmond and the Shenandoah Valley. At the same time General Banks was directed to send an infantry brigade, together with all the cavalry attached to his corps, to march on Culpeper Court

House, seize it, and push the cavalry on toward the Rapidan and Gordonsville. Threatening Gordonsville and Charlottesville would in Pope's opinion be the best way to isolate the Shenandoah Valley and draw troops away from Richmond.

After that mission should be accomplished, Banks was to send forward his entire cavalry force from Culpeper, under Brigadier General John P. Hatch, to seize Gordonsville, destroy the railroad for a dozen miles east of that town, and then move on toward Charlottesville to destroy railroad bridges and disrupt communications as much as possible. Moving out on July 15, Hatch encumbered himself with artillery and trains, found the roads bad, and made so little forward progress that the expedition was abandoned in the face of the arrival of Confederate Major General Richard S. Ewell with the advance guard of Stonewall Jackson's troops at Gordonsville on July 16.

Still hopeful of preliminary success in the unfolding of his remote control strategy, Pope tried again. He instructed Banks to send several thousand cavalrymen, again under Hatch, to move down on the west side of the Blue Ridge, destroy the railroad west of Gordonsville, and continue south to destroy the railroad between Charlottesville and Lynchburg. Hatch made a feeble start on this assignment, but for undisclosed reasons (probably Ewell's presence at Gordonsville) quickly abandoned the movement, whereupon Pope relieved him from command and sent in his stead the able Brig. Gen. John Buford to serve as Chief of Cavalry of Banks' corps.

Buford had been buried in the Inspector General's Department as a major, without influential friends to rescue him from oblivion, when he reported to Pope in the capacity of an Inspector shortly after the latter was given command of the Army of Virginia. Pope offered him a field command which Buford gratefully accepted. His commission as Brigadier General of Volunteers came through promptly and Pope immediately gave him a cavalry brigade in one of his corps.

POPE TAKES THE FIELD
At this stage Pope concluded that the time had come for him to take personal command in the field. It was high time! Jackson's advance

elements had reached Gordonsville and his main body was on the way. The rest of Lee's army was still in Richmond, while McClellan's Army of the Potomac remained at Harrison's Landing. Halleck had arrived in Washington in mid-July to take over and it may be presumed that one of his first official acts was to tell Pope to take himself out of Washington and join his troops, where he belonged. There was of course no objection from Lincoln, who had temporarily used Pope as his military adviser pending Halleck's arrival.

On July 29 Pope left the Capital, reviewed Ricketts' division of McDowell's corps at Waterloo Bridge, and joined Banks at his headquarters a short distance southeast of Little Washington. Pope's strength return for July 31 shows a grand total of nearly 72,000 officers and men, but does not give a true picture of his strength. Banks, for example, had 8,800, not the 15,000 he reported. Actually Pope's three corps including his cavalry and King's division, still at Fredericksburg, totaled about 43,800. In theoretical support but too distant or otherwise engaged to be immediately available were the commands of Sturgis, Cox, and White, which brought Pope's total to 64,000. In the critical Sperryville-Culpeper-Warrenton triangle he had only 34,800.

March orders for the army now directed Banks' corps to advance to the point where the Sperryville-Culpeper Turnpike crosses the Hazel River, McDowell to move with Ricketts' division from Waterloo Bridge to Culpeper, and Sigel's corps at Sperryville to remain in place. By August 8 all of Pope's infantry and artillery except King's division at Fredericksburg were disposed along the turnpike from Sperryville to Culpeper. The cavalry covered the front from Madison Court House to Rapidan Station, with pickets posted along the Rapidan River from the Blue Ridge on the west to the forks of the Rappahannock above Falmouth on the east. Halfway between the cavalry forces under Buford and Bayard, a signal station was established on the top of Thoroughfare Mountain, ten miles southwest of Culpeper, commanding a view of the entire country as far down as Orange Court House.

Pope had misgivings about the First Corps under Franz Sigel, the German-born general who had recently succeeded the politically minded John Fremont, whose military accomplishments had failed to measure up to his reputation as an explorer. Sigel was popular with his men but somewhat controversial in character, and far from compatible with his fellow officers of the Regular Army. "A very insignificant looking man, but a thorough soldier and gentleman," was the way one of his staff described him in a letter to his family. Banks and McDowell on the other hand enjoyed the confidence of the army commander, so it was on these two corps that Pope came to rely more fully than on Sigel's.

TIGHTENING UNION DISCIPLINE

Whether he was influenced by what he had observed of the troops after his arrival, or simply as a matter of sound administration, Pope issued a general order on August 6 whose purpose was to tighten discipline and improve the marching and combat capabilities of his army. Straggling was strictly forbidden, and to make certain that the order would be obeyed, regimental commanders were instructed to habitually march in rear of their regiments, company commanders in rear of their companies. Men could not fall out except by written permission of a medical officer and then only if sick enough to be forced to ride in an ambulance. None but ambulance and ammunition wagons would be permitted in the column of march of the respective regiments, all other wheeled vehicles to follow in rear of the troops. Shelter tents and knapsacks were to be carried in the wagons, and each officer and man would at all times on the march be required to carry two days' cooked rations on his person. Enlisted men would habitually carry 100 rounds of ammunition, and any company commander whose men were found deficient in this respect was to be arrested forthwith and reported to the War Department for dismissal from the service.

The terms of this order implied either a lack of confidence in the efficiency of his subordinate commanders or a blunt recognition of the lack of training and discipline of the troops under their former separate status. Probably some of both. Whatever the reason, Pope must be credited with a determination to put his army in a condition to make the most of its opportunities. It would appear, however, that the language of certain parts of the order was hardly calculated to raise morale, in view of the implication that the General could not trust his officers to perform their sworn duty except under the compulsion of harsh and punitive terms.

On August 7 Pope rode to Sperryville to inspect Sigel's corps. While there he received several reports from the cavalry that enemy troops were crossing the Rapidan at several points between the railroad and the bridge at Liberty Mills. The reports continued to come in on the morning of August 8. Buford and Bayard messaged that the enemy was advancing on Culpeper and Madison Court House, respectively, but Pope was unable to determine which of the two towns represented the principal objective of Jackson's force. In the course of the day, however, he decided to concentrate his full strength in the direction of Culpeper in order to keep his own army between the enemy main body and the lower fords of the Rappahannock. To that end Crawford's brigade of Banks' corps was sent forward in the direction of Cedar (Slaughter) Mountain, to support Bayard's cavalry as it retired before the enemy in the direction of the mountain, and to assist Bayard in determining the strength and dispositions of the hostile forces. Buford was near Madison Courthouse. At the same time Banks and Sigel were directed to move their troops immediately to Culpeper from Hazel River and Sperryville, respectively.

Banks marched promptly, reaching Culpeper the same day, the 8th of August, but Sigel was slow and, judging from Pope's subsequent official report, stupid as well, for he sent army headquarters a note from Sperryville inquiring which road to take, although there was only the single broad turnpike between the two points. Consequently, Sigel's corps reached the assembly area almost a day later than Pope intended and was not ready to be sent in company with Banks to meet the enemy advance on August 9.

Some days earlier Banks had reported an effective strength of some 15,000 men. It turned out, however, according to Pope, that his actual effectives did not exceed 8,800. The reason for the discrepancy was never explained. At the time of the concentration Pope believed Banks' strength to be almost twice as great as it actually was, and the army commander's battle plans were predicated upon that assumption. That at least was Pope's story after the stunning defeat of his army at Second Manassas, and his statement must be judged with subsequent events in mind.

Sigel's unsatisfactory performance up to this time had thrown Pope's logistics off schedule to the extent that Banks' corps on August 8 was the only immediate complete tactical weapon of consequence available for offensive action. McDowell had but one of his two divisions, Ricketts' at Culpeper, the other being at Fredericksburg, covering the Union supply base at Aquia Creek Landing. Pope thereupon took it upon himself to order King's division up from Fredericksburg, a thirty-five-mile march, and so advised Halleck by telegram at 10 o'clock on the evening of August 8. Since Burnside's corps had now arrived at Aquia Creek, it was perfectly proper for Pope to recall King.

In the same telegram Pope summed up his estimate of the situation by advising Halleck that the enemy division (Elzey's—actually a brigade of Ewell's division, commanded by Jubal Early, who had supplanted the invalided Elzey), which had crossed the Rapidan during the day, was probably a reconnaissance in force, which might however represent an advance upon Culpeper. He indicated his intention, as soon as Sigel's corps should join the rest of the army the following morning, of pushing the enemy across the Rapidan and then taking up a strong position in accordance with Halleck's suggestion in an earlier message.

COMBAT IMMINENT

On the morning of August 9, Banks with his entire corps was ordered toward Cedar Mountain to join the brigade of A. S. Williams' division under General Crawford, already well forward. Banks was directed to occupy a strong position at the point reached by Crawford and to halt the advance of the enemy. Ricketts' division of McDowell's corps was posted nearby at Colvin's Tavern, where the Madison Court House-Culpeper Road intersects the Culpeper-Cedar Mountain Road, to hold that tactically important point against a possible advance by a Confederate force reported by Buford to be in strength near Madison Court House. Ricketts' division would thus be in position, three miles behind Banks' corps, either to support the latter or to serve as a strongpoint for a buildup of additional strength to counter the hostile threat from the direction of Madison Court House.

Occasional enemy horse-artillery fire was directed on Banks' position during the day, but there was no evidence in his opinion to justify a belief that the Confederates planned to attack. Enemy cavalry had been making demonstrations, but Banks reported to Pope that in his judgment the supporting Confederate infantry was not strong enough to launch an attack. Later in the afternoon, however, the tempo of artillery fire increased to such an extent that Pope became alarmed and sent Ricketts' division barging toward the front, in support of Banks as a measure of insurance.

It was late afternoon of August 9, before Sigel's corps reached Culpeper, and just about the time Pope was preparing to start for the front to see for himself what was happening. It was bad enough that Sigel was late in arriving at Culpeper, but on top of that he had compounded his earlier mistake by neglecting to enforce Pope's standing order to keep two days' cooked rations on the men's persons on all marches. This failure meant further delay until he could borrow rations from McDowell's trains at Culpeper and have a hot meal cooked for his troops.

Army Commander Pope was having his troubles. It was an inauspicious start for the Army of Virginia, which seemed to be getting off on the wrong foot in its first campaign. Pope was trying hard—that much was evident—but his tools lacked sharpness and his own attitude had not contributed materially to the development of a smooth-working, enthusiastic organization.

Jackson's successes in the Shenandoah Valley and Lee's effective neutralization of the Army of the Potomac on the James had afforded an opportunity for the commander of the Army of Northern Virginia to take the initiative, which he was quick to grasp. He was now in a position to call the turn if he played his cards carefully but boldly.

Operating in widely separated areas, but in accordance with a definite strategic concept, Lee and Jackson between them had successfully frustrated Federal designs on Richmond and the Valley. Lee's immediate task, as the summer weeks passed, was to maintain a close watch on the slow-acting McClellan and at the same time keep Pope's new army preoccupied while he sought an opening to crush the latter before the two Federal armies should succeed in effecting a junction.

Lee was fast becoming an expert in taking calculated risks by splitting his forces and reassembling them in time for the payoff battle. If he could attack Pope, keep Washington on tenterhooks, and hinder or prevent a junction between the armies of Pope and McClellan, it would immeasurably improve the fortunes of the Confederacy. It might even pave the way for an invasion of the North, a project that was dear to Lee's heart and constantly in his thoughts.

It was no secret that Pope's army was being concentrated east of the Blue Ridge in the Warrenton-Culpeper area. Lee learned of it through his efficient spy system almost as soon as Pope arrived in Washington and began to sound off. But even before the Federal Army of Virginia came into being, the "armies" under Banks, Fremont, and McDowell must not be allowed to maneuver at will along the Rappahannock.

It was natural, then, that Stonewall Jackson be ordered to retrace his steps and take up where he had left off when summoned to Lee's aid at Richmond. Lee had learned to respect Jackson's capabilities and, keen judge of character that he was, no doubt recognized—particularly after Mechanicsville—that his spirited lieutenant was at his best when working alone, and without a curb bit.

In mid-July, with the divisions of "Baldy" Ewell and Charles S. Winder, Jackson set out for Gordonsville, which was reached on July 19 after a leisurely march of three days. Ten days later Lee wrote that he was sending A. P. ("Powell") Hill's Light Division to strengthen Jackson's force, adding in diplomatic language that Hill could be trusted with Jackson's plans and implying that so large a force as Jackson would now command was too unwieldy to be handled as a one-man show. The advice was however wasted on the uncompromising Jackson, who persisted to the end of his career in treating his generals as though they were children who could not be trusted to think for themselves.

On August 1 Jackson's force at Gordonsville numbered more than 24,000 men, almost half of Lee's army, and the largest body of troops that **lie** had commanded up to this time. The three infantry divisions, with their artillery components, were led by Hill, Ewell, and Winder. By far the largest, the Light Division, had at least 12,000 men present. Ewell's strength was 7,200, while Winder counted only 4,000 in the relatively weak outfit, which formerly had been Jackson's own division. Brigadier General Beverly H. Robertson's 1,200 cavalrymen completed the roster.

Robertson had succeeded Ashby, Jackson's dashing cavalry leader who had been killed in the Valley campaign, and whose troopers had now been reorganized into four regiments under the West Pointer whom Jackson disliked, preferring "Grumble" Jones to the man selected by President Davis. Robertson's Laurel Brigade, as the consolidated regiments were called, joined Jackson after his arrival at Gordonsville.

Jackson's men were happy to get away from the Peninsula and the swamps of the Chickahominy to the more familiar country with its clear, swift-running streams, modern (by Civil War standards) roads, and wooded country fringed by the towering ridges of the Blue Ridge Mountains. The troops were in good physical shape, the weak sisters having been weeded out in the rapid marches of the earlier campaign. The regiments were below their normal strength, few replacements having been received, but their morale was good and discipline had been restored by a strenuous regime of continuous drilling after the Seven Days Battles. They had yet to face defeat and were ready for the best that Pope could offer.

Acutely aware of Lee's hope that Pope's army might be attacked and destroyed before effecting a junction with McClellan's, Jackson was alert for any information that would enable him to apply his successful Valley technique to a portion of Pope's army if it could be caught before Pope could complete his own concentration. Jackson had his eye on the network of roads at Culpeper, which he correctly believed to be Pope's assembly point. When reports from spies disclosed that only a part of the Army of Virginia had reached Culpeper, Jackson determined to act promptly. In the late afternoon of August 7, on which date Pope's divisions were strung along the turnpike from Sperryville to Culpeper, Jackson's troops took off, bivouacked that night at Orange Court House, twenty miles from Culpeper, and resumed the march at dawn the following morning, initial objective the crossing at Barnett's Ford.

CONFUSION AT ORANGE COURT HOUSE

On August 8 Ewell's division led off, with Powell Hill and Winder to follow in that order. Jackson had issued sketchy written orders for the march the evening before, but neither he nor any of his staff had apparently given any thought to routine logistical factors, such as the relative strength and road distance of the several divisions and the position of organizational trains. To further confuse the issue, Jackson changed his mind about the route of the leading division under Ewell, but neglected to inform either Hill or Winder of the change in orders. Instead of following the Orange Court House-Culpeper Road, Ewell was directed to take the road to the left till he reached the Rapidan at Liberty Mills; there he would split his division and march on parallel roads to north and south of the river till he reached Barnett's Ford.

At Orange Court House, Hill, in position early in the morning, waited for the tail of Ewell's supposed column to clear. The troops he watched however turned out to be Jackson's division, under Winder's command, followed by its division trains. Ewell by this time was miles ahead. When Jackson put in an appearance he promptly inquired the reason for Hill's delay, but even then did not tell him of the change in orders; nor did he make any effort to straighten out the tangle.

The net result of the mix-up, which would never have occurred had Jackson been a bit more communicative, was threefold. Jackson's vaunted "foot-cavalry" made one of its sorriest showings, with Hill's division ordered back to Orange Court House for the night after advancing little more than two miles for their day's work. Jackson's corps, instead of reaching Culpeper on the 8th as planned, covered only about eight miles of the twenty-mile distance with less than half of the troops. Finally, a spark of mutual distrust was struck between Jackson and Hill that, fanned by subsequent winds of misunderstanding, would lead to the arrest of the latter and the filing of court-martial charges by his uncompromising superior within a matter of months. All of these could have been avoided if the close-mouthed Jackson had been more considerate of his subordinates and played his lone wolf role with greater acumen.

The disgruntled Jackson informed Lee of the delay, expressing a fear that because of the slow progress on August 8 the expedition would accomplish little. Federal cavalry had obstinately opposed his forward movement and the enemy now knew pretty well what he was up to. Pope was not the only commanding general having troubles. The honors were consequently about even on the morning of August 9.

The Federal cavalry under Buford and Bayard was doing a fine job of screening the movements of Pope's army, and the chances were now good that Jackson's delayed march had given Pope the additional needed time to concentrate at Culpeper. Nevertheless Jackson optimistically believed the odds were in his favor. These were the same troops opposing him that he had made monkeys of in the Valley. His own strength was much greater now; if he moved fast and took advantage of any opening that might offer, it was still possible that Pope's army could be defeated in detail.

DESTINATION–CULPEPER

A. P. Hill, determined to erase the apparent recent blot on his record, started his march that third morning long before daylight, soon caught up to Ewell and Winder. The entire force quickly put the Rapidan behind them. With part of the cavalry covering the advance and the rest marching on the left flank and toward Madison Court House, the tired Federal cavalry was pushed steadily back as Jackson, with Ewell's division still in the lead, crossed Robertson River at Locust Dale and headed down the home stretch toward Culpepper.

Off to the northeast the troops were able to observe, several miles distant, a long tree-covered ridge known locally as Slaughter Mountain, so called after a minister by that name who lived on its northern slope. The bitter fighting that was soon to take place in its vicinity would serve to confirm the name, but history would call it the Battle of Cedar Mountain or Cedar Run as a more euphonious title and in deference to the twin-forked creek whose branches, originating on either side of the Gordonsville-Culpeper Road, meandered east and south to join at Hudson's Mill, about a mile from the Slaughter home, and thence flowed on to the Rapidan.

CHAPTER 3

The Battle of Cedar Mountain

AUGUST 9 turned hot and sultry as the day advanced. Some of the fast-marching Confederate soldiers, oppressed by the choking dust and enervating heat of midday, were felled by sunstroke. Others, unable to maintain the pace demanded by the driving corps commander, staggered off the road and sank down in the shade to recover. Jackson's preference for losing one man in marching rather than five in battle was being demonstrated in this forced march on Culpeper, and the ratio seemed to be working out according to formula.

Bayard's Federal cavalry, screening Banks' dispositions south of Culpeper and watchfully reconnoitering the Rapidan crossings, had discovered the enemy in force as they crossed at Barnett's Ford on August 8. The Federal pickets had then retired along the Orange Court House Road and rejoined the main body of the cavalry on wooded high ground between the branches of Cedar Run, a mile west of the highway. Here Bayard covered the right flank of Crawford's infantry brigade, which was awaiting the enemy in a concealed position along the valley of Cedar Run, north of Cedar Mountain and protected from direct fire by high ground to its front and rear.

BANKS BLOCKS JACKSON'S ADVANCE

Acting upon the August 8 report of his cavalry, Pope sent forward Banks' corps of two divisions, under Brigadier Generals C. C. Augur and A. S. Williams, with orders to strengthen Crawford's defensive position and to block Jackson's advance until other reinforcements could be brought up. By noon of August 9 Banks was in position on a line running in a northwesterly direction on the high ground east of Cedar Run. The line, including the cavalry on the flanks, extended from Hudson's mill on the south, across the Orange Court House-Culpeper Road to a point somewhat more than a mile north of the pike, Augur's division on the left, Williams' on the right. Jackson's direct route to Culpeper was sealed off. He would now have to fight his way through or around his enemy if he still wished to take Culpeper as planned.

Shortly after noon the forward guns of Banks' artillery opened on the leading elements of Ewell's division as the Confederate advance guard came into view of the Federal batteries posted in front of their infantry on high ground south of Cedar Run, overlooking the highway. The word went back to Ewell and thence to Jackson. Both galloped ahead for a personal look at the terrain where the Union commander had apparently decided to contest Jackson's advance. It was partly wooded, rolling country with occasional fields of grain, but it was not possible at a glance to tell whether the Federals were there in strength. Their position would have to be developed and there was only one way to do that.

Jackson's strength, including Lawton's and Gregg's brigades guarding wagon trains, totaled some 24,000 combat effectives.

If the Union troops in his front were only a part, or even the full strength of Banks' corps, Jackson's initial target, he felt confident of his superiority. Just to make certain, however, and because it was still early in the afternoon, he decided to wait for A. P. Hill's division to come up before launching an attack.

The obvious key to the battlefield, Cedar Mountain, loomed to the right less than a mile from the highway. Ewell was directed to place his batteries on the mountain and his infantry initially on its northern shoulder supporting the guns. Winder was assigned a position directly to the front, along the Culpeper road and on Ewell's left. When Hill's division came up it would form a second line in the rear of Winder.

As the troop deployment proceeded, the Federal guns reopened, firing intermittently whenever the enemy exposed themselves as they moved from column into successive lines or crossed open country within the vision of the alert Union gunners. Development for action of over 20,000 men, marching on one road in a single column seven miles or more long, would take several hours of intense effort. In the process, the Confederate artillery, moving rapidly into firing position, was given the task of neutralizing the Union guns and discouraging any tendency on the part of the Blue infantry to launch an attack that might disrupt Jackson's buildup.

As the opposing forces completed their development for action, the two Federal divisions of Banks' corps, five brigades in all, were aligned along Cedar Run for a distance of two miles, with Bayard's cavalry (less one regiment near Hudson's mill) covering Gordon's right flank brigade. Jackson's three divisions contained twelve infantry brigades, two additional brigades having been left at Robertson's River, two miles in the rear, to guard the trains. They were deployed from the northern tip of Cedar Mountain, on the right, to the Culpeper Road, inclusive, on the left. The divisions of Winder and A. P. Hill, on the left, one behind the other, would be prepared to attack in depth, while two of Ewell's brigades would deny to the enemy the important bastion of Cedar Mountain on the right.

20,000 AGAINST 8,000

With A. P. Hill on hand, Jackson would have 20,000 muskets, Banks only 8,000, the odds greatly favoring the Confederates, unless Union reinforcements should be quickly supplied to achieve a balance. Ricketts' division of McDowell's corps, three miles away, had not yet been ordered forward, and was not under Banks' command. King's division of the same corps was not even in the picture. Sigel's corps, arriving belatedly at Culpeper without rations, could not be counted on till August 10.

Banks was an old opponent of Jackson's, who had suffered more than one humiliation at Stonewall's hands during the Shenandoah Valley fighting. It is not inconceivable that he envisaged at Cedar Mountain an opportunity to turn the tables on the wily fox by attacking quickly before Jackson could get all his troops to the field. Thus he could restore a reputation which had been somewhat tarnished by the Valley defeats. But his close-in infantry scouting from the Cedar Run position was ineffective. While Bayard's cavalry had reported the crossing in force of Confederate troops at the Rapidan, his pickets had been driven back, while Jackson's horsemen evidently did a thorough job of counterreconnaissance as the Gray infantry column advanced. As a result, Banks was simply guessing at the strength of his opponent and he guessed wrong.

Pope's instructions had been perfectly clear and unequivocal; Banks was ordered only to put his two divisions in a posture of defense to block the enemy advance. The last thing Pope wanted was to bring on a general engagement with inferior forces, the outcome of which could easily be that his separated corps would be defeated in detail.

Jackson's advance from the Rapidan, lacking the element of surprise, caused no consternation in the Union ranks. Banks, an aggressive general, welcomed another opportunity to try his luck against his heretofore victorious opponent. He would briefly follow orders and allow the enemy to commit the first overt act, but he had no intention of staying permanently on the defensive if an opportunity should present itself to make an active defense, which to the military means simply to go over to the offensive as soon as it appears profitable to do so.

Early's brigade of Ewell's division, leading the long column as advance guard, and Taliaferro's of Winder's undersized division, edged forward under cover toward the enemy position as soon as the two divisions had completed their deployment about 3 o'clock. They advanced cautiously, putting out skirmishers and taking plenty of time to allow Powell Hill's 12,000-man division to close up in reserve and assure ample support for a decisive attack.

BANKS GUESSES WRONG

Now, at 2:25 P.M. on the 9th, Banks sent Pope a message that revealed a faulty evaluation of Jackson's intentions:

> *General Williams' division has taken position on the right of the pike, the right on a heavy body of woods. General Augur on the left, his left resting on a mountain occupied by his skirmishers. He will soon be in position. The enemy shows his cavalry (which is strong) ostentatiously. No infantry seen and not much artillery. Woods on left said to be full of troops. A visit to the front does not impress that the enemy intends immediate attack; he seems, however, to be taking positions.*

Following the dispatch of the foregoing, an hour and a half passed while nothing much happened that would be likely to cause Banks to revise his estimate. The main bodies of both forces were concealed from the other by dense woods and folds in the ground, as the opposing troops disposed themselves under cover.

The afternoon was pretty well advanced when the opening shots of the infantry skirmishers were pressed off. Banks, having made up his mind that the Confederates were not strong enough to take the initiative, now persuaded himself that his orders were sufficiently discretionary to permit him to take the offensive. He informed Pope of the developments:

> *4:50 P.M.—About 4 o'clock shots were exchanged by the skirmishers. Artillery opened fire on both sides in a few minutes. One regiment of rebel infantry advancing now deployed in front as skirmishers. I have ordered a regiment on the right, Williams' division, to meet them, and one from the left, Augur to advance on the left and in front.*
>
> *5 P.M.—They are now approaching each other.*

The Federal line overlapped the left of the Confederate, with dense woods extending westwardly and affording an opportunity for the Blue to mass troops without the knowledge of the Confederates. That flank was vulnerable; therefore Jackson, with his quick eye for tactical details, ordered the left flank brigade of Lieutenant Colonel Garnett to be on the alert and to ask for reinforcements at that point.

By 5 o'clock the artillery duel was in full swing. Jackson had stretched out for a rest on the porch of a convenient farmhouse, awaiting the arrival of A. P. Hill before launching a coordinated attack. The booming of the guns, heard in Culpeper, became so loud and continuous that General Pope, despite the optimistic earlier messages of corps commander Banks from up front, drew his own conclusions and sent word to Ricketts' division of McDowell's corps to move at once to Banks' support. Although Ricketts had also heard the firing, and was less than three miles distant, he did not reach the field until 7 P.M., by which time the fighting was over. It would seem that this unit wasn't overly anxious to participate in Banks' affray.

35

THE MEETING ENGAGEMENT

Early initially had been to the left of the Culpeper Road, but by 5 o'clock he had moved east of it into the cornfield. Winder's three brigades were in the woods to the left of the pike, two of them being in line parallel to it and facing east. Apparently there were some incipient plans for attacking across the front of Early to capture some Federal artillery which was exposed to a swift advance. About this time the two Federal divisions, less Greene's brigade of Augur's division, which remained in place, were launched in an advance which converged slightly on Early and Winder. Garnett, commanding Winder's leading brigade, saw some of the Federal line in motion, and sent word to the division commander. A courier galloped up to Jackson to report trouble on the left. Winder had been mortally wounded by a direct hit from a Federal gun before he could act on Jackson's warning to Garnett to strengthen his left. In the resultant confusion, with the division commander out of action, an aggressive Union brigade, Crawford's, attacking Garnett from front and flank in a converging drive, had broken through and was exultantly driving before them two of Garnett's regiments.

JACKSON'S LEFT DRIVEN BACK

These serious reverses on Jackson's left occurred at about the time Taliaferro was taking over command of Winder's division, the sequence of events being as follows: The Stonewall Brigade, under Colonel Charles Ronald, had been formed at right angles to the other two, but was a hundred yards or more deep in the woods and not in close contact on its right flank with neighboring units. When the Federal advance was first observed, Taliaferro quickly sent word to Ronald to advance straight forward toward the wheatfield to meet the enemy. Ronald did so, but his lines reached this clearing just in time to receive a volley in the face from Crawford's oncoming regiments. The Stonewall Brigade broke, and (according to Gen. Branch) streamed rearward uttering loud cries of panic. Crawford's regiments, in hot pursuit, arrived at the east edge of the woods, about where the Tenth Maine monument now stands, which put them on the rear and flank of Taliaferro's other two brigades. The latter were still parallel to the road and at that moment were being assailed by Augur's right brigade, which was turning Early's left. Crawford delivered heavy fire into the backs of Garnett's and A. G. Taliaferro's men. The Confederate officers tried to face their rear ranks about, but the commands could not be heard. In a few moments these two brigades also broke and began to stream to the rear. A fine disaster was in the making. It began to appear that Banks' judgment was about to be vindicated.

The news of Winder's serious wound (he died a few hours later) and the accelerated tempo of artillery fire was, however, bringing Jackson himself at an extended gallop to the scene of action.

The turning point of the battle had now arrived. Banks' drive had lost its initial momentum. His units had expended most of their ammunition, and no provision had been made for a corps reserve, with which to deliver the final, knockout punch. So for a few minutes there was this general wild melee of Union and Confederate soldiers, locked in close combat, in the edge of the woods, in the cornfield, and between the road and the clump of cedars. The fight could break either way.

This was the sight that met Jackson's eye as he arrived at the front. It was a part of Stonewalls' genius that he perceived instantly that the time had come, and this was the place, to strike a counterblow. He sent hasty orders to Ewell and Hill, then without waiting for his orders to filter down through command echelons, he galloped to where he knew his reserves were waiting.

The leading brigade, Branch's, of A. P. Hill's division, was resting in the woods and listening to a pep talk by the commander, who in civil life had been a congressman and was an accomplished orator. A few words from Jackson sent Branch and his men dashing to the front. As they hurried through the woods they encountered Ronald's fleeing men but did not falter, merely opening ranks to allow these remnants to continue rearward.

Branch's attack struck in the flank and rear those Federal troops who had nearly surrounded the brigades of Garnett and A. G. Taliaferro. His big regiments drove the bluecoats back toward the north, as Branch slanted off somewhat toward the right so that his advance crossed to the opposite side of the Culpeper road.

By 6 o'clock the battle was raging fiercely all over the field. Hill's Light Division had come up to give Jackson a combat edge of 2.5 to 1. The able combination of Jackson, Ewell, and Hill, despite Banks' early success in flanking the Confederate left, could scarcely lose this battle.

Taliaferro, an excellent general who had assumed command of Winder's division, persuaded Jackson to return to a more appropriate and less dangerous position, as he and Ewell reorganized their confused brigades and made ready for the coordinated attack that Jackson now ordered.

Banks' infantry had by this time all been committed, his only reserve being Bayard's cavalry, which was not strong enough to do much except harassment or pursuit. Gordon's brigade had followed Crawford's into action on the Federal right, while Greene's brigade held the left of the line in support of McGilvery's battery in standing off a possible attack by Trimble and Forno, seen descending Cedar Mountain. The Federal losses were heavy. Crawford had lost every one of his regimental commanders and most of his field officers in the swirling fight with Winder's division. Generals Augur, Geary, and Carroll were badly wounded and Brigade Commander Prince captured.

Jackson's overwhelming strength was now thrown into the battle with the inevitable result. Ewell was directed to attack the Federal left, while A. P. Hill and the remnants of Winder's division went after the Union right. Four of Hill's six large brigades (Field was in "support," Gregg was guarding trains), averaging over 2,000 men each, were sent charging forward in two directions. Branch, Archer, and Pender, with the first-named in the van, were given the mission of turning the enemy right flank, Thomas was sent to help Early's brigade of Ewell's division; Hill's remaining brigade, under Field, was told to form a supporting line in company with Sheffield's brigade of Taliaferro's reorganized remnants, in order to give depth to the attack.

A. P. Hill Saves the Day
The Confederates moved forward all along the line, as the Federals commenced to withdraw toward Cedar Run.

It was now A. P. Hill's turn to show the stuff of which he was made. Stripping off his jacket to reveal the flaming red shirt that was his badge of valor, and drawing his sword as Jackson had done before him, Hill jumped into the middle of the action and led his cheering brigades into the attack.

It was here at Cedar Mountain that Hill and his Light Division set the combat pattern that contributed so greatly to its reputation as a magnificent fighting division. The impetuosity and fearlessness of their leader was reflected in the attitude of the men in the ranks, who admired "little" Powell and would go anywhere that he told them. The Virginia cavalier, a handsome man and finished horseman, had in the few months since he received his second star forged a powerful shining weapon in the form of the Light Division, which even now was on its scrappy way to becoming the best in the entire Confederate service.

Jackson's march order for August 9 originally scheduled A. P. Hill's division to follow Ewell's division, but because of the mix-up at Orange Court House that morning, the Light Division followed Winder, which meant that it would be the last to get into the fight. What effect that may have had on the ardent spirits of the men can only be conjectured, but there was no doubt whatever that they were rarin' to go when they reached the battlefield, deployed rapidly, and hurled their weight of numbers and driving force into Jackson's well-timed, effective counterattack.

There was no stopping the fierce charge of Hill's brigades. The Federals wavered, recoiled, and retreated, unable to stem the avalanche of greatly superior numbers which the Light Division brought to bear against them. Hill's men delivered the knockout punch in short order and completed the pattern which was destined to be repeated again and again as the war progressed.

Jackson's superior strength was quickly felt all along the line. The Federal brigades were being steadily pressed from the front and turned on the flanks. Banks' artillery was hastily withdrawn as the victorious Southerners drove the Federals in every direction. In a vain but brave effort to cover the withdrawal of the guns and stay the Confederate advance, Bayard sent in a 164-man battalion of the 1st Pennsylvania Cavalry. They charged in a column of fours, parallel to the pike and into the spearhead of the Confederate counterattack. Crossfire from Branch's brigade and the remnants of Taliaferro's division emptied many saddles, but the impetus of the charge carried the unit inside the Confederate line. Only 71 men returned, but more must have been rounded up later, since Bayard reported only 61 casualties for his entire brigade.

JACKSON ATTEMPTS A PURSUIT

By 6:30 P.M. the battle was over, but Jackson as usual was determined to reap the fruits of his tactical victory. Having escaped a near disaster in the early stages, by personal intervention at the point of greatest danger his unerring instinct enabled him to turn the enemy's initial progress to his own advantage. He had wisely delayed his attack until his opponent had revealed his strength and position, and A. P. Hill's Light Division, larger than all the other Confederate troops combined, had reached the battlefield. Then it was that he threw everything he had at his weaker opponent. In an hour and a half nearly 4,000 men and officers on both sides were killed, wounded, captured, or missing, and Jackson's successful troops were crossing Cedar Run in pursuit of the retreating Federals.

Although Jackson, who rarely bestowed words of praise on any of his living officers either orally or in his brief reports, gave Powell Hill no credit for the Confederate success, the Light Division and Hill himself had the satisfaction of knowing that it was they who had tipped the scales at the psychological moment, a feat they would duplicate some weeks later at the Battle of Antietam, there again preventing a disaster to Confederate arms.

Jackson and Hill would both prove by their deeds, before meeting a soldier's death on the field of battle, that they were great leaders, courageous fighters, able tacticians, and dedicated patriots to the Southern cause. They would likewise demonstrate that no matter how bitter their official relationship, neither would permit personal animosity to influence his attitude toward the other during combat.

The opportunity was present after Cedar Mountain for Jackson to heal the breach first created between the two generals by the senior's unjustified criticism of Hill at Orange Court House, but it was not in the Jackson character to admit that he may have been a bit hasty in passing judgment on what only appeared to be a disregard of his orders on the part of Hill. Hill's determined and energetic efforts to wipe out the slur by proving himself and his division to an ungenerous superior was met by complete silence on Jackson's part. The latter's message to Lee said simply: "God blessed our arms with another victory," thus allowing the Commanding General to infer that with the help of Providence Stonewall Jackson had added another wreath to the laurels gained in the Valley. It was not until May 1863 that Jackson wrote his official report of the battle, in which the name A. P. Hill appears but once, in the following cryptic sentence: "As General Hill had arrived with his division, one of his brigades (General Thomas') was sent to Early and joined him in time to render efficient service." The heroically significant part played by Branch's brigade of Hill's division, together with the supporting efforts of Archer's and Pender's brigades, also of Hill's division, was factually recorded in the report, but the division commander himself might have been a mere spectator on the scene so far as any recognition by the corps commander was concerned.

On the other side, Pope's report on the Virginia Campaign, verbose as it was, at least handed out a few bouquets to those who served under him in the capacity of general officers. "General Banks' conduct at the battle of Cedar Mountain," wrote Pope, "was marked by great coolness, intrepidity and zeal." To which he added that "Generals Williams, Augur, Crawford, Greene, Geary, Carroll, and Prince, of Banks' Corps, have been already noticed for their gallant and distinguished conduct at Cedar Mountain."

The official reports after the battle showed total casualties of approximately 3,800 out of 28,000 engaged. Of these, 2,377 were Federal, 1,355 Confederate, although there is reason to doubt the numbers reported by the Southerners, who recorded only four men missing despite the panicked rout of Winder's two brigades in the early stages. The fighting along the pike had been the most vicious, and it was there that over half of all the casualties incurred. Crawford's Federal brigade (Williams' division) alone lost 867 men of 1,767 engaged, while Williams' other brigade under Gordon brought that division's total to 1,212. Augur's three brigades suffered 986 casualties.

Winder's Confederate division was the hardest hit on the other side, losing 707 men or close to 25% of those engaged, which exceeded by a good margin the combined losses of Hill and Ewell. The cavalry losses were negligible, 61 for Bayard and 19 for Robertson, most of the Federals falling in the final charge which Bayard launched late in the day, without effect on the outcome.

General Pope arrived with Ricketts' division of McDowell's corps as Banks' defeated troops were on their way back to their original position east of Cedar Run. The Federal withdrawal was made in good order as Pope took charge and disposed Ricketts' fresh troops on a strong position to dispute the Confederate follow-up, while Banks' depleted brigades were massed a short distance to Ricketts' rear in support.

As the Confederates cautiously pursued, with the heretofore unused brigades of Field and Stafford as the spearpoint, Ricketts' artillery opened, bringing Jackson's men to an abrupt halt. Darkness had fallen, Culpeper was still seven miles distant, and a cavalry patrol reported to Jackson that it had taken prisoners from Sigel's Federal corps. It was apparently not going to be easy sailing for the Jacksonians, but the general allowed the artillery duel to continue until almost midnight before deciding that the imponderables of the situation made it impracticable to advance further during the night. Orders were issued to bivouac in place. The Battle of Cedar Mountain had passed into history.

As a matter of fact, Sigel's corps *was* beginning to come up from Culpeper, having put away a good meal in the interim. Banks' corps had been rather badly used up, so Pope fed Sigel's men into the position occupied by Banks, sending the latter several miles to the rear to reorganize.

By daylight of August 10, Pope's Army of Virginia was pretty well concentrated except for King's division of McDowell's corps, still twenty miles away, and Buford's cavalry, which was at Madison Court House. Pope reported results to Halleck, claiming a victory, which must have surprised Banks and his defeated divisions when they heard about it. Nevertheless, and in spite of his tactical victory, Jackson had suffered a strategic set-back in failing to seize Culpeper as the first step toward defeating Pope before the latter could complete his concentration.

In retrospect, Banks' corps, 8,800 against 20,000, had done very well to stop Jackson, which was their primary mission. His troops had fought with bravery and determination. They had broken and routed Stonewall

Jackson's own vaunted division (under Winder) and had battled unceasingly until overwhelmed by vastly superior numbers. Yes, they could look back with pride on that engagement at Cedar Mountain, for in the Valley Jackson had repeatedly whipped them with much smaller forces, while here it took a preponderance of better than two to one in Jackson's favor to effect their defeat.

For two days the opposing armies rested within artillery distance of each other. Jackson had given up any intention of renewing the attack in the face of Pope's evident strength, but he was willing to accept battle again on his Cedar Mountain position if Pope should be interested. The intervening period was used to bury the dead and remove the wounded, after which, when it became apparent that Pope entertained no serious offensive measures, Jackson put his troops in motion to the south and returned to his former camps at Gordonsville.

CHAPTER 4

Lee's Campaign against Pope

THE ALARMED reaction of the North to the defeat of Pope's advance corps at Cedar Mountain confirmed the unhappy suspicion that the unpredictable Stonewall Jackson had done it again. His most recent battle had shown most of the earmarks of his "here he comes—there he goes" maneuvers in the Valley, which a few months earlier had made him a national figure and certainly the most feared of all the Confederate generals. With a somewhat larger force than he had in the Valley, but still greatly outnumbered by Pope's slowly concentrating army, Jackson had repeated his earlier successful tactics, moved to defeat his opponent in detail, and although balked in his hope of taking Culpeper, had managed to again whip Banks' two-division corps before fading back to his base at Gordonsville.

Nevertheless, Jackson's margin of victory this time had been slimmer than in his earlier battles, and he had failed to secure his strategic objective. Banks' Federals had waged a spirited fight, with dogged courage, and in the early stages had come very close to a victory. When Banks, attacking before A. P. Hill's division had completed its deployment, disregarded Pope's order to wage a strictly defensive engagement, he had 8,800 men against Jackson's at that time only slightly greater strength, represented by the divisions of Ewell and Winder. Had Banks' drive to outflank Jackson's left been strongly supported in depth, the Confederate confusion incident to the breakup of Winder's small division might easily have resulted in the rolling up of Ewell's line as well. It might then have been too late for Jackson and Hill in concert to repair the damage and launch their victorious counterattack.

The initial setback at Cedar Mountain failed to discourage Pope, who was still in an aggressive mood and anxious to proceed with his planned

44

offensive, now that his army was concentrated at Culpeper. The fact that two-thirds of Banks' corps had been rendered hors de combat for a period of weeks did not seem to be sufficient reason for postponement. Neither did a personal incident, with respect to which he chose conveniently to overlook the fact that he himself, contrary to his earlier bombastic pronouncement, had indeed "turned his back on the enemy" on the evening of the Battle of Cedar Mountain. That had occurred during the retreat of Banks' corps when Pope, arriving on the scene, personally ran into a hot spot east of Cedar Run at the very moment when Jackson's pursuing divisions were breathing down the necks of the retiring Federals. It was no place for an army commander to be if he wished to continue in that capacity, and Pope wisely chose discretion by participating in the retrograde movement.

It was Halleck who held Pope in check after Cedar Mountain, and it would appear that Halleck's judgment was sound. To the General-in-Chief it was more important that the armies of McClellan and Pope be closed to supporting distance of one another than that Pope should engage in a unilateral adventure by lashing out at Jackson immediately. Quite possibly, in directing Pope not to advance beyond the Rapidan at this stage, Halleck saved him from falling into a trap of Jackson's devising, for Jackson wrote Lee that he was falling back to Gordonsville in the belief that Pope would follow, and that he hoped to meet him on a position of his own choosing, with reinforcements at hand. Since Longstreet's corps was now on the way to Gordonsville from Richmond, an incautious advance by Pope could have brought about his defeat somewhat further south than the area where it actually did occur a few weeks later.

On August 15, six days after the Battle of Cedar Mountain, Pope's army was increased to almost 52,000 men by the arrival of Major General Jesse L. Reno at the head of 8,000 men comprising two divisions of Burnside's force which had just come up from Fredericksburg. Reconnaissance by Confederate cavalry located the Federal divisions resting in positions northeast of Cedar Mountain, their Rapidan River outpost line extending from Rapidan Station on the right to Somerville Ford on the left, a distance of eight to ten miles.

LEE TAKES COMMAND

On that same day General Lee in person arrived at Gordonsville and summoned his chief lieutenants, Longstreet, Jackson, and Stuart, to a conference at headquarters. Longstreet's corps of over 25,000 men had just completed a two-day rail trip from Richmond. Stuart traveled by train to make it on time, while Fitz Lee's cavalry brigade took to the road to join the main army assembled at Gordonsville. All that remained of Lee's army in the Richmond area were the divisions of D. H. Hill and Lafayette McLaws and Wade Hampton's brigade of cavalry, left behind to keep a watchful eye on the Army of the Potomac, then on its way northward by way of Fortress Monroe.

With Lee's arrival on the scene and the junction of his two wings, the Army of Northern Virginia was slightly superior to Pope numerically. The preliminaries were over and the stage set for the main event, but Lee would have to act quickly, if he was to crush the opposing force before additional reinforcements should reach Pope. He outlined his plan of action for the benefit of his lieutenants. From the concealed position of his army behind Clark's Mountain, on the south side of the Rapidan opposite Pope's left flank, he would cross at Somerville Ford, swing around the enemy left and sever Pope's lifeline to Washington. Meanwhile Stuart's cavalry would cross farther to the east, move rapidly to Rappahannock Station, and cut the railroad line northeast of Culpeper by destroying the bridge on Pope's retreat route.

However, it did not work out that way. As so often happens in war, a too-wordy order, sent by Stuart to Fitzhugh Lee, initiated a chain of events that, with overtones of comedy, served again to postpone the day of evil destiny for the braggart who was so sure of himself that he advised his army to forget about their rear. Pope in his delusion was acting much like the overconfident big-league pitcher who in the ninth inning waves his outfielders to the bench as he prepares to strike out the last batter of the opposing team.

The plan was for Stuart's cavalry to precede the forward movement of the infantry-artillery team, Robertson's brigade cooperating with Jackson, Fitz Lee's with Longstreet. The cavalry was directed to move out August 18. Fitz Lee was to meet Stuart at Raccoon Ford, but Stuart's orders neglected to impress on him the urgency of the time factor and it was because of that oversight that the first Confederate plan failed to materialize.

Fitz Lee's brigade had ahead of it almost a thirty-mile march if made directly from the North Anna River at Davenport's Ford to Raccoon Ford on the Rapidan. His wagons had already been sent ahead to Louisa Court House, en route to the original assembly point at Gordonsville, and it was imperative that he replenish his rations before going after Pope. Instead of marching directly to Raccoon Ford, he took the long way around to fill his men's empty haversacks, adding thirty more miles to the trip. Consequently he was out of touch with his commander, Jeb Stuart, for twenty-four hours.

POPE EFFECTS A LIMITED WITHDRAWAL

Pisgah Church, the intermediate rendezvous to which Lee moved his army from Gordonsville as the first stage of his offensive, lies in the shadow of a high hill known as Clark's Mountain, from which eminence it is possible to observe the countryside for many miles to the north. From the Confederate lookout on top of the mountain the Federal camps lay in full view, and, since all the topographical features of the impending battlefield could be studied, the signal station was a priceless adjunct to the mapping genius of Jackson's chief topographical engineer, Captain Jed Hotchkiss.

In Washington General Halleck, seriously perturbed by McClellan's uncooperativeness and snail-like pace in executing the order to transfer his army to Aquia Creek for the planned junction with Pope's army, was prophetically fearful that Lee would attack and overwhelm Pope before McClellan should arrive. On August 16 he telegraphed Pope not to cross the Rapidan but instead to take position north of the Rappahannock, where he could be more easily reinforced.

Although Halleck didn't know it at the time, the captured letter from Lee to Stuart had given Pope an even more compelling reason to fall back to the north bank of the Rappahannock. He now knew for a fact that the bulk of Lee's army confronted him, and, it was reasonable to assume, with a superior force. In pleasant contrast to McClellan, however, Pope did not offer an advance alibi by magnifying the enemy strength beyond all reason.

Nevertheless it was time to pull back, even though a retrograde movement would violate Pope's earlier assurance to his men that there would be no turning of the backs of *his* army to the enemy. The trouble was that the position of the army was strategically as well as tactically unsound, between two rivers, the Rapidan and the Rappahannock, both of which were in the habit of rising rapidly after heavy rains and becoming unfordable in a matter of hours. Nor could there be any further doubt that Lee's purpose was to move to eliminate Pope before the Army of the Potomac could (or would) arrive.

Discretion was clearly indicated for the moment, so Pope shifted his army to the rear the few miles that were necessary, moving by corps echelon on the 18th and 19th of August. By midnight on August 20 there were no Federal troops between the two rivers except a few cavalry regiments and one small infantry support. Pope's new line extended along the north bank of the Rappahannock, with his right near Sulphur Springs and his left, except for part of Buford's cavalry, near Kellys Ford.

The Confederates followed closely on the heels of the retiring Federals, Lee's entire force moving up to the Rappahannock and feeling out Pope's new position. Finding it strongly posted at all the nearby crossings, Lee discarded his first plan and proceeded to develop a new one, as the 21st, then the 22nd of August passed with continuous artillery fire being exchanged along a length of seven or eight miles between the opposing armies on either side of the river.

Lee and Pope were acutely conscious of the passage of time, although for different reasons, for the minds of both were centered on the image of McClellan's Army of the Potomac. On the 21st, Pope had word from Halleck that if he could hold Lee south of the Rappahannock for two more, days he would receive sufficient reinforcements to enable him to resume the offensive. By the night of August 22 General Reno's division, followed by the Pennsylvania Reserves under Brigadier General John F. Reynolds, arrived on Pope's left, in the Kellys Ford area. On the 25th all of Reno's corps was present; and most of Heintzelman's corps (Hooker's and Kearny's divisions) had detrained near Warrenton

Junction. Porter's corps had marched up the Rappahannock to Deep Creek, thirteen miles south of Bealeton. Other divisions of McClellan's army were also on the way, although not very rapidly, as Pope waited for Lee's blow to fall.

On the south side of the Rappahannock, with its many fords, Robert E. Lee was concocting a new scheme to get at Pope. He had already used five days in probing for a soft spot in Pope's defensive armor, but which he had failed to find in that area where he had originally planned to operate around the Union left flank. Because of some heavy rains upriver the stream was now fordable only with difficulty; something had to be done quickly before it was too late. Stuart's cavalry, presently engaged in one of their circuitous rides around the Union army, was looked to for the latest intelligence.

On August 19, after Fitz Lee had arrived, twenty-four hours later than expected and with men and horses jaded by their sixty-mile march, Stuart had moved part of his cavalry to Mitchell's Ford, where he received word from Lee that Pope's army had withdrawn from the Rapidan. Lee had personally climbed Clark's Mountain, that high hill from which the Confederates were able to look down on Pope's camps, and had seen the Blue columns, or at least the tell-tale evidence of marching troops in the long dust clouds, as Pope prudently withdrew from the pocket between the Rapidan and Rappahannock.

On the 20th of August numerous skirmishes occurred between Stuart's cavalry and the Blue squadrons of Buford and Bayard which were covering Pope's withdrawal. On that day an otherwise insignificant railroad building named Brandy Station gained prominence for the first time in the war, when Robertson's Confederate cavalry brigade tangled with Bayard's Union cavalry and drove them back across the Rappahannock after some spirited sparring. Brandy Station was a name that would make headlines in 1863, after Chancellorsville, when Pleasonton's Federal cavalry would for the first time treat Stuart's cavalry with unaccustomed roughness; but the Southerners had it pretty much their own way on this first of several occasions when the important crossroad of Brandy Station would provide the stage for cavalry combat.

49

STUART'S RAID ON POPE'S HEADQUARTERS

For the next two days Lee's infantry remained under cover while his cavalry felt Pope's line across the Rappahannock. Stuart gathered enough information to convince him that the Federals had no discoverable soft spots. On August 22 he asked Lee's permission to ride around the enemy right flank to cut the railroad line to Washington in Pope's rear and secure information that might be useful to the Commanding General in furthering his offensive plans.

With Lee's approval, Stuart at once gathered up Fitz Lee's and Robertson's brigades and started out with 2,000 troopers and several of Pelham's guns, leaving only two regiments on the south bank of the river. Crossing at Waterloo Bridge, the column rode swiftly to Warrenton and there took the road to the east, heading for Catlett's Station, on the line of the Orange and Alexandria Railroad. Stuart was now well to the rear of the Union army and, happy thought, in an excellent position to retaliate for the humiliating blow to his pride in the undignified loss of his hat and papers.

Luck plays an important role in war and some generals have enjoyed more than their fair share. On close study, however, it will be found that the Lady confers her favors on those who by energy and boldness put themselves in the way of opportunity. Jeb Stuart belonged in this category. Pope did not. On the contrary, Pope's braggadocio, his harsh measures toward the Virginia country folk, and such inept and unmilitary policies as leaving his rear to take care of itself combined to make him one of the most universally despised Northern generals ever to move into Confederate territory.

In one respect only was Pope fortunate at the time of Stuart's raid on Catlett's Station. He was away from his headquarters when the jaunty Confederate and his two thousand cavalrymen paid him that surprise visit on the night of August 22. It was raining hard as Stuart and his brigades moved in from the west and prepared to wreak havoc on the supply trains of the Army of Virginia. They picked up a Negro "contraband" whose eyes rolled when he learned what was afoot, but who lost no time in telling all that he knew, including the exciting intelligence that the raiders were within shouting distance of Pope's headquarters and his trains were guarded by a single regiment of infantry.

The Federal camp, not expecting Confederate visitors, was lit up like an amusement park on a summer evening. Halting outside the lighted area, Stuart assigned missions: Fitz Lee's brigade to raid the camps and inflict all the damage possible; Engineer Captain Blackford with one of the regiments as escort to destroy the railroad bridge; Robertson's brigade to stand by in reserve. All outfits were to start simultaneously at the bugle call, whereupon the Rebel yell was to be sounded with such a roar as to scare the wits out of the completely unsuspecting Federal rear echelon.

The attack was literally a howling success. Even in daylight, with advance warning, two thousand wildly yelling troopers at the gallop, fanning out in every direction and disregarding all obstacles, can be a fearful thunderbolt. To receive such a greeting in a place of fancied security, on a dark and rainy night, when some of the officers were just sitting down to a late supper, was adding insult to injury and applying almost unfairly the important principle of surprise.

The affair went off beautifully for the Confederates, disastrously for the Federals. The Pennsylvania Bucktail Regiment, guarding the depot, was quickly overcome. Hundreds of mules, riding horses, and prisoners were rounded up, including several of Pope's staff officers. But the most rewarding of all the booty was the capture of Pope's complete file of orders and correspondence, plus his horses, tent equipage, and a dress uniform. The latter was presented to Stuart, who later paraded it to the delighted troops and then shipped it off to Richmond, where it was publicly displayed in the State Library as mute testimony to the unwisdom of Northern boastfulness. No wonder that Jeb Stuart, for whom such feats as this were all in the day's work, was the dashing idol of the South.

The success of Stuart's massive raid was tempered by only one failure, blame for which did not rest with the Confederate cavalry. In the course of the destruction of the Union depot and camps a terrific thunderstorm broke on the wild scene, quenching all the fires that had been kindled and wetting down the railroad bridge so effectively that it refused to burn. Axes were applied, but as the rifle fire of defending Union infantry became increasingly punishing, the attempt was finally abandoned.

About the time the depot was captured, Captain Blackford heard the sound of an engine starting. A train was pulling out for Washington.

The engineer refused to halt the train, whereupon Blackford, his horse trotting alongside the moving engine, fired into the cab and prepared to leap aboard to execute his own order. At that moment his horse stumbled, pitching him to the ground, as the train went merrily on its way. Blackford reported that it had proceeded out of control, although the skeptical reader may be justified in wondering just how the captain could be so sure that his pistol shot had found its mark, in view of the circumstances.

Just before daylight of August 23rd, with a nearby creek rising rapidly and threatening to interfere with the withdrawal of his column, Stuart gave the order to retire. Recall and assembly were sounded, individual troopers rejoined their outfits, and with more than 300 prisoners and a gratifyingly large number of captured horses, mules, and wagons loaded with loot, the heavily encumbered brigade headed back for Waterloo Bridge via Warrenton.

A mounted messenger galloped ahead with the invaluable intelligence found among Pope's papers. Lee would soon know almost as much about the Federal plans and the expected reinforcements from Aquia Creek as Pope himself. Stuart had certainly turned the tables, with his sixty-mile march and humiliating descent on Pope's rear area.

And how, one may ask, did the absent General Pope react when the news reached him? Strangely enough, his official report estimated the raiders at a strength of only 300 troopers, while berating the Blue defenders for a disgraceful exhibition. It would be only natural for those caught napping to exaggerate the numbers of the invading horde of horsemen. The explanation might be that Pope, realizing the ridiculous position in which he found himself, tried to minimize Stuart's achievement in riding around the Union army with a large body of troops and without opposition or even hindrance.

At this stage there existed a situation most unusual in war. The opposing army commanders were in possession of each other's plans and orders. Both Lee and Pope intended to take the offensive, the difference being that one was ready while the other was not. Lee held the initiative and was sparring for an opening. But he was already behind in his schedule, in which the time element was all-important if he was to succeed in crushing Pope before McClellan should arrive on the Rappahannock.

The Stuart raid served a double purpose in throwing Pope badly off mental balance and in furnishing Lee with solid facts upon which he could act with confidence. He now knew Pope's dispositions, his strength, and how he planned to employ that strength. Even more vitally important, Lee knew that of McClellan's army, both Porter's Fifth and Burnside's Ninth Corps were on hand, with others coming up rapidly. With over 70,000 men already on the line of the Rappahannock or within supporting distance, and the remainder of McClellan's divisions ordered to his support, Pope would soon have 150,000 men under his command or within call. Against that large army Lee could count 52,000 men present, with only D. H. Hill's and McLaws' divisions and Hampton's cavalry brigade as reinforcements when they would arrive from Richmond. It was now or never, and Lee lost no more time in making his decision.

The retrograde movement of Pope's Army of Virginia from the Rapidan to the Rappahannock barrier, strategically sound and executed with little interference from the Confederates, served but to postpone the day of retribution which would soon reveal John Pope as an opponent no more capable of matching wits with the master, Robert E. Lee, than the succession of Union generals who preceded and would follow him in army command—until Grant.

Pope was now definitely on the defensive, dancing to the tune that Lee would choose to play. Nevertheless, his new line along the high east bank of the Rappahannock was skillfully constructed, with artillery and infantry strongly posted to deny to the Confederates the innumerable fords along the entire front. It should also be noted that he had successfully stalled off Lee's offensive probings almost—but not quite—long enough to enable McClellan, never known to move rapidly, to transfer the divisions of his Army of the Potomac from Harrison's Landing by the roundabout water route to Aquia Creek Landing and to dispatch several corps thence to the Rappahannock country.

"Dispute every inch of ground and fight like the devil till we can reinforce you. Forty-eight hours more and we can make you strong enough" wired the distraught Halleck on August 21. To which Pope, still confident, replied that he need not worry; "I think no impression can be made on me for some days."

53

That was what Pope thought, but Lee and Jeb Stuart had different ideas. The Catlett's Station raid was of course not the kind of "impression" Pope had in mind; still it was an unpleasant and fateful one that promised greater repercussions than the ordinary hit-and-run cavalry foray. The unfortunately loquacious general from the west again appeared to have said the wrong thing.

While Stuart was riding around Pope on August 22-23, Jackson, acting on Lee's instructions, was sideslipping to the west, feeling for a place to cross the river. Lee had made up his mind that Pope could not be whipped in his present strong position; main reliance would have to be placed on a maneuvering mass, capable of luring the opposing army out of position and strong enough to fight a pitched battle if it came to that. He reasoned that it would be a mistake to so maneuver that Pope could fall back in the direction of Fredericksburg, because there would be no fruits to gather from that tree; on the contrary, it would merely serve to unite Pope and McClellan, the very thing he was determined to prevent.

JUBAL EARLY HAS A ROUGH TIME

Unable to find any evidence of weakness on the left of Pope's line along the Rappahannock, Lee's efforts met similar frustration on the Federal right. Every ford that Stuart's cavalry investigated found alert Federal horsemen screening concentrations of infantry and artillery, evidence that Pope knew something about war of position and had done an efficient job of prevention.

At Beverly Ford Stuart had gone beyond mere reconnaissance and light skirmishing. Under a heavy Confederate artillery bombardment, his squadrons drove back a regiment of infantry and an artillery battery and immediately fanned out patrols in all directions to examine the terrain. Finding it unsuitable for an attack, and pressed by a large infantry force, Stuart withdrew.

Under continuing pressure from Lee to locate a feasible crossing further up the river, Jackson and Stuart continued their progressive movements to the northwest. Reaching the ruined bridge at Sulphur Springs, they at last found one ford that appeared to be undefended. The leading regiment dashed across and secured a bridgehead, while Early's brigade with two batteries crossed a short distance below and established a position on a ridge near the river's edge.

Night had now fallen and a heavy rain caused the river to rise rapidly as it invariably did. Jackson decided to bivouac his main body on the west shore, but the next morning sent Lawton's brigade to reinforce Early before the swollen river made further crossing impracticable. Although Jackson put pioneers to work rebuilding the bridge, while Longstreet's artillery kept up a brisk fire all along the line to divert attention, Early's isolated detachment would have been lucky to escape capture or destruction if the Federals had been sufficiently enterprising to discover the extent of its predicament. Jackson's calculated risk at Early's expense paid off, however, for no real attack was made by the Federals at any time.

Sigel's corps, further down the river in the direction of Freeman's Ford, could have made it mighty uncomfortable for Early, but his people had just finished an artillery duel with Longstreet's batteries and Sigel's thoughts were centered on defensive tactics at the moment. The crossing by the Confederates at Sulphur Springs conjured up in Sigel's mind the dire possibility that Lee's entire army might be on the move. Whereupon he informed Pope that his right flank was in danger of being turned and he thought it wise to withdraw his troops to a more secure location. Pope's reply was to order Sigel to hold his ground and let the enemy develop in the direction of Warrenton, whereupon Pope would come down on Lee and his whole army.

Early on the morning of August 23 Pope ordered Sigel to advance with his whole corps on Sulphur Springs "to attack and beat the enemy." Banks' corps was ordered to follow and support Sigel, The former was prompt to comply, but the latter was not, with the result that both corps became intermingled on the same road. Sigel's trains interfered with the troop movement, and things generally got pretty thoroughly fouled up. Running into some Confederate skirmishers near a small creek about half a mile from the Rappahannock, the advance regiment of Sigel's corps opened fire; whereupon the Confederates crossed the creek and burned the bridge. Apparently that was all Sigel needed to call a halt, so he bivouacked his entire corps about the middle of the afternoon and ordered the bridge repaired. This important undertaking required the rest of the day, during which the corps made no further effort to comply with Pope's order to "attack and beat the enemy."

In retrospect, the situation had its humorous aspects, even though Early's troops, apparently abandoned to their fate, did not see anything funny about it. The fact was that both Early and Sigel felt themselves to be in a dangerous spot and were anxious to get away from there. The difference was that Early had good reason to be nervous, while Sigel acted the timid soul when he could have gained an easy success if he had shown even a slight dash of the offensive spirit.

Pope reported the affair at Sulphur Springs as a determined attempt by Lee to cross a large force, which he said had been effectively repulsed. Apparently the Federal general had failed utterly to divine the intentions of his able opponent or even to consider the real significance of Jackson's maneuvers along the river.

Satisfied with the results secured, and knowing by that time that Stuart's raid on Pope's rear had been successfully concluded, Jackson relieved the tension of Early's force and permitted it, on the morning of the 24th of August, to return to the main body and the welcome food which had been denied them for most of the period of their isolation.

Lee "Shoots the Works"

The solution to the vexing problem of how to get at Pope appeared to Lee to be a wide flanking movement around the Federal right, well to the west of but parallel to the vulnerable Orange and Alexandria Railroad, the sensitive supply line to Alexandria upon which Pope had to depend for the necessities of military life. If Lee could thus draw him out of his present position into an instinctive reaction to protect his communications, Pope would have to march away from the oncoming Army of the Potomac and an opportunity might present itself to defeat him in the open.

It was a typically bold plan, the kind that appealed to Lee. It was also the sort of thing that delighted Jackson, whose sharp eyes glinted when the scheme was explained to him. Jackson wanted to start early the following morning, but the more stolid and logistically minded Longstreet preferred to wait another day, to allow time for working out the details and provisioning the troops. Lee agreed with Longstreet.

The risks were great and he knew it. Only a general of Lee's caliber would venture to separate the two wings of his army by a gap of fifty miles, with a hostile army between them. Pope now outnumbered him by a considerable margin that would in all likelihood be widened at an increasing rate from day to day as more of McClellan's divisions landed at Aquia and moved inland to join Pope. Lee could of course yield the initiative and retire in the direction of Richmond, or he could attack Pope at once and put everything to the test in a knockdown encounter. Neither idea appealed to him. The plan that he did adopt was the only one that offered promise of decisive results, for his low opinion of Pope's ability, despite the defensive skill the Northern general had shown during the past few days, was such that he did not consider Pope's immediate strength superiority, or the greater risk of dividing his own army, to be particularly significant or dangerous.

Jackson and Longstreet were equally content with the roles assigned their respective corps. The former, with Stuart's cavalry to follow on the second day as a covering force, would on August 25 lead his three divisions, some 24,000 men, in one of his amazingly fast marches in a wide swing well beyond and around the Federal right, via Amissville, Salem, Thoroughfare Gap, and Gainesville, to Bristoe Station, where his force would cut the main railroad and, with luck, destroy the huge Federal warehouses at Manassas Junction.

Lee and Longstreet, with the rest of the army, about 28,000 men, would temporarily stay where they were, to hold Pope to the line of the Rappahannock with Old Pete's four divisions, demonstrating to the extent necessary to persuade the Federals that the Army of Northern Virginia was staying put. The greatest risk was that Pope would learn what was going on and act offensively to deal with Longstreet while Jackson was moving away from Lee. That however was a chance that had to be taken.

The monotonous, unavailing search for an unprotected crossing, as Jackson's men sideslipped to the left and the Federals kept pace with them on the opposite bank of the Rappahannock, was now over. The next move would be more to their liking as they moved into familiar country in one of those unfettered swinging half-lopes which in the Valley had earned for them the cherished designation of Jackson's "foot-cavalry."

On Sunday, August 24, Lee rode out to Jackson's command post at Jeffersonton to give him final instructions and discuss the route, the assembly area for the two wings of the army, and other important details. It was all clear in Lee's mind but he wanted to make certain that Jackson thoroughly understood his plan. Everything must go off like clockwork. Lee was so supremely confident on that score that he informed Jackson the two wings of the army would reunite in the vicinity of Manassas after, not if and when, Pope had been separated from the reinforcements marching to join him. Jackson was specifically told to march north behind the sheltering screen of the Bull Run Mountains to avoid detection, but not to bring on a general engagement. Lee was placing his money on the horse *Maneuver*, and Jackson was his jockey.

Jackson immediately made preparations to march at first dawn Monday, August 25, the troops stripped down to bare essentials, including a small amount of cooked rations. The men would not even carry their knapsacks. Wagon trains were to be limited to ammunition carts and ambulances. Live cattle would accompany the column, other items of food to be gathered from the countryside as they marched.

Jackson's rigorous rules for road marches placed him in a class by himself and way ahead of his time. McClellan considered ten miles a day to be a creditable performance, but "Little Mac" was the antithesis of Stonewall in more respects than one.

Longstreet's guns replaced Jackson's along the Rappahannock under cover of darkness. Early Monday morning Jackson's column moved silently and swiftly up river to an unguarded crossing at Hinson's Mills, five miles west of Waterloo Bridge, where the troops splashed across on the first leg of an adventure that promised plenty of excitement. Meantime, Longstreet kept the Federals in place by demonstrating along the Rappahannock. His artillery played intermittently on the enemy positions across the river, Longstreet's infantry showed itself to the Federals, and Stuart's cavalry skirmished at the important fords.

Although Jackson's column circled widely around Pope's right, Federal observers noted the marching troops. Pope's headquarters, however, interpreted the information to mean that it was a move to the Shenandoah Valley on the part of a flanking column and that Lee's main body would shortly follow, headed for Front Royal. No troops were sent by Pope to dispute the march, not even a cavalry detachment to discover for certain whether the estimate was correct. All he did, apparently, was to speculate on what the move might mean.

By Monday evening Jackson's marching men had put twenty-five dusty miles behind them and halted for the night at Salem, six miles west of Thoroughfare Gap on the Manassas Gap Railroad. At 9 P.M. Pope wired Halleck his opinion, as already stated, adding that he would send a reconnaissance party across the river Tuesday morning to find out whether the main body of Lee's army had in fact moved out. Most of the message, however, was devoted to a long dissertation on the low strength and poor condition of Banks' corps, the fact that Sigel was of no use to him and should be replaced, and that McDowell's corps was the only one that he could depend on to render effective service. It was obvious that Pope was rattled and devoting more attention to worrying about the condition of his army than he was to the pressing problem of how to deal effectively with the Army of Northern Virginia.

True to form, Jackson's men were not told where they were going, as their leader rode tirelessly up and down the column urging it forward. The general opinion was that they were returning to the Valley, a pleasant prospect indeed. That was also Pope's opinion, which made it almost unanimous. On Tuesday morning, August 26, however, as they resumed the march and passed through Salem, the head of the column turned to the right and headed for Thoroughfare Gap. That killed the Valley rumor, but it made no difference to the foot cavalry as they slogged along with complete confidence that "Old Jack" knew what he was doing.

POPE'S REAR AGAIN EXPOSED

Marching straight for Bristoe Station, his initial objective, Jackson's column passed through Gainesville, where Stuart caught up with him, and from there preceded and paralleled the infantry line of march as a covering screen until Bristoe Station hove in sight. The sun was setting when the advance elements reached their destination, Jackson's troops having marched fifty miles in two days, while Stuart's horsemen had covered the same distance since 2 o'clock that morning.

Jackson was now only five miles southwest of Manassas Junction, thirteen miles in rear of Pope's headquarters, and squarely on his road and rail communications to Washington. Munford's cavalry, sweeping ahead of Jackson's column, had gathered in the few enemy patrols encountered on the last few miles of the route, to guarantee that no word of the Confederate surprise should be relayed to Washington or Pope. No organized bodies of the enemy had been met during the two-day march of the infantry. It was almost unbelievable that 24,000 Confederates could circle a Federal army without detection, but it had been done.

Jackson could have taken the direct, shorter route along the Manassas Gap Railroad to Manassas Junction, but that would have left the Orange and Alexandria Railroad open for a quick rail movement to the north with a strong Federal force that could cause trouble. He therefore cut across country to Bristoe Station, where he could destroy the railroad bridge over that stream and use Broad Run as a barrier to hold off any threat from Pope while the stores were being uninterruptedly destroyed at Manassas Junction.

Galloping ahead to Bristoe Station, Munford's cavalry brushed aside a Federal cavalry detachment and mopped up a guard company of Blue infantry, at the same time hastily throwing obstructions on the tracks to block possible train movements in either direction. At that moment an empty train, returning to Alexandria from Warrenton Junction, roared up, crashed through the flimsy obstruction, and escaped. This was the first piece of bad luck the Confederates had experienced since leaving the Rappahannock. Washington would soon know something was afoot.

On the second attempt Hays' infantry brigade did a more thorough job of blocking the rails. Two more trains, also empties, following closely after the first, were derailed and set on fire. Pope's rail communication with Washington was now effectually cut.

Ewell's division, having led Jackson's column the full distance, bivouacked for the night near Bristoe Station and took over from the cavalry shortly after dark. With Jackson's rear temporarily secure against all but a Federal corps or larger, Stuart's horsemen marched the few intervening miles to approach Manassas Junction from the north while General Isaac Trimble with two infantry regiments moved up the tracks to take the depot from the front. Between them, Stuart and Trimble quickly gobbled up the depot against token resistance from the small defending garrison. By daylight of August 27 Jackson arrived with A. P. Hill's division and his own under Taliaferro, leaving the major part of Ewell's division at Bristoe, with several regiments of cavalry, to secure the rear.

As soon as Jackson had placed guards on the supply of liquor, the famished, ragged hordes of Confederates were turned loose on the huge warehouses, horse corrals, and other riches, to forage to their heart's content. The picture is one that defies the imagination. Having lived on meager rations for a long time, mainly the field corn plucked en route during the two-day march from the Rappahannock, the feast of plenty that was theirs for the taking at Manassas Junction was almost reward enough for the weeks of slim pickings that preceded their just completed historic achievement.

Many thousands of gaunt, grimy, unwashed, almost shoeless, hungry soldiers immediately proceeded to gorge themselves on the solid food and inviting delicacies that they found in such abundance. When they reached the point where not another morsel could be forced into already overloaded stomachs, they filled blanket rolls with more than they could carry, hoisted whole hams on their bayonet points, threw sacks of coffee across the saddles of their horses. Fat draft horses, and sleek riding horses were gathered in to fill gaps or replace animals that had given their all in the service of Stuart's hard-riding cavalry and Pelham's horse artillery. The wonder of it is that the whole outfit was able to weather the rare experience without foundering or being forced to sleep off a gastronomical orgy of such vast proportions. Neither is there a record of the envious disappointment with which Ewell's men, holding the fort at Bristoe Station, must have received the news of the good fortune of their comrades in the other two divisions.

Jackson and Lee would have been highly gratified had they known how effective was the disruption of Federal communications resulting from the Manassas raid. The purpose of the Confederates was of course to sever Pope's lifeline, to deprive him of his source of supplies and reinforcements, to prevent the movement of troops, materiel, and food supplies from Alexandria; in short to render him—and his superiors in Washington—both blind and deaf.

There was, however, no panic either among the Union military personnel or the War Department. Possibly the full significance of the event, with all its potentiality for disaster, did not register at once. Still, the Confederates were between Pope and the Capital, only a few miles away, and it wouldn't have taken much to start a panic, if a twentieth-century type of fifth column, armed and sympathetic to the Southern cause, had been planted in Washington to exploit the opportunity.

Colonel Herman Haupt, the ubiquitous, efficient rail transportation chief for the Eastern armies, was undoubtedly the busiest man in the North at this time. Although he was accustomed to meeting and solving transportation crises, this one had occurred at the worst possible time, as he sweated to speed reinforcements to Pope's Army of Virginia. Given a little time, Haupt could justify his well-earned reputation for doing the improbable, but even he couldn't rebuild bridges in nothing flat. Neither could he recover for use at Alexandria Depot empty trains whose return trip from Pope's army found the railroad bridge down at Broad Run. But he strove mightily during the last few days of August, and without him the recovery from the effects of the raid, logistically speaking, might well have occurred too late to affect the campaign.

The Confederates Are Coming!

Alexandria was the first to react on the evening of August 26, when the empty train that had crashed the barrier at Bristoe steamed into the station. Obviously the engineer couldn't have seen much as he dashed through to safety, so the Federal authorities weren't overly excited, believing it to be just another of Stuart's frequent cavalry raids. The excitement in Washington began to mount, however, when Herman Haupt forwarded to Halleck, about 9 P.M., an informative telegram from Manassas Junction, signed by Dispatcher McCrickett, which read:

> *No. 6 train, engine Secretary, was fired into at Bristoe by a party of cavalry—some say 500 strong. They had piled ties on the track, but engine threw them off. Secretary is completely riddled by bullets. Conductor says he thinks the enemy are coming this way.*

To this disturbing message Haupt added that the wire between Manassas and Warrenton (Pope's headquarters) had been cut, and that he had at Alexandria transportation for 1,200 men, who he suggested "might be sent to Manassas to protect the road while we repair it."

It was only a few minutes after sending the foregoing message that the dispatcher at Manassas closed his key and took off to escape capture. Haupt also passed that news on to Halleck, advising him that no more troops should be sent forward in cars. He proposed instead that they be sent by marching in order to provide better security for themselves and at the same time protect the rail communications.

HALLECK'S FRANTIC ORDER TO HAUPT

Halleck's inadequate, almost helpless reaction was to pass the buck frantically to the already overworked but capable Haupt in these words:

> *General Smith, General Slocum, General Sturgis, or any other general officers you can find, will immediately send all the men you can transport to Bristoe Bridge or Manassas Junction. Show this order.*
>
> H. W. HALLECK,
> GENERAL-IN-CHIEF

Haupt wasted two hours trying unsuccessfully to locate a general officer, advising Halleck at 11 o'clock that Cox was in Washington, Sturgis in the field, and Smith nowhere to be found. He didn't mention Slocum, but did locate two regiments of Cox's command and said he would next go to other camps "to drum up some more."

The upshot of Haupt's bird-dogging search was that he finally rounded up two more New Jersey regiments. Placing Brigadier General George W. Taylor, one of Slocum's brigade commanders, in command, Haupt loaded the four regiments and an artillery battery on cars, and sent them packing for Manassas Junction, with orders to seize and hold the Bull Run bridge.

TAYLOR MAKES A NOBLE EFFORT

Taylor was an energetic fellow, but without the least idea what his raw troops were up against. The train was halted at a point above the Junction, the men were de-trained and marched resolutely forward. Placing the battery near Bull Run, Taylor opened an annoying fire on the enemy in Manassas, crossed the bridge, and advanced to drive out the Confederate raiding party, as he vaguely understood them to be.

So far as Jackson knew, this might be a genuine threat. Taking no chances, he sent the better part of A. P. Hill's division to dispose of the brave but hapless Federals. When the Union troops realized the size of the determined force moving to cut them down, they suddenly turned and tried to escape. Taylor was killed, more than one hundred of his men killed or wounded, six guns and over two hundred men captured. To add to their woes, the retreating troops ran into Fitz Lee, who with three regiments of Gray cavalry was returning from a reconnaissance to Fairfax Court House. That finished the Federals as an organization, although some individuals made their way back to Alexandria.

Pope's information at Warrenton had come from a fourth train whose engineer, sensing trouble ahead, jammed on the brakes as the train approached Bristoe Station and quickly backed away to safety. But Pope also accepted this intelligence as of little importance and took no action. The fact was that the Federal commander was fast reaching a stage which, to an objective observer, would suggest a state of bewilderment, although Pope himself believed he had the situation well in hand and was moving his chessmen around the board in clever fashion, all things considered.

POPE OPERATES IN A FOG

Nevertheless, for three days, from the 24th to the 27th, as he shifted divisions here and there for reasons best known to himself, Pope had not the haziest notion of what the Confederates were doing, so careful had been their preparations and so well masked the movements of both Jackson's and Longstreet's wings. As for Pope's cavalry, it might as well have been in Canada or elsewhere, for he had worn down Buford's and Bayard's regiments on inconsequential missions. Now, when they could have been usefully engaged on distant reconnaissance, he failed to assign them to that essential mission, at least not in the early stages when information was needed the most.

While all this was going on behind the curtain of Federal ignorance that Lee had so effectively rolled down around three sides of the area occupied by the Union forces, just what was Pope's strength at sunset August 27, when Jackson's 24,000 men had finished making a shambles of his rear; and what were the positions and dispositions of the opposing armies?

It had finally penetrated Pope's consciousness, on the morning of August 27, that affairs had taken a more serious turn than he had at first supposed. Upon discovering that the strength of the Confederate force on his rear indicated far more than a mere raid, he had ordered up an infantry regiment and followed it with Hooker's entire division, which engaged Ewell in a brisk encounter that developed more fully the character of the Confederate opposition. Pope was now aware that Lee had, recklessly it seemed, divided his army. It appeared that his own Army of Virginia lay between the two Confederate wings. Exultantly, therefore, Pope concluded that Lee had worked himself into a dangerous position and that Jackson's exposed position presented him with "the only opportunity which had offered to gain any success over the superior forces of the enemy," as he stated in his official report.

"I determined, therefore," Pope's report continues, "on the morning of the 27th of August to abandon the line of the Rappahannock and throw my whole force in the direction of Gainesville and Manassas Junction, to crush any force of the enemy that had passed through Thoroughfare Gap, and to interpose between Lee's army and Bull Run. Having the interior line of operations, and the enemy at Manassas being inferior in force, it appeared to me, and still so appears, that with even ordinary promptness and energy we might feel sure of success."

HEAVY UNION REINFORCEMENTS ARRIVE

It was a reasonable evaluation, and the opportunity was even better on paper than Pope believed. For he now had at hand, under his immediate command, more than half again as many men as Lee; for the purpose of defeating each of the separated Confederate wings in detail his superiority was 3 to 1 against Jackson, as well as against Longstreet.

Pope's strength had expanded to approximately 77,000 men, his own army augmented by two two-division corps from the Army of the Potomac and Burnside's Falmouth troops, under command of Major

Generals Fitz John Porter, Samuel P. Heintzelman, and Jesse L. Reno respectively, in addition to Reynolds' division of Pennsylvania Reserves and a brigade of Cox's Kanawha troops, which had been transferred from West Virginia and were awaiting transportation at Washington. Instead of being confronted by the superior forces of Lee's army, as he reported, his own strength exceeded Lee's by 25,000 men. The disparity was not nearly great enough to bother Lee; the difference between the two men being that Lee was not only the better general, but knew exactly what he was doing and precisely how to achieve the desired result.

When darkness fell on August 27, Jackson's force was concentrated at Manassas Junction, Ewell having broken off a sharp fight with Hooker's division below Bristoe Station and joined Jackson on the latter's instructions. Longstreet's wing was strung along the road from Salem to White Plains, the head of his column seven or eight miles to the west of Thoroughfare Gap.

POPE PLANS TO CRUSH JACKSON

Pope issued movement orders to accomplish his purpose of crushing Jackson. By evening of August 27, his army was well north of the Rappahannock, moving by several different roads on Gainesville and Manassas Junction. That night the Federal troops were disposed as follows: Sigel's and McDowell's corps, in that order, with Reynolds' division attached, on the Warrenton turnpike, almost to Gainesville; Kearny's division and Reno's corps at Greenwich, south of Broad Run, and several miles to McDowell's rear; Hooker's division of Heintzelman's corps west of Bristoe; Porter's corps on the line of the Orange and Alexandria Railroad northeast of Warrenton Junction; and Banks' corps on the same rail line two miles back of Porter. Banks' orders were to guard the army trains, shepherding them to Manassas Junction or as far as the condition of the tracks and bridges permitted. When Banks reached Warrenton Junction, Porter's corps was under orders to proceed in the direction of Greenwich and Gainesville to support the spearhead corps of Sigel and McDowell in company with Heintzelman and Reno.

Buford's cavalry was operating west of the Bull Run Mountains, in the direct path of and only a few miles south of the head of Longstreet's column. Bayard's brigade was also reconnoitering in the vicinity of Thoroughfare Gap, which on August 28, he was directed by McDowell to occupy until Rickett's division could come up to relieve him and close the Gap.

When Pope finally learned, about dark on the evening of August 27, that the divisions of Ewell, A. P. Hill, and Taliaferro, Jackson's entire force were all at Manassas, he appears to have become so excited at what struck him as a glorious opportunity to bag the valuable prize that he lost sight of every other consideration. Whereupon he swung the order-changing department of his headquarters into high gear, sending orders to all the corps commanders that in effect threw into the discard the half completed movement by which a position was being developed that would face west on the line: Gainesville to the railroad crossing at Cedar Creek. The new plan was to concentrate the entire army in the Manassas-Bristoe area, but nothing was said as to what it would do on arrival. Pope probably expected to play it by ear, hoping to crush Jackson instead of Lee, if indeed he was capable of thinking in two dimensions at the same time, which one may at this stage be pardoned for doubting.

It is enlightening to read the revised march orders that Pope sent out by courier in all directions from Bristoe, to which point he had accompanied Hooker's division of Heintzelman's corps and witnessed the short but spirited engagement with Ewell's Confederate division. Pope's widely scattered corps commanders were all urged to move their forces expeditiously in the direction of Manassas Junction to support McDowell, temporarily in command of Sigel's corps as well as his own. McDowell was directed to proceed eastward from Gainesville and would presumably be the first to arrive at the Junction. It seemed to Pope, still optimistic, that all he had to do was converge on the wily Stonewall and "we shall bag the whole crowd"—a phrase that tickled his fancy, for he repeated it in practically all of the messages to his corps commanders that evening.

It would seem from these dispatches that the threatening position of Longstreet's divisions was being overlooked, for no mention is made of enemy troops other than Jackson's. If Pope remembered his morning telegram to Halleck, that Lee's main striking force was marching by the same road that Jackson had taken, and was even then within a few miles of Thoroughfare Gap, it is strange that he would order the whole army to proceed forthwith to Manassas Junction while turning its collective back on the approaching enemy main body.

Pope's last message to Halleck before Jackson's raiders cut the telegraph line was the long telegram of August 25. In that dispatch he had admitted his ignorance of the strength of Lee's army, but did indicate that his opponent's intentions appeared to be directed toward his (Pope's) right. The next bit of information came from the train, engineer who ran the gauntlet at Bristoe the night of August 26, news that gave no hint of the size or composition of the enemy force on Pope's rear. Then for four days not a word from the Army of Virginia, which first puzzled and then worried Halleck, who was at first not aware that the telegraph line had gone dead at Pope's end.

Pope was a busy general during the last few days of August, as events on the plains of Manassas hastened to a climax. Nevertheless one may be permitted to inquire why it was that communications between Pope's headquarters and the War Department at Washington were not routed through Falmouth when the direct wire through Manassas went out. Fitz John Porter was able to and did send frequent messages to McClellan at Aquia, through Burnside's headquarters at Falmouth, even after he came under Pope's command along the Rappahannock. Pope could have used that channel, with staff improvisation, had he wished. Perhaps it just didn't occur to him.

McCLELLAN MUDDIES THE WATERS

Meanwhile, as division after division of McClellan's army was fed to Pope in successive installments from Aquia, McClellan and Halleck continued to bicker, as they had been doing ever since Halleck took over in Washington and began issuing orders to "Little Mac." With McClellan's arrival at Aquia on August 24, the interchange had taken on a different tone, however, for now McClellan saw his army slipping out from under him and wanted to know if Halleck intended to make good his promise that McClellan should command the two armies when they were joined. The war of nerves apparently didn't bother McClellan, but it was beginning to get under the skin of the harassed Halleck, who had plenty on his mind.

From Porter's messages, relayed through Burnside to Halleck and Lincoln, it began to look as though Pope was in trouble. Franklin's corps had reached Alexandria and Sumner's was at Aquia Creek. Maybe Pope would need both. So Halleck invited McClellan to come up to Washington to talk things over. He evidently managed to smooth McClellan's ruffled feathers, because the latter ordered Franklin to move his corps out toward Manassas Junction and summoned Sumner's to Alexandria to be in readiness to follow. Then the little general had second thoughts and regaled Halleck with reasons why both corps should be retained in the Washington defenses. The relationship between the General-in-Chief and one of his principal army commanders had developed owing to Halleck's pussy-footing, which had permitted the problem child to get completely out of hand at a most critical time. Halleck was now so dominated by his recalcitrant subordinate that his words and actions became almost childish. He couldn't seem to make up his mind how to solve what was after all a perfectly simple problem. The obvious solution was to send McClellan with his remaining corps to the theater of operations, take command of the combined armies himself, and make the necessary decisions in the field as required.

News travels fast through armies in the field; traditionally the ranks quickly learn through the grapevine what is transpiring, and guess its probable meaning. The troops grasped the significance of Pope's withdrawal to the line of the Rappahannock, followed shortly by a rash of skirmishing and an exchange of artillery fire between the opposing batteries stationed on either side of the river. Finally came Pope's order to his divisions to march in the direction of Manassas. None of this escaped the attention of the men who carried the muskets; to many of them it brought forebodings.

"Events are fast approaching a crisis in this neighborhood," wrote Lieutenant Gillette in a letter to his father, postmarked Warrenton Junction, Va., August 27, 1862. "The enemy have, with their usual rapidity of action and daring, completely surrounded our forces on the front, right and rear; leaving the road to Alexandria across country the only one open. The Rebels have burned the bridge in our rear over Broad River, thus cutting off exits that way. A heavy force goes up to dislodge the enemy and make a hole for us to get out of, when Bull Run will be the line of defense."

It was on that same day, August 27, that Pope reached the belated conclusion that enemy interruption of direct telegraph communication to Washington need not prevent him from sending reports to Halleck by way of Falmouth. At 10 o'clock in the morning, after a silence of four days, he got off a message to the General-in-Chief, several significant extracts of which are worth quoting:

> *The enemy has massed his whole force at White Plains, with his trains behind him. A strong column penetrated by way of Manassas Railroad last night to Manassas, drove off a regiment of cavalry and one of infantry, and I fear destroyed several bridges. My position at Warrenton is no longer tenable. I am now moving my whole force to occupy the line from Gainesville to railroad crossing of Cedar Creek, on Alexandria and Central (Orange and Alexandria) Railroad, ... all forces now sent forward should be sent to my right at Gainesville. Whether the enemy means to attack us or not I consider doubtful .... I think it possible he may attempt to keep us in check and throw considerable force across the Potomac in direction of Leesburg. Under all the circumstances I have thought it best to interpose in front of Manassas Junction, where your orders will reach me .... You had best send a considerable force to Manassas Junction at once and forage and provisions, also construction corps, that I may repair the bridge and get the railroad trains to the rear.*

It is clear from a careful reading of that message that Pope's information of the enemy was accurate in part, but his evaluation of their probable intentions, as of 10 A.M., August 27, faulty. Longstreet's corps was in fact within a few miles of White Plains, between Salem and Thoroughfare Gap, but instead of "a strong column" having penetrated to Manassas, it was Jackson's entire corps, almost half of Lee's army. It was not until that evening that the serious character of the Confederate movements was clear to Pope, at which time he issued orders that expose him as ignoring the opportunity to effectually seal off Thoroughfare Gap and prevent the junction of Longstreet's wing with Jackson's isolated force. Corps Commander McDowell had earlier appraised the situation correctly and sent Ricketts' division to occupy the Gap in time to have forced Longstreet to fight for the privilege of passing through the gate in the Bull Run Mountains. But Pope thought he knew better, failed to approve his subordinate's action, and thus played directly into Lee's hands.

Nevertheless Pope must be credited with reacting promptly and commendably in an effort to meet the radically altered conditions that confronted him. His orders to the scattered Union corps and divisions were based on a positive plan to concentrate against an implied threat to Washington, while at the same time cutting off the retreat of the "strong column" of the enemy at Manassas. The major weakness of his decision was that it rested on a foundation of hasty speculation that was somewhat premature.

The lack of adequate mounted reconnaissance during the past few days was being felt by the Federal commander, who apparently still had much to learn of that art from the Confederates. Pope had sufficient cavalry for the purpose but, in common with many of the higher commanders in the Union armies, either did not understand how to make effective use of the mounted arm, more particularly its great potential for gathering enemy intelligence, or else assumed that horses could keep going indefinitely without adequate care, feeding, and rest. At any rate, Pope was playing it half blind on August 27, making false moves, and heading for disaster.

The first phase of the Second Battle of Manassas had virtually been concluded with Jackson's accomplishment of his initial mission by the destruction of the Federal stores at Manassas and the cutting of the main railroad line in Pope's rear. Hooker's brush with Ewell's division at Bristoe Station was an episode of that phase, but without particular significance other than its effect on Pope, who rated it a successful effort to punish the bold Confederate raiders. The fact was that Ewell had voluntarily withdrawn to Manassas in conformity with Jackson's instructions to avoid bringing on a serious engagement. The only reason Ewell had been stationed at Bristoe in the first place was to prevent interference with the job of demolishing the base at Manassas, and that condition he had fulfilled.

Pope's presence at Bristoe with Hooker gave him temporarily a front row seat from which he was able to observe to the north, late in the evening of August 27, the huge fires that lit the skies as Jackson's men put the torch to the Manassas stores that they were unable to carry away. By that time Pope had learned that Jackson's entire corps was in his rear and that Lee's army had thus been divided. He then convinced himself that if his army could be concentrated quickly he would be in position by morning to "bag the whole crowd," meaning Jackson, before Lee's main body should arrive.

The events of August 28 through September 1 appear strangely kaleidoscopic. The freewheeling manner in which Pope whipped corps and divisions back and forth, marching and countermarching in a dizzy whirl, must have seemed to his subordinate generals to have almost nightmarish characteristics. If Pope was aware of the importance of that cardinal rule of war known as the principle of simplicity, it evidently escaped his attention as he reeled off his series of successive march orders in frantic efforts to counter the sure, confident moves of that superbly coordinated team of Confederate generals, Lee, Jackson, Longstreet, and Stuart.

Assuming that Pope's corps and separate division commanders all received and complied with the night orders of August 27, the entire army would at daylight August 28 be converging rapidly on Manassas and Bristoe to swallow Jackson's three divisions which, according to Pope, were "between Gainesville and Manassas Junction." And so they were, as a matter of fact, but that was no guarantee that they would stay there to be gobbled up at will.

McDowell's own large corps of 18,500 men, which if effectively employed might have blocked Thoroughfare and Hopewell Gaps, delayed the advance of Longstreet's wing, and quite possibly ruined Lee's whole risky project, was instead directed to form the spearhead of Pope's lunge against Jackson. Pope could just as well have used a part or all of the corps commanded by Sigel, Heintzelman, Reno, and Porter as his attacking force while McDowell fought a delaying action with Longstreet. Instead of that, the whole army was ordered to fall upon Jackson, leaving no one to engage Longstreet.

McDowell's orders called for him to advance from Gainesville on Manassas with his right resting on the Manassas Gap Railroad, and his left "well to the east." Pope wanted McDowell to throw out a kind of net that would block Jackson's expected attempt to get away to the west.

Time was of course the vital element, whichever course Pope adopted. McDowell was certain to be in the unfortunate position of having to expose his rear to one wing or the other of Lee's army. Pope chose to ignore Longstreet and the larger half of the Confederate army, possibly in the belief (as he wired Halleck that morning) that Lee intended to cross the Potomac at Leesburg and therefore posed no immediate threat. There is no doubt that the Union general's mind was centered on bagging Jackson, to the exclusion of any other consideration, but most particularly that pertaining to the capabilities of his major opponent, General Lee.

Fitz John Porter's corps at Warrenton Junction was ordered to make an early start at 1:00 A.M., August 28, to reach Bristoe at daylight, without waiting for Banks corps to replace him as protector of the army trains. Porter was told, however, to send word to Banks, a few miles south of Warrenton Junction, to get a move on, while he marched north to reinforce Hooker for the advance to Manassas.

Reno's corps received orders similar to McDowell's except that his march would be from Greenwich direct to Manassas, while Kearny's division of Heintzelman's corps (the other being Hooker's) was to make a night march from Greenwich and report to Pope by dawn at Bristoe. Since Hooker's division was already there, he received no movement orders.

Pope's instructions to Banks were originally transmitted to him through Porter, who may or may not have expedited the message, since everything Porter did or failed to do at this time subsequently became suspect. At any rate Pope repeated the instructions in a direct message to Banks on the morning of August 28, directing him to guard well the railroad trains that would all have been run back from Manassas Junction to Kettle Run, where the railroad was obstructed. Pope was going to be sure this time that the elusive Jackson should not add insult to the injury inflicted at Manassas, so he assigned an entire corps to protect what remained of his supplies. And it would appear that a couple of divisions was not too many, judging from the low opinion held by at least one brigade commissary officer in Banks' corps, who wrote home on August 27: "It need occasion no surprise to hear of the capture of a portion, at least, of the trains of General Banks' army. The teamsters invariably abandon their teams in the presence of danger, therefore making it an impossibility to save the train."

JACKSON ESCAPES THE TRAP

Stonewall Jackson and his three divisions at Manassas were at dark on the 27th in a precarious position, to put it mildly. For most army corps a similar situation would be described as desperate. In two days they had marched sixty miles, on an arc of almost 270 degrees from their starting point on the Rappahannock, reached the virtually undefended rear of the Union army, destroyed its major base of supplies, uncovered the enemy's capital, and cut its communication with Pope's headquarters. Those were the favorable aspects. On the liability side, the rest of the Confederate army, marching to rejoin Jackson, was still twenty miles away. The bulk of Pope's 76,000 men, in a potentially favorable tactical position, was squarely on Lee's axis of advance, fully aware of Jackson's vulnerability and confident that this time the elusive fox would be run to ground.

The affair at Manassas had gone off even better than Jackson had hoped, although he knew so well the capabilities of his men and the reliability of his division commanders, Ewell, Powell Hill, and Taliaferro, that it was no surprise to him that the mission had been accomplished so smoothly. Jackson had led them on this perilous adventure with supreme confidence that they could do the improbable. The men had been rewarded by the rich spoils and unaccustomed delicacies with which they had regaled themselves. They also had the extra satisfaction of having again outwitted and discomfited a Union army, this time under a commander who had made himself cordially hated in the South by his braggadocio, but even more by his punitive orders respecting civilians in the theater of operations.

Now it was up to Jackson to get his men out of the predicament which faced them. This would not be easy, for the element of surprise had disappeared. The enemy knew that Jackson was at Manassas with all his divisions, and that he was unsupported. The Federals were certainly not going to sit still and allow Stonewall to retire unscathed at his leisure.

Stuart's cavalry was functioning with its customary facility, watching all the roads radiating from Manassas, reporting Federal troop movements in that direction, and keeping the surrounding country under constant observation. Fortuitously, but not surprisingly for the enterprising Southern horsemen, a mounted messenger from Lee's position on the road to Thoroughfare Gap had successfully ridden through enemy-occupied territory to Manassas to advise Jackson of the progress of the main body. This was vital information, assuring him that Longstreet's corps was following the same route that his own column had taken and was not more than an easy day's march away.

Undisturbed by the certainty that Pope's army, or at least a portion of it, must even now be converging on Manassas, Jackson concluded that it would be tempting fate to remain any longer in his exposed position. There was but one sensible thing to do and only one direction to take: retreat along the roads leading north and northwest from Manassas Junction, and hole up somewhere to await Lee's arrival with Longstreet's wing. The only alternative, with but 24,000 men, would have been to attempt to punch his way through Bristoe Station and circle around to the west, in rear of the advancing Federal columns, to join Lee. That however would have the disadvantage of putting even greater distance between the two wings of Lee's army and would probably defeat Lee's purpose of fighting a general engagement with a united army to crush Pope before all his reinforcements arrived. Moreover, Jackson did not know enough about Pope's strength and dispositions to engage in such an uncertain venture.

Confident as always, Jackson had been sending mounted messengers from time to time to keep Lee informed of his position and the results that were being achieved. In none of the messages was there so much as a hint that his corps was in danger or even threatened. Consequently Lee was able to proceed with the execution of his design, with the assurance that his strategy held every promise of success.

The withdrawal of Jackson's three divisions northward from the flames of Manassas on the night of August 27–28 was reminiscent of his famous Valley maneuvers in the spring. With Stuart's troopers remaining behind to complete the work of destruction under orders to follow as rear guard protection for the infantry and artillery, Jackson started his divisions at intervals on three different roads. His plan had been carefully thought out with intent to deceive Pope as to his real purpose. Believing that when the

Federals should reach Manassas and find the bird had flown, Pope would conclude that the Confederates had retreated in the direction they had come, Jackson calmly decided to add to Pope's bewilderment by doing the unexpected and adopting a typical Jacksonian stratagem.

Three or four miles east of Gainesville, on the Warrenton Turnpike, the small hamlet of Groveton squatted on a crossroad, to the north of which the countryside was covered with groves of trees capable of concealing large bodies of troops. It was there that Jackson planned to hide his three divisions to rest from their strenuous labors and await Lee's arrival by the turnpike. With an eye to a defensive position in case Pope should take it into his head to attack, Jackson liked the looks of the rocky ledge known as Sudley Mountain (or Stony Ridge), that extended in a northeasterly direction about a mile north of Groveton. At its base ran an unfinished railroad that would serve nicely as a front line.

Toward that position Jackson directed his divisions. Taliaferro, accompanied by the corps trains, was sent up the Manassas-Sudley Road, starting sometime before midnight. Ewell moved up the Centerville road, crossed Bull Run at Blackburn's Ford, thence north along Bull Run, and turned west over the Stone Bridge toward Groveton. A. P. Hill was given the long route, with instructions to march to Centerville to mislead the enemy and throw another scare into Washington, then turn back along the Warrenton Turnpike to wind up at Sudley Church.

Although Jackson's general plan to transfer his corps from Manassas to Groveton accomplished its purpose without the knowledge of or interference by any Federal troops, with habitual reticence he refrained from informing his division commanders sufficiently to enable them to exercise more than a minimum of control beyond starting and stopping. As before Cedar Mountain and elsewhere, much was left to their imagination. Ewell, for example, was merely told that a guide would be furnished to lead him. But when the guide showed up with what appeared to be somewhat vague instructions, he took Ewell's division by a more roundabout road than had evidently been intended, for en route Jackson sent a staff officer to pull Ewell back in the proper direction; otherwise he would have followed Hill to Centerville. As it was, his division had to endure a march that was six or seven miles longer than it need have been. Once again

Jackson's reluctance to delegate authority had to be paid for in wholly unnecessary extra effort by troops who were by any standard deserving of greater consideration.

By noon on the 28th Taliaferro was concealed in the woods north of Groveton, and Ewell and Hill were nearing that rendezvous area. The cavalry was screening the movements. Entirely unobserved by the enemy, and well before the converging Federal columns had reached Manassas, Jackson's tired men had gone into concealed bivouac north of the turn-pike at Groveton and become lost to view as completely as though the earth had swallowed them up.

LONGSTREET AT THOROUGHFARE GAP

Longstreet's corps of five divisions, commanded respectively by Major General Richard H. Anderson, and Brigadier Generals Cadmus M. Wilcox, James L. Kemper, David R. Jones, and John B. Hood, had left the Rappahannock on the afternoon of August 26, following the same route taken by Jackson. Longstreet's march was far more deliberate than Jackson's, however, for he took the better part of the two succeeding days to reach Thoroughfare Gap, covering in that time only half the distance that Jackson's corps had marched to reach Manassas in the same period of time.

The Bull Run Mountains, running north and south, are cut by four principal passes, Aldie Gap at the northern terminus, then Hopewell's Gap, Thoroughfare Gap, and the southernmost exit of New Baltimore. The one used by the Confederates, Thoroughfare Gap, was practically a mountain gorge, not long, but several hundred feet high, narrow and winding, with slopes that were rocky and steep. Although its passage could be negotiated swiftly by troops in a hurry, it was conversely sus-ceptible to an obstinate defense by a relatively small force of a division or so, tactically well placed. At the very least the defenders could make it so expensive for even a greatly superior attacker that the latter would be likely to seek another and easier route over the mountains even at the risk of losing valuable time.

The leading elements of Longstreet's corps reached Thoroughfare Gap about midafternoon of August 28 to find the pass unoccupied by the

Federals. Buford's cavalry had been reconnoitering the roads west of the mountain but had pulled back when McDowell sent Ricketts' division to take possession of the Gap. Even though Pope had disapproved the measure when McDowell first proposed it, the latter, to whose strength had been added Sigel's corps and Reynolds' division, all under McDowell's orders, decided to use his own judgment and sent Ricketts anyway.

As Longstreet approached from the west, Ricketts was belatedly moving in from the east. Receiving word from advance scouts that the pass was clear, Longstreet bivouacked his divisions for the night on the west side of the mountain, sending a brigade from Anderson's leading division to occupy the pass. Ricketts had arrived by that time and was in possession of the eastern exit. Longstreet would have to maneuver or fight, and the latter might promise a delay that could not be countenanced while Jackson remained unsupported.

Longstreet chose maneuver as the quickest and least expensive device. During the night, while the main body rested, General Wilcox with three brigades was sent four miles to the north to cross at Hopewell Gap, while General Hood took his brigades over a trail a short distance south of Thoroughfare Gap. The stratagem worked so successfully that Ricketts, to avoid attack from both flanks as well as the front, relinquished his hold on the eastern exit and by daylight had put plenty of distance between the mountains and Gainesville.

Thus McDowell's wise precaution in sending Ricketts to delay Longstreet and cover his own rear came to naught. Longstreet himself wrote later that if Ricketts' force could have been thrown against Jackson's right and rear instead of marching around him, and the Federals in front of Jackson had cooperated, such an attack, well handled, might have given the Confederates serious trouble before Longstreet reached the field. The flaw in that speculation was that neither McDowell nor Pope had any idea that Jackson was elsewhere than at Manassas Junction. Nor could Longstreet on August 28 have had any conception of the bewilderment into which the Federal commander had been thrown by Jackson's confusing in and out movements.

As Longstreet's troops debouched from the hills and headed down the road to Gainesville on the morning of August 29, still feeling no impulsion to speed because the messages from Jackson breathed a confidence that he was in good shape and fully able to take care of himself, all seemed quiet on the distant plains of Manassas, which were plainly visible as the men wound down the slopes of the mountain into open country. The peaceful quiet of the countryside gave no hint during the early hours of the morning that events were shaping, a dozen miles to their front, that would mean bitter fighting before the sun could reach the meridian.

THE CUPBOARD WAS BARE

The movements of the Federal divisions in response to Pope's night orders of August 27 to concentrate in the area of Manassas Junction were slow and uninspired. Much of the inertia was due to the mutual distrust of one another that characterized the relations between Pope and McClellan, whose army was being fed piecemeal to Pope as McClellan bickered with Halleck, Halleck straddled the issue of deciding which of the field commanders was to fight the pending battle, and Pope ran around in mental circles from which emanated hasty orders to all concerned based on incomplete military evaluations. At the very start Pope had irritated his new army by ill-advised, undiplomatic general orders; and his subsequent performance had done little to erase the pronounced unfavorable impression gained by his subordinates, in only a very few of whom, for his part, did he have any real confidence. The right climate for harmonious teamwork was wholly absent, and the fact showed up like a neon light as the Second Manassas campaign moved toward its climax. The army commander had not earned the confidence of his own corps commanders, while most, if not all of McClellan's generals, conscious of the latter's leadership qualifications even though they may not have admired his fighting ability; would naturally be slow to transfer their loyalty and allegiance to an untried leader under the anomalous conditions prevailing at the time.

Looking over the list of Union corps commanders present or on the fringes during the campaign of Second Manassas, there really wasn't much to stir martial enthusiasm. Franz Sigel represented in a sense the Lincoln Administration's concession to the German element in the army, but had little else to recommend him. Banks was somewhat better, but hadn't added anything to his reputation in the conduct of his semi-independent operations in the Shenandoah Valley. Irvin McDowell was the most capable of Pope's three corps commanders, a good solid soldier whose record had been tarnished by the opera-bouffé affair at the First Battle of Manassas, when he was so unfortunate as to be in command of the troops in the defenses of Washington, and was importuned by public opinion and against his better judgment to lead them into action before they had learned what it took to fight a real battle. Now that McDowell was again leading troops on the identical field, the memories of July, 1861 were still fresh in the minds of too many of his men to make them feel securely confident of his leadership.

Of McClellan's lieutenants, Reno and Heintzelman played it straight, conducted themselves in a soldierly fashion and fought their corps bravely. Fitz John Porter, however, a general who was probably as close to McClellan as was Burnside, acted in so cavalier a manner toward Pope, his superior officer, that after the battle he was ordered before a general court-martial and cashiered for failure to move his corps into battle as ordered. The Porter case later became a cause celebré, a subject of controversy for almost a hundred years. On the written record alone Porter stands convicted on the score of his scathing and open condemnation of Pope and all his works in advance of the battle and on the inescapable fact that his Fifth Corps was held out of action for a long time although he was within short marching distance of the battlefield, received repeated orders from Pope to advance (all other corps commanders received the same kind of orders and obeyed them) to meet the enemy, and was faced with no more obstacles to compliance than were any of the other corps. Pope was later to comment that for his non-action in the presence of the enemy Porter had been likened to Benedict Arnold. Lincoln is quoted as having remarked to an intimate friend his conviction that McClellan wanted Pope to be defeated. Porter was a confidante of McClellan's and one of his favorites. All of which suggests the equation: things that are equal to the same or equal things, are equal to each other.

The darkness of the night of August 27 was one of the ex post facto alibis that Pope employed to explain the slow movements of his divisions toward Manassas Junction, where he hoped and expected to bring the career of Stonewall Jackson to a close. But Jackson's divisions marched unerringly and without difficulty in the same pitch darkness to their rendezvous at Groveton.

It was late on the morning of August 28 when the divisions of Hooker and Kearny reached Manassas Junction from Bristoe Station, to be joined shortly thereafter by Reno coming up from Greenwich. Although McDowell's two corps, his own and Sigel's, were supposed to be the first to arrive, it didn't work out that way, for one reason or another. Why McDowell's force was still at Gainesville is not clear, but it would seem that McDowell either did not act promptly on Pope's order to march with his entire force at early dawn on August 28, or decided on his own to wait until Ricketts' division should return from Thoroughfare Gap. It is more likely, however, that McDowell did not concur in Pope's judgment, feeling that he would serve a better purpose by remaining poised at Gainesville, ready to move to Ricketts' support against the possible threat of Lee's main body following Jackson, or to start late in the opposite direction in compliance with Pope's order. In the light of history, McDowell could have been right, except that battles are not won when corps commanders act unilaterally or in contravention of instructions from their superiors, no matter how incompetent or inept the latter might appear to be.

Pope's arrival at Manassas to find the place empty of Confederates at noon of August 28 must have given him an unpleasant surprise, although he neglected to mention it in his report. Actually Jackson had cleared the area by 2:00 A.M. His reaction, however, was typical of the mercurial nature of his actions and orders throughout the campaign—ill-digested plans put into effect hastily and with the unjustified optimism that his alleged strategy seemed to generate; insufficient consideration of the logistics that army commanders simply cannot afford to ignore; woeful indifference to the necessary details of staffwork essential to proper execution of the army orders by subordinate commanders; thoughtlessly boastful letters to Halleck such as the one in which he had earlier written that he "could easily make the position of Gordonsville untenable." Following that sequence would come a change for the worse in the situation of his army, and then the cycle would start all over again.

The wheel started turning again when Pope reached Manassas and learned that Jackson had departed. Word came in that the enemy had been to Centerville and Groveton but had disappeared. Naturally, thought

Pope, the brash Confederate was retreating along the Warrenton Turnpike. Still optimistic that Jackson could not escape him, fresh orders went out at 4:15 P.M., August 28, directing the army to march on Centerville, with McDowell's two-corps force to proceed along the Warrenton Pike. It was to be a kind of double envelopment that would catch Jackson between a Federal nutcracker, each arm of which was superior in strength to the fleeing fugitive.

CHAPTER 5

Second Bull Run I: The Fight Near Groveton

UNTIL the late afternoon of August 28 the principal occupation of the more than 100,000 men presently comprising the armies of Lee and Pope had been marching and bivouacking. For nearly a month elements of both forces had been maneuvering for position while concentrating for a show-down battle. During that time the fight at Cedar Mountain provided the only really bloody interlude between spurts of mobile shadow-boxing. The footwork of the two contestants in the aggregate had been nothing short of prodigious, but except for Cedar Mountain the casualties had been relatively light.

The physically harmless phase of the campaign now came to an abrupt end, as the larger half of Lee's army prepared to move through Thoroughfare Gap and down the road to Gainesville to join Jackson, and the marching corps of the still puzzled Pope moved hither and yon seeking the whereabouts of gadfly Jackson.

Heintzelman's divisions under Hooker and Kearny, together with Reno's and Stevens', both under Reno, were on the road from Manassas to Centerville. Sigel's corps and Reynolds' division followed the Manassas-Sudley road. Porter's corps was still south of the Manassas Railroad and seemingly content to remain there despite Pope's repeated orders to move up to the Junction. The movements of McDowell's two divisions, King's and Ricketts', are more difficult to trace, for several reasons, one being the conflicting successive orders from Pope which would have had McDowell moving in two directions at once; the other, the fact that Ricketts' division had gone up the road to Thoroughfare Gap and then down again, and was now somewhere between the Gap and Gainesville. McDowell himself, riding alone from Gainesville to Manassas on the night of August 28 to consult Pope with a view to clearing up the apparent misunderstanding about his corps' activities, managed to get lost and was unable to recover his bearings until the following morning.

King's division of McDowell's corps spent the night of August 27 near Buckland Mills instead of in the Manassas area, where it was supposed to be. Consequently it was near the Warrenton Turnpike when Pope's afternoon order of April 28 arrived to change the point of Federal concentration from Manassas to Centerville. By pure chance, or perhaps it should be called mischance, King's division was thus destined to have the doubtful honor of drawing the first real blood in the Battle of Manassas.

JACKSON LIES IN WAIT

Carefully concealed in the woods north of the turnpike near Groveton, Jackson's divisions rested and awaited developments. Jackson was no longer the fox seeking cover, but more like a crouched panther awaiting the arrival of its mate and ready to spring on the back of any living thing that should come too close to its lair.

The holed-up Confederates had received only a smattering of information concerning the movements of the Federals which Stuart's troopers were able to pick up by contact. But a Confederate cavalry troop, operating with Taliaferro along the Warrenton Turnpike, captured a courier carrying a night dispatch from McDowell to Sigel and Reynolds that divulged Pope's plan to concentrate at Manassas Junction and furnished detailed information on the routes of the Union corps.

Colonel Bradley T. Johnson, one of Taliaferro's brigade commanders, picketing the side roads leading into the turnpike, collided with Reynolds' division on the Warrenton Pike and a short engagement ensued, with inconclusive results. Reynolds, assuming that Johnson's force was merely a reconnaissance detachment, turned off the road toward Manassas and kept on his way, unaware of the presence of Jackson's corps in the immediate neighborhood.

Jackson had established a temporary command post in the corner of a field not far from the turnpike. Stripped down to bare essentials, as his marauding column had been from the time it left the Rappahannock three days before, there was nothing in evidence to denote a corps headquarters; no train, no camp equipage, no cooking facilities, not even an ambulance—the corps trains and ambulances were parked near Sudley Church, but there was no surplus of baggage.

When Jackson used the word surplus, he meant not only peeling down to the skin, but cutting below the epidermis if that would help speed the march.

DECIDES TO POUNCE

Division Commanders Ewell and Taliaferro were close at hand by Jackson's order, so that immediate action could be taken whenever the situation might demand. All three generals were stretched out sleeping in the shade when Stuart's trooper rode up with the captured dispatch late in the afternoon of August 28.

What happened next was strictly in the Jackson tradition and quite different from the sequence of events one might expect from the normal general commanding. Jackson was an individualist who never followed the conventional pattern if a shorter way could be found. Getting to his feet, he quickly scanned the paper, roused Ewell and Taliaferro, and read Pope's dispatch to them.

There was no conference, no discussion on the best course to pursue, no questions asked and no suggestions invited. Jackson's mind instinctively reviewed the pros and cons. To allow King to pass now would be to interpose no opposition to Pope's concentration and might defeat the whole purpose of Lee's campaign. On the other hand, to attack prematurely could bring the Federal swarms buzzing about his ears before Longstreet arrived, and that too would thwart Lee's designs. It was indeed a fielder's choice, but Jackson never hesitated. When in doubt, attack, seemed the wiser course.

With that rapid mental estimate of the situation, almost an automatic reflex as it must have seemed to the two division commanders, Jackson remarked to Taliaferro, "Move your division and attack the enemy." Turning then to Ewell he employed only three words, "Support the attack." The two short sentences were more meaningful to those accustomed to Jackson's taciturnity than any five-paragraph field order could possibly have been. Taliaferro and Ewell were told what to do but not how to do it. It was unnecessary to indicate the time of the attack, because Jackson was not in the habit of dealing in futures, and it was obvious that the place would be where ever they found the enemy. Jackson himself would give the signal to launch the attack.

A.P. Hill's division was up at Sudley Church, guarding the Aldie road, and would not be engaged initially. Ewell's and Taliaferro's men were sleeping practically in formation. All they had to do was wake up and grab their muskets. By the time the officers' horses were saddled, long lines of infantry were moving toward the turnpike. When they reached a position in the woods from which to see the road, where they expected to find some trace of the Federals, none were to be seen. It was not until the lengthening shadows foretold the coming sunset that a Federal column was observed marching east in the direction of Centerville.

THE MEETING ENGAGEMENT ON AUGUST 28

That would be King's division of McDowell's corps, heading for the Federal concentration point at Centerville, where Pope's latest faulty estimate had established Jackson's location. Furthermore, this outfit had fire in its eye, for the men of the Union army were sick to death of marching, marching, marching, and never seeming to get anywhere. Some real fighting would be a change for the better, and King's division was in the mood to mix it up with the enemy at the earliest opportunity. For that purpose at least two of King's four brigades, commanded by John Gibbon and Abner Doubleday, were ably led to carry the burden of the engagement that in the next few minutes would fall to their lot.

Divisions abreast, Taliaferro on the right, Ewell on the left, the Confederates were formed under cover with five brigades in the front line, under instructions to await the signal to attack, while Jackson himself, unaccompanied even by an orderly, rode forward into the open to observe the enemy column. Jackson's utter disregard of personal danger in establishing to his own satisfaction the basic facts upon which to predicate his actions and orders was never better illustrated than on this occasion. He was in high good humor, greatly relieved by the news that Lee and Longstreet would be up in the morning, and quite ready to show his hand to Pope.

Captain W. W. Blackford, an engineer officer on Jeb Stuart's staff, in whom the cavalry leader had great confidence, was for the time being with Jackson's corps in its Groveton hideout after delivering a dispatch from Stuart. Blackford with several companions had visited a nearby farmhouse to refresh themselves with a supply of buttermilk, only to find a couple of flankers from King's Federal division there for a similar purpose. Outnumbered, the Northerners had chosen to surrender.

Hatch's brigade, the leading element of King's division, passed him on the turnpike as Jackson deliberated. He decided to let them pass, presumably to determine the extent of the Federal column, and it was only when Gibbon's brigade hove into view that he concluded the right moment had come. Satisfied with his close-up inspection of the enemy column, Jackson galloped back to the woods and informed Ewell and Taliaferro that they were free to attack.

The field for the encounter, north of the turnpike, was generally open, with Brawner's farmhouse, an orchard, a patch of woods near the farmhouse, a few stacks of hay and a half-demolished worm fence affording the only available cover. The Southerners moved forward rapidly from their ridge position and the Federals, although surprised, just as quickly deployed to meet them. As the two lines approached one another, off to the west puffs of white smoke and the far-off detonation of artillery shells signaled the meeting between Longstreet and Ricketts at Thoroughfare Gap.

The fight between Jackson and King was fairly static, with both lines slugging it out practically toe to toe. Scarcely a hundred yards initially separated the two forces as the determined antagonists shot it out with neither side gaining or losing much distance. The available cover, however inadequate, was used by both sides, but the fighting was concentrated in a relatively small area and for the numbers engaged it was as sanguinary a battle as any that occurred during the war. Neither contestant was willing to call it a day, even when twilight made it almost impossible to see the target. At such close quarters, with no cover, the casualties mounted at a frightful rate, but in the obstinacy and sheer courage which marked the fight, neither side appeared able to gain a decision.

When the fight started, Gibbon had available only a single battery of six Napoleons against ten Confederate guns. Later in the engagement a second Union battery swung into action, doubling Gibbon's fire power to give him a slight artillery superiority, without which it is doubtful that his outnumbered infantry regiments could have held the field against the five Confederate brigades thrown against him. Taliaferro later reported that the Federal artillery was admirably served and "at one time the annihilation of our batteries seemed inevitable, so destructive was the fire."

NEITHER SIDE WINS

In several respects the opening engagement of the Battle of Second Manassas near Groveton was unique. Only five brigades, about 4,500 men, of Jackson's wing managed to get into the fight, while less than 3,000 of King's division, chiefly Gibbon's brigade of Wisconsin (soon to be known as the black-hatted Iron Brigade) and Indiana regiments, supported by two regiments of Doubleday's brigade, carried the entire burden for the Federals. The Confederates had the advantage of higher ground from which to launch their attack and, in addition, had time to form for attack on the unsuspecting enemy marching in column along the road and with flankers insufficiently extended to give warning of the concealed Confederates. King had been led by Pope's order to believe that Jackson was at Manassas, which of course did not excuse him from taking more effective precautions in enemy country, so the Confederate attack caught King's men completely by surprise.

Furthermore, the battle was fought in fading daylight, entirely by the troops who made the initial contact. No reserves were thrown in by either of the contestants, which would have been a normal expedient except for the rapidly increasing darkness that caused confusion, uncertainty as to the identity of nearby contingents, and loss of direction on the part of both infantry supports and artillery batteries attempting to shift position. The strange fact was that neither side attempted to execute a flanking maneuver, which would very likely, under the circumstances, have proven decisive for whichever commander had been able to manage it.

Finally, two of Jackson's generals were wounded in the action, Ewell and Taliaferro, which of itself was almost enough to swing the balance in favor of the Federals. They were the two division commanders who shared in the attack, and both were seriously wounded. "Old Baldy"

Ewell lost his leg as the result of a shattered knee, was out of action for months, and thereafter had to be strapped to his horse or ride into battle in a carriage.

Aggregate losses exceeded 2,300 men out of about 7,500, an extremely high ratio of almost one-third, the Confederates suffering greater casualties than the Federals. Considering all factors, Gibbon's heavily outnumbered brigade covered itself with glory even though it was unable to claim a decisive victory. But the evidence clearly gives Gibbon the better of the argument, despite the fact that King's entire division, sometime during the night, pulled itself together and, leaving the field to the Confederates, resumed its interrupted march, but toward Manassas instead of Centerville. There wasn't much else for King's division to do, after putting up a heroic fight and suffering approximately 1,100 casualties.

Strategically the honors went to Jackson, who accomplished the purpose of his attack, which was to bring down upon him, if possible, the whole of Pope's army in order to involve it in a general engagement before McClellan could join forces. Jackson had timed his successive moves shrewdly. He knew that Longstreet was only a few hours' march behind him and it now seemed tactically safe to show his hand. Jackson knew also that Pope's entire army was searching for him and it was a reasonable assumption that by morning, finally aware of his location as the result of King's battle at Groveton, Pope would throw into battle every division that could be rushed to the scene.

At 10:45 P.M., after the Groveton game was called on account of darkness, King sent off a message to McDowell, which must have reached Pope one way or another. In that dispatch he reported:

> *From prisoners taken tonight there is no doubt that Jackson's main force is in our immediate front. Our position is not tenable, and we shall fall back toward Manassas, with the expectation of meeting forces sent to our support.*
>
> *If Ricketts should attempt to join us he might be cut off unless he falls back by the way of Greenwich. Prisoners report Jackson has 60,000 or 70,000 men.*

In all probability King's warning reached Ricketts in a separate message during the night at Thoroughfare Gap and may even have influenced the latter's action in hastening his retreat after Longstreet maneuvered him out of position and forced him to head eastward on the Warrenton pike; or else Ricketts just naturally swung off to the south and away from the direct road to Centerville to avoid being caught between Longstreet and Jackson.

The interesting aspect of King's dispatch, however, is the Confederate prisoners' report on Jackson's strength. That was typical of the wily Jackson, whose soldiers were trained to feed misleading information to the enemy if captured. The accounts of his battles are full of similar episodes, in which his strength is magnified many times for his own purposes.

Earlier reports than King's on the affair at Groveton had leached Pope at Manassas, but the information was far from complete, for at 10 P.M., August 28, in a long telegram to Halleck, Pope's only reference to King's fight was contained in two sentences:

"Late this afternoon, a severe fight took place 6 miles west of Centerville, which was terminated by darkness. The enemy was driven back at all points, and thus the affair rests."

The message did not reach Halleck until 6:45 P.M., August 29, the following day, indicating how effective was the disruptions in communications caused by the Manassas raid. By the same token, however, it is not too flattering a commentary on the recuperative powers of Pope's signalmen.

FEDERAL CONFUSION

Pope's field generalship, which had been reasonably effective on the Rapidan and Rappahannock positions, had notably deteriorated as soon as the war of position was changed by Lee's strategy to a war of maneuver. Pope's habit of jumping to conclusions on the basis of insufficient and frequently inaccurate intelligence, together with his consistent wishful thinking, led him to issue a succession of individual march orders to the scattered elements of his army. Thus he had them shifting back and forth until his corps and division commanders must have begun to wonder whether Pope had any idea at all what he was doing. First there was the order to concentrate at Manassas. Next came the change order which made Centerville the objective. And still later he made a shift in the direction of Groveton.

The result was almost universal lack of confidence in the general commanding. Pope himself had only a vague general idea as to the positions of his several corps at any given moment and, conversely, they never knew just where to find him. His troops were leg-weary from marching and countermarching. The Army of Virginia, to put it bluntly, was not in good shape to fight a coordinated battle against an aggressive opponent who knew his business.

The receipt of King's 10:45 P.M., dispatch started again the old familiar cycle in Pope's mind. Jumping to the immediate conclusion that McDowell's corps (King and Ricketts) had intercepted Jackson's retreat and that now he, Pope, had finally pinned the elusive Confederate between two major elements of his own army, Pope lost no time in ordering an early morning attack to wind up the business, as he thought.

Proceeding happily on the assumption that all parts of his army were just where his earlier orders had directed, which unhappily was far from the fact, Pope ordered McDowell's wing (which included Sigel and Reynolds) to hold its ground at all costs to prevent Jackson's retreat to join Lee, advising McDowell that "at daylight our whole force from Centerville and Manassas would assail him from the east, and he would be crushed between us."

Kearny's division at Centerville was ordered to move forward cautiously during the night along the Warrenton Turnpike, drive in the Confederate pickets and keep in close contact with the enemy main body until daylight. At that time Kearny was to make a vigorous assault that would be supported by the divisions of Hooker and Reno.

Porter's corps, which Pope thought was at Manassas Junction, was ordered to move on Centerville at dawn, so that Porter's strength, two divisions made up mostly of Regulars, could be added to the blow to be aimed at Jackson's force in the morning.

That was the night when McDowell was making his personal journey to Manassas to see Pope, who had moved his headquarters elsewhere.

As stated, McDowell lost his way in the darkness, and remained out of touch with both army headquarters and the troops under his command, including his own corps (King and Ricketts), Sigel's corps, and Reynolds' division.

Pope might just as well have "shot an arrow into the air" so far as that half of his plan was concerned which directed McDowell from the west to block Jackson's supposed retreat while the rest of the army attack him from the direction of Centerville-Manassas. For there were no Federal troops except Buford's wearied cavalry brigade and Ricketts' retreating division between Jackson at Groveton and Longstreet at Thoroughfare Gap, since the lost McDowell had not received Pope's order and of course could not comply. Finally, since Sigel, Reynolds, King, and Ricketts were a part of McDowell's command, all were perforce obliged to make their own decisions as to what steps to take in the fluid situation, until McDowell should again be in touch with them.

Toward morning of August 29 Pope learned that his plan has miscarried and that the divisions of King and Ricketts were retiring to Manassas Junction and Bristoe respectively. It must have dawned on him that the road which Longstreet would use to join Jackson was now wide open; therefore it would be necessary to defeat Jackson quickly before the rest of the Confederate army completed its advance to reinforce him.

As it happened, Reynolds' division and Sigel's corps were that night south of the Warrenton Pike and not far from Groveton, which fitted nicely into Pope's plan of attack for Friday morning, August 29. Pope thereupon sent supplementary orders direct to Sigel, shortly before dawn, "to attack the enemy vigorously at daylight and bring him to a stand if possible." And to Fitz John Porter, still in the vicinity of Manassas Junction, about 3:00 A.M. went an order "to move upon Centerville at the first dawn of day."

In the welter of messages that Pope so freely dispatched to his sub-ordinate commanders during the hectic rat race by which he desperately sought to counter the Confederate moves, at no time does there appear to have been any carefully conceived or coordinated plan of action. The messages were mostly fragmentary and incomplete, in virtually every case simply directing the corps commanders concerned to march on a designated point at a specified time. If Pope had a definite plan in his mind other than to move enough troops between Lee and Washington to protect the Capital, following the fright thrown into the Federal camp when Jackson interposed his corps in Pope's rear, he failed utterly to transmit it to his generals.

The state of mind of those subordinate commanders is not difficult to imagine. A good soldier is trained to obey orders, but he doesn't have to like them. The army commander had by this time managed so thoroughly to confuse the issue that it became a serious question whether Pope's army would be able to hold together in a serious test of arms, even against an opponent of lesser strength.

CHAPTER 6

Second Bull Run II: The Main Battle Opens

To AVOID the topographical indigestion that might result from an effort to compare the two battles fought at Manassas, or Bull Run, it would be well to exclude for the time being all thoughts of First Manassas, July 1861, particularly the familiar historic place names. While both engagements were fought on the same Plains of Manassas southwest of Centerville, the 1862 battle, once the two armies were locked in combat, was rather less fluid and certainly more professionally conducted than the 1861 encounter.

The stream itself, Bull Run, played a minor role in the Battle of Second Manassas, except as a terrain feature for reference purposes. The 1862 battle was fought six to eight miles west of Centerville and three miles east of Gainesville, astride the Warrenton Turnpike, in the area about Groveton, where the opening engagement between Jackson and King occurred on the evening of August 28.

The battlefield was singularly free of obstruction that might hamper the movements of troops. The gently rolling ground, criss-crossed by a network of roads and country lanes, made it convenient for lower commanders to shift their units about and for the troops themselves to execute their tasks with a better understanding of the purpose.

It is a mark of good generalship when a commander maneuvers his opponent into a position that forces him to fight on terrain chosen by the former. Stonewall Jackson had commanded a brigade at First Manassas and knew the ground well. He also had in Captain Jed Hotchkiss a peerless, indefatigable map maker, and it may safely be assumed that the two of them had not overlooked the matter of topography when they were doing their homework along the Rappahannock earlier in August, in preparation for Jackson's wide sweep to reach his prearranged target on Pope's rear, the Manassas depot.

That however should not have afforded the Southerners any great advantage, for McDowell was in command of the Union forces at First Manassas and it is a fact that Pope, to whom the area was unfamiliar, relied heavily on McDowell's presumed knowledge of the terrain during the second battle. The major difference was of course the relative ability of the opposing commanders to utilize their knowledge to advantage.

It would be interesting to know just when Jackson chose the position north of Groveton to which he adjourned his corps on the night of August 27-28, when Manassas Junction became too hot, literally and figuratively, for him to hold. But, regardless of when the decision was made, he certainly moved to the new area with speed and precision, as though he had long planned it that way and then executed the movement virtually as an automatic reflex.

The position that Jackson selected was an ideal one for the Confederates, from every standpoint. It was not only strong for defensive purposes, but possessed strategic value of vital importance to Lee's whole campaign. For it must be remembered that the success of the Confederate plan depended on bringing Pope to battle before the armies of McClellan and Pope could join forces in overwhelming strength. Examined in that light, Jackson's decisions and actions were admirable in themselves, but even more so in the highly successful way by which they were fitted into Lee's plan of campaign.

Single handedly Jackson had first conducted his 24,000 men on a grueling sixty-mile march around and to the rear of Pope's army to destroy his base of supply and cut his communications. Then he tarried at Manassas Junction just long enough to fool Pope into thinking that he had the venturesome Confederates in the bag. With exquisite timing, neither too soon nor too late, Jackson next faded back to a concealed position as the Union commander rushed the scattered elements of his army back and forth in a wild fox chase that compounded Pope's confusion and wore down the energy and morale of his equally bewildered troops, while the wily quarry and his own weary men caught up on their sleep in the woods above Groveton.

Still timing his actions on a split-second schedule, Jackson's knowledge that he was in the ideal spot for the purpose, that Lee and Longstreet were by that time only a few hours' march away, and that the time had come to let Pope know where he was so that the latter would do the expected, Jackson attacked King's division of McDowell's corps on the evening of August 28.

It couldn't have worked out better for the Confederates. Call it luck that Pope's confusion and bad guesses prevented McDowell from conceivably ruining the operation for Lee. The point is that Pope *was* confused, McDowell *did* get lost that night, Porter *did* drag his heels, Federal coordination and control *was* deficient. Furthermore, Lee and his principal lieutenants had developed to a fine art the ability to weigh military factors, to appraise the capabilities, probable intentions, and actions of their opponents, and to act quickly and as a rule unerringly on the conclusions to be drawn. It is beside the point that the Confederate moves were so often terribly risky and overly audacious and should by all the rules of warfare have resulted in their own defeat and destruction. For their very boldness and unexpectedness exploited the element of surprise, that most useful principle of war which, when efficiently introduced, could and usually did negate the best laid plans of a less competent but stronger opponent.

THE STAGE IS SET

With the coming of daylight August 29, the Plains of Manassas became the stage for the enactment of another great drama starring the North and the South. All the actors were on hand for the play except Lee and Longstreet, who had been but briefly delayed by the temporary incident at Thoroughfare Gap, which in fact had no ill effect on the Confederate timetable.

Jackson's three divisions, now reduced to about 20,000 men, had resumed their Groveton position, after the surprisingly tough and sanguinary fight with King's Federal division the preceding evening, along the eastern base of Sudley Mountain or Stony Ridge, which extended in a two-mile long arc to the northeast from the vicinity of Sudley Church to a point on the unfinished railroad north of Brawner's.

The Confederate line ran behind the unfinished railroad bed along which Jackson's skirmishers were posted to warn the main body of danger in time for the troops, under cover in the direction of the ridge, to form up for defense or attack.

A.P. Hill's division held the left of the line, its flank strongly anchored on a rocky hill that faced northeast and commanded the road to Aldie Gap. Part of Hill's position included a belt of timber about five hundred yards in width, which afforded concealment but offered a poor field of fire, and to that extent was the weak point of Jackson's position. To offset that disadvantage, Hill's troops were disposed in depth, deployed in three successive lines, with half of the division strength assigned to the third, or reserve line.

Jackson's center was held by two brigades of Ewell's division, now commanded by Lawton, occupying a single line. Ewell's other two brigades, under Early, were detached to guard the right rear of Jackson's position from a wooded knoll overlooking the Warrenton Turnpike, where they could serve the dual purpose of securing the right flank and watching for Longstreet's approach from Thoroughfare Gap.

Jackson's right, in front of Early, was held by Taliaferro's division, now commanded by Starke, also disposed in three lines with half of the division in the third line.

Overall, Jackson's defensive position was approximately two miles in length, supported by forty guns, and with both flanks secured by Stuart's cavalry, one brigade being at Haymarket to maintain communication with Longstreet, the other well out toward the enemy to watch the roads in the direction of Manassas and Centerville.

Jackson's mission was now to wage a strictly defensive battle against the vastly superior force that Pope could amass to crush him. The odds that confronted him were terrific; it would take everything the Confederates had to prevent disaster if the Federals should succeed in exploiting their overwhelming superiority in manpower and artillery. Nevertheless, Jackson's position was a strong one, by nature and troop disposition, for the unfinished railroad afforded a succession of dirt embankments and cuts that were made to order for infantry on the defense.

POPE'S GLASSES STILL CLOUDED

Pope's third plan to catch Jackson before he escaped, following the abortive lunges in the direction of Manassas and Centerville, both of which were countermanded in mid-air, was as hastily conceived as the first two, and based on equally incomplete intelligence.

Compounded partly of his own lack of judgment and partly of just plain bad luck, the conclusion to which Pope quickly leaped when word arrived of King's fight at Groveton was that the latter had run into the head of Jackson's column retreating on the turnpike in the direction of the Gap. Apparently no other possibility entered the consciousness of his single-track mind; the news seemed to him to confirm the accuracy of his earlier evaluation and he immediately triggered orders for a dawn attack in which McDowell with Ricketts' and King's divisions would prevent Jackson from getting away while the rest of the army demolished him in a converging attack from the east and south.

Pope lacked vital information. McDowell had gotten lost during the night, with the result that Ricketts and King were forced to act on their own. Ricketts' report to McDowell on the action at Thoroughfare Gap disappeared in thin air, and King decided to move on to Manassas, and hence out of circulation, when he found that no one else seemed to care what became of him. Thus McDowell's temporarily leaderless corps, instead of blocking Jackson's supposed route of departure, had vacated the area and removed all possible hindrance to the fast-approaching junction between Lee's two wings; for when Ricketts learned of King's departure, it was perfectly natural for him to follow suit, being already on his way in a rather dense fog of war of his own.

So far as Pope's knowledge went, he was all set to achieve his goal of erasing Jackson, who was, he thought, struggling desperately to escape the net. Longstreet must still be west of Bull Run Mountains, and anyway, Pope may have figured that his campaign to date hadn't placed him in too favorable a light in the eyes of the North, and he had better do something worth reading about pretty quickly to remove the possibility that the Administration in their impatience might send McClellan galloping out to take his place.

So the attack orders went out late in the evening of August 28. Sigel's corps of three divisions would attack in conjunction with Reynolds' single division, supported by Heintzelman's two-division corps and Reno's two divisions. McDowell's corps and Porter's, two divisions each, were directed to reverse their direction and push on to Gainesville to make certain that Jackson should not escape. Banks' corps would continue its job of protecting the army trains.

The brief direct order from Pope to Porter to change direction and shoot for Gainesville preceded a lengthier joint dispatch to McDowell and Porter on the 29th: "Push forward with your corps and King's division, which you will take with you, upon Gainesville. I am following the enemy down the Warrenton turnpike. Be expeditious or we will lose much."

Pope then penned a weird document to McDowell and Porter, that same morning of August 29. Since become famous, or perhaps infamous, as the "Joint Order," its contents raise a serious question as to the state of Pope's mental apparatus at that stage of the proceedings:

> You will please move forward with your joint commands toward Gainesville. I sent General Porter written orders to that effect an hour and a half ago. Heintzelman, Sigel, and Reno are moving on the Warrenton turnpike, and must now be not far from Gainesville. I desire that as soon as communication is established between this force and your own the whole command shall halt. It may be necessary to fall back behind Bull Run at Centerville tonight. I presume it will be so, on account of our supplies . . . .
>
> If any considerable advantages are to be gained by departing from this order it will not be strictly carried out. One thing must be had in view, that the troops must occupy a position from which they can reach Bull Run to-night or by morning. The indications are that the whole force of the enemy is moving in this direction at a pace that will bring them here by to-morrow night or the next day. My own headquarters will be for the present with Heintzelman's corps or at this place.

The order exuded uncertainty and wishful thinking, gave misleading information, directed an offensive while implying that it would end in a withdrawal, and finally closed on the one thing that Pope was sure couldn't be criticized—the occupation of the line of Bull Run. It was indeed a pathetic piece of writing which couldn't help but confirm Porter's already well-established, adverse opinion of John Pope. The order speaks for itself and little purpose would be served by pointing out its obvious defects, misinformation, and omissions.

The receipt of the joint order late in the morning found Porter's Fifth Corps near Dawkin's Branch, a tributary of Broad Run, with twin forks running south from their source just north of Manassas Gap Railroad. Porter had received Pope's earlier message and already reversed his snail-like movement toward Centerville, so that his arrival at Dawkin's Branch placed him about three miles from Gainesville, the objective assigned by Pope.

McDowell had caught up again with his divisions near Manassas Junction, where he discussed with Porter the joint order that had just arrived from the commanding general. It was decided, because of the exhausting marches of Ricketts and King and the latter's fight at Groveton, that McDowell's divisions would follow Porter on the Manassas-Gainesville Road, and so it was arranged.

As the column inched its way toward Gainesville, McDowell rode on ahead to join Porter. On the way a courier handed him two messages from cavalry brigadier John Buford, who had been keeping in touch with Longstreet's advance and was now observing from the vicinity of Gainesville. The first, addressed to Ricketts at 9:30 A.M., read:

> *Seventeen regiments, one battery, and 500 cavalry passed through Gainesville three quarters of an hour ago on the Centreville road. I think this division (Ed. note: Buford apparently includes Bayard's Brigade in this reference) should join our forces, now engaged, at once. Please forward this.*

The second, to McDowell, read: "A large force from Thoroughfare Gap is making a junction through Gainesville up the Centreville road with the forces in the direction of the cannonading."

Immediately after reading Buford's informative dispatches, McDowell joined Porter on a small rise of ground near the head of the latter's halted column at Dawkin's Branch. The two generals, looking in the direction of Gainesville, could see clouds of dust rising above the treetops, a sure sign of marching troops, and no doubt the advance elements of Longstreet's wing moving east on the Warrenton Pike to join Jackson. No enemy troops were visible in the open country to the west and there seemed to be no reason why Porter should not move rapidly forward to strike the marching enemy columns in flank.

STUART EMPLOYS AN ARTFUL DODGE

Stuart's cavalry, according to General Lee's official account of the situation on Longstreet's front on August 29, reported that a large enemy force was approaching the Confederate right flank from the direction of Bristoe, in reacting to which three brigades under Wilcox—Pryor's, Featherston's, and Wilcox's, were sent to reinforce Jones' division on the right of the line. Lee added that the supports were not needed, however, since the enemy merely fired a few shots in the direction of the Confederates and then withdrew. The shots referred to evidently came from the skirmishers thrown across Dawkin's Branch from Porter's corps.

Stuart's report also mentions the brief but bloodless long-range contact with Porter's corps by a portion of the Confederate cavalry. The cavalryman remarked with obvious satisfaction that, while awaiting the expected approach of the enemy corps, he kept several detachments dragging brush down the road from the direction of Gainesville in a ruse to deceive the enemy. Recalling that McDowell and Porter had observed dust clouds to the west and believed that they indicated the approach of the Confederate main body in their direction, it may well be that Stuart's stratagem proved to be a significant element in diverting an offensive Federal move on the southern flank.

In any event, the actions of both McDowell and Porter were definitely influenced by the signs of dust. Ex post facto, the stories told by McDowell and Porter differed materially from what they had agreed upon at their conference. McDowell, who was senior to Porter, later testified that he directed Porter to advance to the attack at once, and that he would lead his own corps directly north on the Sudley Springs Road, to add his strength to the battle that had been raging intermittently beyond the turnpike for some hours between Jackson and the Federal divisions under Sigel and Reynolds.

It is important, in light of the subsequent court-martial which found Porter guilty, to note that the conference between McDowell and Porter at Dawkin's Branch took place late on the morning of August 29, when Longstreet's wing was coming up on the Warrenton Turnpike, Jackson's right flank north of the pike was in the air until Longstreet deployed, and for the time being a terrain vacuum existed that Porter's corps was in position to fill if he had done nothing more than briskly obey Pope's order to move on Gainesville.

VIOLENT CLASHES

Pursuant to Pope's orders, shortly after sunrise Sigel's corps on the right, with Reynolds' division on the left and somewhat to the rear, deployed for action as the Federal artillery opened on Jackson's stronghold along the unfinished railroad north-west of Groveton. As the Union skirmishers marched warily forward, Jackson's troops also moved up to their firing positions, to await the attack. For several hours the Federals jockeyed for position but, except for a succession of sharp skirmishes, a large-scale attack was held up until the leading divisions of the Union corps of Reno and Heintzelman, Reno's own and Kearny's, could come up to extend the line to the north in the direction of Bull Run and Sudley Church. The delay was of incalculable advantage to the Confederates, for whom every hour of additional time brought that much closer the fortunate moment when Lee's army would be reunited on the field of battle.

Pope established his field headquarters at noon on Buck Hill, a short distance north of the Warrenton Turnpike—Sudley Springs crossroad, from which eminence his field of vision included a large part of the battlefield. The situation looked good to the army commander, who had, as he thought, issued orders that would soon result in a happy solution to the problem that had been vexing him for several days. So far as he knew, Longstreet was still far removed and, if his divisions acted expeditiously, the firm of Jackson and Company would shortly be dissolved.

By early afternoon the Federal divisions assigned to this zone were all up, dispositions for battle completed, and the troops ready to engage in the serious fighting that Pope had hoped would begin at daybreak. Kearny and Hooker of Heintzelman's corps held the right of the line. Behind Hooker was Reno, then Sigel's corps astride the turnpike, and on the extreme left stood Reynolds, south of the Warrenton Pike and southwest of Groveton.

Sigel held the center of the line. His men had been involved during the morning in sporadic but fairly severe fighting, carrying out Pope's instructions to hold Jackson in position till Heintzelman and Reno could reach the scene from Centerville. Reynolds' division, operating on Sigel's left, about 1:00 P.M. was briefly in contact with Longstreet's leading elements without realizing they were from Longstreet's wing, following which he moved back to Chinn Ridge.

Reynolds was in a state of some uncertainty as commander of an independent division attached to McDowell's corps. Theoretically he was acting under McDowell's orders, but that peripatetic general seemed to be all over the field, hard to locate, and apparently acting as Pope's roving deputy-at-large, without a recognizable portfolio. A message that Reynolds sent to Pope's Chief of Staff, Colonel Schriver, at 3:30 in the afternoon, shows how far communication and control had deteriorated:

> *Colonel: General Sigel is moving on Gainesville down the pike, with my right near Groveton. My left toward the railroad.*
>
> *I do not know where anybody is but Sigel. Please let me hear from you.*

Two of Sigel's divisions (his corps was composed of three divisions under Schenck, von Steinwehr, and Schurz, with Milroy's independent brigade attached) bore the brunt of the morning attacks over a broad front, and were roughly handled by the defending Confederates, protected as the latter were by the railroad cuts and embankments. Never a particularly aggressive fighter, Sigel's customary procedure seemed to be to look for reasons why immediate battle for his troops should be deferred. This time he had no choice in the matter, but true to form reported to Pope, about noon, that his line was weak, Schurz' division and Steinwehr's had been badly cut up, and ought to be pulled out of the line to recover. Pope was aware that Sigel was a weak reed and could not be strongly relied on, but without any other troops at hand there were no replacements, so Sigel was told to stay put. Feeling perhaps that his subordinate's morale could stand a little boosting, Pope confidently informed him that McDowell and Porter were even then moving in on Jackson's right flank (which of course was premature and inaccurate despite Pope's orders), and would quickly relieve the pressure on Sigel. That was pretty helpful medicine, thought Pope, who then rode the line to pass the same good word on to Reno and Heintzelman.

JACKSON TAKES PUNISHMENT

From about 1:30 to 4:00 in the afternoon, Pope's divisions launched piecemeal but vigorous attacks against Jackson's intrenched position all along the line. Artillery roared continuously and there was scarcely a time when an infantry attack was not in progress at one point or another. Yet there was no directing genius to coordinate the brave but successive advances of the Union divisions, or to take advantage of any favorable opportunity which might offer, as would certainly have been the case if Lee, or Jackson, or Longstreet had been directing the Federal effort in place of Pope.

In fairness to Pope it may be contended that his battle plan was sound enough had it been properly executed. Pope could say that the frontal attacks by Sigel, Heintzelman, and Reno were directed as a pivot for the purpose of fully occupying the attention of Jackson's corps, which Pope believed to be the only force at that time on the field, while the corps commanded by McDowell and Porter represented the maneuvering mass that was ordered to press the attack against Jackson's flank to assure the victory.

That was fine on paper, except that it underestimated the ingenious battlefield capabilities of Lee and his chief lieutenants, allowed no margin of safety in case any part of the plan failed to work, and completely overlooked the necessity of using the auxiliary arm, the cavalry brigades of Buford and Bayard, for close-in reconnaissance and counter-reconnaissance when the two armies met on the battlefield. Even after giving the devil his due it must be concluded that Pope himself has to bear the major responsibility for the Union defeat at Second Manassas, with however a very powerful assist from a reluctant corps commander by the name of Fitz John Porter. All of which is getting a bit ahead of the story while forming impressions that cannot help but force themselves on one's consciousness as the play progresses.

With three full corps, reinforced by a separate division plus an independent brigade, in line from Bull Run on the right to a point half a mile south of the turnpike and about a mile west of Groveton on the left, Pope's attacking line covered a good three miles of front with a strength of about 33,000 men. The line paralleled Jackson's along the unfinished railroad and overlapped it slightly at either end. The Federal offense therefore mustered twice as many men as Jackson had available to stave them off, but Pope would need the additional 26,000 of McDowell's and Porter's corps if he was to have any success in dislodging Jackson's obstinate fighters.

Pope in person took command of his army for the afternoon phase on August 29. The possibility of turning Jackson's left in conjunction with McDowell's expected flank attack on the Confederate right prompted him to order Heintzelman to make an all-out effort, since Sigel's hand had been played out in the center without result, although one of his attacks through a patch of woods had created a temporary gap in the Confederate line which the Federals were unable to exploit. Reno was directed to attack concurrently on his front, while Sigel would be given a respite for the time being.

A. P. Hill's Light Division, which held the left of Jackson's position, was one of the best, if not the best fighting division in the entire Confederate Army. It would need all its courage and determination this day to withstand the violent attacks made on it by the divisions of Kearny, Hooker, and Reno. Fortunately for the fiery Ambrose Hill, the Federal divisions made their attacks successively, a tactical defect which one might suppose to have been a military policy of the Federal corps and army commanders, judging from the consistency with which they adhered to that policy in so many battles during the first half of the war.

The intention however had been for all three divisions, Kearny, Hooker, and Reno, to attack simultaneously, which in a sense contravenes the statement made in the preceding paragraph. But something more positive than intentions is necessary to put driving force into the unpleasant task of marching troops into a hail of antagonistic shells and bullets. It was the higher command echelons, superior to the individual division and brigade commanders, which somehow failed to provide the essential ingredient of minute-by-minute coordinating control on the battlefield.

Jackson's massed artillery on the north flank poured a galling fire into Kearny's division on the right, to prevent his advance, while Hooker and Reno moved disjointedly but impetuously into the attack, the Confederate skirmishers falling back rapidly to the railroad embankment as the Blue masses pushed resolutely forward through the underbrush.

Hill's veterans met them with heavy volleys of musketry that set fire to the dry underbrush, but still the determined Federals came on, in spite of losses. This was Hooker's division, and "Fighting Joe" was at his best as a division commander. The no-man's land between the two forces quickly disappeared as the on rushing brigades ate up the intervening distance to engage in hand-to-hand combat. A gallant Federal charge penetrated Hill's line, took possession of the railroad at that spot, and drove the Confederates out. But only for a moment. Then the defenders' second line came forward at a run and it was the Union's turn to retire. Hooker's men fell back, re-formed, and again rushed forward to repeat their earlier success. Once again Hill's supports drove them out, and so it went at close quarters for some time.

Inevitably, when a supposedly irresistible force meets an immovable body, the mobile element loses out, and so it was with the stout-hearted brigades of Hooker and Reno. Despite the protecting railroad embankment for the Confederates, and the rolling ground which afforded partial cover for the advancing Federals, the slaughter was terrific on both sides and could not be sustained indefinitely. The local victory would fall to that commander who would throw in his last reserve at the psychological moment. That commander was the red-haired, red-shirted Hill, and his ace-in-the-hole was Pender's brigade, which crossed the railroad and hit

Hooker's weary men at an angle that sliced through the ranks with sufficient fresh force to turn the tide. The still unwounded Federals broke for
the rear.

But Hooker also had an unused reserve, Grover's brigade, which he
now threw into the swirling fight. Grover had been watching the battle
all along and done some thinking. When his turn came, he told his
men to advance at a walk until the Confederates opened fire, when they
would make one rush, halt and deliver a single volley, and then cover the
remaining distance in a second rush to drive the attack home with the
bayonet.

Grover had already formed four of his regiments in two lines, with
the fifth in the lead, and had reconnoitered the ground over which he was
to advance. His direction of attack ran through a copse into a 50-yard
gap in the railroad bank, called "The Dump." One volley, one irresistible
rush, and Grover's force poured through The Dump and into the woods
beyond. They kept right on going, and Lawton's second line at that point
was swept away. The Confederates were in real trouble, but help was at
hand. Stonewall Jackson, who always seemed to see what was going on,
observed the impetuous Federal charge and took prompt steps to neutralize it. Pulling a brigade from another part of the line nearby, which
was not in action at the moment, he threw it at the victorious Federals
and the extra weight of the fresh troops in turn caught Grover's men in
the flank. It was more than they could manage, weakened as they were
by heavy losses sustained in the assault. Grover fell back, fighting gamely,
through the woods, and rejoined his division, leaving 25 percent of his
men on the field as casualties.

The fighting spirit of the men of both sides had been deeply stirred in
this first major clash of the Manassas battle that involved large forces of
either army. Memories of First Manassas played a part, undoubtedly, for
many of the officers and men had fought over this same ground in July
1861. There were old scores to be paid off; the Federal troops animated by
the urge to erase the memory of the wild panic that had seized so many
of the raw Union levies in their first defeat of the war; the Confederates
equally determined to show that they could repeat the performance. It
was a knock-down, drag-out affair from beginning to end, lasting from

mid-morning to dark, up and down the line, in fragmentary encounters without at any time developing into a general engagement involving all the troops in contact.

The casualty lists grew longer by the hour, but neither side showed the slightest evidence of giving up. Dead bodies cluttered the railroad bed where the close-in encounters mostly took place. The afternoon phase was mainly A. P. Hill's battle, with assists when needed from Lawton's (Ewell's) neighboring division, for it was on Hill's front that the driving attacks by Hooker's and Reno's divisions were directed. The Light Division had lost heavily; thousands of its members were down to their last cartridge. Federal marksmen from wooded cover kept up the firing pressure unceasingly so that resupply of ammunition was a hazardous undertaking.

At 4 o'clock, almost as though by unanimous consent, occurred a lull in the booming of artillery guns and the clatter of musketry fire that had been practically continuous for more than six hours. But not for long. Pope had ordered a fresh attack by Kearny and Reno, again directed against the left of Jackson's line where Hill's undefeated but badly depleted Light Division had already withstood the driving attacks of Hooker and Reno. Five Federal brigades, shoulder to shoulder, charged through Confederate gun fire, captured the railroad in their zone, and pushed Hill's exhausted men steadily backward several hundred yards within their own lines. The critical moment had arrived; Jackson's line was bent back on the center; if supported in depth the Federal attack could be decisive.

Sometime earlier the brigades of Early and Forno, of Lawton's (Ewell's) division, posted on the extreme right of Jackson's line near the Warrenton Turnpike, had been relieved of their vigil by the arrival of Longstreet's leading division. They had then rejoined their own outfit in the center and were ready for business. Jubal Early seemed marked by destiny to be Johnny-on-the-spot at critical junctures, particularly when a counter-attack was called for. His troops had turned the trick at First Manassas; and now they would do it again.

Summoned by the hard-pressed Hill in a desperate effort to stave off disaster, Early's reinforced brigade came charging through the weakened Confederate line with leveled bayonets. Kearny's Federals had by this time lost some of their impetus and cohesion. These fresh, determined, onrushing Confederates threw the Union troops into confusion, cold steel had its customary effect on morale, and the attackers turned about and fled to shelter, with Early's avengers in hot pursuit.

The final Federal attempt to break Jackson's line had failed as did the first four. Pope made no further effort on August 29 to destroy Jackson, and the battle ended on that front with both Federals and Confederates occupying the same general positions between the turnpike and Bull Run each held when the serious fighting had started early in the afternoon.

Meanwhile, King's division of McDowell's corps, now commanded by Brigadier General Hatch (King was still sick and had to be relieved), had completed its march up the Sudley road from Manassas Junction and was led into the line on Reynolds' left. As they were taking position, however, McDowell pulled them out, having just received a message from Pope that the enemy was falling back and he wanted Hatch's division to pursue down the Warrenton Road. The day was almost spent, but the division responded enthusiastically, quickly got under way, and ran smack into a reconnoitering Confederate column (one of Longstreet's divisions) coming from the opposite direction. Both outfits were somewhat surprised at the unexpected meeting. They engaged in a spirited and extended exchange in the gathering dusk and then called it off for the day. Ricketts' division, following in trace of Hatch, was assigned to a position in reserve, north of the turnpike, as Hatch, after his brush with the enemy, moved into the Union line on the left of Sigel's corps.

Most of the fighting on the 29th was north of the turnpike between Jackson's corps on the one side and the Union corps of Sigel, Reno, and Heintzelman on the other. Both armies lost heavily in killed and wounded, but neither could claim a victory, although Jackson was clearly entitled to the honors of the day for having maintained his position in the face of repeated and heavy Federal attacks. Now he was no longer isolated and alone, for Lee and Longstreet had arrived on the field along toward noon, when Longstreet's divisions, as they came up, filed off the road in successive increments and were fed into an extension of Jackson's line, astride the turnpike and to the south of it.

Pope, wholly unaware that Lee's army had been reunited and now confronted him in its entirety, and still operating under the delusion that only Jackson's wing opposed him, was as determined as ever to knock him out by means of the flank attack that he had earlier in the day directed Porter and McDowell, working together as a unit, to mount.

In pursuit of that objective, the hopelessly optimistic commander of the Army of Virginia at 4:30 P.M. sent Porter an order "to push forward into action at once on the enemy's flank, and, if possible, on his rear." Unfortunately for Pope's hopefully ambitious plan, Porter's corps was not where he thought it was, advancing steadily on Gainesville, but instead was halted in place, still east of Dawkin's Branch, doing nothing much but marking time where it had been all day. Porter himself was back at Bethlehem Church, near the tail of his column and not much over a mile west of Manassas Junction. It was about 6:30 P.M. when he received the order, rather late in the day to initiate an attack under the circumstances as Porter understood them. Nevertheless, and probably chiefly for the record, he ordered Morell's division to prepare to attack, but cancelled the order as soon as he found that the entire division was ready to move.

A RISKY CONFEDERATE VENTURE

Lee's plan of campaign, that led to Pope's disaster at Second Manassas, was unbelievably bold; could even be called a reckless adventure that offered only a slim chance of success. Yet it was well on its way to fruition as Jackson completed its first phase by throwing Pope into a dizzy whirl on August 27-28. Notwithstanding Pope's setback, the danger to Lee's army would continue to be critical until it could be reassembled to present a united front against Pope's ever-increasing strength.

The almost casual, unruffled manner in which Lee and Longstreet brought the main body of the Confederate army through Thoroughfare Gap to join Jackson's isolated wing at Groveton revealed a calm confidence in the joint Confederate ability to safely effect the reunion. It likewise implied an almost contemptuous disregard of Pope's capability to prevent it.

Pope's forces, chiefly through his own neglect, offered only negligible opposition to Longstreet's advance. Ricketts' well-intentioned but token resistance at the eastern end of the pass through Bull Run Mountains turned out to be a half-hearted measure, directed by corps commander

McDowell on his own volition and without orders from or even the knowledge of the army commander, who was so obsessed with the idea of bagging Jackson that he seemed to have forgotten about Longstreet.

After Ricketts, maneuvered out of position the evening of August 28, had moved rapidly away from the Gap to make his way back to Bristoe, the Federal cavalry under Buford was all that stood between Longstreet and Jackson except an eight-mile road march. Although the Confederates in the Gap heard the sounds of battle between Jackson and King, the music struck Lee as a reason for rejoicing rather than a cause for worry, in the sense that it was convincing evidence that Jackson's divisions were nearby and apparently quite able to take care of themselves. Had the reaction been otherwise there can be no doubt that Longstreet's force would have been ordered to push ahead without a halt, in a night march to Jackson's support.

Early on the morning of August 29 the Confederate divisions resumed their journey, passing through Haymarket and Gainesville, near which latter point Buford was keeping the road under observation and from where he sent his 9:30 message to Ricketts (see page 176). As Longstreet's reinforcements neared the battlefield, Sigel's corps was attacking Jackson's position from the east and the pace of Hood's leading Confederate division accelerated as the noise of battle grew louder. In fact Hood moved so fast that he outdistanced the divisions in rear, so that Longstreet had to slow him down.

The evidence points to the arrival of Hood's division, preceded by part of Stuart's cavalry, in rear of Jackson's line about 10:30 or 11:00 o'clock in the morning. As succeeding units came up they were turned off to right and left of the turnpike, deployed and moved forward. When the entire corps (less Anderson's rearguard division, with the trains, which came up later) had arrived and formed up on the right of Jackson's line, the Longstreet order of battle from left to right was as follows: Hood's two brigades (on either side of the turnpike) with Evans' independent brigade in support on the turnpike, Kemper's small division, and D. R. Jones' division. Wilcox's three brigades, in column formation, were disposed on the north side of the turnpike on Hood's left rear, apparently as corps reserve. Jeb Stuart with Robertson's cavalry brigade moved out to Jones' right, a half-mile south of the Manassas Gap Railroad, to cover the army right flank, while Fitz Lee's brigade covered Jackson's north flank.

The entire Confederate line now covered a front that extended for a distance of almost five miles, from Jackson's left in the vicinity of Sudley Church to Longstreet's right on the Manassas Gap Railroad, not including the cavalry, which operated still further out on each flank. The line was shaped like a V, the apex pointing west, affording an excellent opportunity to emplace artillery on a commanding elevation where the two wings joined about half a mile north of the turnpike near the bed of the unfinished railroad. There Longstreet massed a heavy concentration of guns, so placed as to enfilade the open spaces along the front line in either direction. The afternoon was enlivened by an artillery duel which continued for several hours, to inflict material damage on the unprotected troops of both sides.

The movement of Longstreet's corps into a position that should long before have been preempted by Porter's and McDowell's two corps, according to Pope's plan, was accomplished without Federal opposition, for the reason that Porter was cooling his heels on the far side of Dawkins Branch and McDowell was getting ready to march north on the Manassas-Sudley Road, some 2½ miles to the east.

Battlefields are usually marked by one or more terrain features of particular tactical value to the troops that first take possession. North of the turnpike it was the Stony Ridge line in front of which ran the unfinished railroad. When he first arrived Jackson occupied that position and could not be budged from it by the most intense Federal attacks. South of the turnpike the key was still another stretch of high ground called Stuart's Hill, probably a prolongation of Stony Ridge, studded with woods and extending almost due south for several miles from a point near the turnpike, to the Manassas Gap Railroad and beyond. On the northern extremity of Stuart's Hill, several hundred yards south of the turnpike, Lee established his field headquarters and from that central point prepared to direct the battle.

LONGSTREET COUNSELS DELAY

Porter's failure to seize the tactically important ridge south of the turnpike, upon which were situated the Munroe (or Monroe) and Cole houses, gave Longstreet an opportunity that he was quick to seize. As it happened, no offensive measures were attempted by the Federals against Longstreet's position, in consequence of which Lee was persuaded by Longstreet to bide his time on the premise that Jackson, while battling fiercely, was not in serious trouble, and there would come an opportunity to decisively employ the massive army reserve of four divisions (five when Anderson arrived) after the Union divisions were given the privilege of wearing themselves out in repeated attacks. Although Lee's anxiety to assist the embattled Jackson was understandable, his desire to press for a conclusion, now that a general engagement seemed inevitable, was influenced more by the belief that every hour of delay would bring more of McClellan's divisions to bear on the outcome. At the same time, however, the presence of Longstreet's 30,000 men now (August 29) gave him 50,000 to Pope's approximately 65,000 actually on the field, instead of an army of 100,000 or more, which could so easily have been at Pope's command except for McClellan's consciously dilatory execution of Halleck's orders. The knowledge that the opposing forces were now on practically even terms undoubtedly was a factor in Lee's decision to delay the immediate commitment to action of Longstreet's wing.

LEE DEFERS TO LONGSTREET

As Pope shifted the weight of his attacks from Jackson's center to his left, where A.P. Hill's division was about to carry the major burden of the defense, Lee watched the battlefield and deliberated. Uncertain as to the extent of Pope's reinforcements from McClellan's army, and reluctant to bring on a general engagement between the Federals and his own entire army until the relative strengths and dispositions were more accurately determined, Lee discussed with Longstreet the question whether the time was not ripe for the right wing, now in position, to attack down the turnpike to assist in relieving the pressure on Jackson's somewhat depleted ranks.

Longstreet demurred, adhering to his firmly established tactical conviction that it was more profitable to maneuver his troops into a position that would force the enemy to attack from a less advantageous position.

Beside which, he said, he had not yet had time to study the ground to his front, and until he could do so, it were better to refrain from what might prove to be a premature effort.

Returning from his reconnaissance, Longstreet expressed himself in favor of further delay, in support of which he described the terrain as unfavorable, adding that the Federal line extended a long way to the south of the turnpike, and heavy reserves might well be coming up from the direction of Manassas. As Lee and Longstreet talked, a courier arrived from Stuart to report a Federal column marching up from Manassas and another, estimated as an army corps, moving up the Manassas-Sudley Road. That seemed to confirm Longstreet's fears, and it was then that Lee ordered Cadmus Wilcox's division over from Longstreet's left to reinforce D. R. Jones on the extreme right.

Lee continued to wait, while Longstreet again rode off to reexamine the situation in light of the new information. When he returned the second time, Jackson had arrived at Lee's command post to bring the Commanding General up to date on his own situation. Lee again indicated to Longstreet his opinion that an attack was indicated, but Longstreet advised still further delay until the intentions of the Federal troops that were advancing could be determined. It might be expected that Jackson, who up to now had done most of the work and taken all the losses, would support Lee's opinion, but whether from pride or because to be taciturn was strictly in character, he offered no comment, and soon left the conference to get back on the job where the noise of battle was increasing up Sudley Springs way.

A few moments later Stuart himself rode up and confirmed the approach of a Federal corps, presumably McDowell's. Impatient at Longstreet's continued unwillingness to commit his divisions to action, Lee mounted Traveler and rode forward to look the situation over for himself. After an hour or so he was satisfied that the Confederate line was secure, that the Federals reported by Stuart did not pose an overwhelming threat, and that his original idea of a strong attack along the turnpike held excellent promise, including the possibility of splitting off the approaching Union reinforcements. The discussion with Longstreet was resumed, but the latter remained obdurate in opposing an attack.

It was an interesting picture—Lee in his quiet, firm way indicating a positive wish that Longstreet should get going—Longstreet just as firmly sticking to his guns in favor of a defensive attitude, for the time being. Two men of strong character, neither of whom was convinced by the other; surely a commentary on the way in which Lee dealt with his chief lieutenants, each according to his character. Lee knew Longstreet too well to insist on action against Old Pete's considered judgment. Yet it was not a sign of weakness on Lee's part, simply a realization that the results that he wanted would not be forthcoming at the hands of an unwilling general. Nevertheless, as Douglas Southall Freeman has observed, the seeds of the failure at Gettysburg were planted on August 29, 1862, when Lee permitted Longstreet to differ with him, and Longstreet in turn realized the extent of his safety in opposing the judgment of his commanding general.

Hours had passed since Lee had first indicated his wish that Longstreet attack, and the afternoon of August 29 was nearly spent. Longstreet suggested that there would now be insufficient daylight to initiate an offensive, and proposed instead that he institute a reconnaissance in force down the turnpike to develop the situation preparatory to a possible concerted Army attack the following morning. Lee reluctantly approved, so about sunset Hood's division moved out, ran into Hatch's (recently King's) Federal division, and late at night withdrew with a number of prisoners to its original line. The effect on Longstreet was to convince him that the Federal strength was such as to preclude success in an early morning attack, even though R. H. Anderson's division and the reserve artillery had reached the field during the day to give Longstreet five divisions under his immediate command. Old Pete had made up his mind that an active defense was the correct prescription and he was going to do it his way so long as Lee continued willing to defer to his subordinate's judgment.

On the record it would seem that Lee's original plan of campaign, to cut Pope off from McClellan's reinforcements before their arrival and then crush him with more nearly equal strength, had been somewhat modified when he learned how many of McClellan's divisions had already reached Pope since the latter's retrograde movement from the line of the Rappahannock to counter Jackson's threat to his rear. The battle urge which in the presence of the enemy at Groveton led Lee to advise Longstreet to attack was a temporary adherence to the original conception, but his readiness to go along with Longstreet's defensive psychology indicated a revision of his basic thinking. Now it became Lee's policy to again depend rather on maneuver than offensive fighting to defeat his stronger opponent, as evidenced by his early morning dispatch of August 30 to President Davis, in which he said; "My desire has been to avoid a general engagement, being the weaker force, and by maneuvering to relieve the portion of the country referred to (the Rappahannock frontier). I think if not overpowered we shall be able to relieve other portions of the country, as it seems to be the purpose of the enemy to collect his strength here. . . ."

Little if anything can be proven by speculating on who was right, Lee or Longstreet, insofar as an attack by Longstreet's wing on the afternoon of August 29 was concerned. At the very least it would have taken much of the pressure off Jackson, whose left was bent back upon itself and came perilously close to being broken by Heintzelman and Reno. It might also have resulted in throwing Pope into a complete state of confusion, for even at that late hour he was still unaware that Longstreet's wing had joined Jackson and continued to believe that Jackson's three divisions were all that faced him. Finally, a well-supported drive down the turnpike might very well have driven a wedge through Pope's fluid position, to catch his supports coming up to attack Jackson and possibly also to hit McDowell's two tired divisions as they plodded north on the Manassas-Sudley Road. As for Porter, who played the timid soul on this occasion, and was scarcely acting in character as a part of McClellan's army (or was he?), it is not unlikely, considering his attitude on that day, that an "I told you so" reflex would have led him to seek safety in a retrograde movement.

Longstreet's fear that his own force might be overwhelmed if he attacked was of course unfounded in view of Porter's reluctance to engage. There were in fact no Federal troops whatever directly in front of Longstreet, between the turnpike and the Manassas Gap Railroad, a two-mile wide frontage, except Reynolds' lone division, and Reynolds' position was wide open on both flanks. Sykes and Morell of Porter's corps had not even deployed south of the railroad, and McDowell was leading the divisions of Hatch and Ricketts up the Manassas-Sudley Road, which was a good 2½ miles distant from Longstreet's front line.

From Longstreet's standpoint, to be sure, Porter's corps was a potential threat to the security of his own line and could have caused the Confederates a lot of trouble had Porter chosen to act aggressively. Longstreet could not have anticipated how supinely Porter would act. In his estimate of the situation he would naturally assume that so large a body of Federal troops would be utilized to the best advantage. Porter's two divisions happened to be so disposed that by moving rapidly straight to the front they could, assuming a quick overthrow of Drayton's brigade, have moved easily around and behind Longstreet's right flank.

That would not necessarily have had fatal results for Longstreet, who preferred the defensive and was far more adept than Porter in his tactical reactions and in shifting brigades and divisions on the battlefield. Longstreet's strength at the moment was three times that of Porter, and even if the latter had committed his corps to a flank attack, his major contribution to the Union cause would in all probability have been to disrupt Confederate plans for their successful counterattack on the second day. That, however, would have been military teamwork of a high order, to which Fitz John Porter was not disposed to contribute, with John Pope calling the signals.

McClellan Fiddles While Pope Burns

While Pope's army fulfilled its ill-fated destiny on the Manassas plains, twenty miles from Washington as the crow flies, a disgruntled McClellan kept sending a steady stream of telegrams to Halleck from Alexandria, where he remained in an unhappily anomalous position as the titular commander of an army that was fast melting away from his control.

Halleck for several days had been importuning McClellan to speed the two corps of Franklin and Sumner to Pope, while McClellan sought every excuse and expedient to hold them in Alexandria. Whether that additional strength would have been effectively employed by Pope or not is beside the point, which was that the General-in-Chief, the official head of all the armies, had ordered them to be sent, and it was not McClellan's prerogative to circumvent Halleck's direct and increasingly peremptory orders to that effect.

Pope Claims a Success

The Confederates, during the heavy fighting on Jackson's front on Friday afternoon, had pushed their line ahead of the unfinished railroad in several places, and Hood's scrap with Hatch's division on the turnpike ended late in the evening with the former's division parked some distance ahead of Longstreet's ridge line. During the night, however, it seemed best to Lee to pull the advanced units back to their former position, which resulted in what looked to the Federal troops in contact to be a wholesale withdrawal. That in any case was the way Pope chose to interpret the movements, and he so advised Halleck in a 5 A.M. telegram:

> We fought a terrific battle here yesterday with the combined forces of the enemy, which lasted with continuous fury from daylight until dark, by which time the enemy was driven from the field, which we now occupy. Our troops are too much exhausted yet to push matters, but I shall do so in the course of the morning, as soon as Fitz John Porter's corps comes up from Manassas.

CHAPTER 7

Second Bull Run III: The Climax

WITHDRAWAL of the Confederate lines to their initial battle position as a stronger one upon which to receive the expected, and hoped-for, attack by Pope's army on Saturday, August 30, was misinterpreted by the Federal commander to mean that Jackson declined to take further punishment and preferred to retire from the field. Dawn reconnaissances by Federal parties found that the Confederates had in fact relinquished their advanced lines, which when coupled with similar reports by two of his corps commanders, McDowell and Heintzelman, confirmed Pope in his optimistic appraisal and stirred him to lay plans for a vigorous pursuit.

At 3:00 o'clock in the morning, Porter received Pope's latest order to bring his command immediately to the field of battle. This time he responded with alacrity, possibly in the belief that he had already carried his indifference to orders too far, especially if his information of the evening before was correct, that the battle was going well for the Federals in the area of the turnpike and to the north. His prompt compliance with the new directive meant that there would be no Union troops opposing Longstreet's divisions in the direction of the Manassas Gap railroad, but that was Pope's concern, not his. Without losing any time, he started north on the Sudley Road and upon arrival at the center of the army position reported to Pope in person for instructions.

Pope's latest strategic brain-child, compounded as usual of grossly insufficient knowledge of his opponent's dispositions and strength and his own wishful thinking, played directly into Lee's hands. With his customary skill at interpreting the advantages of terrain and its utilization for the benefit of his own forces, Lee had set up for Pope's reception a vise-like set of jaws, at whose hinge stood the mass of his reserve artillery, with a clear field of fire to front and flanks. The Warrenton Turnpike, natural avenue of approach, led through the center of the position, and it was quite probable that troops advancing on either side of the road would tend to gravitate in that direction, and thus funnel directly into the very place Lee wanted them, and from which he could inflict the heaviest damage. Pope's contribution to the Confederate desideratum, by the act of weakening his own left to bring Porter's two divisions to the center of his planned attack, was as a result quite pleasing to General Lee. The fact was that Pope still acted as though he had only Jackson to deal with, that the latter was now retreating, and that Porter would be of no earthly use to him way down there on Dawkin's Branch.

Strange as it may seem, Pope thought Jackson might get away from him and at the same time Lee was worrying lest Pope fall back in the direction of Washington and escape the destruction that the Confederates had in store for him. On August 29 Lee had discussed with his lieutenants what measures they might take to encourage the Federals to attack if Pope should stall for time. In fact, Lee's fear of Pope's possible withdrawal was so well defined that he made plans that evening to resume the march next day by way of Sudley Ford and the Little River Turnpike to get between the Federals and Washington to prevent the very thing he feared. On the other hand, Pope maintained later that because he was short on rations he had no choice but to attack on August 30 or fall back to meet up with his supplies. In substance, then, it appears that Lee was mighty anxious for Pope to attack, while Pope was equally anxious to do so, but with no intent to accommodate Lee.

Lee Awaits Pope's Next Move

Saturday, August 30, started out hot, with a hint of rain to come. The Confederates rested on their arms, leaving the initiative to the Federals, who spent the morning in preparation for another go at their obstinate opponents, who the day before had seemed so determined to retain for themselves every foot of the terrain they had acquired. The Confederates could clearly see from their own lines the vast troop movements by which the Federals were rearranging themselves for the new attack. Jackson was especially intrigued by the amount of marching that took place in the enemy zone during the morning, much of it seeming to indicate a shift of emphasis to the south and away from his own left, where A. P. Hill still held the line, but with far fewer fighting men than the number with which he had thrown back twice his own weight on Friday.

Jackson is reported to have made the observation that appearances indicated the unlikelihood of an attack that day, but he decided to wander over to Lee's headquarters to compare notes. There he found Lee already discussing the outlook with Longstreet and Stuart, and considering what steps might be taken to needle Pope into action if that should be needed.

Generally speaking, the morning passed quietly, except for a sharp exchange of gunfire on the north flank, where a Confederate battery took appropriate steps to discourage several enemy guns from becoming too venturesome, and an infantry exchange when several regiments of Ricketts' division ran into a hornet's nest and were given a lively time. Pope's sketchy reconnaissance during the morning had failed to discover Confederates where they had been the day before. From this he jumped to the erroneous conclusion that Jackson had withdrawn and was retreating toward Thoroughfare Gap. What had actually happened was that Gregg's brigade had pulled back to replenish ammunition, then returned to its former position. Had Pope made an effort to confirm his hasty impression by consulting his front line troops, Ricketts for one could have assured him that the Confederates were still very much in evidence.

POPE'S INADEQUATE RECONNAISSANCE

Pope's sorry reconnaissance on his north flank was duplicated on the south flank. Where Hatch and Hood had collided on the turnpike on the evening of April 29 Pope again found no Confederates, which seemed to confirm his belief that Jackson had in fact pulled out. Pope still hadn't learned that Longstreet was on hand. Had the Federal commander pushed his reconnaissance a few hundred yards farther he would have been unpleasantly surprised to find Longstreet's corps ready and waiting where Pope was sure there were no enemy troops at all. Without exaggeration, it may be doubted that there was ever in the history of American armies a better example of inadequate reconnaissance.

By noon Pope's plan of action had matured, and orders went out for all commanders:

SPECIAL ORDERS

NO.— —

The following forces will be immediately thrown forward in pursuit of the enemy and press him vigorously during the whole day. Major-General McDowell is assigned to the command of the pursuit.

Major-General Porter's corps will push forward on the Warrenton turnpike, followed by the divisions of Brigadier-Generals King and Reynolds. The division of Brigadier-General Ricketts will pursue the Hay Market road, followed by the corps of Major-General Heintzelman. The necessary cavalry will be assigned to these columns by Major-General McDowell, to whom regular and frequent reports will be made. The general headquarters will be somewhere on the Warrenton turnpike.

In preparation for further heavy work, Pope wired McClellan, Halleck, and any others that he could think of, to rush extra artillery ammunition to him. Halleck in turn telegraphed Banks, at Manassas Junction, in charge of Pope's trains, advising that ammunition would be sent as soon as possible, but meantime "Cannot you send him some from Manassas?"

Banks' 1:45 P.M. reply to Halleck was a gem, indicating as it did the low state to which Pope's system of communication and supply within the army had fallen:

Your dispatch received. There is artillery and other ammunition in my train near Centerville, Sixteen wagons went up last night. I have many more wagons on the road now near this place, which can be moved directly to him if I knew where to send them.

Please inform me.

Halleck took time to reply to the helpless Banks, advising him that Pope's headquarters were at Groveton that morning, and adding, with what must have been a wry smile: "You can judge best from the firing where he is now. The enemy this morning was said to be falling back toward the mountains."

Halleck Tries to Reassure Pope

Ineffectual as his efforts to date had been to expedite through McClellan the prompt transfer to Pope of the divisions of the Army of the Potomac as they debarked at Aquia and Alexandria, Halleck must be credited with making strenuous efforts in that direction. Predicated on the unwarranted assumption that McClellan was following orders and had already sent Franklin's corps to Pope, Halleck telegraphed the latter at 2 P.M. that afternoon:

> *Yours of 5 A.M. is received. All matters have been attended to. Thirty thousand men are marching to your aid.*
>
> *Franklin should be with you now and Sumner tomorrow morning. All will be right soon, even if you should be forced to fall back. Let your army know that heavy reinforcements are coming.*

But Franklin was at that moment still a long way from Bull Run. He had gone only so far as Annandale, a mere five miles from Alexandria and a good eighteen miles from the battlefield. McClellan, who was applying the curb bit, gave Halleck the lame excuse that Franklin was unable to get transportation for his extra ammunition, implying that it was all the fault of the quarter-masters. Halleck expressed his dissatisfaction in a caustic message to McClellan:

> *I am by no means satisfied with General Franklin's march of yesterday. Considering the circumstances of the case, he was very wrong in stopping at Annandale. Moreover, I learned last night that the Quartermaster's Department could have given him plenty of transportation if he had applied for it, any time since his arrival at Alexandria. He knew the importance of opening communication with General Pope's army, and should have acted more promptly.*

On receipt of the last message McClellan capitulated, directed Franklin to proceed, and ordered Sumner to "march immediately to the relief of General Pope." About the same time he informed Halleck that Couch's division had arrived in part, that the remainder would soon be there, and requested instructions as to the disposition of the additional reinforcements. Halleck replied that Couch should be immediately sent to Pope, and directed McClellan to send transports to Aquia to bring Burnside's command up to Alexandria as well.

Halleck, apparently not trusting McClellan to impress on his corps commanders the urgency of the situation, made still another effort to rush aid to Pope, telegraphing McClellan at 2:10 P.M.:

Franklin's and all of Sumner's corps should be pushed forward with all possible dispatch. They must use their legs and make forced marches. Time now is everything. Send some sharpshooters on the trains to Bull Run. The bridges and property are threatened by bands of Prince William Cavalry. Give Colonel Haupt all the assistance you can, The sharpshooters on top of cars can assist in unloading the trains.

If it was any satisfaction to McClellan, his protracted delay in sending Franklin and Sumner to join Pope, which should have given the Army of Virginia 30,000 more rifles and close to a 2 to 1 superiority over Lee on the field of Bull Run, had withheld the vital reinforcements just long enough for Lee's army to achieve the victory that sent Pope's divisions reeling back in defeat that very afternoon.

Brigadier General Jacob D. Cox, commanding the Kanawha Division, having made a well-regulated move from West Virginia and finally succeeded in reassembling his division at Alexandria, was now occupying a position at Upton Hill, west of Annandale, from which point his cavalry patrols reconnoitered the country to the front and on both sides of Fairfax Court House. As Pope was about to initiate his alleged pursuit of Jackson on the afternoon of August 30, Cox reported to his superior, McClellan, that all was quiet and no enemy were reported in the country about Fairfax Court House.

The impression prevailed in Washington at this time that Pope was doing all right, but could use the additional troops to clinch the matter. Still there were plenty of wild rumors floating about, as there always are when a major battle impends or is occurring, and it was not beneath the dignity of certain major generals to speed all such on their way for the benefit of others.

General Banks, who was playing a sedentary role as guardian of the army trains at Manassas Junction and Centerville, had plenty of time on his hands while his fellow corps commanders were marching and fighting. Judging from the pages of the Official Records, Banks improved his time by penning messages to all and sundry, including President Lincoln, as though he were an official war correspondent charged with responsibility for disseminating all the news that came his way. One particular telegram to McClellan, on the morning of August 30, was typical:

> *There was a camp rumor as I came in from Bristoe that Jackson had moved toward Alexandria. Col. J. S. Clark, one of my aides, who has been out to the front, reports that Jackson has fallen back about 5 miles toward the mountains. He judges mainly by the sound of the guns. There has been an entire change of position, I judge. A scout reported to me at 10 A.M. that Jackson was at Gainesville with about 30,000. He said he saw and knew him. My corps is moving up from Bristoe. No enemy near.*

POPE HAS MISGIVINGS

Pope's private thoughts on the morning of this third day of battle were somewhat less optimistic than his orders to pursue the "retreating" Confederates indicated, if his subsequent official report is to be accepted as entirely objective. Therein he presents a dismal picture of the condition of his army on the morning of August 30, stating that the troops were "greatly exhausted by marching and fighting almost continuously for many days," but without mentioning the fact that much of the countermarching was for the reason that the army commander himself was operating in a fog of war more or less created by his own ineptitude.

Pope also declared, in his ex post facto bill of particulars, that the War Department failed to speed rations and forage to the army from Alexandria, with the result that his men and horses had but little food for two days and were consequently in a weakened condition for further marching and fighting. The fact that Lee's army managed to live and fight at considerably greater distance from its supply base was disregarded, as Pope sought for alibis.

Porter's successful effort to keep his corps from participation in the battle and in so doing to deprive Pope of a possible victory over Jackson on the 29th became increasingly disloyal, almost treasonous, the more Pope thought about it, and his dark mood was not brightened by the continuing failure of McClellan's two corps, Franklin's and Sumner's, to come to his support. "It was not until I received this letter (referring to Franklin's slow pace in coming to his support) that I began to be hopeless of any successful issue to our operations; but I felt it to be my duty, notwithstanding the broken-down condition of the forces under my command, to hold my position," he wrote.

In spite of such forebodings, Pope prepared to renew the engagement on August 30, although it is difficult to understand his mood of the moment, if he was honest in so describing it, when at that time he was under the impression that his opponent was actually marching away from the battlefield. "Every indication during the night of the 29th and up to 10 o'clock on the morning of the 30th, pointed to the retreat of the enemy from our front." Those are Pope's own words, and his 12 noon pursuit order was issued in that belief. It may well be asked, in view of the fact that the Confederate line was again exactly where it had been all during the previous day's fighting, what kind of scouting and patrolling Pope's army had undertaken between the night of August 29 and midday of August 30. Pope had castigated Porter for failing to initiate a reconnaissance in force the previous day, to ascertain whether the Confederates were in such strength as Porter claimed, without corroborating evidence. Now the shoe was on the other foot, but Pope kept very quiet on that aspect of the situation.

There was one additional incident that occurred that Saturday morning which centered about whipping-boy Porter and, compounding that general's other sins of omission and commission, was duly recorded in the evidence introduced at Porter's later trial by court-martial. Porter's corps of two regular divisions had been reinforced by a brigade of Sturgis' division, dispatched from Washington, which gave it a strength of about

11,000 men. As Porter's troops were marching up in the early morning from Dawkin's Branch to join the center of Pope's army, Griffin's brigade of Morrell's division and Piatt's brigade of Sturgis' division missed a turn in the road and shortly found themselves with division commander Morrell himself at their head in Centerville, some miles east of the battlefield.

When Piatt discovered that his brigade was headed away from the battlefield, he reversed his brigade's direction of march and rejoined the army in time to participate in the action. Griffin's brigade, however, in company with Morrell, remained at Centerville all day, within hearing of the battle and without making any move to join its own outfit in the fight. "On the contrary," wrote Pope bitterly, "the brigade commander made requisition for ten thousand pairs of shoes on one of my aides-de-camp who was at Centerville in charge of the headquarters train." Was it possible that Porter had authorized the side jaunt? If so, it was not inconsistent with his freely written expressions as to how he really felt about his superior officer.

The Attack is Launched

Between 12 noon and 2 o'clock the Federals moved forward to what purported to be a pursuit but which at once became an attack, on a three-mile front which extended from the Warrenton Turnpike near Groveton on the left, to Bull Run near Sudley Church on the right. The Confederates were fully prepared and waiting along their prepared position of the previous day, on a line that was four miles in length, and which consequently overlapped the attackers by a mile or more on Longstreet's southern flank.

Porter's corps on the Federal left, Heintzelman's on the right, moved forward abreast, under Pope's instructions to push forward generally along the turnpike, which to observers indicated that the main effort would be made against the Confederate center. This was what the doctor (Lee) ordered, or rather hoped for, as the Federals obligingly advanced directly toward the point where Lee had massed the weight of his artillery.

Preceded by the usual skirmishers and followed by great numbers of guns and heavy concentrations of reserve troops, the imposing Federal mass advanced in three waves at approximately a hundred yard distance. McDowell's corps was given the mission of direct support for the two leading corps, Hatch's division backing up Porter on the left, Ricketts' division to follow Heintzelman on the right. Pope's ephemeral "pursuit" proved to be so short-lived, however, in view of the Confederates' failure to cooperate, that hasty improvisation by the lower echelons was necessary to adapt the forward elements to the unexpected situation.

Skirmishers from both Porter's corps and Hatch's division almost at once came in contact with Jackson's line in the Groveton woods north of the Pike and the main bodies immediately deployed for combat. Somewhat misled by the woods, Hatch swerved to the north, losing contact with Porter, whose right brigade complained that Hatch failed to lend support as ordered. But Hatch had his hands full, what with the heavy woods and Confederate volleys from behind the railroad, and there was nothing much that he could do about it.

The corps commanded by Sigel and Reno constituted the third echelon under Pope's plan for the advance, Sigel on the left, Reno on the right, both north of the turnpike. Reynolds' division, covering the army left on the south side of the turnpike, was in fact the only Federal force actually facing Longstreet's corps, but McDowell and Pope in their ignorance chose to transfer Reynolds to the north side just prior to the Confederate counterattack, in spite of Reynolds' reports that he was in contact with enemy infantry in the woods on his front!

Only the tread of thousands of feet, the rumble of gun carriages and the creaking of harness broke the uncanny silence on the field where yesterday had resounded the roar of guns and the cries of the wounded. There was something ominous about it, and it is to be doubted that many of the troops believed that they were engaging in a merry chase of retreating Confederates. Those who may have accepted Pope's pursuit order at face value were soon to be disillusioned.

Here and there, from behind protective cover, an occasional Confederate head popped up to get a better look at the impressive scene as the Union lines swept forward. It was just the sort of picture that Civil War artists loved to paint, but other thoughts were passing through the minds of Jackson's men, who it seemed were again to be the principal target of the stubborn Unionists, as they had been all the preceding afternoon.

The advancing lines were allowed to come forward without a shot or sound from the waiting Confederates. Suddenly an authoritative signal was given and the artillery at the center of the line opened fire with a crashing roar that brought Jackson's men at the double to their fighting positions. At once the attackers poured a hail of bullets into the woods in front of them, and the fight was on.

The sweeping bursts of artillery fire staggered the Blue front line, but the attack had been mounted in depth and the lines in rear pushed steadily ahead, ignoring losses. It soon became apparent that the Federal advance was aimed at Jackson's right center, where the divisions of Lawton and Starke held forth, with the Stonewall brigade, of First Manassas and Valley fame, as part of Starke's division.

Longstreet's line, mostly south of the Warrenton Turnpike, appeared to have been left out of Pope's calculations entirely, as though it didn't exist. Improbable as it may seem, that Longstreet's 30,000 men had been on the field for twenty-four hours without Pope's knowledge, no evidence can be found to disprove such an opinion. On the contrary, the dispositions that Pope made for attack on the second day, completely ignoring the southern sector, are confirmatory, unless Pope is to be charged with complete tactical ignorance.

Longstreet's desire to get a close-up view of the attack and to prepare for his own participation in the battle caused him to ride forward to his front line while the fight raged along and to the north of the turnpike. In his own words: "I reached a point a few rods in front of my line on the left of the pike where I could plainly see the Federals as they rushed in heavy masses against the obstinate ranks of the Confederate left. It was a grand display of well-organized attack, thoroughly concentrated and operating cleverly. So terrible was the onslaught that Jackson sent to me and begged for reenforcements. About the same time I received an order from General Lei to the same effect."

Porter's troops were evidently anxious to show that they could fight as well as relax, when the spirit should move them. Composed largely of Regular troops, they had demonstrated their combat ability on the Chickahominy in the Peninsular campaign. As the spearhead of the August 30 attack, they appear to have aroused Longstreet's admiration as they pushed doggedly ahead in determined attempts to penetrate and overwhelm the right and right center of Jackson's line behind the unimproved railroad, although the official reports of several general officers of other Federal corps, contiguous to Porter's zone of advance, were somewhat less complimentary. Sigel, for example, criticized Porter for masking his own troops and bunching in the open, as well as having retreated before he need have, with the excuse on the part of several regiments that they were out of ammunition.

The pressure of Sykes' Regulars on the left and a part of Morell's division under Daniel Butterfield on the right (Morell himself was calmly passing the time in Centerville, as previously noted) carried the aggressive Federals almost to the railroad bed at a point a mile north of Groveton and west of the Groveton-Sudley road. The Stonewall Brigade, ranks badly thinned by casualties taken the previous day, fought grimly to hold their position, as the attackers pressed relentlessly forward until the two lines were only a few yards apart, when it became a hand-to-hand struggle.

After a time Jackson's old division ran out of ammunition, but still the men refused to give up. Instead they seized rocks from the railroad embankment and from that vantage point hurled them at their opponents. The effect of such non-lethal but unpleasant weapons on the Federals has not been recorded, but the fact remains that the "Deep Cut," where the last-ditch stone throwing occurred, marked the farthest advance of Porter's corps and the Stonewall Brigade was credited with turning the Federals back. It is more reasonable to assume, however, that Lee's reserve artillery, massed only a short distance off, had the range of Porter's advanced units, took them in flank, and made the place too hot to hold.

When Porter's corps was repulsed and driven back, the Confederates figured the time had come to do a bit of attacking themselves. With their advance the whole battle line north of the turnpike became seriously engaged. Ricketts' Federal division was pulled out from support on the right and sent around to strengthen the line threatened by Porter's withdrawal. Sigel's corps, backing up Porter's position, took the Confederate blows with stubborn resistance, as Ricketts came up to help. For several hours the battle continued between Pope's army and Jackson's smaller force plus Hood's division. The latter was in position astride the turnpike and became engaged when Porter retired, with a view to speeding his departure. Porter's troops retreated in good order, were halted farther back, re-formed and after a while were returned to the battle and, according to Pope, rendered distinguished service.

LONGSTREET'S TACTICAL JUDGMENT VINDICATED

From the moment Longstreet had come on the field, about midday August 29, his tactical sense, as well as his confirmed predilection for the active defense, told him that it would be the part of wisdom to put off the commitment of his divisions until the psychological moment should arrive when he could deliver a devastating blow to produce the decisive result that Lee sought. Longstreet was a determined, even stubborn, character, but a rugged fighter when the chips were down. What he wanted, and insisted upon almost to the point of occasional insubordination, was that the conditions should be as nearly right as possible before he would consent to throw his divisions in.

The extent to which the troops of his colleague, General Jackson, were forced to suffer while his own remained unengaged, seemed not to enter his mind. Repeated urging by Lee, short of direct orders, failed to budge him. Let's wait some more, was the burden of his song, even when Jackson's line cracked ominously. At Second Manassas it turned out that Longstreet would withhold the weight of his counterattack with impunity, but when the performance was repeated at Gettysburg the following summer, Lee lost the battle to Meade.

Longstreet laid his plans carefully. His divisions were alert and waiting for the moment when all of Pope's divisions should be committed and many of them had reached the stage where they may be said to have been fought out. The battle on Jackson's front had gone on and on for hours. His own division had narrowly escaped defeat in fending off Porter's corps. Stephen Lee's reserve artillery had been in action all morning on the high ground in front of Jackson's right; it was that battalion which was largely instrumental in turning back Porter's early attack. Ewell's division on Jackson's center had had little to do, but A. P. Hill's on Jackson's left, weakened by its severe fight on August 29, faced odds and came close to breaking.

It was then that Jackson, unaccustomed to admitting that his corps needed help, swallowed his pride and sent to Lee for support from Longstreet. Lee immediately ordered Old Pete to send a division to Jackson's aid on the left. "Certainly," responded Longstreet, even though he was confident that the artillery would halt the Federal attack with their guns. Longstreet's instinct, and what he could see with his own eyes from his vantage point at the center of the army line, told him that the advanced guns, with the ability to deliver a plunging enfilade fire, could stop the attackers in their tracks long before he could get the supporting division into position to be of help.

The artillerymen had their own observers forward on the ridge in rear of which their eighteen guns stood ready, horses hitched, waiting only to be unleashed. The Federal attacking line, now aimed toward the left center of Jackson's position, marched with its exposed flank within easy gun range, offering a target that occurs but once in a lifetime for the average gunner.

At just the right moment the teams galloped forward to the crest and opened fire with shattering effect. The attack melted away. Lee messaged Jackson to inquire if he still wanted reinforcements. Jackson took his time in replying, to make certain that the artillery had in fact done more than hold the Federals in check. As soon as he was convinced by what Lee and Longstreet had already observed, that the disruption of Pope's second and third waves had left the front line unsupported and that the leading attackers, finding their supports escaping from the deadly gunfire, had promptly followed suit—Jackson withdrew the request. Almost at the same moment, his men, sensing instinctively that the tide had turned, dashed out in pursuit.

LEE COUNTERATTACKS

The climactic moment had arrived! It was what Longstreet, long on patience but a terrific fighter when aroused, had been waiting for. The enemy had been repulsed, his reserves had been thrown in and driven back, his whole force was probably in a state of confusion and must not be allowed to recover. It was the psychological moment to hit them hard while off balance, with everything the Confederates had.

Lee saw the golden opportunity at the same time. An order was sent to Longstreet to counterattack immediately with his whole force of five divisions, including that of R. H. Anderson, who had been assigned to the reserve since his arrival. Longstreet had however anticipated Lee's action and already ordered the advance, shortly before 4:00 P.M.

Now the V-shaped Confederate vise was about to close on the disordered ranks of Pope's array. The lines swept forward, Longstreet's right bearing northeast as his center and left headed directly east. At the other end of the line, Jackson's right would move straight ahead while his left bore southeast. There was naturally some confusion, with Longstreet's fresher divisions making better time against lesser initial opposition, except on the turnpike, than Jackson's men, who had been defensively engaged at close quarters for several hours. Indeed only a small part of Jackson's force actually took part in the early stages of the pursuit.

Reynolds' division, at first posted on Chinn Ridge, had been moved to the north to support Porter's attack on Lee's center, leaving that important terrain feature unoccupied. Chinn Ridge, a prominent landmark and obviously a key position on that part of the field, protected Henry House Hill, on the next ridge to the east, and should have been held at all costs. For Pope to order Reynolds elsewhere was the height of folly, although typical of the Army Commander's tactical handling of his battle. Reynolds was complying with Pope's order to cross to the north side of the turnpike when Longstreet struck. Two of Reynolds' brigades had completed the move, but the third, commanded by Lieut. Colonel Robert Anderson, was caught in motion and wrecked.

Despite the disconcerting set-back there was no evidence of a Federal rout. The heavy pressure of Longstreet's impetuous advance against the Union left caused Pope to order a wholesale shifting of divisions to meet the threat of an envelopment. Sigel first sent McLean's and Milroy's brigades to Chinn Ridge, followed soon after by Koltes and Krzyzanowski, who took position somewhat to McLean's right. Finally came Tower with his own and Hartsuff's brigades. McLean's and Milroy's brigades of Sigel's corps, and Tower's brigade of Ricketts' division offered strong resistance to Longstreet's determined effort to effect a penetration west of Chinn Ridge. The Confederates had to fight for all of their gains, but with five divisions in line, fired with the hope of a solid breakthrough, the advantage lay with Longstreet, who made the most of it. When Longstreet's advance seized Chinn Ridge to threaten Henry House Hill, a short distance to the northeast, Porter, Reno, and Reynolds were all rushed to the latter historic ridge in a desperate effort to prevent the Confederates from rolling up the entire left flank of Pope's army.

CAVALRY COMBAT

Jeb Stuart, upon whom Lee relied almost exclusively to keep him informed on troop dispositions of his own as well as the enemy divisions, was not one to remain on the sidelines if opportunity offered to put his troopers and horse artillery into action. Longstreet's counterattack provided just such an opportunity, one that fitted the role of horse cavalry in the pursuit and harassment of a retreating opponent.

When Longstreet's divisions moved forward in the assault that broke the back of Pope's army, Stuart managed to get hold of four batteries, Stribling's, Roger's, Eshelman's, and Richardson's. Detaching Colonel Tom Rosser from his cavalry regiment, Stuart put him in temporary command of the artillery contingent and turned him loose on Longstreet's right to enfilade the Union lines. Rosser's detachment, supported solely by horse cavalry, moved to positions near the Chinn House from which point the Confederate guns caused consternation in the unstabilized Union ranks with their raking enfilade fire. Displacing forward by battery as the Federals fell back, Rosser shortly found his leading guns near the Wheeler House, half a mile in front of Longstreet's advancing line.

While Rosser with his artillery was having a field day on Longstreet's extreme right and in front of his infantry, Robertson's cavalry brigade, with Munford's regiment in the lead, engaged Buford's Federal cavalry in a spirited mounted fight near Lewis' Ford. Robertson had moved his brigade up to the Lewis house in order to be in position to circle the Union rear at Stone Bridge if the opportunity should occur. The opposing cavalry were near enough to hear each other's commands. Buford's brigade, in column of regiments, moved forward at the trot. Munford charged at the gallop, passed through the first Union line, encountered the second, and a fierce hand-to-hand struggle ensued, in which Munford, greatly outnumbered, was driven back. Soon, however, the two remaining regiments of Robertson's brigade came up, whereupon the Union cavalry in turn retired, leaving 300 prisoners in Confederate hands. It was one of the handsomest mounted engagements of the war to date, according to eye-witnesses, and as such received glowing reports at the hands of Munford, Rosser, and Stuart, all of whom seemed rather pleasantly surprised at the unaccustomed spirit shown by the heretofore reluctant Union cavalry.

POPE'S LAST STAND

The losses were heavy on both sides as Longstreet's scythe relentlessly cut a wide swath in its curving northeasterly attack. A mile and a half the Confederates advanced, but there was no penetration and no outflanking, and Pope's divisions still held possession of the Warrenton Turnpike as the Union left was folded slowly but surely back toward the field of First Manassas. Several Confederate brigades south of the pike made repeated charges to carry the Henry House Hill, bitterly defended by Reynolds' brigades under Meade, Seymour, and Anderson, in company with one of Sykes' brigades and other assorted troops. The famous landmark of First Manassas might be called Pope's Last Stand at Second Manassas, for it was there that Longstreet's spear was blunted long enough for darkness and a handful of hard-fighting Federal brigades to save Pope from complete rout and to permit the rest of the army to retreat, across Bull Run at the equally famous Stone Bridge and the nearby fords, to the temporary safety of a defensive position at Centerville.

Bull Run for the first time during this campaign now attained greater prominence than a mere geographical reference point of no tactical significance. Except for a few places where it could be forded with some difficulty, the famous Stone Bridge on the turnpike to Centerville became the bottleneck through which Pope's retreating army for the most part had to pass. The stream was fifty to sixty feet wide, with vertical sandstone bank on the east side, some twenty or thirty feet high in the vicinity of Stone Bridge, thus constituting a real obstacle. The bridge itself, part of which had been reconstructed, was less than nineteen feet in width, but it was possible for the troops to march in two files on one side while artillery and wagons simultaneously used the other half of the bridge. That is, under conditions of discipline and control, which in a retreat are usually lacking. Fortunately for Pope's army, the victorious Confederates had equally expended their energies, and Reno's rearguard discouraged any real effort on Longstreet's part to turn the retreat into a rout, so that the withdrawal was in fact effected with virtually no interference by the victors.

The battle of August 30 came to a close only when the shades of night were drawn, by which time Longstreet's men were winded by their energetic pursuit and his units, becoming intermingled during the race, required time to become unshuffled. At the same time it started to rain, which served to dampen martial enthusiasm. Pope's army had taken a licking, that was certain, and the army commander decided to throw in the sponge, while putting as good a face on the matter as possible.

POPE'S ARMY RETIRES TO CENTERVILLE

At 8 o'clock that night, almost as soon as the shooting ended, Pope sent written instructions to the corps commanders "to withdraw leisurely toward Centerville," the route each corps was to follow being indicated in the orders. Reno's two divisions were designated as a rear guard to cover the retirement. An order was sent to Banks at Bristoe Station to bring the army trains to Centerville after destroying the railroad trains and such other stores as had not already been transferred therefrom to the army wagons. Banks was specifically told to leave no ammunition behind, and to take along all of the sick and wounded for whom transportation could be found.

The retirement was somewhat inaccurately reported by Pope to have been made quietly and in good order, without interference from the Confederates, who made no effort to press the pursuit. Pope himself rode back to set up his headquarters at Centerville, from where, at 9:45 P.M., he wired the bad news to Halleck.

We have had a terrific battle again to-day. The enemy, largely re-enforced, assaulted our position early today. We held our ground firmly until 6 P.M., when the enemy, massing very heavy forces on our left, forced back that wing about half a mile. At dark we held that position.

Under all the circumstances, both horses and men having been two days without food; and the enemy greatly outnumbering us, I thought it best to draw back to this place at dark. The movement has been made in perfect order and without loss. The troops are in good heart, and marched off the field without the least hurry or confusion. Their conduct was very fine. The battle was most furious for hours without cessation, and the losses on both sides very heavy. The enemy is badly crippled, and we shall do well enough. Do not be uneasy. We will hold our own here. The labors and hardships of this army for two or three weeks have been beyond description. We have delayed the enemy as long as possible without losing the army. We have damaged him heavily, and I think the army entitled to the gratitude of the country. Be easy; everything will go well.

Whistling in the dark and figuratively shrinking from the unpleasant duty of reporting another failure instead of the victory which Washington had been led by earlier dispatches and other miscellaneous intelligence from various sources to expect, one can sympathize to some extent with the dejected general whose initial boasting just prior to the campaign would now be thrown back at him from every direction.

The distortions in his dispatch, including the part where he speaks of being greatly outnumbered and reports the troops "in good heart," were in the McClellan tradition and had come to be routine on the part of Union army commanders, but the latter portion of his message is the one that stands out, particularly the absurdly inaccurate postscript. Poor Pope, a recognized failure in his trial of strength with an opponent whose apparent invincibility had seemingly again been confirmed, and torn between dashed hopes and the feeling that he had been double-crossed by the unfriendly, uncooperative McClellan, said nothing in this message about success being snatched from him by Porter's action in absenting his corps from the battle at the crucial moment. That would come later.

Right now he sought vindication, although doubtless feeling deep down that he was fighting a losing cause. The rather pathetic effort to ward off a scathing rebuke from Halleck brings to mind a friendly dog, expecting punishment, as he extends his body close to the ground and advances toward his master with an appealing look in his hurt eyes.

Halleck had to think over the nature of his reply, which reached Pope the following day, as his army took up its defensive position at Centerville. He was probably touched by the tragedy of Pope's situation and rates an accolade for the diplomatic manner in which he tried to put heart into the Army of Virginia through its commander.

> *My Dear General: You have done nobly. Don't yield another inch if you can avoid it. All reserves are being sent forward. Couch's division goes to-day. Part of it went to Sangster's Station last night with Franklin and Sumner, who must be now with you. Can't you renew the attack? I don't write more particularly for fear dispatch will not reach you. I am doing all in my power for you and your noble army. God bless you and it.*
>
> *Send me news more often if possible.*

CHAPTER 8

The Battle of Chantilly

SUNDAY morning, August 31, Pope called his corps commanders together to receive his orders for the posting of their troops on the somewhat higher ground in the Centerville area, where six roads converged to a point five miles east of the recent Bull Run battlefield. Franklin's corps of 8,000 men, much smaller than expected, had arrived during the night, and 11,000 troops of Sumner's corps were close by and should be up by the end of the day.

According to Franklin's official report, his divisions reached Centerville Saturday afternoon, August 30, after he had detached one of the brigades of Slocum's division with a battery of guns to guard the point where the Little River Turnpike joins the Warrenton Pike between Centerville and Alexandria. Passing through Centerville without stopping, the balance of Slocum's leading division had advanced three miles in the direction of the Bull Run battlefield and crossed Cub Run, when Franklin rode up to find Slocum, his division formed across the road, endeavoring to stem a massive tide of retreating men, horses, guns, and wagons, "all going pell-mell to the rear in an indiscriminate mass," as Franklin described it. Slocum expressed the opinion that it was as bad as the Bull Run retreat of 1861. There was no stopping the majority of the frantic horde, but Slocum's officers did manage to herd about 3,000 of them into a nearby yard; the rest ran to the rear as one man; nothing could stop them." All of which indicated that at least one corps commander disagreed with Pope's statement that the army withdrew quietly and in good order.

The ordered dispositions at Centerville were as follows: Porter on the right, north of Centerville, with Franklin next on the left; then Sigel south of Centerville, with Reno on his left and rear. Behind the four corps on the semicircle covering the crossroad and facing west, Heintzelman was posted, east of Centerville, as army reserve. McDowell was stationed two miles to the east on the Centerville—Fairfax Court House Road. That accounted for all but Sumner and Banks, who were on the way but had not yet come up, and the cavalry brigades under Buford and Bayard, whose horses had been so badly used up that Pope no longer had any cavalry that could be effectively employed. Banks' assignment would be on the north side of Bull Run, covering the bridge on the Manassas-Centerville Road, while Sumner would move immediately upon arrival to a position between Centerville and Chantilly, which latter place he would occupy in force.

From right to left, under Pope's defensive plan, the army would be disposed along a seven-mile front, on commanding ground, covering all approaches from the direction of the enemy. Assuming a prompt distribution of the troops as indicated, and since Lee's tired soldiers were not supermen, there might still be a chance for the Army of Virginia to turn the tables on the Army of Northern Virginia, *if* Pope should prove capable of providing the necessary leadership and *if* his officers and men retained any respect for or confidence in their leader.

It was still raining that Sunday morning, the streams were rising, the dirt roads fast becoming paths of soft muck, and the Stone Bridge over Bull Run had been destroyed. Dead bodies of men and horses, Blue and Gray alike, cluttered the scene of the recent battle in company with broken fences, trampled fields, and the usual flotsam and jetsam of discarded equipment, broken rifles, upturned wagons, and other memorabilia of a fiercely fought battle.

Lee's united army, reduced in numbers by some 9,000 killed, wounded, missing and captured, was not far from being at the end of its string, despite its decisive victory over Pope's larger army and the indomitable spirit of the ragged veterans who had just added one more glorious page to the battle history of the Confederacy. Lee's ammunition was down to the danger point. His food and supply problem had become acute. The effect of the windfall that Jackson's depot raid had acquired had by now worn off. A resurvey of the situation was indicated.

Fitz Lee's cavalry, which had been reconnoitering to the east, reported the arrival of Pope's reinforcements at Centerville, including the corps of Franklin and Sumner and the divisions of Cox and Sturgis. Lee was fully conscious of the fact that his troops had not been able to pursue the retreating Federals, in consequence of which it was reasonable to assume that Pope would not be likely to keep running, but would occupy the most logical nearby position from which to oppose any further effort on Lee's part to drive for Washington. That would probably be the road center at Centerville, where the Confederates had worked hard the previous year to construct impregnable defenses that could still be useful.

Lee rode out through the rain Sunday morning with Stonewall Jackson for a personal survey. A short distance beyond Bull Run his party came under the fire of Federal pickets, indicating the possibility that Pope had come to a halt and proposed to bicker further with his victorious opponent.

Reverting to his heretofore highly successful reliance on maneuver, Lee decided that he would once again move to circle Pope's right in the hope of striking his line of communications to Washington and thus pry him loose to finish the job of winding up his military career. Jackson's corps, worn out though it was by this time, unfortunately occupied the logical position on the north flank from which to make the attempt. "Good, good," was all that Jackson remarked when Lee gave him the mission; there is no record, however, that his soldiers used the same polite four-letter words to express *their* reactions.

With Fitz Lee's cavalry covering the column, Jackson's three divisions slowly took off in the direction of Sudley Springs, where they would cross Bull Run, move north to the Little River Turnpike and follow that road toward Fairfax Court House, while the rest of Stuart's cavalry made a demonstration on the Warrenton Pike east of Bull Run. Longstreet's corps was detailed to remain where they were to bury the dead and remove the wounded, and then follow Jackson's route.

During the afternoon, after Jackson's corps had departed, Lee was again riding over the field when he suffered a painful accident. Wearing coveralls to protect him from the rain, while he was dismounted his horse shied at a sharp noise nearby. Lee grabbed for the bridle, caught his foot in a fold of his unaccustomed garb, and was thrown to the ground, breaking the fall with both arms. A sprain of one wrist and a broken bone in the other hand required splints, forcing him to take to an ambulance for transportation. The usual rumors reached the Northern papers, which reported Lee to have been wounded in the battle, several imaginative accounts going so far as to give the precise details.

With A. P. Hill's division in the lead, the long column started out, weary, hungry, soaking wet from the continuing rain, and slipping crazily in the narrow, muddy road. The unhappy foot soldiers, showing little resemblance to a victorious army on parade, can scarcely be said to have put their hearts into the renewed march, so that progress was painfully slow. The troops bivouacked for the night at Pleasant Valley, along the Little River Turnpike near Cub Run, still several miles from Pope's rear, which now for a change was being guarded almost as strongly as his front and all other portions of the army's anatomy. Longstreet's divisions were equally apathetic as they took to the road, spending the night on the west side of Bull Run.

Jackson resumed the march on the morning of September 1, by which time the rain had ceased, but the roads were still muddy, the hunger of the men unsatisfied, and the rate of march continued slow. It was mid-afternoon when the head of the column passed through Chantilly, which boasted a fine old mansion on the turnpike about four miles due north of Centerville and the same distance west of Germantown. The Confederates were marching east along Little River Turnpike (now U.S. 50), with A. P. Hill's division again in the lead, followed by Jackson's division (under Starke) and Ewell's division (under Lawton). The troops moved in double column, half the brigades off to the right of the road and the others to the left, leaving the road itself for artillery, wagons, and couriers. This method of marching, used often by both sides, was usually more pleasant for the men, who thus traversed meadows instead of tramping in a cloud of dust. More important, it provided a tight, closed-up formation from which deployment could be effected quickly to the front or either flank.

The terrain was rolling, the low ridges running generally at right angles to the road. Pastures and fields of grain, with occasional clumps of woods, lay on either side of the highway. About four miles east of the hamlet of Chantilly was a ridge called Ox Hill which, like the other low ridges in this area, intersected the highway roughly at right angles. To the casual traveler Ox Hill is scarcely to be distinguished from the rest of the terrain, though it is nearly a hundred feet higher than the other ridges in this area. It is crossed by the Ox Road coming in from the north. At the point where Ox Road intersects the turnpike, an unnamed road runs south to the Warrenton Turnpike.

The battlefield of Chantilly, or Ox Hill, lies immediately south of Little River Turnpike, and on both sides of the unnamed road mentioned above. There was a narrow clearing along the pike adjacent to the crossroads, from which the wooded slopes of Ox Hill extended south for some 400 yards to an open field nearly a half-mile wide and deep, part of which was in corn. A rail fence bordered this field on the north, and the trace of the unfinished branch of the Manassas Gap Railway ran roughly along its southwestern edge.

Confederate skirmishers moving south of the column, along the railway bank, reported that the Federals in considerable strength were coming up from the general direction of Centerville. Though Jackson did not know it, an inhabitant of the Chantilly-Ox Hill area, a man named Campbell, had gone south to report to Pope near Centerville that the Confederates were moving in strength along Little River Turnpike toward Fairfax Court House. They had advanced to the point, Pope thought, where it began to look like a serious effort to turn the Federal right flank at Centerville. He thereupon prepared to meet the new situation and to fight a general battle if that should become necessary. Hooker was detached and sent to Fairfax with instructions to take command of all the troops in that vicinity and move them to Germantown, while McDowell's corps was sent in the same direction to form on Hooker's left. Stevens' reinforced division of Reno's corps was dispatched in the direction of Ox Hill with part of Heintzelman's corps in support.

Stevens' guide, Campbell, led the column off to the northeast of the Warrenton Pike, following an obscure wagon track through the woods. A battery of field artillery and Kearny's division followed. The leading units emerged into the clearing across the unfinished railroad southwest of the Reid house, the battery being placed in firing position on a low knoll in that vicinity. The battery began to shell the woods to the north, where smoke puffs from the muskets of Jackson's withdrawing skirmishers were seen.

When Jackson became aware of the threat on his flank he at once deployed his divisions, facing south, on either side of the road running south. The brigades began to advance slowly through the woods, the left of the line being refused to give flank protection.

At Jackson's direction A. P. Hill peeled off Branch's brigade, followed by Brockenbrough's, to move through the woods on the right of Lawton, to feel out the enemy. From the firing it appeared that the Federals were in greater strength on that flank. After advancing 400 yards below the turnpike the men came to a rail fence, with the clearing beyond—from which they received small arms and cannon fire. The two brigades halted along the fence, while three more brigades came up to their support. The Confederates placed a battery in position on the high ground near Stuart's house, on the pike, but it was unable to fire because the woods to the south of the highway prevented the gunners from seeing the cornfield in which the battle was raging.

After watching the action for a time from the knoll where his Federal battery was firing, Stevens concluded that he could gain nothing by remaining in position, but must attack. About 4:30 P.M. he formed his division, now reduced to some 2,000 muskets, in a column of brigades, and leading them in person, he charged toward the rail fence where the Confederates were in position. As he climbed over the fence Stevens was killed. About this time a tremendous thunderclap exploded and a torrential rain descended in the mens' faces. In a short time many of the soldiers on both sides could not fire, their powder being water-soaked. Nevertheless the fighting grew heavier, and somewhat confused, both sides taking considerable losses.

During Stevens' charge, the Confederate lines on the east of the side road fell back. But there were no fresh Federal units on hand to exploit this success. The fighting in the edge of the woods, the loss of their commander, and the heavy rainstorm demoralized Stevens' units, so that Kearny, who came up about this time, was unable to get them to move forward again in support of his leading brigade, Birney's. Kearny was informed by one of the regimental commanders at the south end of the field that his men were out of ammunition and that the enemy were in the cornfield a few yards ahead. Despite this warning, Kearny, in a rage, rode forward alone to reconnoiter. In a moment the nearest Federals heard some firing, from which they concluded that Kearny was dead or captured. Soon the heavy rainfall and gathering darkness took the starch out of everyone, so that the fighting was not renewed.

The mercurial John Pope apparently had had one of his better moments when he moved that afternoon, with a surprising show of resoluteness, to counter the threat of the new Confederate flanking maneuver in the direction of Fairfax Court House. The possibility of just such an attempt as Jackson made had been foreseen, for as early as 3 A.M. Pope had ordered the newly arrived Sumner, whose corps was the last detachment from the Army of the Potomac to come up, to send a brigade of infantry to reconnoiter the Little River Road beyond Germantown. His subsequent troops dispositions were initiated hours before Jackson's slow moving column hove into sight. The Confederates' last view of their enemy had been a confused mass of men and vehicles all trying to cross the Stone Bridge at once, in what many accounts have described as a disorderly rout. Hence the discovery that Pope's divisions were no longer retreating, but on the contrary were moving against them with obviously aggressive intent, must have come as an unpleasant shock. Although the two Federal divisions that had blocked Jackson were greatly outnumbered, the fierceness of their attacks and the fact that the violent storm and darkness discouraged further conflict combined to convince the Southerners that further efforts were potentially too costly to undertake.

It was chiefly the divisions of Stevens and Kearny which had stopped Jackson in his tracks in the relatively short but deadly encounter in the vicinity of Ox Hill. Although Longstreet had come up late in the day at the head of his column, insufficient daylight remained for his corps to develop for action. Therefore the engagement ended in a stalemate. Later that night the Federals withdrew in the direction whence they had come, having accomplished their mission of protecting the north flank of the retreating main column

The importance of the action lay in the fact that the stiff Federal resistance at Ox Hill prevented Lee from achieving the crowning success that would otherwise have been his as an aftermath to the second Confederate victory at Bull Run, in the form of a final humiliation for the despised Pope; while the latter, acting with surprising resilience, had shown his teeth instead of his tail in warning Lee that he had better let well enough alone. The Federals lost about 1,000 men and the Confederates 500. But for the North it was an expensive battle, resulting in the loss of two of its best division commanders, Stevens of Reno's corps and Kearny of Heintzelman's.

The affair at Chantilly, in which only a relatively small part of Pope's army succeeded in turning back Lee's final attempt to exploit his clean-cut victory west of Bull Run, convinced the Confederate commander that the Union army not only was not running away, but still had some fight left in it. Furthermore the position at Centerville had its advantages and, since the Confederates themselves had labored to strengthen the works the preceding year, they were fully aware that the defenses could not easily be breached. The latest Confederate turning movement had been thwarted, and it seemed to Lee that it would be a most difficult matter for his tired troops to gather in any more fruits except by means of another major engagement, which he was not prepared to demand of them. Human endurance can be stretched to extraordinary lengths under stress of battle, but sooner or later a physical reaction sets in that nothing but rest can overcome. That extra something, a reserve of energy called up from the untapped resources of the spirit, had already been expended. As for the cattle, the living embodiment of Civil War commissary stores, they and the mules seemed to have lost interest in life and could not be persuaded to stir even when tempted by the abundance of captured hay and corn, but only lay dejectedly on the ground.

Lee's decision not to press the advance would have been good news to Pope, a badly defeated general whose earlier boldness and will to fight had by this time completely evaporated. All Pope wanted now was to get back safely to the defenses of Washington. From his new headquarters at Fairfax Court House he reported to Halleck on September 2 that "we had another pretty severe fight last night, in which Reno's and Heintzelman's corps were engaged," and expressing the fear that the enemy "will again turn me as soon as he brings up his forces again." It is not difficult to sense Pope's depressed state of mind:

> *I will give battle when I can, but you should come out and see the troops. They were badly demoralized when they joined me, both officers and men, and there is an intense idea among them that they must get behind the intrenchments. The whole force I had for duty yesterday was 57,000 men, exclusive of Couch's.*
>
> *The straggling is awful in the regiments from the Peninsula. Unless something can be done to restore tone to this army it will melt away before you know it. . . . The enemy is still in our front. It is his undoubted purpose to keep on, slowly turning our position so as to come in on our right. You had best decide at once what is to be done. The enemy is in very heavy force and must be stopped in some way. . . .*
>
> *If you knew the troops here and their condition I think it would be well. You had best look out well for your communications. The enemy from the beginning has been throwing his rear toward the north, and every movement shows that he means to make trouble in Maryland.*
>
> *Wherever I have attacked him he is in greatly superior force. I would attack today, but the troops are absolutely unable.*

It was all over; nothing remained for Halleck to do but tell Pope to come on in to the defenses of Washington, which he did in a politely cryptic telegram that for all practical purposes placed the defeated general and his routed but still sullenly defiant army under the command of General McClellan.

After the fight at Chantilly, Lee discontinued the pursuit and turned his thoughts toward an invasion of Maryland, paying no further attention to his recent antagonist except to direct Stuart's cavalry to engage in harassing tactics with the double purpose of making it as unpleasant as possible for the defeated army and to cover such movements of his own army as he proposed shortly to initiate.

Brigadier General J. D. Cox, commanding a brigade at Upton's Hill, was directed to cover the last stages of the retrograde movement of

Pope's army to Alexandria and vicinity, when the march from Centerville was resumed on the morning of September 2. In the absence of further pressure from the Confederates, the better led and disciplined divisions were gradually restored to some semblance of order, but thousands of stragglers had to be rounded up between the scene of the late battle and the Washington fortifications.

To the best of the War Department's knowledge, the danger to the Capital was still acute and there was no assurance that Lee's army, flushed with victory, might not still drive around or through Pope's apparently disorganized mass of troops in an attempt to capture Washington. So real was the fear that orders were issued to promptly ship all ordnance to New York and, by direction of the President himself, to immediately organize all clerks and employees of the Government into companies and to arm and supply them with ammunition for the defense of the Capital. Masses of freshly recruited Union soldiers were milling around in Washington, many of them completely new to soldiering.

POPE HOPES TO RETAIN COMMAND

Arriving at Ball's Crossroads, Pope reported to Halleck that by morning September 3, all of his troops would be in camp within the intrenchments and that the enemy showed no signs of making further attacks. Then, after a day's rest, Pope began to take account of stock and to speculate on what was in store for Major General John Pope, late of Manassas, Virginia and points south and west. Halleck's last message had been far from reassuring, so Pope tarried at Ball's Crossroads, putting off the evil hour when command should pass to McClellan. Taking up his pen, he put out an indirect feeler, through a friend in the War Department, to ascertain how far McClellan's authority extended and to suggest again that Halleck exercise command in person.

Getting no satisfaction through indirect channels, Pope tried a new approach direct to Halleck, to whom he made the suggestion that the army should attack again with fresh troops "while the enemy is weakened and broken down." But Pope was finished, his ideas no longer worthy of even a polite brush-off, although Halleck did extend the courtesy of a reply, in which he made it plain that McClellan was in command, would exercise general authority over all the troops, and directing Pope, as soon as all his troops had come within McClellan's jurisdiction, to report in person at Halleck's headquarters. It was the army's unique way of saying, in effect, come on over and get the axe.

Pope, however, seemed to have a fairly tough hide and, although it was clear to everyone else that he was going down for the third time, he submitted on September 4 a proposal for a reorganization that would give him an army of about 50,000 men with a lot of new regiments, organized into four corps under Banks, McDowell, Reno, and Hooker. That gratuitous suggestion was not even given the dignity of an acknowledgment, instead of which Halleck informed McClellan that Pope was to be relieved of command.

Querulous letters kept flowing from Pope to Halleck, while McClellan issued orders direct to Pope's former subordinates, completely ignoring the crestfallen commander of the erstwhile Army of Virginia. It finally dawned on Halleck that the decent thing to do would be to end Pope's suffering, which was accomplished by a terse order, dated September 5, which simply said: "The Armies of the Potomac and Virginia being consolidated, you will report for orders to the Secretary of War."

Exit John Pope!

McClellan's Comeback

The last days of August and the first few days of September afforded many anxious moments for the amateur strategist in the White House. President Lincoln had brought Halleck in from the west to provide, as he hoped, unity of command and a coordinating force that might accomplish for the Union what separate army commanders seemed incapable of achieving—a clean-cut victory over the enemy.

McClellan had failed in his Peninsular Campaign, following which Pope had been given his chance with the Army of Virginia, into which were fed the several corps of the Army of the Potomac as they arrived from the James River. Halleck, however, proved unable to handle the situation, which degenerated rapidly to the point where Lee's army, with 50,000 more men, might well have destroyed Pope's Army of Virginia, broken the defenses of Washington, and conceivably dictated a negotiated peace from the national capital.

McClellan's hostility to Pope, coupled with his callous readiness to do everything possible, by whatever means, to facilitate the downfall of his military rival, was a shocking thing in Lincoln's view. Despite McClellan's resistance to Halleck's efforts to speed the forces of the Army of the Potomac to reinforce Pope at Manassas, enough of them had joined Pope to enable him to defeat Lee's separate wings in detail if the Union Commander had been enough of a field general to employ his augmented army effectively.

The anomalous position in which McClellan found himself, with his own army pulled out from under his control and nothing to take its place until he was finally placed in command of the Washington defenses, was an unhappy one for the little Napoleon, who continued to regard himself as the only general who could "save the country." McClellan was a determined character, however, and lost no opportunity to advance his own cause, whether it be by chipping away at Pope or feuding with Halleck.

As the Battle of Second Manassas mounted in fury, Lincoln watched developments anxiously. Direct information from Pope's headquarters was nonexistent. The President daily visited the telegraph office to read the sparse items of news that came in from other sources, chiefly Porter's biased telegrams to Burnside, and the reports which the indefatigable Colonel Haupt sent in a steady stream to the War Department from Alexandria. The latter were fragmentary in character, however, and could furnish only certain pieces of the jigsaw puzzle. Impatient to learn more, Lincoln finally wired McClellan on August 29 to inquire if he had any news of Pope. It was McClellan's reply to that telegram that badly shocked the President, for McClellan took it upon himself to offer advice, suggesting that one of two courses should be followed, either concentrate all available forces to establish connection with Pope, or "leave Pope to get out of his scrape" as best he could and use all other available troops to secure the Capital against attack.

Pope's wire of 5 A.M., August 30 (pp. 211-12) suggested that he had won a partial victory and would make it a total one the following day.

That sounded encouraging, and Lincoln's spirits rose. Unfamiliar with Pope's habit of wishful thinking and inadequate generalship, Lincoln can scarcely be blamed for accepting at face value a battlefield report that in actuality was founded on a complete misconception of the real facts.

The hopes that Pope raised in Washington were dashed the following day, when the news of the Union army's defeat arrived, followed by other reports which recorded the progress of the retreat in the direction of Washington. But it was not until after Pope had obliquely invited Halleck to order his army back into the defense of Washington and Halleck had obliged him, that McClellan was placed in command of the defenses and all troops therein. As usual, Halleck waited until a critical situation had become a fait accompli and then made it official; Old Brains simply lacked the ability to exercise the functions of general-in-chief and to direct events with a firm hand.

The cocky McClellan now believed the Administration had turned to him because he was the man of destiny who would save the country. Nothing could have been farther from the truth. Lincoln had become convinced that McClellan wanted Pope to be defeated, no matter what the cost to the country, and that he had passively, if not actively, contributed to that result. On the other hand, Lincoln knew also that McClellan was a skilful organizer and that no other general officer was better able to whip the troops into fighting trim, even though he was not a fighter himself. The President's decision was therefore in the nature of a temporary expedient to carry the country through a crisis, with no intent to allow Little Mac to again lead the army in a field campaign. The proof of the latter statement is found in the fact that command of the Army of the Potomac was offered to Ambrose E. Burnside when Lee a few days after Manassas moved into Maryland, and it became evident that another campaign was imminent.

McClellan's hold on the imagination and affection of his army was amazing. It is said that when the disheartened and dejected troops were threading their way back to the Washington defenses from Centerville on September 2, McClellan rode out from Alexandria with a single staff officer to meet them. Catching the first glimpse of the familiar figure on horseback, some of Porter's men raised a cheer. The magic word passed swiftly down the line. "The army is now better contented than it was," wrote Lieutenant Gillette to his parents on September 8. "General McClellan, their idol, is restored to command. He is, in the opinion of all soldiers, the only honest and skilful leader we have had. None other can replace him in the affection of the men. To take from an army the leaders it loves and to substitute those who are to them unknown or disliked, is to defeat that army at once."

CHAPTER 9

Lee Invades Maryland

THERE were rumors afloat in the Confederate ranks, even before the action at Chantilly, that Lee's next move would be to cross the Potomac, to carry the fight to enemy territory. Many were of the opinion that the order had already been issued and the march for Edward's Ferry begun, when on September 1 Jackson led his divisions north through Sudley Springs, only to turn right instead of left when the head of the column reached the Little River Turnpike leading through Germantown to Alexandria.

The speculation of the men in the ranks was well-founded. The area of Virginia over which the armies had ranged in recent weeks had been pretty thoroughly drained of supplies, whereas Maryland and Pennsylvania offered a rich territory not only for restocking Lee's army with food and clothing, but with much other needed materiel as well, such as livestock, and especially riding and draft horses as replacements for Stuart's cavalry and the artillery.

While it served Lee's purpose admirably to keep official Washington in suspense and fearful for its safety, he had no intention of going the whole distance to the capital. Although he had not succeeded in destroying Pope's army, he had so clearly crippled it that after Second Manassas it ceased to exist as an organization, its constituent elements being absorbed into the Army of the Potomac.

It is one of the measures of Lee's superior talents as an army commander that he would not take foolish risks; what appeared to less able generals as audacious ventures were in Lee's mind calculated with an eye to the relative capabilities of his own army and that of his opponent, with particular emphasis on the abilities of the Union commander as Lee himself evaluated them. Also there must be potential gains commensurate with the risks for the latter to be taken. He was too shrewd a strategist to push his luck too far; consequently his plans did not at any time contemplate an attack on the Washington fortress.

The gratifying results of his campaign against Pope had however exceeded Lee's expectations. Starting out with the hope that he could inflict a crushing defeat upon that hated general, the plan was altered, by Pope's stubborn opposition on the Rappahannock, to become a campaign of maneuver; and was again modified to launch a successful counteroffensive when the opportunity was offered by the failure of Pope's battle tactics. Lee felt that the brilliant Confederate victory deserved to be exploited, in fact it had to be, or the enemy would recover his balance, renew his strength, and make ready to stage a new offensive on Virginia soil. The Army of Northern Virginia could not afford to stand still or rest on its laurels. It must either go forward to press the advantage just gained at Second Manassas, or pull back to refit.

There was considerable justification for optimism in Con federate circles. Much had been accomplished in the three months that had elapsed since Lee took command. At the start, McClellan had been within sight of Richmond, Jackson was facing greatly superior odds in the Valley, and the Federals controlled all of West Virginia and the North Carolina coastline; the initiative rested with the North and everywhere the pressure had thrown the Southerners on the defensive. Now all that had been changed. Richmond was saved, the Valley cleared, the Army of the Potomac had withdrawn to Washington, Pope's army had been defeated, virtually all of Virginia and most of West Virginia cleared of enemy troops. The Confederates had seized and now held the initiative, with Washington rather than Richmond in fear for its very existence.

Invasion of the North had been in Lee's mind for some time. He believed it would have international implications in creating an atmosphere favorable to the Confederacy in England and France, an extremely important factor in view of the strong Federal naval blockage of Southern ports. The presence of his army in Maryland might swing that doubtful State into the Confederate column. It would also be most helpful if the Northern countryside should take over the burden of sustaining his 50,000-man army for a time. Finally, the morale of the army had been given a lift by its recent victory, its confidence in its leaders and itself was at a high pitch, and neither must be allowed to decline.

Nevertheless, Lee knew perfectly well what the great exertions of the summer had done to his army. The losses before Richmond and at Manassas had been heavy. A number of his better generals had been killed or wounded. His divisions were admittedly not in condition to invade, as Lee stated in a letter to President Davis: "The army is not properly equipped for an invasion of an enemy's territory. It lacks much of the material of war, is feeble in transportation, the animals being much reduced, and the men are poorly provided with clothes, and, in thousands of instances, are destitute of shoes."

Again, however, it was desirable to take a calculated risk. The advantages of a successful invasion, in Lee's judgment, outweighed the disadvantages. The possibility existed that the Baltimore and Ohio Railroad could be destroyed, which would be a disaster of some magnitude to the Northern armies. If all went well, the Confederates might even push on into Pennsylvania to cut the Pennsylvania Railroad, in which event the supply route to the west via the Great Lakes would remain as the only connecting link between East and West. There was indeed great promise in an invasion. And so the die was cast and the orders issued.

Two routes were open to Lee. He could take the sheltered roadway by way of the Shenandoah Valley, or the more exposed approach east of the Blue Ridge Mountains. The second would be quicker and, being closer to Washington, more likely for that reason to have greater psychological impact on the North. Practical benefits might accrue as well, in causing the Administration at Washington, if sufficiently alarmed, to make hasty, ill-advised decisions.

McClellan Resumes Command

McClellan's resumption of command was far from being the result of a universal belief that he was the man of the hour, whose leadership of the Union armies of the East would restore their fallen fortunes and carry them forward to victories. By and large that may have been the attitude of the rank and file of the Federal soldiers, as demonstrated by their spontaneous enthusiasm when he rode out into their midst as they trudged dejectedly back to the capital. They knew, as did their Confederate opponents, that they had fought with as much bravery and determination as Lee's men, but they were also well aware of the incompetent general-ship which had brought about their defeat. It was their conviction that Pope and McDowell had not given them the chance for victory which, rightly or wrongly, they believed with all their hearts could be theirs under General McClellan.

Lincoln and the members of his cabinet however viewed McClellan in a very different light and were in better position than the army to appraise his attitudes and actions in the light of the overall situation. There were some members of the cabinet whose objections to "Little Mac" were based largely on political considerations, but his record of achievement in the purely military spheres, unimpressive as it was, overshadowed the polit-ical implications. Secretary of War Stanton and Secretary of the Treasury Chase were more vocal than the rest in their opposition to McClellan's restoration to power. In Chase's view, it was a matter of life or death for the government, while Stanton, who by virtue of his position had a more intimate knowledge of the day-by-day military situation, worked desper-ately on his colleagues to convince them that only disaster could be antic-ipated if McClellan were again to be given a command of any importance.

That McClellan was a controversial national figure is to put it mildly. The historical accounts vary widely as to how it actually came about that he was in the top military spot when the Army of the Potomac moved out from Washington to counter Lee's invasion of the North. Lincoln him-self had been at no pains to conceal his growing distaste for McClellan as a fighting commander, believing that he had rendered the country a distinct disservice by his lack of cooperativeness with Pope's army and his superiors in the War Department. On the other hand, the President's custom of keeping his ear to the ground and talking freely with mili-tary visitors from the Army, regardless of rank, enabled him to keep his finger on the army pulse, so he knew how strongly the troops felt about McClellan. Consequently, when affairs reached the point where civilian clerks were pressed into service and armed to repel the imagined attack on Washington, and it became apparent that the armies were floundering in an almost leaderless morass of uncertainty, Lincoln concluded that all personal feelings must give way before the critical emergency should dissolve into irretrievable disaster.

Burnside's refusal to accept the post left no general of sufficient experience in army command, in Lincoln's opinion, to turn to except McClellan. It is perfectly clear, however, that the President's decision was to put McClellan in command only of the troops *in the defenses of Washington.* He had no intention of allowing the general to lead the army into the field or to fight a battle, and said so, without any reservations, to a number of intimates. The idea was to use McClellan's genius for organization to again whip the army into a sound state of organization and thus gain time to figure out who would take over when it became necessary to wage a campaign. "If he can't fight himself," said Lincoln, "he excels in making others ready to fight."

Lincoln's decision, then, was to place McClellan in charge of the Washington defenses, and it was made on his sole responsibility in spite of the opposition of a majority of the Cabinet. When on September 2 the President announced the decision at a Cabinet meeting, it is said that Stanton, trembling with rage that his advice was being disregarded, burst out with the statement that no such order had been issued by his authority. To which the President, putting aside for once his gentle manner, remarked curtly that the order was his own and he would be responsible for it to the country.

Interestingly enough, the one-sentence order: "Major-General McClellan will have command of the fortifications of Washington and of all the troops for the defense of the capital" was the *only* formal order that McClellan received from the War Department until, early in November, six weeks after the battle of Antietam, he was again relieved from command, this time for good. A gesture in the direction of officially creating a new field army was made by the War Department on September 3, when Halleck was directed to "prepare an army to take the field." But Lee's invasion of Maryland had so soon created a new crisis that, insofar as the chain of command was concerned, all administrative considerations were of necessity shelved in face of the needs of the moment.

McClellan was not the man to act coyly in such a situation, and so it came about that he assumed limited command as ordered, got busy, ignored Pope, absorbed the Army of Virginia into the Army of the Potomac, and then marched at the head of that unofficial army to meet Lee. All this was without specific orders; but on the other hand it was not repudiated by Halleck or the War Department. There are times in the affairs of men when unilateral action by one individual may be the only answer, and this appears to have been one of those times.

McClellan's first action, on receipt of Halleck's written orders confirming the President's oral statement to the general on the morning of September 2, was to ride out to show himself and to receive the plaudits of those of the army who felt so disposed. His second was to bring order to the defenses and restore a sense of discipline, which was effected simply by telling the experienced corps and division commanders what they were to do.

Three corps, Heintzelman's Third, Fitz John Porter's Fifth, and Sigel's Eleventh, were assigned to the fortified line on the Virginia side. Sumner's Second Corps, Burnside's Ninth, and Mansfield's Twelfth covered the city on the Maryland side. The Sixth Corps under Franklin and the First, shortly to be commanded by Hooker, had not yet been reshuffled and were consequently in a semi-state of reserve. In numbers of bodies the eight corps exceeded 100,000 men by a substantial margin, seemingly more than enough to protect Washington and defeat Lee's 50,000 at the same time. In addition, 26,000 other troops, including newly arrived contingents and the regular garrison, manned the remaining forts that ringed the city, with 120 field pieces and 500 heavy guns in position to provide a powerful deterrent to a possible enemy attack. As it turned out, an attack on Washington was never seriously undertaken or even planned at any time during the war.

Among McClellan's notes that were published in the Century Magazine shortly after his death, he referred to the concern with which in early September 1862 he viewed Halleck's insistence that the Federal garrison of some 12,000 men at strategic Harper's Ferry be kept there. Although outside of his jurisdiction, McClellan felt strongly that the post should be abandoned and the troops brought to Washington to augment those already within the defenses. It was typical of "Little Mac" that his overriding theme of bringing every available man under his own wing was again foremost in his mind, but the reasons given on this occasion were that the garrison was isolated, could not be expected to avoid capture or destruction if attacked, and if Harper's Ferry should be occupied by the Confederates the matter would be of little consequence since his army, if successful, could easily effect its recapture.

Halleck gave McClellan's views a brusque brush-off, terming them erroneous. He refrained from using the word gratuitous, which he might very well have done, since McClellan's responsibilities were specifically limited to the defenses of the capital, and Halleck had informed him in no uncertain terms, on several occasions, that he was not to command troops beyond the line of demarcation. Furthermore Halleck had stated that the general who would command the troops when they should move had not yet been selected. He might as well have saved his breath so far as McClellan was concerned, for the latter coolly proceeded with his own plans, which included the assumption of field command without Halleck's specific approval.

The ironic factor involved in McClellan's belief that Harpers Ferry should be abandoned was yet to be disclosed. As will appear later, that vital position loomed importantly in Lee's thinking, so that its influence on the forth-coming battles would be tremendous. Had McClellan been clairvoyant, he would have foreseen that Federal possession of Harpers Ferry was the very thing that led Lee to divide his army, and barely escape destruction as a result. As it turned out, advance reinforcement of the garrison at Harpers Ferry by the Federals might have proven to be the decisive factor, by holding that strategic area just a few hours longer, in utterly destroying the separate wings of Lee's army instead of recording the Battle of Antietam as a stalemate.

LEE CROSSES THE POTOMAC

Without waiting for the reinforcements that had been dispatched from Richmond on Lee's request to President Davis, the Confederate army on September 3 started out on its new and exciting adventure into enemy territory. Moving west in the direction of Leesburg, to cross the Potomac at shallow White's Ford, thirty miles upriver from Washington, the bands blared forth with "Maryland, My Maryland," as the column headed for

Frederick City, Lee's first objective thirteen miles north of the river. There he hoped to rally to the Confederate cause the people of Maryland, thousands of whose sons were already serving in the armies of the South.

Dirty, unshaven, ragged, and barefooted as so many were, the Confederates were lighthearted and cheerful as they swung along the invasion route. Three fresh divisions under Lafayette McLaws, Daniel H. Hill, and John G. Walker, together with Wade Hampton's cavalry brigade and the reserve artillery, caught up with the column on the way, adding 20,000 additional troops to Lee's army. Most of these units crossed the Potomac at Cheek's Ford, at the mouth of the Monocacy River, several miles above White's Ford. But to Lee's disappointment, even with these reinforcements he could count no more than 50,000 in all, for his stragglers duplicated the experience of Pope's army after Second Manassas, and in such numbers as to nearly offset the gain in strength from the newly arrived contingents from the capital.

By September 7 the entire army was across the Potomac, had disrupted traffic along the Chesapeake and Ohio Canal, paralleling the Potomac River, and looked forward to the early breakup of the Baltimore and Ohio Railroad, which latter was one of the major purposes, or at least scheduled byproducts of the invasion. The previous day Lee had issued his proclamation to the people of Maryland, but neither the invitation nor the presence of Confederate troops on their soil had the desired effect, for Maryland remained loyal to the Union. It was Lee's first setback, and it made the invasion an even more hazardous affair with respect to communications, although there is no reason to believe that Lee made any change in his schedule, despite the chilly reception from the inhabitants.

LEE'S PLAN OF CAMPAIGN

Major General John G. Walker, commanding one of the three reinforcing divisions, has left an interesting account of his reception when he reported to General Lee upon his arrival in the vicinity of Frederick on September 8. The Commanding General evidently had confidence in Walker's judgment and discretion, for he told him that his division would probably be ordered on detached service during the campaign and it was therefore necessary that he know its "ulterior purposes and objects."

"Here," said Lee, tracing with his finger on a large map, "is the line of our communications, from Rapidan Station to Manassas, thence to Frederick. It is too near the Potomac, and is liable to be cut any day by the enemy's cavalry. I have therefore given orders to move the line back into the Valley of Virginia, by way of Staunton, Harrisonburg, and Winchester, entering Maryland at Shepherdstown.

"I wish you to return to the mouth of the Monocacy and effectually destroy the aqueduct of the Chesapeake and Ohio Canal. By the time that is accomplished you will receive orders to cooperate in the capture of Harper's Ferry, and you will not return here, but, after the capture of Harper's Ferry, will rejoin us at Hagerstown, where the army will be concentrated. My information is that there are between 10,000 and 12,000 men at Harper's Ferry, and 3,000 at Martinsburg. The latter may escape toward Cumberland, but I think the chances are that they will take refuge at Harper's Ferry and be captured."

Lee seems to have been more loquacious than usual on that occasion, if Walker did not embellish the account by antedating some of the facts, because the commanding general is reported as having gone to some length to divulge his entire plan of campaign, even to the extent of explaining why he felt that he was safe in executing his plans without fear of interruption by the Federals.

"McClellan is an able general but a very cautious one. His army is in a very demoralized and chaotic condition, and will not be prepared for offensive operations—or he will not think it so—for three or four weeks. Before that time I hope to be on the Susquehanna."

"In ten days from now," Lee continued, "if the military situation is then what I confidently expect it to be after the capture of Harper's Ferry, I shall concentrate the army at Hagerstown, effectually destroy the Baltimore and Ohio road, and march to this point," placing his finger at Harrisburg, Pennsylvania. "That is the objective point of the campaign. You remember, no doubt, the long bridge of the Pennsylvania railroad over the Susquehanna, a few miles west of Harrisburg. Well, I wish effectually to destroy that bridge, which will disable the Pennsylvania railroad for a long time. After that I can turn my attention to Philadelphia, Baltimore, or Washington, as may seem best for our interests."

Parenthetically it may be noted at this point that Walker's division, in carrying out Lee's instructions, made an effort to destroy the aqueduct near the mouth of the Monocacy River, but found its construction to be such that neither by the use of picks or crowbars could his men make any impression on the solid granite structure, and the drills available to his engineers were too dull to pave the way for blasting. Consequently that part of his mission had to be written off as a failure.

SPECIAL ORDERS NO. 191

At Frederick, on September 9, Lee issued the now famous order to his army, the purpose of which was to take Harpers Ferry out of Federal control and at the same time advance the main body of the army to Boonsboro, a reconcentration point that was subsequently changed in order to halt D. H. Hill's division of 5,000 men at South Mountain, while Longstreet's corps continued on to Hagerstown. It was a copy of this order, carelessly dropped in Frederick, that was picked up by a Union soldier when the Federal Twelfth Corps reached there at noon on September 13. The premature disclosure of the whereabouts and planned movements of Lee's army, the inadequate use to which McClellan put the information thus fortuitously acquired, and the later fact that Lee himself attributed his loss of the Battle of Sharpsburg (Antietam) to the incident of the "Lost Dispatch," gives to Special Orders Number 191 a significance greater than that of any single event in the entire campaign.

Special Orders No. 191	Headquarters, Army
	of Northern Virginia.
	September 9th, 1862.

The army will resume its march tomorrow, taking the Hagerstown road. General Jackson's command will form the advance, and after passing Middletown, with such portions as he may select, take the route toward Sharpsburg, cross the Potomac at the most convenient point, and by Friday night take possession of the Baltimore and Ohio Railroad, capture such of the enemy as may be at Martinsburg, and intercept such as may attempt to escape from Harper's Ferry.

General Longstreet's command will pursue the same road as far as Boonsboro, where it will halt with the reserve, supply, and baggage trains of the army.

General McLaws, with his own division and that of General R. H. Anderson, will follow General Longstreet; on reaching Middletown he will take the route to Harper's Ferry, and by Friday morning possess himself of the Maryland Heights and endeavor to capture the enemy at Harper's Ferry and vicinity.

General Walker, with his division, after accomplishing the object in which he is now engaged, will cross the Potomac at Cheek's Ford, ascend its right bank to Lovettsville, take possession of Loudoun Heights, if practicable, by Friday morning, Keys' Ford on his left, and the road between the end of the mountain and the Potomac on his right. He will, as far as practicable, cooperate with General McLaws and General Jackson in intercepting the retreat of the enemy.

General D. H. Hill's division will form the rear guard of the army, pursuing the road taken by the main body. The reserve artillery, ordnance, and supply trains, etc., will precede General Hill.

General Stuart will detach a squadron of cavalry to accompany the commands of Generals Longstreet, Jackson, and McLaws, and with the main body of the cavalry, will cover the route of the army and bring up all stragglers that may have been left behind.

The commands of Generals Jackson, McLaws, and Walker, after accomplishing the objects for which they have been detached, will join the main body of the army at Boonsboro or Hagerstown.

Each regiment on the march will habitually carry its axes in the regimental ordnance-wagons, for use of the men at their encampments, to procure wood, etc.

By Command of General R. E. Lee,
R. H. Chilton, Assistant
Adjutant General.

Major General D. H. Hill, Commanding Division.

The preceding reprint, quoted in McClellan's official report, shows that it was the copy sent to General D. H. Hill, whose division was assigned to form the army rear guard. From that fact stemmed a historic controversy among the surviving Confederate generals as to where the responsibility rested for the loss of the order. Hill always maintained that he never received a copy directly from Lee's headquarters, the implication being that it was dropped by a staff officer en route. However the loss came about, its vital effect on Lee's first invasion of the North is a matter of history.

The gratifying outcome of Lee's calculated risk in dividing his army as a prelude to defeating Pope in the latter days of August was fresh in the Confederate leader's mind. Although he had a greater respect for McClellan, he was also familiar with his opponent's uniformly cautious attitude and believed that a repetition of his own strategy in the present case would allow sufficient time for the detached portions of his army to accomplish their mission and reunite with the main body in ample time to forestall what otherwise could be an extremely dangerous situation.

Longstreet and Jackson each reacted in his accustomed manner when Lee first discussed his plans with them at Frederick. Jackson was enthusiastic at the prospect, remarking that it was about time that he pay his friends in the Valley another visit. Longstreet, however, who in his own written account of the campaign said that when Lee first proposed the Harpers Ferry division as a project for a special force under Longstreet himself, he objected to dividing the army at that stage. He argued that the troops were not yet in condition to undertake any more marching in enemy country than was absolutely necessary, that the Federal army was *not* as disorganized as it had been pictured, and that it would certainly come after them. Since Lee was anxious to take Harpers Ferry, and found Jackson equally in favor, Longstreet's objections were ignored.

The movement order was issued on Tuesday, September 9. In it Lee mentions Friday morning as the time when the separate detachments under McLaws and Walker were expected to be in position on Maryland Heights and Loudoun Heights, respectively, to prevent a possible escape by the Federal garrison until Jackson's corps of three divisions could come in from the west to close the trap. Jackson was given three days, until Friday night, September 12, to travel a circuitous sixty-mile route, capture the Federal garrison at Martinsburg, and close the escape route of the

Harpers Ferry garrison to the west. Upon completion of the converging movement of the three detachments, Jackson as the senior would automatically take command of the whole, but it will be noted that the two-division force under McLaws was given the mission of actually capturing the troops at Harpers Ferry.

The importance that Lee ascribed to the seizure of Harpers Ferry may be judged by his action in sending six of the ten divisions in his army, including two of Longstreet's, on that diversionary mission, leaving but four divisions with the main body, three of them in Longstreet's corps, and D. H. Hill's separate division. Walker's division was small, mustering only about 2,000 men, but even so, less than half the army would be forced to contend with McClellan's Union army if things should go wrong. On the other hand, both Confederate wings would be sheltered by the high mountain ranges, and could unite rapidly in either direction via Martinsburg. If worst came to worst, the entire army could retire via Harpers Ferry to the safety of the Shenandoah Valley, a defensive contingency to which Lee's psychology did not particularly lend itself under the circumstances.

McClellan Moves to Counter Lee

As soon as it became apparent that the Confederate army was committed to operations in Maryland and cherished no designs on the city of Washington, the unofficially reconstituted Army of the Potomac moved warily out from the defenses of the capital to regain contact.

The anomalous position in which Halleck had placed McClellan did not seem to faze the latter, who proceeded to take charge of military affairs as fully as though he had been given carte blanche by the War Department. The situation was unique, since neither the President, the Secretary of War, nor the General-in-Chief, wanted to restore McClellan to field command, but were prepared to hand the reins to another general in his stead. Nevertheless McClellan acted on his own authority, leaving his superiors, however they may have felt about it, to acquiesce passively. After all, when the house is on fire, the owner is not likely to throw obstacles in the path of the fireman, even though he may not think well of him.

Lee's army had faded from the vicinity of Washington, commencing on the third of September, and it looked as though they would cross the Potomac. When the probability became a certainty, McClellan progressively redisposed several corps in positions at Rockville, Tennallytown, Offutt's Crossroads, and Leesboro, holding those of Heintzelman, Porter, and Sigel within the lines at Washington. General Pleasonton, given command of the cavalry, was ordered out on September 6 to establish and maintain contact with the enemy cavalry. The army was organized into two wings and a center column under Burnside, Sumner, and Franklin; and Banks was assigned to command the defenses of Washington. On September 7, by which date all of Lee's army had crossed the Potomac, McClellan opened field headquarters at Rockville and prepared to follow Lee.

Now that McClellan had relieved in a measure the nervous strain under which the indecisive Halleck had been laboring, the General-in-Chief revived his accustomed fears for the safety of the capital. In the current circumstances he expressed the belief that Lee would double back across the Potomac to come in on McClellan's left rear, which would again place Washington in jeopardy. McClellan was cautioned to make haste slowly, which in the light of Little Mac's record to date might be termed gratuitous advice. It may be doubted, however, that McClellan would now pay any more attention to Halleck than he had heretofore.

Cavalry Skirmishes

The Army of the Potomac was preceded in its advance by an entirely different cavalry team than the one which had served with Pope in the Virginia campaign. In that campaign three brigades, a total of fourteen regiments, had been attached to the three corps of the Army of Virginia, each brigade commander being responsive to the orders of his corps commander. By the end of the campaign the horses were so broken down by the excessive demands made on them that for all practical purposes the organizations concerned had become inoperative, for the time being at least.

McClellan put together a group of cavalry regiments, from his former army and elsewhere, in an organic division under the command of

Brigadier General Alfred Pleasonton, a dapper little horseman who was an old dragoon, knew how to use cavalry in its proper role, and proceeded to do so. He divided his division into five brigades, each under a colonel except the First, which was commanded by a major. Each of the brigades was composed of two regiments except the Second, which had four; that one was commanded by Colonel John Farnsworth, a fine young Regular who was destined to die in a fruitless charge at Gettysburg ten months later. Pleasonton counted twelve regiments in his division, none of which had participated in the Manassas campaign.

Moving out as a body, the Federal cavalry quickly fanned out over the Maryland countryside to scout thefords and seek out the enemy cavalry, which was similarly dispersed over a wide area, screening Lee's army. Initial contact was made September 7 at Poolesville. Thereafter, for three days, frequent skirmishes occurred between opposing detachments, as the Federals pushed westward toward Lee's main body in the Frederick area.

The Confederate cavalry under General J. E. B. Stuart, after crossing the Potomac at Edward's Ferry, had swung off to the right and were disposed along a line twenty miles in length, with Munford's reduced brigade on the right at Poolesville, Wade Hampton's in the center at Hyattstown, and Fitz Lee's on the left at New Market. Stuart established his headquarters at Urbana, a central point from which roads radiated to the several brigade command posts to the front, and to army headquarters at Frederick.

Sugar Loaf Hill, an isolated ridge five miles southwest of Urbana, which rose to a height of 700 feet to dominate the surrounding area, was an excellent observation point from which the Confederates could watch the roads which McClellan's army would have to use in coming to Lee's position. Pleasonton marked this prominent landmark as his objective and made strenuous efforts to take it, driving Munford's defending brigade out of Poolesville in the process. But Stuart's cavalry cordon managed its counter-reconnaissance mission with such skill that McClellan was unable to learn what Lee was up to in the early stages of his advance.

For several days, Stuart's troopers had an easy time of it until the Federal cavalry pressed closer, when the skirmishing became more brisk and the Union infantry began to add their weight of numbers. It would only be a matter of a few days before McClellan's superior strength would be felt and Lee would have to decide whether to meet the challenge east of the mountains.

During the peaceful period before the Union infantry in strength forced the Confederate cavalry screen to withdraw, the fun-loving Jeb Stuart at Urbana organized one of those dances which he enjoyed almost as much as a saber charge. There were plenty of attractive Maryland girls in the vicinity, and Stuart's staff lost no time in rounding them up. The merriment was at its height when the report came in that enemy cavalry was attacking the Confederate pickets. Buckling on their swords and taking a hasty farewell, Stuart and his officers assured the ladies the interruption would be temporary and please to wait. The business of discouraging the overzealous Federal patrols having been accomplished, the dancing cavalrymen returned as promised, the party was resumed, and a good time was had by all.

Frederick City Changes Hands

The Army of the Potomac moved slowly forward at the rate of only six miles a day for the first few days, reflecting Halleck's "go-slow" policy. Each of the three columns was assigned a different route on parallel roads that diverged more widely to cover a broad front as Washington faded into the background. Burnside's right wing, which included the First Corps under Hooker and the Ninth under Reno, marched on the Brookeville-New Market Road. The center under Sumner, including his own Second Corps and Mansfield's Twelfth, advanced along the Rockville-Frederick Road. Franklin's left wing, composed of his own Sixth Corps and Couch's division of the Fourth Corps, followed the Offutt's Crossroads-Seneca Road. Porter's Fifth Corps would later be reassigned to McClellan's army to constitute the reserve, but for the time being it was held in Washington. In all, McClellan had seventeen veteran divisions at his disposal, some 90,000 men altogether. This gave him almost a two-to-one superiority over Lee, which, however, it was not in McClellan's nature to admit. As usual, he overestimated Lee's strength by more than 100 percent, insisting that the number of Confederate troops exceeded his own by a large margin.

On the morning of September 10 Lee's Army of Northern Virginia, pursuant to Special Orders No. 191, resumed the march in accordance with the mission assigned to the several fragments, Jackson's corps in the lead and moving west on the Boonsboro road. As division after division crossed Catoctin Mountain, Stuart's cavalry screen, still skirmishing here and there with the aggressive Federal cavalry, prepared to follow. covering the rear.

Pleasanton informed McClellan of the Confederate departure, whereupon the march tempo of the Union army was stepped up. On September 12 and 13 the leading elements of Burnside's right wing and Sumner's center column entered Frederick.

CHAPTER 10

The Battle of South Mountain

As THE Confederate columns debouched from the shallow passes over Catoctin Mountain, only the most phlegmatic in the ranks would have been unimpressed by the imposing sight of the long, towering South Mountain range that reached skyward at a distance of seven miles across the intervening valley to the west. To the men in Jackson's corps, thoughts of their own Shenandoah Valley would be uppermost, for this fertile Maryland valley as well as the bordering mountains had a familiar look, except that this Northern valley was closed in at its upper end where the two mountains merged in a graceful, lofty horseshoe curve.

General Lee would not fail to note the scenic grandeur, on this his first invasion of Northern sail. But the esthetic features would quickly be subordinated to the military implications as he contemplated the possible developments of the next few days. The bastion of South Mountain might well prove to be a shield against McClellan's oncoming army, now that he was committed to the Harpers Ferry diversion. It had been his expectation, when he crossed the Potomac, that the Federals would relinquish Harpers Ferry rather than permit the garrison to be sacrificed, but Halleck had decided otherwise.

Lee was taking a huge gamble by dispatching divisions in all directions, dividing his army into four separate parts, and offering an enterprising opponent the opportunity to destroy him on the installment plan. That is, if McClellan should be alert enough to discover what great risks Lee was taking, and quick enough to take advantage of the opening. Lee did not believe that McClellan would react that speedily; on the contrary, he was confident that Jackson would quickly take Harper's Ferry and rejoin the main body in the Hagerstown-Boonsboro area before the Union army could or would do anything about it. And it would in all probability have worked out just as Lee planned had it not been for the "lost dispatch," which so completely changed what had started out as a promising invasion to a near disaster at Antietam.

MCCLELLAN LEARNS OF LEE'S PLANS

The 27th Indiana Volunteers, a regiment of the First Division of Mansfield's Twelfth Corps, Army of the Potomac, reaching Frederick on the morning of September 13, bivouacked in the same field that had been occupied the evening before by D. H. Hill's division, the rear guard of Lee's army. A few minutes after the regiment had stacked arms, First Sergeant John M. Bloss and Private B. W. Mitchell reported to their regimental commander that Mitchell had just picked up an order signed by Colonel Chilton, General Lee's Chief of Staff, which had been wrapped around three cigars.

The order was immediately taken to General A. S. Williams, the division commander, whose Adjutant General, Colonel Pittman, had known and served with Colonel Chilton before the war. Pittman stated that the signature was authentic. The important document was rushed to General McClellan.

The excitement at army headquarters caused by this unexpected windfall can only be imagined. For once McClellan was galvanized into prompt action. The news was almost too good to be true! Orders were quickly dispatched to the several corps commanders and within a matter of hours the army was ready to resume the march. The left column was directed to force the South Mountain pass at Crampton's Gap in an advance on Rohrersville, the center and right columns were to proceed through Turner's Gap on the Middletown-Boonsboro Road in the direction of Hagerstown.

McClellan was now in the enviable position of knowing exactly where all elements of Lee's army were, what course each had been instructed to follow, and the exact timetable for each. Through the almost criminal carelessness of an unknown Confederate staff officer, Lee at one stroke was deprived of the advantage of surprise, and lost the initiative gained by his invasion of Maryland. To his opponent he must have appeared to be a veritable sitting duck, ripe for the kill. From the viewpoint of the Federals,

Lee had taken one calculated risk too many, with Jackson's force of four divisions in the vicinity of Harpers Ferry south of the Potomac, separated from Lee and Longstreet by twenty-five miles and a broad river; and with the five Confederate divisions on the Maryland side of the Potomac divided into three parts, each part a half day's march from either of the others.

Such an opportunity to defeat an enemy in detail has rarely occurred in the history of war. It remained to be seen whether McClellan was enough of a general to turn the opportunity to his own advantage.

McClellan's plan of maneuver contemplated the seizure of the principal passes through South Mountain, followed by the occupation of Pleasant Valley. If the plan succeeded, the left wing under Major General William B. Franklin would take Rohrersville, cut off, destroy, or capture the two Confederate divisions under McLaws on Maryland Heights, and relieve the garrison under Colonel Miles at Harpers Ferry. As McClellan phrased it in his evening order of September 13 to Franklin: "My general idea is to cut the enemy in two and beat him in detail."

In spite of the great good fortune that had come to the Union commander in the form of a copy of Lee's orders, his chronic incapacity to move with alacrity led him to defer the starting time for the movement until the following morning. Why he failed to order a night march, which would have brought his army to the gaps by daybreak, is hard to understand. His army was relatively fresh, time was all-important, and possession of the passes over South Mountain would enable him to effectively dominate the situation. Although McClellan did not know it, Lee had no intention of defending them until he learned that the Army of the Potomac was closing in. All the mountain passes were in fact McClellan's for the taking, with only Stuart's light cavalry force to be brushed aside. But the Union commander allowed the afternoon and night of September 13 to pass before he moved, a delay which was to be a godsend to the Confederates.

Today's students of the two separate struggles for the South Mountain gaps, and certainly the Confederate generals who defended them in September 1862, have been puzzled as to why McClellan made his main effort through the pass leading to Hagerstown, assigning twelve divisions to that mission and only three to the reduction of Crampton's Gap, seven miles to the south. Possession of Lee's march table for the scattered troops of his army had given McClellan as much information as the Confederates themselves had, and his announced plan was to cut Lee's army in two. It would seem logical for McClellan to have reversed missions, sending a small corps to engage Longstreet at Boonsboro while the Federal main body was marched through the lower pass at Crampton's. That was the more direct route, which not only would have encouraged the Harpers Ferry garrison to hold out till relieved, but more certainly would have achieved the object of cutting the Confederate army in two.

McClellan may have reasoned that if he should take his army too close to the Potomac, Lee might somehow pull his divisions together and sideslip to the east in the direction of Washington, which would again cause a near-panic among the civilians at the capital. Or, he may subconsciously, or even consciously, have still harbored resentment because of his alleged cavalier treatment at the hands of the War Department, compounded by Halleck's rejection of his earlier recommendation that Harpers Ferry be abandoned. It was not beyond the realm of possibility that the general who had suggested to the War Department that Pope be allowed to "get out of his scrape as best he could" might harbor similar thoughts about Harpers Ferry. Also it is probable that, according to his custom, he estimated Lee's strength at twice its actual size and based his tactics accordingly. However McClellan may have figured it, the results fell woefully short of an effective exploitation of the glorious opportunity that was afforded him to whip the invader to the point of impotence if not final destruction.

THE ACTION AT CRAMPTON'S GAP

Franklin's Sixth Corps, followed by Couch's division of the Fourth Corps, reached Burkittsville, a small town at the base of South Mountain near the eastern end of Crampton's Gap, about noon on September 14. There the advance guard encountered the Confederates posted on both sides of the mountain road, protected behind stone walls and fence lines, with artillery sited above the junction of the two roads leading into the pass. Franklin assigned Major General Henry W. Slocum's division to a position on the right, Major General William F. Smith's division on the left, whereupon the two divisions, on a frontage of about 2,000 yards, advanced promptly to the attack.

Colonel T. T. Munford, temporarily in command of Robertson's brigade of General Stuart's cavalry division, had played a prominent part in screening the southern flank of Lee's army before Frederick and in delaying the forward movements of Pleasonton's Federal cavalry. It was now Munford's task to hold Crampton's Gap as long as possible, in company with similar action by D. H. Hill's rearguard division at Turner's Gap, seven miles to the north.

Munford had been given a man-sized job, which was in effect to block the advance of a major element of McClellan's army with a mere handful of men, initially two small Virginia cavalry regiments aggregating less than 300 troopers. In addition, he was expected to hold the Brownsville Pass, two miles south of Crampton's. His only artillery support consisted of Chew's battery and several guns each from three other batteries, all of which were posted halfway up the mountain in positions to cover both Crampton's and the Brownsville Pass.

As Munford's small rearguard fell back through Jefferson and Burkittsville before the Federal advance, to take position on either side of the mountain road, Mahone's infantry brigade of R. H. Anderson's division, a part of McLaw's force charged with the capture of Maryland Heights, was called back across Pleasant Valley to Munford's support.

About 3 o'clock on the afternoon of September 14 Slocum and Smith advanced to the attack. In overwhelming numbers the Federals pressed their advantage, and although Munford's combined infantry-cavalry-artillery command fought every step of the way and held Franklin's corps to a slow and painful advance for three solid hours, the weight of numbers of the determined Federals proved too much for the defenders. Munford retired slowly up the mountain, his force dwindling steadily. When near the crest, his line broke. At that moment reinforcements from McLaw's division, Semmes' and Cobb's brigades, hastened up from Pleasant Valley. But the rout, once started, could not be stemmed. The entire Confederate force, original defenders and reinforcements alike, retreated in disorder into the valley below, the infantry to Brownsville, the cavalry to Rohrersville. Losses amounted to several hundred on each side, including a sizable number of prisoners, several colors, and at least one gun captured by the attackers.

The gateway to Pleasant Valley was now open and South Mountain breached at the lower pass. Events at that point were moving according to McClellan's plan, but General Franklin failed to follow up his initial success. A dispatch from McClellan, at 1 o'clock on the morning of September 15, directed him to occupy the road from Rohrersville to Harpers Ferry, take possession of Pleasant Valley, open communication with the Federal garrison at Harpers Ferry, and then join the main body of the Union army at Boonsboro, which McClellan said he would attack the following day.

Franklin's reply at 8:50 A.M. indicated that the enemy was drawn up in line of battle across Pleasant Valley and that the cessation of firing at Harpers Ferry made him suspect that it had already been captured by the Confederates. If so, he added, he would need reinforcements before he could attack. Two hours later, he sent McClellan a second message to the effect that the Confederates then had two lines of battle across the Valley, in a very strong position, and since he was "outnumbered two to one" he felt that he was not justified in attacking.

The accuracy of Franklin's observations as to the relative strength of the enemy and his own corps of three divisions is open to doubt, but in view of McClellan's own habit of vastly overestimating his opposition, Franklin was simply following the leader's example. Be that as it may, Franklin did *not* attack. He merely held his force in position until Lee moved his troops behind Antietam Creek; the Sixth Corps then followed, to join McClellan's main body on September 17, two days later, on the line of the same creek east of the town of Sharpsburg.

McCLELLAN'S MAIN BODY MOVES WEST

The Federal troops of the center column under Major General Edwin V. Sumner, his own Second Corps and Mansfield's Twelfth, were united at Frederick on September 13 with Major General Ambrose E. Burnside's right wing, composed of Hooker's First Corps and Reno's Ninth. This large force of twelve divisions, four times as strong as Franklin's left wing, was given the task of seizing Turner's Gap, through which ran the old National Road from Frederick to Hagerstown. Passage of the gap would bring McClellan's main body into contact with Lee and Longstreet, who according to Lee's dispatch should have with them only three of the nine Confederate divisions of Lee's army, not counting Stuart's cavalry division; the other six being engaged in the Harpers Ferry adventure. Preceding the infantry-artillery column were three brigades of Pleasonton's cavalry division, one brigade having been detached to cooperate with Franklin at Crampton's Gap, and another sent on reconnaissance in the direction of Gettysburg, thirty miles to the north.

The fortunes of war, however, were not to smile exclusively on the Union army. McClellan's delay in moving his army out from Frederick until the morning of September 14, eighteen to twenty hours after digesting Lee's order, to a large extent nullified the rare military advantage afforded him in the knowledge of his opponent's troop dispositions and intentions. Had he gone beyond the mere dispatching of advance elements on the night of September 13, Lee would have been deprived of the time necessary to plug the two mountain gaps with infantry and artillery in support of the thin cavalry screen. McClellan's army could have been through the passes and spreading out in the valley beyond before the Confederate units ordered back to South Mountain could have reached it.

It so happened that when Lee's lost dispatch was handed to McClellan during the morning of September 13, a citizen of Frederick who was secretly a Southern sympathizer, was at McClellan's headquarters and of course picked up the startling news of the disclosure of Lee's plans. As soon as he could get away without arousing suspicion, the volunteer spy rode hard to South Mountain to advise Stuart, who in turn immediately relayed the intelligence to Lee at Hagerstown.

Longstreet's presence at Hagerstown rather than Boonsboro had been brought about as the result of a rumor that Federal troops were coming down on Hagerstown from Pennsylvania. The word had gotten around that Lee's first attempt in the direction of Pennsylvania had so alarmed the authorities in Harrisburg, the capital city, that Governor Andrew G. Curtin hastily called up 50,000 militia and wired President Lincoln for help to secure the State against the expected Rebel invaders. In reply, the War Department pulled Major General John F. Reynolds away from his regular assignment with troops and dispatched him to stiffen the backbones of the raw volunteers. Although the rumor had no foundation in fact, Lee decided that he could protect McLaws' operations in the vicinity of Maryland Heights more effectively from the road center at Hagerstown, twelve miles north of Boonsboro. In addition, that position would facilitate the reconcentration of his army after Harpers Ferry fell, and would afford him, as well, greater flexibility of maneuver in carrying out the later phases of the invasion.

D. H. (Harvey) Hill's Confederate division, the army rear guard, had been left at Boonsboro to block the anticipated retreat of the Harpers Ferry garrison up through Pleasant Valley and to assist Stuart in holding Turner's Gap. Hill had managed, as a result of a somewhat critical temperament and occasionally grumpy attitude toward others, to antagonize a number of his colleagues among the general officers. Like many others, then and now, he hated administrative chores to such an extent as to sidestep his responsibilities in that direction. Another weakness was an apparent lack of assurance in making decisions when not in combat, although in battle he was to grow in stature with experience. Hill had clashed with Stuart on several occasions because he had spoken contemptuously of the cavalry arm, and the relations between the two generals were far from cordial. There may have been no significance in that fact insofar as Hill's sense of duty was concerned, but for some reason he left the defense of the gap largely to Stuart's cavalry. Meanwhile Hill remained at Boonsboro, keeping an eye on what he considered his principal mission, and in that respect neglected his additional responsibility at Turner's Gap.

When Stuart reported to Hill that the cavalry was being pushed back to South Mountain by the advancing Federals, the rearguard commander made a gesture of support by sending one of his brigades under Colonel A. H. Colquitt to support Stuart at the Gap, while at the same time another brigade, Garland's, was alerted but not dispatched. The rest of Hill's division remained at Boonsboro, three miles from Turner's Gap. Colquitt moved his brigade to the eastern face of the mountain and there, in the darkness of the night of September 13, he looked down into the broad valley between South and Catoctin Mountains. As far as the eye could see, innumerable enemy camp fires indicated that the Federals were in vastly greater strength than the two cavalry brigades which Stuart had reported as the only troops that had been pressing him. This startling intelligence was likewise quickly forwarded through Hill to Lee.

Thus by midnight of the 13th the situation had been drastically altered. Lee knew that a copy of his orders had fallen into McClellan's hands. Harpers Ferry had not yet capitulated as expected on September 12. The Confederate army, widely scattered, was an easy prey for an aggressive adversary. It was now clear to Lee why the Army of the Potomac seemed to be moving with unaccustomed celerity, a matter that had been puzzling him for some hours.

The Confederate strategy would have to be changed, and at once. The ambitious plan to move into Pennsylvania must be shelved, temporarily at least. Lee's earlier idea, not to defend the passes of South Mountain in order to lure McClellan farther from his base of supplies, had now lost its attraction, coupled as it was with the timetable upset caused by the prolonged delay in capturing Harpers Ferry.

Having lost the initiative through no fault of his own, and through sheer luck so far as McClellan was concerned, Lee reacted with customary firmness in the face of adversity. His situation had suddenly become so critical that he began to think seriously of the wisdom of calling the whole program off and returning to Virginia. His orders and dispositions for the next two days were planned and executed with that possibility in mind.

The immediate requirement was to meet the Federal threat by delaying McClellan's advance through South Mountain, and to safeguard the status of that portion of his own army that remained in Maryland. For it must be remembered that Stonewall Jackson's corps and Walker's division were by this time south of the Potomac, carrying out their instructions to throw a net around Harpers Ferry prior to taking it over in conjunction with McLaws' force, which was operating from the Maryland side of the river.

By midnight September 13, Harvey Hill had received from Lee confirmatory orders to cooperate with Stuart in holding the passes at Turner's Gap and vicinity, which included three crossings: the National Road through Turner's Gap; Fox's (Braddock's) Gap, where the old Sharpsburg

Road crossed the mountain a mile to the south; and still another gap a mile to the north, where a second road led to Hagerstown. Hill was informed that Longstreet's troops, the divisions of D. R. Jones and John B. Hood, would be sent back from Hagerstown the following day to add their strength to the defense of the passes.

THE FIGHT AT TURNER'S GAP

The morning of Sunday, September 14, was bright and clear. The Union troops, advancing on all the roads leading west to the South Mountain gaps, were in a cheerful mood. Their favorite general was again leading them, Lee's army was retiring before them, and this time they would be fighting to drive the brash invader from their own Northern soil.

Pleasonton's cavalry had the preceding day driven the Confederate cavalry back into the mountains, but Pleasonton, after making a reconnaissance up the mountain, concluded that as the enemy position was too strongly held, it would be wise to let the infantry and artillery catch up before attacking.

At Pleasonton's request, Brigadier General Jacob D. Cox, in command of the Kanawha division of Reno's corps, assigned Scammon's brigade to join the cavalry in storming the pass. Suspecting that his entire division might be needed, Cox personally brought his other brigade, under Colonel George Crook, to follow Scammon, who about 9 o'clock in the morning had reached the foot of the mountain and started to make the ascent on the old Sharpsburg Road.

The right wing of the Union army advanced with corps abreast, Reno's Ninth and 'Hooker's First, which together totaled seven divisions, moving in the lead in columns of divisions on parallel roads. When Reno was advised that Cox's division was on its way up the mountain, he sent word that the entire Ninth Corps, three additional divisions commanded respectively by Willcox, Sturgis, and Rodman, would support the attack. Two batteries of twenty-pounder Parrott guns were placed near the turnpike to cover the advance from a position that enabled them to effectively reach the enemy guns near the crest.

Scammon's brigade proceeded in a deployed formation to the left of the Sharpsburg road with the mission of turning the enemy right. The going was not too difficult for the first mile or so, across cultivated fields, but when, farther up, the slope became steeper and more wooded, the troops found it necessary to halt frequently to recover their wind. As they neared the crest, Hill's Confederate infantry opened fire, while at the same time a battery poured in canister and case-shot from a still higher position. The Southerners, protected by portions of a stone wall paralleling the rough country road that connected the Sharpsburg road with the old National turnpike, were apparently there to stay; it would take cold steel to drive them out. The Federals were in the mood, so, with Crook's column in close support, the attacking line fixed bayonets and advanced with loud cheers.

The regiment on Scammon's left, the Twenty-third Ohio, was commanded by Lieutenant Colonel Rutherford B. Hayes, later a President of the United States. Hayes' regiment, moving through the woods, was given the task of outflanking the enemy. Unseen by the Confederates, Hayes passed the crest and came in on their right and rear as the other regiments of his brigade charged frontally. The fight was close-in and vicious, both sides losing heavily, but Scammon's men were not to be denied the fruits of their laborious climb. The combined troops of D. H. Hill and Stuart fought doggedly and bravely. It was not until Confederate General Garland, whose brigade was defending Fox's Gap, was killed that the Confederates broke and yielded the crest on that part of the mountain to the victorious Federals of Cox's division. Even then Hill's men fought on, attempting in repeated counterattacks to recover the lost ground, but without success. Finally, about noon, both sides had lost so many men in the hand-to-hand combat in the woods, and were so exhausted by their continuous efforts over the entire morning, that a lull in the battle occurred, almost as though by mutual consent an unspoken truce had been declared until both contestants should receive reinforcements to enable them to again be at each other's throats.

HILL GETS A REPRIEVE

General D. H. Hill, charged by Lee with the responsibility of holding Turner's Gap as long as possible, had foolishly relied on Jeb Stuart to inform him of the tactical features of the mountaintop and neglected to even visit the Gap until the early morning of September 14. His first shock upon arrival was to learn that the peripatetic Stuart had ridden down to see how things were faring at Crampton's Gap. The second shock, when he and Colquitt rode along the crest on a reconnaissance, occurred when they distinctly heard the rumble of artillery carriages and the voices of Federal officers giving commands on the road leading up to the crest. Colquitt's brigade was the only one of the five brigades in Hill's division that was at hand, although Garland's was climbing fast. Hill concluded that his entire division, if present, would not be strong enough to block the Federals, but his uncertainty was so marked that all he did was to order up G. B. Anderson's brigade and direct one regiment of Ripley's brigade to move to the next pass north of Turner's Gap, leaving the balance of Ripley's and all of Rodes' small brigade to continue the watch at Boonsboro. Consequently, when Cox attacked shortly after 9 o'clock, Hill had only two brigades in line to receive him, but those two did their best for three hours, and their best was extremely good.

It was not until late in the morning, when Garland's brigade was shattered, losing 200 men as prisoners in addition to a large number of killed and wounded, that Hill could bring himself to the point of abandoning the Boonsboro part of his mission. Finally he sent word to Rodes and Ripley to bring their brigades up the mountain. But it would be mid-afternoon before they could arrive and then it might be too late, since Hill had no idea when Longstreet had left Hagerstown nor how long it would take his two divisions to cover the twelve-mile march to the foot of the mountain. While Hill was gloomily dwelling on the critical situation in which he found himself, welcome aid came from an unexpected source—the enemy, in the person of General Burnside.

BURNSIDE TAKES CHARGE

General Burnside, commanding the Federal right wing, and General Reno, Ninth Corps commander, met at the foot of the mountain for a brief conference. Hooker's First Corps had not yet reached the field, but Reno's corps was on hand, and Willcox's division had already joined Cox, forming on his right and extending across and to the north of the old National Road leading through Turner's Gap. In the process

Willcox had lost many men from Confederate direct and enfilading artillery fire.

Burnside now took command of the battle and directed Reno to send the remaining two divisions of the Ninth Corps, Sturgis' and Rodman's, to join Cox and Willcox, but not to make a general attack until Hooker's corps had arrived and was well on its way up the mountain in the zone north of the Hagerstown Turnpike. It was this reprieve which proved such a boon to D. H. Hill's thin line of defense at the summit, but it is doubtful if either Burnside or Reno had the remotest idea that their delay would forfeit the opportunity for Cox and Willcox with their superior numbers to sweep the top of the mountain clear of Hill's three depleted brigades.

BURNSIDE'S WEIGHT BEGINS TO TELL

During the midday breathing space of several hours thus afforded Hill, the two remaining brigades of his division, Ripley's and Rodes', scaled the mountain and were fed into the defensive line, Ripley to the south, Rodes to the north of the turnpike. Longstreet also, approaching Boonsboro with the divisions of D. R. Jones and John B. Hood, would reach the crest in the nick of time to redress the balance late in the afternoon and prolong the battle until far into the night.

With the arrival of Sturgis' and Rodman's Federal divisions at the scene of action, the Ninth Corps commander, Reno, took over from Cox in a continuation of the attack on the Sharpsburg Road leading through Fox's Gap. Major General Jesse L. Reno, graduate of the Class of 1846 at West Point, age 39 and a Virginian by birth, had fought in the Mexican War and distinguished himself with Burnside in the latter's successful invasion of North Carolina, which led to the capture of Roanoke Island in early 1862. In the Battle of Second Manassas he had again conducted himself in a manner to win the unstinting commendation of General Pope, who seemed to take a rather dim view of so many of the other corps and division commanders who served under him in that ill-fated campaign.

By the time Sturgis and Rodman were in position, McClellan had arrived and was in consultation with Burnside and Reno at Pleasonton's command post, on a central knoll in the midst of the curving hills on the south slope of the mountain. The conference resulted in a decision to press the attack in the direction of the Mountain House, west of the turnpike, a key position which commanded the road through Turner's Gap at its most sensitive spot. Before the coordinated corps attack could be launched, however, Longstreet's reinforcements had come up. The combined divisions of Hood, Jones, and Hill pitched into Reno's divisions. The fight was bloody and prolonged, swirling back and forth without a decision for several hours.

Just before sunset, General Reno came forward to the front line to see what was holding up progress toward the summit objective—the Mountain House. As he exposed himself to get a better view, an enemy bullet found its mark and he fell, mortally wounded, the highest ranking officer of either army to lose his life in this battle. As he was being carried to the rear, Reno managed with his last breath to gasp out a final message to his men: "Tell my command that if not in body, I will be with them in spirit." One of his fellow officers has recorded the opinion that "the hero's body was small, but his spirit was mighty."

The head of Hooker's corps reached Mount Tabor Church about the middle of the afternoon, pausing while the corps commander looked over the terrain. His three divisions, led by Generals Meade, Hatch, and Ricketts, all veteran commanders, were successively deployed as they arrived, Meade on the right, Hatch on the left, and Ricketts, last to come up at about 5 o'clock, in rear as reserve. The right of Meade's line was posted about 1½ miles beyond the old National Road. Three roads were available for the ascent, partly through woods and partly over farm lands, the two country roads (other than the turnpike) winding through ravines or depressions between the rounded mountain peaks which towered several hundred feet above the turnpike on either side.

Advancing abreast, Meade and Hatch soon encountered the Confederates, when the battle became general all along the line east of the turnpike. Pushing steadily forward and upward, Meade's division succeeded in turning the Confederate left. Soon the first ridge, which commanded the pass on both sides of the mountain, was in Federal hands. Gibbon's brigade of Hatch's division was then sent directly up the turnpike in a brisk engagement which forced the Confederate center back to the crest; at that point reinforcements braced the line, but Gibbon managed to hold his gains.

Longstreet Moves to Hill's Support

On receiving the news from D. H. Hill late in the evening of September 13 that McClellan's army was present in strength in the valley east of South Mountain, Lee at Hagerstown called Longstreet to his tent to inform him that on the following morning he would have to take his two divisions back to the mountain to support Hill. Longstreet demurred, on the premise that the proper strategy was to adhere to the original plan not to hold the passes. Old Pete argued that it would be better to retire to Sharpsburg where the army could be reunited in safety, but Lee insisted that the order be carried out so that McLaws' two divisions on Maryland Heights would not be jeopardized.

As Longstreet's column on September 14 plodded along the dusty road to Boonsboro, the sounds of furious fighting on the mountain heights came clearly to the ears of the men. When they neared Boonsboro a dispatch rider galloped up to Lee, riding as usual at the head of the column, with an appeal from Hill to hurry Longstreet's reinforcements if the crest was to be held against a greatly superior Federal force. Shortly after 3 o'clock, when the head of the column reached the foot of the mountain and began the ascent, Hood's Texas brigade strode by and spied General Lee sitting on his horse beside the road, watching the troops breaking from column into extended order for the climb.

"Give us Hood" they shouted. Lee nodded his head in acquiescence, a reaction that twentieth century military men might have some difficulty in understanding. But Lee, who knew his soldiers, appraised their apparent lack of discipline sympathetically. Their division commander, John B. Hood, one of the South's best fighting generals, had been placed under arrest by Longstreet back at Manassas for insubordination in connection with a wrangle between General N. G. "Shank" Evans and himself over some captured Federal ambulances, which had been claimed by both parties to the controversy. Hood had been permitted to accompany his division on the march into Maryland, but without command authority, and now that his men were again going into battle they wanted their trusted leader at the helm. Acting on the spur of the moment, and without consulting Longstreet, Hood was summoned by Lee, his status of arrest suspended until after the battle, and the restored division commander rode to the head of his troops with their cheers ringing in his ears.

Longstreet's reinforcements arrived barely in time to prevent a repetition of the Confederate rout at Crampton's Gap. Hill's five brigades had been fighting all day to hold off two Union corps with a strength of seven divisions, and they had about reached the limit of endurance. Hill's right had been turned, but the line had somehow been restored further up the mountain. Several hours later Hooker's troops were massed to turn Hill's left, where Rodes' undersized brigade was fighting stubbornly against overwhelmingly superior strength. Daylight was almost gone before Longstreet's divisions under D. R. Jones and Hood, with Evans' brigade attached, tuckered by their tiring march from Hagerstown and the climb to the top of the mountain, moved into position for the relief of Hill's exhausted troops. Longstreet immediately took charge of the defense and, even before he had examined the terrain, sent back word to Lee that South Mountain could not be held. Nevertheless the Confederates, strengthened by Longstreet's divisions, hung on until night brought an end to the bitter fighting. All the troops, on both sides, were more than ready to flop down on the ground for some blessed rest, no matter what the next day should demand of them.

About the time the battle on the heights ended, two more Union corps, Sumner's and Mansfield's, the latter under the temporary command of the senior division commander, Brigadier General A. S. Williams, reached the eastern base of the mountain and went into bivouac. McClellan's army was now fully concentrated, but when the Federal skirmishers up on the crest moved forward at daylight, September 15, to feel out their opponents, they discovered that the Confederates had withdrawn during the night, leaving their dead and wounded behind.

Some 5,000 casualties, including those missing and captured, represented the cost to both armies of the engagements at Crampton's and Turner's Gaps. That was the penalty the Confederates had to pay for delaying McClellan's army for twenty-four hours; it was McClellan's price for gaining the passes too late to save Harpers Ferry or to cut Lee's army in two as planned. The Union casualty reports show losses of 533 at Crampton's and 1,813 at Turner's for a total of 2,346, practically all killed or wounded. The Confederate reports, as usual incomplete and unofficial, group South Mountain and Antietam as one and are virtually impossible of separation. Douglas Southall Freeman placed the Confederate killed and wounded at some 1,800 at Turner's Gap only, exclusive of Garland's brigade, the greater part of which was captured. Adding the losses at Crampton's, it may safely be assumed that the aggregate of losses at South Mountain for Lee's troops exceeded 2,500. Since the Union strength was far greater than the Confederate, the percentage of loss of the Southerners was consequently substantially higher than that of their opponents, a rather unusual occurrence because the Confederates had the advantage of a stronger position and the defense normally inflicts greater damage on the attackers than it receives.

It is an intriguing picture that presents itself in studying the Confederate maneuvers at this stage of Lee's campaign. With a small force of only two divisions, barely one-fifth of the manpower of his army, General Lee bivouacked at Hagerstown with supreme confidence as McClellan, with an army almost twice as large as the entire Confederate invading army, moved west in pursuit. With his right arm, so to speak, Lee reached out to gather in Harpers Ferry and safeguard his line of supply to Virginia. With his left arm, when he learned that McClellan's unaccustomed rate of march posed a threat to his own safety, Lee straight-armed to bar his opponent's passage of the mountain gaps long enough (he hoped) to assure the fall of Harpers Ferry and enable him to reconcentrate his full strength farther west, probably in the Sharpsburg area.

It would be a close thing, but the Confederate leader figured all the angles and, as happened time after time on other battlefields such as Richmond, Second Manassas, Fredericksburg, Chancellorsville, and Gettysburg, his precision timing brought the desired results. Invariably, in taking his calculated risks, Lee counted on the inability of his opponent to match his own mental agility and the quick reactions, to his orders, of his subordinates and their brigades and divisions. In the case of the Battle of South Mountain, it was McClellan's tardiness in forcing the gaps rather than superior Confederate battle proficiency that gave Lee the vital extra time that he needed. From his standpoint, the strategic gains outweighed the losses, without which it is more than probable that he would have retreated to Virginia without fighting the Battle of Antietam.

CHAPTER 11

The Harpers Ferry Diversion

WHAT HAPPENED at Harpers Ferry in mid-September 1862 is reminiscent of the favorite strategy of American Indians on the warpath in frontier days. Every reader of "westerns" or confirmed movie-goer is familiar with the Red Man's preferred method of attack, in which a horde of almost naked savages, hideous in their brilliant war paint, would race their ponies in wide circles around the objects of their attack, shooting arrows and firing rifles until the defenders were softened for the kill.

Lee's plan for the investment by encirclement of the Federal garrison at Harpers Ferry followed that pattern. He sent close to 30,000 soldiers, almost 60 percent of his army, to make certain that the overwhelming Confederate superiority should force the capitulation of the relatively small garrison without loss of time. For it would prove a losing gamble if McClellan should surprise Lee by closing in on his scattered divisions before they could reassemble as an operational army.

Lee's timetable as set forth in Special Orders No. 191 of September 9 called for the occupation of Maryland Heights and Loudoun Heights by McLaws and Walker respectively by Friday morning, September 12, at which time Jackson was expected to be at Martinsburg, in position to prevent the Federals from escaping in that direction. If all went smoothly, the sideshow should be concluded so that the traveling Confederates would be able to rejoin Lee at Hagerstown or Boonsboro before the Union army could interfere.

The strategic importance of Harpers Ferry, which changed hands periodically during the Civil War, lay in the fact that its possession was essential to that army, Union or Confederate, whose operations included the use of the Shenandoah Valley either for offensive or defensive purposes. It was a sensitive area, located at the confluence of the Shenandoah and

Potomac Rivers, where the Baltimore and Ohio Railroad, so vital to the North, crosses the Potomac.

Squatting at the base of the Blue Ridge Mountains, which tower a thousand feet above the Potomac to look down directly from that imposing height on the little town, Harpers Ferry does not strike the observer as the best place to fight a battle. The small community nestles in the angle formed by the two rivers, which in conjunction with the massive bluffs hem it in on all sides except the west, where the lesser but still formidable Bolivar Heights provide access to the town. Loudoun Heights loom rocky and steep directly to the east on the far side of the Shenandoah River and the lofty Maryland Heights complete the impressive picture across the Potomac as the northern arc of the mountain perimeter.

Harpers Ferry is only eighteen miles west of Frederick by the most direct road, but Lee's orders required Jackson's three divisions to take a long, roundabout, sixty-mile march through Middletown, Boonsboro, Sharpsburg, across the Potomac and through Martinsburg in order to dispose of the Federal detachment reported to be at the latter place, to intercept escapees from Harpers Ferry, and to approach that town from the west. With McLaws' two-division command blocking the escape route to the north from his position on Maryland Heights, and with Walker's division closing the route to the east from Loudoun Heights, the 11,000-man Federal garrison at Harpers Ferry would have the choice of surrender or death.

The Federal garrison, under command of Colonel Dixon S. Miles, included two regiments and several additional squadrons of cavalry, a dozen or more regiments of infantry, and about six batteries of artillery, but formal defenses were practically nonexistent. Several pseudo-forts on Maryland Heights and lines of rifle pits and earthworks here and there on Bolivar Heights made a pretense of fortifications that were scarcely worthy of the name. There were no Federal troops on Loudoun Heights, Miles had disposed 7,000 men on Bolivar Heights, manning a curving line about a mile and a half long from the Potomac to the Shenandoah; 2,000 on Maryland Heights; and about 1,800 to guard bridges and other points on the rivers and the fringes of the town itself.

Brigadier General Julius White was in command of the small Union force of 2,500 men at Martinsburg. Exercising his discretionary authority, on receipt of word that the Confederates were approaching from the north on September 12, he moved his detachment to Harpers Ferry, raising the strength of the garrison there to approximately 13,000 men. Normally White would by reason of rank have assumed command of the combined forces, but since Colonel Miles had specific orders from General Halleck, White's position became largely that of an observer. Halleck was seriously intent on holding Harpers Ferry. On September 7 he had telegraphed Colonel Miles to advise him that McClellan's army was in motion and emphasizing the importance of holding the town as long as humanly possible.

MCLAWS FIRST TO ARRIVE

To Lafayette McLaws, whose division had reached Manassas from Richmond too late to take part in that recent battle, Lee assigned the leading part in the three-way undertaking to reduce Harpers Ferry. With "Dick" Anderson's division added to his own, under McLaws' command, the latter was instructed to take the road from Middletown to Harpers Ferry and by Friday morning, the twelfth, to seize Maryland Heights "and endeavor to capture the enemy at Harpers Ferry and vicinity." The topography being what it was, Maryland Heights seemed to be the key to the tactical success of the overall mission. It so dominated Harpers Ferry that with the Confederates occupying the mountain peak on the Maryland side and Loudoun Heights in Virginia, the town would be next to untenable for the defenders. Nevertheless, McLaws' two divisions would be exposed in rear to a possible sudden appearance of a strong Union force approaching through the mountain gaps from the east. It therefore behooved him to work fast and carefully in discharging his difficult double mission of attack in one direction while guarding his rear from another.

McLaws started from Frederick early on the morning of September 10, with less than a twenty-mile march ahead of him; but his movements were slow, requiring two days to cover about twelve miles. Thursday night, September 11, found him encamped at Brownsville, at the western exit of the South Mountain pass of the same name, some six miles north of the Potomac where it passes the base of Elk Ridge, a tall mountain range whose southern extremity was known as Maryland Heights. Possibly McLaws preferred not to reach his objective too early lest he stir up a Federal hornet's nest prematurely and thus risk the escape of the garrison at Harpers Ferry before Jackson and Walker could reach their designated positions to close the circle.

From his bivouac at Brownsville, the mountain peak from which McLaws had been directed to eject the Federal occupants loomed as a formidable obstacle from which plunging fire could be expected from the Union guns that would certainly be located on Maryland Heights. McLaws reasoned that the best approach would be to scale the heights by way of Solomon's Gap, four miles north of Maryland Heights and only two or three miles from his present camp. Once having gained the ridge, he would proceed south along the crest, following a mountain road that he was told led directly to the Federal artillery position.

Having thus decided, McLaws split his command into two parts, Kershaw's brigade supported by Barksdale's to follow the mountain road, while the remaining eight brigades would be disposed in Pleasant Valley in a central position that would enable them to challenge any enemy who might cross South Mountain. The latter force would at the same time block the valley route against troops from the Harpers Ferry garrison who might attempt to escape in that direction.

McLaws himself led the advance of his main body to the Potomac, which was reached by nightfall, September 12, in the vicinity of Weverton. This small town at the southern extremity of South Mountain, derived its significance chiefly from the fact that the road from Harpers Ferry along the north bank of the Potomac, the Baltimore and Ohio Railroad, and the Chesapeake and Ohio Canal all pass that point in the narrow space between the river and the mountain. Kershaw concurrently climbed the mountain, but the route was so rough and steep and full of boulders that he found it necessary to halt for the night about a mile from his objective.

Saturday morning, September 13, Kershaw's two brigades pushed forward along the ridge, Barksdale working around the precipitous eastern face of Maryland Heights to outflank the enemy, whose outposts had already been driven in. One of Barksdale's companies opened fire at close range, which seemed to disconcert the Federals. In any event, they started down the mountain and were promptly joined by the entire force of the defenders, so that by mid-afternoon all of Maryland Heights was in the hands of the Confederates, most of the Union troops returning to the town of Harpers Ferry. The Federal troop commander, Colonel Ford, claimed later that he abandoned the position on order of Colonel Miles, who denied that he had issued any such order. There was no doubt that the Federals had failed to put up a vigorous defense and the evidence seemed to point to Ford as the culprit. The result was that McLaws was able to take Maryland Heights with ease, while Colonel Ford was later tried and convicted on a charge of neglect of duty.

The dramatic collateral features of the Confederate investment of Harpers Ferry and its influence on the Battle of Antietam, which turned Lee back into Virginia, will appear later in the narrative. At this point, however, it is of interest to note that military strategists have enjoyed speculating on what might have resulted had Miles made a more serious effort to hold Maryland Heights, the dominant terrain feature in the area. It is reasonably certain that 10,000 Federals on that side of the Potomac could have prevented McLaws from accomplishing his mission, but Miles' instructions were to hold Harper's Ferry as long as possible, which obviously would be impossible if he should transfer the bulk of his troops to the other side of the Potomac. By adhering strictly to his orders, even though Maryland Heights was evacuated with untimely speed by a none too courageous colonel, the resistance offered by the Federals in the town made it necessary for Lee's converging columns to tarry in the vicinity of Harpers Ferry several days longer than Lee had planned, with almost disastrous effect on the Confederate fortunes.

While McLaws on September 13 was completing the first half of his mission by taking possession of Maryland Heights, Walker without opposition occupied Loudoun Heights and Jackson arrived with the leading elements of his corps to the west of Bolivar Heights. Much work was still to be done, however, before the attack could commence. Pioneers must cut paths along the mountain tops, so that the guns could be placed to deliver maximum fire on the town below. Communications must be established between Jackson's force, which included the divisions of A. P. Hill, A. R. Lawton, and John R. Jones, and those of McLaws and

Walker across the Potomac and Shenandoah Rivers. The cordon around Harpers Ferry must be made tight in Jackson's zone, which meant disposing troops in a wide arc paralleling the Federal rifle pits and earthworks from the Potomac to the Shenandoah. All of which took time, so that it was not until the afternoon of September 14 that Jackson was ready to advance his troops to Bolivar Heights preparatory to signaling the order for the converging, coordinated artillery bombardment to open simultaneously from the two mountaintops and from his own position west of the town.

During the time that Jackson was making his preparations and trying with indifferent success on September 14 to establish flag signal communication with McLaws and Walker across the two rivers, McLaws was having his troubles. While getting his artillery into position for the second part of his mission, the capture of Harpers Ferry, things began to pop at the northern end of Pleasant Valley, where Semmes' and Mahone's brigades had been posted in a dual mission to protect the road taken by Kershaw to reach Maryland Heights, and to guard the passes through South Mountain. It was Semmes whose alert reconnoitering discovered that there was no Confederate infantry in position to secure Crampton's Gap. On his own authority Semmes dispatched several regiments of Mahone's brigade with a battery to occupy the gap. From then on events moved rapidly.

McLaws heard the firing on South Mountain and rode back with Jeb Stuart to investigate. As they neared the western exit of Crampton's Gap, they met General Cobb, who in some excitement informed them of the loss of the Gap and the rout of the Confederates, who were even then streaming down the western side of the mountain. McLaws was at that moment in a very difficult position. It was impossible for him to hold off the Army of the Potomac, if the Federal troops now in the Gap should prove to be the advance elements of McClellan's army. Furthermore, the brigades of Semmes, Cobb, and Mahone would probably be quickly cut to pieces if the Federals pressed their advantage in superior force. That in turn would mean the reoccupation of Maryland Heights by the advancing Bluecoats, the relief of Harpers Ferry, Lee's army cut in two, and possible destruction of the divided wings.

Fortunately for McLaws and the Confederate army as a whole, Union General Franklin, whose corps it was that took Crampton's Gap, proved to be somewhat less than enterprising. Hence McLaws was able, during the night of September 14, to recall all of the troops who had captured Maryland Heights except one of Barksdale's regiments and two guns. By morning he had five brigades less one regiment disposed in two lines across Pleasant Valley below Crampton's Gap, and it was this force which led Franklin to inform McClellan that he was outnumbered two to one. McLaw's bold front at a critical moment was thus sufficient to bluff a timid Franklin to gain the time necessary for Jackson to force the surrender of Harpers Ferry and for Lee to change his mind about calling the show off by withdrawing his army to Virginia.

Jackson Slow to Act

There were times in Stonewall Jackson's military career when his customary sense of urgency was lacking. Most of the time he was a driver who gave his men no rest, nor spared himself in marches or battles until victory was achieved or his immediate mission accomplished. Occasionally, however, his actions seemed uninspired, a fact which in his case attracts attention for the simple reason that his standards of performance were so high that any deviation, however slight, became notable because it was so unusual. The investment of Harpers Ferry was one of those times.

Lee's directive of September 9 contemplated the capture of the Federal garrison at Harpers Ferry by Friday night, September 12. He believed that McLaws' force could bring it off with Walker's assistance from Loudoun Heights, while Jackson's corps was cutting the Baltimore and Ohio Railroad and closing the Federal escape route to the west. The schedule may have been a bit ambitious in point of time, because the three columns did not reach their assigned areas on the perimeter around Harpers Ferry until Saturday the thirteenth, on which day Jackson, by virtue of seniority, assumed the direction of affairs. Lee had not specifically stated in his order that Jackson should take command, probably because of his familiarity with Harpers Ferry and its environs and his realization of the difficulty of achieving unity of action in a tactical situation of that character.

The only means of communication between the Confederates on Bolivar, Maryland, and Loudoun Heights was by flag wigwag or messenger. Since the Federals controlled the town of Harpers Ferry and the bridge over the Potomac, Jackson's couriers would have to cross by distant fords, which would consume more time than could be spared. Flag signal's were therefore utilized, but that also took time, assuming that the signal personnel on all three peaks were on the alert and functioning perfectly, which was not fully the case on this occasion. So far as Jackson could see by personal observation from his position west of Harpers Ferry, when he arrived late on the morning of September 13, there was no visible evidence of the occupation of either Maryland or Loudoun Heights, on the opposite side of the Potomac and Shenandoah Rivers. Jackson then tried flag signals, but they evoked no response from McLaws or Walker. Toward the end of the afternoon the sound of firing on the crest of Elk Ridge was heard, but Jackson could only guess what it meant. Failing to rouse McLaws and Walker by signal flags, he reverted to messengers, who returned after dark to report that both commanders had reached their objectives. Obviously nothing further could be undertaken till morning.

On the morning of September 14, which ushered in the battle for South Mountain at the two Gaps, Turner's and Crampton's, Jackson resumed his efforts to establish two-way communication with Walker and McLaws. Walker responded, advising that he had six guns in position on Loudoun Heights, but Jackson directed him to wait until fire could be opened from both sides of the river at once. Still unable to contact McLaws, a message was finally received through Walker to the effect that McLaws was occupied with the enemy in his rear, implying that his Harpers Ferry mission would have to be sidetracked for the time being.

So it came about that another whole day, Sunday, September 14, passed while Jackson fussed with inadequate communications. At the same time McClellan's army was pressing inexorably toward a full-scale battle with Lee's army, still widely scattered two days after Lee had hoped to have it reconcentrated, with Harpers Ferry safely in the bag. Jackson had not sent in a report to Lee since they had separated on the morning of September 10, nor had Lee dispatched any additional instructions to Jackson. Consequently both were in the dark as to the fortunes of the other.

Sunday evening, when the fighting had ended on South Mountain, and word reached Lee that McClellan's main body had crossed the valley to a position from which to effectively support the troops on the mountain, the Confederate leader dispatched a message to McLaws telling him to abandon his position on Maryland Heights and in Pleasant Valley, and with his two divisions to recross the Potomac. McLaws was further informed that the commanding general had resolved to withdraw the rest of the army that was still in Maryland by way of Sharpsburg to Virginia, crossing the Potomac at Shepherdstown.

Lee's disappointment at the failure of his optimistic invasion plans was not allowed to show, but it must have been intense. Gone was the bright hope that by this time his reunited army would be on its way to Harrisburg and the Susquehanna. Instead he must now salvage what he could in order to escape disaster in the process of reconcentrating on Virginia soil. On the other side of South Mountain was the entire Army of the Potomac. He could not hope to oppose that massive force with but three divisions, two of Longstreet's and what was left of D. H. Hill's. Worse still, the rout of the Confederates at Crampton's Gap meant that the Federals now threatened him from two directions, even though the prompt withdrawal of McLaws should succeed in bringing his two divisions to safety. There seemed to be no alternative. Lee and Longstreet must also retire, and a night movement was thereupon ordered. Longstreet and Hill were informed of the decision, but were not told of Lee's intention to withdraw across the Potomac. That bad news was probably withheld for psychological reasons, or Lee may still have held the remote hope that some unforeseen circumstance might arise to improve his fortunes.

FEDERAL CAVALRY RUNS THE GAUNTLET

As the clouds of apparent doom lowered on the Federal garrison at Harpers Ferry, Colonel B. F. "Grimes" Davis, commanding the 8th New York cavalry, conceived the idea of breaking through the Confederate cordon to join McClellan's approaching army. It was obvious that cavalry was of no use to the garrison in the present circumstances, and it made sense to try to save the horses and horse equipment, which would be of great value to the Confederates if they should fall into their hands.

The project was discussed with General White, Colonel Miles, and the commanding officers of the three cavalry regiments, the 8th New York, 12th Illinois, and. 1st Rhode Island, on the evening of September 13. The possibility that the entire garrison might make the effort to escape the trap was considered, but Miles would not consent on two counts, that it would be in violation of his orders, and his belief that the infantry and artillery could not march fast enough to get away with it.

Miles hesitated, but after a heated exchange with Colonel Davis, who was determined to save the cavalry, he gave his approval of the attempt, which was to be made the following night. Preparations were carefully made; every officer and man was thoroughly briefed so that there would be no slip. Some hours after dark on the evening of September 14 the three regiments moved out with "Grimes" Davis at the head of the column, crossed the pontoon bridge over the Potomac and turned left on the road leading around the nose of the mountain to Sharpsburg. Taking up a fast trot, the cavalry found their route unopposed, chiefly because McLaws' force, which would certainly have been covering the east bank of the Potomac at the foot of Maryland Heights had they not been so busily engaged in Pleasant Valley, couldn't be two places at once.

It was a daring undertaking for so small a force to make a dash through country that would in all probability be swarming with Confederates. And as so often happens when a determined officer leads men of spirit in a bold gamble, the escape of the cavalry was completely successful, without the loss of a single horse or man. Even better, the Federal horsemen had the good fortune to come across a Confederate train (Longstreet's ammunition train) of 97 wagons, under escort of a detachment of 600 men on the Hagerstown Road, all of which they captured and led triumphantly into the lines of the advancing Army of the Potomac.

THE SURRENDER OF HARPERS FERRY
Confederate accounts of the final phases of the investment leading to the surrender of Harpers Ferry on the morning of September 15 vary

somewhat. General Walker, in command on Loudoun Heights, contended that Jackson informed him the garrison would be given twenty-four hours to remove civilians or surrender before the artillery bombardment commenced. In Walker's account, he stated that a further delay of that length would be fatal to Lee's plans; consequently, on the afternoon of September 14 he took advantage of the latitude afforded in Jackson's instructions by inviting Federal gunfire on two regiments that he exposed as a decoy. When the Federals responded, Walker had the excuse that he sought. He ordered his guns to open fire; whereupon the other batteries of Jackson's artillery promptly followed suit.

Colonel Henry Kyd Douglas, of Jackson's staff, was emphatic in denying that Jackson intended to grant a 24-hour delay. Brigadier General Bradley Johnson, who was also present, definitely refuted Walker by quoting chapter and verse from the official file of Jackson's messages. The dispute over that particular matter is only of academic interest except for the impact of the additional delay on the smaller half of Lee's army confronting McClellan. If Harpers Ferry had not fallen on September 15, it is quite possible that McClellan could have destroyed Longstreet and D. H. Hill at Sharpsburg before McLaws, Anderson, and A. P. Hill reached the battlefield.

Soon after daylight on the 15th, fifty guns commenced a converging bombardment on the town of Harpers Ferry from Loudoun and Bolivar Heights. Many of the batteries enfiladed the Federal lines from the Charlestown Road to the Potomac. Others fired directly to the front, while those on the crest of Loudoun Heights took the Union line in reverse. The artillery fire continued until 8:30 A.M. with almost no reply from the overwhelmed Federal guns. About that hour Colonel Miles, the garrison commander, called a council of war of the brigade commanders, in the course of which he expressed the opinion that their case was hopeless, that further sacrifice of life would be fruitless. With evident reluctance on the part of some of the officers, the council voted unanimously in favor of surrender if honorable terms could be arranged. Miles appointed General White to negotiate with the Confederates, the officers separated, and almost immediately thereafter Miles was struck by a Confederate shell and mortally wounded.

TO STAY OR NOT TO STAY!

The night of September 14 was a difficult one for General Lee. Crampton's Gap had been lost to Franklin's Federal corps and it was clearly no longer possible to hold back McClellan's army at Turner's Gap. A message had gone to McLaws directing him to withdraw from Pleasant Valley as best he could and return to Virginia. Longstreet and D. H. Hill were told that South Mountain was to be abandoned, that their division would march to Sharpsburg. The ultimate destination was not mentioned.

Shortly after these decisions were taken, a courier from Jackson reached Lee with a note that started a new and more hopeful train of thought in the commanding general's mind. Jackson's report intimated, but did not make the positive statement, that Harpers Ferry would be captured the following morning (September 15). If that should happen, it might still be possible to salvage something from the wreckage of Lee's ambitious invasion plans. It was not in character for him to give up without a fight, so long as even a tiny chance to retrieve a situation remained to him. The message from Jackson was the first rift in the dark clouds of misfortune which had befallen the smaller wing of Lee's army in the past few hours.

Instead of withdrawing across the Potomac Lee revised his plan. He would concentrate at Sharpsburg, a small town west of Antietam Creek where a number of roads converge. Only three miles from the Potomac, Sharpsburg was seven miles southwest of Boonsboro and twelve miles from Harpers Ferry. With luck, and *if* Jackson's implied promise should be fulfilled, it might still be possible for the Army of Northern Virginia to be fully reassembled behind Antietam Creek by nightfall September 15, or the following day.

McLaws would face greater hazards than Longstreet and Hill, who would be unlikely to encounter Federal opposition in their direct march down the road from Boonsboro. Lee had not received any word from McLaws, who may or may not have gotten the earlier message directing him to retire to Virginia. The Federal corps that had taken Crampton's Gap was considered a serious threat to McLaws' rear, for Lee could hardly expect Franklin to be so unenterprising as actually proved to be the case.

With his new plan in mind, Lee sent modified orders to McLaws to cross the mountain (Elk Ridge) or follow the river road, his destination to be Sharpsburg; he would cross the Potomac only if forced by circumstances to do so. The cavalry was directed to cover McLaws' rear from the vicinity of Rohrersville. Longstreet and Hill would accompany Lee to a new position at Keedysville (midway between Boonsboro and Sharpsburg, designated by Lee as "Centerville"), three miles northeast of Sharpsburg. The original orders to Jackson and Walker, to rejoin the main body after the fall of Harpers Ferry, were modified only to the extent of substituting Sharpsburg for Hagerstown or Boonsboro. The dead and seriously wounded would unfortunately have to be left behind on South Mountain.

Longstreet and Hill withdrew that night from South Mountain under cover of darkness without the Federals becoming aware of their departure. As the column took the road to Sharpsburg, preceded by the wagon trains (which incidentally put a portion of Longstreet's trains in an unprotected position to be captured by Colonel Davis' Federal cavalry following their escape from Harpers Ferry), Lee sent still another message to McLaws, instructing him to go directly to Harpers Ferry if its surrender had been effected by the time the message was received. En route Lee decided not to stop at Keedysville, but to move on to Sharpsburg, which offered a better tactical position for disposing the army.

During the morning of September 15 the so-called "main body" of Lee's army completed its night march, crossed Antietam Creek, and moved into positions assigned by General Lee on either side of the Boonsboro road north of Sharpsburg. Hood's, D. R. Jones', and D. H. Hill's divisions, Evans' brigade, Stuart's cavalry, and the reserve artillery were all that Lee had on hand, some 18,000 men, a pitifully small force to meet McClellan's Army of the Potomac if Little Mac were to press his advantage. That, however, he had never been known to do, nor would he make the most of this opportunity, the last he would ever have as a soldier.

Toward noon a message arrived from Jackson announcing the surrender of Harpers Ferry. He reported that A. P. Hill's division would be left to complete the details, while the rest of Jackson's force would be ready to march after they had received their evening rations. Jackson inquired to what place they should move.

Although not unexpected, the good news was promptly passed on to the troops. It had arrived at an opportune moment; something had happened to the supply wagons and the soldiers were hungry. The fall of Harpers Ferry would not fill empty stomachs, but it did serve to boost morale with its assurance that the rest of the army would soon be on hand to join the three divisions already at Sharpsburg in fighting off the pursuing Federals.

THE LOST OPPORTUNITY

This was McClellan's great opportunity, to strike with overwhelming force to crush the smaller half of the Confederate army at Sharpsburg before the Harpers Ferry troops could reinforce Longstreet and D. H. Hill. McClellan had for several days known all about Lee's troop dispositions and plans, but even with that knowledge he was so dilatory in his movements that the most he was able to accomplish by the night of September 14 was to capture one pass only through South Mountain. And so far as that success was concerned, it might just as well not have been achieved, because Franklin failed to exploit the breakthrough, and, so far as the record shows, McClellan did absolutely nothing to capitalize on his possession of Crampton's Gap.

The machinery of the Army of the Potomac was not too well synchronized. It was strongly built and could take a lot of punishment, but it moved slowly and somewhat ponderously. In comparing the skillful maneuvers and rapid marches of Lee and Jackson with the manner in which McClellan and Pope shifted their chessmen, the image of the lion and the elephant comes to mind. The conclusion is inescapable that McClellan, a topnotch organizer and administrator, was ineffective as a field general. His good fortune in having a copy of Lee's orders fall into his hands was dissipated because of the interminable time lag in putting the knowledge to good use. Reverse the roles and it is a good guess that

Lee in McClellan's position would have given the Confederate army the worst licking of the war.

Where was McClellan's imagination? He had said that his plan was to cut Lee's army in two and defeat him in detail. Why did he fail to use his cavalry under Pleasonton, either to harass Jackson's force at Harpers Ferry, or to circle around South Mountain at its lower end and attack McLaws in Pleasant Valley? Why did he allow an entire corps, Franklin's, to sit idly by for several days doing nothing after the capture of Crampton's Gap? Even more to the point, how was it that, with virtually his entire army in hand at the foot of South Mountain, and only a part of D. H. Hill's division of 5,000 men holding Turner's Gap, McClellan was so deficient in the spirit of the offensive that he made little effort to brush Hill aside by weight of numbers or outflanking maneuver. Again, at daylight on September 15, when he learned that Lee had withdrawn from Turner's Gap during the night, why did he not immediately send at least Sumner's fresh corps pouring through the gap in pursuit?

The Army of the Potomac resumed the march on the morning of September 15 and commenced crossing South Mountain. Soon the Blue column was flowing toward Sharpsburg in a seemingly endless stream along the Boonsboro Road that the troops of Longstreet and Hill had followed only a few hours earlier.

McClellan's troops were no more than a three hour march behind Lee, but that unruffled general didn't seem to feel at all hurried. McClellan had never been known to act impetuously and Lee had little reason to believe that the Union commander would adopt a different course in the present circumstances. The Confederates were still on the road and approaching Antietam Creek when the Union soldiers appeared on the horizon six miles to the northeast.

Antietam Creek, although not too formidable a military obstacle, since it could be forded at a number of places except during spring or summer freshets, was a sufficiently prominent terrain feature to afford an excellent reference point and a natural dividing line between the two armies that were now taking position for battle. Flowing almost due south, but following a winding course, it passes Sharpsburg about a mile to the east. Four stone-arched bridges crossed the stream within a few miles of the town, but only one would achieve distinction in the battle, and be known thenceforward as Burnside's Bridge. No effort was made by the Confederates to destroy any of the bridges, a rather surprising circumstance in view of the military situation which led Lee to make his stand there. However, he may not have had sufficient time for his engineers to place demolition charges, although it is more likely that he purposely refrained from destroying the bridges. The Federals, making their first move to cross, were permitted to do so without serious opposition, almost as though Lee wanted them to come in close for their assault, where his infantry and guns could mow them down as they crossed the open fields on the upgrade approach to the higher ground near Sharpsburg. The creek, varying in width from 60 to 120 feet, runs through a small valley, with the west bank more steep and broken than that on the east, where the slope is more gradual. Hence the advantage of terrain rested with the troops occupying the west bank, particularly at the two center bridges, where rugged bluffs and hillocks afforded an even more marked advantage to the occupants. Farther to the east rose a line of prominent hills that promised excellent artillery positions for the Union troops on that side of the stream.

The town of Sharpsburg, where five important roads converge, is situated near the center of what was to become the battle area, which varied from 2.5 to 4 miles in width between the Potomac River and Antietam Creek. The town itself rests on the western side of high ground, in a saucer-like formation, and all around was farmland, mostly under cultivation, with an occasional patch of woods. These woods, identified in accounts of the battle as East, West, and North Woods, were destined to play an important role in the battle; as would the Dunker Church, on the Hagerstown Road at the eastern edge of West Woods, about a mile north of Sharpsburg.

The position upon which Lee had chosen to resist any further advance by McClellan was tactically sound. Strategically, however, it was vulnerable in the extreme, for in the event of a serious reversal, which would not be surprising in view of the disparity in relative strength, Lee could be thrown back into the Potomac at his rear, with the lone ford at Shepherdstown his only immediate retreat route. The peninsula between the Potomac and Antietam Creek was so shallow, averaging not more than three miles, that it barely provided room for the development of his army, leaving but little additional space for maneuver.

McClellan had his army, close to 90,000 troops, well in hand on the morning of September 15, with the major portion advancing without opposition against Lee's 18,000, and with only seven miles to cover before reaching the Antietam. On the face of it, an objective observer would be disposed to write Lee off as a bad risk on that day.

THE CONFEDERATE POSITION

As the Confederates filed across Antietam Creek, Lee disposed them in position along the high ground that includes the town of Sharpsburg. Facing to the east the line generally paralleled the creek, but well back from it, no effort being made to secure any of the bridges except the one southeast of the town (Burnside's Bridge), where a detachment was assigned to guard that crossing. North and east of Sharpsburg, where the center and left of the line were posted, the troops were placed to the east of the Hagerstown Road, which during the battle served the useful purpose of an avenue of communication between the several parts of Lee's command. West of the Hagerstown Road the ground was broken and uneven, in contrast to that on the east, which was rolling and unobstructed, much of it marked off in cultivated fields which afforded to the Confederates a highly effective field of fire for infantry and artillery.

The initial line of defense was about three miles in length, with most of Stuart's cavalry and horse artillery occupying the extreme left flank, anchored on a prominent hill about six hundred yards northwest of Dunker Church and only a short distance from the Potomac River. From Stuart's right the line curved in a gradual arc to the south—the arc held by the divisions of John B. Hood and D. H. Hill in that order; the brigades of both, except Rodes' brigade, facing generally northeast. Evans' brigade was next in line, then D. R. Jones' division, on the high ground of Sharpsburg and the ridge south of the town. On the extreme right flank stood Colonel Munford's brigade of cavalry. The Confederate artillery, consisting of 125 pieces, all that were present on the fifteenth of September, were emplaced along the line wherever a profitable firing position offered itself.

The advance of McClellan's massive force, clearly visible to the Confederates throughout the better part of the day, seemed not to worry General Lee in the slightest. So confident was he that McClellan would be slow to fight that he expressed the opinion there would be no attack on *either* the fifteenth or sixteenth, although he had known for several days that McClellan had a copy of his own detailed orders of September 9. Lee believed that by the morning of the sixteenth Jackson, McLaws, and Walker would all be on hand, and in the meantime his Federal opponent would insist on taking precautions to make certain that every man and gun was placed to his own satisfaction before engaging in battle. It seemed that Lee's remarkable ability to evaluate his opponent's intentions would once more be proven, because his estimate of the situation was to be confirmed in all respects almost exactly in accordance with his forecast.

THE FEDERAL ADVANCE

On the night of September 14 McClellan's strength had been augmented by the arrival of half of Porter's corps, Sykes' Regular division, from Washington. Porter's other division, under Morell, was scheduled to join the rest of the army on the 15th. Humphrey's division of new troops had also reached Frederick, but did not depart for Sharpsburg until 3:30 P.M. on the 17th. McClellan now had at his disposal six corps in addition to Pleasonton's cavalry, giving him odds of substantially more than two to one, if he should delay until Lee's entire army was concentrated. Were he to act at once, as he should have, his superiority would be at least four to one. Of course McClellan didn't see it that way. According to his custom, he had estimated Lee's strength in Maryland at 120,000 men, an almost inconceivably gross exaggeration. Whether he believed his own estimates may be questioned, but exaggeration served his purpose, and on that score he was consistent throughout his military career. If on the other hand he really believed, as he stated on so many occasions, that Lee had two or three times the actual Confederate strength, always outnumbering his own, only then do McClellan's actions and orders make any military sense. On that assumption alone, however, McClellan is disqualified as a general charged with the responsibility of leading an army.

McClellan's orders for the pursuit directed Pleasonton's cavalry to lead off through Boonsboro, followed by the corps commanded by Sumner, Hooker, and Mansfield. Burnside and Porter would follow the old Sharpsburg Road. Franklin's corps was directed to move off the mountain at Crampton's Gap, into Pleasant Valley, and endeavor to relieve Harpers Ferry. As previously related, Franklin allowed himself to be unnecessarily stymied by McLaws in the Valley, and even when the Confederate general pulled his brigades out and marched to Harpers Ferry on September 15, Franklin did nothing but sit and wait for further orders. Thereafter McClellan either forgot about him, or purposely allowed him to mark time, because his corps failed to move until he was sent for on the evening of September 16. Even then he did not reach the battlefield until late in the morning of the seventeenth.

The Army of the Potomac appears to have been habituated, by their commanding general, to slow, short marches. McClellan consistently underestimated the capacity of his troops. If ever an opportunity for rapid marching and speedy development for attack was offered, this was it. Instead of which, with but seven miles to march, McClellan himself stated in his report that September 15 was too far spent when he reached the Antietam for him to consider an attack until the following day. No excuse was possible for such snail-like action, the only extenuation being that Burnside was even worse, for he dallied on the mountain until past noon, and it was not until McClellan personally pried him loose that Burnside's corps finally got under way.

The assignment of bivouac areas for the night appears to have satisfied McClellan that he was doing all that could reasonably be expected. No effort seems to have been made, by cavalry or otherwise, to reconnoiter the Confederate position, or gain some idea, by capturing prisoners, as to the strength and composition of the Confederates in front of him. We do not know, from anything McClellan has written, whether he had as yet a plan of action; if he did, it was only partly formulated, for no orders were issued that night, nor were any troop dispositions made that would place them in a position to attack.

That part of the Army of the Potomac, 70,000 strong, that had completed the march or would shortly arrive were massed in the vicinity of Keedysville, on either side of the Boonsboro Road, except for Burnside's corps, which went into bivouac opposite but some distance east of Burnside's Bridge, on the left of the army. The corps of Sumner, Hooker, and Porter were at Keedysville, with two divisions advanced in the direction of Antietam Creek, Richardson's and Sykes', one on either side of the turnpike. Mansfield was still marching on the road from Boonsboro, while Franklin, as already noted, was back in Pleasant Valley with 20,000 men. Artillery was sited along the hills looking down on the Antietam, and several long-range guns fired a few experimental shells into the Confederate lines. But the preparation of a comprehensive plan of operation for the army was deferred until the following morning.

McClellan and Burnside

On the morning of September 16, McClellan, accompanied by Artillery Commander Hunt and several other staff officers, rode the length of the Federal line on a reconnaissance to effect such realignment of positions as appeared necessary. He particularly liked the looks of the area in the vicinity of Burnside's Bridge, remarking that from the viewpoint of the Federals it was favorable for both offensive and defensive action, and that it covered as well the road from Harpers Ferry to Sharpsburg. But he noted also that Burnside was too far back from the bridge to be effective. He thereupon ordered him to move his corps forward to the bridge, occupy the heights immediately to the rear, and be prepared to interdict the Harpers Ferry Road.

In his postwar accounts, McClellan states that the preceding order was given to Burnside at noon, but that night had fallen before it was executed. This was the second occasion in two days upon which McClellan saw fit to criticize Burnside for being slow to respond to orders. The third occasion would be on the afternoon of September 17, when Burnside, according to McClellan, was many hours late in attacking the Confederate right, with results that would deprive the Union army of a decisive victory. If McClellan was seeking an alibi for his own shortcomings, Burnside was as convenient a candidate as any, more particularly in view of the fact that Lincoln had offered him the army command in preference to

McClellan. That may have rankled somewhat in the mind of the latter, and been a contributory cause of his critical attitude toward his good friend and Supporter, whose own subsequent failure as army commander was to become even more notorious than McClellan's.

LEE'S ARMY RECONCENTRATES

General Lee's composure on the night of September 15, when with only 18,000 men he held a thin line at Sharpsburg against the overwhelming strength of the Army of the Potomac, assembled on the opposite side of the Antietam, reflects in great measure the quality and character of that superb leader of men. His attitude had completely changed overnight. The misgivings which had disturbed him the previous night on South Mountain, when the probability of a retreat to Virginia was uppermost in his mind, had vanished. His hope that the fall of Harpers Ferry would occur in time for his reunited army to oppose McClellan with at least a fighting chance for survival had blossomed into a conviction that the reliable Jackson would certainly be up on the morning of September 16. Lee was accustomed to odds of two to one in his opponent's favor, so that was no real handicap. McClellan had never been known as an aggressive campaigner, and in the past few days, even though he had shown unusual evidence of rapid (for him) movement, Lee felt sure that an attack, when it should finally come, would be preceded by the time-consuming measures that invariably characterized the Federal commander's prelude to action. Lee was equally confident, and with justification, that McClellan would telegraph his punch and thus allow the defense to counter from whatever direction the attack should be launched.

Nevertheless, Lee's decision to stand and fight on the Antietam was one of the boldest, all factors considered, that he had made up to this time. To risk disaster with the broad Potomac at his back was a gamble that few generals would have the courage to take. Longstreet considered it a foolish and unnecessary risk. It is doubtful that Lee would have so decided had Grant been in McClellan's place, or if he had foreseen the heavy losses to be sustained by the Confederates, with no compensating advantage. But Lee was first of all a fighter, with a keen understanding of human nature. The stakes inherent in bringing to a successful conclusion his invasion of Northern soil were huge; he did not wish his army to suffer the loss of morale that would inevitably follow a withdrawal from Maryland without a general battle; and he badly needed the supplies and material captured at Harpers Ferry, which might otherwise be recovered by the Federals. Moreover, he still believed that the Army of the Potomac was disorganized after Second Manassas and could not as yet meet his own army with a real chance of success. In his eyes, therefore, the risks that he was willing to take did not appear nearly so great as events would actually prove them to be.

From the position on the southwestern edge of Sharpsburg where Lee had pitched his headquarters tents in a grove of trees near Shepherdstown Road, the commanding general kept an anxious eye on that road to the south. Momentarily expecting the arrival of Jackson's corps on the morning of September 16, Lee chafed at the delay, for Jackson had advised him of his intention to start his troops on the fifteen-mile march from Harpers Ferry after they had finished their supper on the evening of the fifteenth. Stuart had visited Jackson at the Ferry after the surrender of the Federal garrison and then ridden to Sharpsburg to recount to Lee all the gratifying details. Lee had every reason to anticipate a night march by the normally fast-moving Jackson, who on this occasion must have weighed the need for haste, indicated in a message from Lee, against the condition of his troops. His ragged veterans had been marching or fighting continuously ever since they had left the Rappahannock prior to the Second Battle of Manassas, only a few weeks previously, and had been standing under arms most of the night of September 14, preparatory to attacking the Federal garrison at the Ferry at daylight, September 15. It was also a fact that straggling, after the fight at Manassas, had grown to immense proportions, and although Lee's army had been partly reequipped from captured Federal stores, it was still sadly in need of properly fitting shoes and other items of clothing. Even Jackson could not demand and continuously receive superhuman efforts from his vaunted "foot cavalry."

At midday September 16 Lee's period of watchful waiting came to an end as Jackson and Walker rode up to report their troops coming up behind them. McLaws, Anderson, and A P. Hill were still absent, but Lee expressed confidence that the three divisions would arrive before the day was over, and, with the added strength of Jackson and Walker, that the situation could be kept under control. Jackson was directed to bivouac his troops on the army left, in rear of the line occupied by Hood's division, while Walker was told to place his division on the army right by daylight on the seventeenth.

During the morning the Confederate batteries expended considerable ammunition taking potshots at groups of Federal officers busy on reconnaissance across the Antietam. General McClellan, with members of his staff, was one of the targets upon whom the Confederate guns tried unsuccessfully to register. McClellan subsequently stated that he had been personally successful in getting the enemy to expose the position of battery after battery as he rode along the Federal line on the morning of September 16. However, the ineffective gunfire from the Sharpsburg heights led Lee, as he went along the line, to caution the gunners not to waste their shells, but to save them for the Federal infantry; a wise bit of advice on another count, for the Confederate guns could not hope to match Henry J. Hunt's better trained and equipped Union artillery, at Sharpsburg or elsewhere. Lee was too perceptive a general not to realize that his smaller number of guns would clearly get the worst of it in an artillery duel with the Federals, such as the one that his gunners had initiated and in which the Union gunners cheerfully joined. A great admirer of the effectiveness of the Union artillery, Confederate General D. H. Hill is credited with the remark that "the Confederate guns could not cope with the Yankee pieces—the contest was one of the most melancholy farces in the war."

McClellan's Battle Plan

For his battle headquarters McClellan had his wall tents pitched near the Pry House, situated on top of a hill on the north side of the Boonsboro Road, midway between Keedysville and Porterstown. The farmhouse overlooked Antietam Creek and commanded an excellent view of the terrain to the west of the stream, including those portions of the Confederate position that were not obscured by woods and the north-south ridge that prevented a view of most of the town of Sharpsburg, on the reverse slope of the heights.

Having completed his morning reconnaissance and issued orders for certain troop realignments, McClellan was ready to give some thought to the business of readying his plans for the impending battle. Shortly after noon he had reached a decision on the general character of the attack. As stated in his preliminary post-battle report to Halleck:

> *The design was to make the main attack upon the enemy's left—at least to create a diversion in favor of the main attack, with the hope of something more, by assailing the enemy's right—and, as soon as one or both of the flank movements were fully successful, to attack their center with any reserve I might then have in hand.*

When McClellan's army had marched out from Washington in search of Lee's army, it was divided into two wings and a center column. Burnside had been given command of Hooker's First Corps and Reno's Ninth; Sumner his own Second and Mansfield's Twelfth Corps; and Franklin his own Sixth and Couch's division of the Fourth Corps (the rest of this corps having been left on the Peninsula). When Porter's Fifth Corps joined the army at South Mountain, McClellan kept it under his own command as a reserve.

So far as official orders went, there had subsequently been no modification in the chain of command, other than the elevation of Brigadier General Jacob D. Cox to temporary command of Burnside's Ninth Corps following the death of General Reno at Fox's Gap. Nevertheless, when the army reached the Antietam, Burnside found himself unceremoniously shunted off to the army left flank with only his own Ninth Corps, while Hooker's First Corps was held on the right under McClellan's direct supervision. Something had occurred to cool the intimate relationship which had long existed between McClellan and Burnside, ever since their West Point days together. Burnside suspected that Joe Hooker, who was not above conniving whenever it might suit his ambition for independent command, may have been the cause of McClellan's changed attitude, but on the other hand there is indisputable evidence that Burnside was strangely lethargic in all his movements and actions from South Mountain to the end of the campaign. It is also possible that McClellan intended the grouping of corps into wings to be solely for purposes of control on the march, and believed that greater flexibility would be achieved, when battle should be joined, by dispensing with the cumbersome wing formation and issuing his orders direct to the corps commanders. If so, it would have been a simple matter, and the part of wisdom, to make his decision official and so inform the three general officers most concerned.

At 2 o'clock on the afternoon of September 16, in accordance with orders from McClellan, Hooker's First Corps moved out from its position at Keedysville, crossed Antietam Creek at the upper bridge and two nearby fords, and, about 4:00 P.M., advanced to the Hagerstown Turnpike, where the column turned south. Marching along and on both sides of the road, with Meade's division in the lead, the advance elements about sunset ran into Confederate pickets, who were quickly driven in.

Lee, Jackson, and Longstreet were engaged in a discussion of tactical plans for the next day and studying the maps in the commanding general's headquarters in Sharpsburg when the Federal artillery in the late afternoon opened fire from the hills across the Antietam. Shortly thereafter a report came in that the Federals were crossing the creek at Pry's Mill. Longstreet was immediately directed to send Hood's division to meet the threat and Jackson was told to move into line on Hood's left.

What McClellan may have had in mind beyond putting Hooker's corps, unsupported, in an attack position for the following morning can only be conjectured. The disadvantage from the Federal viewpoint was that McClellan informed Lee by this action exactly where his attack would be aimed and thus gave timely warning of his intentions. Hooker's isolated position was an uncomfortable and dangerous one for a few hours, for it was not until almost midnight that Mansfield's Twelfth Corps followed Hooker across the Antietam, going into bivouac for the night about a mile or so northeast of Hooker's bivouac.

When the clash between the outposts of the opposing forces failed to develop into more serious fighting because of the darkness, the troops settled down for the night. McClellan sent word to Franklin in Pleasant Valley to bring his corps to the battlefield, while Lee, becoming more and more concerned over the non-arrival of McLaws and A. P. Hill, dispatched couriers with urgent messages to them at Harpers Ferry to rejoin with all possible speed.

CHAPTER 12

Antietam I: The Bloodiest Single Day

FOR SOME inscrutable reason, the commanding generals of the Union armies during the first two years of the Civil War, almost without exception, habitually fed their corps and divisions into battle in a piecemeal and consequently wasteful, inefficient manner. Whether this was because they didn't know any better, or had so little confidence in their corps commanders that they were unwilling to allow them discretionary authority for effective troop leading, the failure of Northern leaders to gain victories against smaller and less adequately equipped Confederate forces may be attributed as much to that rigid concept of generalship as to any other single factor. One might have expected the Union leaders to learn something from Lee's repeated successes in the battles of 1862. But McClellan, Pope, Burnside, and Hooker, one after another, employed the piecemeal method of attack as though it were official doctrine. Unfortunately it was the men in the ranks who paid with their blood for such inept field generalship.

McClellan's initial tactical dispositions in the Antietam battle afforded a foretaste of the manner in which he would fight his troops. Instead of a coordinated, mutually supported troop movement, he sent Hooker's First Corps of three divisions across the Antietam all by itself, beyond supporting distance; it was not until nine or ten hours later that he ordered Mansfield's Twelfth Corps of two divisions to follow. Each corps commander was on his own; teamplay under such conditions was unlikely; McClellan at his headquarters was too far back to exercise timely and effective control. Although Lee had no intention of initiating an attack in the late afternoon of September 16, there was no reason why Hooker and Mansfield should not have advanced on a time and space schedule that would have permitted mutual support, under specific orders from the army commander in the form of a coordinated mission. No such orders were issued. So far as the record shows, Hooker and Mansfield were left to open the Battle of Antietam as semi-independent commanders, with Hooker in the lead and Mansfield in distant support.

In his final, lengthy official report on the battle, written months after the event, McClellan expanded on his preliminary report by stating specifically that his plan was to attack Lee's left with Hooker's First and Mansfield's Twelfth Corps, supported by Sumner's Second Corps, and if necessary by Franklin's Sixth Corps (which at the time was still on South Mountain); and, "as soon as matters looked favorable there" he would have Burnside's Ninth Corps attack the enemy right to carry the Sharpsburg heights. There was also an intimation that the final blow would be struck by the troops of McClellan's center, presumably Porter's Fifth Corps, after the attacks on Lee's left and right had gained the proper double-enveloping momentum. It all read very well indeed, *after* the battle, but it would have been more helpful had he told his corps commanders what he had in mind before they were committed, so that they might have executed their respective assignments intelligently as elements of the army team.

THE PRELIMINARY SKIRMISH

The opening skirmish in the Battle of Antietam occurred in the late afternoon of September 16, between a detachment of Stuart's cavalry on the Smoketown Road and Confederate General John B. Hood's two brigades, hastily shifted to the open wood later known as East Wood, and Union General George G. Meade's division of Pennsylvania Reserves (the vanguard of Hooker's corps). This fight, which took place near the D. Miller house, was a short, sharp, feeling-out process on both sides, with the artillery playing a supporting role. Hooker, who did not desire to make an all-out assault until morning, was merely getting set by jockeying for a strong position. He contemplated a movement aimed at Lee's extreme left flank, similar to his action as a division commander in the Battle of Second Manassas, when Pope's divisions on the Union right hammered successively at Jackson's left near Groveton.

Lee's left was in fact his more vulnerable flank, even though it rested on the Potomac River, which completed its final looping turn in the Sharpsburg area only a few hundred yards from the Confederate left, where General Stuart had posted his horse artillery batteries on a low ridge immediately north of Nicodemus Run. The Hagerstown Turnpike was less than a mile to the east of the Potomac at that point, allowing only limited space for maneuver, with the result that the position could be defended with less men than normally required per yard of front. By the same token, however, a successful penetration by the Federals there could conceivably pay off, for the reason that the river ran in a southwesterly direction for several miles at Stuart's rear, to open up maneuver space in which an aggressive Federal commander might operate to roll up Lee's line or attack him from the rear.

Hooker's First Corps bivouacked the night of the sixteenth on the northern slope of the ridge which dominates the area, the divisions of Doubleday and Ricketts inline, with Meade's division covering the front of both. Hooker himself passed the night at the farmhouse of J. Poffenberger, east of the Hagerstown Turnpike, in rear of Meade's division. But he was up before daybreak Wednesday, September 17, for an early look at the terrain over which he would shortly launch his divisions. The day dawned gray and misty, through which could dimly be seen gently rolling country, the most striking feature of which was the Dunker Church with its white brick walls, standing out like a gleaming pearl against the dark green background of the West Wood, not more than a mile from his point of observation. The church, on the west side of the Hagerstown Turnpike, rested as it were "at the apex of a large V, the left side of which (looking north) was the Hagerstown Road, the right the Smoketown Road, which merged with the Turnpike about where the church stood. The Smoketown Road passed through the western fringe of the East Wood; the West Wood paralleled the western edge of the turnpike. Between the two roads as they approached a junction, the apex of the V, Hooker could see a large field of high corn, which would become as famous as the Dunker Church or the sunken farm road (soon to be called Bloody Lane) that angled off in an easterly direction from the turnpike 600 yards or so south of the church. The upper portion of the V was covered in part by the

North Wood, which reached out from the Hagerstown Road toward the East Wood to practically close the north side of the triangle of terrain above described.

The North Wood and the woods 400 yards to the east had been occupied by Hooker's corps in the course of its approach march. The Dunker Church, together with the East Wood and West Wood, were within the Confederate lines. From the standpoint of tactical maneuverability and troop concealment, the terrain at the point of contact of the opposing forces offered infinite possibilities for alert, observant troop leaders.

In round numbers, Lee's army on the field of Sharpsburg numbered at the most 28,000 men, supported by 200 guns, at daylight on September 17. McClellan's strength, disposed along the ridge across the Antietam and in contact with the Confederates north of the town exceeded 70,000, with Franklin's corps the only one that had not yet come up. Lee's still absent divisions, those of McLaws, Anderson, and A. P. Hill, together with Hampton's cavalry brigade, would give him 15,000 additional men for a total of approximately 43,000, if they should arrive before it was too late. McClellan's exaggerated estimate that more than 100,000 Confederates confronted his slightly smaller army may have made him feel quite heroic, if he actually believed his own inflated figures, but the false image could not help but distort his tactical judgment and adversely influence his battle actions. By September 17 his knowledge that Harpers Ferry had succumbed was forty-eight hours old, long enough for most of Lee's army to have been reunited at Sharpsburg and to neutralize the once-in-a-lifetime opportunity that the slow-moving McClellan had been too lethargic to exploit.

HOOKER VS. JACKSON

General Hooker was at this stage enjoying his role as a semi-independent commander of the Union army's attack echelon, a responsibility that McClellan had reposed in him with assurance of support from Mansfield's, Sumner's and even Franklin's corps if the army commander's plan to make the principal effort against Lee's left flank showed promise of fruitful results. It was "Fighting Joe's" big opportunity to prove that the sobriquet was something more than a typographer's error made in a newspaper correspondent's dispatch from the Peninsula which had correctly read: "still fighting—Joe Hooker"; but the euphonism had stuck and it was up to Hooker to make it good.

Hooker's three divisions had slept on their arms the night of September 16, astride the Hagerstown Road. As soon as it was light enough to see where they were going, the attack was launched, Seymour's brigade of Meade's Pennsylvania Reserves on the left and in the lead. The objective, the whitewashed brick Dunker Church, was a reference point that could not be missed by the most unobservant soldier, even though some may have wondered about the vagaries of human existence which required church attendance under such unusual circumstances.

Practically simultaneous musketry fire from keyed-up skirmishers in both the Federal and Confederate lines was followed immediately by the artillery from Hooker's batteries, several of which from well-sited positions poured their shells over the heads of the advancing blue-coats into the Confederate position. Across the Antietam Henry Hunt's rifled Parrotts, anxious to aid Hooker's attack, poured a devastating fire on that part of Jackson's line against which the Federal infantry advance was pointed. Hood's Texans, who the evening before had resisted Meade's probing attack, had been pulled out of the front line to cook a long-delayed hot meal, with the result that the Confederate defensive line was somewhat further to the south when the battle opened at daylight on September 17.

During the night the reduced divisions of McLaws and Anderson, which had been marching, climbing mountains, and fighting on various fronts including Maryland Heights and Pleasant Valley ever since September 10, had responded to Lee's urgent message to join the main body at Sharpsburg as quickly as possible. Shortly after dawn the straggling, wearied column reached the town at the end of a toiling march from Harpers Ferry, fifteen miles distant. The arrival of these reinforcing brigades meant that the Army of Northern Virginia, now fully reassembled except for A. P. Hill's Light Division, which was still paroling prisoners at Harpers Ferry, had a fighting chance to block the Union army, despite McClellan's superiority of more than two to one, counting Franklin's advancing corps as present.

Hooker advanced with his three divisions abreast, in the order, right to left—Doubleday, Meade, and Ricketts, with Meade's division somewhat advanced,—each division disposed by brigades in depth, the flanks (theoretically at least) overlapping the Confederate line so far as could be seen. The corps formation was such that, assuming the attacking line could proceed without breaking, it would sweep to the south through the West Wood, the East Wood, and Miller's thirty-acre cornfield which lay between the woods. Mansfield's Twelfth Corps, which had bivouacked a mile or so northeast of the First Corps, heard the noise of the opening engagement, sprang to arms, and moved promptly in support with the divisions of Williams and Greene.

In the early stages of Hooker's aggressive attack the Confederates were driven back in confusion. Brigade after brigade, including those of Stonewall Jackson's own division under Starke, was broken up or swept aside as the determined Federals pushed grimly ahead into the cornfield and the woods on either flank. Then it was that Jackson, rising to the occasion as he usually did when the going was tough, sent for Hood's division, busily engaged in cooking the first hot meal the men had anticipated for several days. Annoyed at the interruption, the fiery Texans came charging out of the West Wood to catch in flank Gibbon's Federal brigade, which had outrun the other First Corps troops through the tall corn. The fight had by this time become a general engagement, as the battle lines surged forward and back, with local successes and failures occurring in such rapid succession that it was impossible for the fighting units to know whether they were winning or losing. Losses on both sides were enormous, shells crashed indiscriminately into Federals and Confederates alike, blue and gray regiments melted into scattered fragments, as the early morning hours passed and the casualties steadily mounted.

Ricketts' division, on the left of Hooker's attacking force, together with Meade's division in the center, made slow but steady progress and gradually drove the Confederates into the West Wood, on whose edge the fighting became even more terrible. All of Jackson's two divisions, excepting only Early's brigade, were thrown into the battle. "The two lines almost tore each other to pieces," wrote Palfrey.* "Ricketts lost a third of his

---

*The Antietam and Fredericksburg, by Francis W. Palfrey. New York, 1882.

division, having 153 killed and 898 wounded. Phelps's brigade lost about forty-four per cent. Gibbon's brigade lost 380 men. On the Confederate side the carnage was even more awful. General Starke, commanding the Stonewall division, and Colonel Douglas, commanding Lawton's brigade, were killed. General Lawton, commanding Ewell's division, and Colonel Walker, commanding a brigade, were severely wounded. More than half of the brigades of Lawton and Hays were either killed or wounded, and more than a third of Trimble's, and all the regimental commanders in these brigades, except two, were killed or wounded."

The Confederate defense line was necessarily thin, because Lee didn't have enough strength to man a continuous cordon throughout the position he had selected, with each flank resting on the Potomac River. To the Federals, however, the Confederate left appeared to be solidly held, an illusion created by the guns under Stuart, who was in command on that flank. Manned by such able artillerymen as Pelham, Poague, and Pegram, the gunners kept shifting positions between bursts of fire in a successful endeavor to convince the enemy that there were no open holes through which to attempt a major penetration.

Much can happen in a thirty-acre cornfield whose stalks rise above the average man's head, particularly when hundreds of men using lethal weapons and with blood in their eyes are waiting in its invisible depths for the unwary to venture into the trap. Hooker seems to have realized that his attack was not progressing according to plan and that something had to be done quickly about that cornfield.

"From the sun's rays falling on their bayonets projecting above the corn I could see that the field was filled with the enemy, with arms in their hands, standing apparently at 'support arms,'" wrote Hooker in his official report. He thereupon ordered every available battery, five or six as he said, to open at once with canister. "In the time I am writing every stalk of corn in the northern and greater part of the field was cut as closely as could have been done with a knife, and the slain lay in rows precisely as they had stood in their ranks a few moments before."

Disaster loomed for Lee's army by 7 o'clock. Hooker's divisions had breached Jackson's line and the spearhead was being followed up from McClellan's seemingly inexhaustible reservoir of manpower.

Hood's impetuous counterattack had temporarily halted the Federal advance, but Lee knew that it could be for a short time only, unless troops were shifted from other positions. Without hesitation he pulled G. B. Anderson's brigade of D. H. Hill's division out of the line east of Sharpsburg, and soon thereafter ordered Walker's division over from the right flank to Jackson's support. Lee's instinct would prove sound, however risky the decision to employ more than half of his available infantry, in addition to most of Stuart's cavalry, in defending only one-quarter of his four-mile line. Hood's Texans were the finger in the dyke, but there was no telling how soon the Federal flood waters would cause other cracks that could so weaken the defense structure as to cause it to crash in ruins. Jackson's situation was extremely critical, even though Hooker's attack had crested and then receded in the face of Hood's counterattack.

MANSFIELD'S ATTACK

Mansfield's Twelfth Corps had moved forward promptly from its bivouac at the opening of the battle, guiding on the Smoketown Road. His two divisions deployed to form a single line, Williams on the right, Greene on the left, and then paused to await an opening to join Hooker's battle. Before the corps entered actively into the fight and while still in the act of deploying Mansfield fell, mortally wounded.

Major General Joseph K. F. Mansfield, Class of 1822 at the Military Academy, was a Christian gentleman of high character. It was he who planned the Battle of Buena Vista in the War with Mexico, during which he rendered conspicuous service and was rewarded by being made Inspector General of the Army. He was 59 years of age in 1862, and his towering form and flowing white locks made him a conspicuous figure on the battlefield. Many of his troops were raw recruits, which may have been one of the reasons why he rashly exposed himself in leading them forward into their first battle.

As the Twelfth Corps was approaching the East Wood, Hooker rode up, shouted a few words to Mansfield, in order to be heard above the sound of the gunfire, and then galloped off. The sense of Hooker's message was that the Confederates were breaking through and pushing

Hooker's divisions back, and that Mansfield must hold the East Wood to check them. The reason for the First Corps commander's haste was no doubt the impelling necessity to do something to halt the wild panic that had infected some of his men as an aftermath to the slashing counterattack spearheaded by the fiery Hood.

Mansfield was startled by the news, having been led to believe that Hooker's attack was succeeding handsomely and that the mission of his supporting corps would be to exploit the initial success by knocking the Confederates even more off balance. Instead of this it was now his task to restore the Union line and salvage all that he could of the advantage which appeared to be slipping from the Federal grasp.

His leading regiments had reached a rail fence bounding the last field to be crossed before reaching the East Wood, which Mansfield thought was still in the hands of Hooker's corps. The men had deployed along the fence and opened fire on dimly seen figures moving through the woods. Mansfield spurred his horse forward and lifted him over the fence, shouting to the men to cease firing at their own comrades. When he had managed to halt the fire he started forward toward the woods to find out which Union division held it, but was stopped short by a captain and sergeant of the 10th Maine Regiment, who insisted that the general was heading for the Confederate lines. About that time the graycoats opened fire, one bullet striking Mansfield in the stomach, another wounding his horse. Dismounting, he attempted to lead his horse to safety, but his wound was so serious that four men made a stretcher of their muskets to carry him off the field.

With Mansfield gone, the senior division commander, Brigadier General Alpheus S. Williams, assumed command of the Twelfth Corps, but before launching his attack consulted General Hooker to ascertain the lay of the land, Hooker had just time enough to give Williams a few general directions when he received a slight wound in the foot and retired from the field, to be succeeded by General Meade. Hooker's First Corps had been badly shattered, losing almost 2,500 men in killed and wounded, so that for all practical purposes the corps was out of action. When Williams' two divisions pushed ahead to renew the attack, Meade withdrew the remnants of the First Corps to the ridge north of the

Poffenberger house, where they had bivouacked the night before, to reorganize.

There were as usual conflicting reports on the condition of the First Corps after its attack and repulse. One account had it that Hooker's outfit had been completely shattered and that thousands of the men ran away from the battle. When Sumner came on the field he said that he was unable to locate any one from the First Corps except General Ricketts, who informed him that "he could not raise three hundred men of the corps." On the other hand, General Meade, who succeeded Hooker as corps commander, reported something less than 7,000 men that evening, which number still represented a rather tidy body of men. There was certainly confusion and plenty of straggling when the corps was pulled out of the line, but it was still an organized body and far from being "completely dispersed."

In occupying the West Wood and East Wood, the defensive positions of the Confederates, in addition to the cover afforded by the foliage, were greatly strengthened by the outcroppings of limestone whereby nature provided the same protection as breastworks. Furthermore, the Southern generals, experienced in utilizing terrain to advantage, had so disposed their brigades on Jackson's front that the Federal attacks were channeled directly into a funnel from whose sides the Confederates were able to fire from cover into the flanks of the attacking brigades. The same sort of reverse salient which Lee had set up for Pope at Second Manassas was again used to invite first Hooker's corps, then Mansfield's, to put their heads in the lion's mouth. Here at Sharpsburg, however, although McClellan repeated Pope's error of feeding his troops into battle in piecemeal fashion, the receptive lion lost his own teeth so fast in the chewing process that he escaped complete destruction by a hairsbreadth.

The massive Federal attacks against Lee's left were taking a heavy toll of lives on both sides in the early hours of the morning. Hooker's corps had failed to push its attack to a conclusion and was forced to withdraw, but Jackson's smaller defending force, although badly mangled, still fought on. D. H. Hill's division on Jackson's right was battling tenaciously, and now reinforcements from the center and right of Lee's line were thrown in to stem the attack by the Federal Twelfth Corps.

The confusion incident to the change of corps commanders resulting from the loss of General Mansfield was temporary, but undoubtedly took some of the strength out of the second Union attack. Williams was a good general, who led the fight as well as any could have done. Nevertheless, his attack, like Hooker's, failed to break the Confederates. The angle of attack of his two divisions, his own on the right, Greene's on the left, was in a southwesterly direction and more diverging than converging. Williams headed for the West Wood as Greene followed the ridge leading to the East Wood. The former took heavy losses from Confederates on his left and front, but Greene, meeting less opposition, was able to drive the defenders completely out of the East Wood. Greene even gained a precarious foothold near the Dunker Church, Hooker's original objective, a position which he was able to hold until early afternoon, when a Confederate counterattack drove him back.

By 9:00 A.M. the violent struggle north of the Dunker Church, and in and between the woods on either side of the cornfield, had been waged continuously and bloodily for four hours. Then came a lull in the battle, during which the manipulators of the human chessmen studied the board as they planned their next moves. Four thousand officers and men of Hooker's and Mansfield's corps had fallen; the Confederate losses, while not so heavy, were equally great in proportion to the numbers engaged. The Federal tide had carried Greene's division through the East Wood and across the cornfield to effect a lodgment in the West Wood north of the Dunker Church, and Sumner's fresh Federal corps was advancing to take part in the battle.

But the Confederate line had not given way. Lee's left, badly shattered, had been bent but not broken. The resiliency of the Southern brigades was amazing. Jackson had even strengthened his defensive posture as a result of the forced retirement of Hood's division and a part of D. H. Hill's. Every available man had been thrown into the battle, yet the redoubtable Stonewall, far from admitting failure as the result of being driven back and having suffered a temporary break in his line, was watching the struggle from the West Wood and planning an aggressive counterattack with the help of troops that Lee had withdrawn from other parts of the line and placed at his disposal.

One wonders at the lack of imagination and ingenuity displayed by General McClellan, as he watched the battle through binoculars from the garden of the Pry House on the far side of Antietam Creek. The superior, long-range Federal artillery, massed on the ridges paralleling the creek, had been pouring metal into the Confederate line since daylight, but not a single Union infantryman of three unused corps totaling tens of thousands massed behind the guns, had been sent across the stream for any purpose. There was no reconnaissance, no probing attack, no flanking maneuver, no anything. Lee's center and right were allowed to rest peacefully in place, hour after hour, without even a threatening gesture from McClellan to prevent the Confederate brigades from being moved about at Lee's pleasure.

There can be but one plausible explanation of McClellan's reluctance to take advantage of the most favorable opportunity in two years of war for a Union army to wipe out Lee's army and bring the war to a close. It was that the commander of the Army of the Potomac lacked a fighting heart, a defect from which it naturally followed that he would magnify the Confederate strength and play it so safe that tactical advantages would be frittered away. When the history of Lee's first invasion of Maryland is analyzed, it is difficult to credit the great Southern leader's postwar comment that McClellan was the Union army commander for whom he had the greatest respect. It may be questioned whether the remark was not quoted out of context, or possibly even with tongue in cheek.

Sumner's Corps Joins the Fray

The bloody fighting in which the First and Twelfth Federal Corps had engaged since daylight failed to accomplish its purpose of turning the Confederate left. The Federal line had made some progress, to be sure, but at a terrific cost in casualties, including many general officers. Greene's division of the Twelfth Corps had succeeded in seizing a portion of the West Wood and holding it, but without sufficient strength to do more than grimly hang on and hope for support.

Jackson's troops had been so badly chopped up during the early hours of the morning that the Federals could without question have overrun the line and rolled it up if only McClellan had staged a coordinated, simultaneous attack along the entire front. He had the men to accomplish it; his powerful artillery had been in position along the high ground east of Antietam Creek for almost two days; and Lee was still short three of his divisions when the battle opened. Instead, McClellan sent in one corps at a time, over the same route, against the identical target, at lengthy time intervals that precluded mutual support and served only to give Lee the time he needed to shift forces from right to left to parry the blows.

It had been 7 A.M. before the Federal Second Corps, commanded by Major General Edwin V. Sumner, received orders to cross the creek in support of the two corps already engaged. There were three divisions in this corps, Sedgwick's, French's, and Richardson's, but only the two first named moved out together, Sedgwick at 7 and French at 7: 30. Richardson didn't receive his orders until 9:30. Staff work at Union army and corps levels seems to have been somewhat less than efficient in this campaign.

Sumner's approach march to the battlefield followed pretty much the same pattern as had Hooker's corps—across the upper bridge and fords in a northwesterly direction, Sedgwick's division leading. Each division marched in three brigade columns, directly across country after crossing the creek, with intervals of approximately 70 yards between columns. These two divisions accounted for about 10,000 men, and their advance was made in so orderly a manner, with colors flying as though on parade, that the Confederates, awaiting the shock of their attack, watched the martial display with unconcealed admiration.

When the center of the corps reached a point opposite the Dunker Church, the columns at a given signal changed direction by the left flank and were at once in attack formation with divisions abreast, Sedgwick on the right, French on the left, each division in columns of brigades at 70 yards' distance between each brigade line. It was a picturesque maneuver, but its effectiveness may be open to question since the Confederates could see the whole show and prepare their reception in advance. As it happened, however, Jackson had formed a new line on a position some-what farther to the south and there were no Confederates to prevent French from forming up on the left of Greene's division, still holding near Dunker Church, or to keep Sedgwick from moving his division into line on Greene's right.

Ewell's division, now commanded by Jubal Early, who succeeded Brigadier General A. R. Lawton after the latter was wounded, was just about all the infantry Jackson had left at the moment to meet this fresh assault, and Early was busily engaged, farther on the left of the Confederate line, opposing Williams' division of the Twelfth Corps. Greene advanced on the Dunker Church. Early struck him in the flank and Greene recoiled. But now Sedgwick's division was driving ahead, unopposed, and unless stopped would in a few moments be in position to take Lee's main line in flank.

Early's division, down to not more than 600 men, could not hope to deter Sedgwick's 6,000, but help was coming from General Lee. McLaws and Walker came swinging up from Sharpsburg in the nick of time and Jackson, watchfully awaiting the appropriate time, saw that this was the moment for which he had planned.

Lack of coordinated direction of the three Federal corps engaged had much to do with the repeated failure to achieve any conclusive results against Lee's left. There was no guidance or direction from McClellan. One corps commander, Mansfield, had been killed; another, Hooker, was wounded; and the third, Sumner, came on the field absolutely cold, unbriefed, depending entirely on his own eyes and guesswork. As a result, the divisions of the Twelfth and Second Corps became sandwiched together, so that it is unlikely that the right hand knew what the left was doing, or vice versa.

JACKSON COUNTERATTACKS

The climax of the first phase of the Battle of Sharpsburg was reached about 10:30 o'clock with the arrival of McLaws and Walker. Hood's badly battered but still defiant division was withdrawn in favor of the reinforcing divisions, which deployed for attack as they moved swiftly into action. This was the psychological moment for Jackson's counterattack. Orders that had been drafted in anticipation of just such an opportunity were carried by galloping staff officers to McLaws and Walker to clear the West Wood, drive the Federals back and turn their right. Passing through the woods north of the Dunker Church, the Rebel yell signaled the advance as McLaws' brigades rushed impetuously ahead to hit Sedgwick's division in a driving flank attack that took that steady general by surprise and gave his strong division no opportunity to change direction. The effect on Sedgwick was disastrous, 2,200 men being shot down like sheep, and the remainder thrown into confusion. In a very few moments Sedgwick himself received his third wound, whereupon his leaderless troops faded rapidly to the rear. There they were halted, to re-form under the protection of a solid phalanx of artillery batteries judiciously placed in the forward edge of the North Wood and the ridge to the east.

"God has been very kind to us this day," remarked Stonewall Jackson as he rode along with Lafayette McLaws, observing the gratifying effect of his timely counterstroke. Part of Walker's division had in passing become engaged, in company with D. H. Hill's division, reinforced by that of R. H. Anderson, somewhat farther to the southeast. French's division of Sumner's corps, diverging from the direction of Sedgwick's advance, had encountered the left center of Lee's line rather than Jackson's. Consequently it was for the most part McLaws' division which followed Sedgwick's retreating brigades across the corpse-strewn cornfield, in a vigorous attempt to turn the retreat into a rout.

As it turned out, however, Jackson's gratitude was premature. The Federal artillery was not to be shaken. As they poured destruction into McLaws' hot pursuit, the Confederate ranks wavered, became more and more demoralized, and finally, having suffered casualties that totaled almost 40 percent of the strength with which McLaws had entered the action, they were forced to give up and withdraw to the cover of the West Wood.

Nicely timed and bravely undertaken as Jackson's counterattack had been by McLaws' hard-fighting division, the scales were weighted against it by the fortuitous appearance of still another Federal division, which put in an appearance just in time to aid the artillery in depriving McLaws of a resounding victory on that part of the field. McClellan's plan had been to hold Franklin's Sixth Corps, when it should arrive, in a position of readiness on the east bank of the Antietam, to be put in where needed. Three Union corps in succession had been thrown piecemeal into the battle, at intervals throughout the morning, but neither singly nor together were they able to break Jackson's ever-dwindling but desperately fighting troops. The remnants of J. R. Jones' and Lawton's Confederate divisions, after a bitter fight, had finally succeeded, about 12 o'clock, in driving the obstinate Federal General Greene from Dunker Church, to which his division had so bravely clung while the tide of battle shifted on either side of him.

Coupled with McLaws' success, there is every reason to believe that Jackson could have put the Union forces to flight, in spite of the dogged defense by their artillery, if he had been able to call up a few additional brigades to push the pursuit. The fact that every unwounded man was already engaged, and McClellan had summoned Franklin's two-division corps to aid the Union effort against Lee's left, was too much for the badly shot-up, weakened Confederates of Jackson's wing. They had done their level best, had in fact achieved almost miraculous results against what should have been overwhelming odds, but they were not supermen. Jackson therefore pulled what remained of them back to the West Wood, where he placed the shattered remnants along its eastern border for rest and reorganization, as the battle shifted southward in its second phase.

Longstreet's description of the morning battle pictured the Confederate line as "swaying forward and back like a rope exposed to rushing currents. A force too heavy to be withstood would strike and drive in a weak point until we could collect a few fragments, and in turn force back the advance 'til our lost ground was recovered. Thus the battle ebbed and flowed with terrific slaughter on both sides. Federals fought with wonderful bravery and the Confederates clung to their ground with heroic courage as hour after hour they were mown down like grass. The fresh troops of McClellan literally tore into shreds the already ragged army of Lee, but the Confederates never gave back."

Franklin's Sixth Corps, composed of two divisions under reliable, experienced commanders, Major General William F. Smith and Major General Henry W. Slocum, had been marking time in Pleasant Valley after their success at Crampton's Gap, supposedly keeping Confederate General McLaws' division out of circulation. While they relaxed in that pleasant area two days, September 15 and 16, McLaws had withdrawn to rejoin Jackson at Harpers Ferry and later to follow him to Sharpsburg. We have just seen how busy McLaws had been since his arrival at the latter place after he had joined the battle. Franklin had at long last been summoned by McClellan, his two divisions reaching the Antietam during the morning of the seventeenth. For some strange reason McClellan's order to Franklin directed him to send Couch's division, which was attached to the Sixth Corps, to Maryland Heights. Presumably the purpose was to guard against a surprise attack on the army rear, an extremely remote possibility but a typical McClellan decision in the light of his habitual exaggeration of his opponent's strength and capabilities. Not that it made any real difference, since Couch would simply have increased the army commander's unemployed reserve at the Antietam. Couch reached the lower end of Pleasant Valley before being recalled, too late to participate in the battle on the 17th.

When Franklin found that he was needed to assist the three stymied corps who had preceded him across the Antietam, he moved promptly. Smith's division was the first to reach the field, and although only one of his brigades became engaged it was enough to restore the balance and bring the exhausted Confederates to a halt. Franklin joined Sumner to talk things over and find out what had happened. What he learned led him to believe that the situation was made to order for a strong counter-attack, in the belief that the Confederates on that flank were played out and his fresh corps, despite its forced march, could bring it off successfully. Sumner disagreed, influenced unduly by the lack of success of his own three divisions following those of Hooker and Mansfield. Franklin had more than 10,000 fresh troops, and they were good divisions, in position and ready for immediate use. They could almost certainly have put the finishing touches to Jackson's decimated divisions and it was nothing short of a military crime that the attempt was not authorized. Here again McClellan remained in character, supported Sumner's view, and refused Franklin's request that he be permitted to attack. The disappointing result was that Smith and Slocum sat the battle out in relative peace and quiet just as they had been doing for two days in Pleasant Valley.

"THE BLOODY LANE"
The Battle of Antietam is accurately recorded in Civil War history as the bloodiest single day's engagement on any front. In achieving that doubtful

honor, it may be equally accepted that THE famous "sunken road" about 600 yards southeast of Dunker Church (sunken lanes were characteristic of farmlands in the vicinity of Sharpsburg) led even the famous corn-field in the competition to attain high score in number of casualties per square yard.

The bitter struggle on Jackson's part of Lee's line, which continued with practically no pause from dawn to nearly midday, came to a halt mainly because of mutual exhaustion. The Confederate bulldog had managed to chew up without actually destroying the major part of three Union corps, the First, Twelfth, and Second, a feat that could not possibly have been accomplished if those three corps had been utilized in a coordinated attack under a competent, aggressive army commander actually present on the field. On the other hand, almost half of Lee's infantry had been rendered temporarily hors de combat in the course of denying McClellan the privilege of throwing the Army of Northern Virginia into the Potomac.

The stage for the second phase of the battle centered on the sunken farm road which, leading out from the Hagerstown turnpike at a point about a third of a mile south of the Dunker Church, ran east for half a mile to the farm of H. Piper, and then continued around Newcomer's cornfield. This was the Confederate sector entrusted to D. H. Hill's division, on whose right extended two of Longstreet's divisions under "Shank" Evans and D. R. Jones, manning the original defense line that Lee had prescribed upon the army's arrival at Sharpsburg.

Sumner's Federal Second Corps, as previously noted, included the divisions of Sedgewick, French, and Richardson. Sedgwick and French came on the field together, but Sumner's information was incomplete and faulty, with the result that the direction of his attack was at right angles to the route Hookers and Mansfield's corps had taken in their successive assaults on Jackson's position. The quick fate that overtook Sedgwick has been described, but what of French and Richardson?

It seems that while Sedgwick was advancing unopposed through the East Wood, across Miller's cornfield, and into the West Wood, French led his division too far to the south and found himself, rather than attacking the left of Lee's line, in conflict with D. H. Hill's division, which occupied the left center of the Confederate position between Jackson and Longstreet. French's spirited attack on Hill was making progress when R. H. Anderson, who had just completed with McLaws his forced march from Harpers Ferry, and was on the way to join Jackson by Lee's order, was informed that D. H. Hill was in trouble and needed help. Anderson, together with one of McLaw's brigades, turned aside to support Hill and the desperate encounter around Bloody Lane was in full swing.

McClellan had planned simultaneous attacks against Lee's left and right. When those attacks should be progressing according to plan and, presumably, Lee's flanks were in process of being rolled up toward the center, McClellan expected to launch a third assault at the center and that would be it. But McClellan wasn't doing much of anything to effectuate his plan. About all that can be said of his actions and orders on the morning of September 17 is that he directed his corps commanders, one after another, to cross the creek and attack Lee's left flank. By 10:30 o'clock the fight on Lee's left had scored a staggering total of almost 13,000 casualties, 7,000 of which were Federal, the rest Confederate losses. Even before the flames on that flank had died down, however, the battle center of gravity had spontaneously shifted farther south. It was not planned that way, but battles are seldom tidy affairs that work out as intended by the guiding hand of army headquarters. In this instance French's aim was inaccurate and his blow landed on D. H. Hill.

From then until 1 o'clock the fighting raged in the new area with mounting intensity as one side or the other received reinforcements. For the Confederates, several brigades of Walker's division had joined the fight, and Richardson's division of Sumner's corps came up to add his strength to French's. Since Longstreet now had a number of his divisions engaged, he took command of the battle as it swung back and forth, now swirling close to the Dunker Church, then around the Roulette house and barns, and in the sunken road (Bloody Lane) and Piper's cornfield just south of the sunken road, flanking it on the south.

The heavy Federal guns had for a long time been concentrating from the far side of the creek on the Confederate batteries and the Union gunners had done their work well. So much of Lee's artillery was put out of action that at the height of the battle on this part of the line there remained but twelve guns to raise feeble outranged voices. French and Richardson between them forced the Confederates back until the sunken road became their main line of resistance, to which they clung with fanatic heroism. The depressed road proved to be almost as effective as a trench for defense, its natural strength reinforced by protective fence rails that were piled in place by the defenders.

The tenacity of the Confederates in their efforts to hold the sunken road was matched by the gallant persistence of the Union attackers. For more than an hour repeated efforts were made to take the desired objective, as the masses of the dead were stacked like cordwood in the narrow lane. The weight of the Union drive, with the arrival of Richardson's fresh division, eventually proved too much for the Confederates. Several of their regiments broke. The Federals rushed up to the lane and from the upper bank poured in such a devastating fire as no group of human beings could hope to sustain. The extent of the carnage was appalling. Then and there the name Bloody Lane was coined; no more apt description could be applied. French and Richardson cleared the field of Confederates and seized the ridge beyond the cornfield, but the two Federal divisions had paid a high price for their success. Division commander Richardson was mortally wounded, and the Union losses reached a figure in excess of 2,900. The Confederates suffered even greater losses and except for their artillery, organized defense in that area had ceased to exist.

McClellan Misses His Greatest Opportunity

Here was the opportunity of a lifetime for McClellan to drive a wedge through the center of Lee's position. But he not only wasn't there, it is also doubtful if at his remote command post he had more than a hazy notion of the tactical situation, where the actual fighting occurred. The Pry house, McClellan's choice as his field headquarters, had the advantage of being on high ground east of the Antietam, overlooking the Sharpsburg area to the west and south. It was a perfectly safe spot, but it was much too distant from the battlefield for the Union commander to be able to react instantaneously and effectively, as Lee was wont to do, when it was minutes, net hours, that counted. At a distance of two miles as the crow flies, and somewhat further by road, to the key areas such as the Dunker Church and Burnside's Bridge, the position selected was at least consistent with McClellan's philosophy of never moving faster than a figurative slow walk.

Franklin was on the field, however, with the divisions of Slocum and Smith, and although he saw the opportunity to cut through at the hinge where Jackson's position connected with Longstreet's, he was unable to sell the idea to McClellan. Why the army commander sent Franklin's 10,000 troops to the front and then refused to let them get in the fight must remain one of the unsolved mysteries of the Battle of Antietam. At the very least it struck a new low in army generalship.

The Confederate loss of the sunken lane brought to an end the second phase of the battle, with Lee's battered divisions, bloody but still defiantly unbowed, holding grimly to their somewhat retracted original line. They were "badly whipped," in Longstreet's own words, but they wouldn't admit the fact, and since McClellan hadn't the least idea that Lee was in such desperate straits, and seemed incapable of making the kind of effort necessary to disclose the facts, the Southern commander was far from being licked at this stage of the battle.

CHAPTER 13

Antietam II: Final Phase

OF THE three stone bridges that crossed Antietam Creek within the battle area, the only one to become a bone of contention was the bridge farthest south, three-quarters of a mile southeast of Sharpsburg, where the Rohrersville-Sharpsburg road crosses the creek. The ridges bordering both sides of the stream at that point were wooded and quite steep, creating a canyon-like area that was ideal for defense but decidedly unpromising for an attacking force.

The right of Lee's line, manned by D. R. Jones' division of Longstreet's corps, rested on the wooded bluffs above the bridge, with three batteries judiciously placed where they could effectively rake the bridge to discourage any Federal attempt to run the gauntlet of direct, plunging fire. McClellan's engineers after a reconnaissance had reported that the only ford in the vicinity of this crossing, which would go down in history as Burnside's Bridge, was located half a mile below, in a deep bend of the stream. The Union force to whom was assigned the task of attacking Lee's right consequently faced the unhappy prospect, if it was to use the bridge, of approaching along a narrow roadway in column formation under the concentrated fire of Confederate artillery and musketry, with no chance of fighting back until the bridge was crossed and the troops that managed to escape destruction fanned out in battle order on the far side.

CARELESS RECONNAISSANCE ON BURNSIDE'S FLANK

The Union failure to reconnoiter the Antietam thoroughly for available crossings was sheer criminal negligence, for there were any number of places where infantry could cross, even if they should have to hold their rifles above their heads. Crook's men found a ford 250 yards upstream from Burnside's Bridge, and Scammon's brigade crossed a quarter of a mile downstream and about half-way from the bridge to Snavely's Ford, where Rodman's division was ordered to cross. There were other crossings as well, so it would appear that McClellan's engineers must have made merely a superficial reconnaissance. That however does not exonerate Burnside, Cox, or any of their division commanders for accepting at face value what must have been obvious to anyone who took the trouble to examine the creek for a few hundred yards in either direction.

Burnside's Ninth Corps was selected by McClellan to execute the attack on the south flank, but the orders were not issued until September 17. The only instructions given Burnside on the fifteenth, when the Army of the Potomac reached the Antietam, directed him to go into bivouac on the army left. Burnside's choice of a camp area, in rear of the hills along the creek and about a mile below the bridge, did not suit McClellan, who considered it too far removed from the battle area. Burnside was told to move his divisions closer to the bridge, which was accomplished in due course, although the corps commander was criticized for taking too long to effect the change of position.

FEDERAL COMMAND CONFUSION

The command situation in McClellan's army had become somewhat anomalous in the course of the campaign. Burnside was originally designated as commander of the Right Wing, composed of Hooker's First Corps and Burnside's Ninth, the latter temporarily under Cox, who normally commanded the Kanawha division. The order prescribing the wing organization had never been rescinded, but McClellan chose to ignore that fact when Hooker was directly ordered to attack Lee's left while Burnside, with only his own corps, was sent to the other end of the Union line. Burnside chafed under what he regarded as an affront, but placed the blame on Hooker's well-known ambition for independent command, on the assumption that "Fighting Joe" had wangled the post of honor from McClellan, more or less at Burnside's expense.

From Washington to South Mountain, Jesse Reno led the Ninth Corps until he was killed at Fox's Gap. Since then, the senior of the four division commanders in the corps, Brigadier General Jacob D. Cox, had been acting corps commander. Cox suggested to Burnside that the latter resume command of the corps, whose staff had accompanied Reno's body to Washington for burial, but Burnside, reluctant to vacate the higher wing commandership, declined to act on the suggestion. This made for ineffective control on the south flank, with Burnside and his wing staff breathing down the neck of a nominal corps commander whose own division staff was inadequate for its dual mission.

During the day, September 16, McClellan had visited the Ninth Corps, ordered Burnside to move his divisions closer to Antietam Creek, and later wrote that he had advised Burnside "he would probably be required to attack the enemy's right on the following morning." But Burnside received from McClellan's remarks the impression that the Ninth Corps would be expected merely to create a diversion of sufficient strength to hold the Confederates on Lee's right in place, in order to prevent them from being shifted elsewhere to bolster the line.

McClellan seems to have lost some of his usual confidence in his close friend Burnside as a result of the latter's unexplained delay in moving his troops off South Mountain in the direction of Sharpsburg on the morning of September 15. The impression was sharpened when McClellan found the Ninth Corps in too withdrawn a position east of Antietam Creek on the sixteenth. It may have been that combination of events that prompted the army commander to virtually ignore Burnside on the latter occasion by having the army staff directly assign the divisions of the corps to the positions which McClellan thought they should occupy. At any rate, before settling down for the night, the corps had been redisposed as follows: Rodman's division at Snavely's Ford a half-mile below Burnside's Bridge; Sturgis' division covering the bridge, on either side of the road leading to it. Cox's division was split, one brigade attached to Rodman, the other to Sturgis. Willcox's division was placed in reserve a short distance to Sturgis' left rear.

Toomb's brigade of D. R. Jones' division, somewhat isolated from the rest of the division, held the hill mass closest to the bridge on the Confederate side of the stream, which effectively covered the crossing. Supported by several batteries, sited to enfilade the bridge and its eastern approach, Toombs' small force of 600 infantrymen would be endangered chiefly by being outflanked in the event a Federal division should cross by the lower ford and come in on Toombs' rear. Lee was aware of the danger, but had no troops to spare until Walker's division arrived from Harpers Ferry on the afternoon of September 16. At daylight on the morning of the battle, September 17, Walker was ordered down to guard Snavely's Ford, until the situation on Jackson's front became so tense that Lee pulled Walker out, about 9 o'clock in the morning, to lend his strength to the left and left center where McClellan was making his main effort.

Burnside chose for his field headquarters a high knoll northeast of Burnside's Bridge, which boasted a haystack that afforded a prominent landmark for messengers to spot. The location proved to be a front row seat for watching the battle to the north, for from that position the observer could see as far as the Dunker Church and up to that point at least could follow the movements of the troops of both armies as the fighting surged back and forth.

BURNSIDE'S CORPS ALERTED

During the early morning hours of the 17th McClellan sent Burnside a message to form his troops and hold them in readiness to assault the bridge, but not to initiate the attack until McClellan should give the word. Evidently the army commander wanted to wait until the attack on the army right had registered a success before committing the Ninth Corps. General Cox was with Burnside at his hilltop headquarters when an officer of McClellan's staff rode up with the order to attack:

Major-General Burnside:

GENERAL,—General Franklin's command is within one mile and a half of here. General McClellan desires you to open your attack. As soon as you shall have uncovered the upper stone bridge you will be supported, and, if necessary, on your own line of attack. So far all is going well.

The distance from the Pry house, McClellan's headquarters. to Burnside's command post was about two miles, which would indicate that the above order was received by Burnside sometime between 9:30 and 10:00 o'clock, depending on the speed of the courier's horse and the rider's sense of urgency. In view of the subsequent controversy over the delay on Burnside's part in responding to McClellan's "repeated orders to attack," as the latter described it, the timing of the order is significant. Acting corps commander Cox has written that the actual attack order dated 9.10 A.M. was the first that Burnside received, McClellan's allegations as to an 8 o'clock order to the contrary notwithstanding.

Two things are clear. In the first place, McClellan missed a great opportunity by not ordering the Ninth Corps to attack simultaneously with Hooker's First Corps at daylight, against Lee's respective flanks. There was nothing to lose and everything to gain, including a ten to one chance to inflict a decisive defeat on the Confederates before midday. In the second place, Burnside was unconscionably slow in initiating and carrying out his part of the army mission. Whether the attack of the Ninth Corps was to be a diversionary or full-fledged effort makes little difference, for it is quite obvious that Burnside on September 17 was operating in what was either a mental vacuum or a state of suspended animation.

As a matter of fact, not one of McClellan's three wing commanders had much to recommend him for what would today be referred to as army command. Each of the three had been placed by McClellan at the head of two army corps, each corps comprised of either two or three infantry divisions. Neither Major General William B. Franklin nor Major General Edwin V. Sumner had demonstrated in their earlier assignments that he possessed unusual talents for high command or more than average military competence to mark him for advancement. Length of service and their respective positions on the army officer list offer the logical explanation for their assignments. McClellan's popularity with the men in the ranks of his army cannot have failed to cause him to analyze the reasons therefor, and it is just possible that a desire to win friends may have caused him to be less critical of the performance of his generals than the welfare of the army required.

Franklin and Sumner, the latter over sixty years of age, were "present or accounted for" during the Maryland campaign, but that was about all. Neither seems to have influenced the action to any extent in a constructive way. On the negative side we have seen how uninspired was Franklin's leadership at Crampton's Gap and subsequently. Nevertheless both generals managed to retain their positions as corps commanders through the rest of the year 1862 and until after the Battle of Fredericksburg, following which heads rolled in great profusion. Although Sumner, a fine, loyal, fire-eating, old-school type of Regular Army officer escaped the axe which caught Franklin and Burnside in the aftermath of that great December disaster to Union arms, Sumner died in the early part of the year 1863, and there is some reason to believe that his death was hastened by more than physical causes stemming from the Maryland and Fredericksburg Campaigns.

McClellan and Burnside

Major General Ambrose E. Burnside's case was of a far different character. His career was intertwined with and to a certain extent paralleled that of McClellan. They attended West Point at the same time, were intimate friends then and later, and were associated as corporation officers in a western railroad after both had resigned from the Army. Each commanded the Army of the Potomac at different times, but neither was successful in that capacity. Both possessed inventive ability of a sort, McClellan having developed the McClellan saddle and Burnside having created an early model of the breech-loading rifle. The blood of the politician ran through the veins of both; McClellan aimed high to seek the Presidency and failed; Burnside set his sights lower and after the war won the governorship of Rhode Island for three successive terms, and then moved on to the United States Senate.

Burnside's chief asset was a winning personality. He possessed an unusual charm of manner and knew how to turn it on to his advantage. It may not be fair to attribute his rise to prominence in the Union Army entirely to his personal magnetism, but there is little doubt that he would have been just another Civil War general without it. Even more than that, perhaps, for in the absence of such a powerful aid to recognition, Burnside's weakness of character would almost inevitably have been discovered before, rather than after, the historic military blunders associated with his name. The most penetrating analysis of Burnside's character came from General Palfrey, an army officer who knew him well, and who wrote that "nobody could encounter his smile and receive the grasp of his hand without being for some time under a potent influence. . . and yet his presence was an element of weakness where he was a subordinate, and was disastrous when he held a great command." What more apt comment on Antietam and Fredericksburg could be offered!

INEFFECTUAL UNION TACTICS

Noting that McClellan was feeding his troops against Lee's left in corps driblets, Burnside adopted a similar plan on a small scale against the Confederate right—if indeed his feeble initial effort, when finally undertaken after an interminable and inexcusable delay, can be dignified by the use of the word plan.

The morning hours of September 17 were the critical ones; critical in the sense that McClellan's hope of victory rested on a coordinated attack, the only kind that offered a real chance for success against Lee and his capable lieutenants, all of whom were highly skilled in taking advantage of every opening and in extracting the maximum gain from any demonstrated weakness or false move on the part of their opponents. The inconclusive effect of the successive attacks by Hooker's First Corps, Mansfield's Twelfth, and finally Sumner's Second, can fairly be charged to McClellan's inadequate planning and direction of the battle, once started. Nevertheless, the three attacks had taken a heavy, almost insupportable toll from Lee's army, less than half the size of McClellan's and therefore unable to sustain equal numerical losses with the Federals.

The Union fortunes would have been best served by the battle plan which McClellan stated in his official report he intended to carry out, namely a double envelopment of the Confederate line. The army commander's failure lay more in the execution than the conception, for the battle as actually fought by the Union army was a disjointed series of corps attacks, uncoordinated by army headquarters and generally unrelated to one another. The men and officers of the various divisions fought as bravely and well as the Army of the Potomac ever had—the fault certainly does not belong on their doorstep.

The manner in which Pleasanton's cavalry division of five brigades was employed after the arrival of the Union army at the Antietam was a piece out of the same cloth. McClellan knew what had happened at Harpers Ferry and must be credited with the intelligence to realize that Lee's missing divisions would be coming up to Sharpsburg by one or the other of the only two available roads, both of which could and should have been covered by Pleasonton's horsemen, between Sharpsburg and the Potomac to the south. It was the only logical assignment that could be given to the cavalry under the prevailing tactical conditions, and it would have served a four-fold purpose, to secure the army left flank and open Snavely's Ford for an easy crossing of the Antietam by the troops of the Ninth Corps; to harass Lee's line of communication to the Potomac; to keep McClellan informed of Confederate movements in that direction; and to delay the arrival of Lee's reinforcements. Any one of the four missions would have served a constructive purpose; combined they could mean the difference between victory and defeat. Instead, except for a brief skirmish across the middle bridge, the Union cavalry was relegated to bleacher seats opposite the center of the battle area where they watched the game in a dismounted status, together with Porter's reserve corps and Franklin's two immobilized divisions, while the rest of the Army of the Potomac fought and bled and died in fragmentary fashion until the sun went down, with the Confederates still holding approximately the same positions to which Lee had assigned them on the morning of September 15.

In spite of the inability of three Union corps, half of McClellan's army, to achieve the objective of cracking Lee's left or breaking the hinge between Jackson and Longstreet on the left center of the Confederate line, the punishment dealt out by those Union divisions was so severe, and the margin of Confederate disaster so thin, that a determined Union effort at either end of the line, or at the center, or at all three points, must have accomplished Lee's downfall long before A. P. Hill's absent Light Division could reach the field. McClellan had at his disposal three practically unused corps, Franklin's, Fitz John Porter's, and Burnside's, a total of eight divisions. With the exception of one brigade of Smith's division, not one of them had been thrown into the battle during the fierce fighting of the early morning, or at any subsequent period during the entire battle, which can only mean that McClellan had no conception of the extent to which the contest on the north flank had weakened Lee's much small army. When affairs came to a pass that found D. H. Hill fighting in the ranks with a rifle, and General Longstreet personally helping to serve a Confederate gun, both of which phenomena actually occurred during Sumner's attack against Hill's sector, one is likely to wonder at the lack of competent Northern leadership that could so utterly fail to exploit such an opportunity.

Contrast the moral courage and aggressive fighting spirit of General Lee at the very moment when his center had been swept so clean of defenders that a Union army corps could have driven through the huge hole with but few losses. D. H. Hill had set the example by staging a "lost cause" counterattack with a few hundred men, which of course got nowhere as attacks go, but which did apparently have an important psychological effect on Sumner's divisions, who had just driven the Confederates back from Bloody Lane. For Sumner, conscious of his own heavy losses and ignoring what his men had done to their opponents, chose that moment to dissuade Franklin from pushing his own two divisions into the vacuum which neither Sumner nor McClellan, who had ridden over for a few minutes for a close-up view of what had happened during the morning hours, had the vision to recognize.

It was then that the alert, quick-thinking Lee decided that the moment was opportune for an attempt by Jackson and Stuart to turn the Federal right and, in Jackson's words, "drive McClellan into the Potomac." What Lee was going to use for men and guns was apparently unimportant—surely his lieutenants could scrape together a few regiments and a couple of guns for the purpose. Jackson was all for it, and managed to locate a regiment and two batteries of Walker's division who were given the mission of working around McClellan's right when Stuart's guns opened as a starting signal. Simultaneously with the flank movement, several thousand other Confederates would support the advance on the left. When, however, after a careful reconnaissance Stuart's cavalrymen discovered that the Federal right was solidly anchored on the Potomac, the projected attack was abandoned. It wouldn't have had the chance of a snowball in the nether regions, but the point was that Lee and his key generals, the flaming spirit of the offensive still burning brightly, never seemed to know when they were licked. This explains in part why they seldom failed to outgeneral and outfight their slower-witted, heavier opponents.

BURNSIDE'S DUBIOUS PERFORMANCE

Without exonerating McClellan from full responsibility for failure to achieve a clean-cut, ringing victory over Lee's army in the Battle of Antietam, which by all the rules of warfare should have been the outcome, the corps commander who had it in his power to turn the trick in spite of the army commander's hesitant tactics and ineffective battle leadership was Ambrose E. Burnside, the wingless wing commander who permitted his personal feelings to control what little military judgment he may have had.

If Burnside, smarting over the apparent affront which McClellan had administered by detaching Hooker from Burnside's wing and giving Hooker the mission of leading the attack on the Confederate left, made a conscious decision to emulate McClellan's slow pace in committing his troops to action, he certainly succeeded. The four divisions in the Ninth Corps were just as good as those of the other divisions of the army, and deserved better leadership than Burnside could furnish. Several of them had demonstrated their fighting qualities only a few days earlier on South Mountain. Except for a couple of hours in the early morning of September 17 their only Confederate opposition across the Antietam above Burnside's Bridge was the small brigade of Brigadier General Robert Toombs, who was more of a Southern politician and orator than a general, at least by Confederate standards. It was true that Toombs' thinly held line occupied a tactically favorable defensive position, but that applied only to an attempt to storm it by a frontal charge over the small bridge, an unimaginative maneuver that any experienced platoon commander would have avoided in favor of an enterprising flank attack by using the available, nearby fords.

Burnside had been alerted by McClellan in person on September 16 to the probability that he would be ordered to attack Lee's right the following morning. Early on the morning of the battle Burnside received a message from army headquarters to form his divisions and be prepared to launch his attack when McClellan should give the word. At 9:10 the attack order was signed and on its way to Burnside.

The sequence of the series of orders leaves no doubt that Burnside was fully aware of McClellan's intentions and should have had his divisions on their marks, like sprinters, awaiting only the starter's pistol to send them speeding down the track. All the alibis in the world cannot excuse Burnside for delaying his attack a minute beyond 10 o'clock, which was the very hour that marked the critical phase of the battle north of Sharpsburg. Had the Ninth Corps jumped into the fight at that time, the psychological effect alone might very well have served as the last straw for the embattled, wearied, decimated Confederate divisions, who with the exception of Stuart's cavalry and artillery on Lee's extreme left flank had all fought their hearts out in the magnificent struggle against McClellan's vastly greater numbers and clearly superior artillery. As of that hour, and for the five hours that followed. Lee had no reserves that he could call upon, in contrast to McClellan's nine fresh divisions, which up to that time had not participated in the fighting.

BURNSIDE'S BRIDGE

The stone-arch bridge over the Antietam in front of Burnside's corps was the major obstacle to getting the Union attack under way mainly because Burnside lacked imagination and ingenuity in planning how to put his divisions across the stream. He knew of the existence of Snavely's Ford a half-mile downstream, but made no effort to reconnoiter above or below the bridge for possible additional fords, an inexcusable oversight because several such crossings did in fact exist, as the troops were later to discover for themselves. The corps commander appeared to be hypnotized by the bridge, the approach to which was under the direct fire of Toombs' Confederates from the opposite hill. The more Burnside tried to figure out what to do, the more bemused and confused he became. He couldn't seem to make up his mind to attack directly across the narrow bridge, so he temporized and tried out a few probing advances with small detachments, with no success. Each time the Federals moved out toward the bridge Toombs' Georgia regiments opened with everything they had and drove them back. It was supremely important to the Confederates that they discourage the bluecoats from becoming too zealous, for they knew full well that once they were over the bridge it would be impossible to hold them back with the small force under Toombs' command.

Rodman's division was given the mission of crossing by Snavely's Ford, to come in on the Confederate flank and rear. For several hours, until about 9 o'clock, Walker's Confederate division guarded that point, but it had then been recalled by Lee to strengthen the defenses above Sharpsburg. Consequently from 9 o'clock on the way was open for Rodman to advance unopposed, but it took his division a long time to march down to the ford, so long in fact that several regiments of Sturgis' division were finally able to force a crossing at the bridge itself before Rodman had completed his relatively short march.

While Burnside watched from his hilltop headquarters, General Cox as corps commander directed the Union efforts to carry the bridge. Crook's brigade of the Kanawha division made the first attack, moving out a short distance above the bridge, covered by a firing line from Sturgis' division. Coming under heavy Confederate fire as soon as the troops showed themselves, Crook was stopped in his tracks and had to withdraw. The second attack was made by a brigade of Sturgis' division, supported by artillery, with no better success.

600 CONFEDERATES PIN DOWN 13,000 FEDERALS

Precious hours were passing while a comparative handful of Confederates on Lee's right flank held up an entire army corps of four Union divisions, 13,000 strong, thereby buying the priceless time that Lee desperately needed for A. P. Hill to come up from Harpers Ferry. The fighting at the northern end of the line had practically ceased, with the exhausted troops of both sides lying on their arms and glaring at each other like two badly wounded animals without energy to renew the fight, before the final and successful attempt was made to cross Burnside's Bridge.

Meanwhile, as Burnside in his indecision continued to put off the hour of the concerted attack that McClellan had directed, messenger after messenger galloped over from army headquarters with urgently repeated orders for Burnside to get on with his assault. That general was either in a blue funk, or had made up his mind to ignore McClellan, for all he did was to brush off the messengers as though they didn't exist. Finally it was borne in on the impatient army commander that something was wrong with his friend Burnside. What he should have done was to ride over to see for himself why his lieutenant was acting so strangely, and to exercise his own authority on the spot. Instead of which he continued his policy of fighting the battle by remote control, contenting himself this time with sending his inspector general, Colonel D. B. Sacket. Sacket was told to order Burnside "to take that bridge, at bayonet point if necessary" and to stay right with the reluctant general until the order was executed.

That did it, but it was almost 1 o'clock when Sacket delivered his message, three long hours after Burnside had first received the order to launch his assault. Still disgruntled, Burnside evidently realized that he could stall no longer if he wished to hold his job. Sending for General Cox, Burnside told him to carry the bridge at all hazards, a decision that could just as well have been reached three hours earlier, with results that might have changed the course of the war.

TWO UNION REGIMENTS CROSS THE BRIDGE

Cox directed Sturgis to select two regiments from Ferrero's brigade, which had not yet seen action in the battle, form them in a double column so that after crossing the bridge they could fan out to right and left while on the run without losing their regimental integrity, and charge the bridge. Sturgis chose the Fifty-first New York under Colonel Robert B. Potter, and the Fifty-first Pennsylvania under Colonel John F. Hartranft, and to lend weight to the charge, a light howitzer was set up to deliver point-blank fire on the far edge of the bridge. When everything was set, Federal skirmishers all along the line laid down a heavy musketry barrage, the howitzer blasted the further side of the bridge, and the two regiments dashed across. The casualties, as expected, were fairly heavy, bunched as the men were on a narrow front, but there was no hesitation, and Toombs' Confederates fled to the safety of their division line.

The precipitous heights on the Confederate side of the stream, for-midable as they appeared, were heavily wooded and therefore useful for sharpshooters only at the edge nearest the bridge. Nevertheless, volley fire directly on the road paralleling the creek, by which the Federals were forced to approach the bridge, and on the bridge itself, achieved a shotgun effect that was plenty lethal in spite of the interfering trees and foliage.

At the base of the hills, which were almost vertical for the last few feet, was an area of defiladed space, free from the Confederate musketry fire but still enfiladed by artillery fire, where the attacking Federals paused momentarily to deploy after rushing the bridge and before starting to climb the hills.

The Union spearhead having penetrated the Confederate defense, it was easier sailing for the rest of the Ninth Corps for awhile. Rodman's division crossed at Snavely's Ford, Sturgis and Crook and Willcox by the bridge and the two additional fords that had by that time been discovered 250 yards north of the bridge, and 400 yards south of it. Under Cox's direction the heights above the Antietam were occupied by the Union forces, as they prepared to advance on Sharpsburg along the ridge to the north. However, all these movements had taken time, because of the narrow defile of the bridge, and it was 3 o'clock in the afternoon before the corps dispositions were completed, the light artillery in position, ammunition resupplied, and the troops properly placed for an extension of the advance.

The Maryland Campaign was a historic one in several ways, one of its more unique aspects being the fact that two future Presidents of the United States were combat participants. Even more unusual is the fact that both were members of the same regiment, the 23rd Ohio Volunteers. The regimental commander, Lieutenant Colonel Rutherford B. Hayes was wounded when his regiment, a part of the Kanawha Division of the Ninth corps, made its successful attack at Fox's Gap. Sergeant William McKinley, age 19, in charge of the commissary department, distinguished himself during the Battle of Antietam in a less flashy, but nonetheless heroic manner, when on the erstwhile Confederate heights above Burnside's Bridge he personally and without orders carried hot coffee and food across the bridge and up the hill, under fire in both directions, until every man in his regiment had been served. One has only to have had a similar experience to appreciate the stimulating effect on the morale of that particular Ohio regiment.

Lee's battered divisions on the left and center of his position had with almost unbelievable tenacity held their sagging line against the superior weight of men and metal thrown against them during the long hours of the morning. Few battles in history have recorded such bloody carnage as that of the Antietam. More than 10,000 men had been killed or wounded in the early attacks by Hooker and Mansfield, and additional thousands of casualties were added in the struggle between Sumner and D. H. Hill in and around the sunken road. Confederate reserves were nonexistent, but still McClellan held out two army corps, Porter's and Franklin's, as well as Pleasonton's cavalry division, while he waited impatiently for the slow-thinking and even slower moving Burnside to swing into action with his Ninth Corps on the southern flank.

McClellan himself had been fumbling the ball ever since the fortunate circumstance which had given him Lee's blueprint for action back at Frederick on September 13, four days earlier. General Grant was later to describe McClellan as "one of the mysteries of the war," a characterization that only partly explains why he missed *all* of the opportunities gratuitously offered him by General Lee, master of the calculated risk. McClellan's explanation as to why he did not commit Franklin and Porter with their four divisions, at the moment when Lee was figuratively staggering on the ropes, was that he felt it necessary to hold out a strong reserve in case Lee should mount a counterattack, which, obviously, was the last thing that the Confederates could have managed.

Nevertheless, and in spite of McClellan's martial timidity and Burnside's lethargy, it looked, at 3:30 in the afternoon, as though the boom was about to be lowered on the Army of Northern Virginia. The Confederates still holding the line north and east of Sharpsburg were about fought out, McClellan was holding five unused divisions in that same area that could be thrown into the final phase on short notice. while Burnside's four divisions under Cox, across the creek and deployed in battle formation, were moving steadily up the southern slopes of Sharpsburg, squarely on Lee's right flank.

THE NINTH CORPS ENTERS SHARPSBURG

With Willcox's division on the right, Rodman's on the left, each supported by a brigade of the Kanawha division, Cox advanced to meet D. R. Jones' Confederate division, which, having shifted position, was disposed diagonally across the Federal front and guarding the approaches to the town of Sharpsburg from the south. Sturgis' division was held in reserve on the high ground recently vacated by the Confederates. On the other side, Jones' six brigades were strongly posted behind the stone fences and crests of the crossridges, supported by all the artillery Lee was able to transfer from the now quiet other sectors.

As soon as Willcox's men came into view on the open ground between Antietam Creek and Sharpsburg, the battle opened with a fury that matched the earlier struggle to the north. Over fields and through farmyards the fiercely fighting Federals slowly but steadily pushed Jones' hard-pressed, outnumbered brigades until Cox had effected a lodgment in the lower end of Sharpsburg and occupied the high ground southeast of the town. About that same time, Pleasonton's dismounted cavalry crossed the creek at the middle bridge, drove back the Confederate skirmishers at that point, and cleared the way for four horse batteries to move across and engage the Confederate artillery in the vicinity of Cemetery Ridge, on the eastern edge of Sharpsburg. Still later in the afternoon, while the Ninth Corps continued its forward progress on the south flank, several battalions from Sykes' division crossed to lend support to the horse batteries that were still in action (Pleasonton's cavalry had been withdrawn). The pressure from two sides was more than the few Confederate guns on the crest could resist; Cemetery Hill was abandoned to the Federals.

In the heat of the battle, as Willcox inclined to the right in his advance, Rodman moved somewhat to the left to face the Confederates occupying the ridges to his left front, and thus diverged from Willcox's line of advance. It was now 4:30 o'clock. The ammunition wagons had been unable to keep pace with the Federal advance, due partly to traffic delays over the Burnside Bridge, so that it became necessary to call a temporary halt to Willcox's thus far successful assault while the ammunition was hurried forward to replenish empty cartridge boxes.

A. P. HILL TO THE RESCUE

The dramatic climax to the Battle of Antietam had within itself all the ingredients for a bestselling historical novel. Although the leading characters were too engrossed in the problems of the moment to give any thought to histrionics. George B. McClellan, Thomas J. Jackson, Ambrose E. Burnside, and Ambrose Powell Hill had all been cadets together at West Point, McClellan and Jackson in the Class of 1846, Burnside and Hill in the Class of 1847. McClellan and Powell Hill were roommates, but Hill lost a year on account of illness and graduated a class behind McClellan. "Tom" Jackson as a cadet displayed many of the characteristics which, then as later, kept other men at arm's length, but McClellan and Hill were warm friends, while Burnside and Hill, also close friends, led their class in undergraduate escapades if not in scholarship.

Nellie Marcy, attractive daughter of Colonel Randolph B. Marcy, later Chief of Staff to General McClellan, was one of the most popular of the "army brats" and quite naturally caught the eye of the young army officers in Washington, among them George McClellan and Powell Hill. The former roommates and intimate friends both fell in love with Nellie. Ambrose Burnside, admirer and loyal supporter of McClellan, did all he could to assist him in the competition for Nellie's hand, while father Marcy, learning that McClellan was about to resign from the Army and enter the railroading business, allowed as how that afforded more promise for the future. So that was one battle that McClellan won and Hill lost. Nellie became Mrs. McClellan and Powell Hill, concealing his disappointment, attended the wedding.

The scene now shifts to a small town in Maryland, some years later. Lee's Army of Northern Virginia, locked in a deadly struggle with McClellan's Army of the Potomac, has been bled white and is hovering on the brink of disaster. Outnumbered more than two to one, it is standing on the defensive and with no reserves at hand to meet a possible final thrust from McClellan's powerful and as yet uncommitted reserve of five divisions. Lee's first invasion of the North, at 4:30 o'clock on the afternoon of September 17, stands a good chance of coming to an inglorious end. Jackson's veterans had succeeded in chewing up two Federal corps and assisted Longstreet in fending off a third. The fourth, Burnside's Ninth Corps, after a long delay was now pushing close to Sharpsburg and threatening the safety of Lee's entire defense line. Had McClellan only known it, Lee's army was ripe for the coup de grace.

There remained the remote possibility that the Confederate army could be saved by a miracle, but the time was getting awfully short within which even a miracle would prove effective. Lee's one last hope was A. P. Hill's Light Division of 3,000 effectives, whom Jackson had left behind at Harpers Ferry to wind up the task of paroling the thousands of Federals who had surrendered in time to free most of Jackson's corps for the more important task of fighting McClellan at Sharpsburg.

An urgent message from Lee to Hill, which the latter received at 6:30 in the morning, aroused him to the danger facing the army on the Antietam. Leaving Thomas' brigade to wrap up the remaining details of the Harpers Ferry job, Hill promptly put his five other brigades on the road to Sharpsburg. Dressed largely in Federal uniforms, which were a vast improvement over their erstwhile conglomerate wearing apparel, the hard-bitten veterans of many a tough march and battle moved at a rapid gait along the dusty road to Shepherdstown, with hardly a pause for breath.

Why Hill took the long seventeen-mile route via the Shepherdstown Road rather than the much shorter route across the Potomac at Harpers Ferry is not known. He may have figured that the Federals would make him fight to reach Lee if he chose the latter, whereas it was pretty certain that he could cross the Potomac without opposition at Boteler's (Blackford's) Ford, and an additional march of five miles would be preferable to not getting there at all. Thanks to his old friend Burnside, the extra two hours of marching were not wasted, although by a very slim margin.

Major General Ambrose P. Hill, age 36, a native Virginian with a fiery temper, loved a fight, preferably against the Yankees. Between battles, however, he apparently had no scruples against taking on his superiors in the Confederate army, to keep his hand in as it were. There was the time after the Peninsular Campaign, for example, when Hill tangled with General Longstreet and challenged him to a duel in the fashion of a true Cavalier, but that affair was smoothed over. It was Stonewall Jackson, however, who most frequently rubbed Hill the wrong way. A feud between the two generals, which started at Orange Court House during the march that preceded the battle at Cedar Mountain, was only concluded at Chancellorsville, nine months later, when Jackson's career was brought to a close through an accidental volley from his own men.

Jackson was a stern disciplinarian who would brook not the slightest deviation from the letter of his orders, whether by a private in the ranks or a major general commanding a division. He could be uncompromisingly unpleasant in exerting his authority, and there were occasions when he carried matters to extremes by jumping to unfair conclusions without permitting the object of his wrath to explain what might only appear to the general to be a violation of his orders. There were times when Jackson criticized Hill for marching too slowly, and others when he objected that the Light Division traveled too fast for units in rear to keep up.

The crisis between the two occurred on September 4, 1862, after the Battle of Second Manassas, when Jackson's corps was crossing the Potomac at Leesburg, on the way to Maryland. Jackson's standing orders were that division commanders must see to it that their units moved out at the hour Jackson ordered, no later, and that the division commander himself would ride the column to prevent straggling, which plagued the Confederate army so badly after Manassas. On the day in question, Jackson found that his orders were not being followed in Hill's division; there was straggling in the rear and the division commander in Jackson's opinion was doing nothing to prevent it. So Jackson rode forward and halted Hill's leading brigade without notifying the division commander. Hill rode back to see what was wrong, inquiring angrily as to who had ordered the halt. The brigade commander pointed to Jackson, sitting his horse and watching the tableau. The enraged Hill rode up to Jackson and, informing him that if he proposed to issue orders directly to brigade commanders he had no need of a division commander, offered Jackson his sword. "Keep your sword," responded Jackson curtly, "and consider yourself under arrest." Jackson then rode off.

From that time on, and until Jackson's corps approached Harpers Ferry on September 14, A.P. Hill rode at the rear of his division without exercising command. It was only when action was imminent that Jackson lifted the arrest status temporarily to restore Hill to command of his division for the purpose of battle.

A. P. Hill, the impetuous man of action, was little given to putting his thoughts on paper, unlike the many generals who at the drop of a hat recorded their views before, during, and after battle. For that reason he has until recently been the forgotten general of the Confederacy, despite his magnificent record as commander of the Light Division, which he molded and led throughout the war until his promotion to corps command after Chancellorsville. Lee considered Hill his best division commander, and it was his name that hovered on the lips of both Stonewall Jackson and Robert E. Lee in the last moments of their lives.

THE CLIMAX

The battle on the south flank, along the Sharpsburg ridge and in the lower part of the town, was being conducted ably and with dogged persistence by Burnside's divisions under Jacob Cox, once the bridge had been crossed and maneuver space made available. There was no glamour in this particular fight, just hard, killing work, uphill from Antietam Creek, in the face of heavy gun fire from the artillery Lee was able to assemble from all parts of the field. The Confederates had been given plenty of advance notice of Burnside's obvious intentions, so there could be no surprise. The Federals of Willcox's, Rodman's, Sturgis', and Cox's own Kanawha division had to endure a hurricane of fire from Longstreet's Confederates, who were just as determined to stop this new outfit as Lee's divisions on the north and east sectors had been against McClellan's first and second attempts on their left and center.

Field commander Cox, directing the Union effort from the center of the corps position, quickly became aware of the gap caused by the diverging attacks of Willcox and Rodman. The configuration of the ground and the Confederate movements were such that the Federals were given little choice; but a gap could be dangerous, so Cox ordered Sturgis forward from reserve to fill it. The leading Federal brigades at this stage had advanced more than a mile beyond the bridge; their forward progress had been slow but steady, and although their casualties were heavy the divisions were understandably elated that they had broken the Confederate defense on its right and appeared on the verge of achieving a victory over the vaunted Southerners of Lee's famous army that had so far never met defeat.

Cox's attack on his right had succeeded in occupying the high ground southeast of Sharpsburg and a part of the town itself. The effort on the left was also making progress and had reached a point about 1,200 yards from the Sharpsburg-Shepherdstown Road, Lee's return route to the Potomac if a retreat should become necessary. Should that road be cut before Hill's division arrived, even the slow-to-fight McClellan would then, at long last, commit his powerful reserve—against which there could be but feeble resistance, and it would then be all over.

It was 2:30 o'clock when A. P. Hill galloped ahead of his troops to meet Lee and inform him that five of his six brigades were making a forced march and should be up in one and one-half hours. They had been on the way since 7:30 that morning and the road they were following required a seventeen-mile march, if everything went well. There was more than the usual straggling because of the heat and dust, to say nothing of the killing pace at which their red-shirted general had been driving them. Hill was going to get his troops there if only half of them should make it by the time the grueling foot race was over.

The word of his arrival quickly spread through the ranks, with electrifying effect. This meant that there was still hope, though why only one more half-size division could be expected to balance the scales against the overwhelming strength of the Union army would seem to defy all logic. The answer lay in the fighting spirit of Lee's army, together with the unsurpassed leadership of its commanding general and his principal lieutenants, when disaster threatened even more than in times of victory.

No help could be looked for from Jackson or D. H. Hill, while Longstreet's divisions had been whittled down at the center to the point where they would be lucky to merely stay alive. With the exception of D. R. Jones' brigades, and the artillery, now using antipersonnel canister to slow Cox's assault on the Confederate right, Lee hadn't a single unit to help the hard-pressed Jones, who was fighting desperately to prevent his line from giving way at the seams.

An anxious Lee kept looking to the south, as the inexorable minutes passed, wondering whether Hill's men would come up in time. Everywhere he looked there were only Union troops and they were pushing the weary Confederates all along the line, almost—but not quite—to the point of no return, that psychological moment when the bravest spirits falter, a few men panic, and the game is up.

Toombs' Confederate brigade, the same that had immobilized Burnside's four divisions on the heights east of the Antietam, opposite Burnside's Bridge, all morning and well into the afternoon, had fallen back when the stream was crossed and was now fighting on the right of Jones' division. To Toombs' rear, in the open fields between the two important roads leading south from Sharpsburg to Harper's Ferry and Shepherdstown respectively, fields of tall Indian corn along the right provided partial screen from observation by those north of Sharpsburg and to the east.

As General Lee watched, suddenly a column of troops appeared out of nowhere, moving at a fast gait across the fields and along the road from Boteler's Ford. Calling to his side a lieutenant who happened to be carrying a telescope, Lee told him to take a good look to see if he could identify the troops. If they were Federals, it could mean the end, because this new mass of fighting men were in the rear of Jones' line— and they wore blue uniforms. The lieutenant took a long look, turned to the General, and informed him that the units were carrying Confederate flags. A. P. Hill's division at last! The men couldn't be from any other organization; the battle was not yet lost!

As Hill's division reached the combat area, two of the five brigades, Field's and Pender's, were detached to cover the approaches by Snavely's Ford and the lower reaches of the Antietam. The other three, under Branch, Gregg and Archer, moved into line at the double and charged. In the mad scramble, Branch was killed, Gregg wounded, and 374 casualties sustained by the three attacking brigades, but a loss of 20 percent of Hill's effectives, far less than many of the other Confederate divisions which had stood on the defensive, was a low price to pay for what the short, fierce, flank attack achieved. A. P. Hill again at the psychological moment saved the day for Lee's army, tottering on the brink of complete disaster as it had been just a few moments before the Light Division came up.

Scammon's Federal brigade of the Kanawha division, in reserve behind Rodman's division on the left of Cox's line, saw the Confederate reinforcements about the same time, changed front to the left and drove the leading skirmishers back on their main body. One of Rodman's brigades included a regiment that was receiving its baptism of fire. Becoming confused in the cornfield this regiment lost its cohesion and was struck at the same time, at an angle, by the rush of A. P. Hill's men, who charged to the tune of the wild Rebel yell. Division Commander Rodman, in an effort to restore the line, was mortally wounded. Cox managed to realign his divisions to repair the break, but the sudden, unexpected counterattack by Hill's 1,800 yelling demons unnerved the Federals and forced them back. The retirement was made in good order, but it was a decisive check, and on that note the Battle of Antietam ended. Burnside's divisions remained on the west side of the Antietam, holding the high ground they had won at a cost of more than 2,300 casualties, while the Confederates, wisely deciding not to push their good fortune too far, busied themselves in intrenching the line of the road to Shepherdstown with a view to securing that vital withdrawal route, Lee's lifeline to Virginia.

LEE DEFIES MCCLELLAN

As the merciful darkness settled over the blood-soaked fields north, east, and south of the little town of Sharpsburg, lantern carrying litterbearers threaded their way among the dead and wounded, sorting out the latter for removal to the barns, churches, and other buildings designated as temporary hospitals. There the overworked surgeons of the two armies administered first aid, amputated arms and legs, or gave what relief they could to those who were beyond saving. It was of course impossible to immediately gather up all the wounded, of the many thousands who lay where they had fallen, calling piteously for water, for the loved ones at home, or, stoically silent, waiting and hoping for help or even death to end their suffering.

The famous Dunker Church, at the very heart of the heavy fighting in the morning, was one of the houses of worship to serve as a hospital.

Wounded soldiers of both sides sought and found sanctuary there, in spite of the Federal shells which found a mark in its white brick walls. The church was badly damaged, but the thrifty parishioners of German decent rebuilt it in 1864, only to have it blown down by a heavy windstorm in the year 1921, so that today's visitors to the Antietam battlefield can see only its foundation stones.

Lee's headquarters tent was in the same grove at the southwestern edge of town where he had first set it up upon the arrival of his army from South Mountain. One after another his generals rode in from their several posts to report the status of their corps and divisions and to confer on plans for the next day. Their feelings can only be imagined. All knew how close to disaster the army had been, nor were they under any illusions as to the fate that still hung over their heads. They could be and were justly proud of the way their troops had thrown back the massive Federal attacks, but they were all realists enough to know that a well-planned and skillfully executed Union assault on September eighteen could, and probably would, drive them into the Potomac or cut to pieces what remained of their army.

Almost 11,000 of their men and officers had become casualties in a single day at Sharpsburg, in addition to nearly 3,000 at South Mountain, Boonsboro, and Harpers Ferry. Other thousands had fallen out during the hard marches since the Battle of Manassas and were still among the missing. The army would be fortunate if it could now muster 30,000 men able to wield a musket or yank a lanyard, while McClellan's army, after its cumulative losses of somewhat more than 13,000, still had over 62,000 able bodied soldiers, half of whom had not been engaged at Antietam.

Jackson, the two Hills, Hood, Stuart, Early, and D. R. Jones, among other generals, were all there. It was not a council of war—Lee was in the habit of consulting his lieutenants and then announcing his decision—but it was obvious from the character of the reports that all the generals, Jackson included, believed that a retreat across the Potomac was not only logical but inevitable, if the army expected to remain intact to fight another day. Lee talked with each in turn, calmly gathering information and seemingly unmindful of the distressing situation which the successive reports managed to portray. Concerned over the safety of Longstreet, who had not arrived, Lee inquired if any had seen him. About that time Old Pete put in an appearance, to Lee's evident relief, for he put his arm on Longstreet's shoulder with the remark: "Here is my old war horse at last."

After sifting the reports, and much to the amazement of the assembled generals, Lee announced calmly that the army, clearly incapable of offensive action, would not retreat, but remain in its present defensive position; if McClellan chose to attack, they would meet it. The men were to remain in the lines and cooked meals would be carried to them. Stragglers between Sharpsburg and the Potomac were to be gathered up and returned to their units. The Maryland campaign was not yet over. On that note the generals were dismissed to return to their organizations.

Psychological warfare? In a sense it was, but it was more than that. Lee was supremely confident that his army, defeated as it was, could still outfight McClellan if the latter should at this late date overcome his timidity and dare to risk all in a second day's battle. Perhaps Lee still hoped that an opportunity might offer for that outflanking maneuver which he had wanted to try with Stuart and Jackson on the afternoon of the first day. Clearly he hated the thought of retreat, an admission that the Maryland invasion was a failure, even though his hard-fighting army had deprived McClellan of a victory. For Sharpsburg was certainly a stalemate-a new experience for the Army of Northern Virginia and one which was not relished by its commanding general.

McClellan Still Hesitates

The wounded Confederate tiger, at bay and still dangerous, stood fast on the night of September 17 and throughout the following day, daring the still hesitant McClellan to attack if he had the courage and the will.

During the morning of the eighteenth, two reinforcing Union divisions, Couch's and Humphreys', arrived on the field with over 12,000 men, but according to McClellan the boys were tired from marching and "needed rest and refreshment" before he would think of asking them to fight! The contrast with A. P. Hill's Confederates needs no comment.

History records that McClellan lacked both courage and character. His official report of the battle reveals his indecision and the reasons why he allowed the second day to pass without lifting a finger to exploit what he alone considered a victory. In his own words, wherein he kept alive the fiction that Lee's strength was 100,000 or more men (2½ times the actual Confederate manpower), McClellan reveals his inadequacy as a fighting army commander:

> *Night closed the long and desperately contested battle of the 17th. Nearly 200,000 men and five hundred pieces of artillery were for fourteen hours engaged in this memorable battle. We had attacked the enemy in a position selected by the experienced engineer then in person directing their operations. We had driven them from their line on one flank and secured a footing within it on the other, The Army of the Potomac, notwithstanding the moral effect incident to previous reverses, had achieved a victory over an adversary invested with the prestige of recent success. Our soldiers slept that night conquerors on a field won by their valor and covered with the dead and wounded of the enemy (no mention of the even greater Federal losses).*
>
> *After a night of anxious deliberation, and a full and careful survey of the situation and condition of our army, the strength and position of the enemy, I concluded that the success of an attack on the 18th was not certain. I am aware of the fact that under ordinary circumstances a general is expected to risk a battle if he has a reasonable prospect of success; but at this critical juncture I should have had a narrow view of the condition of the country had I been willing to hazard another battle with less than an absolute assurance of success.*

There was much more of the same, a rationalization ad nauseam to bolster McClellan's case for deferring a resumption of the battle, but the quoted section is sufficient in itself to contrast the character of the opposing commanders, Lee and McClellan, and to justify the former's willingness to take the calculated risk that he did.

Lee Withdraws

Although Lee had indicated to McClellan his willingness to continue the battle, he had probably learned of the arrival of Union reinforcements, and had another day to think over what his generals had advised on the evening of the seventeenth. It would be prudent, however disappointing, to retire to Virginia and seek a more favorable opportunity to accomplish the purpose which the now fruitless invasion of Maryland had failed to achieve.

The word was passed to his lieutenants. After midnight, September 18-19, the retrograde movement was initiated, with Longstreet in the lead and Fitz Lee's cavalry brigade to cover the withdrawal. All night long and well into the morning the Confederate columns plodded south and splashed through the waters of the Potomac at the ford a mile and a half below Shepherdstown. There was no interference from the Union army, not even an attempt by the cavalry to harass the retreat, which suggests rather strongly that McClellan had permanently surrendered the initiative to his "defeated" opponent.

Safely across the Potomac with all his troops, wagons, and wounded, Lee moved the army a short distance back from the river and went into bivouac, leaving the reserve artillery with forty-four guns and a couple of small infantry brigades to discourage a possible Federal attempt to effect a crossing by the ford the army had just used.

Shortly after midnight of the 19th, General Pendleton, whom Lee had charged with the responsibility of guarding the ford, woke the Commanding General with an alarming report that McClellan had sent Porter's corps across the Potomac at an upper ford while the Federal artillery pounded the rear guard with a heavy bombardment. The excited minister-turned-general told Lee that the infantry had retreated and all the Confederate guns had been captured.

Lee, although disturbed by the news, was reluctant to undertake a counterattack in the darkness, but Jackson, when summoned, took a more serious view of the matter. With Lee's permission, he sent A. P. Hill's division back to the river at once. Having turned back Burnside's corps on the afternoon of the seventeenth, Hill's men were keen to add a few more laurels to those already earned by the Light Division. Hill found that Pendleton had been badly misinformed, in that a Union brigade had crossed at Boteler's Ford and had captured only four rather than forty-four guns, all the others having been safely brought off by the retreating Confederate rear guard. On seeing the approach of Hill's whole division, the Federal brigade commander at once started to pull back across the river. Unfortunately one of his regiments, the 118th Pennsylvania, failed to get the order, and remained to receive the full impact of A. P. Hill's customary fiery assault. The Federal soldiers, who had been in the service only three days prior to Antietam, stood their ground bravely for a short time, but presently broke and poured back over the steep embankment, almost a cliff. Some were impeded by fallen timber, others floundered in the river. The Confederates rushed to the top of the bank and poured destructive fire into the fugitives, hitting many in the act of trying to clear the timber and others in the water. A number who took refuge in a mill building were killed by their own artillery, which was firing with defective fuses. The regiment lost 71 killed, and several hundred wounded and captured.

After this sad affair, McClellan made no further effort to pursue the Confederate forces. For all practical purposes the campaign was over.

The North, at first, accepted McClellan's victory claim at face value. Later, when all the facts emerged, there was a less enthusiastic reaction. But for President Lincoln, patiently waiting and hoping for even a quasi-victory to afford an excuse to issue his Emancipation Proclamation, the fact that Lee's invasion had been turned back and the Confederate army had been the first to leave the field was believed sufficient to establish a foundation for the historic pronouncement. The bloodiest single day's battle of the Civil War was therefore not fought in vain. For it was made the vehicle whereby the War Between the States was transformed from a family dispute into a crusade for human freedom. Truly it can be written, of that famous battle on the banks of the Antietam, that God works in a mysterious way His wonders to perform.

CHAPTER 14

Lincoln Tries Another General

THE ARMY of Northern Virginia spent the early autumn of 1862, after Antietam, on the banks of Opequon Creek in the lower Shenandoah Valley about twelve miles northwest of Harpers Ferry. The Army of the Potomac rested north of the Potomac in Maryland, with its base at Harpers Ferry. In order to find out what McClellan might be planning, Lee in early October sent J.E.B. Stuart with 1800 troopers on a sweeping raid around the Union army.

This business of circling the Federal army was a specialty of the dashing Stuart. He had done it once before to McClellan near Richmond and now he staged a dramatic repeat performance with startling results. Crossing the Potomac at McCoy's Ford, the Confederate horsemen rode rapidly northward through Mercersburg, Chambersburg, across South Mountain and then, turning south through Emmitsburg and Frederick, recrossed the Potomac at White's Ford east of Leesburg, only a little more than two days after they had started out.

It was a fruitful expedition. Stuart's men gathered in several hundred good horses from Pennsylvania farms; wore Pleasonton's Federal cavalry to a frazzle in horse-killing marches in a continuous but unsuccessful effort to head off the Confederates and break up the raid; and shook badly the new, bright confidence that the North had reposed in the person of General McClellan. Of supreme importance to Lee, Stuart had learned during the raid that McClellan was getting set to move back into northern Virginia—an accurate intelligence report which had the added advantage that Lee was given several weeks to prepare for his opponent's return because the latter's timetable had been upset as a partial result of the exhausted condition of the Federal cavalry.

McClellan ascribed the success of the enemy raid to "the deficiency of our cavalry," and urged upon Washington "the imperative necessity of at once supplying this army with a sufficient number of horses to remount every dismounted cavalry soldier within the shortest possible time." To this the sorely tried Lincoln sent through Halleck an appropriate riposte: "The President has read your telegram and directs me to suggest that if the enemy had more occupation south of the (Potomac) river, his cavalry would not be so likely to make raids north of it."

LINCOLN JOLTS McCLELLAN

As McClellan continued to stall with one excuse after another in an effort to explain why he was not following Lincoln's October 6 order "to cross the Potomac and give battle to the enemy or drive him south," the President dispatched a long letter to the general which evidently jolted him and in all truth should have caused him to blush with shame. This is what Lincoln wrote in his inimitable fashion on October 13:

> *You remember my speaking to you of what I called your overcautiousness. Are you not overcautious when you assume that you cannot do what the enemy is constantly doing? Should you not claim to be at least his equal in prowess, and act upon the claim?*
>
> *As I understand, you telegraphed Gen. Halleck that you cannot subsist your army at Winchester, unless the railroad from Harper's Ferry to that point be put in working order. But the enemy does now subsist his army at Winchester at a distance nearly twice as great from railroad transportation as you would have to do without the railroad last named. He now wagons from Culpeper Court-House, which is just about twice as far as you would have to do from Harper's Ferry. He is certainly not more than half as well provided with wagons as you are. I certainly should be pleased for you to have the advantage of the railroad from Harper's Ferry to Winchester; but it wastes all the remainder of Autumn to give it to you, and in fact ignores the question of time, which cannot and must' not be ignored.*
>
> *Again, one of the standard maxims of war, as you know, is, "to operate upon the enemy's communications as much as possible without*

exposing your own." You seem to act as if this applies against you, but cannot apply in your favor. Change positions with the enemy, and think you not he would break your communication with Richmond within the next twenty-four hours? You dread his going into Pennsylvania. But if he does so in full force, he gives up his communications to you absolutely, and you have nothing to do but to follow and ruin him; if he does so with less than full force, fall upon and beat what is left behind all the easier.

Exclusive of the water line, you are now nearer Richmond than the enemy is by the route that you can and he must take. Why can you not reach there before him, unless you admit that he is more than your equal on a march? His route is the arc of a circle, while yours is the chord. The roads are as good on yours as on his. You know I desired, but did not order, you to cross the Potomac below instead of above the Shenandoah and Blue Ridge. My idea was, that this would at once menace the enemy's communications, which I would seize if he would permit. If he should move northward, I would follow him closely, holding his communications. If he should prevent our seizing his communications, and move toward Richmond, I would press closely to him, fight him if a favorable opportunity should present, and at least try to beat him to Richmond on the inside track. I say "try," if we never try, we shall never succeed. If he makes a stand at Winchester, moving neither north nor south, I would fight him there, on the idea that if we cannot beat him when he bears the wastage of coming to us, we never can when we bear the wastage of going to him. This proposition is a simple truth, and is too important to be lost sight of for a moment. In coming to us, he tenders us an advantage which we should not waive. We should not so operate as to merely drive him away. As we must beat him somewhere, or fail finally, we can do it, if at all, easier near to us than far away. If we cannot beat the enemy where he now is, we never can, he again being within the intrenchments of Richmond.

Recurring to the idea of going to Richmond on the inside track, the facility of supplying from the side, away from the enemy, is remarkable, as it were by the different spokes of a wheel, extending from the hub toward the rim, and this, whether you move directly by the chord·

or on the inside arc, hugging the Blue Ridge more closely. The chord-line, as you see, carries you by Aldie, Haymarket and Fredericksburg, and you see how turnpikes, railroads, and finally the Potomac, by Aquia Creek, meet you at aid points from Washington. The same, only the lines lengthened a little, if you press closer to the Blue Ridge part of the way. The gaps through the Blue Ridge I understand to be about the following distances from Harpers Ferry, to wit: Vestal's five miles; Gregory's, thirteen; Snickers, eighteen; Ashby's, twenty-eight; Manassas, thirty-eight; Chester, forty-five, and Thornton's, fifty-three. I should think it preferable to take the route nearest the enemy, disabling him to make an important move without your knowledge, and compelling him to keep his forces together for dread of you. The gaps would enable you to attack if you should wish. For a great part of the way you would be practically between the enemy and both Washington and Richmond, enabling us to spare you the greatest number of troops from here. When, at length, running for Richmond ahead of him enables him to move this way; if he does so, turn and attack him in the rear. But I think he should be engaged long before such point is reached. It is all easy if our troops march as well as the enemy, and it is unmanly to say they cannot do it. This letter is in no sense an order.

More than ample time had now elapsed for McClellan again to put his army in fighting trim. The morale of the troops was good, they were well supplied and equipped, and they easily outnumbered Lee's army two to one. Federal cavalry reconnaissance had informed McClellan that the two wings of the Confederate army were now sixty miles apart, Longstreet's First Corps at Culpeper and Jackson's Second Corps in the Shenandoah Valley.

In late October McClellan moved. Advancing with his usual caution, and in accordance with his plan to attack Longstreet and drive him back or at least keep him from forming a junction with Jackson, the Army of the Potomac crossed the Potomac at Berlin and on November 6 reached Warrenton, Virginia.

In view of McClellan's vast numerical superiority, Lee decided to employ maneuver rather than force. In conformity with that decision he left Jackson in the Valley to threaten the Union flank and rear. This was a dangerous calculated risk on Lee's part, but the sort of thing for which he was famous.

By this time, however, McClellan's luck had run out. Stuart's second free-wheeling raid around the Army of the Potomac, each time with impunity, had left a decidedly unfavorable impression on the public mind. Lincoln had carefully read the Antietam battlefield reports and accurately interpreted them as reflecting an unexploited opportunity because of McClellan's lack of aggressiveness. Secretary of War Stanton and General-in-Chief Halleck had evaluated McClellan and found him wanting. So once again, and this time for good, on November 7, 1862, George B. McClellan was removed from command.

CHANGING HORSES IN MIDSTREAM

The practice of changing horses in midstream was hardly characteristic of the man whose "horse sense" was almost legendary, yet Lincoln was guilty of doing just that on at least two historic occasions. The first was in early November 1862, when he supplanted McClellan with Burnside, and the second in late June 1863, when Meade replaced Hooker in the presence of the enemy only three days before the Battle of Gettysburg. Lincoln may not have been aware of the danger involved in such a procedure, or, if he were, he may have considered the administrative and command obstacles to be the lesser of two evils.

It was a sad blow to the enlisted men of the Army of the Potomac when the word came down that McClellan had been relieved. He was extremely popular with the men, who never failed to cheer him to the echo whenever he passed them on the road or in camp. There is no doubt that they had a blind faith in Little Mac and their feelings were probably fairly expressed in the letter of a Massachusetts soldier to his family dated November 10, 1862, in which he wrote: "As sure as George B. McClellan leaves, the courage, enthusiasm and pluck go with him."

It is doubtful that either President Lincoln or the people of the North understood the great test of loyalty and patriotism to which the Army of the Potomac was being subjected in the summary removal of the popular

McClellan, who cherished thinly veiled political ambitions of his own and was not above he wrote: "The order depriving me of the command created a deep feeling in the army, so much so that many were in favor of my refusing to obey the order, and of marching upon Washington to take possession of the Government." This implied that McClellan and some of his headquarters staff were toying with the idea of a military coup détat, but thought better of it and then made it appear that there was a spontaneous grassroots movement in the army that he himself found it necessary to quell for the sake of the country. The truth is that there was just too much intelligence and hard common sense in the ranks of the volunteer regiments that made up by far the greater part of the Army of the Potomac, for such a mutinous sentiment to get very far even if it had been carefully nurtured as a planned project; and there is no real evidence that such was the case.

The McClellan supporters insisted that the President waited until after the fall elections (which went against the Lincoln cohorts) to remove McClellan. This may have been partly true, but even so there was sufficient justification for the ax to fall without further delay. Longstreet's corps, half of Lee's army, had already crossed the Blue Ridge and Lincoln had every right to conclude that McClellan's slow pace in crossing the Potomac and moving south was advertising his punch so effectively that Lee was being given time and space to maneuver in a way that could easily nullify all the advantage of Federal surprise and initiative.

McClellan's removal is easy to understand. Month after month of favorable summer and early fall weather had slipped by without visible evidence that McClellan intended to make a move of any sort, least of all an offensive one. Obviously Lincoln couldn't wait indefinitely, but it does seem strange that he delayed issuing his removal order until a few weeks after McClellan had been told in no uncertain terms to commence his offensive without further delay. Possibly the President cherished the despairing hope that this time it would be different; he would give it another try and if nothing else should be accomplished, the Army of the enemy and the new commander spared the task of overcoming the inertia of starting the ponderous machine.

AN UNPROMISING SELECTION

The selection of General Ambrose E. Burnside to succeed George B. McClellan is more difficult to understand, for it was an appointment that by no stretch of the imagination could be termed full of promise. The real truth was that Lee and Jackson, Longstreet and Stuart were just too good for the Federal generals at that stage. The Administration at Washington had been unable to find the right combination to give the Confederates a taste of their own medicine, possibly for the reason that by comparison with the Confederate commanders no Union leader had emerged to stir the popular imagination by winning a notable victory.

But why Burnside? Why not Reynolds or Hooker, or Meade, or Couch, or anyone of the other corps or division commanders who had better fighting records than the man whose name seems almost to have been pulled out of a hat? The only explanation that makes any sense, and that very little, is that Burnside was closely identified with McClellan, was known to be opposed to the latter's relief by any other general, least of all himself, and was chosen in the belief or hope that his elevation to army command would cause a minimum of dislocation and disharmony in the ranks of the army. True, Burnside had a charming personality and made friends easily with his warm smile and engaging address, and as a graduate of the U. S. Military Academy was naturally presumed to have been thoroughly grounded in the military arts and sciences.

This was a faulty assumption. The law governing admission to the Military Academy of the Civil War period precluded entrance examinations on subjects beyond those taught in the rural common schools, which in most cases were reading, writing, and arithmetic. Consequently the average young man who secured an appointment to West Point would be found, at the equivalent to qualifying him for the freshman year at one of the civilian colleges.

The intellectual education acquired at West Point was approximately the same as that of any polytechnic school, while that pertaining to the military arts and sciences, aside from the courses on engineering, was confined to the school of the soldier and close order drilling of smaller units.

No instruction whatsoever was given in strategy or grand tactics, in military history, or in "the art of war," and consequently little if any incentive was afforded for individual collateral reading of the kind that would be likely to develop the qualities essential to generalship. The four-year course of study specifically covered two years of work in mathematics, one in physics and chemistry, one in the construction of fortifications, to which was added a little English, philosophy, elementary law, one year of basic Spanish, and two of French.

Furthermore, the opportunity for professional improvement in the Regular Army after graduation was completely absent, because of the small size of the Army and the fact that duty with troops was restricted to the frontier posts of the West, where the normal complement of units was several companies of infantry at the most.

It is not surprising that, with a few exceptions, those graduates of the Military Academy who attained subsequent distinction as corps and army commanders had left the service shortly after graduation to find greater outlets for their energies and abilities, nor should their lack of preparation for the responsibilities of high command be solely charged to their own unwillingness to educate themselves by study and the reading of military history. They were in large part the victims of a system which failed to stimulate any real interest in the art and science of warfare, which in the last analysis had to be learned the hard way after the shooting started.

Furthermore, there was an absence in Washington of militarily well-educated officers of broad experience, capable of and ising officer personnel of the Army, appraisng their several potentials for higher command, and giving the Administration a wider choice from which to select the all-important army commanders. Unfortunately, it appears that it was by a system of trial and error that the commanding generals of the Union Army were selected and catapulted into their posts of responsibility. On occasion they didn't like it, and at least in the case of Burnside and Meade they protested to no avail.

Burnside's Background
Burnside was born in Liberty, Indiana on May 23, 1824 and graduated from West Point in 1847, one year after McClellan, whom he admired and whose friendship he cultivated. The Mexican War was in progress and his first assignment was Vera Cruz, but the war had ended before

he arrived. He spent several uneventful years of soldiering, except for a brush with Apache Indians in New Mexico, in the course of which he was wounded. Having reached the conclusion that the cavalry carbine was unsuitable for warfare on the Plains, he invented a new breech loading rifle. He became so enamored of his creation that he resigned from the Army in October 1853, organized the Bristol Firearms Company, built a plant in Rhode Island to manufacture the rifle in quantity, and went broke in the process. It seems that he had not completed his contract to supply rifles to the United States, so after an uphill fight of several years he gave up the struggle and turned everything over to his creditors, including his sword and uniform.

McClellan had also left the Army and was serving as Engineer-Vice President of the Illinois Central Railroad. Through his friendship with his former schoolmate, Burnside landed a job with the railroad, later became treasurer of the company, and was able to discharge all his old debts. Thus two kindred spirits were brought into an intimate business relationship, for McClellan had already achieved the distinction of having invented the saddle which bore his name from then on until changing times and mechanized warfare relegated the American horse cavalry to a final state of oblivion in the year 1941.

Possibly because Burnside's brief manufacturing experience had been in the State of Rhode Island, he re-entered the Service in 1861 as colonel of a Rhode Island regiment of infantry. On October 13, 1864 he was relieved from his command and in April 1865 resigned his commission in the military service to engage in railroad and steamship enterprises. Soon thereafter the people of Rhode Island elected him to the governorship for four consecutive terms and then sent him to the United States Senate, where he served from 1875 until his death in 1881 at the age of 57 years. Despite this evidence of politics in his blood, there is nothing in his military record to show that he cherished any political ambitions while in uniform, nor was he in any sense an intriguer. On the contrary, he was regarded by his military associates as a loyal and honest officer and gentle man. But few of them had any illusions on the score of his capacity for high command.

Burnside As a Troop Leader

In the early stages of the war Burnside commanded a brigade in the disastrous First Battle of Bull Run, with neither credit nor discredit to himself or his troops. Following this he was given the rank of brigadier general of Volunteers and directed to organize a coast division of the Army of the Potomac for an expedition to invade North Carolina. With his independent command of some 15,000 men he conducted a campaign along the coast, seized Roanoke Island, and performed other successful feats which seemed to impress the Administration with the fact that here was a general with promise of considerable ability.

Burnside's bold and aggressive campaign in North Carolina having resulted in the capture of seventy-nine guns and 3,600 prisoners, he was rewarded by a promotion to major general in March of 1862. Further exploits in the South were prevented by the recall of his command to reinforce McClellan's army on the Virginia peninsula. After Pope's defeat at Second Manassas Burnside was given command of the Ninth Corps and subsequently of the right wing of the Army of the Potomac as it marched into Maryland in pursuit of Lee.

As a corps commander with the rank of major general at Antietam, Burnside was considered by his friend and superior McClellan to have been inexcusably slow in getting his troops into action on the second day. The Army of the Potomac was divided tactically into three wings for that battle and Burnside given command of the left wing. McClellan had, however, pulled Hooker's corps away from Burnside for action on the right, leaving the latter with but a single corps, which was adequate for the accomplishment of his mission had he moved promptly when directed. Burnside's orders were to attack across Antietam Creek against the right of Lee's line, which as it happened was lightly held, but the Confederates made the most of their artillery, enfilading the stone bridge in front of Burn side's troops, and the unimaginative general was unable to figure a way to cross except over the narrow bridge, despite the fact that several fords were available in his sector. Repeated oral orders kept coming down from Army headquarters to get going, from about 9 o'clock in the morning till well past noon, with but little effect on Burnside, whose mental reflexes, never overly rapid, appeared to become even more sluggish in the heat of combat.

Finally a peremptory order from McClellan caused sufficient reaction to force him to move; with the result that two regiments from New York and Pennsylvania, respectively, dashed across the bridge, pierced the Confederate line, reached the heights overlooking Sharpsburg, and forced Lee to throw in his last reserves to bring the Federals to a halt.

That was McClellan's clue to throw in his unused reserves, 20,000 of them, to exploit the partial success on Burnside's front, which, typically, he failed to do. Whereupon A. P. Hill's Confederate division, arriving about the middle of the after noon from Harpers Ferry, was thrown into the battle, drove the Federals back to the creek and saved Lee from utter defeat.

CHAPTER 15

The Strategy of the
Fredericksburg Campaign

MCCLELLAN's temporary headquarters were at Rectortown, fifteen miles north of Warrenton, when on November 7 he and Burnside (at Orlean) received separate copies of the order for the farmer's relief. It was snowing heavily, as though nature were symbolically confirming Lincoln's fear that McClellan would delay his march until winter weather and bad roads should make it impracticable. Burnside's first action was to confer with McClellan. By mutual agreement the transfer of command was deferred for several days until the army could reach the Warrenton area. This gave Burnside a breather during which to collect his thoughts, consider the implications of McClellan's plan of campaign along the line of the Orange and Alexandria Railroad, and decide whether to adopt it or develop a new plan of his own.

After studying the situation for several days, Burnside informed Halleck that McClellan's plan of operations was un acceptable. He stated that as soon as the concentration in the Warrenton area was completed he proposed to make a feint toward Culpeper or Gordonsville to deceive the enemy, then within a few days, after stocking up with reserves of food and ammunition, move the entire army rapidly to Fredericksburg en route to Richmond. He reasoned that by establishing a new base at Aquia Landing and taking the Fredericksburg route he could more effectively cover Washington and assure better protection for his lines of supply and communication, by land and water. Historic Aquia Creek, which empties into the Potomac River at Aquia Landing, was for ten years after the Indian War of 1676 the northern frontier of Virginia. This stream was an important supply route for the Army of the Potomac in 1862-63, during the campaigns of which it served as the army base, a logistical fact which must have influenced Burnside's plan to a certain extent.

The on-to-Richmond fallacy clearly obsessed Burnside as it had his predecessors. In his post-battle report which followed the Fredericksburg campaign he maintained that he had chosen to go by way of Fredericksburg on the premise that it was the shortest road to Richmond, "the taking of which, I think, should be ·the great object of the campaign, as the fall of that place would tend more to cripple the Rebel cause than almost any other military event, except the absolute breaking up of their army."

The destruction of the hostile army, it will be noted, would in Burnside's words admittedly deal the heaviest blow to the rebels, but he chose the lesser objective, Richmond, with a bit of specious reasoning that falls somewhat short of giving him an A for audacity.

Burnside argued that it would be a simple matter to move rapidly to Falmouth, cross the Rappahannock to Fredericksburg on pontoon bridges, and advance on Richmond before Lee could effect a junction of his two widely separated wings. He failed to indicate what he hoped to accomplish by seizing Richmond while Lee's army was still intact and at large to the west, nor did he explain why he was going at the task of crossing the Rappahannock the hard way rather than by the innumerable fords above Fredericksburg.

If it was simply a foot race that he envisaged, that was one thing. But it would have been more sensible, if he was looking for a fight, to move directly toward his opponent than to circle around him with the objective of seizing upon the inert mass of bricks and mortar, and the practically unarmed civilians, which_ comprised Richmond. The only valid prize there, in fact, was the principal cannon factory available to the Confederacy, which was located in Richmond. The new route offered the possibility that his opponent might show up unexpectedly and belligerently before his own schedule called for the enemy's appearance. If Burnside believed that by beating Lee to Richmond he would succeed in cutting him off from his base of supplies, he misjudged his shrewd opponent, who had already taken care of such a contingency by establishing an alternate base at Staunton in the Shenandoah Valley.

It is not likely that McClellan had shown Burnside Lincoln's letter of October 13, in which the President had suggested the line of operations that he would follow were he the army commander. That Lincoln's strategic sense had developed markedly was evident in the forementioned letter, which displayed a surprisingly sound grasp of the logistical facts of life and which spelled out in a simple but convincing manner the several strategic moves that were open to the opposing armies and the advantages inherent in the course which he favored but refrained from putting in the form of an order.

Lincoln's theory of moving on the inside arc via Culpeper and Gordonsville was designed to bring on an early clash with Lee, and it was that plan which McClellan was slowly following when he was taken out of the game. Had Burnside had the opportunity to read and heed Lincoln's suggestions, he might have had second thoughts and felt less sure of the soundness of his own decision to discard McClellan's plan in favor of moving on Fredericksburg by the north bank of the Rappahannock.

He may have been influenced unduly by the fact that a railroad line ran from Fredericksburg to Aquia Creek, where river steamers had carried passengers on to Washington in pre war days. This line had been repeatedly destroyed and rebuilt, as the armies surged back and forth, but now it seemed to be firmly under the control of the Federals, at least for the time being.

HALLECK DISAGREES; LINCOLN APPROVES CONDITIONALLY

Having already approved the McClellan plan, which Burnside now wanted to change, Halleck reacted unfavorably. On November 12, he visited Burnside at Warrenton, accompanied by two staff officers, Generals Meigs and Haupt, Quartermaster General and Chief of Military Railroads, respectively, and urged him to follow the original plan. But Burnside was unyielding, and finally, still demurring, Halleck announced that the President would have to make the decision. He then returned to Washington, while Burnside for two days waited impatiently for the green light. The word came on November 14, in the form of a terse message from Halleck which simply said: "The President has just assented to your plan. He thinks it will succeed if you move rapidly; otherwise not."

It is always easier to judge the quality of strategic decisions after the event. But if, as appears from the evidence, Burnside's primary reason for an end run rather than a line buck was merely greater security for his supply lines back to Washington, historians may be justified in concluding that the specter of Lee's superior generalship must have weighted the scales, in Burnside's estimate of the situation, to such an extent that he chose caution rather than boldness in this his first great test as army commander. Burnside's vast superiority in combat strength should in all conscience have given him sufficient moral courage to hazard the remote possibility that Jackson would move in on his rear, which was already adequately protected by an entire corps, Slocum's Twelfth, at Harpers Ferry, in addition to strong contingents along the Potomac between Harpers Ferry and Washington, and a powerful reserve of armed manpower in the Capital itself. Certainly this danger would be a small one if the Army of the Potomac should move rapidly and aggressively to keep Lee's two wings from consolidating. By his decision to march away from his weaker opponent, rather than toward him, Burnside compounded even McClellan's perennial timidity in a proposal that was hardly calculated to elicit cheers from Washington.

Lee's Strategy

Several days after McClellan had been superseded, Lee outlined his strategy in a letter to Confederate Secretary of War Randolph at Richmond:

> As long as General Jackson can operate with safety and secure his retirement west of the Massanutten Mountains, I think it advantageous that he should be in position to threaten the enemy's flank and rear and thus prevent his advance southward on the east side of the Blue Ridge. General Jackson has been directed accordingly, and should the enemy descend into the Valley, General Longstreet will attack his rear and cut off his communications. The enemy is apparently so strong in numbers that I think it preferable to attempt to baffle his designs by maneuvering rather than to resist his advance by main force.

Debating in his own mind where best to fight Burnside, Lee seemed to prefer a position on the North Anna River, which ran east and west about thirty miles south of the Rappahannock. In a dispatch to Richmond written shortly after the Battle of Fredericksburg, he stated that his plan had contemplated a retirement to the North Anna position if the enemy should cross in force at Port Royal, which is situated about seventeen miles downriver from Fredericksburg. In this dispatch he added:

My design was to have done so in the first instance. My purpose was changed, not from any advantage in this position, but from an unwillingness to open more of our country to depredation than possible, and also with a view of collecting such forage and provisions as could be obtained in the Rappahannock Valley. It will, therefore, be more advantageous to us to draw him further away from his base of operations.

Lee's strategy was clearly not to fight on the Rappahannock, but along the line of the North Anna River, where in his opinion the defensive could be turned into a counteroffensive more rapidly and effectively than at Fredericksburg, with the added advantage of causing the Federal line of communications and supply to be appreciably lengthened. Jefferson Davis, however, favored a position at Fredericksburg, and it was doubtless the Confederate President's attitude that tipped the scales in Lee's decision to make a stand there.

Lee had known by November 7 that advance elements of the Union army had reached Warrenton and that its cavalry was maneuvering along the Rappahannock. As the Federal build-up in the Warrenton area continued, Lee was undecided as to McClellan's next move, but thought he might still turn west to the Shenandoah Valley.

Longstreet has noted in his own account of the Battle of Fredericksburg that Lee knew of the Federal change in army command within twenty-four hours of the time the word reached McClellan and Burnside, presumably through spies or by courtesy of General

Stuart's capable cavalry scouts. Longstreet has recorded that when the news reached Lee, the latter remarked that he "regretted to part with McClellan, for we always understood each other so well; I fear they may continue to make these changes until they find someone whom I don't understand."

COMPOSITION AND DISPOSITION OF THE OPPOSING FORCES

On November 9, several days after Burnside received the order from Washington relieving McClellan, the opposing forces were situated as follows:

The Union army, with a total strength of some 140,000 effectives and 320 guns, was largely disposed along the western base of Bull Run Mountains, with three corps and the Reserve Artillery near Warrenton; two corps in the New Baltimore area; one corps, the Ninth, with Stoneman's and Whipple's divisions attached, near Waterloo; Pleasonton's and Bayard's cavalry covering the army front on the line: Amissville-Jefferson-Rappahannock Station (the junction point of the Rappahannock River and the Orange and Alexandria Railroad). The Twelfth Corps remained at Harpers Ferry.

The Confederate army, numbering approximately 90,000 present for duty with 275 guns, was as previously noted widely separated. Longstreet's First Corps was at Culpeper, to which place it had moved from the Valley when McClellan crossed the Potomac in late October. Jackson's corps of almost equal strength was in the Shenandoah Valley between Berryville and Charlestown; and Stuart's cavalry was operating partly on the Rappahannock and partly in the Valley with Jackson.

Lee in addition had a small detachment, composed of a regiment of infantry and a battery of artillery, occupying Fredericksburg, while elements of Stuart's cavalry patrolled the river above the town. The Fredericksburg garrison was promptly directed to destroy the railroad between Falmouth and Aquia Creek, as insurance against the possibility that the Federals might take it into their heads to shift eastward, in which event they would need that short stretch of rails to extend their new water-borne line of supply from Washington.

BURNSIDE CREATES THREE GRAND DIVISIONS

One of Burnside's first acts upon taking command was to reduce the number of generals reporting directly to the army commander by reorganizing the seven infantry-artillery corps into three grand divisions, in effect making the commanding general of the army an army group commander in today's type of army organization, with three subordinate army (grand division) commanders, each of whom was given direct control of a wing composed of two infantry corps, each corps consisting of three infantry divisions and organic artillery, with at least one cavalry brigade attached.

In naming Sumner, Hooker, and Franklin as his three chief lieutenants for the campaign upon which the Army of the Potomac was about to embark under its new general, Burnside had seemingly accepted the judgment of his predecessor McClellan. Sumner and Franklin had each commanded wings, as he himself had, during the recent Antietam campaign. Hooker, commander of the First Corps at Sharpsburg, was moved up a peg doubtless because he had by that time earned quite a reputation as an aggressive division and corps commander in the Peninsular Campaign, the battles before Richmond, Second Manassas, South Mountain, and finally Antietam, where he was severely wounded and subsequently on convalescent leave from September 18 to November 10, when he rejoined the command.

Major General Edwin Vose Sumner was the only one of the three who had not attended the United States Military Academy. A native of Boston, he entered the Army in 1819, in the infantry, later served in the cavalry during the Indian Wars in Kansas, and was a veteran of the Mexican War. By Civil War standards he was an old man at the start of the war and despite his brave spirit clearly should never have been retained in an active combat role in competition with division and corps commanders who were his juniors by many years, even by decades. Sumner was a loyal and devoted officer, however, a gentleman of the old school, who lacked neither character nor courage, and his superiors probably did not have the heart to shelve the old soldier.

Major General William B. Franklin graduated from West Point in 1843, was assigned to the Engineer Corps, saw action as a brigade commander in

First Manassas, as division commander and later commander of the Sixth Corps in the Peninsula, at South Mountain and Antietam. In the latter fight his corps, which had been stymied watching McLaws' Confederate Division opposite Harpers Ferry, was not recalled to Antietam until the major battle on the Federal right was over. McClellan, having directed Burnside to take up the fight on the left, had held Franklin's and Porter's corps in reserve for a projected later drive through Lee's center. This final punch never materialized, however, because Burnside's protracted delaying in getting underway permitted A. P. Hill to come up from Harpers Ferry to save the Confederates from what should have been a stinging defeat.

There is nothing in the record to suggest that either Franklin or Sumner was more than an average field commander. Neither of them had achieved distinction in the early part of the war and it will be seen later that Franklin in particular failed to make the most of his big opportunity at the Battle of Fredericksburg. Following that engagement he was put in cold storage for a period of six months and then transferred to the less important Department of the Gulf where he served until the end of the war.

The reshuffle resulted in the formation of grand divisions as follows:

Right Grand Division

Major General Edwin V. Sumner, Commanding

Second Army Corps, under Major General Darius N. Couch, composed of three divisions commanded by Brigadier Generals Hancock, Howard, and French.

Ninth Army Corps, under Brigadier General Orlando B. Willcox, composed of three divisions commanded by Brigadier Generals Burns, Sturgis, and Getty.

Attached cavalry division commanded by Brigadier General Alfred Pleasonton.

Center Grand Division

Major General Joseph Hooker, Commanding

Third Corps, under Brigadier General George Stoneman, composed of three divisions commanded by Brigadier Generals Birney, Sickles, and Whipple.

Fifth Corps, under Brigadier General Daniel Butterfield, composed of three divisions commanded by Brigadier Generals Griffin, Sykes, and Humphreys.

Attached cavalry brigade commanded by Brigadier General William A. Averell.

Left Grand Division

Major General William B. Franklin, Commanding

First Corps, under Major General John F. Reynolds, composed of three divisions commanded by Brigadier Generals Doubleday, Gibbon, and Meade.

Sixth Corps, under Major General William F. Smith, composed of three divisions commanded by Brigadier Generals Brooks, Howe, and Newton.

Attached cavalry brigade commanded by Brigadier General George D. Bayard.

The Eleventh Corps, under Brigadier General Franz Sigel, constituted the reserve corps, located first at Centreville, later at Dumfries.

The Twelfth Corps, commanded by Brigadier General Henry W. Slocum, was on detached duty guarding Harpers Ferry.

FULL SPEED AHEAD

Burnside was full of steam and rarin' to go when Halleck's telegram arrived on November 14, putting Washington's stamp of dubious approval on the Fredericksburg adventure. The army staff leapt into action, fortunately without the aid of mimeo graph machines, which would likely have burned out their bearings as the pent-up impatience of the army commander was suddenly released like a coiled spring.

Early on the morning of the following day, November 15, General Edwin V. Sumner, newly appointed commander of the Right Grand Division, took off from Warrenton like a sprinter at the bark of the starter's gun. In a surprisingly rapid march of two and one-half days his wing, which constituted almost one-third of the Army of the Potomac, covered the forty miles to Falmouth and took a position from which they could have gobbled up Fredericksburg in a matter of hours.

The march to Falmouth, averaging more than fifteen miles per day, would be considered acceptable by World War I standards, though not in World War II when they were trained to march twenty-five miles per day. For the Army of the Potomac, accustomed to McClellan's five or six miles a day, it was unheard of. But it had the happy result that the North took heart, the President breathed a sigh of relief, and the men and officers themselves no doubt held their heads higher with that warm feeling of achievement that comes from doing more than anyone, including themselves, believed possible.

Lee was for a moment caught flat-footed. For once his excellent intelligence system had failed to keep up with the vital "enemy information," and Sumner's troops reached Falmouth a good twenty-four hours before Lee was even certain of the direction in which Burnside's army was headed. On this occasion the much maligned Federal cavalry succeeded admirably in screening the march of Burnside's army down the Warrenton pike along the Rappahannock, and it was not until the advance elements of Sumner's grand division had actually reached Falmouth on November 17 that Lee became convinced of Burnside's intentions. By that date the rest of the Union army was on the march, reaching the Fredericksburg area November 19-20.

Longstreet was immediately directed to start one division in the direction of Fredericksburg, his other two divisions and the corps artillery to follow shortly.

JACKSON PREFERS THE VALLEY

Jackson's reluctance to leave the Shenandoah Valley, on the theory that his threat to Washington and to the flank and rear of the Union army would yield greater fruits than an immediate consolidation with Longstreet, persuaded Lee to allow him that discretion for the time being. One may be permitted in passing to wonder whether Jackson's earlier independent successes in the Valley and his rugged individualism may not have contributed something to his thinking in this instance, when he persuaded Lee to let him remain where he was, to play the game in his own inimitable way.

For a long period of time Jackson had been successful in pinning down enemy troops of as many as three and four times his strength, and in keeping the North off balance and in mental turmoil by his frequent maneuvering. But this time Lincoln was doing his own strategic thinking and was disposed to discount the Jackson threat.

Even after Lee had put Longstreet's corps into motion, he delayed sending for Jackson, influenced somewhat by later and inaccurate, information that it was only Sumner's grand division which had marched to Falmouth. However it soon became apparent that Burnside's whole army was marching eastward, so on November 19 Lee sent word to Jackson to join him at Fredericksburg. Lee himself mounted and commenced his own journey for the same destination on the 20th, the same day that Jackson's corps took off on its last long march through the familiar and beloved Shenandoah Valley, the scene of so many of his early triumphs, and which would never see him again.

Eight days of road marching brought the Confederate Second Corps on November 27 to Orange Court House by way of Strasburg and New Market, a distance of 120 miles, which still left 36 miles to travel before they would reach Fredericks burg. The Army of the Potomac had for some time been fully concentrated across the river from Fredericksburg, impatiently and strangely marking time for a solid week. This in turn led Lee to take his time in the hope that delay in effecting a junction of his two corps might lead Burnside to launch an attack that would afford the canny Southerner an opportunity to repeat the tactics which he had successfully demonstrated against Pope.

Finally, however, after allowing Jackson's weary men a much appreciated three days' rest, Lee became disturbed lest the next storm should make the roads a difficult obstacle for Jackson's corps. Accordingly Jackson on November 29 was ordered to continue the march, cover the remaining thirty-six miles, and take position on Longstreet's right below Fredericksburg.

CHAPTER 16

Interlude on the Rappahannock

IT IS NOT clear whether Burnside had entirely ruled out in advance the crossing by the fords of Sumner's division to occupy Fredericksburg and establish a bridgehead for the subsequent passage by pontoons of the rest of the army with their trains. But there was finally no doubt in his own mind that his plan of campaign contemplated a rapid march to Falmouth and an equally prompt crossing of the Rappahannock *on pontoon bridges,* to be followed by the march on Richmond. There is likewise some evidence to indicate that he considered sending a portion of his cavalry south of the river to approach Fredericksburg from the west for the purpose of seizing the heights of the town to facilitate the crossing of the main army. The details of the program following the occupation of Fredericksburg were to be spelled out later. But Burnside was clear as to the first two steps, and was under the distinct impression that he had out lined his pontoon requirements explicitly in his conference with Halleck at Warrenton on November 12, and that Halleck understood the importance of having the bridging equipment shipped immediately to Falmouth so that it would arrive concurrently with the Army of the Potomac and be available for expeditious employment.

Sumner's grand division reached Falmouth November 17. Two days later, on November 19, Burnside himself arrived with the main body of the Union army and looked around for his pontoons, which had not arrived. As soon as Sumner had brought up his troops and examined the fords above Fredericks burg, where his men had observed stray cattle crossing the river without difficulty, he urged Burnside to let him cross at once, assuring him that he could take the town with little effort, which was obviously true at that time when the Confederates were only strong enough to offer token resistance. Burnside however had his mind fixed on crossing by pontoons, was fearful of risking the danger of threatening rains which could cause a rapid rise in the river and perhaps split his army in two, and seemed confident that the quick arrival of the pontoons would enable him to carry out his plan without a hitch.

Had Burnside displayed the mental flexibility which history associates with great military commanders, there is little doubt that he would have exploited the opportunity afforded him by the time, space, and weather factors and safely crossed the entire army, less trains, before the subsequent rains made the fords temporarily impassable for foot troops. In this case the delay in the arrival of the pontoons would merely have caused some supply inconveniences for a matter of days and the engineers could have placed the bridges without the interference from the Confederates which, made their task so difficult and costly later on.

Poor Burnside! The new general had gotten off to a flying start, and his army had established a speed record for the Federals in a march of which Stonewall Jackson need not have been ashamed. Lee had been given a bit of a surprise, and everything looked promising for the Union forces, with Longstreet nowhere in sight and Jackson still in the Valley.

THE LOST OPPORTUNITY

Longstreet has recorded the fact that "when word was received, about the 18th or 19th of November, that Sumner with more than 30,000 men was moving towards Fredericksburg," two of his (Longstreet's) divisions, ordered flown to meet him, "made a forced march and arrived on the hills around Fredericksburg about three o'clock on the afternoon of the 21st." Indisputable evidence, indeed, from the commander of the leading Confederate contingent to reach Fredericksburg, that Burn side had been given three whole days during which Sumner's divisions could with but little interference have occupied the Fredericksburg heights and established such a strong, fortified bridgehead that the story of the Battle of Fredericksburg might never have been written. But Burnside passed up that opportunity and thus lost the first round in the battle of wits between Lee and himself.

Where were the pontoons? What to do? Burnside was a good soldier, not overly burdened with brains, but a reasonably deter mined character when things went along as planned. His mind had been made up to cross the river on pontoons and in no other way, so—no pontoons, no crossing. Sumner's idea of going would have separated the troops from their wagon trains, which to Burnside was unthinkable. Besides, it soon started to rain, which doubtless comforted Burnside with the thought that he had been right in refusing Sumner's earlier request for permission to ford the river.

In the last analysis, however, and even after charging Halleck with the responsibility for the early delay due to lack of administrative energy, and the resultant further delay because of rain and mud and the shift from road to water-borne travel for the pontoons, the cold fact stands out that sufficient bridge equipment did actually reach Burnside on the morning of November 24. Yet it was not until December 11, two and one-half weeks later, that the move to lay the bridges was initiated. And for that no one can be blamed but Burnside himself.

Had the pontoons reached Falmouth when Burnside had every right to expect them, the Army of the Potomac would have faced Lee south and west of Fredericksburg with both flanks resting securely on the Rappahannock River above and below the town, and with little fear for supply and communications lines, despite the fact of having a river at its back. Burnside ·outnumbered Lee by almost 40,000 men, not counting Sigel's reserve corps, Slocum's Twelfth Corps at Harpers Ferry, or additional reinforcements from Washington upon which the Union general could call if the situation should warrant. Longstreet with about 41,000 men, approaching Fredericksburg from Culpeper, would have encountered 120,000 Federals at a time when Jackson was still 150 miles away, and even Lee would hardly have attacked under such circumstances.

But it didn't happen that way, because the pontoons had not arrived, Burnside was still cooling his heels at Falmouth, and Longstreet's corps was able to move calmly and without opposition into a strong defensive position on the heights of Fredericksburg, to the obvious relief of the townspeople who had understandably become rather nervous as they waited helplessly for something to happen.

Sumner Demands that Fredericksburg Surrender

Shortly before Longstreet's troops arrived on the afternoon of November 21, Sumner sent an officer across the Rappahannock by boat under a flag of truce from Stafford Heights, which looked down on Fredericksburg from the opposite side of the river. The letter, addressed to the mayor and common council, demanded the surrender of the town on the grounds that Confederate troops had fired on his men from the streets of the town and that its mills were manufacturing supplies for the armed forces of the Confederacy. The ultimatum stated further that if the demand was not met by 5 o'clock that same after noon, sixteen hours' grace would be allowed for the removal of women and children, sick and aged, after which the town would be shelled as a preliminary to occupation by the Union forces.

It may be doubted, in view of Burnside's refusal to allow Sumner to use the fords, that the plan would have been carried out, particularly since the Confederates moved in before the deadline was reached. In any case Longstreet on his arrival was shown the letter from Sumner and advised the mayor to send a reply to the effect that the Confederates did not propose to make Fredericksburg a base of military operations and there would therefore be no justification for the Federals to shell the town. The result of the exchange of greetings was that the shelling did not then occur, possibly because the arrival of Longstreet's corps and the non-arrival of the pontoons had put an entirely new face on the tactical situation. Sumner at that time gave the mayor no positive assurance that the town would not be shelled, however, so on that night Lee advised the townspeople to evacuate their homes. On the 22nd the sad exodus of women, children, and old men started. Even the Federals were touched by the sight, to such an extent that Sumner sent word to Longstreet that the town would not be shelled so long as it remained militarily inactive.

The second favorable opportunity to take Fredericksburg before Lee's arrival thus went the way of the first. Now Burnside really was in hot water, with his schedule shot to pieces, an unfordable river yet to cross, nothing in sight to use for by adding strength both to his defensive position and to the troops to man it.

If the result had not proved so tragic, the delayed arrival of the vital pontoons would have qualified as a comedy of errors. Had Halleck merely been careless or slow in carrying out his part of the plan, or if someone down the line misunderstood or was dilatory in carrying out his instructions, it would not have been the first or only time in the history of warfare. If on the other hand Halleck was annoyed by Burnside's unwillingness to be guided by his advice, an annoyance intensified by the further fact that Lincoln had overruled Halleck and approved Burnside's plan, and Halleck consciously allowed the transfer of the pontoons to be stalled for more than a week, then indeed his actions deserved the strictest kind of censure.

General Oliver O. Howard, one of Sumner's division commanders, termed the story of the moving of the bridge trains to Falmouth "a strange one." "It seems to indicate," he wrote, "that Halleck himself was playing a part, possibly hoping to get Burnside well into winter quarters without anybody being particularly to blame. As it required thirteen days to do a piece of work which could easily have been done in three days, it would be a marvelous stretch of charity to impute it to mere bungling."

BURNSIDE MARKS TIME

Nearly two weeks had passed since Lincoln's telegram to Burnside had unleashed the new army commander. The Army of the Potomac, having completed an impressive march and neatly accomplished a change of base without the fanfare or extravagant claims to unusual achievement that McClellan would inevitably have trumpeted, had for the second of those two weeks been idly passing the time doing little but fight off the cold in its camps immediately across the Rappahannock from Fredericksburg.

The winter of 1862-63 failed to measure up to the record breaking American winter of 1740, when most of the Atlantic coast harbors were frozen solid, or even the less severe Revolutionary War year of 1780 when oxen were used to haul cannon across Long Island Sound to the mainland, and Chesapeake Bay froze solid at Annapolis.* Just the same, the weather at Fredericksburg in December 1862, if not notable for unusual severity, was rugged enough for those Confederates whose shoes and overcoats, if any, required considerable imagination on the part of their unfortunate wearers to rate them as adequate against the wintry blasts, the snows, and the ice-covered ground.

Burnside's soldiers on the other hand were comfortably supplied and warmly clad, thanks partly to an energetic Quartermaster General, and to an equally capable railroader general by the name of Haupt, who kept the railroads of the North in repair and running all through the war. Haupt was the kind of man who got things done and had little time for the lazy or incompetent.

Burnside's reputation for looking after the welfare of his men when he was a division and corps commander had been well established. He was noted for his habit of snooping around company messes and enlisted men's quarters, checking on his subordinates to make certain his men were being properly cared for. His elevation to the post of army commander stopped all that because he had his hands full with other duties for the short period of time that he retained the top position, virtually all of it in movement, contact with the enemy, or actual combat. After the Battle of Fredericksburg, during the winter of 1862-63, a notorious food shortage occurred in the Army of the Potomac, with disastrous effect on a morale that was already weakened by the depressing defeat and unnecessarily heavy casualties. Burnside as the Commanding General was naturally and rightly held responsible, and there were many who, convinced from the start that he was out of his depth as an army commander, were not surprised at the outcome.

It is recorded that time hung heavy on Confederate hands, after they had taken such steps as Lee directed to strengthen their defenses on the high ground west and south of Fredericksburg. So the soldiers, many of whom were teenagers, understandably helped to keep themselves healthy by engaging in snowball fights and similar youthful diversions as they waited for the Union general across the river to break the monotony of the long period of watchful waiting.

He Who Hesitates—!

The thoughts that passed through the active mind of amateur strategist Abraham Lincoln during this trying period of waiting have not been recorded, but they are not difficult to imagine. Burnside was meticulous in reporting to Halleck from day to day, and it must be presumed that his reports were passed along for the President to read. But action was at a standstill, vital time was slipping away, and finally, unable to stand the suspense any longer, Lincoln wired Burnside an invitation to meet him at Aquia Creek at dark on the evening of November 26 in these under-standing but rather wistful words: ". . . could you, without inconvenience, meet me and pass an hour or two with me?"

The record is silent as to what passed between the two men at the Aquia Creek meeting or at the subsequent conference two days later, when Burnside journeyed to Washington to continue the discussion. Jackson's corps had not yet reached Fredericksburg, but the other half of Lee's army was strongly posted on the high ground at the western edge of the town. It is reasonable to assume that the new situation facing Burnside was analyzed from every angle with a view to developing a revised plan that might promise success as soon as the bridges could be placed.

There was no question as to Union preponderance of manpower, and for a refreshing change from McClellan, Burnside did not besiege the authorities at Washington with calls for reinforcements. The stra-tegic position of the Union army, now directly covering Washington, did result in releasing 15,000 of the large body of troops stationed in the capital for transfer to Burnside's command, giving him a combat strength of more than 120,000 men. Burnside, aware of his over-whelming superiority, had initially held Slocum's Twelfth Corps at Harpers Ferry and Sigel's Eleventh at Centreville but on December 9 he ordered both corps, totaling over 26,000 men, to Dumfries, twenty miles north of Fredericksburg, as army reserve. There was such a thing as over congestion of an area, and it was at this late date not at all certain that a formidable river crossing against a strongly posted veteran army such as Lee's would be the comparatively simple operation that it had promised to be only a few days earlier.

One of the considered plans that seemed to hold promise was to move a strong maneuvering force to a point opposite Port Royal, about seventeen miles south on the Rappahannock, throw one or more of the pontoon bridges across and attack upstream, on the south side of the river, concurrently with the crossing of the main body in the vicinity of

Fredericksburg. This scheme would have the advantage of disrupting Lee's line of communication to Richmond and at the same time serve as the flanking left prong of a pincers movement against the Confederate position.

As the Rappahannock flows seaward below Fredericksburg it gradually widens and, with its wooded banks, presents from Port Royal south a formidable obstacle to an army wishing to cross either there or below. At Port Royal which was first established in 1744 and subsequently developed into one of the main shipping points on the river, the Rappahannock is over half a mile wide and it is doubtful that Burnside had sufficient excess pontoon equipment to throw even a single bridge across at that point at the same time that he would be effecting a crossing at Fredericksburg. It may even be doubted that he had taken steps to reconnoiter that far south, for he certainly failed to scout D. H. Hill's Confederate Division at Port Royal. Seemingly he was content to rely on the long distance vision of his balloon observers.

Even if Burnside had decided to attempt a crossing at Port Royal, Hill's Division, concealed in the dense woods that fringed the river on the Port Royal side (now a part of the A. P. Hill Military Reservation), could easily have nullified all his efforts by concentrating merely a portion of its infantry and artillery firepower on the narrow column of Federal troops crossing the pontoon bridge. It may be questioned, indeed, that the engineers could have succeeded in laying the bridge.

In addition to its importance as a shipping point on the navigable Rappahannock, Port Royal and the small village of Port Conway on the opposite bank had their moments in history. The latter was the birthplace of James Madison, fourth President of the United States. It was there, too, that Lincoln's assassin, John Wilkes Booth, crossed the river on April 24, 1865, as he fled from the pursuing Union soldiers, across the river and into the Garrett barn, a few miles above Port Royal, where two days later he was killed while resisting arrest.

Confederate Troop Dispositions

As December was ushered in and the troop development phase of the Fredericksburg campaign came to an end with the arrival on the field of

Jackson's corps from the Shenandoah Valley, Lee's army at first occupied a widely extended, unconnected curving line with its left resting on the south bank of the Rappahannock opposite Falmouth and its right at Port Royal, twenty miles downstream. Although the official returns of early December showed 91,760 present for duty at Fredericksburg, the cavalry brigades of Wade Hampton and W. P. Jones were on detached missions so it is doubtful if Lee had more than 88,000 combat effectives on the field.

Longstreet's corps was posted along the range of hills west of Fredericksburg and extending in a southerly direction paralleling the Rappahannock, from a point opposite Falmouth almost to Massaponax Creek. The depth of the positions occupied by his troops varied in accordance with the natural strength or weakness of the terrain features along the line of defense. While awaiting the arrival of Jackson's corps, Lee stretched Longstreet's divisions to Hamilton's Crossing where Lee set up his own headquarters for the time being. Ranged in order from left to right of the position were the divisions of R.H. Anderson, Lafayette McLaws—with Robert Ransom in direct support—George E. Pickett, and John B. Hood. The defensive strength of the occupied hills in Longstreet's sector was such that his corps occupied a frontage of more than six miles, with but little depth.

CHARACTER OF THE BATTLEFIELD

In front of Longstreet's sector was the upper end of a broken plain which, between the Confederate position and the river, widened out from about 600 yards opposite Falmouth to two miles in the Deep Run area, and then narrowed to a mile at the lower end.

The range of heights below Fredericksburg is broken by ravines and small streams, two of which—Hazel Run and Deep Run—are definite obstacles in the path of a deployed, advancing body of troops—especially if covered by enemy rifle or artillery fire. In December 1862 both streams flowed through ravines that were thirty feet deep and were hidden by woods and dense undergrowth.

Hazel Run in particular was an important tactical feature that was to influence strongly the outcome of the Federal attack against Marye's Hill. Twenty feet in width at the point where it is crossed by the Telegraph Road, it was more of a psychological and physical obstacle in the dead of winter than would have been the case in warm weather, when the effects of a thorough soaking could be accepted by the soldiers with greater equanimity.

The hill slopes of the Confederate position were covered with woods that afforded the occupying troops exceptional ad vantages of observation. The two hills at the north end, Taylor's and Marye's, are together known as Marye's Heights, which at its lower extremity is cut by Hazel Run. Marye's Hill rises steeply and abruptly from the flat ground below, a mental as well as physical hazard for the boldest attacker. The most prominent features of the whole ridge are known as Stansbury's Hill, Cemetery Hill, Telegraph (Lee's) Hill, and Prospect Hill. All these hills are from forty to fifty feet above the lower level.

The town of Fredericksburg at the time of the battle extended from the river bank perhaps a quarter of a mile in the direction of Marye's Heights. The generally open terrain between the western limits of the town and the strong Confederate defensive position on the heights would appear to offer room for maneuver, were it not for the canal that bisected the area and the wide, neighboring drainage ditch that carried off the waste water from the canal.

In 1862 there was a dam several miles above Fredericksburg, where the canal originated. The canal is still very much in evidence, with a full, rapid flow of water. The diversion of water through the canal, together with the rapids below the dam and a fine collection of big rocks in the river bed, combined to discourage troop crossings of the river or the canal, which by itself was destined to be a serious handicap to the maneuver of the Union divisions.

Three main roads and several minor ones led from the streets of Fredericksburg across the battlefield-to-be. The Plank Road, of later Chancellorsville fame, crossed the ditch over a wooden bridge in front of Marye's Heights, and, ascending the ridge, kept on to Chancellorsville and Orange Court House. The Telegraph Road crossed Hazel Run and, passing around the base of Marye's Hill, headed southward to Richmond. At the foot of Marye's Hill it became a sunken road, with a stone wall on either side, which continued for over 500 yards and was destined to prove the major stumbling block to Federal success.

The old Richmond stage road and the main railroad to Richmond ran south between the river and the foothills to the west. The bridges by which these two crossed Deep Run had been either destroyed or damaged, as had those by which the Plank and Telegraph Roads crossed the ditch obstacle in front of Marye's Heights. The Confederates apparently had no intention of making Burnside's task any easier.

Disposition of Jackson's Divisions

Although Lee had definitely decided to fight on the Rappahannock, if and when Burnside should advance, rather than fall back to the North Anna, he was uncertain where the Union army would cross. He rather expected the perfectly natural move of a flank action by a crossing either above or below Fredericksburg. The latter now seemed more logical, since Burnside had already passed up the opportunity to cross above Fredericksburg when his army marched down from Warrenton. Port Royal, seventeen miles downriver in a direct line from Fredericksburg, and that much closer to Richmond, was very much on Lee's mind. When Jackson came up in advance of his column he was directed to spread his troops over a wide area, with D. H. Hill's Division at Port Royal, Early's (Ewell's) at Skinker's Neck, twelve miles southeast of Fredericksburg, A. P. Hill's at Yerby's house, three miles to the right rear of Longstreet's right flank, and Taliaferro's at Guiney's Station, four miles further to the south on the line of the Richmond-Fredericksburg Railroad. Stuart's four cavalry brigades were posted to move wherever they might be useful. D. H. Hill's Division reached Port Royal just in time to encounter and drive back several Federal gunboats steaming up the river. Jackson had no liking for the position at Fredericksburg, insisting that it could easily be outflanked by the use of the fords above the town. He was in favor of the North Anna position, but Lee, while of the same opinion, had yielded to Jefferson Davis and that was the way it had to be despite Jackson's strong objections.

Burnside's Tentative Plan

A few days after the Union army had been fully concentrated near Falmouth, Burnside called his generals together, communicated to them his intention of crossing a maneuvering force in the vicinity of Skinker's Neck, and asked for comment. True to form, Hooker was the only one who took issue with what was presented to them as a decision, stating that it was preposterous to talk about crossing the Rappahannock in the face of Lee's army.

This was the same Hooker who only a short time before had urged Burnside to let him take his Center Grand Division across the Rappahannock on an independent drive in the direction of Bowling Green, presumably to the glory of Joe Hooker, whose ambitious soul caused him so to ignore the hierarchy of command that he sent a direct communication to Secretary of War Stanton inquiring whether rations could be made available to his command at Port Royal within three days. Burnside's disapproval of Hooker's request on the ground that the move would be premature was undoubtedly registered without knowledge of Hooker's irregular, if not downright insubordinate letter to Stanton. One wonders how Burnside would have reacted had he been in possession of all the facts. In any event, he ignored the objection, stating that his mind was made up and the proper orders would issue in due course.

A few days after that conference, Major General William F. Smith, commanding the Sixth Corps of Franklin's Left Grand Division, accompanied Burnside on a short ride along Stafford Heights immediately below Fredericksburg, on the Federal side of the river. On that occasion Burnside is reported by Smith to have told him that his earlier plans had been changed and the crossing would be effected much closer to Fredericksburg than Skinker's Neck. Smith was admonished to keep the information strictly to himself. He volunteered the opinion that Burnside would have no difficulty in crossing at the upper point but his troubles would begin after he was across, because of the range of hills, about a mile back from the river, presumably occupied by the enemy. Burnside's over-confident reply was that he knew where Lee's forces were and expected to surprise them and occupy the hills before Lee could bring anything serious to bear against him.

Burnside's thinking at that stage seems to have been based on the fact that Lee was widely dispersed and could be outwitted by a rapidly executed surprise crossing that would drive a wedge between his two wings, forcing him to withdraw from Fredericksburg in order to consolidate the wings and remove the threat to Richmond. There were however at least two major flaws in that estimate; first, there could be no surprise in laying pontoons and crossing a large body of troops; second, Lee was a past master of the art of rapidly concentrating widely separated elements of his army at the point of impact at the psychological moment, as at First and Second Bull Run, and Antietam. Burnside should have known this and given the possibility due weight.

The Commanding General of the Army of the Potomac had by this time painted himself into a corner where there was no visible door. The longer he waited the worse his situation became; none of his tentative plans seemed to meet with wholehearted approval from his grand division and corps commanders. The truth of Lincoln's remark that the Fredericksburg move could succeed only if the army moved fast had been con firmed. Now that Lee's army was all present or accounted for, there was a foreboding among Burnside's officers and even many of the enlisted men that the forthcoming attack already had two strikes against it. The third strike would be imposed principally through the incapacity and ineptitude of a confused army commander who just couldn't make up his mind either what to do or how to do it. Confidence in Burnside had reached an understandably low ebb!

CHAPTER 17

The Curtain Rises at Fredericksburg

THE LENGTHY prelude to open combat at Fredericksburg, which was extended well over a week after both armies were fully assembled and facing each other across the Rappahannock, was reminiscent of the bear and the bees; the massive Federal army of 120,000 men in the role of the bear and the relatively smaller Confederate army of 90,000 defending the hive. The former, wanting badly to get at the honey, had been stung so many times that it was somewhat wary of stirring up the bees, and was taking no chances on disturbing them without making certain that the first blow of its massive paw would be a lethal one.

THE UNION ARMY PREPARES TO CROSS THE RIVER

Lee was quite aware of the fact that he could not prevent the Union army from crossing the Rappahannock because Stafford Heights, which confronted Fredericksburg from the opposite shore, dominated both the town and the plain below. Conversely the Federal guns could not, without displacing forward, reach Marye's Heights and the ridges to the south where the Confederates planned to make their main defense.

General Hunt, able Chief of Artillery of the Army of the Potomac, had skillfully placed 147 of his 312 guns at appropriate intervals along Stafford Heights, from which they could individually and collectively deliver their fire on the just and unjust alike, in the unfortunate event that any of the former civilian inhabitants of Fredericksburg should choose to remain in or return to their homes after Lee had advised them to evacuate.

McLaw's Division of Longstreet's corps had upon its arrival on November 25 been ordered to occupy Fredericksburg with part of the command. Accordingly Barksdale's Mississippi Brigade of 1600 men was assigned the mission of occupying Fredericksburg and picketing the river bank with detachments, under instructions to dig rifle pits and loop-hole the houses along the river from which the men could with relative impunity pick off the engineers of the Union army when they should finally reach the point of laying their pontoon bridges.

One evening during the period of watchful waiting, several Union bands, assembled near their end of the railroad bridge, decided it would be a good idea to keep their instruments in working order by playing a few patriotic airs such as "Hail Columbia" and "The Star Spangled Banner," which they did with great gusto but without eliciting a response from the suspicious Southerners. Finally the bands struck up "Dixie." That broke the ice, figuratively, for there is no record of its having melted the half-inch crust ice that covered the river at the time. There was much cheering and laughter on both sides of the river, but the entertainment proved to an expensive lark for the Federals. General McLaws, whose suspicions were aroused, promptly caused his men to construct even more of the rifle pits from which the Mississippians would shortly create havoc.

HALLECK WITHHOLDS APPROVAL

Burnside meanwhile was feverishly burning the midnight oil at his headquarters in the Phillips house, sending off dispatches to Halleck in Washington in a rather pathetic invitation for some encouragement from the General-in-Chief which might assist the army commander in reaching a decision and perhaps, collaterally, shift some of the responsibility for the attack plan to higher headquarters.

The telegraph wires carried the following message· to Washington on the night of December 9: "All the orders have been issued to the several commanders of grand divisions and heads of departments for an attempt to cross the river on Thursday morning [December 11]. . . . If the General-in-Chief desires it, I will send a minute statement by telegraph in cipher to-morrow morning. The movement is so important that I feel anxious to be fortified by his approval." The next day Halleck made the following pointed reply: "I beg of you not to telegraph details of your plans, nor the times of your intended movements. No secret can be kept which passes through so many hands." Clearly the hopeful general in the field was to receive neither encouragement nor suggestions from topside! Still, a more perceptive or less calculating general-in-chief might at such a moment conceivably have taken a quick rundown to Burnside's headquarters at Fredericksburg at least to talk things over.

THE CROSSING POINTS ARE FINALLY DETERMINED

Burnside's vacillation as to where his army would cross at long last came to an end with his decision to effect crossings simultaneously at three points: at the northern and southern extremities of Fredericksburg for Sumner's right wing, and just below the mouth of Deep Run, a mile or so below the town, for Franklin's left wing. Burnside's message to Halleck December 9 and his decision to cross at and just below Fredericksburg, rather than at Skinker's Neck, meant that his mind was made up that Lee's two corps were widely separated, and that Franklin's grand division could be neatly inserted in the opening as the first step in turning the *left* flank of Jackson's corps. The precise locations and other tactical instructions were determined for army headquarters by the Chief Engineer of the army, a brilliant young lieutenant by the name of Comstock, whose order to his engineers was a model of brevity and conciseness:

> *Two pontoon bridges to be thrown at site of old pontoon bridge, one of them to have approaches for artillery. One pontoon bridge at site of old canal-boat bridge; approaches for artillery.*
>
> *Two pontoon bridges just below mouth of Deep Run, a mile below Fredericksburg; one to have artillery approach.* Major Spaulding to throw three upper ones; Major Magruder to throw the next, and Lieutenant Cross the lowest one.*
>
> *Bridge equipage, now at White Oak Church, to move up and go into park near Phillips' house by dark. At mid night trains to move down within 400 yards of river, and to move down and begin unloading at 2 A.M.*
>
> *If enemy's fire is kept down, bridges to be thrown as soon as boats are unloaded; if too hot, wait till artillery silences it.*

Upper two bridges to be covered by two regiments of infantry; canal-boat bridge by one regiment; two lower bridges by two regiments and a 12-pounder battery.

Corduroy at Skinker's Neck to be laid during to-morrow night; woods to be felled, etc.

As soon as pontoons are on bank of river, all teams to be taken away.

LACK OF CONFIDENCE IN BURNSIDE

A search of the official records fails to reveal a transcript of what transpired at Burnside's conference with his major commanders on December 10, following their receipt of his warning order of late afternoon the preceding day. The preliminary order, dated 5 A.M., December 9, had merely prepared them for an early movement to cross the river, directing that they put their divisions in readiness with cooked rations for three days and sixty rounds of ammunition to be carried by each soldier, and report to army headquarters at the Phillips house next day at noon, when more detailed oral orders would be issued for the movement of the infantry and cavalry.

Without doubt Burnside at the December 10 conference outlined to his grand division commanders initial missions for their commands, but he was silent or at least vague as to precise blueprints for their subsequent actions after crossing to the Fredericksburg side of the river.

Sumner's Right Grand Division was assigned the north zone, including Fredericksburg; Franklin's Left Grand Division was directed to cross on the two lower bridges and operate in the open plain to the south; Hooker's Center Grand Division was designated as army reserve, to remain on the left bank in readiness to throw its weight wherever the developing situation might require.

Burnside's subsequent orders and written memoranda to his grand division commanders for the most part were postmarked at ungodly hours in the early morning, long before daylight, a time of night when man's vitality is supposed to be at its lowest ebb. It has never been suggested that Burnside did not try, only that he lacked the gray matter that an army commander must have to handle a major task that requires top-flight mental capacity, imagination, moral courage, and experience in charting the battle course of a complex army of over 100,000 officers and men. Burnside didn't spare himself, but it is possible that he would have thought his problems through more clearly had he taken the proper amount of sleep, unless indeed he was the sort of character who prefers to work at night and sleep in the daytime.

Be that as it may, Burnside gave his grand division commanders precise instructions as to the actual crossing of the river. Beyond that his orders were indefinite, conditional, and completely devoid of positive, specific attack missions. There seemed to be only a hazy, general picture in his mind which he passed on to them in fragmentary form. At no time was the combat mission of either wing defined specifically so that the corps and division commanders could feel a surge of confidence that the architect at the top had blueprinted the job to be done in such a way that they in turn could embody in their orders a definite task for their divisions, brigades, and regiments.

Generals Sumner, Hooker, and Franklin must have had their earlier misgivings intensified at the December 10 conference, because a new and puzzling Burnside confronted them. All were professional soldiers and had known the army commander socially and officially for a long time. Since his elevation to army command, Burnside's relations with his principal lieutenants had apparently been cordial and understanding. Franklin and Sumner were honorable officers and gentlemen, and, so far as Burnside knew, loyal to his leadership. But there is nothing in the military record of either to suggest that they were exceptionally gifted leaders, or that there was anything like the Damon-Pythias rapport that existed between Lee and Jackson, Lee and Stuart, or even Lee and Longstreet.

BURNSIDE'S BATTLE ORDERS VAGUE AND INDECISIVE
Assuming that the conference of generals was held at noon December 10 as planned, and that the grand division commanders were given some inkling of what was expected of them after they had crossed the river, Burnside required the rest of that day and most of the following night to piece together the mosaic of his forthcoming attack plans in his own mind sufficiently to enable him to convey the makings of a potential attack order to his worried subordinates. But that was as far as the orders went, as disclosed by a careful reading of the predaylight messages of

December 11 to Sumner, Hooker, and Franklin, all of which have the characteristics of postscripts to letters. The timing, it must be noted, was almost simultaneous with the hour when the engineers were scheduled to start laying the bridges.

> *December 11, 1862–4.20 A.M.*
> ### Maj. Gen. E. V. Sumner,
> *Commanding Right Grand Division:*
> *In addition to the verbal orders already given you, I will add the following:*
> *Your first corps, after crossing, should be protected by the town and the banks of the river as much as possible until the second corps is well closed up and in the act of crossing; after which you will move the first corps directly to the front, with a view to taking the heights that command the Plank road and the Telegraph road, supporting it by your other corps as soon as you can get it over the river. General Hooker will immediately follow in your support, and will see that your right flank is not troubled.*
> *General Franklin crosses below, as you are aware, thus protecting your left. The extent of your movement to the front beyond the heights will be indicated during the engagement.*
> *Please inform me if you propose to change your headquarters before the head of your column reaches the river, that I may send you guides for the roads. I send one with this. If you desire further instructions, please send word by the orderly.*
> *I have the honor to be, general, very respectfully, your obedient servant.*

> *December 11, 1862–4.45 A.M.*
> ### Maj. Gen. Joseph Hooker,
> *Commanding Center Grand Division:*
> *General Sumner is ordered, after crossing the river to move immediately to the front, with a view to taking the heights commanding*

the Plank and Telegraph roads. After crossing, you will hold yourself in readiness to support either his column or General Franklin's which crosses below Deep Run, and will. move down the old Richmond road, in the direction of the railroad. Should we be so fortunate as to dislodge the enemy, you will hold. your command in readiness to pursue by the two roads.

My headquarters will be at the Phillips house, where, if you will send an aide at 8 o'clock, guides will be furnished you to lead your column. I will be glad to see you at head quarters before the head of your column reaches the river.

I have the honor to be, general, very respectfully, your obedient servant.

December 11, 1862–5.15 A.M.

Major-General Franklin,

Commanding Left Grand Division:

General Sumner will, after crossing the river, move immediately to the front, with a view to taking the heights which command the Plank and Telegraph roads. I have ordered General Hooker to hold himself in readiness, as soon as he has crossed the river, to support either General Sumner's column or your own. After your command has crossed, you will move down the old Richmond road, in the direction of the railroad, being governed by circumstances as to the extent of your movements. An aide will be sent to you during your movements.

My headquarters will be at the Phillips house.

Observe that Sumner was ordered "after crossing the river, to move immediately to the front, *with a view to taking* the heights commanding the Plank and Telegraph roads."

Hooker was told: "Should we be so fortunate as to dislodge the enemy, you will *hold yourself in readiness* to pursue by the two roads."

And to Franklin: "After your command has crossed, you will move down the old Richmond Road, in the direction of the railroad, being governed by circumstances as to the extent of your movements."

These were march orders, nothing more.

THE BRIDGES ARE LAID UNDER ENEMY FIRE

The engineer troops, thoroughly briefed on their duties, were well organized and efficient, as engineers usually are. Burnside could count on an
excellent performance, despite the half-inch of ice that coated the river
and made the bridge-laying more difficult. The idea was that they would
move into position during the night, prepared to start the actual bridging
as soon as there was enough daylight.

The throwing of the bridges was scheduled to start simultaneously
at the three points selected for the crossings, at daylight December 11;
with luck the job could be finished in a couple of hours, at which time the
grand divisions would be on their way.

At Skinker's Neck the Federals essayed a bit of deceptive strategy
that might have proven effective had the overall program moved along
with reasonable speed. But it did not turn out that way. Down there,
where Early's Confederate Division held forth, and in the general vicinity
of which Burnside erroneously still believed that Jackson's entire corps
was massed, husky and experienced Northern woodsmen were at work
throughout the night cutting down trees by the light of numerous fires
and laying a corduroy road, with a view to persuading the Confederates
across the river that a major crossing at that point was imminent. It was
love's labor lost, of course, because the success of such strategy depended
on quick Federal surprise action at other points while the enemy was still
mentally off balance. Whatever Early's troops may have thought, General
Lee failed to get excited, made no change in his dispositions, and simply
continued his policy of alert, watchful waiting for more positive evidence
of Burnside's intentions.

The preparatory movement into position of the bulky pontoon
equipment on the night of Wednesday, December 10, naturally could
not be carried out in complete silence. During the night the pickets
on the Confederate side of the river became suspicious and reported
preparations underway on the opposite shore. General Lafayette McLaws
of Longstreet's corps, in command of the defense of the Fredericksburg
sector, convinced by 4:30 on the morning of December 11 that the
long-awaited crossing was about to start, ordered the two designated
Confederate guns to fire the prearranged signal. The element of Federal

surprise promptly went up in the smoke from the muzzles of the two guns as the Confederate rank and file seized arms and leaped to their posts, while the prebattle tenseness that every veteran knows descended grimly on the more than 200,000 men facing each other across a few hundred feet of water.

THE SHOOTING STARTS

A thick early morning haze covered the river and the valleys so that visibility was limited to a few yards. Confederate sharpshooters on the edge of town strained their eyes and tensed their trigger fingers as they watched for the pontoniers to come into view through the fog. Finally they appeared and the crackle of musketry rang out, toppling the leading Union engineers into the water and driving the rest back into the protection of the fog. As the haze thinned out and visibility improved, Barksdale's picked men commenced firing at human targets who were not even armed and hadn't the ghost of a chance at that short range of less than a hundred yards. Repeatedly the nervy engineers rushed to the leading pontoons in an effort to extend the bridges, but each time they were driven back. Cover fire from infantry on their own side of the river was ineffectual since the Confederates were sheltered in cellars or rifle pits and presented only fleeting targets that were difficult for the Union soldiers to hit.

The tense situation on the waterfront at Fredericksburg continued until the morning was half spent. Hunt's Federal artillerymen on Stafford Heights were unable to depress their gun muzzles sufficiently to deliver plunging fire on the annoying Confederate sharpshooters, and Lee's artillery along the heights beyond the town withheld its fire to avoid killing Confederates and damaging the homes of their own people. As a result, the bridge layers suffered mainly from the sharpshooters.

At 10 o'clock the Federal artillery opened with a terrific bombardment in the hope of driving out the annoying Mississippi contingent that was so successfully blocking all attempts to get the bridges laid at the three selected crossing points opposite Fredericksburg. Soon houses were burning fiercely and the resulting smoke, added to the still present fog, created a Dante's inferno that made the town a decidedly undesirable place in which to remain. A newspaper correspondent who was present wrote that "the earth shook beneath the terrific explosions of the shells, which went howling over the river, crashing into the houses, battering down walls, splintering doors, ripping up floors. Sixty solid shot and shells a minute were thrown 'till 9,000 were fired." The bombardment failed however to dampen the spirits of Barksdale's indomitable sharpshooters, for as soon as the guns ceased firing, the musketeers popped out of their holes and resumed their deadly work.

VOLUNTEERS CROSS IN BOATS

General Hunt, a realist as well as a keen artillerist, let it be known finally that his artillery simply couldn't do the job. He suggested that the only solution seemed to be to call for volunteers to ferry across a couple of regiments in the pontoons by rowing, if the bridges were ever to be completed. The nearest candidates were those infantry outfits which had been attempting from the left bank to cover the bridge layers by firing on the Confederate sharpshooters. At the upper bridge the 7th Michigan, 19th Massachusetts, and 20th Massachusetts accepted the challenge and the two first named regiments made their preparations. At the center bridge it was the 89th New York that volunteered.

The first party to cross, about sixty men from the 7th Michigan, jumped into pontoons and paddled rapidly across the river, with ample intervals between boats to minimize casualties. The plan worked beautifully, with a loss of but one man killed and several wounded. Quickly outflanking the Confederates in a rush, they captured a sizable batch of prisoners and established a bridgehead. The rest of the volunteers rowed quickly to the Fredericksburg side while Hunt's artillery laid down what would be known in World War I as a box barrage—a curtain of artillery fire in a protective arc that enabled the two regiments to get across without further loss and enlarge the bridgehead so the engineers could finish their job. This was accomplished in a short time without further interference from the Confederates. The 20th Massachusetts followed the other regiments in the boats, through a misunderstanding of orders which contemplated that they would be the first to cross on the finished bridges. Similar results were accomplished by the New York regiment at the lower bridge.

Even then General Barksdale was not ready to yield Fredericksburg. Bitter street fighting continued through the few remaining hours of daylight on Thursday, December 11, as the Federal infantry fanned out from their bridgeheads and proceeded to clear the area of Confederates. It was not until 7:00 P.M., after darkness had fallen, that Barksdale concluded his mission had been accomplished, and his men had done all that could reasonably be expected of them. This is something of an understatement in face of the fact that 1,600 Confederates had stalled the entire Army of the Potomac for a full day and quite possibly ruined the chances for a Union victory which would have been achieved under more able leadership and more effective coordination of effort.

Couch's Second Corps was to be the first across, followed by Willcox's Ninth Corps, on the upper bridges. Because of Barksdale's bulldog tenacity, only Howard's division and Hawkins' brigade of the Ninth Corps crossed on the 11th, bivouacking for the night in the streets of the town. The other five divisions of Sumner's Right Grand Division marched over on the morning of December 12.

THE CROSSING BELOW FREDERICKSBURG

The spirited and successful Confederate delaying tactics at the three upper bridges were not to be duplicated at the three lower bridges at the mouth of Deep Run, where Franklin's Left Grand Division, composed of Reynold's First and Smith's Sixth Corps, three divisions each, were directed to cross. Lee had expected a crossing further south, when he placed Early's Division at Skinker's Neck and D. H. Hill's at Port Royal. To that limited extent Burnside sprang a mild surprise on his opponent, for the lower bridges were thrown with negligible interference from a few Confederate pickets, who were quickly disposed of, and two bridges were completed by 11:00 A.M., December 11. The third bridge was laid that night.

Franklin appears to have been instructed to synchronize his crossing with that of Sumner's at Fredericksburg, a fact which should be closely scrutinized, for thereby hangs a tale. There was nothing, absolutely nothing, to prevent Franklin from quickly passing over a couple of divisions or even his whole force, the mere presence of which on the Fredericksburg side would have caused Barksdale to evacuate Fredericksburg at least a half-day earlier than he actually did. The lower bridges were only a mile or so below the town, and it would have been a simple matter for Franklin to clear the waterfront to the north in short order so that the coordinated development of both grand divisions could proceed concurrently as Burnside had planned.

An interesting parallel to the opportunity which opened to Burnside on this occasion is found in the historic affair of the Remagen Bridge over the Rhine River in World War II. The difference was that General Eisenhower thought fast in 1945 whereas Burnside's mind was turning over slowly in 1862. Such fleeting opportunities occasionally occur in war; in most cases no one ever hears about them unless they are skillfully exploited or miserably bungled. Burnside's failure to take advantage of his opening reflected the agonizingly slow mental processes which he exhibited after he first sat down at his headquarters in the Phillips house. There were plenty of horses available, but Burnside's sole visit to his grand division commanders, after the army had been committed, occurred during the night of December 12–13, some time after the river crossing operations had commenced.

One wonders indeed why several regiments were not rowed over under cover of darkness the preceding night to seize bridge approaches and facilitate the rapid laying of all six bridges at daylight rather than be forced to perform the task the hard way the next afternoon. If Burnside really expected to employ the principle of surprise in his Fredericksburg adventure, he went about it in a strange way, with the unfortunate result that his own grand division commanders, not the enemy, were the ones upon whom most of the surprise was inflicted.

The lower bridges were not used until 4:00 P.M., when the leading brigade of Franklin's Sixth Corps trudged across, followed by several other brigades, only to receive countermanding orders to retrace their steps because the three upper bridges had been delayed. The result was that all the troops retraced bridgehead to cover the crossing of the entire grand division the next day, December 12.

The ponderous machinery of the Army of the Potomac badly needed oiling, plus some other things which commander Burn side failed to provide simply because it wasn't in him. One of the most important was the ability to make clean cut decisions and issue understandable directives for their execution, leaving some discretion to subordinate commanders so that they would be granted at least a modicum of flexibility in carrying out their assigned missions.

Hamilton's Crossing was one of two key positions at the Battle of Fredericksburg. The other was the stone wall along the sunken road at the foot of Marye's Heights.

The tactical significance of Captain Hamilton's landmark lay in the fact that it was the southern terminal of the seven-milelong range of hills whose northern end rested on the Rappahannock River west of Falmouth. As its name implies, it was contiguous to the road fork by which the Mine Road from the west, close by the nose of the ridge, joined the new military road and another road which led directly from the south, across the railroad to the Fredericksburg-Bowling Green-Richmond Pike that parallels the course of the Rappahannock midway between Hamilton's Crossing and the river. The Richmond, Fredericksburg and Potomac Railroad, traveling the eastern base of the ridge, paralleled the Richmond Road for some distance and then turned directly south at Hamilton's Crossing. Massaponax Creek, a half mile to the south, rounded out the tactical picture at that vital point in the battle area.

LEE CONCENTRATES ON HIS RIGHT FLANK

General Lee had promptly selected Hamilton's Crossing for his initial command post when he reached Fredericksburg on November 21. Entirely satisfied that Longstreet's dispositions along the ridges west of Fredericksburg had provided adequately for the defense of that sector, Lee now concentrated his attention on the more vulnerable, sensitive, maneuverable area to the south, where anything could happen. As previously re counted, he had widely dispersed Jackson's four divisions and Stuart's cavalry brigades in such a way as to throw dust in Burnside's eyes without too greatly impairing his own ability to reconcentrate his army for the payoff battle. Lee, a skillful exponent of the art of taking calculated risks, had supreme confidence in both Jackson and Stuart. This wasn't the first time he had taken long chances and gotten away with them, nor was it the last.

Hamilton's Crossing was a rather exposed spot for the person of an army commander, one might think; and so it would have been except that Jeb Stuart's cavalry was covering the flank. The Federal cavalry, on the other hand, managed to play a most insignificant part in the Battle of Fredericksburg, being conspicuous chiefly by its absence or at least inactivity on the Confederate side of the river. The fault lay not with the mounted troops themselves, but with the high-ranking Federal generals who had never taken the trouble to learn how to employ cavalry as a combat arm and who concealed their ignorance by using the mounted regiments in fragmentary detachments on vague reconnaissance missions, as escorts to army and corps commanders, and as individual couriers. The Federal cavalry was destined to be rejuvenated and given appropriate combat missions in 1863, but such was not the case at Fredericksburg.

Calm and confident, Lee bided his time, employing his abundance of military gray matter in an unhurried, continuous evaluation of the situation from the standpoint both of his own forces and those of the enemy, with particular attention to possible plans open to Burnside. Unlike the Federal commander in his new role of army commander, Lee was a strong believer in seeing as much as possible for himself. He spent much time in the saddle visiting his corps and division commanders, examining battery positions, checking the advantageous and disadvantageous features of the terrain over which his men would have to fight. Thus he familiarized himself, personally and in advance, with any tactically favorable factors which might and usually did contribute to his apparently uncanny knack of being able to defeat his adversaries each time.

Early on the morning of December 11, Lee rode to Telegraph Hill, the highest elevation on Longstreet's line, which afforded an ideal observation post which overlooked the Rappahannock and the intervening open terrain south of the town, as well as the southern and western exits of Fredericksburg. It was the logical spot for a forward battle command post, not only because there was no better place from which to keep an eye on unfolding events in the maneuver area, but also because it was practically the center of the line which Lee had determined in his mind to occupy if and when the tactical situation should call for a wholly defensive battle by his army. Since it turned out just that way, Telegraph Hill became the spot where Lee spent most of his time after the battle was joined, and It became known thereafter as Lee's Hill.

TWO HISTORIC PLANTATIONS

Lee's forward command post afforded an excellent view of Stafford Heights across the Rappahannock, now covered for its full length by the yawning guns of Burnside's artillery. Even without his field glasses Lee couldn't fail to see George Washington's boyhood home. But in all probability his glance rested more often and with greater feeling on Chatham, otherwise known as the Lacy house, where in earlier years Lee was a regular visitor and in the garden of which he courted his bride to-be, Mary Custis. Chatham, which served as Sumner's headquarters, was a plantation of several hundred acres that had been built about 1750 by William Fitzhugh. Situated on high ground overlooking the river and the town of Fredericksburg, opposite its north end and directly above the highway bridge over the Rappahannock, it served as a convenient Federal observation post during the battle. It was less effective than Lee's Hill, because of its location on the extreme right flank of the Union army. Visitors to the site of the Lacy house today will be disappointed to see, from the main highway, nothing recognizable of the famous old plantation. Nevertheless the original mansion, which has been remodeled in recent years, is still standing somewhat back from the present highway.

Only a few hundred yards down river from Chatham, on the same Stafford Heights, is the site of Ferry farm. It is situated off the highway in the direction of the river and, like Chatham, looks down on the Rappahannock and across it to the center of present-day Fredericksburg. The original manor house has been superseded by a later model, built on the foundations of the home in which young George spent the better part of his boyhood—but the foundation outlines of the smokehouse and other outbuildings can be seen, together with a still standing, aged two-story frame building that proclaims to the believers and the skeptical alike that here was the first office in which the future President pursued his chosen profession of surveyor.

A cherry tree proudly spreads its branches within a few feet of the very spot where its famous ancestor allegedly bit the dust at the hands of the youthful hatchetman. A trip down the hill to the river bank will bring the curious visitor to the very spot where Washington threw a Spanish silver dollar across the intervening 275 feet of water, probably aiming it at the old ferry wharf which once marked the upper limit of navigation on the Rappahannock.

While on Telegraph Hill, Lee watched and listened to the Federal artillery bombardment of Fredericksburg, remarking bitterly on the destruction of the homes of civilians. He received with evident pleasure the periodic reports from Barksdale on his success in rebuffing the efforts of the Federal engineers to lay their bridges. Federal success in completing the two bridges at Deep Run before noon, and the upper bridges in the late afternoon, seemed to have little effect on Lee's immediate plans for the redisposition of Jackson's four divisions, still at Port Royal, Skinker's Neck, Guiney's Station, and the Yerby house below the Massaponax.

Why didn't Lee react more positively to make Franklin pay a higher price for the privilege of crossing at Deep Run? Mere token resistance was offered by the Confederates at that point; Stuart's cavalry was available and the redoubtable Pelham alone, with his artillery battery, could have made Franklin's move to the south shore an expensive piece of business. There is only one answer that makes sense; Lee **wanted** the Army of the Potomac to come across and put the river at its back so that its attack would be made against a strongly defended line of hills. Such an assault would be launched from a narrow zone in which it would be difficult for large troop units to maneuver, and would cause the normal development from column to line to become a difficult if not extremely hazardous undertaking. It probably would have pleased Lee had Franklin come across while Sumner and Hooker were still on the other side, although that is mere speculation.

Darkness had fallen on the evening of Thursday, December 11, before the town of Fredericksburg was given up by McLaws' Confederate Division and taken over by Howard's Second Division of Couch's corps and Hawkins' brigade of Getty's division. The marching and countermarching at the Deep Run bridges was over for the night and one Federal brigade (Devens') manned Franklin's bridgehead on the south shore.

Then and only then did Lee make the first move to pull in any of Jackson's corps. A. P. Hill's Division was ordered up from Yerby's and Taliaferro's from Guiney's Station, with instructions to occupy the ridge immediately behind the railroad, extending Longstreet's line to the south and relieving Hood's Division which had been temporarily overextended to cover the right of the position.

The situation as it was developing began to have all the earmarks of another Antietam, on the occasion of which battle Jackson's corps was engaged in taking over Harpers Ferry as McClellan moved against the other half of Lee's army at Sharpsburg, some fifteen miles away. Here at Fredericksburg it just didn't make sense to Lee that Burnside would seriously consider a concentrated frontal attack with his entire army against the prepared and natural defensive position occupied by Longstreet, and thus forfeit the opportunity to use his preponderance of manpower by executing a turning movement against Lee's vulnerable right.

Lee naturally gave Burnside credit for a reasonable amount of intelligence. He was still unwilling to believe that the Deep Run crossing was intended as anything more than a feint and that the principal mass of maneuver would operate from the direction of the Skinker's Neck-Port Royal area. Therefore he allowed the divisions of Early and D. H. Hill to remain where they were determined that they would stay until Burnside should lay all his cards on the table.

Heavy fog again covered the area on the morning of December 12, forming a curtain that prevented the Confederates from observing enemy movements on their front. Sporadic Federal shelling of Fredericksburg punctuated the morning calm, but Lee did not reply. He was conserving his ammunition and sticking to his decision not to shell the town, so the explosives came only from the guns of the attackers. During the morning A. P. Hill and Taliaferro moved into their new positions. When the fog lifted about noon Lee rode over to the right with Jackson on a personal reconnaissance to see what might be going on down by the Richmond Road in Jackson's sector.

Von Borcke, a huge Prussian volunteer who was a member of Stuart's staff, joined the generals and reported that the Federals were massing in front of the Confederate right, that he. had personally been close to their advance units and seen them himself. This was important intelligence, but Lee still wanted the more positive confirmation that his own eyes and ears would give him. So off they rode, Lee, Jackson, and von Borcke, in the direction of Deep Run. Approaching the point that von Borcke had recently left, the distinguished entourage dismounted and on foot crept along a ditch to within rifle range of the Federal troops, from which covered approach they were able to observe through their field glasses a panorama of Blue troop movements of such magnitude as to convince Lee that a general advance was underway. As far as the eye could see, regiment after regiment of infantry was moving steadily down to the river and across two of the pontoon bridges, while on the other, artillery and wagon trains were following one another in closed-up formation.

That was enough for Lee and Jackson. It was almost unbelievable, but the evidence before his own eyes was what Lee had been waiting for. It was now apparent that Burnside's pivot would execute a holding attack to keep Longstreet pinned down at Fredericksburg, while the major attack would be made against Lee's vulnerable right flank. In Lee's estimation that was in finitely better than a turning movement at Port Royal, which would inevitably have forced him into the more difficult maneuver of having to disengage in the face of a superior force and fall back on his originally conceived line on the North Anna River, thirty-six miles further south in the direction of Richmond.

As Lee and Jackson retraced their steps and remounted, Jackson was dismissed with instructions to order Early and D. H. Hill to lose no time in rejoining the main body. The two generals went their separate ways with minds turning over rapidly as they digested this fresh information and mentally weighed the tactical plans that would be formulated promptly to prepare for the passage-at-arms now clearly forecast for the following day.

History Repeats Itself

Thanks to Burnside's slowness in effecting the development of his army and initiating the attack even after the bridgeheads had been safely secured, Lee was given an additional day and two nights to evaluate his opponent's plan and make his own dispositions to meet it. Just as at Antietam, where Lee had succeeded in concentrating his army at the point of impact at the psychological moment to turn imminent defeat into a stalemate, so at Fredericksburg he waited patiently for Burnside to reveal his intentions. Then he moved with confident alacrity to consolidate his two wings on an almost impregnable defensive position whose Achilles' heel could be pierced only by a general with more ability than the ill-fated Burnside could bring to bear.

D. H. Hill had much the longer march to bring him back to the main position, but both Early and Hill made good time in forced marches, so that shortly after daylight on December 13 the Army of Northern Virginia was snugly posted on the high ground all the way from Longstreet's left on the Rappahannock to Jackson's right at Hamilton's Crossing, with Stuart's two brigades of cavalry and horse artillery hinging the door and covering the flank in the mile-wide space between Hamilton's Crossing and the Rappahannock, at right angles to the main Confederate line and astride the Richmond Road.

As finally placed, Longstreet was covering about five miles of front, while Jackson's frontage was less than two miles. But Longstreet could defend with very little depth, while Jackson had a more difficult assignment which called for a flexible defense in depth and a readiness to shift his forces on short notice to counter possible penetrations or turning movements by the Union army.

The actual troop density was about nine men per yard of front in Jackson's sector, three per yard along the two miles of Marye's Heights, and approximately six per yard spread over the remainder of the line, including Stuart's flank position. However, the new military road which the Confederates had constructed along the rear of their position nullified the military significance of such academic calculations, for Lee was able to shift troops readily from one place to another whenever and from whatever direction the threat should come.

Infantry entrenchments and earthworks for artillery positions were traced lightly, but strong fortifications were not constructed. These were built after the first day's fighting was over, when Lee confidently expected the Union army to renew the attack. The trenches with their parapets are even today clearly defined, from the left flank to the right, along the military crest of the ridge in some places and at the foot of the ridge in others, particularly along the line held by McLaws' Division.

Jackson put A. P. Hill's Division in the forward position, in two lines, with the front line along the railroad, while the divisions of Taliaferro and Early were placed side by side as a third line. D. H. Hill was posted south of the Mine Road, as corps reserve in a position of readiness, with the possibility that his division might become the front line if the Federals should succeed in penetrating Stuart's screen and coming in on the rear around Hamilton's Crossing. Jackson's battle command post was on Prospect Hill, behind A. P. Hill's second line and in front of Early's Division, where he was in position to observe the front and exercise close control of his several divisions.

Thus massed on the wooded hills on Lee's right flank, 39,000 men of Jackson's corps waited for the fog to lift on December 13.

CHAPTER 18

Across the Rappahannock at Last

Major-General BURNSIDE.

Permit me to suggest the importance of pushing re-enforcements across during the night, so as to be able to resist any attack during the morning. This seems to me of vital importance.

H. W. HALLECK,

THE MOST surprising thing about this message, sent on December 11, is that it should have been necessary for Halleck to even think of sending it. It failed its purpose nevertheless. Earlier in the evening of December 11 Burnside had sent two dispatches to Halleck which informed him that *four* bridges had been laid and the fifth was expected to be completed during the night; that one division was across and occupying Fredericksburg, and he "hoped to have the main body over early tomorrow." Though not reported at this time, Burnside had six bridges laid by the morning of December 12.

Something was seriously wrong with Burnside. Either his mental apparatus wasn't functioning or he was grossly incompetent. Probably both. One would expect an untrained junior officer to exercise sounder judgment than to talk, as Burnside had, about springing a surprise on Lee by an expeditious crossing at Deep Run that would catch him with his saddlebags down, and then, after taking all of one day to lay his bridges and cross a token force, to allow the succeeding night to pass without pouring over as many additional divisions as the logistical factors would permit.

Burnside appears to have had inhibitions about river obstacles and may still have been obsessed by the fear that had caused him in mid-November to withhold approval when Sumner first arrived and wanted to cross the river by fording. Such a move was entirely feasible at the time because the rains had not started, but Burnside was fearful of a situation which might split his army and leave Sumner's 30,000 troops unsupported and at the mercy of the Confederates.

In any case, willingness such as characterized Lee to take a calculated risk wasn't one of the fixations which troubled Burnside. Neither, apparently, was experience in or even a desire to attempt a night operation. Yet a movement across the river under cover of darkness, with a short march to a jump-off position, would have permitted an attack on Jackson before Early and D. H. Hill arrived at the defensive position. It would have been a potential asset that could have chalked up a credit line on the Burnside balance sheet, which up to this time had already recorded quite a number of liabilities, with only the initial and praiseworthy march from Warrenton to Falmouth on the asset side.

We are not told what impression, if any, Halleck's message urging that reinforcements be pushed across the river during the night may have made on Burnside's mind. Presumably he had already decided not to do so, and, since Halleck hadn't shown much interest in his tactical plans, Burnside ignored the suggestion, and went back to sleep. Whatever he may have thought, no change was made in the orders and the night passed uneventfully for the shivering soldiers on both sides of the river.

The weather early on the morning of December 12 was a duplicate of that of the day before—a heavy, damp mist which served the Union army well in concealing its movements. The infantry and artillery columns moved up unmolested to the crossings in accordance with the prearranged time and space table.

Burnside was keeping a tight rein on his three grand division commanders, allowing them little discretion. After the battle was over, and he had had time to think back over it, he made it appear in his report that his plan had been to fight a holding action against the heights west of Fredericksburg, with Sumner's right wing, while Franklin with the left wing would envelop the Confederate flank. Even in that report it is not clear whether Burnside meant the right flank of the Confederate ridge position or the left flank of Jackson's corps which he thought was waiting for him down around Port Royal.

Everything might have worked out nicely had Lee been more accommodating and played the game the way Burnside planned it. No doubt the latter consoled himself with the thought that he was controlling his corps and divisions in a masterly, flexible manner to prevent them from getting themselves involved in uncoordinated piecemeal attacks until the master mind should be fully ready to turn them loose. The fact was that it was an *indecisive* mind and an unsure hand that was directing the destinies of the Army of the Potomac. One could feel sorry for Burnside at Fredericksburg if he could dismiss from his mind the holocaust of death that Burnside's fumbling strategy was to visit on so many thousands of Union soldiers on December 13.

The morning of December 12 was a busy one for Federal commanders and staffs. A thrilling sight would have been presented to the Confederates had the fog permitted their observers to watch the Union army as it marched by the tens of thou sands over the six swaying pontoon bridges. At the corps and division levels were experienced generals who knew their way around, and under whose watchful eyes the brigades and regiments were directed, via the upper bridges, across the river and forward into the streets of Fredericksburg, and by way of the lower bridges on to the plain below the town.

The Confederates were satisfied to mark time on December 12 as they waited for Jackson's last two divisions to rejoin them, so Burnside's forces were not attacked as the columns poured in unending procession across the six bridges and into the limited area between the hostile defense line and the river.

The Federal march table provided that Couch's Second Corps would be the first to cross at Fredericksburg, followed by Willcox's Ninth Corps, the former to fan out for occupation of the center and northern portion of the town, the latter to extend the line to the south, without any indication as to the position on which his left flank should rest. Next day however Willcox did receive orders to extend to the left and connect with Franklin's right at Deep Run. Hazel Run was designated as the dividing line between the two corps.

At the lower bridges where Franklin's grand division crossed, Smith's corps led the way, followed by Reynolds' corps. By late afternoon the entire force had completed the passage of the river and formed in a continuous arc composed of four divisions in two successive lines, Smith's right resting astride Deep Run, Reynolds' left on the Rappahannock; one division of each corps, Doubleday's and Newton's, being held in reserve near the river. There they bivouacked for the night, halted in place, without orders from higher up for further movement or action and with nothing to do but wait for Burnside to release another fragment of his fuzzy tactical plan.

Six divisions were thus crowded into and immediately south of Fredericksburg and six more bivouacked below Deep Run, while across the river Hooker had been directed to send two divisions (Birney's and Sickles') of Stoneman's Third Corps, and Willcox to move one of his divisions down to the vicinity of the lower bridges, as potential support for Franklin's grand division. Including Bayard's cavalry of 3,500 troopers, his own grand division, and the three support divisions from Hooker and Sumner, Franklin now had available on both sides of the river upward of 54,000 men for the major effort that he was to be called upon to make on the following morning.

Sumner's strength was now down to 27,000 and Hooker had 31,000 more, but all three of the major commanders were still in a state of uncertainty as to just what Burnside expected them to do now that most of them were parked within less than a mile of the dug-in Confederates on their comfortable treecovered ridge.

FEDERAL ARTILLERY SKILLFULLY HANDLED

General Henry J. Hunt, Chief of Artillery of the Army of the Potomac, was indisputably the ablest artillerist of the Civil War, on either side. In preparation for Burnside's crossing of the Rappahannock, he withdrew temporarily all division artillery except one battery which was retained by each division, and attached the mass to the Artillery Reserve, under his own immediate control. Through this organizational device, he was able to arm Stafford Heights, one hundred and fifty feet above the water-line, with 147 guns, extending all the way from Falmouth to Pollock's Mill downriver. As usual, under Hunt's direction, the Federal artillery was emplaced with great skill, prepared to consider all conceivable fire missions, including counterbattery fire, protection for the laying of the bridges, prevention of the movement of possible Confederate reinforcements into Fredericksburg (had they undertaken it), and providing flank protection for the army. When the divisions crossed the river their light artillery rejoined them.

Having graduated from West Point in 1839 in the same class with Henry W. Halleck, Hunt won his initial battle spurs as a battery commander in the Mexican War, in which he fought with conspicuous gallantry through every battle of Scott's great campaign from Vera Cruz to the capital of the Montezumas. During the four years preceding the outbreak of the Civil War he served as a member of the Board charged with revising the system of light artillery tactics, and so well did he perform that task that the Federal artillery functioned throughout the war at a high pitch of efficiency, proving itself superior to the Confederate artillery in a majority of the important battles. Hunt, who directed the Union artillery in all the early battles of the war, was elevated to Chief of Artillery of the Army of the Potomac in September 1862 and held that high position right through to the end at Appomattox.

All the guns on Stafford Heights were rifled; twenty-two were twenty-pounder Parrotts, seven were 4.5-inch siege guns, fourteen were light twelve-pounders, thirty-four were three-inch rifles, and the remaining eighty-four guns were light rifles. The Parrotts were not as effective as they were cracked up to be. Hunt was most critical of their performance in his post-battle report, when he informed the Ordnance Department that they had functioned unsatisfactorily because of the imperfection of the projectiles, which he complained were almost as dangerous to the Union troops as to the enemy and also because the guns themselves were unsafe and frequently burst near the muzzle. He added that they were too heavy for satisfactory use and were suitable chiefly as batteries of position, since they required just as many horses and as many drivers to move them as the heavy 4.5-inch siege guns.

Nineteen batteries, a total of 104 guns, crossed the river with Sumner's grand division, although during the battle the greater number of the guns could not be used because they were shielded by the buildings. Only seven batteries with Sumner's divisions were either wholly or partly engaged on December 13. Seventeen batteries for a total of eighty-six guns crossed with Franklin, and when Sickles' and Birney's divisions of Hooker's grand division were assigned to reinforce Franklin's wing, five additional batteries of thirty guns crossed the river. The battle on the south flank was more open and in that area practically all the guns were effectively employed.

Campfires at night in close proximity to the enemy were not permitted on this occasion, so about all the soldiers in the town had to occupy their attention was the pleasure of looting the houses, which they proceeded to do on a grand scale until their officers put a stop to it. Huge piles of furniture and other household goods were stacked on the Fredericksburg side of the river when details from the Provost Marshal's Detachment picketed the crossings and halted the spreading vandalism.

Burnside Temporizes as His Generals Mark Time

During the late afternoon of December 12 Gen. Franklin, commanding the Left Grand Division, and his corps commanders Reynolds and Smith, all of whom were on the closest official and personal terms, assembled for a conference at the "Bernard house," Franklin's field headquarters.

This place, which Franklin had selected as the command post from which to direct the operations of his reinforced grand division, was a large plantation originally known as "Old Mansfield." At the time of the battle the proprietor was named Bernard, a large slave owner. Bernard objected violently to the Union occupation of his residence, whereupon he was unceremoniously hustled across the river, at Reynolds' order, by a brace of pleased soldiers. The Bernard cabins, incidentally, which housed the plantation's slaves, were some distance farther away, at the northern extremity of A. P. Hill's position, and so were not similarly disturbed. The ruins of the plantation can still be seen near the river a half mile north of Smithfield. The latter sounds as though it should have been a village; actually it was merely another plantation which was converted into a Federal hospital after the battle, and is today the Fredericksburg Country Club.

Franklin, Reynolds, and Smith discussed the situation and compared notes. They were in agreement that the only sensible attack plan for their wing would be to form their divisions into two assault columns on either side of the Richmond Road and to turn Lee's flank at whatever cost.

About 5 P.M. Burnside showed up, was taken on a quick gallop along the lines, and then sat down with Franklin for a talk, at which time he was urged to authorize the latter to carry out the aforementioned plan. When Burnside left, the other three generals were under the distinct impression that he had given tacit approval and was returning to his headquarters to compose the orders. They proceeded to work out the details for the attack which they thought they were authorized to launch, and then sat around for hours waiting for the order so that they might issue last-minute instructions to their subordinate commanders and get a few hours of sleep.

But nothing happened, so at 3 A.M., December 13 Reynolds turned in for the night and after a further period of frustrating delay the other generals did likewise. It was not until 7:45 A.M. that the long awaited order was delivered to Franklin by General Hardie of Burnside's staff, who had been dispatched with instructions to stay with Franklin during the battle in order to keep the army commander informed of its progress. The delay in drafting and issuing this order was one of the most serious mistakes made by Burnside.

These are the "attack" orders issued by Burnside over the signature of his chief of staff, General Parke:

December 13, 1862–5.55 A.M.
Major-General Franklin,
Commanding Left Grand Division, Army of the Potomac: General Hardie will carry this dispatch to you, and remain with you during the day. The general commanding directs that you keep your whole command in position for a rapid movement down the old Richmond road, and you will send out at once a division at least to pass below Smithfield to seize, if possible, the height near Captain Hamilton's, on this side of the Massaponax, taking care to keep it well supported and its line of retreat open. He has ordered another column of a division or

more to be moved from General Sumner's command up the Plank road to its intersection with the Telegraph road, where they will divide, with a view to seizing the heights on both of these roads. Holding these two heights, with the heights near Captain Hamilton's, will, he hopes, compel the enemy to evacuate the whole ridge between these points. He makes these moves by columns distant from each other, with a view of avoiding the possibility of a collision of our own forces, which might occur in a general movement during a fog. Two of General Hooker's divisions and in your rear, at the bridges, and will remain there as supports. The Bernard house may be seen dimly in the grove at the upper right.

Copies of instructions given to Generals Sumner and Hooker will be forwarded to you by an orderly very soon. You will keep your whole command in readiness to move at once, as soon as the fog lifts. The watchword, which, if possible, should be given to every company, will be "Scott."

December 13, 1862–6 A.M.
Maj. Gen. E. V. Sumner,
Commanding Right Grand Division, Army of the Potomac: The general commanding directs that you extend the left of your command to Deep Run, connecting with General Franklin, extending your right as far as your judgment may dictate. He also directs that you push a column of a division or more along the Plank and Telegraph roads, with a view to seizing the heights in the rear of the town. The latter movement should be well covered by skirmishers, and supported so as to keep its line of retreat open. Copy of instructions given to General Franklin will be sent to you very soon. You will please await them at your present headquarters, where he (the general commanding) will meet you. Great care should be taken to prevent a collision of our own forces during the fog. The watchword for the day will be "Scott." The column for a movement up the Telegraph and Plank roads will be got in readiness to move, but will not move till the general commanding communicates with you.

December 13, 1862–7 A.M.
Maj. Gen. Joseph Hooker,
Commanding Center (Grand) Division, Army of the Potomac: The general commanding directs that you place General Butterfield's corps and Whipple's division in position to cross, at a moment's notice, at the three upper bridges in support of the other troops over the river, and the two remaining divisions of General Stoneman's corps in readiness to cross at the lower ford, in support of General Franklin. The general commanding will meet you at headquarters (Phillips house) very soon. Copies of instructions to General Sumner and General Franklin will be sent to you.

THE ARMY ORDERS ARE STILL INDECISIVE

The orders to General Sumner in Fredericksburg involved for the time being merely an extension of the current deployment of his divisions in preparation for an assault by a single division, and that only when Burnside should give the signal. Hooker's order told him only that he was to place his divisions near the bridges on the east side of the river, prepared to support the forthcoming attack by the two grand divisions already across. The wording of this order was so phrased as to keep the troops under Hooker's immediate direction, which meant control by Burnside.

It was the order to Franklin, who was to make the major attack with more than half of the army at his disposal, that caused the greatest consternation in the minds of Franklin, Reynolds, and Smith, because it was entirely different from their own conception, which they had been confident Burnside had accepted the evening before. Obviously Burnside was sending a boy to do a man's job when he ordered one division from each wing to initiate a pseudo-coordinated attack under conditions of poor visibility, at a time when everybody else was convinced that their only hope lay in a powerful flanking assault against Lee's right, the sole weak spot along his entire position.

The phrase "if possible," the use of the verb "seize" rather than "carry" or "capture and hold at all costs," the timid caution to "keep the line of retreat open," and the reference to possible collision with friendly troops in the fog—these were milquetoast terms that could hardly be expected to put confidence and the offensive spirit into the minds and hearts of able corps and division commanders, and an aggregation of stout fighting men who had already, and for quite some time, been convinced that they were being led down a blind alley by a blindfolded leader.

Franklin's own plan was indeed the one that made sense, and by all the rules of warfare it should have succeeded handsomely. If Burnside had been less enamored of his own brain child, which unfortunately was an anemic cripple even in the embryo, he would have· approved Franklin's plan, issued by 9 P.M. a simple army attack order effective at daylight December 13, and gone to bed, with justifiable confidence that the next day Lee and not he, Burnside, would have to do the worrying.

With their hands thus untied, Sumner, Franklin, and Hooker could have coordinated their attack orders at an hour's conference, crossed two of Hooker's divisions at the lower bridges to replace Smith's corps as bridgehead security (as Franklin had vainly urged Burnside to do), moved their assault divisions to the jump-off positions before daylight, and thus have faced at daylight a hopeful set of circumstances that would in all likelihood have resulted in a battle with the odds heavily weighted in favor of the Union army.

Instead of which, Burnside shackled his subordinate commanders to a role of virtual rubber stamps, delayed interminably the use of the stamp, and when he did finally apply it to the ink pad, the resulting impression was so difficult to read that the Union cause would have been better served had Burn side in his youth never learned to read or write.

CHAPTER 19

Fredericksburg I: Union Failure on the Southern Flank

THE ADVANTAGE of terrain lay with the defending Confederates, not only because nature had provided a range of wooded hills and complementary stream obstacles that cut across the plain over which the Union army was ordered to attack, but also because General Lee had a keen sense of terrain appreciation and an incomparable team of corps commanders in Longstreet and Jackson. These two distinguished generals had fought many a successful battle under every conceivable combination of circumstances, were completely *en rapport* with their army commander, and were old hands at the game of making the most of what they had in materiel and manpower, in the character of the terrain, and the errors of their opponents.

Lee's ability to appraise the favorable and unfavorable aspects of the ground features and to dispose his forces to take full advantage thereof was never better exemplified than in his defensive strategy at Fredericksburg. By far the greater extent of his seven-mile-long position was occupied on the left by Longstreet's five-division corps of about 41,000 men, a line thinly held because Lee and Longstreet were both confident that the Federals could not successfully storm the heights or achieve a penetration on that front. For that reason, coupled with the fact that the ground was frozen hard and digging was difficult, little effort was made on Longstreet's section of the line to throw up infantry entrenchments· or to emplace the guns in depressed pits except in very exposed locations.

In Jackson's sector the situation required a different type of defensive treatment. There, in the two mile stretch between Deep Run and Hamilton's Crossing, Lee massed Jackson's entire Second Corps of 39,000 men, exclusive of Stuart's cavalry and artillery, disposed in depth to make the best possible use of cover, elevation, ravines, and streams. The heights were covered with a dense growth of timber, which was heavier than on Marye's Heights and the other hills to the north. While some attention was paid to building breastworks, in the time Burn side thoughtfully allowed him, Lee gave first priority to the important task of cutting roads through the woods in rear of the position, for lateral communication and to facilitate rapid movement of regiments or brigades in order to be prepared to meet the enemy with superior numbers at threatened points.

Jackson's theoretically vulnerable right flank may not actually have been so easy to turn, because the valley of the Massaponax Creek, which cut the line of hills at Hamilton's Crossing, had some marshy characteristics. Also, the creek itself, running east and west about a half mile below his battle command post on the extreme right, was a positive obstacle not easily surmounted by enemy troops under battle conditions. In those days troops attacked in parade-ground formation, and, when a line was broken, confusion and loss of control resulted.

The canny Lee shrewdly anticipated and prepared for every possible tactical maneuver that Burnside might conceive, personally directing the posting of many of the 306 artillery guns which were skillfully sited along the seven-mile position, while on the right flank, where a turning movement seemed to be the most logical move for the Union army, Jackson's corps and Stuart's cavalry were ready and willing.

The Union army, on the other hand, found itself in a most unenviable position, awkwardly straddling an unfordable river with only a handful of tenuous lifelines against a possible disaster that might necessitate a hazardous withdrawal. Six narrow, shaky threads that were the bridges were capable of being destroyed by Confederate artillery fire if Lee should change his mind and decide that the loss of property along the eastern fringe of Fredericksburg was not too high a price to pay for a Federal debacle.

An army of over 100,000 men even moving in close order requires plenty of space in which to maneuver for effective work. It takes a lot of marching and deployment and the intelligent transmission and understanding of a succession of orders down through the chain of command to prepare such a large body of troops for a coordinated assault, if the attack is to attain any measure of success.

It may be unkind to say it, but in retrospect it appears that Lee had not two, but three corps commanders to help him, and the name of the third was Burnside. Burnside's bungling had finally put the Army of the Potomac in a position where nothing but sheer guts and the stout hearts of a mighty host of fighting men would serve to extricate them. He had managed to maneuver them into a serious pocket, a relatively shallow oval-shaped area, with a narrow open end at the south between Hamilton's Crossing and the Rappahannock; except that it wasn't a real opening for the reason that Stuart's cavalry and Pelham's artillery were blocking a possible end run on that flank. At the backs of the Union army was the Rappahannock River and directly to their front rose a formidable row of hills bristling for seven miles with gray-clad soldiers who were figuratively licking their chops as they waited, poised, for the "blue bellies" to "come and get it."

The preliminaries were now out of the way and the gladiators were on the battlefield, over 200,000 of them, facing one an other and ready to spring. Some 90,000 confident Confederates, knowing exactly what they intended to do and determined to add one more to their string of victories, were pitted at close quarters against 120,000 Federals, with 26,000 more in reserve a few miles away and about 50,000 others protecting the upper Potomac and the defenses of Washington.

Historians have always experienced great difficulty in reconciling Confederate strength figures as given by the various generals in their own written accounts, frequently long after the event, with the strength reports in the *Official Records of the Rebellion.* This may be partly explained by the fact that straggling was even more a matter of concern to the Confederate high command than to the Federal. Among the Southern soldiers it was not so much a matter of malingering as it was a privilege which many enjoyed, with considerable impunity in the early part of the war, of taking French leave between campaigns to fall out and visit with friends and acquaintances in home territory. There they could find food and shelter which was an improvement over the army ration and the open fields and woods. Consequently the custom became widespread, al though most of the AWOL's were in the habit of rejoining their outfits whenever a battle appeared imminent.

Straggling has of course always been a serious headache in every army composed of a preponderance of untrained recruits who have not been physically hardened in campaign and have yet to learn how to take proper care of themselves. Even under a strict disciplinarian it always presents a problem that can be eradicated only by time and intensive training and marching. It must be concluded, therefore, that the official returns for the Confederates as a rule exceeded, by varying amounts and de pending on other circumstances, the numb r of combat effectives under arms and present in person for any particular engagement. In this book the *Official Records* are used for strength figures wherever possible, without making allowance for stragglers, men on sick call, or engaged in administrative duties.

FRANKLIN GETS UNEXPECTED ORDERS

Once again the valley was covered with an early morning fog on Saturday, December 13, a day that was soon to terminate the career of many a good man. A high wind and bitterly cold night had caused such discomfort to the thousands of men resting on their arms on that congested battlefield-to-be that the chance to get into blood-warming action, even if it should hasten death or dismemberment, was preferable to freezing to death from numbing inaction.

Burnside was at least correct in expecting that there would be a fog, as on previous mornings, but that it would be dissipated in a couple of hours, as indeed it was. Meanwhile, as of commanders Reynolds and Smith were given the bad news, and the Left Grand Division began to stir.

Since Burnside had refused to release any of Hooker's divisions on the eastern shore, which would have freed Smith's Sixth Corps for use as Franklin might see fit, without worrying about bridgehead security, Franklin assigned the attack mission to Reynolds and his First Corps. Reynolds in turn selected Meade's division, with Gibbon's in support, to spearhead the advance "to seize if possible the heights near Captain Hamilton's, on this side of the Massaponax, taking care to keep it well supported and its line of retreat open."

Scarcely an inspiring attack order, to say the least! Meade was an excellent division commander, who had one of the best out fits in the army, although the smallest at Franklin's disposal, with a strength of only about 4,500 men. It is assumed that he and Reynolds kept the wording of Burnside's order to them selves; they must have if they expected the men of Meade's regiments to put their hearts into the effort. Imagine telling a bunch of two-fisted soldiers to *try* and grab those hills up there by the crossroads *if possible,* with a promise to hold a path open for retreat!

Gibbon's division, slightly larger than Meade's, was directed to support Meade on the right, while Doubleday, commander of Reynold's remaining division, was held in reserve. By 8:30 A.M. Meade was ready to move out, a creditable piece of work considering the fact that only forty-five minutes had elapsed since Hardie reached Franklin with the unexpected order.

A BREATH-TAKING MILITARY PAGEANT

The deployment of Reynold's corps began while the plain between the river and the Confederate heights as well as the town of Fredericksburg was covered by the dense fog of early morning. Aided by the low visibility, the forward movement of Meade's and Gibbon's divisions made excellent progress against only sporadic enemy gunfire which had no targets upon which to sight. The Confederates were aware that something interesting was afoot, for they could hear the sharp bark of commands all along the front even though they could see nothing through the heavy curtain of fog.

About 10 o'clock the brilliant rays of the sun struggled through the mists, which were quickly dissipated to reveal to the startled but admiring eyes of thousands of watchers on the hill a panorama that must have been breath-taking in its scope and grandeur. Like a suddenly rising curtain at the opening of a play, there was displayed Franklin's huge force of over 50,000 men, rank on rank, foot, horse, and artillery pieces, with the bright sun reflecting from thousands upon thousands of flashing bayonets, and with officers dashing up and down on galloping horses. The Left Grand Division covered the plain and presented a martial pageant that would never be forgotten by those who had the fortune to occupy front-row seats.

While it may sound like an anachronism to twentieth century veterans, adjutants were observed moving to the front of their regiments and reading battle orders, after which the successive lines of Federal troops, standards flying, moved out to battle as though on parade. The show was on!

MEADE'S DIVISION SPEARHEADS THE ATTACK

Paced by bursting shells from scores of heavy field pieces which swept the plain before the advancing regiments, Meade's columns, two brigades in line abreast, with the third in column echeloned to the left rear and the artillery advancing between the two leading brigades. They crossed the Smithfield ravine and turned sharply to the right across the Richmond Road. From Deep Run to the far end of Meade's line this road was sunken, in places six feet deep. The road offered protection, but also was an obstacle to forward movement, consequently there was a delay at this point while the men tore down the hedge fences flanking the road and bridged the drainage ditches on either side to provide a passage for the artillery. While this work was in progress the division was badly hurt by converging artillery fire from Jackson's batteries on the crest above Hamilton's Crossing and from Pelham's guns on the left. Reynold's field guns promptly rushed forward to the rise of ground between the Richmond Road and the railroad and replied briskly to the Confederate artillery fire, dividing their attention between Jackson's guns on the heights and Stuart's on the flank.

After crossing the Richmond Road at a point approximately a mile south of the Deep Run or Lansdowne Valley Road, Meade's advancing columns paralleled that road which cut through the line of hills occupied by the line of Confederates. Following Reynolds' instructions, their immediate objective was a point of woods which jutted out like a salient into the open end of the plain. That particular section of woods, as it turned out, offered a more gradual ascent for the attackers than did other portions of Jackson's line. It was Reynolds' plan that Meade's division would gain the crest and then turn left along it toward Jackson's right flank at Hamilton's Crossing, where the bulk of the enemy artillery appeared to be massed. Gibbon's division advanced on Meade's right, echeloned to the rear, brigades in successive lines. Gibbon's had suffered equally with

Meade's from the Confederate shelling, especially from batteries near Bernard's cabins. At the same time, Reynolds directed Doubleday's division to change front to the left facing Stuart's cavalry on the flank, in order to take the weight off Meade's advancing left flank and to prevent a surprise attack from that quarter. Meade also took similar precautions by facing his reserve brigade to the left.

The Federals hugged the ground as the artillery duel raged for well over an hour. The redoubtable Pelham, commanding Stuart's artillery on the extreme Confederate right, stood well out in front of the cavalry with two venturesome guns exposed, far to the front in the triangle formed by the junction of the Mine Road with the Richmond Road. Nimbly shifting his guns each time the Federals found his range, the young officer kept many times his own number of Federal guns engaged until Stuart, fearing to lose the brave but rash artilleryman, issued peremptory orders that he give up the unequal gun fight and retire to a safer position.

As Meade and Gibbon advanced, none of the Confederates on the crest or forward slope of the wooded ridge were visible. The attacking Federals were allowed to approach the railroad, within 800 yards of the crest of the ridge, before running into trouble. At that stage all the Confederate batteries opened with a crash, with such effect that Meade's men were stopped in their tracks, wavered, and pulled back. It began to appear that the Federals had been stopped almost before they started, because several hours now passed before they pulled themselves together for a second attempt. About 1 o'clock the Federal batteries laid down a strong and well directed concentration of fire on the woods that were Meade's initial objective and the Confederate guns on either side of it. Under the protection of this fire Meade and Gibbon resumed their advance, crossed the railroad, and drove the Confederates back into the woods and up the hill.

Along the one and one-half mile front held by A. P. Hill's Confederate Division, the left of Archer's Brigade was separated from the right of Lane's Brigade by 500 yards of swampy woods which the Confederates had failed to reconnoiter carefully or which they negligently assumed could not be crossed by the enemy, overlooking the fact that the ground was frozen sufficiently to make it possible. In rear of the swamp Hill had placed Gregg's Brigade, as a part of the second defensive line, but the open space between Lane and Archer proved too wide for mutually supporting fire.

The swampy woods, which Jackson's generals thought would be a deterrent, proved to be nothing if the sort; Meade's brigades surged through the woods, taking between them several hundred prisoners, smashing Gregg's Brigade and mortally wounding its commander. Gibbon, on Meade's right, advanced only to the Confederate front line. In the dense thicket the divisions lost contact and opened a gap, whereupon the Con federate brigades promptly rallied, counterattacked, and drove Meade's men back in great confusion. Although Taliaferro's Division was in direct support of Gregg's Brigade, it was Early's that rushed over from the right to meet the crisis and turn the tables on Meade. Lane's Brigade put the damper on Gibbon's assault which had reached the railroad but not much further, except for small groups and individual soldiers who followed Meade's example and advanced into the woods.

Enthusiastic rebel cheers, coupled with rapid footwork and vigorous musket fire, followed the retreating Federals down the hill and over the railroad. Gibbon was wounded and forced to retire. Brigadier General C. F. Jackson, one of Meade's brigade commanders, was killed. Reynolds, Meade, and officers of lesser rank did their best to halt the backward drift of the broken regiments, but the troops of both divisions had had all they wanted and there was no stopping them in their sullen withdrawal, particularly those of Meade's division, through the hastily formed line which Birney's division of the Third Corps brought up in support. Birney had fortuitously arrived on the scene at the critical moment; he struck the Confederate right flank and in turn drove the counterattackers back into the woods with a loss of more than 500 killed and wounded. His own casualties were heavy, but his brigades fought magnificently as the retreating elements of Meade and Gibbon streamed through their lines to the rear. Had it not been for Birney, there is no telling what might have happened.

At 2 o'clock Reynolds' corps, strengthened by Birney's and then by Sickles' division, both of Stoneman's Third Corps, which had finally been summoned from the east shore, still held the railway line. But they were unable to make progress against Jackson's strong defense. Later in the afternoon the entire line was withdrawn to re-form in the shelter of the Richmond Road from whence the attack had been launched in the morning.

THE FEDERAL ATTACK LACKED POWER AND DEPTH

Franklin's failure to make better use of Smith's corps was as much a reflection on his generalship as on Burnside's. Granted that the latter's directive was vague and inconclusive, a more energetic wing commander, having committed two divisions to the attack against the Confederate heights, would and should have utilized Smith's 25,000-man corps, the largest in the Union army, to better advantage. As it was, that corps remained virtually static deployed along the Richmond Road from Deep Run on the right, two divisions in the line and one in support. When Meade and Gibbon were repulsed, Newton's support division was shifted to the left to back up Birney, but remained in column of brigades in a position of readiness on equally true of Doubleday, who had deployed and advanced a short distance toward the flank, but who played a virtually in active role throughout the battle.

About the only actual fighting in which Smith's corps engaged was a lively succession of artillery duels with the Con federates in the Deep Run area, and a spirited advance and bayonet charge by a portion of Colonel Torbert's brigade of Brook's division, which in the middle of the afternoon attempted to drive the Confederates from a railroad cut in the Deep Run (Lansdowne) Valley where the railroad crossed a deep ravine. Torbert's troops succeeded in driving back a regiment of Pender's Brigade of A. P. Hill's Division, and capturing several dozen of the enemy. Torbert in turn was counterattacked and forced to retire by Law's Brigade of Hood's Division. Lansdowne Valley was a well-known landmark at the time of the battle and since it was approximately the dividing line between the two Confederate corps, and appeared to be a natural avenue of attack along the upper reaches of Deep Run, the sortie might have had important results had it been launched with sufficient strength and depth.

What should have been a major and decisive turning movement by Franklin's 54,000-man force, against not much more than half that number of Confederates on Lee's right flank, thus turned out to be a relatively inconclusive although very sanguinary engagement in which a majority of the forces avail able to each of the opposing commanders was not fully engaged. The reported casualties significantly tell the story; Meade's division lost 1,853 officers and men; Gibbon's losses were 1,267; Birney's were 950; Doubleday and Sickles suffered, respectively, only 218 and 100 casualties, mainly from Confederate artillery fire; while the other four divisions lost a mere 473 men altogether, for a grand total of 4,861 casualties among the troops under Franklin's command. The opposing Confederates lost approximately 3,400, mostly in the divisions of A. P. Hill and Jubal Early.

As the afternoon waned, Stonewall Jackson made preparations for a counterattack which he judged it would be safer to launch under cover of darkness, just in case it might be necessary for his divisions to retire to their secure haven on the heights after making the attack. The plan called for his artillery to precede the infantry, but nothing came of it because, in Jackson's own report: "The first gun had hardly moved forward from the wood one hundred yards when the enemy}s artillery reopened, and so completely swept our front as to satisfy me that the proposed movement should be abandoned."

CHAPTER 20

Fredericksburg II: Slaughter at the Stone Wall

LONGSTREET'S CORPS, having moved in and occupied the ridge bastion west of Fredericksburg shortly after the Army of the Potomac had reached the vicinity of Falmouth, had, through Burnside's inability to make up his mind on his next move, been granted over three full weeks in which to improve and strengthen its already naturally strong defensive position.

The selection of artillery gun positions, which received Lee's careful personal attention, was made with meticulous care. There can be little doubt that all five of the divisions of Longstreet's First Corps were not only thoroughly briefed on the individual and collective combat roles they would be called upon to play, but were in all probability put through terrain exercises, by way of rehearsal, that would serve to counter every conceivable tactical maneuver open to the Federal forces once they had bridged the river.

COUCH'S CORPS LEADS OFF

General Couch and his Second Corps were selected by Sumner to make the attack against the heights. The written order, received at 8: 15 A.M., directed that he extend his right to prevent the possibility of a Confederate occupation of the upper end of the town, and then alert two divisions, one to be prepared to advance in three lines "in the direction of the Plank and Telegraph Roads for the purpose of seizing the heights in rear of the town," the other to be held in readiness to support the movement of the leading division.

Couch at once designated French's division for the advance, with Hancock to follow, each division in brigade columns of battalions with 200 yards distance between brigades. By 11 o'clock, Burnside had evidently despaired of the early success which he had anticipated on Franklin's front, for at that hour Couch received from Sumner the order to advance, transmitted over a field telegraph line which the Federal signalmen had run from the Lacy house, Sumner's headquarters on the opposite side of the Rappahannock, to the Fredericksburg courthouse building in which Couch had set up his command post.

Under modern battle conditions a unit the size of a division normally moves into its jump-off position by regiments or battalions in columns of fours, twos, single file, or in squad or platoon columns, depending on the nature of the available cover and the configuration of the ground over which the development takes place. When within enemy machine gun and rifle fire the modern deployment into skirmish formation is effected to present a minimum of bunched targets, while the friendly artillery lays down a stationary or rolling barrage ahead of the troops to keep down the enemy fire.

It didn't happen that way at Fredericksburg, for the reason that Hunt's guns on Stafford Heights for the most part were unable to reach the Confederate position, and the debouchment from the streets of the town presented a difficult problem in itself. At 12:00 noon French's brigades moved out from the shelter of the town by the two streets which led into the Plank and Telegraph Roads. As they emerged from the cover afforded by the buildings they found themselves descending a gradual slope on an open plain with Marye's Heights at the far end and about 800 yards distant from the town's western edge. This plain, obstructed in spots by an occasional house and garden, was bisected at right angles to the direction of the Federal advance by the canal drainage ditch, which could be conveniently crossed only at the bridges. Beyond the ditch the ground rose slightly toward the Confederate ridge and provided cover of a sort, behind which the troops could deploy before charging the heights. The entire plain was exposed to converging artillery and musketry fire, and the advancing Federals suffered many casualties while in column before they could be hurried over the two bridges to the slight cover on the far side.

The Grim Reaper Has a Field Day

The Confederate guns on Lee's Hill commanded the valley of Hazel Run and were effectively sited to cover the plain which the Union forces had to cross to reach Marye's Heights. The attacking Federals came under the fire of these guns and others from the heights on Lee's left as soon as they moved out from the cover of the town buildings. Most of their early losses were caused by Lee's artillery. Two Confederate siege guns in particular were much in evidence during the early stages of the battle; these were the "thirty-pound" Parrott rifles, weighing 4,200 pounds and throwing a twenty-nine-pound projectile, which had recently been transferred from the defenses of Richmond for use at Fredericksburg. Enfilading Couch's left flank in the attacks on Marye's Heights, these heavy guns created havoc in the Federal lines from their positions on Lee's Hill until both blew up in the faces of the Confederates, one on the thirty-ninth discharge, the other after fifty-four rounds had been fired. The first to go was firing within a few feet of where Lee, Longstreet, and Pendleton, Lee's Chief of Artillery, were standing when it burst at the muzzle. But by a miracle no one was touched by the flying fragments.

As soon as the advancing lines came within musket range a sheet of flame greeted them from behind the four-foot stone wall at the foot of Marye's Hill, where Cobb's Georgia Brigade of McLaws' Confederate Division and a North Carolina regiment of Ransom's Division were posted. The withering fire cut the attackers down by the hundred. But the grim advance continued, ignoring casualties, until the leading wave was within sixty yards of the wall. At that point flesh and blood could take no more. In truth, even if the spirit had been willing, there just weren't enough soldiers remaining to cover the last stretch of open ground before closing in hand-to-hand combat.

The Second and Third Brigades of French's division followed the First, but they too were stopped in succession at sixty yards and the survivors faded back to the rear, leaving three regimental flags to mark their furthest advance. French's division was out of the fight, leaving a third of its men on the ground.

The turn of Hancock's division came next. The safe attraction of the stone wall, breast-high for the average man standing upright, was such that Confederate reinforcements had in the meantime crowded into the sunken road until they were firing in four ranks as fast as men could change places, and at a resultant cycle of fire that was more than four times the normal rate. As a result, Hancock's reception was worse than French's and although his brigades passed the high water mark of their predecessors and got within forty yards of the wall, they couldn't quite reach it.

By this time the plain was literally covered with the blue-clad dead and wounded. With these prone figures were others who could go no further but still had the intestinal fortitude to stay where they were and inflict such damage as they might with rifle fire to collect partial payment from the securely posted Confederates behind the stone wall, from which the hail of death kept spouting at every head that was raised.

Two Union divisions within an hour had with supreme battle courage offered themselves as a fruitless sacrifice to the stupidity of an incompetent army commander whose capacity for compounding his initial lack of tactical judgment seemed limitless. Having made the decision to spearhead with a single division a frontal attack over open ground against what was obviously an almost impregnable position, the stubborn Burnside could think of nothing better than to keep pouring other divisions with endless monotony into the same funnel regardless of losses. Casualties in the divisions of French and Hancock alone amounted to 3,200 men and officers killed, wounded, and missing. Before the day was over, 6,300 Federal soldiers would become casualties at the base of Marye's Heights out of more than 10,000 for the battle as a whole.

The Stone Wall as a Magnet

Corps Commander Couch, observing such portions of the battle as could be glimpsed through the haze and clouds of smoke which shrouded the field, from the cupola of the court house with General Howard at his side, concluded that it was time to vary the monotony by adopting a new tack. Howard's division was the only one remaining to him, so to Howard he gave instructions to move his division off to the right where he might find it easier going with the possibility of flanking that devilish stone wall. Apparently the idea didn't occur to either Couch or Howard to send a few officer scouts and skirmishers ahead to test the ground and determine in advance that the plan was feasible.

Howard moved promptly to carry out the order, but his regiments, after crossing the ditch as the others had done, and then slanting off by the right flank, ran smack into a marshy lowland caused by seepage from the drainage ditch. Forced to the left by this obstacle, Howard's troops found themselves heading for the same stone wall that seemed like a magnet to draw the successive waves of Federal attackers inevitably into its field of influence.

Now all three of Couch's divisions were immobilized in a small area from which they could move neither forward nor back without stopping a Confederate bullet or shell. Howard's 900-odd casualties brought the Federal total in Sumner's zone to more than 4,000. But the orders kept coming over from the remote army commander to continue the attack, as though by sheer repetition or a miracle of some sort he could pluck a victory from what had by now become crystal clear to the lowliest private—that the Army of the Potomac was taking another terrible licking in trying to achieve the impossible.

Dead horses, dead comrades, rocks, fragments of demolished fences, all were used as parapets by individual soldiers as partial shields against the point-blank musketry fire which continuously battered them from behind the stone wall.

The official report of Confederate General McLaws, in command of that part of the line which included Marye's Heights, stated that "the body of one man, believed to be an officer, was found within about thirty yards of the stone wall, and other single bodies were scattered at increased distances until the main mass of the dead lay thickly strewn over the ground at something over one hundred yards off, and extending to the ravine, commencing at the point where our men would allow the enemy's column to approach before opening fire, and beyond which no organized body of men was able to pass."

Meantime, about noon, Willcox (Ninth Corps) had ordered Sturgis to support Couch's attack. Sturgis moved forward in two columns along the railroad, his brigades echeloned to the left rear of Hancock. The leading brigade deployed, came under enfilade attack from the guns on

Lee's Hill firing down the railroad cut; it was stopped behind Hancock's shattered units. The second brigade was ordered to deploy on the left but it too suffered from the enfilade fire, obliqued to the right, and, like the first, took cover behind the slight rise in the middle of the plain.

Several Federal batteries dramatically galloped across the bridge over the ditch and made a heroic effort to counter the Confederate fire. General Couch himself rode the length of his line, courting death the whole distance and bringing considerable comfort to his men, who understandably were more enheartened to see their corps commander take the same chances for punishment as themselves.

Whipple's division of Stoneman's Third Corps (Birney and Sickles having been released to Franklin), had been sent across the river to free Howard's division on the right to join in the direct attack, and Griffin's division of Butterfield's Fifth Corps was sent in to support Sturgis, while the divisions of Humphreys and Sykes, of the Fifth Corps, were ordered across to support Couch.

In desperation and somewhat wildly Burnside now ordered Franklin to charge the enemy on his front with his whole force in an effort to take some of the weight off the bogged-down divisions on the right; at the same time he ordered Hooker to renew the attack on the stone wall, with two of his remaining reserve divisions of the Fifth Corps. While these divisions were crossing the river, Hooker himself went on ahead to look the situation over and confer with Couch and Hancock. What he saw decided him to try to dissuade Burnside from sacrificing any more men. By the time he had ridden back to the Phillips house, made his plea, been flatly turned down and returned to the front, it was after 4 o'clock. The early December twilight was beginning to reduce visibility with its promise of blessed relief to the endangered Federals lying in the open before the stone wall.

Burnside's order to Franklin to charge with his whole force was the subject of considerable subsequent controversy between the respective headquarters of the two generals. The former took the position that Franklin had disregarded the order, while the latter maintained that it was received too late to be of any use. In any event Franklin did *not* make a general advance, which may or may not prove that the general who is under fire on the actual ground is in better position to appraise the possibilities for success or failure.

Nevertheless, two more divisions—Getty's and Humphreys—were thrown against the stone wall. Willcox had held Getty's division as a reserve and to guard the left of the town. But at 4 P.M. he decided to advance this division, hoping thereby to relieve the pressure on the right. Getty got under way at 5 o'clock, just about dusk, advanced to the right oblique in column of brigades toward the point where the railroad curves off to the left. His second brigade stopped at the railroad embankment, but the leading brigade continued on, through enfilade fire from Lee's Hill, across a small tributary of Hazel Run, until it reached a line within less than a hundred yards of the left portion of the stone wall. Here it was stopped by fire from the front and the left. The survivors lay down, then were withdrawn, first to the shelter of the railroad embankment, then into the town.

While Hooker was on his way to talk with Burnside, Han cock's men had mistaken a troop movement on the Confederate heights, involving the replacement of the Washington Artillery by Alexander's battalion, for a retirement. Hancock reported this to corps commander Couch who in turn told Humphreys: "Now is the time for you to go in!" Humphreys was quick to act. Apparently under the impression that the Confederates were withdrawing and his assault would not involve the fire fight which had halted the earlier attacks, or because he may have figured that an attack with cold steel might succeed where all previous attempts had failed, he directed his troops to fix bayonets without waiting to load their muskets. He promptly led forward the two brigades, composed of Pennsylvania boys who were experiencing serious action for the first time.

Humphreys' division succeeded in getting closer to the stone wall than any other. But that was all, because the alleged Confederate withdrawal was a false alarm; the fresh artillery battalion of six batteries took position in time to open on Humphreys' men. Furthermore the riflemen behind the stone wall were present in even greater numbers than before. The result was a casualty list of over 1,000 for Humphreys. This brought the score for the stone-wall Confederates to approximately 6,300 Federals killed, wounded, and missing, almost as many men as Lee was to lose in Pickett's charge at Gettysburg six months later.

Humpheys' assault, which terminated in semidarkness, was the last of six massive but unsupported Federal attacks on the fortified heights. It marked the end of the day's fighting. Hooker ordered the men to fall back from their advance position with this rather morose and sardonic thought, which he later embodied in his official report: "Finding that I had lost as many men as my orders required me to lose, I suspended the attack."

The order from Hooker for the troops in front of Marye's Heights to retire from their advance position on the open plain was something akin to Falstaff's boast that "he could call up vasty spirits from the deep," and the retort of his companion "Yes, but will they come?" Withdrawal under Confederate fire was a ticklish business even in the twilight. It wasn't until night had fully come that it was practicable to effect the relief of the able-bodied survivors, who were greatly relieved at being able to again move about freely in the comparative safety and com fort of the streets of Fredericksburg.

Under cover of darkness, then, some semblance of order was introduced among the badly mixed up and exhausted thou sands of still living Federals, both walking-wounded and unhurt, who remained in the open plain before Marye's Heights. Accuracy of fire was of course out of the question, so the Confederates used their ammunition sparingly, but with sufficient regularity to prevent their enemy from carrying out salvage operations with any degree of effectiveness. Some units were relieved and replaced by those which were still fairly intact, and it became possible to do something for the wounded.

SYKES' DIVISION TAKES OVER

Sykes' division of the Fifth Corps, the only one in Sumner's or Hooker's grand divisions that had not been in action during the battle of December 13, was sent forward late in the day to relieve a portion of Couch's corps which had been so badly mauled in the succession of frontal attacks on the stone wall. The division reached the western edge of the town while there was still enough daylight for them to see. The field in their front was full of soldiers, living and dead. The sun, about to set, showed red through columns of smoke and haze.

The battle was over. In a short time the shooting and the tumult of battle sounds died away except for desultory artillery fire. As the men watched and waited for further orders in the gathering darkness, shells from the Confederate battery positions etched bright lines with their burning fuses as they streaked across the black sky.

There Sykes' men remained under arms, catching what sleep they could, until they were roused shortly before midnight, when they formed into line and marched away from the town toward Marye's Heights. Moving quietly, with whispered commands, they were then formed in two lines and bivouacked for the few remaining hours of the night within a stone's throw of the stone wall, finding considerable difficulty in locating places on the ground where they could lie down because of the shattered forms of those who had already died or who were so badly wounded that they could neither be moved nor expect to see the sun rise on the morrow.

THE BATTLE AS SEEN FROM THE CONFEDERATE SIDE

The crest of the ridge along which the Confederate guns had been posted with such care and foresight, and below which ran the sunken road lined fore and aft by the stone wall, afforded an incomparable vantage point from which to observe the drama about to be enacted on the stage below.

A small group of Confederate artillery officers, lounging comfortably in the yard of the Marye House in the sector as signed to the Washington Artillery, were smoking their pipes late on the morning of December 13 as, in company with the rest of Longstreet's corps, they waited expectantly for the Federals in Fredericksburg to reveal their intentions.

The fog had cleared and from their lofty position some fifty feet above the open plain they were able to see everything on two feet or four that moved in the open fields between the ridge and the town a half mile to the east.

It was close to noon when a courier came up to the artillery commander, saluted, and handed him a dispatch from General Longstreet to be read before he carried it down to General Cobb of McLaws' Division whose brigade was charged with the infantry defense of Marye's Hill. Hardly had the messenger started down the hill when rifle fire broke out from the direction of Fredericksburg. As the artillerymen watched, a Federal column emerged jogging in double time from one of the streets of the town, arms at the right shoulder, crossed the bridge over the canal ditch, and disappeared from sight behind a rise in the ground. The Confederate skirmishers fell back, firing as they ran, to the cover of the sunken road.

The fight was on. Having deployed, the Federals reappeared over their own low crest. They advanced in columns of brigades, bayonets flashing in the sunlight in a way that one of the Confederates reported "made their line look like a huge serpent of blue and steel." The Washington Artillery, opening with shell and solid shot, tore great gaps in the compact Federal lines, which flowed over and through the garden and farm fences as though they didn't exist. Now the attackers were close enough for enemy canister to get in its deadly work. The blue mass slowed perceptibly, but still came on, until Cobb's infantry, sighting over the stone wall, loosed a terrific hail of bullets at close range. The Federals faltered, seemingly dazed, then broke and sought cover behind the bank to their immediate rear. Almost at once a second line of blue appeared from behind the crest and came gallantly forward. This line was thinned out rapidly, but reached a point a little closer to the stone wall. Soon those who were still standing broke ranks and commenced drifting to the rear, singly or in small groups.

At this stage an additional Confederate brigade was moved into the sunken road to reinforce Cobb. About 2 o'clock the third Federal attack was launched, with the same spirit and an even stronger determination, apparently, to carry the position. This attack crested even closer to the stone wall than the second; but the murderous fire from the sunken road and the plunging artillery fire from the heights was too much for them.

The Confederates by this time were beginning to be a little worried lest succeeding assaults, of which there seemed to be no end, might by sheer weight of numbers smother the defenders in spite of their protective shield and deadly fire. To make certain that wouldn't happen, three more regiments were ordered up from Ransom's Division, which was serving as a backstop for McLaws' front line. Casualties were increasing in the Confederate ranks. General Cobb had been mortally, and General

Cooke seriously wounded. The Federal sharpshooters had gotten the range and the number of dead and wounded on the hill and even behind the stone wall began to mount.

Still the Federal attacks continued, but always with the same final result. Confederate artillery ammunition was running low, the frozen ground had thawed and turned to mud and slush, and the artillery had to call on the infantry to help man the guns. At 5:30 in the afternoon the last of the Federal attacks was launched and repulsed. The Confederate defenders breathed heavy sighs of relief, understandably indeed in view of the long period of fighting and strain they had undergone for five solid hours. For unbelievable as it may sound, only 6,000 muskets and no more than twenty guns had borne the defense of Marye's Heights against the driving weight of seven Federal divisions whose aggregate battle strength exceeded 40,000 men, a ratio of almost 7:1.

During the early afternoon it appeared to General Longstreet that the pressure had mounted to such an extent that a reinforcement of the line which had borne the brunt of the Federal attacks was advisable. The inactivity in front of Pickett's Division, on the far side of Hazel Run and in front of Lee's Hill, seemed likely to continue. So Lee shifted one of Pickett's brigades over to Anderson's front on the left flank of his sector to serve the dual purpose of assisting the defenders at the foot of Marye's Hill if needed, and to be prepared to meet a night attack with the bayonet. He regarded this as a possibility in view of the dogged and completely effective resistance being offered by his troops to the repeated but fruitless frontal attacks across the plain.

THE DEPRESSING AFTERMATH OF BATTLE

The night of December 13 was bitterly cold, which caused extreme suffering for the wounded who could not be evacuated. Many died of their wounds and exposure and, wrote General Couch, "as fast as men died they stiffened in the wintery air and on the front line were rolled forward for protection to the living. Frozen men were placed for dumb sentries."

On the morning of December 14 a macabre sight met the eye. Where the night before the plain had been covered with hundreds of blue-clad dead bodies, the field at daylight was dotted with white figures; thinly clad Confederate soldiers having decided apparently that the corpses would never miss their clothing and that their own needs should take precedence.

The attitude of mind of the men of Burnside's army can be easily imagined. They knew they had been unsuccessful, were depressed by their huge losses, and aside from the normal reaction after the strain of battle, the men in the ranks had joined their high-ranking officers in having completely lost confidence in the army commander.

How Not to Fight a Battle

Sykes' division on the front line found themselves in a most unenviable position when the sun broke through the fog on Sunday morning, December 14. The men were chilled to the bone from having lain for hours on the cold, damp ground. Protected from the view of the nearby Confederates by the early fog, some of them found temporary solace in the warming effect of a pipeful of tobacco and all were able to stretch their aching joints and improve their circulation by limited movements within their assigned positions as they peered through the misty veil at the wreckage on the battlefield.

With the passing minutes the fog grew thinner. Soon the surprised infantrymen spotted through the haze, about eighty yards away, the stonewall which had proven the nemesis of Couch's divisions the day before. Behind the wall were men in gray uniforms walking carelessly about, cooking breakfast, cleaning muskets, and performing the usual chores which occupy soldiers when not in actual combat. The first startled impression of the Federals was that they were prisoners of Lee's army, so close did yesterday's victors appear and so isolated from the rest of the Union army did Sykes' men feel themselves to be.

The Confederates saw their enemy at the same time. As the whistle of bullets shocked the Federals into reality, they hit the dirt as one man and there they lay, two lines of blue in their shallow depression, trying to figure out what they should do and what the Confederates *would* do. The fields behind them were flat and obviously subject to converging fire that would make retreat even more dangerous than to remain where they were. The black muzzles of the enemy guns frowned directly down at them from the heights and from them there would be no shelter once the guns opened up. So long as the men kept the prone position, musket balls couldn't reach them, but any movement, even to shift position on the ground in order to gain slight relief from cramped muscles, drew fire from watchful sharpshooters behind the wall.

Apparently the Southerners were enjoying the situation. They whiled away the time in target practice on such stray chickens, loose horses, broken artillery caissons, and live pigs as were to be seen. Their accuracy was such at the short range that the men of Sykes' division almost with one accord reached the conclusion that to lie low and make as few movements as possible was the only sensible guarantee of continued existence.

Men who left the line to get water or for other necessary purposes, before the lines were pinned to the earth, were either killed or wounded on the return journey, almost to a man. But after several hours of this nerve-wracking experience, the limit of patience was reached by a few tobacco-loving souls who had run out of their supply, and had friends in other companies who they felt sure could fill the need. Occasionally one of these bold spirits would suddenly leap to his feet, sprint in a crouching position to another part of the line and throw himself flat on the ground. As moving targets they were not always hit, and the one who was able to run the gauntlet in both directions safely was heartily applauded and congratulated by his comrades as though he had accomplished a feat worthy of a Medal of Honor. All day long the men of the division sweated it out, the more philosophical ones in fitful catnaps, until finally, but almost hesitatingly as it seemed to the impatient Federals, the red ball that was the sun stood poised on the western horizon. Strained faces turned toward it as to a savior in their eagerness for the short December twilight to arrive and free them from their long and painful bondage.

As the sun disappeared the Federal line sprang to its collective feet. In a moment the Confederates opened fire, but it was then too late for aimed shots. The Federals returned the fire, more to relieve their frustrated feelings than in the expectation of hitting anything, and that was it. A messenger from Fredericksburg brought the welcome recall orders, the troops formed up, and 85 percent of those who had come out from the town just twenty-four hours earlier formed ranks and marched back to comparative peace, leaving 15 percent of their number as casual ties for removal by litter bearers.

Burnside Is Dissuaded from Another Suicidal Assault

About 9 o'clock on the night of the battle, Colonel Rush C. Hawkins, commanding a brigade in Getty's division of the Ninth Corps, sat in on a conference of generals in Fredericksburg which included corps commanders Willcox and Butterfield, division commanders Humphreys, Getty, and Meade, and several others. All seemed to expect that the attack would be renewed the following day, but Hawkins has written that he protested emphatically against even considering another attack. He was evidently successful in persuading the others to adopt his views, and was delegated to represent them in attempting similarly to convince Burnside. Hawkins reached the Phillips house commanders, Sumner, Hooker, and Franklin were there, so Hawkins explained his mission to them and they in turn urged him to await Burnside's return, which occurred about 1 o'clock in morning. But let Hawkins take over at this point:

> As he (Burnside) came through the door he said: "Well, it's all arranged; we attack at early dawn, the Ninth Corps in the center, which I shall lead in person"; and then seeing me he said: "Hawkins, your brigade shall lead with the 9th New York on the right of the line, and we'll make up for the bad work of today."
>
> When he had ceased there was perfect silence, and he was evidently astonished that no one approved. With hesitation and great delicacy General Sumner then stated the object of my visit, and suggested that General Burnside should examine the rough drawing then upon the table, and listen to some reasons why the attack contemplated ought not to be made. After I had explained the enemy's positions, called attention to several pertinent circumstances, and made something of an argument, General Burnside asked General Sumner what he thought, and he replied that the troops had undergone such great fatigue and privation, and met with such a disaster, that it would not be prudent to make another attack so soon. General Hooker, who

was lying full length upon a bed in one corner of the room, upon being appealed to by General Burnside, sat up and said in the most frank and decided manner that the attack ought not to be renewed that morning. Then a general consultation took place, in which all who were present joined, the result of which was a verbal order, transmitted through me, countermanding the arrangements for a second attack.

Evidently Burnside had been convinced, the second day's attack was canceled, and on the morning of the 14th the soldiers were put to work digging trenches along the western edge of the town. The army was very much on the alert against an expected counterattack by the Confederates, even though the order to stand by but not renew the attack had not yet filtered down through the chain of command.

Sunday noon Burnside called another council of war to ascertain the views of his grand division commanders about falling back but retaining Fredericksburg. Hooker was positive in his opinion that it would be a mistake to retreat, while others felt that if the fight was to be renewed, it would be foolish to yield Fredericksburg and then have to re-take it. The consensus of opinion was that Fredericksburg should be held and the council was dismissed with instructions to Hooker and Couch to arrange for a better defense of the town.

So the Army of the Potomac sat it out in the streets of Fredericksburg and on the plain to the south all day Sunday the 14th, and Monday the 15th, as Burnside paced the floor of the Phillips house, wondering what to do.

The Army of Northern Virginia also remained quiet on their secure ridge, as Lee pondered the situation and awaited further evidence of Federal offensive operations, which all the Confederate generals except Hood were sure would be attempted. Lee had advised Richmond by telegram at the end of the first day's fight that he expected a renewal of the attack on the 14th, expressing the belief that the disastrous frontal assaults would be discarded in favor of a more likely turning movement, which he had credited Burnside with the intelligence to undertake in the first place. In preparation for such an eventuality, Lee issued orders which resulted in a reshuffle of his divisions with a view to holding his defense position with reduced strength, while assembling a large reserve that he could use for maneuver, counterattack, or any other measure which might require quick and flexible troop employment.

When the sun dissipated the fog on the second morning, the Confederates could see that the Federals were still occupying the ditch in front of Marye's Heights, but had also barricaded the streets leading west from the town, which in itself implied defensive preparations. On Jackson's end of the line the enemy could with equal facility be observed resting on their arms, row after row of them, but giving no indication whatsoever of an intention to resume the offensive. Thus the second day passed with only an occasional exchange between skirmishers and a few desultory shells from Federal batteries. General Lee was puzzled and scarcely able to believe what his eyes told him.

On the afternoon of the 15th, Burnside sent a flag of truce to suggest time out for burial of the dead and relief for such of the wounded as still managed to survive. Lee consented and the burial parties and medical corpsmen from Fredericksburg commenced their gruesome task, encountering here and there an avaricious Confederate soldier evidently hoping it was not too late to salvage a pair of good boots or other useful bit of clothing or equipment from the fallen Federals.

That night it rained. All who could naturally sought what shelter was available. The next morning the usual haze covered the fields and buildings and there was no sign of the men of the Army of the Potomac. They had folded their theoretical tents and silently stolen away. Burnside had concluded there wasn't much point in just passing the time in in effectual idleness on a field where he had been so soundly defeated. He had ordered a night withdrawal which, needless to say, was accomplished with alacrity and with commendable efficiency by his army. The Confederates, not having been informed of his plan, were for their part able to derive little satisfaction from their lack of alertness in allowing such a huge force to sneak away and with impunity take up its bridges under their very noses.

The successfully executed withdrawal helped slightly to restore the shattered equanimity of the Union army and, conversely, caused a natural chagrin on the part of Lee and his generals. The gratification of the latter over their decisive victory with inferior numbers, and with casualties of only 5,588 against Burnside's 12,660, was tempered by disappointment that they had not been able to exploit the victory.

The strategic fruits were of no real value to the Confederate cause, and nothing much had been accomplished except another setback for the Union, which was better able to replace its man power losses and equipment, and would soon recover its breath and try again.

Lee's feelings were reflected in his very brief initial report on the Fredericksburg action which disposed of the action on Longstreet's front in a few words:

> *Soon after his repulse on our right, he [the enemy] commenced a series of attacks on our left with a view to obtaining possession of the heights immediately overlooking the town. These repeated attacks were repulsed in gallant style by the Washington Artillery, and a portion of McLaws' Division, which occupied these heights. The last assault was made after dark, when Colonel Alexander's battalion had relieved the Washington Artillery and ended the con test of the day.*

In the last analysis, and in retrospect, it was the townspeople of Fredericksburg who suffered most grievously, other than the 2,000-odd soldiers of both armies who had lost their lives. The buildings had been thoroughly shelled by Hunt's artillery, and in the latter stages by Longstreet's, many had been burned, and all were thoroughly ransacked by a Federal army which by now had apparently given up all pretense to the chivalrous attitude with which the war had started out. War was indeed assuming a grim aspect.

CHAPTER 21

Burnside Is Relieved of Command

BURNSIDE'S telegraphic report to Halleck, dated December 17, 1862, recounted the major features of the Battle of Fredericksburg, assumed full responsibility for its failure, and commended in terms of high praise "the extreme gallantry, courage and endurance shown by officers and men," which he said were never excelled. "The fact that I decided to move from Warrenton on to this line rather against the opinion of the President, Secretary, and yourself, and that you have left the whole management in my hands, without giving me orders, makes me the more responsible," added Burnside humbly, yet with a rather keen sense of psychology, for it brought a letter to the Army of the Potomac from President Lincoln which referred to Burn side's report of the battle, praised the courage of the army, and applied consoling salve with the statement: "Although you were not successful, the attempt was not an error, nor the failure other than accident."

No such letter arrived from the taciturn and consistently disapproving Halleck. But the President's acceptance of the defeat without recriminations or jerking Burnside out of the driver's seat must have bucked him up considerably, for he immediately started making plans for another offensive.

LINCOLN APPLIES A CHECKREIN
On December 26, the day after Christmas, Burnside ordered the entire army to stock up with three days' cooked rations and sufficient additional rations on the wagons and on the hoof, plus forage for the animals, to carry the army for an additional ten days. The requisite amount of ammunition for the campaign was ordered loaded and the army directed to be ready to move on twelve hours' notice.

Although the army commander knew what he intended to do, he was afraid that word would leak to the Confederates, so he confided his plans only to those officers who were required to make initial reconnaissances in order to carry out their part of the project. Burnside's plan was to cross the Rappahannock on pontoons at Banks Ford and U.S. Ford, enroute to an attack from the west against the Confederate heights above Fredericksburg.

In the hope of deceiving Lee, a special cavalry expedition of 2,500 troopers, 1,000 of them picked men, was organized and started out before Christmas under command of Brig. Gen. William W. Averell. Averell's instructions were to proceed to Kelly's Ford, some eighteen miles above Fredericksburg, cross the Rapidan, fan out in several directions, including Warrenton and Culpeper, cut the railroad at Louisa Court House, blow up the locks of the James River canal, destroy bridges, and finally assemble at Suffolk, where steamers would be waiting to return the cavalry to Aquia Creek. Thus the cavalry would have circumnavigated the Army of Northern Virginia and possibly given Lee a few bad moments.

The detailed orders for the grand divisions had all been composed and were about to be issued for the movement when this message was received from the President: "I have good reasons for saying that you must not make a general movement without first letting me know of it."

Burnside immediately countermanded the orders, halted Averell's cavalry, and dashed off to Washington, where he was informed by Lincoln that several of his general officers (Lincoln did not divulge their names) had told the President that the army was not in shape to move, and that was the reason for his telegram. It may be assumed that Burnside, now convinced that it was the part of wisdom to take the President into his confidence even if Halleck were not willing to share with him the responsibility of making major tactical decisions, outlined his plan for the new adventure and was given permission to go ahead as soon as the army had been granted a few weeks for rest and refitting.

There was much more to the conference than that, however, because while Burnside was not overly burdened with brains, he wasn't altogether stupid and quite properly expressed his indignation that a couple of his generals had come to Washington behind his back to tell tales out of school. He wanted to know who they were, so he could prefer charges for insubordination and disloyalty. When the information was denied him he suggested to the President that perhaps the country would be better off if he should resign, adding that his generals lacked confidence in him and as a matter of fact were practically unanimous in opposition to any further offensive operations at Fredericksburg. The lonely general must have appeared to the President somewhat like the fictional little boy in the Fourth of July parade whose doting mother noted that "everybody's out of step but Johnnie."

The "disloyal" brigadiers, John Newton, a division commander, and John Cochrane, one of Newton's brigade commanders, both of W. F. Smith's Sixth Corps of Franklin's Left Grand Division, were neither court-martialed nor even reprimanded, because Burnside failed to learn who they were at that time. They had informed both Smith and Franklin in advance of their purpose in going to Washington, when they were granted leaves of absence. Later developments reveal that in due course Burnside did learn their identity.

Newton and Cochrane, whose trip to Washington to tip the President off to the fact that the situation in the army had deteriorated and needed looking into, failed to do more than muddy the waters. The long-suffering Lincoln considered them suspect and took the occasion to smooth down the ruffled Burn side temporarily, while Halleck, for once agreeing with Burnside that the plotters deserved to be dismissed from the Service, pontificated with a few meaningless platitudes and after several days' delay sent the army commander back to his headquarters on the Rappahannock with the assurance that the Administration approved another advance but that Burnside would have to decide the where and how.

THE MUD MARCH

The cavalry of the Army of the Potomac, consolidated under Pleasonton's command, had for some time after the Battle of Fredericksburg been energetically reconnoitering the north bank of the Rappahannock for miles above and below Fredericksburg, reporting what their scouting parties could see of the Confederates here and there on the other side, with particular attention to the fords above Fredericksburg.

The ill-fated army commander now made ready to undertake the last of four attempts to gain the upper hand over his able opponent from Virginia, before finally accepting what was already quite evident to both armies, that he was over his depth in his current role.

His orders to the three grand division commanders, dated January 20, 1863, called for a march along the north side of the Rappahannock, crossings by boats for the leading division of each wing, and throwing of the bridges under the direction of Engineer General Woodbury. These preliminaries were to be followed by the crossing of the entire army and subsequent development leading to a turning movement against the familiar Confederate heights west of Fredericksburg, this time in reverse, however, and at the northern end.

The grand divisions of Hooker and Franklin were directed to cross at points just above and below Banks Ford, about a mile apart from each other and eight miles west of Fredericksburg. This modified plan eliminated the crossing at the U.S. Ford, where the Confederates were reported to be in strength sufficient to block the attempt, in favor of the more concentrated one near Banks Ford. The troops were to be in position at the designated crossing points at 7:30 A.M. in the morning of January 21, ready to expedite the passage as soon as the bridges should be laid. Sumner's grand division was directed to follow the other two when Burnside should give the word. After crossing, the leading grand divisions were to develop in the direction of Fredericksburg, Hooker on the right, Franklin on the left, and initially to seize the high ground and the roads leading to Fredericksburg south of the Rappahannock to and including the Plank Road. To assure adequate artillery protection for the river crossing, and after a careful reconnaissance, Burnside's Chief of Artillery, General Hunt, planned a strong line of batteries along the north bank, aggregating a total of 184 guns (37 more than he had posted on Stafford Heights for the attack of December 13), all the way from Falmouth to a point several miles beyond.

Predicated upon a successful crossing and development, Burnside duplicated his earlier underestimate of Lee's capabilities by indicating his opinion that a vigorous flank attack around the north end of Marye's Heights would cause Lee to evacuate the position. In his mind's eye the hopeful Burnside pictured the army as sweeping eastward between the Rappahannock and the Plank Road, with Franklin making the main effort on the left, Sumner in close support, and Hooker advancing steadily on the right. Between them Franklin and Sumner would out-flank Lee's right (formerly his left), take Taylor's Hill and extend to the Plank Road as Hooker swung down the Mine Road which angled off to Hamilton's Crossing. What Hooker was to accomplish by the latter tan-gential maneuver was not indicated.

It was an ambitious and complicated plan which didn't stand a ghost of a chance of succeeding, even if the corps and division commanders had been cooperative. Burnside's wordy orders to Franklin and Hooker spelled out tactical details that depended progressively on the precise exe-cution of a complicated series of movements by a vast number of units. They would have been difficult of fulfillment without the opposition of an already victorious Confederate army.

Fortunately for the Army of the Potomac, Old Man Weather provi-dentially intervened just at the right moment to save it from still another humiliating battle experience. Rain started to fall on the evening of the 20th, the night Burnside's army was moving toward its new positions preparatory to again crossing the river. Several corps and division commanders, disinclined to allow Hunt to take their artillery away from them at will, delayed the movement of their organic artillery batteries, as the roads quickly became quagmires which upset all march schedules. And the rains continued to descend for two days while the long suffering Federals struggled manfully but hopelessly to carry out the march orders of their army commander.

General Lee was taking Burnside's ambitious new campaign with his customary calm, having been kept adequately informed of the Federal preparations through cavalry scouts, spies, and his own acute powers of deduction. His report of the latest abortive efforts of his opponent showed that by January 19 he was aware of Burnside's intentions. This was one day before the latter had even issued the march orders to his grand division commanders.

Fredericksburg, January 29, 1863.

SIR: On the 19th instant, being satisfied that General Burnside was massing the larger portion of his army in the vicinity of Hartwood Church; that his artillery and pontoon trains were moving in the same direction, and that General Slocum's command was advancing from the vicinity of Fairfax toward the Rappahannock, our positions at Banks' and United States Mine Fords were strengthened and reenforced, these being the points apparently threatened.

The movements of the enemy on the 20th confirmed the belief that an effort would be made to turn our left flank, and that Franklin's and Hooker's corps were the troops selected for that purpose. About dark that evening the rain, which had been threatening during the day, commenced to fall, and continued all night and the two following days. Whether the storm or other causes frustrated the designs of the enemy I do not know; but no attempt as yet has been made to cross the Rappahannock, and some of the enemy's forces have apparently resumed their former positions.

A second storm commenced before day on the 27th, and continued till this morning. The ground is covered with at least 6 inches of snow, and the probabilities are that the roads will be impracticable for some time.

As the long columns plodded forward at a pace that became ever slower as the rains persisted and the roads became slippery mud holes, tempers flared, march schedules lost all meaning, caissons and wagons became hopelessly bogged, units were inter mingled, and prostrate animals smothered in the apparently bottomless pits of Virginia clay. The weak gave up the struggle, dropped out along the road, and some died there, while the subsequent sick rolls recorded a large number of cases of pneumonia and other pulmonary diseases.

By the time the second day was half spent, Burnside, convinced that the prospects were hopeless, called the whole thing off. The pontoons never had reached their destination, hundreds of soldiers had disgustedly taken things into their own hands and deserted, stragglers were all over the countryside. The Confederates on the other side of the river were greatly enjoying themselves jeering at the Federals within range of their voices. The problem of the Union army was no longer one of crossing the river to do battle, but just how they were going to reverse their steps, recover some semblance of military order, and be able to function at all, let alone stage an aggressive battle.

The return to their former camps near Falmouth of the disgruntled, bedraggled, disheartened soldiers of the Army of the Potomac was in sad contrast to the outgoing march, two days earlier, with regimental colors flying and bands playing in a revival of the martial spirit which was no doubt induced by order, but which by the same token was a necessary and useful device so soon after the Fredericksburg defeat.

It would be a long time before that army would again be ready to do battle. Had Lee's strategic plans permitted, he might have taken advantage of the condition of the Union army to undertake a crossing of his own at the upper fords, to add injury to insult at a time when Burnside's army was in the depths of physical and mental despair. Stuart's cavalry and horse artillery alone might have managed to strike terror into the Federal camp, but they too had to wait for the roads to improve before they could do any effective maneuvering. On the other hand, Burnside seemed to be so unsuccessful on his own, without help from the Confederates, that Lee may have reached the conclusion that he could accomplish more by standing pat for the time being.

BURNSIDE LOSES ANOTHER BATTLE

After the abortive "mud march" was concluded, and within twenty-four hours of the army's dejected return to their camps near Falmouth, Burnside seemed to go to pieces. The combination of frustrating events had finally gotten under his skin, and he determined to strike out in all directions against his imagined detractors and disloyal subordinates. He thereupon composed General Orders No. 8, the purpose of which was to accomplish a thorough housecleaning in the Army of the Potomac, with a view to eliminating grand division commanders Hooker and Franklin, corps commander Smith, and a couple of division and brigade commanders, including the two tale-bearers who had gone to Lincoln to complain of Burnside's incapacity.

It is to be noted that the name of General Sumner, who commanded the right wing more or less in absentia during the Battle of Fredericksburg, was missing from Burnside's list of scapegoats. Sumner was a loyal old soul, a nonpolitical, nonscheming officer of the old school and so Burnside, having nothing against him, naturally excluded him from the sweeping denunciations which, with the exception of Hooker and two generals of Burnside's old Ninth Corps, were directed at Franklin and a select group of generals in his Sixth Corps, including the corps commander. General Sumner's death occurred just two months later, in March 1863, and it is fair to wonder if there was any connection with the Fredericksburg.

This was the order which marks the final disintegration of General Burnside:

I. General Joseph Hooker, major-general of volunteers and brigadier general U.S. Army, having been guilty of unjust and unnecessary criticisms of the actions of his superior officers, and of the authorities, and having, by the general tone of his conversation, endeavored to create distrust in the minds of officers who have associated with him, and having, by omissions and otherwise, made reports and statements which were calculated to create incorrect impressions, and for habitually speaking in disparaging terms of other officers, is hereby dismissed the service of the United States as a man unfit to hold an important commission during a crisis like the present, when so much patience, charity, confidence, consideration, and patriotism are due from every soldier in the field. This order is issued subject to the approval of the President of the United States.

II. Brig. Gen. W. T. H. Brooks, commanding First Division, Sixth Army Corps, for complaining of the policy of the Government, and for using language tending to demoralize his command, is, subject to the approval of the President, dismissed from the military service of the United States.

III. Brig. Gen. John Newton, commanding Third Division, Sixth Army Corps, and Brig. Gen. John Cochrane, commanding First Brigade, Third Division, Sixth Army Corps, for going to the President of the United States with criticisms upon the plans of their commanding officer, are, subject to the approval of the President, dismissed from the military service of the United States.

D. It being evident that the following named officers can be of no further service to this army, they are hereby relieved from duty, and will report, in person, without delay, to the Adjutant-General, U.S. Army: Maj. Gen. W. B. Franklin, commanding left grand division; Maj. Gen. W. Sturgis, commanding Second Division, Ninth Corps; Brig. Gen. Edward Ferrero, commanding Second Brigade, Second Division, Ninth Army Corps; Brig. Gen. John Cochrane, commanding First Brigade, Third Division, Sixth Corps; Lieut. Col. J. H. Taylor, assistant adjutant general, right grand division.

After the war, General Smith, the Sixth Corps commander, made a written record of the fact that he had had several conversations with Burnside after the Battle of Fredericksburg, in one of which he quotes Burnside as having said: "I made a mistake in my order to Franklin; I should have directed him to carry the hill at Hamilton's at all hazards." Smith also quoted Burnside as having told him at one time that he had it in mind to relieve Sumner from command, place Hooker in arrest, and put Franklin in command of the army. In appraising these comments, it must be recognized that they were written after the war, and it would be natural for one of the generals who had been listed for removal in General Orders No. 8 (G.O.8), to have something less than friendly feelings for Burnside. But it also suggests Burnside's mercurial character. The conclusion is that Burnside talked too much at some times and too little at others. Franklin's reaction to Burnside can best be summed up by his quoted remark that "the man had lost his mind."

Whatever else may be thought of G.O.8, it was exceedingly presumptuous. Burnside lacked the authority to dismiss officers at will, without first ordering them before boards of inquiry or general courts-martial. The insertion of the phrase "subject to the approval of the President," in several paragraphs of the order, was made at the suggestion of Burnside's staff, who likewise advised that publication be delayed until it could be presented to the President in person for approval. Burnside accepted the recommendations and accordingly journeyed to Washington where he laid the order before the President. In requesting that he sanction its publication, the President was told that it was essential if Burnside was to maintain proper authority and discipline over the army, and that his resignation was the only alternative. Lincoln declined to approve the order without consulting a number of his advisors, whereupon Burnside, insisting that delay would result in disapproval, requested that his resignation be accepted at once. The President no doubt informed Burnside that he would do it in his own way, and the general was requested to return that night to receive the President's decision.

When Burnside again called upon Lincoln the President in formed him that he would not approve G.O.8, and had decided instead to relieve him from command of the Army of the Potomac and to appoint General Hooker in his place. The brief but historic January 25 order of the War Department likewise disposed of Generals Sumner and Franklin, in the following language:

I. The President of the United States has directed:

1st. That Maj. Gen. A. E. Burnside, at his own request, be relieved from the command of the Army of the Potomac.

2nd. That Maj. Gen. E. V. Sumner, at his own request, be relieved from duty in the Army of the Potomac.

3d. That Maj. Gen. W. B. Franklin be relieved from duty in the Army of the Potomac.

4th. That Maj. Gen. J. Hooker be assigned to the command of the Army of the Potomac.

II. The officers relieved as above will report in person to the Adjutant General of the Army.

CHAPTER 22

Hooker Plans a Campaign

It was snowing heavily on the afternoon of Saturday, April 4, 1863 as a little steamer carrying a distinguished cargo glided down the Potomac River from the Washington Navy Yard. President Abraham Lincoln, accompanied by Mrs. Lincoln, Tad, and a small group of friends, was on his way to pay his first field visit to the Army of the Potomac under its new commander, Major General Joseph Hooker. Following Burnside's defeat at the Battle of Fredericksburg in December the army had, since Hooker assured command on January 25, been undergoing a period of reorganization and rehabilitation in its camps near Falmouth, on the north shore of the Rappahannock River.

Poor visibility caused the steamer to put in for the night in a protected cove. The next day the journey was continued, with the snow still falling. Dropping anchor at Aquia Creek Landing, the army supply base, the party completed the trip in a gaily decorated open freight car equipped with wooden benches. Lincoln was greeted at Falmouth by Hooker's chief of staff, Major General Daniel Butterfield. Then the presidential party, snugly ensconced in two army ambulances, was escorted by a large cavalcade of mounted officers to the headquarters of the commanding general.

At the time of removing Burnside from command, the Commander-in-Chief had put aside his misgivings about Joe Hooker and had given him full responsibility for restoring that potentially powerful but badly mismanaged army to a fine edge of efficiency. This Hooker had done with considerable success, and now the army was ready for a final inspection before beginning the spring campaign.

HOOKER'S MILITARY BACKGROUND

The appointment of General Hooker has been the subject of considerable speculation and widely varying reports, but there is little doubt that the final choice was Lincoln's and his alone. Secretary of War Stanton was outspokenly opposed to Hooker as was the General-in-Chief, Henry W. Halleck. Stanton's choice for Burnside's successor was Major General John F. Reynolds, who took himself out of consideration by expressing doubt that he would be allowed the necessary liberty of action as army commander. Generals Meade and Rosecrans were also supposed to have been considered, but Hooker, who wanted the job badly for himself, behind the scenes pulled all available stops in his efforts to secure the appointment. He is believed to have had friends in high places at Washington who were backing Secretary of the Treasury Chase to succeed Lincoln as President. These friends, sounding Hooker out to determine whether he had political ambitions of his own, were said to have been reassured on that score. They promptly made Hooker their candidate for army commander.

Hooker graduated from West Point in 1837, Halleck in 1839. Something may have occurred to arouse enmity between the upper classman and the plebe. Additionally there is a story to the effect that Halleck had uncovered some unfavorable tales about Hooker when they were both living in California as civilians in the late 1850s. However that may be, the President went over the list of senior commanders, disregarding the strong objections of Stanton and Halleck, and chose the handsome but vainglorious forty-eight year old Hooker, despite a record of disloyalty to superiors the counterpart of which is not to be found elsewhere in American military history.

With all his faults, Hooker had proven himself to be an able fighting man. The Mexican War, in which he had won a brevet as lieutenant colonel for distinguished services, was his first combat experience. After sixteen years of service, however, following his graduation from West Point, he had resigned his commission and moved to California. Here, with little success, he undertook farming and civil engineering. At the start of the Civil War he took off for Washington, where the elderly General-in-Chief,

Winfield Scott, gave him such a cool reception that he was still in civilian clothes when the first Battle of Bull Run passed into history. It seems that during the Mexican War Hooker's habit of talking out of turn and criticizing his superiors had made him permanently unpopular with General Scott, who just happened to be the General-in-Chief of the Army of the United States in 1861.

As the defeated Federals streamed back into Washington from Bull Run, it was a propitious moment for Joe Hooker to play his only remaining card. Bypassing General Scott, he secured an appointment to pay his respects to the President. At that meeting Hooker did most of the talking, informing Lincoln that he had at one time been "Lieutenant Colonel Hooker of the Regular Army," was returning to his home in California since he did not seem to be wanted in the Army, and had been an interested observer of the recent Manassas affair. Hooker closed his remarks by suggesting, with doubtful modesty, that "he was a damned sight better general than any you had on that field."

Whether Lincoln was intrigued by his handsome, ruddy face and soldierly bearing, appraised his brash self-assurance as an evidence of confident ability, or was simply hard up for capable combat leaders is not clear. But the result was that Hooker walked out with a commission as brigadier general of volunteers. He was on his way. Hooker's rise was rapid. He commanded a division through the Peninsular campaign and during Pope's Northern Virginia campaign and the Second Battle of Bull Run; led his corps at South Mountain and in heavy fighting on the Federal right at Antietam; and commanded the Center Grand Division of two corps under Burnside in the Fredericksburg campaign. Possibly the sobriquet "Fighting Joe" may have contributed something to his legendary fighting qualities, but he himself disliked the appellation because he probably knew, as few did, that the name had been attached to him as a result of a compositor's error in failing to place a hyphen in a dispatch from the Peninsula. The item in question should have read: "(still) fighting-Joe Hooker" but it came out in print as "Fighting Joe Hooker."

Lincoln's famous letter on the occasion of his appointment to army commander would seem to show that the President, fully aware of Hooker's weaknesses, knowingly took a calculated risk because he wanted leaders who would fight and win battles, regardless of personality, or even character deficiencies. The letter has been printed many times, but is included here as an essential part of the record:

I have placed you at the head of the Army of the Potomac. Of course I have done this upon what appear to me to be sufficient reasons. And yet I think it best for you to know that there are some things, in regard to which, I am not quite satisfied with you.

I believe you to be a brave and a skillful soldier, which, or course, I like. I also believe you do not mix politics with your profession, in which you are right. You have confidence in yourself, which is a valuable, if not an indispensable quality. You are ambitious, which, within reasonable bounds, does good rather than harm. But I think that during Gen. Burnside's command of the Army you have taken counsel of your ambition, and thwarted him as much as you could, in which you did a great wrong to the country, and to a most meritorious and honorable brother officer. I have heard, in such way as to believe it, of your recently saying that both the Army and the Government needed a Dictator. Of course it was not for this, but in spite of it, that I have given you command. Only those generals who gain success can set up dictators. What I now ask of you is military success, and I will risk the dictatorship. The government will support you to the utmost of its ability, which is neither more nor less than it has done and will do for all commanders.

I much fear that the spirit which you have aided to infuse into the Army, of criticising their commander, and withholding confidence from him, will now turn upon you. I shall assist you as far as I can, to put it down. Neither you, nor Napoleon, if he were alive again, could get any good out of an army, while such a spirit prevails in it.

And now, beware of rashness-beware of rashness, but with energy, and sleepless vigilance, go forward, and give us victories.

Noah Brooks, a close friend of the President, happened to be present at Hooker's headquarters when he received Lincoln's letter. Brooks has reported Hooker's reaction:

> *He finished reading it almost with tears in his eyes; and as he folded it and put it back in the breast of his coat, he said, "That is just such a letter as a father might write to a son. It is a beautiful letter, and although I think he was harder on me than I deserved, I will say that I love the man who wrote it."*

CHAPTER 23

The Strategy of
the Chancellorsville Campaign

Two YEARS of war had passed when the Battle of Chancellorsville was fought. The Army of the Potomac had yet to win a decisive victory over the Army of Northern Virginia, although the North had gained strategic advantage in winning the doubtful or border states of Tennessee and Kentucky, and in retaining Maryland and western Virginia. The Federal Navy was throttling the South's overseas trade with its effective blockade of the Confederate seacoast, despite merchant marine losses at the hands of daring Confederate raiders on the high seas. But the North had troubles in addition to its consistent failure to win battles—the difficult problem of recruiting by short-term volunteer enlistments, the reluctance of many citizens to discard their business-as-usual attitude in the face of all-out war, the embarrassing machinations and harmful propaganda of the anti-war contingents, and the diplomatic tug-of-war which the South came close to winning through the early efforts of its overseas agents to bring England and France to a recognition of the Confederacy.

Briefly stated, the political objective of the South, having seceded from the Union, was to secure recognition as a permanent nation. The original objective of the North was to restore the Union, with or without slavery. The military objectives were even more clear cut: conquest of Southern arms by the North, defense of its sovereign territory by the South.

The Battle of Antietam, a strategic although not a tactical victory for the Union, afforded Lincoln the awaited opportunity to issue his Emancipation Proclamation. Although the terms of the proclamation were known in the fall of 1862, the document itself was not officially promulgated until some weeks later, effective on January 1, 1863.

The line of demarcation between the proclamation's political and military implications may be a bit hazy, but its impact was tremendous. European sympathy swung strongly to the North, and the people of the Northern states came to the electrifying realization that they were fighting a crusading war. That made all the difference. Lincoln's stroke of political genius had created a favorable climate for military success if only he could find a general capable of breaking the stalemate in which the Army of the Potomac was gripped on the banks of the Rappahannock.

The important change for the better in the North's political climate imposed on the Union a compulsive responsibility for exercising the initiative and for waging a strong military offensive. Military success had become a vital essential for the Lincoln administration if the fruits of the crusade against slavery were to be gathered in, the favorable opinion of the European nations sustained, and the Northern peace party suppressed.

The South, however, did not give up hope that England and France would ultimately recognize it as an independent Confederacy. Strategic opinion was divided as to the proper military course to pursue. It seemed clear, however, that if the Northern armies could be held off long enough, and the economy of the South held together, a stalemate might result in a negotiated peace that would bring recognition from Europe, preserve the integrity of the Confederate States, and in effect result in a political if not a military victory at the end of hostilities. Anything that the South might do to buy time would be advantageous to it and correspondingly discouraging to the war party of the North. It therefore made strategic sense for the Army of Northern Virginia to remain on the defensive, and so to maneuver that the fighting would take place on battlefields of Lee's choosing, thus conserving his waning manpower through defensive tactics.

Lee Faces Hooker Across the Rappahannock

The position of the Army of the Potomac was the same that it had occupied just prior to and after the Battle of Fredericksburg, on the Stafford Heights that looked down upon the river and the town. Hooker's main supply base was at Aquia Creek Station, fifteen railroad miles northeast of Fredericksburg, to which railhead supplies from Washington were floated down the Potomac and thence transported by rail to Falmouth and other conveniently located advance depots.

The Army of Northern Virginia was standing fast on its strongly fortified natural bastion along the hills west of Fredericksburg. Lee's supply lines were still the Richmond, Fredericksburg, and Potomac Railroad, which carried supplies from his main base at Hanover Junction, a few miles north of Richmond, and the Virginia Central Railroad which ran east and west across the theater of operations and served his army as a convenient advanced base upon which he could retire and procure supplies when necessary. Hanover Junction and Gordonsville were the key points which he could not afford to lose, and the security of which largely influenced his strategy.

Serious combat on a large scale was not even considered during the winter months of early 1863 because the condition of the roads precluded mass movements by either army. There were, however, occasional hit-and-run cavalry raids to secure prisoners, confirm the presence or absence of major enemy units, and maintain contact while waiting for the weather to improve, the streams to return to their banks, and the roads to harden.

Lee had elected to remain on the tactical defensive for the time being to see what his new opponent might be planning. The defensive strategy which had proven successful against Hooker's predecessors was far less expensive to the Confederacy, less able than the Union Army to take and absorb losses. So long as the pressure from Washington continued and the Federals kept on beating out their brains against Lee's strong positions, any other Confederate policy would be unnecessarily wasteful. Lee required time to study Hooker and to learn how much of his boastfulness was sheer bluff. He therefore decided to give Hooker until the first of May to show his hand. If by that date Hooker had not put his army in motion or given a clear indication of his intentions, Lee would take the offensive himself to bring matters to a head.

Hooker assumed that Lee would either remain supinely in a defensive position or withdraw when threatened by Stoneman's encircling maneuver or the main flanking attack planned for the Army of the Potomac. In this Hooker made a fatal mistake. As it turned out, Lee was, as ever, offensively minded. Not only was he to sally out of his trenches and attack Hooker at Chancellorsville, but already, early in 1863, he was considering a new campaign into the North. It is doubtful that Lee at such an early date definitely intended to launch such a strategic offensive, but was simply making tentative plans and preparations in case opportunity should present itself.

Further evidence of Lee's early desire, if not intention, to assume the strategic offensive, is his letter to Seddon on April 9: "Should General Hooker's army assume the defensive, the readiest method of relieving the pressure upon General Johnston and General Beauregard would be for this army to cross into Maryland . . ." In the meantime, Hooker held the initiative, so Lee had to be content with endeavoring to divine the probable course of Federal action and to shape his own plans and actions accordingly. Most of his correspondence and reports at this time indicate that he expected Hooker to advance, generally by means of a river crossing somewhere between Port Royal and United States Mine Ford.

HOOKER'S MISSION AND STRATEGIC CONCEPT

"Go forward and give us victories," Lincoln had written, and that in brief was Hooker's mission. The North desperately needed a tonic that only a resounding military success could provide. The Army of the Potomac had been reorganized and restored to fighting trim. It was once again full of confidence and needed only an inspired guiding hand at the helm to convert a long-range hope for a victory into an actuality.

General-in-Chief Halleck had embodied his strategic views in a letter to Burnside on January 7, following the fiasco at Fredericksburg. On January 31, only a few days after his appointment as army commander, Hooker was given a copy of the Burnside letter and told that the overall strategy remained the same as outlined therein-offensive operations to be undertaken elsewhere than at Fredericksburg. He was to keep particularly in mind the importance of covering Washington and Harpers Ferry, because the troops stationed at both places were not strong enough of themselves to withstand a heavy Confederate attack. Halleck reiterated the sensible doctrine that Hooker's objective was not Richmond, but the defeat and scattering of Lee's army. He ventured the suggestion that the objective should be "to turn the enemy's works or to threaten their wings or communications in order to keep them occupied until a favorable opportunity offered to strike a decisive blow." Specifically Halleck advised Hooker to use his cavalry and light artillery against Lee's communications in an effort to cut off his supplies.

There was an urgency about these instructions, but they failed to move Hooker to precipitate action before he believed his army to be ready. Halleck wanted Hooker to commence operations as soon as possible, and the injunction was repeated toward the end of March, when Halleck accurately pointed out that Lee's forces were pretty well scattered, foraging for supplies. If there should be undue delay in launching an offensive, he said, the favorable opportunity might be lost.

It may be doubted that Hooker had enough humility in his makeup to study the campaigns of his four principal predecessors, McDowell, McClellan, Pope, and Burnside, in order to compare their performances with that of General Lee, and to evaluate the major battles of 1861 and 1862 objectively. By so doing he might have profited by the Federal mistakes, learned something from the strategic and tactical methods of the major Confederate commanders, and applied the lessons constructively to achieve a happier result than any of the first four army commanders had been able to accomplish.

Hooker unfortunately was not the student that the present situation called for. His temperament was such that he thought he had all the answers already. Not only did he have no use for Halleck, his superior in Washington, but there is little evidence that he was even moderately impressed with Lincoln's views on how to fight the army. He does seem to have been thinking fairly straight by April, however. Some of the advice proffered by Lincoln and Halleck may have rubbed off from their letters and conferences, for on April 11 Hooker wrote the President a letter which in part transmitted his current views and foreshadowed the final program which was later polished off and refined to become the plan of operations for the Chancellorsville campaign. Pertinent extracts from the letter follow:

I have concluded that I will have more chance of inflicting a heavier blow upon the enemy by turning his position to my right and, if practicable, to sever his communications with Richmond with my dragoon force. . . . I am apprehensive that he will retire from before me the moment I should succeed in crossing the river. . . . I hope that when the cavalry have established themselves on the line between him and Richmond they will be able to hold him and check his retreat until I can fall on his rear. . . . while the cavalry are moving I shall threaten the passage of the river at various points and after they have passed well to the enemy's rear, shall endeavor to effect the crossing . . .

HOOKER FASHIONS A GIANT PINCERS

Hooker's plan of action for the entire army was beautifully simple in its basic conception, as all great plans must be. In effect the Army of the Potomac would move in on the Army of Northern Virginia from two directions, like a giant pincers closing its jaws, while the army cavalry closed the escape route. This would militarily be called a double envelopment, with half the army advancing from the west, the other half from the east (either wing of equal strength to Lee's whole army), to meet in the open country a mile or so from Chancellorsville. Together they would put the finishing touches on Lee's presumably cringing Confederates, if indeed the latter had not by that time become so petrified with fear of what Joe Hooker might do to them that they had already fled in panic from the scene of their intended destruction. In the latter event Stoneman's cavalry would be Johnny-on-the-spot to "cut off large slices from his column," as Hooker confidently phrased that possibility in his directive. In Hooker's mind's eye Lee's army would be trapped like a fox, with dog packs hemming him on three sides and the Rappahannock River serving as a Federal ally to close the only remaining avenue of escape.

The plan in general had been soundly conceived, conformed to the fundamental principles of war, and gave every reason to hope that it would succeed handsomely if the logistics of time and space should prove valid, and the unpredictable Lee would stay put. There was only one serious flaw in Hooker's line of reasoning. That was his confident assurance that Lee would withdraw toward Richmond or Gordonsville as soon as he should discover that Hooker had unexpectedly outflanked his left and at the same time crossed the Rappahannock and attacked him at Fredericksburg. An additionally disturbing fact to Lee would be that a large body of Federal cavalry would be loose between him and the capital. Hooker knew perfectly well what he would do if the positions were reversed. He apparently could not conceive of his opponent outguessing him when unexpectedly confronted with the successful execution of that magnificent turning movement, which could not fail to give Lee the surprise of his life and leave him no alternative but "to ingloriously fly," as Hooker was to phrase it a few days later.

We do not know the thoughts that passed through Lee's mind as he sized Hooker up and evolved his own tactical concepts to counter the forthcoming Union offensive. It is quite probable that Hooker's overconfident boasts to his officers, indicating what he intended to do to Lee, had filtered into Lee's intelligence nets, and were duly evaluated as the premature mouthings of one of the generals who had shared repeatedly in the defeats which Lee had consistently inflicted on the Army of the Potomac. Robert E. Lee was a keen judge of character and so far had not encountered a high ranking opponent whose probable course of action under a given set of circumstances had been too difficult to predict. In Lee's experience the loudly boastful character had usually been found to have certain weaknesses which he would attempt to conceal even from himself by putting up a bold front. Lee may already have evaluated Hooker's overconfidence as in reality a form of inferiority complex which would result in the pendulum swinging him to the other extreme of overcautiousness if events failed to work out exactly according to schedule. Hooker had not made any secret of his satisfaction with his winter's effort to put his army in fighting trim and his boasts had undoubtedly reached Lee's ears.

Possibly Hooker was whistling in the dark, or felt that to raise the morale of the army after Fredericksburg and concurrently assure it that the nickname "Fighting Joe" was no misnomer, he had to give forth with a few such aphorisms. Time would tell, and soon, what effect his attitude would have on the canny Lee, who was not given to developing obsessions and had managed pretty successfully in the past to weather heavy winds generated by Union army commanders whose military gray matter and strength of character under the stress of battle never seemed to come even close to matching his own.

Hooker's Plan in Detail

Meade's Fifth Corps, Howard's Eleventh, and Slocum's Twelfth, constituting the right wing of the army under the temporary command of Major General Henry W. Slocum, would make a wide turning movement, cross the Rappahannock at Kelly's Ford, above the mouth of the Rapidan and about twenty-one miles west of Falmouth. This force would turn southeastward and cross the Rapidan at Germanna and Ely's Fords, then follow the south bank of the Rappahannock below its junction with the Rapidan to uncover United States Mine Ford and Banks Ford for the crossing of Couch's Second Corps (less Gibbon's division), which latter corps would meanwhile take position prepared to cross at the first-named ford. These four corps, after a forced march of over forty miles for three of them, would then assemble at Chancellorsville with a strength of 60,000 men, as many as Lee had on the field in his entire army. At that point Hooker would take command in person.

Sedgwick with his own Sixth Corps, Reynolds' First, Sickles' Third, and Gibbon's division of the Second Corps, was concurrently directed to cross the Rappahannock below Fredericksburg at the same time and make strong demonstrations with a view to persuading Lee that this was to be the main effort. Sedgwick's specific mission was spelled out in detail. He would first show his 59,000-man, three-corps wing along the high ground opposite Fredericksburg, south of the town at Franklin's Crossing and Pollock's Mill. Then on April 29 engineer General Benham would throw four pontoon bridges over the river; Sedgwick's wing would cross and either pin Lee's army in its present lines or induce him to withdraw to the south. The principal object of Sedgwick's maneuvers would be to prevent Lee from spoiling Hooker's strategy by blocking the principal effort of the right wing and interfering with the surprise outflanking march on Chancellorsville. In the paraphrased words of the late General George S. Patton, Sedgwick would hold Lee by his nose while Hooker kicked him in the pants. If Lee stood fast at Fredericksburg Sedgwick was to attack. If Lee retired on Richmond, Sedgwick would pursue him; if he moved a considerable part of his force toward Chancellorsville, Sedgwick would "carry the works at all hazards, and establish his force on the Telegraph Road." In the latter case, a full-fledged advance by Sedgwick's wing on Chancellorsville, to attack Lee's flank and rear, would have to await Hooker's arrival at that point and his estimate of the situation as of that time. The record suggests that Hooker's move in that event would be to hold the right wing on the defensive and let Sedgwick make the principal attack.

Stoneman's cavalry corps was scheduled to make its sweep around Lee's army two weeks ahead of the movement of the infantry, to cut Lee's communications with Richmond and, in Hooker's mind, so disrupt the Confederate army as to cause Lee to hastily evacuate his present defensive position in a retreat to the south, with Hooker's infantry in hot pursuit. Stoneman's route was to be generally along the line of the Virginia Central Railroad, destroying everything along that road; he would then select strong positions on the roads paralleling the Richmond and Fredericksburg Railroad, prepared to harass Lee's columns as they retired on the Capital. Hooker's theory was that Stoneman would be able to pin Lee in place while the Army of the Potomac assailed him from the direction of the Rappahannock.

As later events were to prove, Hooker was as inexperienced in the proper employment of cavalry as were most of the Union generals. Otherwise he would have been less profligate in sending the bulk of it beyond hope of recall, and retaining only one small brigade of five regiments, about 1,000 troops, under General Pleasonton, for such vital missions as battle reconnaissance, army flank security, and close-in exploitation of local successes. Stoneman would take with him 10,000 men, while the rest of the cavalry, about 1,500, were to be held in reserve to guard the camps and communications north of the river, where their fate would be to play no part in the battle.

Hooker's conception of the role of his cavalry corps was in effect a Civil War forerunner of the "vertical envelopment" of World War II, in which paratroopers, followed by airborne units, were dropped far behind hostile lines to seize and deny to the enemy strategic positions from which to harass them in rear. The fallacy of Hooker's plan lay in the fact that it was a premature use of the horse cavalry before, rather than as collateral to, or following the action of the main army in forcing the enemy into a retrograde movement. In other words, it was imprudently uneconomic and impracticable to attempt to exploit a success in advance of its achievement.

The months of preparation were over the roads drying rapidly, and the Army of the Potomac, sharpened to a keen cutting edge, was poised and waiting only for the word from Joe Hooker that would release the pent-up energy of a long winter in the form of a new thunderbolt of destruction against the battle-hardened but gradually weakening Army of Northern Virginia on the other side of the Rappahannock; or so Hooker figured.

Even as Lincoln wired his approval of Hooker's plan on April 12, orders were going forward to Stoneman's cavalry to be in readiness to move at daylight Monday, April 13. Each trooper was to carry on his horse not less than three days' rations and grain, with at least forty rounds of ammunition for his carbine and twenty for his pistol. The pack and supply trains were to be loaded and ready to roll with additional rations, grain, and forage to subsist men and horses for an additional period of eight days.

The invaders would not have to live off the country in order to survive, at least not for the first eleven days, assuming that all went well and the trains kept up to avoid capture or destruction. But the extra load would be a heavy burden for the individual trooper's mount, averaging between 250 and 300 pounds, depending on the variable weight of the soldier himself; there was no doubt that Stoneman's cavalry horses were greatly overloaded for the ambitious undertaking.

The cavalry commander was given written instructions in the form of sealed orders which directed him to march with his entire corps less one brigade, about 10,000 strong, at 7 A.M. on April 13: "for the purpose of turning the enemy's position on his left, throwing the cavalry between him and Richmond, isolating him from his supplies, checking his retreat, and inflicting on him every possible injury which will tend to his discomfiture and defeat."

The directive was wordy and in great detail, telling Stoneman just where to go, the precise strength of the enemy detachments he would encounter and where they would be found, and stressing the ease with which he would be able to overcome all obstacles. A few additional missions were thrown in, such as the destruction of depots, bridges, ferries, and rail facilities. In grandiloquent terms it laid upon the hapless Stoneman the injunction to let his watchword be "fight, fight, fight, bearing in mind that time is as valuable to the general [Hooker] as the Rebel carcasses."

Stoneman was assured that "you may rely on the general being in connection with you before your supplies are exhausted," but the directive neglected to say how or where Hooker expected to reach him miles away to the south on the opposite side of Lee's army. The order finally concluded with the statement that it devolved on Stoneman "to take the initiative in the forward movement of this grand army; on you and your noble command must depend in a great measure the extent and brilliancy of our success."

The Union cavalry had long wanted a man-sized mission to prove its competence. Now it had it and with a vengeance. It was a broad and imaginative conception, couched in sweeping terms, but a rather more ambitious project than the recently reorganized cavalry corps was as yet capable of carrying out. Hooker, in company with virtually all of the high ranking generals of the line who were without cavalry experience, was unfamiliar with the capabilities and limitations of that arm except in a very general way. He and they seemed to think that because a horse could travel at a rate of six to ten miles an hour for hours on end, there was no limit to the capacity of a mounted organization to range widely over enemy territory and perform a myriad of concurrent missions. Nobody, however, and least of all Hooker himself, took the trouble to explain how only 10,000 men and twenty-two guns could keep Lee's army of 60,000 from exercising an initiative of its own, or how it could be driven into the hands of the Army of the Potomac simply by trotting around the countryside between the Confederates and Richmond. Nevertheless the opportunity was afforded for the Federal cavalry to cause Lee considerable embarrassment and, if Stoneman's force should prove to be sufficiently enterprising and aggressive to cut the Confederate supply line, to offer a serious handicap to the Army of Northern Virginia.

Hooker, no doubt recalling the two occasions when Jeb Stuart boldly led his cavalry brigades on wide sweeps around McClellan's army, figured the Stoneman raid as a shrewd opening gambit for his forthcoming spring offensive. What he overlooked, in drawing premature conclusions on the sure success of this project, was the fact that it was Lee and not McClellan who was the intended victim. And it was Stoneman, not Stuart or Sheridan, who would spark-plug the raid with a still unproven cavalry corps that had yet to cut its eyeteeth on such a grandiose adventure.

An Inauspicious Start

Stoneman and his 10,000 cavalrymen moved out April 13 on schedule and headed for the upper fords. It was his purpose to plant for Confederate consumption the rumor that he was after Jones' Confederate cavalry operating in the Shenandoah Valley. Actually he intended to turn sharply south across the river above the Rappahannock bridge and at Beverly Ford, dash across the Rapidan at Raccoon Ford or other nearby crossings, and then split his force, as directed by Hooker. One element under Averell would aim for Louisa Court House to cut and destroy as much as possible of the Virginia Central Railroad, after disposing of Fitzhugh Lee's cavalry at Culpeper. The other and larger element, under Stoneman's personal command, would follow the road through Gordonsville to Lee's main supply base which was believed to be at Hanover Junction, a few miles north of Richmond, with the primary object of cutting the railroad, destroying all possible communications, and fulfilling the major function of the raid as conceived and spelled out in Hooker's directive.

The leading brigade of the corps was under the command of an aggressive colonel by the name of Benjamin F. Davis, who had first gained prominence as a cavalry commander when he refused to be bottled up with the rest of the Union forces at the time Stonewall Jackson took Harpers Ferry prior to the Battle of Antietam. Davis on that occasion had chosen to make a dash for it across the pontoon bridge to the Maryland shore, which he accomplished with distinction to himself and his cavalry troopers, and was rewarded by capturing some of Longstreet's trains a few hours later. Davis' brigade was now sent ahead by Stoneman to cross the Rappahannock and clear the area on the south bank for the rest of the corps to cross without hindrance. This mission he achieved without much opposition. On the south bank, after driving away the Confederate detachment guarding the ford, he waited for the main body to come across and get on with the war. But for some unjustifiable reason, possibly because his columns contained too many wheeled vehicles, Stoneman was unconscionably slow in getting started. While he dallied, a heavy rain started and kept falling until the wooden Rappahannock bridge was tugging at its shaky foundations, as the river rose rapidly and almost submerged it. Thereupon Stoneman decided he had better wait a bit, which he did to the unconcealed disgust of the aggressive Davis, who finally swam his horses back to the north side of the river to keep from being permanently cut off from the rest of the corps.

It was an inauspicious start for the cavalry's great adventure. With a little more dash and energy, such as Davis had demonstrated, the entire outfit could have been across both rivers and on their way to Richmond before the streams had risen to the danger point. Obviously their return by the same route would have been cut off for the time being. But that was of little moment since they were headed away from the fords anyway and had a long journey ahead of them to get in position behind Lee's army by the time Hooker's schedule called for the infantry corps' to close on Chancellorsville.

Hooker, as yet uninformed of the delay, sent off a confident letter on April 15 to Lincoln, in which he advised the President that Stoneman's cavalry had already crossed the river and was on its way, having had two days of good weather before the rains started. Later that day Hooker was forced to telegraph the President that the cavalry was still north of the river. So far as its strategic value was concerned, it would not be surprising if both Lincoln and Hooker had by now written off the projected Stoneman raid as a loss, if we may judge from Lincoln's letter to Hooker, written immediately after receipt of the disappointing telegram:

It is now 10:15 P.M. An hour ago I received your letter of this morning and a few minutes later your dispatch of this evening. The latter gives me considerable uneasiness. The rain and mud were, of course, to be calculated upon. General S is not moving rapidly enough to make the expedition come to anything. He has now been out three days, two of which were unusually fair weather, and all three without hindrance from the enemy, and yet he is not 25 miles from where he started. To reach his point he still has 60 miles to go, another river to cross, and will be hindered by the enemy. By arithmetic, how many days will it take him to do it? I do not know that any better can be done, but I greatly fear it is another failure already. Write me often; I am very anxious.

HOOKER'S FINAL PLAN

Hooker was enraged. After giving the cavalry the chance to demonstrate its capabilities, Stoneman's timidity had compromised the opportunity and forced the army commander, whose march schedule for the main body was already set, to revise his program. The cavalry was now immobilized near Warrenton Junction, thirteen miles northeast of the Rappahannock. It remained there for practically two weeks, held up by the heavy rain and the resulting high water and muddy roads. Hooker decided on the next round he would not depend on Stoneman's cavalry, but would make their activities secondary to the infantry. If the cavalry could still show its mettle, well and good, but the main dependence would have to be placed on the foot soldiers to flank Lee out of his fortified lines.

Hooker's original plan had been to cross the Rappahannock below Fredericksburg and move against Lee's right and rear. If successfully accomplished this would place the Federal army squarely across Lee's communication and supply lines to Richmond. The second plan, which Lincoln approved, shifted the Federal turning movement to Hooker's right and Lee's left, and gave Stoneman's cavalry the mission of getting around Lee to cut his communications and prevent him from withdrawing to the south before Hooker could administer the anticipated coup de grace. The third and final plan differed from the second solely in placing on the infantry rather than the cavalry the responsibility of leading the great flanking maneuver across two rivers to put the army on the left rear of Lee's cohorts at Fredericksburg.

In line with his determination to prevent any leak to the enemy and thus reveal his intentions, Hooker kept his plans so secret that Stoneman and Sedgwick were the only corps commanders who received written instructions which went further than the initial objective. Nothing was said, even to them, about Hooker's complete plan for the main army. Hence Stoneman was to be cut loose on his ambitious undertaking without a hint as to what the Army of the Potomac was going to do, other than what he himself might deduce from the character of his own assignment.

STONEMAN'S RAID

On April 28, from his advanced headquarters at Morrisville, Hooker had sent brief supplemental orders to Stoneman which amended the original April 12 directive in several particulars. The cavalry commander was told that the operations of that portion of his command which would move on Louisa Court House and the line of the Orange and Alexandria Railroad were intended to mask the main column, which would "move by forced marches to strike and destroy the line of the Aquia and Richmond Railroad." The order recommended that the point selected for the two columns to unite be on the Pamunkey (a few miles north and east of Richmond), and directed that the entire force be across the Rappahannock by no later than 8 o'clock on the morning of April 29.

The adventures of the Federal cavalry during the succeeding week, while interesting and no doubt instructive to the participants, made little impression on the Confederate army and had no direct effect on the Battle of Chancellorsville. Indirectly, however, the Stoneman raid was important, and to the disadvantage of Hooker's army. There is little disagreement among historians that Hooker's decision to detach the major portion of his large cavalry corps for an independent mission was a strategic error. The raid failed to excite Lee, who virtually ignored Stoneman's maneuvering in his rear and avoided making the same mistake as Hooker by allowing his own depleted cavalry to harry and pursue the Federal cavalry.

It can only be conjectured as to what the outcome of the Battle of Chancellorsville might have been, had Hooker retained Stoneman's 10,000 troopers to cover his flanks. It is reasonable to conclude that Stonewall Jackson could never have sprung his historic surprise if the Federal cavalry had been on that flank to reconnoiter widely and reach well out, before the battle, along the roads leading from Chancellorsville.

The Confederates were not aware of the planned Stoneman raid until the movement was actually under way. By means of feints and planted messages that were allowed to fall into Confederate hands, Lee and Stuart were persuaded that the objective of the Federal cavalry was the Shenandoah Valley. This was confirmed by a dispatch from Lee to Stuart as late as April 25, and nothing that transpired subsequently appears to have modified their expectation, until Stoneman's divisions were across the rivers and headed toward Gordonsville and Richmond.

Stoneman's corps finally got moving. It was across the river on April 30, about the same time that the advance elements of Hooker's three infantry corps reached Chancellorsville. The only opposition encountered were the small cavalry brigades of Fitzhugh and W. H. F. Lee, totaling between them about 3,000 troopers whose attention had to be divided between the Federal cavalry and Hooker's right wing. A few minor skirmishes occurred, and some prisoners were captured, but there was no effective opposition to the far-ranging Federal cavalry, which proceeded to carry out its mission of tearing up railroad tracks and causing as much rear area damage as possible.

While the Battle of Chancellorsville was being fought, the main column under Stoneman's personal command continued on its way, but Averell's division of 3,400 sabers was held up at Rapidan Station mainly because of the exaggerated fears of its commander that he was heavily opposed. Averell marked time in the vicinity of Rapidan Station so long that his division was recalled by General Hooker on May 2 and spent the rest of the campaign north of the Rapidan. Averell himself was relieved of command and his division placed under General Pleasonton.

Gregg's division and Buford's reserve brigade, with Stoneman's column, proved more effective in the course of their depredations, but without achieving any practical result beyond the temporary destruction of property, bridges, depots, and other war material. Colonel Judson Kilpatrick's regiment penetrated within two miles of Richmond, traveled 200 miles and captured substantial enemy detachments. Colonel Hasbrouck Davis' regiment had almost as arduous a march, but there was practically no resistance and therefore little glory to be derived from the raid. All the columns except Kilpatrick's and Davis's safely returned to the Union lines by May 11, with men and horses pretty well jaded, but with more experience back of them than most of the cavalry troops had previously been allowed to acquire. Kilpatrick and Davis ended their marches within the Union lines near Yorktown.

THE ARMY MOVES INTO POSITION

Hooker's April 26 orders for the movement of his seven infantry corps from their winter camp near Falmouth to the jump-off positions along the Rappahannock were brief and concise. The instructions prescribed secrecy for the right wing. No fires would be permitted and special precautions would be taken to keep the men from approaching the river after their arrival at the fords. Not so for the divisions of Couch's Second Corps, however, since Hooker wanted Lee to believe that a major crossing would be made at United States Mine Ford and Banks' Ford. The three corps under Sedgwick, whose orders directed them to be in position before daylight April 29, were cautioned not to expose their initial movements, but to be prepared to make an open demonstration in full force on the morning of the 29th. By these various devices, all of which were calculated to preserve the secrecy of the projected crossing at Kelly's Ford, Hooker hoped that Lee would misjudge his real intentions and conclude that the troops seen at Banks' and United States Mine Ford, and opposite Fredericksburg, presaged a turning movement via the aforementioned fords, in conjunction with a main attack against Fredericksburg.

One brigade of Howard's Eleventh Corps had been sent to Kelly's Ford several weeks ahead of the main body as an advance guard, and to secure the north bank at that point. The remainder of the right wing, after a short march on April 27, bivouacked in the vicinity of Hartwood Church, no farther than a three hour hike from the base camp, and approximately fifteen miles short of Kelly's Ford. For the first day's march, apparently, a shakedown was considered desirable, as a mild prelude to the tough days ahead.

Sickles' Third Corps received special instructions. Hooker earmarked it as a sort of army reserve, to be employed wherever the developing situation might require, either with Sedgwick at Fredericksburg, as support to Couch at Banks' Ford, or to strengthen the right wing at

Chancellorsville. Sickles was told, however, to hold his command in readiness to move early April 28, with eight days' rations and ammunition (as prescribed for the right wing), which suggests that Hooker· had already practically made up his mind to use the Third Corps at Chancellorsville.

By twilight on Tuesday evening, April 28, Hooker's army was poised on the designated positions at the several crossings of the Rappahannock. His three-corps right wing was massed north of Kelly's Ford. Stoneman's cavalry corps, two weeks behind schedule, was bivouacked near Warrenton Junction on the Orange and Alexandria Railroad. Cavalry detachments were out front, engaged in screening the infantry until the last minute before the actual crossing, to prevent Stuart's alert scouts from determining what was behind the Federal cavalry.

Couch's Second Corps, minus one division, had arrived opposite Banks' Ford, with advance detachments out toward United States Mine Ford, while Sedgwick's three-corps left wing was moving into position on the east bank of the Rappahannock opposite the lower end of Fredericksburg.

One pontoon bridge only had been ordered laid at Kelly's Ford, although the Rappahannock at that point, about 300 feet wide, was too deep and swift for the men to ford and was difficult even for horses. This bridge was completed by 7:45 P.M., April 28 without opposition from the Confederates, and everything was now in readiness for the second phase, the crossing of the two rivers and the advance on Chancellorsville.

The army commander, with his staff, established an advance command post at Morrisville, five miles east of Kelly's Ford, on the morning of April 28, leaving his Chief of Staff, General Butterfield, at Falmouth to coordinate the activities of the troops under Sedgwick and Couch, to keep Hooker currently posted on developments in that area, and to expedite communication between the two wings.

Except for the abort by the cavalry corps everything had gone smoothly, according to plan, and in good time. The curtain was now about to rise on "Operation Movement," to give it a twentieth century flavor. The morale of the Army of the Potomac rose perceptibly.

THE FEDERAL CONCENTRATION AT CHANCELLORSVILLE

The Eleventh, Twelfth, and Fifth Corps, the first two under Slocum's temporary command, commenced the crossing of the Rappahannock on the night of April 28, in accordance with instructions issued to Slocum and Meade during the afternoon. Preceded by elements of Pleasonton's cavalry, which Hooker had broken up for assignment to the respective corps, one regiment to each, Howard's Eleventh Corps crossed first and then halted to cover the corps of Slocum and Meade, which, in that order, marched across the swaying pontoons commencing at daylight April 29. All three corps were under instructions to then move rapidly across the neck of land between the two rivers, the Twelfth and Eleventh Corps in one column on the Germanna Ford road, while the Fifth Corps would take the shorter road through Richardsville to Ely's Ford.

The advance cavalry meanwhile trotted ahead to seize the Rapidan fords. The two columns were instructed to maintain contact and, should Meade's corps meet opposition at the Rapidan crossing, Slocum was to send one of his corps along the south bank, after crossing, to disperse the enemy and clear the way for Meade's corps to cross. All three corps would then resume the advance on Chancellorsville.

Under Hooker's revised plan, Stoneman's cavalry had been scheduled to precede Howard's Eleventh Corps in crossing the Rappahannock on April 28. But Stoneman did not reach the river until 8 A.M. on the 29th, fourteen hours later than Hooker expected. By that time the Eleventh Corps had already crossed and the Twelfth was using the bridge. The cavalry was thus forced to mark time some hours longer until Slocum and Meade with their respective corps had gotten across. The cavalry was, however, allowed to cut in ahead of Humphrey's rear division of Meade's corps, which division as a result was the last to reach Chancellorsville.

In extenuation of his failure to cross according to Hooker's time schedule, Stoneman claimed, with considerable justice, that the army staff had miscalculated the time required for him to assemble his scattered corps, put it on the road, and march the intervening distance over muddy roads. It was thirteen miles from Warrenton Junction to the crossing, and many of Stoneman's patrols were operating another dozen miles from his bivouac area. The weight of evidence favors Stoneman's contention. There was reason to believe that Hooker himself, who had not taken his own staff into his confidence, purposely delayed notifying Stoneman until the very last minute, in the interest of secrecy, and that he miscalculated badly on the logistics of the situation. However that may have been, the Federal cavalry was placed in the position of having been relegated to a secondary role, with two strikes against it.

Had Hooker been a more quick-thinking and less inflexible army commander, he would have been better advised to make a virtue of necessity at this stage, cancel the raid, and give the cavalry a new mission that would have kept the corps at hand and under his control to cover the army right flank in the advance against the Confederate army. The thought does not seem to have even crossed Hooker's mind. If it had, the Battle of Chancellorsville could have been quite a different story. In spite of the delay, Stoneman's original orders remained virtually unchanged, presumably in the belief, or at least the hope, that the greater mobility of the cavalry would permit it to make up the lost time and still arrive in position to prevent Lee's escape when confronted by the Army of the Potomac.

The crossing of the Rappahannock on the 29th took longer than expected because it started to rain. The muddy roads made marching difficult for the heavily laden foot soldiers, many of whom felt no compunction about throwing away overcoats and other impedimenta to lighten their loads, which exceeded 53 pounds without counting the clothing they wore. Historically the soldier in the ranks takes little heed for the needs of tomorrow until he has learned from bitter campaign experience the wisdom of holding on to his blanket and other essential equipment, burdensome as the extra weight frequently becomes. Small bodies of Confederate cavalry caused the flanks of the marching columns some annoyance, but they were not strong enough to make any real impression. In any event Stuart's job at this stage was to secure information and relay it to General Lee rather than to engage in combat.

Brushing aside Stuart's pickets and other small cavalry detachments, 42,000 men of the three Federal corps, preceded by Pleasonton's cavalry, plodded steadily forward across the pontoon bridge at Kelly's Ford and on to the Rapidan. Slocum, on the right, reached that river at Germanna Ford at 3 P.M. A Confederate detachment of over a hundred men were on the opposite bank, but were subdued and most of them captured by leading Federal units which waded the river. The Confederates had collected timbers to construct a bridge. This work was at once undertaken by Slocum's pioneers, so that the remainder of his corps and all of Howard's was able to cross the river dryshod. Slocum's men were on the south bank and in bivouac by 9 P.M. Howard started across in the moonlight at 11 P.M., completing his movement by 4 A.M. on the 30th. On the left, Meade's Fifth Corps reached the Rapidan at Ely's Ford at 5 P.M. There was no bridge, and no bridging material. So the weary soldiers plunged into the stream, which was up to their armpits, cold, and running swiftly.

The two leading divisions continued fording the river, completing the movement by midnight. Humphreys' division, which had been held up at Kelly's Ford by the passage of Stoneman's cavalry, did not reach the Rapidan until 1 A.M. April 30. Humphreys continued marching until he reached Hunting Creek.

Meade reached the initial phase line at Chancellorsville at 11 A.M., April 30, three hours ahead of Slocum's Twelfth Corps. He must have made a faster march, for he did not get across the Rappahannock at Kelley's Ford until after Slocum, and he did not have the benefit of a bridge at the Rapidan crossing. However, in fairness to Slocum it must be pointed out that Meade had the shorter route, and that Slocum was delayed briefly near Wilderness Church by Jeb Stuart's flank demonstration.

INITIAL ACTION ON SEDGWICK'S FRONT

Pursuant to Hooker's orders, Sedgwick's Sixth Corps, Reynolds' First, and Sickle's Third, all under "Uncle John" Sedgwick's temporary command, broke camp early on April 28 and quietly moved into position on Stafford Heights below Fredericksburg, prepared to demonstrate openly the next day in the hope of persuading Lee that the main effort would be made there. Meanwhile the right wing was circling Lee's left and driving for Chancellorsville.

BRIDGE LAYING BY THE FEDERAL ENGINEERS

Four pontoon bridges were laid by the engineers, under cover of a heavy fog, by early morning April 29, two at Deep Run (another was added later), where Franklin's Grand Division had crossed in December for the first Battle of Fredericksburg; and two more at Pollock's Mill (Fitzhugh's Crossing) further down river. Following the troop demonstration during the morning, bridgehead troops of Reynolds' and Sedgwick's Corps crossed with but token resistance from the Confederates. Having crossed, they bivouacked on the plain close to the river bank, while Sickles' Third Corps remained in a position of readiness as the main body of the First and Sixth Corps, also on the east shore, awaited orders to cross.

Brigadier General Henry W. Benham, West Point 1837, in command of the engineer brigade of the Army of the Potomac, was a veteran of the Mexican War who had spent most of his years in the army constructing and repairing seawalls, forts, and harbor defenses. An earnest and efficient engineer officer, Benham made his preparations so carefully that the placement of all the pontoon bridges would have been effected smoothly and on schedule had he been given the troop help that he requested and was promised. Not if Benham could avoid it would the engineers be blamed, as they were by Burnside at Fredericksburg the previous November, for fouling up the army attack by arriving late with their clumsy pontoons.

Fifteen bridges in all were to be thrown across the Rappahannock and removed between April 28, when the first was laid at Kelly's Ford, and May 4, when the rear guard of Hooker's army had recrossed at United States Mine Ford after the battle. Actually only ten bridges were used, of which five were taken up and relaid at different points. The bridges at United States Mine Ford and Banks' Ford will be covered later.

Nine bridges were used for the advance and six for the retreat. Benham's engineers rendered valiant service throughout the campaign. They met all of Hooker's demands in spite of several unfortunate delays caused either by misunderstandings or reluctance on the part of two or three generals to make available the troops needed to assist the engineers in hauling the pontoons to the river bank.

Lee Reacts Cautiously

The first intimation Lee received that Hooker was stirring came in a message from Stuart on the evening of April 28. This message merely stated that a Federal force of all arms was moving up the Rappahannock in the direction of Kelly's Ford.

The next day, April 29, Stuart telegraphed that a crossing of the Rappahannock was in progress and that three Federal infantry corps had been identified. Lee also received courier reports from Germanna and Ely's Fords that enemy cavalry had crossed the Rapidan about 2 o'clock in the afternoon, but their strength had not been determined and the reports were vague on the subject of enemy infantry.

Hooker's precautionary measures to enforce secrecy on the march of his right wing had paid off handsomely. Lee was surprised on this occasion, despite the best efforts of the Confederate cavalry to pierce the Federal screen and develop the strength and dispositions of the large enemy force seen moving west on the 28th. Stuart's available brigades were greatly reduced in strength. His horses, many of them inferior replacements and not in the best condition at that, could not function as effectively as they had once been able to do. The real reason for Lee's surprise, however, was that for once Federal security and counter-reconnaissance measures were being efficiently handled.

Lee's information on April 28 and 29 was not sufficiently complete to enable him to fully evaluate Hooker's strategy, although the messages did tell him that a possible threat to his left was in the making. Stuart's cavalry, after the Federal crossing at Kelly's Ford, had managed to pick off enough Union soldiers to identify the Eleventh, Twelfth, and Fifth Corps, but the information was not sufficiently positive to convince Lee that all three corps were present at full strength. He knew only that "a large body of infantry and some cavalry" had crossed the Rappahannock and was headed for the Rapidan. This at least served to satisfy him that the threat was not directed at Culpeper and Gordonsville. Still he had to know much more before he could decide in his own mind the extent to which Hooker may have committed his army to a definite line of action.

In point of fact, Stuart's message identifying the Federal corps estimated their numbers as "14,000 infantry and some cavalry," an underestimate by about 28,000, which was a bit misleading as a basis upon which to make important decisions. On that occasion Stuart made a premature guess which turned out to be only one-third correct.

The dispatches of April 29 came into Lee's hands after Hooker's right wing had crossed the Rappahannock and the intervening strip of land between the two rivers, and was on the point of effecting a night crossing of the Rapidan. Germanna and Ely's Fords are only ten and five miles, respectively, west of Chancellorsville, and the courier messages that Federal cavalry had crossed the Rapidan at 2 P.M., could have indicated several possibilities, all of which would have been mere guesses as to Hooker's main body.

It is doing Lee a disservice to claim that he was not surprised by Hooker's success in getting three corps on his flank so neatly, without opposition from the Confederates. This writer for one does not believe that Lee ever claimed to know exactly where Hooker's troops were and what they were up to from the time the Federal army broke camp on April 27 and fanned out from Falmouth, as claimed by Major General R. E. Colston, one of Jackson's division commanders at the Battle of Chancellorsville. Colston subsequently wrote that Lee had information every day of Hooker's movements and that a letter which Lee wrote Jackson on April 23 was proof of the fact that he expected Hooker to cross the Rappahannock above and not below Fredericksburg. These assertions by Colston were in fact only half-truths. The letter referred to had merely warned Jackson not to send more troops than necessary to meet the expected crossing at Port Royal (Hooker's feint), because he, Lee, thought Hooker's purpose at Port Royal was to draw the Confederate troops in that direction and that the actual crossing would be above Fredericksburg. However, Lee did not say how far above Fredericksburg it would be attempted, and his defense line, terminating at Banks' Ford, obviously indicated that he did not expect a crossing so far west.

Further evidence may be found in Lee's expressed annoyance in a message to Anderson (in command of a division near Chancellorsville) that he had not been informed of the situation sooner. Lee was on record as having stated an earlier opinion that, if the crossing were made above Fredericksburg, as he expected it would, the probable limits would be within the line Port Royal-Banks' Ford, inclusive. These points he thereupon established as the right and left flank respectively of his defensive line, which he directed his subordinates to fortify and man, with outpost troops at United States Mine Ford, a short march north of the Chancellorsville crossroads.

It was probably after receipt of Stuart's second report, on the afternoon of April 29, that Lee's thoughts turned to Longstreet in the Suffolk area with the divisions of Pickett and Hood. He had prepared Longstreet for this very moment, so at Lee's request Secretary Seddon sent a telegram immediately to Longstreet, advising that the Union army had crossed the Rappahannock and that it was time for him to rejoin Lee with his two divisions.

As has been noted, Longstreet did not comply. To those who attribute to Longstreet as much as to any one factor Lee's defeat at Gettysburg two months later, his lack of wholehearted cooperation and subordination to his commanding general at the time of the Battle of Chancellorsville was in sharp contrast to the attitude of Jackson, Stuart, and most of Lee's other generals. Longstreet's propensity for placing his own views ahead of Lee's in spite of the fact that he was operating under orders, provides material for an interesting study of personalities and character.

LEE MEETS A CRISIS CALMLY

One of Lee's most admirable traits, among many, was the calm, unhurried way in which he met critical military situations. This characteristic, the mark of a strong character and superior field general, was never better demonstrated than at Chancellorsville. He never permitted himself to be unduly hurried in making his estimate of the situation, but once having made up his mind, his actions were swift and sure.

Captain James Power Smith, a member of Jackson's staff, was awakened at daylight April 29, in his tent near Hamilton's Crossing, with the news that Federal troops were crossing the Rappahannock within a few miles of Jackson's headquarters, just below Fredericksburg. At Jackson's direction, Smith rode quickly to Lee's headquarters, where the general was still sleeping. Entering Lee's tent, he gently awoke him to break the news. Lee swung his feet out of bed and sat sidewise on his cot with the typical remark: "Well, I thought I heard firing, and was beginning to think it was time some of you young fellows were coming to tell me what it was all about. Tell your good general that I am sure he knows what to do. I will meet him at the front very soon."

This was the situation that confronted him on the evening of April 29. Hooker's army had more than a two to one advantage in numbers. Only half of Longstreet's corps was on hand. His own cavalry had less than half its normal strength, while an entire corps of enemy cavalry, 10,000 strong and more aggressive than usual, was cutting in on the rear of his army and posing a threat to his communication line to Richmond, his main source of food, forage, ammunition, and supplies. His opponent had just sprung a surprise on him by a concealed march of three army corps in a wide swing, miles to the west of the fords where Lee had anticipated a crossing. This enemy was now on his left rear with a large force of infantry, artillery, and cavalry, the actual size of which remained to be disclosed. Other Federal troops had shown themselves at United States Mine Ford and Banks' Ford, the left anchor of Lee's long defense line, while another large troop concentration was threatening Fredericksburg and even now had thrown two bridges and established bridgeheads on the west bank of the river below the town.

Would the main effort of Hooker's army be made from Chancellorsville or was the flank march a feint to draw Lee back from Fredericksburg so that it could be taken by assault from the east, as Burnside had tried to do in December? Was the Fredericksburg maneuver a feint that would enable Hooker to move in on Lee from the rear with overwhelming strength? Or might Hooker, dividing his army into two equal parts, either one of which would be as strong as Lee's entire army, have decided to attack simultaneously from two directions to crush Lee between the strong jaws of the pincers?

Lee himself had ridden out from Hamilton's Crossing that morning and discovered that the Federals, under cover of an early fog, had crossed in boats, driven back the Confederate outposts, and completed the bridges over which an undetermined number of divisions had already crossed and halted. Lee could himself see other large masses of troops on the far bank awaiting instructions to cross.

The information received from Stuart on the 29th, that elements of the Federal Fifth, Eleventh, and Twelfth Corps had crossed at Kelly's

Ford and were headed for the Rapidan, provided Lee with the basis for some preliminary orders. He sent word to Stuart to rejoin the left wing of the army at once, taking care not to be cut off by the Federals, while at the same time protecting public property along the Orange and Alexandria Railroad and delaying the march of Hooker's divisions.

Later in the day he ordered R. H. Anderson to change the disposition of two of his brigades from the vicinity of United States Mine Ford to Chancellorsville, to delay the Federal advance. Jackson's Corps of four divisions was held in place for the time being, south of Fredericksburg, prepared to block any major attack from that direction.

Neither Hooker's earlier feint at Port Royal nor Sedgwick's present demonstration at Fredericksburg persuaded Lee to jump to premature conclusions. When Sedgwick paraded his divisions on Stafford Heights, but before he crossed the river in full strength, Jackson's first impulse was to prepare to attack him as soon as he should get across and occupy the plain south of the town. Lee disagreed, telling his lieutenant that it was just as impracticable now as it would have been at the first battle of Fredericksburg, because of Federal artillery superiority and the devastating fire its guns could pour into the attackers from the heights on the east bank. After Jackson had looked the ground over again he deferred to Lee's judgment and concurred in the undesirability of attacking.

The Army of the Potomac was on the march, gaining momentum as its right wing swept like a fast-moving glacier over the Rappahannock and Rapidan Rivers, through the forbidding depths of the Wilderness, and on to Chancellorsville, its first objective.

General George Gordon Meade, in command of the Fifth Corps, was the first high-ranking officer to reach the Chancellor House, a spacious manor house set back a few yards from the crossroads that marked the reference point designated on the map as Chancellorsville. Meade arrived about mid-day on Thursday, April 30, and within a few hours the entire right wing of three corps, eight divisions, had come up, the men resting on their arms while Slocum and Meade went into conference to discuss the next move.

Hooker's second-phase march orders to his three corps commanders, Slocum, Howard, and Meade, issued from Morrisville about 2 P.M. on

April 28, as they awaited the commanding general's word to start the columns across the Rappahannock, had directed an uninterrupted advance through Chancellorsville. The phase line on which they were instructed to march was in open, maneuverable country several miles east of Chancellorsville, beyond the grim woods of the Wilderness. The objective was an imaginary line running north and south from Banks' Ford on the Rappahannock to Tabernacle Church, located about two miles southwest of Salem Church on the Plank Road, terrain features that could be easily identified.

The plan was well conceived and was in the course of being efficiently executed. It was a foregone conclusion that the Confederates would have to relinquish United States Mine Ford as the Federal right wing advanced. Anderson's Confederate Division promptly and wisely pulled back from Chancellorsville as the leading Federal elements came up, but the Southerners were unhurried in their withdrawal as Pleasonton's advance cavalry ran into enemy rear guard opposition and pressed forward more cautiously.

The business of crossing large military forces over river obstacles by fording sounds easy, but the difficulties encountered in crossing the Rappahannock west of Fredericksburg must be seen to be appreciated. Above Falmouth, where the high bluffs rise at some points as much as hundred feet above the water line, they are close to the river, with slopes that are steep, wooded, and deeply cut by ravines. The first feasible crossing was at Banks' Ford, some six road miles from Fredericksburg, a position of such importance that the Confederates guarded it with extreme care. There they had erected a series of earthen parapets in three successive lines on the south side, with traverses to protect the defenders against hostile artillery fire from the opposite bank. Each line was a higher slope than the one in front, permitting the riflemen to fire over the heads of the men in the forward trenches. Clearly it would be an expensive operation to reduce the defenses other than by outflanking.

Seven miles further to the west was the next practicable crossing point at United States Mine Ford, where the Confederates had also constructed strong entrenchments.

Hooker's plan had taken these defenses into consideration and contemplated forcing a voluntary withdrawal of the Confederates by the process of uncovering them by maneuver, which he was well on the way to accomplishing until he changed his mind.

With the uncovering of United States Mine Ford, Benham's engineers quickly threw two bridges at that point. The two divisions of Couch's Second Corps, under Generals Hancock and French, crossed during the afternoon and went into bivouac at Chancellorsville on the night of April 30. The right wing now had a strength of four corps, ten divisions totaling about 54,000 men.

As Slocum and Meade understood Hooker's directive, there would be only a temporary pause at Chancellorsville to allow the right wing to regroup after its fast march. Meantime the cavalry would push ahead to uncover Banks' Ford and exploit the advantage already gained by the flanking maneuver. The specific instructions were that part of one corps would follow the road which parallels the Rappahannock and in close proximity to the river as it follows its meandering course past Banks' Ford and on to Fredericksburg. This would be Meade's job. The balance of his corps and Slocum's Twelfth would proceed in two columns, one along the Turnpike, the other on the Plank Road, until they reached the second phase line: Banks' Ford-Tabernacle Church, when the two corps would develop from march column into extended order to form a connected front across the three roads, the left flank anchored firmly on the river.

At that point, with everything nicely tidied up and in order, the right wing would be drawn up in battle formation, Slocum's Twelfth and Meade's Fifth Corps abreast, Howard's Eleventh Corps in support, and Couch's Second Corps in reserve, all prepared to open the engagement in coordinated fashion, under the direction of General Hooker, who at this point would ride up and assume personal command. That is, if Lee's army were still there, which Hooker's plan did not really anticipate.

There were several sentences in Hooker's initial instructions to Slocum which did not seem particularly significant when read in context, but which may have provided a clue to the commanding general's intentions:

If your Cavalry is well advanced from Chancellorsville, you will be able to ascertain whether or not the enemy is detaching forces from behind Fredericksburg to resist your advance. If not in any considerable force,

the general desires that you will endeavor to advance at all hazards,
securing a position on the Plank Road, and uncovering Banks' Ford,
which is also defended by a brigade of the rebel infantry and a battery.
If the enemy should be greatly reinforced you will then select a strong
position, and compel him to attack you on your ground . . .

In the light of subsequent events, the implications are unmistakable.
Reduced to its simplest terms, the order meant that, if Lee should decline
to flee and choose instead to oppose Hooker with force, the latter intended
to go over from the offensive to the defensive. That in turn would mean
that he would yield the initiative to his opponent and risk the loss of all
that his army had just gained by surprise and maneuver.

General Meade was an excellent corps commander, experienced in
combat, aggressive, and possessed of other soldierly traits which ranked
him as one of the more dependable leaders in the Army of the Potomac.
Anxious to put the Wilderness back of his corps, he lost no time in
directing his cavalry forward from Chancellorsville to follow the River
Road, establish contact with the enemy, and get on with the important
business of uncovering Banks' Ford. In support of the cavalry he sent
forward an infantry brigade of Griffin's division. The cavalry unfortunately took the Turnpike instead of the River Road, the infantry ran into
a superior Confederate force, two brigades of Anderson's Division, and
neither Federal detachment was able to make any progress.

The Captured Diary

Preceding Slocum's Twelfth Corps to the Rapidan on April 29, to sweep
the roads clear of enemy detachments, the horse regiment attached to
that column had operated in the cavalry tradition with speed, dash, and
enterprising ingenuity. Arriving at Germanna Ford, the advance guard
was confronted on the opposite bank by a party of Confederates who
showed a disposition to contest the crossing.

A small party of Federals promptly moved down river a few hundred
yards, found a stray boat and rapidly crossed a sizable detachment. This
force moved on the surprised Confederates from the rear and took as

prisoners half a hundred of Stuart's cavalry, among them an engineer staff officer of General Stuart's with an interesting diary on his person.

The next afternoon, Pleasonton's cavalry surprised and captured near Chancellorsville a Confederate courier bearing a dispatch from General Lee, dated at Fredericksburg, April 30, and addressed to Division Commander McLaws. It stated that he had just been told, at noon that day, of a strong Federal concentration at Chancellorsville. The letter expressed surprise that he had not been informed sooner, and ended by summoning McLaws immediately to his headquarters.

It may be presumed, from the fact that the courier was seeking McLaws, whose division on the Fredericksburg defense line had been alerted to the possibility that it might be needed to support Anderson's withdrawn position south of Banks' Ford, that McLaws had gone forward to make a personal reconnaissance, and that the courier had not yet caught up with him. But the captured message serves to confirm the fact that the rapidity of Hooker's successful flank march had indeed taken Lee by surprise.

Pleasonton's account, written sometime later, stated that he met Hooker at Chancellorsville at 2 o'clock on the afternoon of April 30 and turned over to him Lee's captured message and the diary which had been taken from Stuart's staff officer. Most reports however place Hooker's arrival on the field as having occurred during the evening, some hours later than Pleasonton indicates. This partly nullifies the timeliness of what the cavalry general regarded as vital enemy intelligence that should have drastically altered the situation from the Federal viewpoint, had Hooker acted promptly. Pleasonton's account of what transpired at that time, whether completely accurate or not, is an interesting commentary on the preliminary aspects of the campaign that was now beginning to take shape.

The captured Confederate officer had kept his diary all through the war. Pleasonton, intrigued by the thought that he might find something of importance in the voluminous document, stayed up most of the night of April 29 reading it from cover to cover. His patience had been rewarded, he told Hooker, when he came across an account of a council of war held at Stuart's headquarters in March, about six weeks earlier, which had been attended by Generals Jackson, A. P. Hill, Ewell, and Stuart. The conference, which had lasted five hours, reached the unanimous conclusion that the next battle would be fought at or near Chancellorsville.

This to Pleasonton was information of the greatest significance. He called Hooker's attention to the opinion which had been expressed by Lee's high-ranking lieutenants, emphasizing the fact that the tables had now been turned and Hooker's army was already on the battlefield the Confederates had selected. He pointed out that Lee had by this time received the news of Hooker's arrival at Chancellorsville and urged that the advantage of surprise would be lost to Hooker if the Chancellorsville locale were not promptly changed in order to negate such tactical plans as Lee may already have worked out in conformity with the expressed views of Jackson and the other generals.

Pleasonton then strongly recommended that the advance of the right wing be hastened, to enable the three corps to clear the Wilderness and move into the open country to the east, where maneuver would be possible. The troops could there see what they were doing, and artillery could be used to advantage. An additional advantage, he said, would be the uncovering of Banks' Ford, thus shortening by a substantial number of miles the line of communication with Sedgwick's wing at Fredericksburg. In effect, Hooker's cavalry commander was repeating the identical instructions that Hooker had given to Slocum in the original order directing the circuitous march on Chancellorsville.

Pleasanton Gets an Unpleasant Shock

Pleasonton's account stated that Hooker's apathetic reaction to his recommendations greatly shocked him, in that the commanding general could see no reason for haste, expressing the opinion that the next morning would be plenty of time to move on toward Fredericksburg and Lee's army.

The captured diary had evidently failed to disclose Lee's attitude and reactions when the conclusions of the council were reported to him, as they surely must have been. But it is almost a certainty that the combat powerhouse represented in the persons of the four major participants, and the length of time that had been devoted to the discussions, were guarantee enough that their views would be important elements in Lee's subsequent strategy.

That Hooker was opinionated, self-centered, and lacking many of the essential character traits that are basic in great leaders, military and non-military alike, is borne out by the historic facts. That he intended to rely wholly on his own judgment and disregard that of his principal subordinates, however, was not fully revealed to them until the evening of April 30. Hooker had had excellent reasons for not divulging his strategic plans to his corps commanders or even to his own staff until the very last minute.

But there were obvious dangers in that policy, such as the slow transmission of tactical instructions based on the overall strategy, or staff miscalculations on the time element required for preparing and distributing contingent orders down through corps, division, brigade, and lower units.

HOOKER APPLIES THE BRAKES

Enthusiasm was running high as division after division of the marching Federal columns moved into the area about Chancellorsville, removed their packs and settled down to relax and swap stories while their generals went into a huddle preparatory to getting on with the war.

Meade was in high spirits as Slocum rode up to the Chancellor House. The two generals shook hands as the usually taciturn Meade greeted his friend with unaccustomed gaiety: "This is splendid, Slocum; hurrah for old Joe! We are on Lee's flank and he doesn't know it. You take the Plank Road toward Fredericksburg, and I will take the Pike, or vice versa, if you prefer, and we will get out of this Wilderness."

Evidently the enthusiastic Meade had not yet received his copy of the dispatch which Chief of Staff Butterfield had signed at 2:15 P.M., by Hooker's order. This is what it said: "The General directs that no advance be made from Chancellorsville until the columns (II, III, V, XI and XII Corps) are concentrated. He expects to be at Chancellorsville tonight." When Slocum showed Meade his copy of the delaying order, the wind quickly went out of Meade's sails, and as the word leaked out to the troops,

Hooker's halt order had the effect of changing optimistic enthusiasm to a feeling of bitter disappointment. Officers and men alike realized instinctively that the golden opportunity to exploit the advantage already gained was being jeopardized by faulty judgment.

It would seem that Hooker's thoughts that afternoon of April 30 were still centered exclusively on the thrilling outcome of his first large-scale operation, as he sat in his command post at Morrisville and penned the congratulatory General Order which he planned to publish with a symbolic flourish to his troops that evening. Doubtless he was planning what he would say to his men when Pleasonton interrupted his pleasant train of thoughts with the urgent exhortation to hustle the right wing on toward Fredericksburg to get the jump on Lee.

Perhaps Slocum and Meade had moved faster than Hooker had expected and were getting ahead of his timetable. It may still have been a map problem for Hooker, but it was high time that he transfer his attention from paper to the actual field of operations, where events were moving fast. It was clear enough, however, that he was not ready to clash with Lee until he could reinforce the three leading corps, already at Chancellorsville, with the additional strength to be added by Couch's Second and Sickles' Third Corps, which between them would add over 30,000 men to the 42,000 of the right wing. Then Hooker would have a force of 72,000 from which he felt sure that Lee would "ingloriously fly," to quote from the order which was read to the troops at Chancellorsville that evening:

It is with heart-felt satisfaction the Commanding General announces to the Army that the operations of the last three days have determined that our enemy must either ingloriously fly or come out from behind his intrenchments and give us battle on our own ground, where certain destruction awaits him. The operations of the V, XI, and XII Corps have been a succession of splendid achievements.

As if that boastful general order were not enough, upon his arrival at Chancellorsville, Hooker saw fit to add a foolishly gratuitous insult to the Lord with the comment that "God Almighty will not be able to prevent the destruction of the rebel army!" One may be sure that such blasphemy must have had only the most depressing effect on thousands of God-fearing soldiers in his magnificent army, superimposed as it was on other unfortunate utterances, such as: "the rebel army is now the legitimate property of the Army of the Potomac. They may as well pack up their haversacks and make for Richmond. I shall be after them;" and "God have mercy on General Lee, for I shall have none."

Hooker's Fatal Delay

As the army commander marked time mentally and physically, the Second Corps moved across the river and went into bivouac while Sickles' Third Corps, lately detached by Hooker's instructions from Sedgwick's wing, moved up from Fredericksburg. Sickles made good time the night of April 30, crossed at United States Mine Ford and went into bivouac Friday morning, May 1, in the vicinity of Bullock's (Chandler's), a mile north. of the Chancellorsville crossroads where the Ely's Ford road crosses the Mineral Springs Road.

Pending Hooker's arrival at Chancellorsville, Slocum, as senior corps commander until Couch should come on the field, was responsible for making the necessary tactical decisions, within the framework of Hooker's directive. The latest message, jerking the machine to a numbing, frustrating, "in place, halt," flatly contradicted the earlier order which said that "the right wing, if not strongly resisted," would advance at all hazards and secure a position uncovering Banks' Ford. In the event the Confederates were found to be in force near Chancellorsville, the right wing was to select a strong position and await attack on its own ground, while Sedgwick would come up from Fredericksburg to assail the enemy in flank and rear, although the Sedgwick move was not divulged at that time.

The key words in the order are found in the phrase "if not strongly resisted." Surely a bit of rear guard skirmishing by a small force of retiring Confederates or even a brigade in position at Banks' Ford would not be construed as strong resistance against an advancing force of 40,000 troops. The fact of the matter was that Hooker intended from the very beginning that Sedgwick should pound Lee against the hard rock of Hooker's main force in a defensive position at Chancellorsville, if his strategic maneuvering should fail to drive the Confederate army to the south without giving battle. In such event, Lee was expected to take the same punishment that he had administered to Burnside at the first battle of Fredericksburg.

Hooker's real intentions had not been revealed to his corps commanders, however, so all of them naturally thought he meant what he had said in his march orders. He later gave out that his reason for suspending the advance on April 30 was to gain time for Couch's Second and Sickles' Third Corps to augment the large mass of troops already on the ground. But the truth was that he had, cravenly in the opinion of his subordinates and most historical critics of his revised strategy, chosen to let Sedgwick carry the burden of the attack with only his own Sixth Corps. For it was not long before Hooker also pulled Reynolds' First Corps away from the left wing to join the main body at Chancellorsville, leaving Sedgwick to figure out for himself what Hooker really expected of him.

Clearly something had happened to Joe Hooker that gave off ominous overtones. Here was a general who had brilliantly executed an amazing military feat and then proceeded, inexplicably, to nullify the advantage gained just at the moment of the payoff battle with an opponent facing almost insuperable odds. Had the mysterious power implicit in the very name of Robert E. Lee paralyzed Joe Hooker as soon as the test of battle impended? Had abstinence from his customary drinking muddled his thinking apparatus? Or had his initial success so gone to his head that he felt he had only to wait patiently for Lee to reveal his intentions, concede that Hooker held all the aces, and solve the problem by pulling out for Richmond?

What is probably nearer the truth is that Hooker could scarcely believe his plan had succeeded so admirably, had not thought much ahead of the present moment, and was as a result uncertain just what his next move should be. For the action of the first three days he had planned superbly, but when it came to prompt, decisive action in which he was face to face with his able opponent, he seems to have become the unfortunate victim of self-hypnosis. It was indeed not self-intoxication, for we have Couch's word for it that Hooker was not drinking at Chancellorsville. Yet Couch, his second-in-command, was far from being one of Hooker's admirers; so far in fact that after the battle of Chancellorsville he refused to serve further under Hooker and was transferred to the Department of the Susquehanna.

There in the clearing around and south of the Chancellor House, within a few yards of the key crossroads from which radiated a network of improved and unimproved roads, the hopes and aspirations of the long-suffering but spirited Army of the Potomac received another shattering setback. And it was not from Robert E. Lee this time, except perhaps indirectly through the medium of thought waves, but at the hands of Joseph Hooker himself, the architect of the offensive campaign. Hooker administered the fatal blow to his army, by remote control from a town on the other side of the Rappahannock. For the twenty-hour delay in the forward movement of his right wing was destined to be a decisive factor in giving to the Army of Northern Virginia the necessary time to concentrate. He played directly into the hands of General Lee, who desperately wanted to keep Hooker penned up in the dense woods of the Wilderness. Hooker's volte-face thus served to yield the initiative to Lee, always ready to seize it, and at the same time to paralyze the movements of his own army while the Confederates gathered their forces along the high ground between Old Mine Road and the Banks' Ford-Tabernacle Church line some six miles to the east in open country.

Having been halted where they were, still in the Wilderness, Slocum and Meade held a conference about 2:30 P.M., April 30, and decided the only thing to do was to halt their advance and forego for the time being what would have been the easy task of uncovering Banks' Ford arid occupying their second phase line in maneuverable country. This was a painful decision for two good generals to have to make, impatient as they were to exploit their initial success by maintaining the offensive with its real promise of a decisive victory. Both were angered as well as disheartened by Hooker's switch to a defensive psychology, however temporary it might seem at the moment. They at least were aware of the importance of keeping moving on that Thursday afternoon, and could see no benefit in postponing the fight, if that should be Lee's purpose.

But orders were orders, so the advance brigade of Griffin's division was told to pull back to Chancellorsville, while Slocum and Meade concocted a revised plan which called for the· advance to be resumed the next morning, Friday, May 1. The order of march would be in three columns as follows: two of Meade's divisions, commanded by Griffin and Humphreys, to take the River Road; the third division of the Fifth Corps, Sykes', the Orange Turnpike; Slocum's two divisions of the Twelfth Corps would march on the Plank Road; and Howard's Eleventh Corps would follow in support of the two leading corps. All three columns were instructed to keep in touch with one another during the advance.

As night fell, the four Federal corps occupied a line extending in an easterly direction, with Howard's Eleventh Corps on the Turnpike from a point about three miles west of Chancellorsville, the right flank refused a short distance to the north, and the left flank connecting with the right of Slocum's Twelfth Corps, which formed an arc that ran south and east and enclosed the open country around Fairview. Slocum's left rested on the Plank Road a half mile south of the Chancellorsville crossroads. Meade's Fifth Corps, with the exception of Humphreys' division, which came up the next morning, remained in a position of readiness in the vicinity of the crossroads, while Couch's Second Corps went into bivouac about a mile north of Chancellorsville.

CONFEDERATE COUNTERMEASURES

As stated earlier, General Anderson had been ordered by Lee, late on April 29, to withdraw Mahone's and Posey's Brigades from United States Mine Ford to Chancellorsville. On his arrival at Chancellorsville about midnight that day Anderson found that the movement had already started. The withdrawal continued, under Federal pressure, during the morning of the 30th, the two brigades taking up a defensive line from Zoan Church to Tabernacle Church. In falling back, one of the brigades lost some men to the fast-moving cavalry preceding the Federal corps, but the enemy advance was retarded sufficiently to permit Anderson to pull back his brigades intact.

Lee now directed Anderson to form and strengthen a line of defense east of and facing Chancellorsville, at right angles to the river. He was told to rest his right on the river to cover Banks' Ford, and to anchor his left somewhat south of the Plank Road in such a position as would serve temporarily to cover the roads to Lee's left flank until more troops could be brought up. McLaws' Division, the only other one of Longstreet's Corps with Lee, was told to prepare to move the next day from the Fredericksburg position to support Anderson, if needed.

Anderson's Division spent the rest of the day in digging trenches and throwing up breastworks, under the supervision of Lee's Chief Engineer, Colonel W. P. Smith, sent out for the purpose. The position ran from below the unfinished railroad, on the left, to a point three-quarters of a mile north of the Turnpike, then curved back along Colin Run. It was extended further north as far as the vicinity of Banks' Ford by a line of rifle pits. While the work was progressing, Anderson waited for McLaws' Division to come up to support and strengthen his defense.

Toward evening Lee received a message from Stuart that four and a half hours earlier, or about 2 P.M., three Federal Corps had crossed the Rapidan at Germanna and Ely's Fords, headed southeast. Stuart probably meant that the reported corps had completed the crossing; if Lee so interpreted the message, he would know that the heads of their columns had reached Chancellorsville early in the afternoon, if not sooner. No more time was to be lost. Lee's decision was to attack, and the orders to put his army into position were quickly made ready.

Lee now knew for a positive fact that Hooker had divided his army, where most of its elements were, their objectives (in part), and approximate strength (also in part). It was at that point that he had decided once more to take another of his famous calculated risks and leave Jubal Early with 10,000 men, his own division reinforced by Barksdale's Brigade of McLaw's Division, on the Fredericksburg heights to oppose Sedgwick's. vastly superior force; reverse Anderson's direction to move on Chancellorsville; send McLaws at once to Anderson's support at Salem Church; and start Jackson's Corps (less Early's Division) of 30,000 men on the march to Chancellorsville, to reinforce Anderson and McLaws; and take command of the battle.

Lee's decision was a courageous one, in the Lee tradition. His army had already been divided by the detachment of one corps commander and two divisions to Suffolk. It was further potentially divided by the danger that Stuart's cavalry might be cut off by Hooker's right wing. Who but

Robert E. Lee would have had the strategic insight and moral courage to assume the heavy risk of further dividing his forces? On the other hand, who but he had such perfect confidence in his officers and men and such calm assurance that with God's blessing all would be well?

With unerring instinct, despite the fully recognized and seemingly overpowering threat to his left rear, Lee chose the offensive and elected to attack in the direction of the greater danger, while he turned his back on Sedgwick's threat without the slightest trace of panic or sense of being cornered. Nor is it deprecatory to the reputation of other great army commanders to remark that not one out of ten would have had the courage or wisdom· to make the same decision under similar circumstances.

Never had Lee's exquisite skill and sense of timing been better demonstrated than on this occasion. His ability to utilize to his own advantage and the discomfiture of his opponent the time, space, and psychological factors that are so essential in planning and executing the movements of large military forces, was again to be revealed in what many historians have proclaimed to be his greatest victory—the Battle of Chancellorsville.

His strategy was simple and easily understood. He would hold Banks' Ford to keep Hooker's army divided, entertain Sedgwick with a small holding force, and move to attack the main threat by bearding the larger part of the Union army in the Wilderness den.

STUART REJOINS LEE

Lee need not have worried overly, when he directed Stuart to rejoin the main army, about Stuart's ability to do so. But the cavalry leader's task would have been more difficult, if not impossible, had it not been for Stoneman's apathy. After crossing the Rappahannock on April 29, Stoneman's corps had bivouacked in two areas: Averell's division a few miles west of Kelly's Ford in the direction of Brandy Station; Stoneman's column at Madden, five miles northwest of Germanna Ford. Before splitting into two columns, Stoneman had called all his commanders together to give them final instructions, which caused further delay and should have been thoroughly understood before the corps left Warrenton Junction. Stoneman still had much to learn if he wished to compete with the fast-thinking, fast-moving Jeb Stuart and the two Lees.

Stuart's mission was a complicated one. Lee had directed him to take the greatest care not to be cut off by Hooker's advancing divisions in his effort to return to the army. At the same time he was told to protect public property, presumably against Stoneman's raid, and concurrently, as he marched to rejoin, to impede the progress of the Federal column crossing at Germanna Ford. This was a large order for such a small cavalry force as Stuart had under him, but his energetic actions did cause some annoyance without actually interfering with the progress of Slocum's column.

Stuart assigned to Rooney Lee's Brigade the mission of covering Gordonsville and, to the extent practicable, of protecting the Orange and Alexandria Railroad, which would probably involve him with at least a part of Stoneman's cavalry. General R. E. Lee, at the time he directed Stuart's return, still feared that Hooker's purpose was to strike for Gordonsville, which led him to wire repeated messages to Richmond urging the dispatch of any force that might be available from that point to Gordonsville.

Stuart himself, with Fitzhugh Lee's Brigade, would march at once to the Rapidan, cross at Raccoon Ford, delay the Federal infantry, and then rejoin Lee's army. Lee's Brigade crossed on the night of April 29 and proceeded to carry out its mission. One real effort only was made in strength to effect a delay of Slocum's Federal column. That was when Fitz Lee's Brigade blocked the road with a part of his cavalry and attacked the Federals as they passed Wilderness Tavern, but Slocum detached a couple of regiments to dispose of the Confederates and kept going. Learning about that time that Meade's corps had already reached Chancellorsville Stuart directed Lee's small detached holding force to fall back on Anderson's infantry at Salem Church while he, with the main portion of Lee's Brigade, took a round-about route via Todd's Tavern and Spotsylvania Court House on his way to join up with the army.

It was bright moonlight when the brigade reached Todd's Tavern, where at Stuart's suggestion the troops went into bivouac for the night while he and his staff rode on to report to army headquarters. Stuart's party had traveled only a short distance when they ran into the Sixth New York Cavalry, 350 strong, under Lieutenant Colonel Duncan McVicar, sent by General Pleasonton on a night reconnaissance to learn, what they could of the enemy dispositions, and on the off: chance they might be able to destroy Confederate supplies believed to be stored at Spotsylvania Court House.

While Jeb Stuart and his staff galloped back to Lee's Brigade to rouse them to action, the Federal regiment pulled off the road and drew up in line in Hugh Alsop's field. The Fifth Virginia Cavalry came pelting down the road to find them, and as the Confederates passed, McVicar's troopers charged them in the rear, firing from the saddle, captured some prisoners and moved on to the road junction to protect their return route. Here they were charged in turn by the Third Virginia Cavalry and there occurred a lively little fight, with Federal and Confederate units hopelessly intermingled in the shadows caused by the woods along the side of the road. Finally unscrambling themselves, the several regiments pulled apart to reorganize. The Sixth New York, minus its commander, who was killed in the charge, and their prisoners who had managed to escape in the confusion, made their way back to Chancellorsville.

With a number of killed and wounded in each outfit the honors were even, and in due course Fitz Lee's Brigade continued on its way to rejoin the main army. Major von Borcke, the big Prussian who was a member of Stuart's staff and very outspoken, was with Stuart on this adventure and frankly described the confusion that the charge of the New York cavalry caused in the Confederate ranks. He said that for once Stuart's troopers refused to obey their officers and galloped wildly off in all directions.

As to the value of the Federal reconnaissance, the regiment was able to report only that it had driven through a body of enemy cavalry without being able to state whether the troops were alone or part of a larger force, for the prisoners had all made good their escape. The information turned in was therefore inconclusive, but may have had the effect of making Hooker even more cautious, if that were possible.

Hooker kept his plans so secret that even his chief signal officer was not told what would be expected of him and could therefore take no precautions to spot the necessary material to keep his wire communications open in case of damage from artillery fire. Truly the Chancellorsville campaign, for the Federals, was a case of the right hand not knowing what the left was doing, and vice versa. Under such uncertain circumstances, whatever instructions the signal officer may have issued to his signal personnel must have lacked both clarity and conviction. All that the observers could do was to report what they saw, when the fog and rain would permit, with little idea of its importance or significance. The inevitable result, human nature being what it is, would be apathetic execution of orders that probably appeared routine to the men.

Great pains had been taken by the Federal Signal Corps to install flag signal stations on their side of the Rappahannock, and there is evidence that these were used to advantage, although perhaps not as extensively as they might have been. The field telegraph line between Butterfield's headquarters at Falmouth and United States Mine Ford rendered efficient service except for delays in restoring the line when it failed; and Professor Lowe's two captive balloons opposite Fredericksburg were up and down like jumping jacks on April 29 and 30, sending in frequent items of accurate intelligence with what the aeronauts messaged as from "Balloon in the Air."

The most portentous news came from "Hill and Brooks," at Sedgwick's headquarters dated April 29, 1863—3:30 P.M., addressed to Captain Cushing, Chief Signal Officer. The message from these signal men stated that "about 8,000 or 10,000 infantry and four batteries, followed by an ammunition train and' ambulances, have just passed along in the direction of Fredericksburg, opposite this point."

That would be part of Jackson's Corps, probably Early's Division, but it is impossible to determine how Hooker evaluated the information or whether it had an influence on his action in summoning Sickles' corps on April 30 and Reynolds' corps the following day, from Sedgwick's wing to Chancellorsville to augment the growing force that Hooker was concentrating at the latter point.

Visibility on April 29 had been good all through the afternoon, with the result that at Fredericksburg both the balloon observers and signal stations kept Butterfield informed of enemy movements, as the Confederates reacted to Sedgwick's demonstration and partial crossing of the river. Professor Lowe reported such interesting happenings as the movement of enemy wagon trains to the rear; the apparent strength of the units that were visible; the forward movement of two infantry regiments from the Fredericksburg heights into the rifle pits opposite Sedgwick's bridgehead troops; and other information of solid value to Sedgwick and Hooker, if correctly evaluated and utilized.

The following orders had issued from Hooker's headquarters on the afternoon of April 30:

> *To Benham: to secretly take up two bridges, at Franklin's and Fitzhugh's Crossings respectively, during the night and move them to Banks' Ford before daylight. This order was consistent with the initial instructions to the right wing to advance beyond Chancellorsville for the purpose of uncovering Banks' Ford, but which had not yet been accomplished.*
>
> *To Sickles (12:30 P.M.): to march to United States Mine Ford and cross by 7:00 A.M. May 1. Two additional pontoon bridges had already been laid for the use of his Third Corps.*
>
> *To Sedgwick: if the enemy should expose a weak point, attack and destroy him; if he appears to be falling back, pursue him by the Bowling Green and Telegraph roads.*
>
> *To Gibbon: be ready to move at daylight to rejoin his corps (Couch's).*

To further confuse the situation for Sedgwick, Chief of Staff Butterfield in a letter to Sedgwick quoted Hooker as having told him that when he (Hooker) left Chancellorsville (presumably on the morning of May 1), he expected, if there should be no serious opposition, to reach the heights west of Fredericksburg by noon or shortly after; if opposed strongly, then by nightfall.

That certainly sounded as though the Army Commander intended to act on the offensive, but the letter is a direct contradiction of Hooker's well-advertised attitude of defense in his latest instructions to the corps commanders of the right wing.

Vital time was slipping away for the Federals on the morning of Friday, May 1 as Hooker continued, hour after hour, to mark time in the Wilderness while Lee concentrated his army at Tabernacle Church to meet the Federal threat. Every minute counted, but Hooker had made up his mind not to advance until Sickles' corps should arrive, despite the fact that he had already massed 54,000 men at Chancellorsville and, when Sickles' three divisions would come up, at any moment, his strength would exceed 70,000.

May 1 had dawned clear and cool as the men of the right wing of the Army of the Potomac pulled themselves up from the hard ground and gathered around their campfires to absorb some heat in their chilled bodies. Hooker's army was still resting in the woods and clearings around Chancellorsville, while the generals of corps and divisions waited impatiently for their commanding general to give them the signal to get started on the road to Fredericksburg and out of the dense wilderness that imprisoned them and hampered their movements.

It would be only a question of a few hours until the opposing forces would clash somewhere between Chancellorsville and Fredericksburg. Confederate division commander McLaws had marched at midnight April 30 to Anderson's support on the Tabernacle Church ridge, while Jackson's Corps (less Early's Division) left their bivouacs during the night and were well on their way toward Chancellorsville before daylight.

By this time Lee was pretty well informed as to the strength and dispositions of the divided Federal army. His cavalry had functioned with its usual energy and resourcefulness, so that he knew at least the outline of the positions occupied by the enemy at Chancellorsville. Hooker, on the other hand, having dissipated his major means of mounted reconnaissance, was only vaguely aware of what was in front of him. The reports that had reached him the preceding day from Sedgwick had proven somewhat contradictory, but gave the impression that Lee's main body was still within its established lines west of Fredericksburg, as in fact it was.

There was even the possibility that Lee had been reinforced at Fredericksburg, if Hooker believed the rumor that Sedgwick had passed along, to the effect that Longstreet's two missing divisions had arrived from Suffolk. It seems that several Confederate "deserters" (doubtless under instructions from Jackson) had voluntarily entered the Federal lines below Fredericksburg and given out the information, to which some credence was given by the heavy movement of Confederate troops and trains that had been observed during the afternoon of April 30 by the Federal balloons and signal stations.

Hooker was clearly failing to give proper consideration to the seriousness of Lee's critical position between Hooker's own strong troop buildup at Chancellorsville and Sedgwick's large concentration at Fredericksburg. He seemed strangely reluctant to exploit the important advantage accruing from the favorable fact that his pincers had already closed the gap between his two wings from forty to not more than ten miles. Somewhere between the pincer's jaws were Lee and his 60,000 men, the potential victims of a crushing pressure from front and rear if only Hooker would shake off his odd lethargy and move confidently to finish what had been so beautifully initiated and executed up to the time of his halt order in the Wilderness.

Lee's intentions, as distinct from his actions, were apparently beyond Hooker's capacity to fathom, for the latter was still vacillating on the morning of May 1. He had received telegraphic reports from the Signal Corps that large enemy troop columns were observed about 9 A.M., moving rapidly west from Fredericksburg. The early morning fog had thinned sufficiently by that time to permit occasional balloon observations, but a light rain had started to fall, which reduced visibility for a time until the sun came out later in the morning, after Jackson's Corps had pretty well completed its night march. Coupled with the planted rumor that Longstreet's two missing divisions had arrived, the additional intelligence seems to have added to Hooker's indecision, for he delayed ordering the advance until about 11 o'clock, by which time more precious hours had been wasted and Jackson given time to unite his corps with the divisions of Anderson and McLaws at Tabernacle Church.

Finally, at 11 A.M., Hooker released to his corps commanders a circular which directed a regrouping of troops to put them on two of the three roads leading to Fredericksburg, essentially as planned by Slocum and Meade the evening before, with this exception: Hooker's circular was static, whereas the corps commanders were thinking dynamically:

The Fifth Corps on the River Road, with its head midway between Mott's Run and Colin Run, movement to be completed by 2 P.M.
The Twelfth Corps to be massed below the Plank Road, head resting near Tabernacle Church and masked from the view of the

enemy by small advanced parties; the movement to be completed by 12 o'clock to enable the Eleventh Corps to take its position.

The Eleventh Corps to be masked [sic] on the Plank Road, one mile in rear of the Twelfth, its movement to be completed at 2 o'clock.

1 division of the Second Corps to take position at Todd's Tavern and to throw out strong detachments on the approaches in the direction of the enemy. The other divisions of the corps to be massed out of the road near Chancellorsville.

The Third Corps to be massed on the United States Ford road about 1 mile from Chancellorsville, as fast as it should arrive, except for one brigade which would take position at Dowdall's Tavern.

General Pleasonton to hold his cavalry command at Chancellorsville.

The circular ended with the remark: "After the movement commences, headquarters will be at Tabernacle Church."

It is possible that Hooker had issued oral orders earlier than 11 A.M., the hour at which his circular was authenticated, for Meade's report states that the movement actually commenced about 11 A.M. Also, Hooker's circular does not mention the fact that Sykes' division of Meade's corps was to advance initially on the Turnpike, until after it had crossed Mott's Run. Thereafter Sykes was supposed to move to the left, deploy, and open communication with Griffin on his left and Slocum on his right. None of this beautiful coordination was effected, however, as Sykes ran into the Confederates when he had advanced not more than a mile.

Hooker later testified before the Committee on the Conduct of the War that the above orders were in conformity with his intention of advancing for the purpose of uncovering Banks' Ford to shorten communications between the two wings of his army. It will, however, be noted that there was no intimation, in the phraseology of the orders or in Hooker's testimony, that he was going out to attack the enemy. If the English language means anything, all Hooker was telling his generals in this circular was that they were to place their troops in certain advanced positions. If Hooker had developed any sort of an operational plan in his own mind, there is no indication of it in the circular; no attack mission, no instructions to occupy a defensive line, no orders on what to do when the troops should reach the new positions. Even the closing sentence was ambiguous in stating that army headquarters would be at Tabernacle Church "after the movement commences."

What movement was Hooker talking about—the shift of troops to the new position or a subsequent advance? The latter might possibly have been deduced by the corps commanders, since the designated command post was in front of the assigned position of the massed troops. But army commanders should not have to depend on crystal balls for the interpretation of their orders by subordinates. In point of fact, the Confederates were actually occupying the area around Tabernacle Church at the time Hooker issued the circular. It was a strange document for an army commander to issue under the circumstances, and the effect on the recipients can only be imagined. Conversely, they may have reasoned that half a loaf was better than no bread—at least some of them would be clear of the Wilderness!

THE CONFEDERATES MOVE FORWARD

Stonewall Jackson reached Tabernacle Church in advance of his 30,000 men at 8 A.M., May 1 to find 16,000 other troops under Anderson and McLaws, busily engaged in fortifying their position, a north–south line on a low ridge that ran for three miles from Duerson's Mill on the right, to the unfinished railroad below the Plank Road on the left. This line cut across and effectively blocked Hooker's route from Chancellorsville to Fredericksburg by the, three available roads. Jackson's decision was reached almost immediately; to disregard the entrenching job and advance on Chancellorsville. His plan contemplated the withdrawal of Wilcox's Brigade from Banks' Ford and Perry's Brigade from opposite Falmouth, for Jackson's thought was to advance his whole force to the attack, and that included all the troops under his temporary command. Jackson had his occasional blind spots; the decision would have resulted in his playing right into Meade's hands if Hooker had just kept hands off. When Lee came up a few hours later, he noted the mistake and promptly corrected it by returning Wilcox's Brigade to Banks' Ford.

Aside from the fact that Jackson's instinct was offensive, he was thoroughly aware of the possibility that Sedgwick might break through Early's thin line at Fredericksburg, and was anything but intrigued with the idea of fighting in two directions at once. Two hours were required for his troops to form, and it was 11 o'clock before the advance got underway, Fitz Lee's cavalry brigade covering the left flank in the woods. Anderson's Division took the lead with one brigade on the Turnpike and two on the Plank Road, both preceded by a strong cavalry regiment and infantry skirmishers who were spread well out. McLaws' Division followed with Anderson's two remaining brigades, marching on the Turnpike, while the three divisions of Jackson's Corps, commanded respectively by Rodes, A. P. Hill, and Colston, followed by the main body of the artillery, took the Plank Road behind Anderson.

The two armies at this point were separated by a distance of not more than six miles. They could, therefore, be expected to meet head-on in a matter of two hours or less, either in column on the Turnpike or Plank Road, or in the fields and woods on either side, depending on how rapidly the leading elements would deploy in extended order. The situation had all the earmarks of an interesting meeting engagement fraught with a variety of possibilities. The advantage of numbers rested with the Union forces, but they were uninformed as to either the strength or disposition of the Confederate troops. Consequently they were obliged to advance blindly to a prescribed position without orders either to attack or defend if and when they should run into opposition.

The Confederates, on the other hand, moved out confidently to attack a known foe in a determined effort to repulse and drive him back to the Rapidan. Their commander, for the time being Stonewall Jackson, was marching with them in a position to make the best use of his men instantly and effectively as the battle developed. There would be no dilly-dallying on his part, while the Federal corps commanders, in the circumstances confronting them, would be obliged to send back to Hooker's headquarters at the Chancellor House for orders or they would have to do the best they could, in the absence of on-the-spot decisions, in a fight which inevitably would be as uncoordinated as could possibly be imagined.

CONTACT!

The Confederate column on the right had covered little more than a mile along the Turnpike when its advance cavalry ran into a small force of Federal horsemen, followed closely by a strong body of infantry from Sykes' division of the Fifth Corps. Both outfits deployed promptly, engaged in a sharp fight, and Sykes pressed the Confederates steadily back until he gained the position east of Mott's Run that he had been directed to seize.

Jackson acted immediately to aid McLaws on the right, sending in a brigade from the Plank Road. Similar coordination, however, was lacking among the Federal corps commanders, with the result that Sykes, to avoid envelopment of both his flanks, reported his critical salient to Hooker and was told to withdraw in the direction of Chancellorsville.

The situation developed more slowly on the Plank Road, where Slocum's Twelfth Corps was proceeding with his two divisions abreast. The advance elements encountered Confederate skirmishers almost at once. The Federal divisions thereupon received orders to develop, that is, move from division column into columns of regiments or brigades, from which they could deploy quickly into line. This took almost two hours, so that it was nearly 1 o'clock when they resumed the advance. It is no wonder Sykes found his flanks in the air, with no supporting Federal troops in contact on either right or left.

To meet Slocum's threat to his own left, Stonewall Jackson again reacted promptly to send in a brigade of infantry along the unfinished railroad, which endangered Slocum's right flank and forced his leading elements back on the main body.

While the meeting engagement along the Turnpike and Plank Roads was being fought, the two divisions of Meade's corps on the River Road were advancing with virtually no opposition until they came within two miles of Banks' Ford, the uncovering of which was a major objective of the entire movement. This development afforded a remarkable opportunity for Hooker to exploit what was obviously Lee's weak flank, had he energetically pushed either Couch's two-division corps or Sickles' three-division corps rapidly down the river road in support of Meade, with the mission of turning the enemy right. But

Hooker's thoughts were defensive, and no effort was made to exploit Meade's easy progress.

It would appear that Corps Commander Meade was having too easy a time on the River Road, or his system of communications was inadequate. Certainly he did nothing to help Sykes, whose division was part of his own corps, when the former ran into difficulties on the Turnpike. Hooker had a right to expect Meade to maintain a working liaison with all of his divisions and to coordinate their efforts. For all of Meade, Sykes might just as well have been conducting an independent operation all by himself.

It was at 11:30 in the morning that Hooker had issued the following order to Sedgwick's left wing at Fredericksburg, through Chief of Staff Butterfield: "Direct Major General Sedgwick to threaten an attack at full force at 1 o'clock, and to continue in that attitude until further orders. Let the demonstration be as severe as can be, but not an attack."

Obviously Hooker was not yet aware of the fact that most of Lee's army had shifted during the night and was now moving against the advancing divisions of his right wing. Otherwise he would not have issued orders whose purpose could only have been to threaten the Confederates at Fredericksburg and to cause Lee to hold them there rather than to detach them to confront him at Chancellorsville. Nor was Sedgwick at Fredericksburg any better informed as to the strength of the Confederates on his front.

His lack of enterprise in failing to make at least a reconnaissance in force to determine what was before him, after having crossed the Rappahannock, can scarcely be excused on the basis of Hooker's orders, despite their indecisive character. It was certainly his responsibility to feel out the enemy sufficiently to find out whether Jackson's Corps was or was not still on his front. With a bit more aggressiveness, Sedgwick should have ascertained that only 10,000 men, not 40,000, were now occupying a thinly held seven-mile front on the heights west of Fredericksburg. Instead of this he sat tight.

At 12:30 P.M. Butterfield informed Hooker: "The enemy will meet you between Chancellorsville and Hamilton's Crossing. He cannot, I judge from all reports, have detached over 10,000 or 15,000 men from

Sedgwick's front since sun cleared fog." Yet at the very moment that Butterfield was authenticating that message, Jackson's Corps had met and was pushing back the right wing a couple miles from Chancellorsville.

At 1:30 P.M. Hooker sent word to Slocum, concurrently with his retirement order to Sykes, to call off the advance and return to his former position at Chancellorsville. Howard's Eleventh Corps, ordered to follow Slocum, had scarcely gotten started from camp when it was ordered by Hooker to stand fast. Meade's Fifth Corps was ordered back about 1 P.M., when it seemed apparent to Hooker that his plans had gone awry, but the order failed to reach Meade. A second order followed the first. The latter was delivered to Meade at 3 P.M., when his column had arrived at a point not far from Banks' Ford, almost within reach of his objective. Humphrey's division responded immediately by returning to Chancellorsville at a rapid pace, but Griffin's division did ·not receive the order until after 5:00 P.M. Evidently realizing by that time that they had been isolated, the units of the division practically double-timed back to the Federal lines, still without being molested by the enemy, who appeared to be devoting all of his attention to the area of the Turnpike and Plank Roads.

General Couch, commanding the Second Corps, had been directed to go to the aid of the advance units, with particular attention to support of the sorely pressed but hard-fighting Sykes. Couch detailed Hancock's division for the job, and as usual Hancock performed handsomely and efficiently. Shortly after Hancock's men were in position, however, Couch received an order from Hooker "to withdraw both divisions to Chancellorsville." Couch has written that on receipt of the order he conferred with Hancock, Sykes, Warren, and others who were present; all agreed that the ground should be held because of its commanding position and the open country in front. Warren even went so far as to suggest to Couch that he should ignore the order, and took it upon himself to ride back to try and persuade Hooker to withdraw it. In the meantime, Slocum's corps had been ordered back, thus exposing Hancock's right, and Couch had no alternative but to carry out the order.

After Sykes' men had passed to the rear through Hancock's newly formed line, the latter complied with the orders to retire, a regiment at a time. By 4:30 P.M. all had withdrawn but two regiments, when Couch received a countermanding order from Hooker to hold his position until 5 P.M. Although no reason was given, Hooker's intention may have been to protect the withdrawal of Griffin's division on the left, but now it was too late. Couch, disgusted with Hooker's vacillations, understandably exploded, advising the courier to take this message back to the commanding general: "Tell General Hooker he is too late. The enemy are on my right and rear. I am in full retreat." The depressing effect on the Federal generals can best be described in Couch's own words:

> *Proceeding to the Chancellor House, I narrated my operations in front to Hooker, which were seemingly satisfactory, as he said: "It is alright, Couch, I have gotten Lee just where I want him, he must fight me on my own ground." The retrograde movement had prepared me for something of the kind, but to hear from his own lips that the advantages gained by the successful marches of his lieutenants were to culminate in fighting a defensive battle in that nest of thickets, was too much, and I retired from his presence with the belief that my commanding general was a whipped man.*

LEE'S INSTRUCTIONS TO EARLY

Lee was still on Lee's Hill opposite Fredericksburg on the morning of May 1, after inspecting Early's defensive preparations and before riding west to join Jackson, now in command of all the troops at Tabernacle Church. Lee had told Jackson the evening before that he was to take charge of McLaws' and Anderson's Divisions as well as his own and "make arrangements to repulse the enemy."

Before leaving Marye's Heights, Lee ordered up more artillery in order to give Early powerful gun support. It was vital that the latter's small force of 10,000 men should prevent Sedgwick from crashing through the line while Lee was dealing with Hooker's greatly superior force to the west. There was real danger that Lee's new line, halfway between Fredericksburg and Chancellorsville, might have to face strong attacks from both directions if Early should fail to hold Sedgwick in place. Early was told explicitly that, if forced to retreat, he was to move south; if however the enemy on his front turned out to be merely a diversionary holding force, then Early should send all the men he could spare to join Lee.

Having satisfied himself that everything was shipshape in Early's hands at Fredericksburg, Lee rode down the Plank Road early on the afternoon of May 1 to join Jackson and plan his next move.

LEE IS PUZZLED

The relative ease with which the Confederates were able to turn back the Federal divisions east of Chancellorsville caused Lee some concern. Could Hooker be baiting a trap that might snap shut if the Confederates should become too venturesome? Was it still possible that Hooker's major objective was Gordonsville after all, in spite of Stuart's positive identifications and the obvious objective, Chancellorsville, toward which his right wing had been headed the preceding day? Could it be that the meeting engagement of May 1 had been engineered by a portion of the right wing while the main body was being diverted on Gordonsville? It seemed improbable that Hooker would have come the long route by Kelly's Ford to Chancellorsville only to back away from Lee and head in the opposite direction, but it was possible.

The truth was that Lee did not know just what troops had crossed at United States Mine Ford, nor the extent to which Hooker had been reinforced. That he was now somewhat puzzled is evidenced by this message to General Stuart at 4 P.M.:

> *The captured prisoners agree in stating that this is Meade's corps with which we are now engaged, and that Howard's corps preceded them across the Rapidan, and has taken some other road. This is the only column that we can find in this direction. What has become of the other two?*
>
> *Meade appears to be falling back.*

It would appear from the above that Slocum's divisions had not become sufficiently engaged on the Plank Road to lose any prisoners, that Howard's corps had not even been spotted in rear of Slocum, and that Hancock's division of Couch's corps had succeeded in extricating Sykes without losing a man to the advancing Confederates. Furthermore, the fact that two of Meade's three divisions, which had almost reached Banks' Ford on the River Road before they were recalled, had entirely escaped Lee's notice, was of itself convincing proof that a golden opportunity was being missed by the Federals in that zone of the potential battlefield.

JACKSON'S NARROW ESCAPE

As was his custom in the heat of battle, Jackson prowled around the front lines like a bird dog, looking for openings and observing the action of all elements of his command, to the extent possible for a single man on a horse. Meeting engagements were always a challenge to the austere instructor-turned-general, who was a strong believer in the advantages to be gained by personal reconnaissance, which he had so often utilized to ferret out the weak spot in his opponent's armor and then exploit it to the satisfaction of his own troops and the glory of Confederate arms.

About 4 P.M. in the afternoon, when the Federal divisions had withdrawn along the Turnpike and the Plank Road and disappeared from view in the woods, Jackson rode off to the left with an aide to examine the ground south of the Plank Road and to see for himself how his troops on the left were faring. About two miles south of Chancellorsville he met Jeb Stuart with a cavalry regiment in the vicinity of Catharine (Wellford's) Furnace. One of his infantry brigades was in the act of deploying and moving north to gain contact with the Federals.

Jackson and Stuart rode ahead to a wooded crest to get a better view of the terrain to the west, but there was little to be seen because of the dense woods. About that time a nearby Confederate battery opened up and in reply received a shattering and well-aimed volley from close-in, concealed Federal batteries, indicating that the Confederates were not to have everything their own way. Canister and shell smothered the knoll upon which Jackson and Stuart were standing, as the terrified artillery horses a few yards off to the right screamed, reared, and fell in their traces. Jackson's aide was mortally hit, but the two generals miraculously escaped untouched. It was too hot a spot in which to linger. Jackson began to have second thoughts about his confident belief that Hooker would be found north of the Rappahannock come morning.

Meanwhile Lee had sent out reconnaissance detachments to ascertain, if possible, what the enemy might be up to at United States Mine Ford and whether the indications were that he intended to make a strong stand on the Chancellorsville line. Jackson's eyes were looking west, where Fitz Lee's cavalry was probing to map out the contours of the Federal line and to uncover any weak spots which might exist.

After Jackson and Stuart had terminated their little adventure to the south, Jackson and his staff joined A. P. Hill to take a look at the situation north of the Turnpike. What he saw there assured him that the Federal retrograde movement had come to an end, but he was still unconvinced that Hooker might not pull out under cover of darkness. Just before dark he galloped back to the Plank Road, followed it to its junction with the Furnace Road and there, at Decker's, met General Lee, who was anxious to talk and consider plans for the morrow.

By nightfall Jackson's troops, advancing steadily with little opposition from the Federals, occupied a line from the Mine Road on the right to Catharine Furnace, almost two miles southwest of Chancellorsville. McLaws' Division occupied the crest which topped the higher ground paralleling Mott Run; Anderson prolonged the line to the left across the Turnpike east of Great Meadow Swamp; while Jackson's Corps, disposed in depth along the Plank Road, bivouacked in the order, Rodes, A. P. Hill, and Colston, from front to rear.

The Meeting in the Woods

The sun had now set and the twilight shadows merged into the darkness of night, a blackness intensified by the density of the woods. The skirmishing was over for the day as Lee and Jackson moved off the crossroad, a particular target of a Federal sharpshooter who had apparently zeroed in during daylight, and was busily sniping from a convenient tree-perch from which the Confederates had had no success in dislodging him.

Moving into the pine thicket a few yards off the road, the two famous generals turned up discarded Federal hardtack boxes and went into a historic huddle from which great events were soon to stem. The flickering light from a campfire threw shadows in the dark woods to provide an eerie setting that drew the curious eyes of the handful of soldiers who can always be found on the outskirts of a conference. When such a meeting occurs in the vicinity of a crossroad close to the front and with such prominent central figures as Robert E. Lee and Stonewall Jackson playing the leading roles, it offers a special attraction.

Jackson reported to Lee that all the information he had been able to gather, coupled with his own observations, indicated that Hooker's left was firmly anchored on the Rappahannock, east of United States Mine Ford, and that the entrenchments along the center of his position were being energetically strengthened by earth parapets and abatis. He knew little about Hooker's right, however, and was waiting for the intelligence that Fitz Lee had been amassing during the afternoon. Jackson ventured to assert that all of Hooker's preparations were merely a cover-up to a planned further withdrawal during the night, but Lee had a different opinion. He just couldn't picture Hooker giving up quite so easily as all that.

As the moon slowly rose, within a few miles of where they sat some 70,000 Union soldiers and 50,000 boys in gray worked and loafed and fed themselves, while the conversation between Lee and Jackson canvassed the possibility of turning the Federal right flank, since the prospects for such a maneuver on the Federal left, so near the Rappahannock, appeared dim.

As they talked, Jeb Stuart rode up, dismounted, and was invited by Lee to join the conference and state what he had learned. Stuart, who had just come from Fitz Lee, with the collected reports of his cavalry scouts, was bursting with news. It seemed that his resourceful brigadier had been carefully feeling out the right of the Federal line, and discovered that it was definitely "in the air," did not extend to the Rapidan, or even rest on any substantial intermediate strong point. From the cavalry observations it was clearly apparent that the Federals expected danger chiefly from the south, for their right was but slightly refused north of the Turnpike and no Federal cavalry had been encountered in strength. The picture was almost too good to be true!

Lee and Jackson exchanged glances. It was good news that Stuart brought, and the case for a flank maneuver became a determination in the minds of the two leaders. After that the words tumbled fast. There had to be a road that would lead beyond the Federal right, it couldn't be too long, and it must be under cover. Secrecy was essential for the launching of a surprise attack. Without further ado, Stuart started out to learn if such a road existed.

Before midnight Lee's engineer officers returned from a moonlight reconnaissance to report that the Federal line was so strongly held under cover of the woods, and so generously supported by masses of artillery, that a frontal attack was in their opinion inadvisable, with little chance of success. The evidence for a flank attack was building up. All that remained to convert Lee's strategy into orders was assurance that the mythical road that would meet the requirements for the flank march had been found. Jackson was still with Lee and now Lee made up his mind. Confident that Stuart would find a road, Lee turned to Jackson and informed him that the task was his. The tactical details would be left to Jackson, who was instructed to return before daylight to receive final instructions before putting his troops on the road. The response was brief and to the point: "My troops will move at 4 o'clock," said Jackson, as he saluted and went off by himself to snatch a few hours of sleep before calling his division commanders together to give them the word.

The night was chilly and the ground cold and hard. Unbuckling his sword Jackson leaned it against a tree and lay down with only his coat to cover him. Staff officers had occasion to remember later that Jackson that day had a heavy cold in the chest and that he shivered when he arose stiffly to seek warmth from the dying embers of the fire kindled for him. They also recalled what in retrospect seemed to be a portent of personal disaster when, without being touched by human hand, his sword slipped sideways and fell to the ground with a loud clang!

FEDERAL DISPOSITIONS, NIGHT OF MAY 1–2

At 4:20 P.M. on the afternoon of May 1, when practically all of his troops except Griffin's division had returned to their former positions, Hooker published an order that reads almost like an apology to his disgruntled army for having jerked it back on its haunches: "The Major General commanding trusts that a suspension in the attack today will embolden the enemy to attack him."

"Fighting Joe" indeed! The order can hardly be described as a clarion call to battle, calculated to stir the blood of the fighting men who composed the Army of the Potomac. It was a far cry from the flamboyant language with which Hooker had regaled the army only the day before. Hooker was in truth a beaten man, as Couch said, and all his generals knew it and couldn't do a thing about it.

The position Hooker had selected for his troops to fortify and defend must be examined for a proper understanding of the events of May 2–3. Evidently the crossroad at Chancellorsville loomed large in Hooker's planning, for he disposed his four corps, in front of and extended in two directions from the edge of the U-shaped clearing which enclosed the Chancellor House, Fairview, and Hazel Grove, all three on terrain of a higher elevation than the rest of the nearby landscape.

From the prominent enemy-pointed salient thus formed at the center, the defense line ran northeast to parallel Mineral Springs Run from in front of the clearing at Bullock's (crossing of the Ely's Ford and Bullock Roads) to a point on the Rappahannock several miles southeast of United States Mine Ford. This sector was in the main assigned to Meade's Fifth Corps, with one brigade of the Second Corps at the extreme left of the line. The main portion of the Second Corps occupied the line from Meade's right at Bullock's to the Orange Turnpike.

Slocum's Twelfth Corps rested both flanks on the Turnpike, in a curving bow which formed the southern face of the Chancellorsville salient to encompass Fairview and a part of the open neck of ground connecting Fairview and Hazel Grove. The perceptive student, looking at the map, may wonder, since Hooker had no objection to forming a salient jutting out from Chancellorsville, why he didn't establish a more effective one by including Hazel Grove in Slocum's defensive perimeter as well as Fairview. This would have given him possession of all the high ground in the area, with Scott's Run offering an obstacle to the enemy, and at the same time closed off the corridor of observation from Hazel Grove directly onto the very front porch of the Chancellor House. A short distance north of Hazel Grove, Birney's division of the Third Corps connected Slocum's Twelfth Corps on the left with Howard's Eleventh on the right. The other two divisions of Sickles' corps bivouacked as army reserve in the woods north of the Chancellor House.

The ill-fated Eleventh Corps, slated to be the villain of the Federal piece in the early evening of May 2, was drawn up along the southern edge of the Turnpike from Dowdall's Tavern, which Howard occupied as his headquarters, to a point more than a mile west of the Tavern. There the line bent north across the Turnpike for a pathetically short distance, while two and a half miles of Wilderness, and a nice ridge at that, offered a tempting hole as big as a herd of elephants between the Turnpike and the Rapidan. All the Confederates had to do was to reconnoiter and then act, nor were they slow in doing both.

A line of Federal pickets was strung along the entire front, a mile or so out, to give timely warning of any hostile movement. This was of course a normal formation and served a purpose, but the line of observers would be of little use against a fast-moving, determined aggressor who could brush the screen to one side or overrun it almost before the word could be gotten back to the main position in the rear.

The Battle of Fredericksburg had introduced a new feature which, strangely enough, had never seemed to occur to either army during the earlier battles of 1862. That was the very sensible procedure of using earth and other protective materials to make it more difficult for the enemy to trample the defenders in an attack. Lee started it and both sides quickly learned its advantages; the individual soldier being quite ready to do a little digging when he found out how helpful a parapet or a depression in the ground could be in warding off bullets and shells. The Federals worked like beavers the night of May 1 to make their position as strong as possible; that is, most of them did so in the center and on the left, but on the right of Howard's corps there was apparently no real effort made to fortify the position. The oversight, or neglect, or whatever it was, couldn't have occurred at a worse spot, and the denouement would take a long time for the ill-starred Eleventh Corps to live down.

Hooker's last official act on the night of May 1–2 was to send orders to Butterfield at Falmouth, directing him to send Reynolds' First Corps at once to join him at Chancellorsville. The message was marked 1:55 A.M., but it didn't reach the Chief of Staff until 5 A.M. One division of the First Corps had already crossed the river below Fredericksburg and was operating under Sedgwick's command, where it was holding a small bridgehead. It was then necessary for Reynolds to assemble his divisions northeast of the river, and march by concealed routes (in ravines) to United States Mine Ford, where they would cross the Rappahannock again and continue the march to Chancellorsville.

CHAPTER 24

Chancellorsville I: Jackson's Flank Attack

THE BOLD Confederate plan to turn the Federal right flank has been variously attributed to both Lee and Jackson, but more likely it was a joint conception, arrived at independently. While the decision of course rested with the commanding general and his was the major risk, it was a triple play from Fitzhugh Lee (via Stuart) to Robert E. Lee to Stonewall Jackson that set the stage. For it was the cavalry brigadier whose thorough reconnoitering first discovered Hooker's exposed right flank; while Jackson's staff officers, Tucker Lacy and Jed Hotchkiss, made a vital contribution when they ran down the local resident who provided the intelligence as to the available road, without which the "concealed" march would have been impossible.

Nevertheless it was the army commander whose strategic sense and moral courage were the vital forces which sparked one of the great flank marches of military history. The specific blueprint and the execution were entrusted to Stonewall Jackson.

Faced with an opponent of vastly superior strength, Lee already had twice divided his force. Now he would subdivide the reduced segment for the third time. Not only that, he was about to march a number of divisions across the front of a strongly posted enemy, an undertaking considered by the professional tacticians to be the rankest kind of military heresy.

That however was the sort of thing that made Lee the great Captain that he was. Supreme master of the calculated risk, Lee had acquired the habit of daring greatly, with absolute confidence in his generals and troops. So far they had never failed him. True, his army had come close to disaster on more than one occasion, but each time his opponent had failed to exploit his opportunity, the Battle of Antietam having been the most recent example. It cannot be doubted that in every one of the battles in which Lee took chances that would in all probability have boomeranged on a lesser chieftain, he had been careful to measure the deficiencies of the opposing Federal commander and accurately evaluate his probable reactions. Up to now the successive commanding generals of the Army of the Potomac had consistently accommodated him, and we may be sure the implications of Joe Hooker's surprising reversal were not lost on Lee.

The Reverend Beverly Tucker Lacy, Stonewall Jackson's favorite chaplain, had preached in and was familiar with the Fredericksburg-Chancellorsville area, where the name Lacy was an honored one. The chaplain's brother, Major Horace Lacy, was married to Betty Churchill-Jones, who inherited historic Chatham, situated on Stafford Heights directly across the river from Fredericksburg and within shouting distance of Ferry Farm, where George Washington spent a dozen years of his boyhood. Chatham was known as the Lacy House when General Sumner used it as his headquarters during the Battle of Fredericksburg, but it was Ellwood Manor, owned by Betty Lacy's father, and situated a few hundred yards south of Wilderness Tavern, that would figure in a dramatic aftermath of the Battle of Chancellorsville.

Tucker Lacy of all people would know about the roads south of the Turnpike. Earlier that night he had given General Lee such information as he possessed, but the responsibility for marching the troops to the jump-off position for the flank attack now rested with Stonewall Jackson. Lee and Jackson understood each other perfectly—Jackson must himself solve the problem.

As Jackson was warming his hands at the pre-dawn fire and sipping the coffee that a thoughtful staff officer had wangled for him, Chaplain Lacy rose from among the recumbent forms of the staff and joined the general, who made room for him on the log upon which he was seated. Unmindful of the fact that he was conversing with his chaplain, Jackson talked about the military problem confronting the army. Almost casually he inquired if Lacy might know of a road by which the Confederates could get around Hooker's flank. Having already informed Lee, the chaplain told Jackson that such a road did in fact exist, and he traced it on the map that Jackson handed him. "Too close to the Federal line," was Jackson's comment, "wasn't there another road farther removed, by which they could march unobserved?"

Lacy didn't know, but remarked that the owner of Catharine Furnace, Colonel Wellford, would surely have the answer. Besides, he had a young son who could serve as a guide. Jackson lost no time in rousing Jed Hotchkiss, his dependable engineer officer and resourceful mapmaker. The two staff officers rode off posthaste on their mission.

By the time they returned, General Lee had joined Jackson. The generals eagerly received from Hotchkiss the news that a road had been found that met the specifications, that it was suitable for artillery, and was under cover all the way. Producing the rough sketch that he had made, Hotchkiss explained that the Furnace Road ran south from where they stood, past Catharine Furnace, to join the larger Brock Road, which ran slightly east of south for three-quarters of a mile after crossing the unfinished railroad. The marching column would turn into the Brock Road there, and follow it for about a half mile to a point where a dirt road wound around to reconnect with the Brock Road below its junction with the Orange Plank Road. By following this route, a distance of something less than twelve miles, the column could debouch in rear of the Federal right flank.

The missing piece of the puzzle had now been found. But it was approaching the hour of dawn. No more time could be lost—Jackson was already way behind the schedule that he had set when he told Lee he would march at 4 A.M.

> "What do you propose to do?" was Lee's question.
> "Go around here," replied Jackson, pointing
> to Hotchkiss's tracing.
> "What do you propose to make the movement with?"
> was the next, and more important question.
> "With my whole corps," said Jackson, not batting an eye.
> "And what will you leave me?" inquired Lee, drily.
> "The divisions of McLaws and Anderson," was the reply.

The dramatic exchange defies adequate description. Here was a subordinate commander telling his commanding general that he proposed to risk the possibility that Hooker's powerful army of over 70,000 men and 182 guns would move a short distance to the front and annihilate the 12,900 men and 24 guns left with Lee, while Jackson with 31,700 men and 112 guns was winding his way a distance of twelve miles through the Wilderness to get on the Federal right and rear.

Lee must have been momentarily stunned at the bold conception, which went farther than even he had envisioned. But Lee possessed the capacity to think on a large-dimensional scale. Jackson's plan, if it should succeed, could achieve major results far beyond a diversionary effort that might merely serve to throw Hooker off balance temporarily. Jackson's plan could lead to a disaster for Federal arms. Lee was quick to recover and react. "Well, go on," was all Lee said, calmly. But it was enough. Jackson moved rapidly to issue his orders and put the troops on the road: Fitzhugh Lee's cavalry in front and on the right to screen the column, to be followed by the divisions of Rodes, Colston, and A. P. Hill in that order.

The ammunition wagons and artillery would follow immediately in rear of each division, but the supply and ambulance trains must take a longer and more roundabout route to Todd's Tavern and west, so the troops would be between the enemy and the trains, while the latter would not delay the march of the combat elements.

Considerable time was taken in organizing the march and making certain that every man knew just what was expected of him. There was to be no noise, no straggling. Just to make sure of the latter, officers were instructed to use the bayonet on any laggards. The grim Jackson thought of everything—this was to be the march to end all marches—nothing would be left to chance. Stonewall Jackson was in his element, and his men rejoiced with him at the prospect.

It was shortly after 7:30 A.M., three and a half hours later than Jackson had planned, when the head of the column passed Decker's, near the junction of the Plank Road and the road running southwest to Catharine Furnace. The roads were still damp from a previous rain, which meant there would be no dust clouds to disclose the movement. Lee stood at the crossroads to observe the start. As Jackson came by, mounted on "Little Sorrel," the two generals conferred briefly. Jackson rose in his stirrups, eyes gleaming, and pointed down the road. Salutes were exchanged and Jackson trotted forward. It was the last time Lee would see him alive.

The troops plodded steadily and cheerfully ahead. Soon they were spotted by the enemy as they crossed the high ground east of Scott's Run.

Below Catharine Furnace the tree-covered road climbed a low hill and was also exposed above the tree tops to the view of the Federals a mile to the north. Federal artillery threw in a few bursts, whereupon officers were stationed on the near side of the open stretch of road, and the troops were directed to double-time across the opening. A trail entered the road from the north at that point, and by Jackson's orders an infantry regiment was moved onto the trail and halted to provide security for the column against a sudden lunge by the Federals.

LEE CONCEALS HIS WEAKNESS

There would be no halfway measures on the part of the small force of two divisions and supporting artillery which remained under Lee's control, in their efforts to divert Hooker's attention from Jackson's flank maneuver. No doubt remained in Lee's mind that Hooker wanted him to launch an attack. His tactics were therefore to encourage Hooker in that belief, and the best way would be to keep things stirred up all along the front. It would be fatal to Confederate hopes if Hooker were to discover what a weak force remained to oppose him; Lee would therefore keep him off balance and in a state of suspense until Jackson should achieve his expected success against the Federal right.

In accordance with that plan, several batteries opened on the Federals as Jackson's column took up the march, and the skirmishers of McLaws and Anderson introduced a hot musket fire from their positions on the Plank Road. All morning long, at intervals, the firing was aggressively kept up, with apparently satisfactory effect, since the Federals showed no disposition to assume an offensive posture.

At 8 A.M. Birney's division at Hazel Grove, some two miles southwest of Chancellorsville, had spotted Jackson's column crossing the exposed ridge, about a mile to the south. It was a long column and many wagons were observed sandwiched between the foot soldiers. The Federals were puzzled, however, by the fact that the Confederates were headed away from the front, for the road Jackson's troops were traversing ran south at that point and it looked to the Federals as though they were withdrawing. That was the way Hooker interpreted the reports, at any rate, no doubt highly pleased at this apparent confirmation of his prophecy that

Lee must withdraw his army. It looked very much to Hooker as though Sedgwick's threat to Lee's direct communications with Richmond, by the railroad and Richmond Stage Road leading south from Fredericksburg, had forced Lee to retreat on Gordonsville.

THE AGGRESSIVE DAN SICKLES

Dan Sickles was a colorful character whose civilian and military traits revealed few if any inhibitions. He alone of Hooker's corps commanders was not a professional officer or a graduate of West Point, his prewar career having included active participation in politics, business, and a long series of amorous involvements, some at least of which were rather notorious. The most publicized of his extracurricular activities was probably his shooting to death of Philip Barton Key, not far from the Capitol in Washington, for having an affair with Sickles' wife. It was an interesting sidelight of that incident that Sickles' attorney was Edwin M. Stanton, who was soon to become Lincoln's Secretary of War.

Sickles, a proponent of offensive action, was not averse to expressing his own individual views whether or not they happened to conform to the overall tactics of his superior. He was on intimate terms with Hooker and did not hesitate to press his viewpoint on the army commander. When Generals Meade, Slocum, and Couch experienced the frustrating checkrein which Hooker applied to the right wing on the afternoon of May 1, Sickles' Third Corps was still en route from Fredericksburg to Chancellorsville, so his outlook on the strategic situation was presumably less restrained. The strength of his corps was almost 19,000 men, second in size to the largest corps in the army, Sedgwick's Sixth, and he was all for getting his divisions into action. Upon arrival at Chancellorsville his corps was posted as army reserve. This prospect did not appeal to Sickles' combative nature. In scouting around he discovered what looked to him like a weak link in the chain of defense between the Eleventh and Twelfth Corps, so with Hooker's approval he moved Birney's division into the line to strengthen the gap.

Again it was Sickles who took the initiative early on May 2 when he moved Birney forward to occupy the important clearing on the high ground at Hazel Grove, from which observation point the lateral movement of Jackson's Corps was first discovered by several of Birney's observers posted in tall trees. While it was a fact that the advance of Birney's division left a gap of one mile on Howard's left, the defect was not particularly serious in view of Hooker's great strength.

No matter what opinion may be held as to Sickles' military competence as a corps commander, he was an aggressive general who held to the view that the army was there to fight and not to sit on its haunches waiting for the enemy to make all the moves. During the morning, Birney reported on the Confederate column that was crossing his front in a never-ending procession of men, vehicles, and guns, all in full view. Sickles repeatedly importuned Hooker to allow him to move against the enemy with a view to cutting his column. But it was not until noon, four hours after the Confederates were first observed, that permission was finally and grudgingly granted. Sickles was told to "advance cautiously" to "harass the enemy," an insipid form of order that was scarcely couched in language to inspire the troops to heroic effort.

The persistent way in which Hooker was throwing away opportunity after opportunity for decisive action against the Confederates passes all understanding. After he had successfully placed his right wing on Lee's left rear, the fight appears to have gone entirely out of him. From that time on Lee took the initiative and pressed it, while everything that Hooker did or failed to do merely compounded his unaccountable failure to pursue his advantage on the afternoon of April 30.

Hooker's reasoning in allowing Jackson to move west, unopposed, for the entire morning of May 2 is obscure. An inviting and vulnerable target passed across the southern front, only a mile away, for four solid hours without interference. If indeed Lee was withdrawing on Gordonsville, as Hooker professed to believe, the logical reaction would seem to have been to attack and turn the retreat into a rout; to cut the column at several points; to send the cavalry at a rapid clip to block the march at the head of the column or at the very least to raise havoc along the flanks; and at the same time to send one or two corps in a driving attack against whatever Confederate force remained on Hooker's front, since it was obvious the latter couldn't be very powerful.

Jackson's Corps of 30,000 troops, confined to a narrow, tree-covered path through the Wilderness, and strung out over ten miles of road, was as vulnerable a target for an aggressive opponent as could be imagined. Weighted down by his division trains, unable to effectively deploy his troops if attacked, incapable of utilizing his artillery, Jackson was courting disaster every step of the way from early morning until late in the day when he came to the end of the trail and his greatest opportunity.

It was the good fortune of Lee and Jackson that the heavy risk they were taking did not end in the destruction of the Army of Northern Virginia. Nor does it detract one bit from the reputation of either to remark that it was Joe Hooker, alone and unaided, whose mental inflexibility and lack of moral courage created the climate which made possible, indeed almost inevitable, the successive actions that culminated in the wholly unnecessary and therefore disgraceful defeat and withdrawal of the Army of the Potomac north of the Rappahannock.

The more one thinks about it, the more amazing does Hooker's apathy appear. Spirited action, positive orders, prompt movements against the enemy-all breathing the spirit of the offensive, were clearly the need of the moment. But the spark was lacking. A smog of inaction, uncertainty, and timidity at the top imprisoned the Federal giant as the Confederate David marched confidently forward with his slingshot at the ready.

SICKLES NIPS AT JACKSON'S HEELS

Preceded by several battalions of Berdan's famed sharpshooters, Birney's advance brigade crossed Scott's Run (Lewis Creek), under orders from Sickles to pierce the Confederate column and seize the road upon which it was marching. Jackson's corps artillery was passing at the time, the main body of the infantry having already cleared. A lively scrap ensued with Colonel Best's 23rd Georgia Regiment, which was covering Jackson's right in the vicinity of Catharine Furnace. Soon Posey's Brigade of Anderson's Confederate Division joined in the fray from the east.

Several captured Confederate prisoners stated that they had been marching to get on the Federal right and that things would start popping over there right soon. Sickles was skeptical, believed they were lying to mislead the Federals, a ruse the Confederates had learned to adopt with some success on other occasions. He felt sure Lee was retreating.

Hooker shared Sickles' opinion, but didn't feel the same urgency to go after Lee, at least not until he had thought it over some more. His compromise decision, after some time had elapsed, was to direct Howard to send his reserve brigade, of all outfits, to support Sickles' advance elements, while Pleasanton was told to take his cavalry down that way. No specific mission was mentioned other than to cooperate with Sickles, so Pleasanton conceived his own objective and decided that what he should do was to cut the Confederate column, establish communication with Sedgwick (a rather ambitious conception), and pursue the retreating enemy (which did make sense). But it would have made better sense if Hooker had placed his cavalry on the army right flank at the outset.

Jackson, informed that the rear of his column was under attack and his trains endangered, directed the two rearmost brigades of Archer and Thomas to countermarch and dispose of the threat till the trains had cleared. While the contestants bickered in the thickets, the major portion of Jackson's column kept going. After a bit Archer and Thomas broke off the engagement and quietly went their way, leaving several score of prisoners, including most of the 23rd Georgia, in Birney's hands as a consolation prize. There was no pursuit by the Federals, either with infantry or cavalry.

The events of the afternoon were sufficient to drive Hooker to at least one major decision. At 4:10 P.M. an order was dispatched to Sedgwick as follows:

> *The major general commanding directs that General Sedgwick cross the river as soon as indications will permit; capture Fredericksburg with everything in it, and vigorously pursue the enemy. We know that the enemy is fleeing, trying to save his trains. Two of Sickles' divisions are among them.*

This message to Sedgwick was slightly less negative than earlier "iffy" directions, but it was still discretionary, leaving it to the commander of the left wing to decide when "indications will permit." Professor Lowe's balloon and the signal stations had been sending a veritable stream of informative observations of enemy movements to Sedgwick and Butterfield. Those on May 2 particularly painted a picture of relative Confederate inactivity at Fredericksburg and the apparent departure of the bulk of the troops that earlier had crowded the hill positions west of the town. Furthermore, several of Hooker's messages during the morning stated positively that only Ewell's (Early's) Division had been left at Fredericksburg. Sedgwick had little excuse for not stirring himself more energetically.

Hooker's Achilles' heel was his right flank, as Jackson would soon demonstrate. But it needn't have been. For in disposing his right wing on the defensive line on the afternoon of May 1, after pulling his divisions back to Chancellorsville, Hooker had sent this order to Slocum and Howard at 4:45 P.M.: "Let the right of your line fall back and rest at the sawmill ruin on Hunting Run, or in that direction, and have everything passed to the rear of it." Hooker evidently forgot that Slocum was no longer the wing commander, with the chain of command down to Howard; otherwise the message would be unintelligible. Applied to Howard's corps on the extreme right it did make sense, although Howard claimed that the order never reached him. Both Howard and Slocum are reported to have protested against the instructions to refuse the right, on the premise that the Wilderness in that sector was impenetrable to troops except on the roads which they would have no trouble in holding. To fall back would in the opinion of the two corps commanders have the same demoralizing effect as a retreat.

The sawmill ruin was located about one and a quarter miles northeast of the extreme right of Howard's line along the Turnpike. A glance at the map will assure any Doubting Thomas that in planning a greater refusal of his line Hooker was right; Slocum and Howard decidedly shortsighted. Nevertheless Hooker allowed himself to be mollified, which probably was not too difficult in the light of his fixation that Lee must attack or withdraw. Hooker thus appears to have given at least passing thought to the possibility of a flank attack. His fatal mistake was in failing to insist on a strong extension of the right to insure strength on that flank, for he had ample troops to extend the line if he had decided to use them for that purpose rather than build up his powerful reserve north of Chancellorsville.

Had Reynolds' First Corps been transferred from Fredericksburg on May 1 instead of the following day, and placed on Howard's right to fill the gap to the Rapidan, Jackson's reception would have been quite a different one. There would still have been time if Hooker's order of 1:55 A.M. had reached Reynolds promptly, but its arrival was delayed until after daylight and the First Corps had a day's march ahead of it. As it turned out, Reynolds himself arrived at 6 P.M., but it was several hours later that his divisions got across the United States Mine Ford and forced their way along the crowded road to reach Chancellorsville. By then it was too late—the debacle had occurred. Furthermore, evidence is lacking that Hooker would have posted Reynolds on Howard's right even if he had arrived during the afternoon.

Having yielded to Slocum and Howard, and in spite of their conviction that the Confederates were physically incapable of penetrating the woods, Hooker was negligent in not checking carefully to make certain that adequate security measures had in fact been taken to prevent surprise, for it was generally conceded that the entrenchments and breastworks of Howard's corps were inferior to those thrown up by the Twelfth, Fifth, and Second Corps.

So far as can be determined, and in marked contrast to Lee's practice, Hooker made only one extended personal appearance among the troops of his army during the entire Chancellorsville campaign. That was a post-breakfast inspection ride which he took on May 2, accompanied by a number of staff officers, around the lines of the Chancellorsville position. What he saw seemed generally to satisfy him, for he was heard to remark at one point, "How strong, how strong"—evidently referring to the character of the protective fortifications of earth and felled trees that his troops had zealously built overnight in accordance with his orders.

That Hooker had misgivings about the security of his right flank, however, was evidenced by a written message dispatched at 9:30 A.M. to the commander of the Eleventh Corps, after he returned to his headquarters. The message called Howard's attention to the fact that his dispositions had been made to meet a frontal attack by the enemy, and directed that he examine the ground to the flank in order to be prepared to meet an attack from whatever direction it might come. The suggestion was added that Howard have "heavy reserves" well in hand to meet such a contingency. Like all Hooker's communications to his lieutenants, this one lacked directness and decision. If Hooker as army commander felt that his right was insecure, he should have said so in no uncertain terms, indicated the corrective measures desired, and sent a staff officer to see to it that they were carried out to the letter, if he had any doubt as to the efficiency of the corps commander concerned.

O. O. HOWARD AND THE XI CORPS

The still inadequately explained mystery of the Chancellorsville campaign was the yawning three-mile-wide Wilderness gap which Hooker allowed to exist on the right of his army between the Orange Turnpike and the Rapidan River to the north.

Hooker's strategic error May 1 in bringing to a grinding halt the gathering momentum of his offensive drive toward the rear of Lee's army at Fredericksburg did not prevent him from making a careful and comprehensive plan for defensive operations in the large, fortified semicircle around Chancellorsville. There in the dense wilderness it was his belief that the conditions of the Battle of Fredericksburg in December 1862 would be reversed and that the Confederate army would destroy itself in an attack against the impregnable line that his troops would construct during the night of May 1.

Hooker's conception must have contemplated solid anchors on either flank—the left on the Rappahannock below United States Mine Ford, the right on the Rapidan above the ford. His action in stripping Sedgwick's left wing of all troops except his own Sixth Corps and Gibbon's division indicated an apparent desire to be prepared at Chancellorsville with overwhelming defensive strength for the best Lee might offer. Nevertheless, since Hooker's intention was clearly to have Sedgwick do all the offensive fighting for the army, and in the next few days two full corps at Chancellorsville were not even engaged, it is difficult to understand just what precise plan had really formed in Hooker's mind.

In retrospect, it is surprising that Hooker placed the Eleventh Corps on the important right flank at Chancellorsville, considering its reputation and the fact that the corps and its commander had only just gotten acquainted. But it is definitely to Hooker's discredit that, having placed it there, he failed to make certain that proper troop dispositions were made to secure so vulnerable a position.

A portent of things to come might have been noted in late April during the march of the right wing from Falmouth to Kelly's Ford. Hooker's orders to his corps were to travel as light as possible, keeping the number of ration wagons to the bare minimum for eight days' subsistence. But it developed that, while the other corps commanders conformed to the letter of the order, Howard's corps exceeded the authorized maximum by a large margin, to unduly clog the roads. and impair the mobility of the entire wing.

Viewed objectively, it appears that both Hooker and Howard must be charged with gross negligence insofar as the security of the right flank of the army was concerned. It is no excuse to say that both generals were convinced that Jackson's observed flank march was to be interpreted as a withdrawal in the direction of Gordonsville. Insurance against surprise, whether expected or discounted, is one of the duties of a field commander. Neither Hooker nor Howard took out even a small policy against such a contingency. Nor can it be said that Howard was not fully warned of the forthcoming threat, hours before Jackson struck.

Howard felt so certain in his own mind that the Confederates could not crash the Wilderness, in the face of the heavy tangle of trees and interlacing underbrush, that he completely neglected to take the most fundamental precautions, apparently believing that an attack could come only from the south, the direction in which he faced the greater portion of his troops along the Turnpike. Only two small regiments, not over 900 men in all, were placed at right angles to the Pike, on the extreme flank, and even those on the Turnpike were unprepared when the attack occurred, for they were preparing for supper with their arms stacked at the edge of the road, no effort apparently having been made to keep even a fraction of each company or regiment under arms in a position of readiness for immediate action. Barlow's brigade, initially in corps reserve near Wilderness Church, was the only organized body that was not strung out in extended order. It was that brigade that Howard personally took forward to Hazel Grove, beyond reach of the right flank, when Hooker directed him to send a brigade to the support of the Third Corps in the course of Sickles' afternoon fight with the Confederate rear guard.

From the time of his arrival at Chancellorsville, Howard had established his headquarters at Dowdall's Tavern, which at the time of the battle was being occupied as a residence by Melzi Chancellor. It was located east of the junction of the Turnpike and the Plank Roads, about a mile from the extreme right of the Eleventh Corps. His main line extended generally along the southern edge of the Turnpike until near the Tavern, where it was several hundred yards south of the Turnpike; from there on it ran in a direction slightly south of east, crossing the Plank Road and hugging the north bank of the small creek that paralleled Scott's Run, some 500 yards further south.

The three divisions of Devens, Schurz, and von Steinwehr were posted from right to left in that order, each division disposed in two lines of varying depth and strength. Schurz' Third Division held the center in the vicinity of Hawkins' Farm, with one brigade on the Turnpike and the other placed to the north in such position that it could face either south or west, although its attention was plainly directed on the Turnpike.

During the latter part of the morning, after Hooker had warned Howard to look to his right, Howard sent this message to headquarters: "From Gen. Devens' headquarters [Taylor] we can observe a column of infantry moving westward on a road parallel with this on a ridge about one to two miles south of this. I am taking measures to resist an attack from the west." The last sentence of the message was pure eyewash, for not only did Howard take no measures worthy of the name to resist attack from the west; he repeatedly discounted the effort of at least a few of his subordinate officers to warn him of the impending danger.

Confederate cavalry during the early afternoon had been feeling out his line on the west, and his own pickets brought in two prisoners who stated they had lost their way from a column that was moving around the Federal right. Infantry patrols sent out from Howard's corps to the front discovered enemy skirmishers about a mile and a half from the Turnpike, and enemy infantry patrols had reconnoitered Howard's front shortly before noon. All signs pointed unerringly to the fact that the enemy was on the move and getting closer all the time.

At 2 o'clock Howard's division commander on the right, General Devens, was told by his outposts that the enemy was moving around his right. The officer of the day made a similar report, but was advised, curtly, not to start a panic. A short time later, in repeating the warning he was told in no uncertain terms not to be a coward—the enemy was retreating!

Devens was a Regular, newly assigned to the Eleventh Corps and regarded askance by the men of the division for the reason that their former commander, Brigadier General Nathaniel C. McLean, had been downgraded in order to make room for Devens to take command of the division. Whether Devens or McLean was the better man is beside the point. A slot apparently had to be created and McLean stood in the way. But the appointment was not a popular one and Devens must have been aware of the fact that he was not welcome.

McLean was given command of the Second Brigade of Devens' division. His regiments were posted at the extreme right of that portion of the Eleventh Corps line that was strung along the Turnpike, with Von Gilsa's brigade occupying the refused angle north of the Turnpike. And it was McLean's officers and men who repeatedly brought the warning reports that Devens chose to treat in so cavalier a fashion, almost as though he had made up his mind that nothing constructive could be expected from the personnel of the Eleventh Corps. Devens would have cause to regret his attitude in a very short time.

At 2:45 P.M. a major from the outpost on the right sent the division commander an urgent message which should have startled him: "A large body of the enemy is massing in my front. For God's sake make disposition to receive him." Devens was sufficiently impressed to forward that intelligence to General Howard, but the latter's mental bloc was so pronounced that he simply brushed the information off. A similar message at 3:00 P.M. received the same treatment.

Is it any wonder that historians have placed the blame for the de bade of the Eleventh Corps equally on Hooker and Howard? Even with their low opinion of the morale and discipline of the Germans, it cannot be said that their attitude was calculated to effect any improvement or to encourage a courageous fighting spirit either among the junior officers or in the ranks.

Confirmatory evidence of Hooker's complacency, and confidence that Lee was retreating, is found in a circular which he sent around to his corps commanders at 2:30 P.M. The order directed them to replenish their supplies and make ready for an early start the next morning, presumably in pursuit of the "retreating" enemy. And it was as late as 4:10 P.M. that Hooker informed Sedgwick by telegram that the enemy was "fleeing." Just how wrong can a general be?

At 4:30 P.M., with Sickles still engaged and the remainder of the army idly sitting it out, Slocum was ordered forward to support Sickles. All he did in compliance was to send forward Geary's division to link up with Sickles' left and close the gap that existed between the two corps as a result of Birney's forward move earlier in the day.

LEE MAINTAINS THE PRESSURE

Lee anxiously awaited the noise of Jackson's guns far to the left. As the afternoon dragged slowly on, he kept up the pressure of McLaws' and Anderson's Divisions against the center of Hooker's line at Chancellorsville. The pronounced salient in the Federal position, greatly enlarged by Sickles' advance from Hazel Grove, would under normal circumstances have been seized upon by the watchful Lee, had his strength permitted, to launch a powerful arrow against the base of the salient, with an excellent chance of severing the Federal troops at Hazel Grove and below from the main body. As will be seen later, just such an effort was made by an energetic Confederate unit shortly before midnight that night, and although it was unsupported and failed to panic Sickles, it did temporarily sever his communications. The important effect of the isolated attack, however, was that Hooker became thoroughly alarmed and, according to Couch, "at once made preparations to withdraw the whole front, leaving General Sickles to his fate."

The skirmishing along the lines was especially severe on the front occupied by Hancock's division of Couch's Second Corps, which held a position between Slocum's left and Meade's right, at the apex of the Federal bulge at Chancellorsville. At no time, however, did it assume the aspect of a decisive attack and consequently, after a number of local exchanges, the Federal troops appraised the Confederate exercises for what they were, mere distractions.

Developments at Fredericksburg

As the calm before the storm continued throughout the afternoon on the Chancellorsville front, a similar situation prevailed at Fredericksburg, where Sedgwick, as the direct result of Hooker's spasmodic, conditional messages, was in the unenviable position of wondering which end was really up.

It appeared initially that his main job had been to hold Lee at Fredericksburg by demonstrations and then to attack if conditions should justify. He had every reason to believe that Hooker planned a two-pronged attack to squeeze Lee to death if he remained. But the real expectation was that Sedgwick would shortly be called on to pursue the fleeing Confederates toward Richmond. Then Hooker sat down at his end of the line and began sapping Sedgwick's three-corps strength until only his own Sixth, plus half of Gibbon's division, remained. Finally, about an hour before Jackson's thunderbolt struck, Hooker wired his left wing commander to capture Fredericksburg and vigorously pursue the enemy, without letting him in on the secret as to which direction Hooker expected the enemy to take or what Hooker's huge troop concentration was going to do about the matter.

Hooker was becoming more and more incoherent as time went on. He became thoroughly enmeshed in the net of his own cerebrations, if such a term is justified in this case, which may be doubted. Although Sedgwick gained no laurels for brilliant planning and execution in this campaign, he was more sinned against than sinning, and it is not too surprising that the uncoordinated performance of his left wing was somewhat short of satisfactory.

From the tenor of Hooker's order, Sedgwick could fairly assume that a Federal victory had been achieved at Chancellorsville, or the message surely would not have spoken so positively of Lee's retreat. The mere fact that Sickles' corps was "among the enemy trains" spoke volumes. It would thus seem that Sedgwick's mission was the comparatively simple pursuit of a fleeing enemy, so he set about the task of fulfilling the mission early on the evening of May 2.

While Sedgwick was in the process of preparing to move, the situation at Chancellorsville had exploded. Another order came in from Hooker about 11 P.M. This one directed Sedgwick to "cross the Rappahannock at Fredericksburg immediately upon receipt of the order" and move in the direction of Chancellorsville until he connected with Hooker. He was told to attack and destroy any force on the road, and be in Hooker's vicinity at daylight.

Confusion still reigned in the area of army communications. Surely Hooker knew that Sedgwick was already across the Rappahannock. But the professional soldier is trained and conditioned to follow orders explicitly, and this order said to cross at Fredericksburg. Sedgwick's reaction was something akin to that of the newspaper man with whom it is second nature to "follow the copy out of the window (if necessary)." The order was a puzzler, sure enough. Should Sedgwick recross the river and follow the north bank of the river to Chancellorsville? That wouldn't make sense, because there were no Confederates there to attack. Well then, should he recross and re-recross a second time, in order to "follow copy" and avoid embarrassment to the major general commanding? Inconceivable as it may sound, that possibility was actually considered, but common sense came to the rescue. Sedgwick decided simply to move northward from the plain on which his entire corps was spread, seize Fredericksburg, and then take off for Chancellorsville by the shortest route.

While Lee's thoughts on the afternoon of May 2 were centered on Jackson's dramatic sweep through the Wilderness, upon which the fate of the Army of Northern Virginia depended, unremitting Confederate pressure was kept up against the Federal position before Chancellorsville. Whether the local action at that point was chiefly to divert Hooker's attention from what was transpiring in the depths of the forest to the west, or Lee anticipated a collateral gain from the effect of pushing Hancock's troops closer to the Chancellor House, in order to extract the maximum advantage from the expected rolling up of Hooker's right at Dowdall's

Tavern, the Confederates did exert unusual efforts against the center of Hooker's position.

Lee's generalship at this critical juncture is pleasant to contemplate. Not for a minute would he yield the initiative that he had seized May 1 from Hooker, who was now so far off balance that light, constant taps were apparently all Lee need administer to maintain the status quo until Jackson should burst from cover in his crashing attack. The god of war was smiling on Thomas Jonathan Jackson in his last great adventure on earth, for the march of his powerful column was not interrupted by the Federals, thanks mainly to Hooker's obsession, which seems to have filtered down through the ranks to the point of paralyzing inaction in the zone where the greatest danger threatened.

Yet, despite Jackson's strict orders against straggling, and the intense eagerness with which he personally repeated his demand that his men "press on, press on," the famous march was conducted at a relatively slow pace for divisions that had by their repeated successes in earlier forced marches become known as Jackson's "foot cavalry."

The conditions were favorable for a rapid gait, for there was no possibility of losing the way, and nothing to slow the column. Yet by 1 P.M. the cavalry advance guard had advanced only eight or nine miles after a lapse of six hours. True enough, the column had been subjected to sporadic shelling as it crossed the clearing at Wellford's Farm, but the effect should have been to accelerate the march rather than retard it. To some extent the great length of the column itself contributed to the slow pace, for there is always a certain amount of telescoping between units, except where perfect march discipline is maintained. And it is unlikely that Jackson's own sense of urgency was reflected in the toiling ranks of the enlisted men, especially on such a warm spring day.

As the leading element of the advance cavalry reached the crossroad ten miles south of the Turnpike, it turned right on the Orange Plank Road, which led directly to Dowdall's Tavern, Howard's corps, headquarters at the junction of the Plank Road and Turnpike, the very heart of the Federal position along the latter. This was the route Jed Hotchkiss had marked in the expectation that it would bring the Confederate column to a jumpoff position beyond Hooker's right flank.

The Confederate cavalry, with the Second Virginia in the lead, continued the march for half a mile to Hickman's, where the Germanna Plank Road from the northwest joins the Orange Plank Road. There the regiment halted and dismounted to give their horses a breather, while one squadron moved down the road a bit further as security for the rest of the outfit. Running into a small body of Federal cavalry on the road, the Virginians drove them back and then returned to Hickman's. But they had galloped far enough in their pursuit to look across the open fields of Talley's Farm to the Turnpike where Federal infantry in considerable strength was posted. The squadron commander returned posthaste to report that he had "gotten a view of the right. of the Federal line."

Half a mile east of Hickman's was Burton's Farm, set on high ground in a clearing to the north of the Plank Road and not over 1,000 yards from the center of Howard's position. The squadron commander's report was quickly relayed to Fitzhugh Lee, at the junction of Brock Road and the Plank Road. At the same moment Jackson himself rode up at the head of his infantry. With suppressed excitement Lee invited Jackson to ride with him to the clearing—he had something interesting to show him. After halting the infantry, the two officers rode on to Burton's to take a good look.

An Expensive Delay

Jackson had no need of his field glasses to disclose what must have been a disappointing sight-Federal infantry all along the Turnpike, as far as he could see, and well to the left (west) of the road upon which he had counted to bring him quickly on to the Federal flank and rear. It was now 2 o'clock and, unfortunately, a lot more marching had to be done before he could place his divisions for the attack. A few minutes of further silent observation was sufficient. Summoning a courier to his side, Jackson sent a message back to General Rodes, commander of the leading division of the Second Army Corps, instructing him to continue on the Brock Road across the Orange Plank Road and halt when he reached the Turnpike. There Jackson would join him and issue further orders.

The additional three or four mile approach march was to prove a serious if not fatal deterrent to the full exploitation of Jackson's forthcoming destruction of the Federal Eleventh Corps. For it would be well after

5 o'clock in the afternoon before the attack commenced, and night came early in the dark forest at this time of year, even though it was springtime.

Lee's cavalry, supported by a brigade of infantry, was placed in observation on the Plank Road, to mask the final phase of the march of the main column, and as insurance against possible aggression by the Federals. By 2:30 P.M. Rodes' leading division had reached the Turnpike a short distance from Wilderness Tavern and moved east for almost a mile toward Chancellorsville to Luckett's, still without running into enemy troops. Seemingly the Federals were entirely oblivious to the threatening storm about to break.

Jackson had sometime before, around 3 P.M., sent off his last message to General Lee, shortly after observing the Federal position from Burton's Farm:

> *The enemy has made a stand at Chancellor's which is about two miles from Chancellorsville. I hope as soon as practicable to attack. I trust that an everkind Providence will bless us with great success.*
>
>

Respectfully,
T. J. Jackson, Lieutenant General.

> *The leading division is up, and the next two appear to be well closed.*

It was high time the corps move off the road and develop an attack formation, if complete success was to be attained before darkness should force a halt. The deployment was effected smoothly and, despite a certain amount of noise, without the Federals becoming aware of the vast troop movement taking place within a mile of them. Preparations for the evening meal occupied the attention of Howard's unsuspecting soldiers, whose arms were stacked and who sat or lolled around in as unprepared a posture as though they were comfortably secure in their camps at Falmouth.

Moving silently off the Turnpike to right and left as they advanced, Jackson's brigades formed in extended order facing east, overlapping the Federal flanks to the north and south in such strength that their attack, when launched, should be irresistible. It was no easy task for some 25,000 men to form battle lines in the tangled forest, but Jackson was determined that the job be done right, despite the passing of the precious minutes,

The lines were carefully dressed as the deployment continued and finally, sometime after 5 o'clock, the preparations were complete.

The character of the landscape was as though made to order for the Confederate dispositions, and they took full advantage of it to assure complete surprise. Dowdall's Tavern was set on the eastern fringe of a large clearing, with Talley's Hill some hundreds of yards to the west, while Hawkin's Farm extended the cleared area to the north. There was open ground as well in the triangle formed by the Turnpike and the Plank Road as far as Burton's Farm, but beyond that the forbidding Wilderness again closed in, to conceal the preparatory maneuvers of the wily Jackson and his corps. It was under cover of the heavily forested area that the thunderbolt was fashioned, ready to be launched in the open terrain the minute Jackson should give the word.

For an overall length of almost two miles the gray lines, three of them, extended on either side of the Pike leading to Chancellorsville. First a line of skirmishers, four hundred yards in front of Rodes' division, which was formed in a single line with brigades abreast. Several hundred yards in rear of Rodes came Colston's Division, similarly deployed. Last of the three lines was composed of A. P. Hill's men, disposed partly in line and partly in column. Jackson's plan for the actual attack had been carefully explained to his three division commanders and additional time allowed for them to give detailed instructions to their brigades and regiments, so there would be no hitch.

There would be depth as well as breadth to the attack and the supporting divisions were told to drive resolutely ahead through the forest, capture the successive objectives which Jackson indicated, and allow nothing to halt the forward push. Flank protection was provided for, and the artillery was prepared to gallop to the front to crack any islands of resistance which the Federals might be able to form Zero hour had arrived. Jackson sat his horse, shoulders hunched, watch in hand, the dial showing 5:15 P.M.

"Are you ready, General Rodes?" he asked.
"Yes, sir."
"You can go forward, sir," said Jackson.

451

That was all. Suddenly a bugle sounded and eager trumpeters, all along the line, sounded the charge. The skirmishers moved out with a rush, as the long lines dashed forward like an uncoiled spring, thousands of excited throats making the dark forest ting with the nerve-shattering Rebel yell.

The surprised Federals heard the shouts and cheering at the same moment the startled denizens of the forest fled in all directions. "Like a cloud of dust driven before a coming shower," wrote General Howard, "the first lively effects of the steady Confederate advance appeared in the startled rabbits, squirrels, quail, and other game flying wildly hither and thither in evident terror, and escaping, where possible, into adjacent clearings."

Howard's two inadequate, small regiments facing west on the north side of the Turnpike had just time enough to seize their weapons and offer token resistance because of the suddenness of the attack, for the Confederate lines so far overlapped the Federal right and left, and the assault struck with such power and depth that the defense crumbled in a few moments, the men falling back in disorder.

At the very moment when the massive attack started, General Howard was returning to his headquarters at Dowdall's after visiting Sickles at Hazel Grove. His absence from the vital right flank at this critical moment was serious, but it is to be doubted that he could have taken any constructive steps to reduce the impact of the Confederate assault even if he had been on the spot. At such a time, the presence of the commander in person is imperative chiefly for its influence on morale, but there would have been no time for Howard to issue effective orders and even less time for them to be transmitted and executed. It was General Couch's opinion, expressed later, that "no corps in the army, surprised as the Eleventh was at this time, could have held its ground under similar circumstances."

There was no stopping the cheering, exultant men of Jackson's big divisions. Wild with enthusiasm, the irresistible Confederates rolled over brigade after brigade of the successive lines of Howard's corps, as the retrograde movement of the overwhelmed regiments quickly turned into a confused rout which gained momentum as the Confederate avalanche ground steadily forward toward Chancellorsville.

The sight that greeted Howard as he galloped up to Talley's Hill was one to cause the heart of the bravest general to turn over. Men in blue were fleeing for their lives in every direction, throwing away their rifles as they ran. Equipment was strewn everywhere, terrified artillery horses were rearing and plunging, men were falling rapidly, and fleeing cattle clogged the road. All efforts to rally and reform the fugitives were unavailing. The panic in that first wild melee was complete.

There were plenty of brave men and courageous officers in the Eleventh Corps, and under a different set of circumstances the corps might have made a worthier stand. But its low morale, as previously explained, and the lack of confidence which the higher commanders displayed in so many of its regiments, were enough to make the corps a sitting duck for the Confederate hunters almost without the assist gratuitously made by the generals of the corps as a result of their wholly inadequate security measures.

Somewhat farther to the east, in the direction of Chancellorsville, Major General Carl Schurz's Third Division of the Eleventh Corps, with a strength of about 5,000 men, had sufficient warning, from the noise of the conflict and the rush of men to the rear, to form a hasty line of defense that extended from the wood opposite Hawkin's Farm, past Wilderness Church, to Dowdall's Tavern on the Turnpike. But the time available was too short to make the position strong or to prepare the men psychologically for the impending shock and the wild flight of their fellow soldiers. The fast-driving Confederate bolt soon hit that line with solid force and it too quickly melted.

By 6 o'clock, less than an hour after Jackson first struck the unprepared Federal right, the Confederates had firm possession of Talley's Hill. One last despairing Federal effort to salvage something from the wreckage was made east of Wilderness Church, but the panic had by now infected the entire corps and this final line was quickly broken and streamed to the rear in company with the others.

THE FEDERALS MAKE A STAND
It was 6:30 P.M. before General Hooker received the news of the disaster to his right. That seems strange until one remembers that this was the year

1863, radio communication was unknown, artillery fire almost nonexistent in the Wilderness except on the roads and from prearranged positions in the clearings, and the sound of musket firing was localized by the very denseness of the forest. Still, it would seem that at least one mounted staff officer might have had the presence of mind to take an extended gallop to warn the army commander of what had occurred. On the other hand, the reception given by Howard's division commanders and Howard himself, earlier in the afternoon, to those who had anticipated trouble, had not been of a kind to encourage further initiative on the part of either the line or staff. Poetic justice seemingly had prevailed.

Hooker was seated peacefully on the porch of the Chancellor House when suddenly the first wave of fleeing men, horses, cattle, and vehicles was seen coming at a run down the Turnpike. The sight struck Hooker like a thunderclap, but it must be said to his credit that he reacted immediately and decisively—a pleasant change from his recent complacency. Quickly mounting his horse, the general galloped out to meet the retreating mass, sized up the situation as the old fighting division commander would have done, and at once snappy orders began to crackle.

Guns were ordered to Fairview, down the road a short distance toward Dowdall's to block the Confederate advance. One of Couch's brigades was posted across the road running north from the Chancellorsville crossroads to halt the rout and the Confederates alike. Hiram Berry's division of Sickles' corps was moved forward to the Fairview area to offer organized resistance. A division of Meade's Fifth Corps was shifted to the crossroads, near Bullock's, and a message dispatched to Pleasonton to send a cavalry regiment immediately to Howard. Order of a sort was being restored.

Meantime Sickles, having become acutely aware of the excitement on both sides of the Turnpike to the north of him, took things into his own hands, broke off the fighting below Hazel Grove which had about petered out anyway, and headed north where things were getting hot. Nor had Pleasonton waited for Hooker's order to exercise his own initiative. Taking two of his cavalry regiments and as many guns as he could quickly get his fingers on, Pleasonton moved energetically to operate against the head and right flank of the Confederates advancing east along the Turnpike. Reynold's First Corps, coming up from Fredericksburg, was crossing United States Mine Ford at this inauspicious moment, just in time for his column to help clog the already crowded road from the ford to Chancellorsville.

Although Hooker had neglected to inform Reynolds where he intended to employ the First Corps, there is reason to believe that it would have been posted on Howard's right, to close the then existing gap and to anchor the right of the Federal semicircular defense line on the Rapidan River. It was now too late for that, and Reynolds was directed "to occupy the ground vacated by the Eleventh Corps." This in itself was a rather weird, hopeless mission which no doubt gave the solid Reynolds some food for thought, particularly after he had learned the extent of the debacle on the army right.

The shades of night were now beginning to fall, to the considerable advantage of the Federal forces, for Stonewall Jackson's divisions were under the strictest injunction to let nothing stop them in their impetuous and so far thrillingly successful drive to inflict a crushing defeat on their old foe. Jackson could well have used a few more hours of daylight to put the finishing touches to his outstanding performance. Despite the superlative achievement of his Second Corps, entirely too much time had been taken in covering the dozen miles from Decker's. Yet the fault was not Jackson's. His blazing spirit seemingly could not multiply itself to accomplish the march and development in less time. But it is not unreasonable to conclude that his corps could have cut through to seize United States Mine Ford if he had started at 4 A.M. as planned. What slowed him down during the early hours of twilight, after the virtual destruction of Howard's Eleventh Corps, was a combination of Confederate troop confusion in the darkness of the forest, weariness, disorganization, and the resulting loss of momentum in the ranks of his attacking divisions, and a stiffening of resistance by the Federal corps other than the Eleventh. The sharp edge of Jackson's penetration had finally been blunted and the Confederate waves were now breaking ineffectually against hard rock in place of yielding sand.

WORTH HIS WEIGHT IN GOLD

His ear acutely cocked to sounds from the west, Lee acted promptly to order into action the divisions of Anderson and McLaws as soon as the noise of the conflict on the Turnpike reached him. The two Confederate generals threw their divisions, or as many of the troops as were in contact, into a vicious attack on Hooker's center at Chancellorsville. This nicely coordinated drive was calculated to overrun the important crossroads, smother the units protecting the Chancellor House, and either cut the Federal line or keep the enemy so fully occupied that no troops could be detached to interfere with Jackson's efforts on the flank.

There was to be no rest for the fleeing fugitives from Howard's corps, who had escaped from the pursuing Confederates at Dowdall's only to run smack into a flurry of fighting on the Chancellorsville front. The frightful confusion can only be imagined. Ambulances, baggage wagons, caissons, loose animals, camp followers, and frenzied soldiers flowed rapidly east in a tide of human flotsam that might have brought to an inglorious end the resolute Army of the Potomac, had it not been made of sterner stuff.

This was not the first time the Confederates had inflicted a near disaster on a Union army. But the Army of the Potomac as a whole did not panic easily, and once again its sturdy regiments rose magnificently to the occasion in spite of the crumpling of their right flank and the write-off, for all practical purposes, of an entire corps of three divisions. Hancock's division of the Second Corps was posted at the center across the Turnpike and thus received the heaviest weight of the collateral Confederate blow, delivered with artillery and infantry by Lee's two divisions. The strongly fortified front line on Hancock's sector was under the command of an unusually keen young officer named Nelson A Miles, whose skillful and determined handling of the battle at that point, in refreshing contrast to much that happened elsewhere that afternoon of May 2, would win for him a retroactive Congressional Medal of Honor. Repeatedly and violently the Confederates concentrated their attack on Miles' regiment, but each time were vigorously repulsed. It was a shining example that the young officer set for the rest of the army and the action was conspicuous in the midst of the infighting which raged over much of the Wilderness.

The months of disciplinary training in the Federal camps above Falmouth were now paying off. The steadiness in the ranks of the Second, Third, Fifth, and Twelfth Corps, and their refusal to panic as Howard's refugees streamed through them to the rear and even beyond

Chancellorsville into the arms of the Confederates, gave assurance that the Confederates had begun to sail into rough waters. These Federal veterans were undisturbed by the tumult and shouting and shooting—it was all in the day's work, and had Hooker only known it, his army was in shape and in sufficient strength to recapture the initiative, launch a counterattack against Jackson's weary troops, and more than cancel the debt.

Perhaps that was too much to expect from the Hooker of April 30–May 2, whose defensive psychology had become a fixed attitude that nothing could shake. The Army of the Potomac would save him from himself, but its personnel were powerless to do any more in spite of their capabilities and the willingness to make the most of them, given competent leadership at the top.

THE FEDERAL CAVALRY HAS AN ADVENTURE

Cooperating with Sickles at Hazel Grove and the Furnace, Pleasonton's cavalry was given the mission of going to the aid of Howard's hard-pressed corps on the Turnpike. Sickles' two divisions, under Birney and Whipple, in company with the 6th New York Cavalry, which covered Sickles' flanks, were pretty well isolated from the rest of the army at Hazel Grove and hence in danger of being cut off. By the same token, however, they were a thorn in Lee's side in holding what may fairly be termed the key position on the battlefield. Sickles for one was keenly conscious of its strategic importance and confident that his corps, properly supported, could hold the position.

Pleasanton had the 8th and 17th Pennsylvania Cavalry Regiments with him at the western and northern edges of Hazel Grove, within several hundred yards of the southernmost element of Howard's Eleventh Corps. Both regiments were relaxing at ease but ready for any contingency, although restricted to the extent that they had been sent there to cooperate with Sickles and thus were not free to go off on independent adventures of their own.

When Pleasonton was informed of the stampede of the Eleventh Corps he has said that he sent the 8th Pennsylvania to find and help Howard, and moved the 17th Pennsylvania off into the woods to the left to hold the enemy in check until he could get artillery into firing position.

By dint of great exertion and considerable good fortune he managed to assemble twenty-two guns in a formidable line and, facing west rather than east, was ready for Jackson's men when they came up about dusk, after forcing their way through the tangled forest.

The 8th Pennsylvania Cavalry, Major Pennock Huey commanding, moved north on the road running to the Turnpike, in a column of twos, with the three squadrons also in column. Huey's account of this and the following action declared that he was told only to assist Howard, nothing having been said of the disaster that had already engulfed the Eleventh Corps. His troopers, laboring under the inspired delusion that Lee's army was retreating, were in high spirits in spite of the gathering darkness and uncertainty of the situation. They were completely unaware that a large force of Confederates was advancing at right angles to their direction of march, and just a short distance away.

The head of the regiment had almost reached the Plank Road, sabers still in the scabbards and pistols holstered, when they were startled to discover the road filled with Confederates, whose skirmishers lapped over on both flanks of the Federal cavalry.

This was one of the unplanned, accidental lethal encounters that constantly occur on battlefields, make their unrecorded impact for good or ill on the plans of the generals, and are forgotten by history unless some participant preserves the episode in writing for the edification of posterity. The charge of the 8th Pennsylvania Cavalry was a great surprise both to the enemy and itself. It had no choice but to charge or surrender, and no one can say whether or not it proved anything, or how long it took for the elements of the regiment who survived to regain the cohesiveness of an organized unit. After receiving the destructive volley the survivors made their way east to Chancellorsville, where they were formed again in line, to intercept stragglers.

Nevertheless, it is not beyond the realm of possibility that the unexpected boldness of a single regiment of Federal cavalry, appearing suddenly in the very midst of the infantry fighting, made a marked impression on the minds of the Confederate foot soldiers. The result could very well have been to cause the latter to be extraordinarily alert to the possibility that other Federal cavalry was prowling about in the forest, and that it was that form of trigger-happiness that led directly to the wounding and subsequent death of Stonewall Jackson.

FEDERAL ARTILLERY AT HAZEL GROVE

The diversion caused by the 8th Pennsylvania Cavalry was of a temporary character. On the Confederates came, through the woods, solid masses of men in skirmish line and column, carrying a Union flag taken from the Eleventh Corps, or possibly picked up off the ground. It was growing darker by the moment as the Confederates burst from the woods into the clearing at Hazel Grove and let loose a volley of musketry from thousands of muskets as they rushed into the open.

The Federal command to fire rang out and twenty-two guns answered almost with a single roar. At pointblank range the carnage among the Confederates was indescribable. Quickly reloading, the guns fired a second time, and then for twenty minutes poured canister into the torn gray ranks and, as Pleasonton remarked, "the affair was over." It was Rodes' Division that tried to take Hazel Grove and failed. Pleasonton was later to record that the Confederates would have succeeded if their infantry fire had been more accurate and aimed lower to take advantage of ricochets. As it happened, most of the musket balls passed harmlessly over the heads of the Federal cannoneers, who for their part aimed low and made their bursts fully effective.

General Henry Hunt, Chief of Artillery of the Army of the Potomac, would have been proud of his artillery that day had he been present. But one of Hooker's many errors of judgment at Chancellorsville had been to relieve the architect of his superb artillery corps of field command, leaving him with only administrative responsibilities, until almost the eleventh hour, when he was again given full charge of all the artillery, both administrative and tactical. The way in which the Federal artillery functioned was a lasting tribute to the years of dedicated, intelligent preparation and training which Hunt had devoted to the guns and those who served them. Hunt would have approved of the way those twenty-two guns stopped cold the attempt of Rodes' Division to overrun Hazel Grove, and he was entitled to share with them the credit for preventing two divisions of Sickles' corps, at the same time, from being irretrievably cut off from the main body of the army.

Hunt would likewise have been thoroughly pleased had he been in position to observe the heroic work of another artillery outfit, Dilger's Battery of Howard's Corps, during the first mad dash of the Eleventh Corps to the rear. Hubert Dilger had learned what makes a good artilleryman tick during service with the horse artillery in his native Germany, which he left to join the Union Army. They gave him command of an Ohio battery and before long, under his skilful and loving care, it became Dilger's Battery, Eleventh Corps. There was none better. Single-handedly the indomitable captain, manipulating his gun crews with tactical skill and courage, denied the use of one of the only two roads open to Jackson and inflicted heavy damage on the advancing Confederates until they managed to swarm in on his embattled guns from the woods on either side of the road and force a withdrawal barely in time to avoid capture. To what extent Dilger's lone battery was able to buy time for Hooker's divisions in rear to readjust their lines to meet Jackson's advance can only be conjectured, but there can be little doubt that his bold conduct accomplished greater results than all the rest of the Eleventh Corps put together.

All during the early hours of the night the Federal artillery, emplaced at Fairview, Hazel Grove, Chancellorsville, and other points to the north, poured shell and canister into the temporarily jumbled brigades of Jackson's Corps, giving them no peace and, in the darkness, making it difficult to reconstitute them as efficient units. In spite of which, Jackson's zeal to "press on" had not abated, and he was prompt to urge A. P. Hill, whose division was in better shape than the other two by reason of having been the tail-ender in the attack column, to rush a brigade to cut Hooker off from United States Mine Ford. Before the attempt could be made, both Jackson and Hill were wounded, and the day's fighting came to an end.

Fighting continued sporadically far into the night of May 2, which was an almost unheard of occurrence during the first half of the Civil War. But the aftermath of Jackson's flank march, the fighting on the right of Hooker's army, and the disastrous foot race of the Union Eleventh Corps, which could have led to the complete defeat of the Army of the Potomac, had keyed up both armies to such an extent that precedent was shattered.

The fierce drive which animated the spirit of Stonewall Jackson, in his famous maneuver and the devastating surprise attack into which it led, had not diminished in the least when darkness closed in over the battle-field. His divisions had taken the initial objectives he had designated; it was the enemy that was "ingloriously flying." The thought uppermost in Jackson's mind at this stage was how best to exploit the victory already so handsomely won on a part of the field.

The none too easy ten-hour march had been followed immediately by a difficult deployment in the Wilderness on a two-mile front, then a raging attack through thickets that the Federal generals regarded as impassable. Who can doubt that the driving force of General Jackson, despite the foregoing, would have pressed the attack through the night, so that he might reap the fruits of victory? It was his hope that by continuing the attack he could squeeze Hooker between Lee and himself, block the Union army off from United States Mine Ford, cut Hooker to pieces in the process, or at the very least link up with Lee's wing before Chancellorsville to drive the Federal army into the Rappahannock.

The mere fact that his own divisions were tired out, could have used some food to advantage, and were badly in need of reshuffling after the wholesale intermingling of organizations during the early hours of the attack, would not deter the impatient Jackson; neither would the increasing resistance of the remaining corps of the Union army which succeeded the confusion attending the roll-up of its right flank. Jackson was the kind of general who would figure that the time to press the attack is when the enemy is demoralized, and he suspected that to be the case with Hooker's divisions, if the example of the Eleventh Corps could be taken as the criterion. Even though his troops were confronted with the tough assignment of further fighting in the darkness, their morale was high and the enemy would be facing equal difficulties. He, Jackson, had gained the ascendancy and was determined to hold the initiative as long as his men were able to remain on their feet.

Rodes' Division, in the van of the attack, had by this time lost all semblance of a cohesive unit, as was to be expected. That level-headed commander decided that the cause would be better served were he to take time out to pull his units together for more effective work, so he called a halt to the advance and requested that A. P. Hill's Division, in the third line, be brought forward to take the lead and continue the attack. That made sense to Jackson, who was up front and in close touch with the forward elements, as he always was in the heat of battle. He at once gave the order to a staff officer, who put spurs to his horse and in a few moments Hill reported to receive the corps commander's instructions.

"Press them, Hill. Cut them off from the United States Ford. Press them!" ordered the taciturn Jackson, the direct actionist who was a believer. in short, concise oral orders. Jackson knew what he wanted done, quickly, and the fiery Hill, his smoldering feud with his corps commander forgotten for the moment, was not one to ask questions. Galloping off, and no doubt enthused by the opportunity for the Light Division to take the place of honor at the front of the corps, Hill sped to his troops to put them in position on either side of the Turnpike, ready to leapfrog the advance brigades.

A bright moon had arisen to throw an eerie light on the Turnpike and the occasional clearings, intensifying the shadows and giving to the terrain and natural objects that unnatural appearance with which every soldier is familiar who has marched or maneuvered at night. Because they were unfamiliar with the Chancellorsville terrain, neither Jackson nor any of his generals knew exactly where they were or the precise trace of their front-line position. The moon helped, of course, and there must be a road or roads that would lead to United States Mine Ford in rear of Chancellorsville. It wouldn't do to push much further ahead without that knowledge, so Jackson, still the direct actionist, decided to find out for himself.

Accompanied by several members of his staff and one of Stuart's couriers, who had brought a message from the cavalry commander and was retained by Jackson as a guide familiar with the countryside, the small cavalcade of mounted men started out on the personal reconnaissance that was to mark Stonewall Jackson's last ride. Moving at a walk along the Turnpike, which coincided with the Orange Plank Road from Dowdall's Tavern to the Chancellorsville crossroads, Jackson halted at an old schoolhouse, one of the more familiar landmarks of the region. Across the road could be seen two roads branching off to the northeast, the nearer of which Stuart's courier identified as the Mountain Road, a spur paralleling the Turnpike for only a short distance and leading nowhere; the other was a road leading to Bullock's Farm, about a mile north of Chancellorsville.

That was important intelligence, but Jackson had to know more. How close was the enemy? What were they doing? Down the Mountain Road went the little group of horsemen, the staff growing increasingly nervous as they found themselves in a no-man's land ahead of their own lines and an unknown distance, perhaps half a mile, possibly only a few yards, from the enemy. It was no place for a lieutenant general to play scout, and one of the staff officers questioned the advisability of going any further. Jackson assured him that all was well, the enemy was on the run, they would continue.

After a bit the general halted, motioned for silence, and cocked his ear. Noises to the east and not too far off! An officer giving a command to some men; the sound of axes! That was what he had come out here for. The Federals were close by and fortifying their position.

Turning their horses, the little group started to retrace their steps to their own lines. Taking up the trot, as though symbolic of Jackson's urgent anxiety to renew the attack, fortifications or no fortifications, and to galvanize A. P. Hill into action, the Confederate horsemen rapidly approached the line of their own out-guards. Trigger-happy and understandably nervous, the Confederate skirmishers out in front along the Turnpike heard the clatter of hoofs, saw the shadowy figures coming toward them at a rapid gait, and mistook them for a detachment of Federal cavalry looking for trouble. A single shot rang out, then another, followed by a volley as Hill's men opened up to repel the imagined threat, killing a captain and a sergeant in Jackson's small party.

"Cease firing. You are firing on your own men!" shouted one of Jackson's staff officers as he leaped from his horse and ran excitedly toward the Confederate lines. But it was too late. Jackson's frightened horse bolted, galloping wildly in the direction of the enemy.

With difficulty the general managed to get the animal under control sufficiently to turn its head toward his own lines, when another volley from a North Carolina regiment on the north side of the Turnpike found its mark, three bullets striking Jackson as he fought to rein in his now almost unmanageable horse. One bullet lodged in his right hand; another passed through the left wrist and came out through the palm of that hand; the third passed completely through his left arm between the elbow and the shoulder, badly shattering the large bone and cutting the main artery, rendering the arm useless. Little Sorrel plunged into the thicket, knocking the general's hat off and badly scraping his face. Fortunately he had by that time reached the line of pickets, where ready hands caught at the reins of the trembling animal and carefully assisted the disabled corps commander to dismount. Already weak from loss of blood and shock, Jackson was placed on the ground in a grove just north of the Turnpike and first aid of a sort administered.

Bad news travels fast, and in a short time A. P. "Powell" Hill, who had also been reconnoitering along the front in close proximity to Jackson, hurried up, to be joined almost at once by other staff officers, including Captain James Power Smith, one of Jackson's aides. Smith had been acting as a communication center between the artillery reserve at the rear and Jackson's moving command post in the saddle, during the attack and pursuit of the early evening.

It was during the heavy Federal bombardment described by Jackson's aide, while the disabled corps commander was being transported to the rear, that A. P. Hill received his wound in company with many another Confederate. Hill's wound, while slight, proved sufficiently disabling to require his removal for treatment. Several shell fragments had struck him in both legs, resulting in painful but not serious injury.

Hill managed to move under his own power a short distance to the rear, where he conferred with his nearby brigadiers. Although Rodes was the senior division commander after Hill, he was not a major general, and all agreed that Hill should send word to Jeb Stuart that he was their choice to succeed Jackson as acting corps commander.

PANDEMONIUM IN THE MOONLIGHT

Conscious of the isolation of his two divisions at Hazel Grove, Birney's and Whipple's, but at the same time aggressively aware of the fact that his position, between Lee's right wing facing Hooker at Chancellorsville and Jackson's Corps driving in from the west, served as a Federal wedge to prevent a junction of the two Confederate wings, Sickles had been urging Hooker to permit him to launch an attack.

His purpose ostensibly was to recover several guns which had been abandoned during the early part of the evening, when Rodes' troops were stopped in their tracks by the artillery Pleasonton had commandeered at the Grove to meet the Confederate assault. But Sickles was full of fight and temperamentally allergic to passive resistance at any time, and besides, his tenuous line of communication with Chancellorsville could stand strengthening, having already been temporarily cut by an enterprising body of Confederates. All in all, a vigorous attack would in Sickles' opinion be a salutary move that should not be delayed till morning lest it then be too late to derive the collateral benefits.

At 10 o'clock the desired permission was received from Hooker and preparations for the attack in the moonlit forest got under way. Staff officers were sent to division commanders Williams, of Slocum's Twelfth Corps, and Berry of Sickles' own, to inform them of the plan and assure their cooperation. Williams' division, which was the nearest, found that his line was at right angles to Sickles' at Hazel Grove. Fearful of confusion in the darkness, Williams requested that the attack be deferred until Slocum, then at army headquarters, could approve, but the courier either garbled the reply on his return to Sickles, or the latter disregarded the request, for the attack proceeded as planned.

With bayonets fixed, Birney's division moved out shortly before midnight, in column of brigades, regiments abreast and formed in line of companies, each company in column of fours. The center regiment of each brigade marched astride the road leading north to the old schoolhouse on the Turnpike, almost a mile distant, which at this time was occupied by the advance elements of Jackson's Corps, although Sickles wasn't aware of that and Birney's regiments only knew that they were likely to encounter the enemy at any moment.

It was not long before pandemonium broke loose in the darkness. Birney's regiments on the right ran into Williams' Federal troops while those on the left overran Lane's Confederates. The regiments on the road reached the Turnpike but failed to hold it. Musketry firing became general all over the lot, friendly and enemy troops shooting promiscuously at one another; at the same time Slocum's artillery opened up on his order, since no one had informed him of the projected Third Corps attack, and he was taking no chances.

As a coordinated attack the effort proved somewhat abortive. If Sickles expected Williams and Berry to make a concerted effort to drive back the Confederates on the Turnpike, he failed to make it clear just what form their cooperation should take. The attack turned out to be a unilateral one on Birney's part, but it did serve a useful purpose. For Sickles was able to improve his position, somewhat further advanced in the direction of the Turnpike, and to secure ground to the right that enabled his pickets to connect with those of the Twelfth Corps. Furthermore, the heavy fire which was directed into the mass of Confederate troops on the left had the effect of cooling their ardor for any further adventures that night.

The confusion in the ranks of Jackson's Corps as a result of the intermingling of units collateral to their impetuous advance, the difficulties inherent in fighting in the darkness on unfamiliar terrain, particularly that of the Wilderness, and the depressing moral effect of the loss of Jackson and Hill within a few minutes, combined to set the Confederates up as likely candidates for a severe reverse at Federal hands. Had Sickles and Slocum taken time to put their heads together to plan a coordinated counterattack with the two corps working together as a team, instead of getting in each other's way and killing each other's men, there would have been a good possibility that the panic of the Federal Eleventh Corps might have been duplicated, with the Confederates on the receiving end. But that was not to be, and the Federals were forced to content themselves with the thought that valuable time at least had been bought and they were still in the fight.

General Rodes, temporarily in command of Jackson's Corps after A. P. Hill was wounded, now called a halt in the attack, countermanding Jackson's earlier order to Hill's Division (presently commanded by Harry Heth) to push on to United States Mine Ford, and the two armies settled down to a few hours of doubtful rest before morning and certain resumption of the fighting.

The interesting speculation presents itself as to what might have happened during the night if Jackson had not been wounded. It is almost certain that the attack by A. P. Hill's Division up the road through

Bullock's would have been continued with the object of cutting in behind Hooker's position at Chancellorsville. But then what? Meade's unused Fifth Corps was ready for action and Reynold's First Corps was now on the field, tired after its forced march but capable of giving a good account of itself.

Without knowing the topography, without any preparation beyond the command to "press forward and cut them off from the United States Ford," without coordination between the three divisions of his corps, and unable to use his artillery in the dense forest, Jackson's chances for an effective nighttime exploitation of his daylight success cannot be said to have been of the best.

A LOST OPPORTUNITY

Hooker's ineptly conceived and ineffectual employment of his cavalry during the Chancellorsville campaign has been mentioned, but little has been said about the activities of the cavalry division of 3,400 sabers, commanded by Brigadier General W. W. Averell, following his duel with Fitzhugh Lee and Averell's failure to destroy the latter in the March affair at Kelly's Ford.

Averell's division ran into advance elements of Rooney Lee's Brigade at Brandy Station, drove them back on Lee's main body at Culpeper, and then continued on to Rapidan Station, pushing the Confederates ahead of them. A packet of mail captured at Brandy Station disclosed a letter which said that the Federal cavalry was being followed by Hooker's whole army and that Jackson's corps of 25,000 men was at Gordonsville preparing to resist Hooker. This "intelligence" Averell had forwarded to Hooker with the comment that it was "believed to be reliable and important."

During these movements Averell received several dispatches from Stoneman which were somewhat ambiguous and in at least one instance at variance with Hooker's original instructions to the cavalry corps. Purporting to guide Averell's actions, they were badly phrased. Stoneman's intentions, as explained in his official report, were not discernible in the wording of the messages. Averell interpreted the instructions to mean that he was to keep the enemy cavalry in the vicinity occupied, while Stoneman avers that the intent of the orders was for Averell to block off his immediate opposition and then promptly rejoin the main army.

The net result of the badly mishandled situation was that Averell remained inactive for two nights and a day at Rapidan Station, with Rooney Lee facing him across the river and apparently quite content with being able to pin down such a large force of enemy cavalry with but a fraction of their strength. Rapidan Station was only twenty miles west of Chancellorsville, less than half a day's march for cavalry. Somehow Hooker got wind of what was going on and sent word to Averell directing him to bring his whole outfit to Chancellorsville (where his regiments could be used to advantage). Nothing happened. A repeat message on the afternoon of May 2 finally brought action, and in due course the cavalry division found its way to Ely's Ford, only five miles distant from the battlefield, where again it came to a halt on the north side of the river and simply marked time. Up to now Averell's score had been only one man killed, and two officers and two men wounded, which explains his ineffectual operations more eloquently than a dozen reports.

Here was a case of another lost opportunity for the Army of the Potomac, which if understood and grasped could have changed the course of the battle. The word "could" is used advisedly, for there can be no assurance that Hooker would have employed Averell's cavalry any more effectively than he did Pleasonton's, which was at hand in brigade strength and could have secured the army right flank if Hooker had so directed. The upshot of the matter was that Hooker relieved Averell of command of his division, but stopped short of preferring charges, merely stating that "in detaching him from this army my object has been to prevent an active and powerful column from being paralyzed in its future operations by his presence."

STUART TAKES COMMAND

With the launching of Jackson's flank attack against Hooker's right, Jeb Stuart, whose cavalry had covered the march of the Second Corps, found time hanging heavy on his hands. His horsemen were now idle, their mission completed for the present. It therefore appeared to Stuart that he could operate more constructively if he should move up to Ely's Ford, where reports had it some Federal wagon trains had been parked. Receiving Jackson's permission, about 6 P.M. Stuart led a force of 1,000 men composed of infantry, cavalry, and a battery of artillery and soon arrived at the Ford where he found Averell's Federal cavalry division occupying the north shore. That was an interesting development, which Stuart decided to exploit by way of a preventive, diversionary attack.

But there was far more important work in store for General Stuart than a night encounter with Blue cavalry. As he was making his dispositions for the attack, a staff officer reported from A. P. Hill with a message that both Jackson and himself had been wounded, that Stuart was now the senior officer in the Second Corps, and that he was to return at once to assume command. Sending word to Fitzhugh Lee to secure and hold the road from Ely's Ford to Chancellorsville, to restrain a possible ambitious move by Averell (about which he apparently need not have worried), Stuart galloped off through the darkness to take over.

TWO ARMS ARE LOST

Several hours after the ambulance arrived that conveyed Jackson to the corps hospital tent, set up several hundred yards east of Wilderness Run in a field along the Turnpike, chloroform was administered by Doctor McGuire and the left arm amputated just below the shoulder. Tucker Lacy and Captain Smith remained with Jackson throughout the night. In the morning the chaplain removed the severed member to the Lacy farm, which was about a mile distant from the hospital, buried it in a spot near the house, and erected a marker for the dubious benefit of posterity.

After Jackson had regained consciousness, Major Sandy Pendleton came to report that Hill had been wounded, Stuart had reached the field to take command, and he had been sent to learn whether Jackson had any instructions. The drugged general brightened, made an effort to concentrate, and seemed about to respond with his customary incisiveness; then his features fell and he answered feebly: "I don't know—I can't tell; say to General Stuart he must do what he thinks best."

Stuart was in a very difficult position at this juncture. He hadn't the remotest idea what Jackson's follow up attack plan might have been, nor was he informed until he arrived on the field as to what shape the corps was in or just where the positions of its several elements might be. General Hill and Captain Boswell, Jackson's Engineer Officer, were the only two who knew that Jackson had directed Hill to advance the Light Division through the darkness to the White House (Bullock's), north of Chancellorsville, to cut Hooker's line to United States Mine Ford; but Boswell had been killed and Hill wounded. Although Stuart must at the first opportunity have consulted Hill on his stretcher and learned of Jackson's plan, common sense dictated a pause for reorganization, with a view to renewing the attack at daybreak. That would give Stuart a few hours to gather up the reins of his unfamiliar steed and to proceed more confidently, instead of jabbing blindly at the Federals with but a foggy conception of the tactical situation.

A note dictated by Jackson was handed to Lee at the Chancellor House after the successful Confederate assault of May 3 had forced Hooker to take up a new line further removed from Chancellorsville. Greatly moved, Lee replied, expressing his deep regret at Jackson's loss in a message that revealed the character of the great leader: "Could I have directed events, I should have chosen for the good of the country to be disabled in your stead. I congratulate you upon the victory, which is due to your skill and energy."

Lee's habitual thoughtfulness for others led him, while the battle was still raging, to direct that Jackson be removed to a safer spot lest through some mischance he be taken prisoner. By a roundabout road, therefore, the wounded general was transported by ambulance to the home of his friend, Mr. Chandler, at Guiney's Station, where he was placed in comfortable quarters which would, it was hoped, afford an opportunity to convalesce in quiet surroundings and with his wife present. For several days his condition showed encouraging improvement, but pneumonia developed and he began to grow weaker. Chaplain Lacy reported to Lee Jackson's turn for the worse and the fear of the doctors that the disease might prove fatal. Lee, who would not accept that dire forecast, sent Lacy with a message to Jackson: "Give him my affectionate regards and tell him to make haste and get well, and come back to me as soon as he can. He has lost his left arm, but I have lost my right."

On Sunday, May 10, Jackson was told that the end was near. Soon he became delirious, and began to issue battle orders. "Order A. P. Hill to prepare for action. Pass the infantry to the front!" Then, calmly, as though in benediction: "No, no, let us pass over the river, and rest under the shade of the trees." With which words the spirit of Stonewall Jackson passed quietly into Immortality.

CHAPTER 25

Chancellorsville II: May 3

THE CONFEDERATES at Chancellorsville were ready for a rest when the fighting ended late on the night of May 2–3. It had been a tough day for all of their divisions. The entire force had been engaged, with Jackson's Corps having borne the heavier burden of marching and fighting. But the right wing—McLaws and Anderson—had also done their share. Hooker's flank had been neatly turned, at a heavy price, to be sure, in the loss of Jackson and Hill, but the morale of the Confederates was heightened by their satisfaction at having inflicted a crushing blow on the enemy. The initiative remained in Lee's hands, and to a man the Southerners were prepared to press their advantage early Sunday morning in a renewal of their driving attack on the Federal positions.

On the opposite side, despite the disaster which had put the Eleventh Corps hors de combat, the Anny of the Potomac had quickly recovered its equilibrium and was full of fight-everywhere but at the top. Out of a total of five Federal corps on the battlefield, only two, the Eleventh and Third, had been fully engaged and, of the latter, Birney's division had seen limited action for but a short time. The Second Corps (except for one brigade), the entire Fifth Corps, and one division of the Twelfth Corps, can hardly be said to have been in action at all. In effect, then, more than half of Hooker's 70,000-man main striking force had merely stood to arms, manning their fortifications. If that was Hooker's idea of how to fight a battle, Lee's mental graph of his opponent's ability must have shown a sharply descending curve.

Reynold's First Corps, having spent the better part of May 2 on the road from Fredericksburg en route to join Hooker, had started to cross United States Ford during the evening. This was just in time to aid in slowing down the mad rush of the terrified fugitives of the Eleventh Corps, who seemed determined to escape by way of the pontoon bridge over which Reynolds' divisions were coming on the field. Marching by way of Hartwood Church, it had occurred to Reynolds to cross at Banks' Ford and take the River Road on the south side of the Rappahannock. But he thought better of it, doubtless because the pontoon bridge that was on hand at that point had not yet been thrown. Had he decided to cross there, it could have led to interesting possibilities, the most intriguing of which was the chance of coming in on Lee's rear from the east, while the latter was preoccupied with a holding attack against the center of Hooker's line at Chancellorsville.

Equally rewarding, by occupying Banks' Ford on the southern side, Hooker's operational flexibility would have been vastly increased, cooperation with Sedgwick assured, and almost anything might have happened. A mentally alert army commander in Hooker's place would certainly have made better use of such a huge, available reinforcement.

The sudden, shocking revelation that Lee's army, instead of retreating on Gordonsville as Hooker had been insisting, was attacking vigorously after a well-planned and executed march that effectively outflanked the outflanker, had the odd effect of increasing Hooker's defensive-mindedness, if that were possible. His smug assurance that Lee, if he should attack, would shatter his army against an impregnable Federal position, had been replaced by fear for the safety of his own army. Hooker had lost confidence in himself, that was certain, but the tragedy of his psychosis was that it implied as well a wholly unjustified lack of faith in the Army of the Potomac, which was ready, willing, able, and even desperately hopeful that some miracle would happen to jolt their bemused, timid commander out of his strange lethargy.

It would seem that Hooker's wing of 70,000 (net after casualties) should have been more than enough to fight a defensive battle against Lee's 45,000 who confronted the Federals at Chancellorsville, without overcrowding the position with Reynolds' added strength of more than 16,000. Hooker had not reckoned with Lee's superb ability to maneuver offensively, but the frame of mind of the Federal commander was such that even 86,000 men would not be sufficient, in the face of his woeful lack of effective combat leadership, to gain the ascendancy over the alert and confidently aggressive Confederates.

Upon Reynolds' arrival in advance of his corps, Hooker issued instructions that the First Corps should take position on the army right "his (Reynolds') right to rest on the Rapidan, on the east bank of Hunting Run, and extending to the crossing of the Chancellorsville and Ely's Ford Roads, and thence along that road in the direction of Chancellorsville." Reynolds' left was to connect with the right of Sykes' division of the Fifth Corps. This order superseded an earlier order for Reynolds "to seize the position vacated by the Eleventh Corps," which had indeed been wishful thinking of a high order.

HOOKER PULLS IN HIS HORNS

The best that Hooker could come up with at the tail end of Saturday, May 2, was the creation of an inner or second defense line, a V-shaped affair with the point at Bullock's Farm, the base the curving line of the Rappahannock, and the sides occupied by three of the six corps present. Reynolds' First Corps occupied the army right, or west side of the new line, along Hunting Run; Meade's Fifth Corps was shifted to the center, generally along the Ely's Ford-Chancellorsville Road; the remains of Howard's shattered Eleventh Corps occupied the army left or east side of the line along the Bullock Road, somewhat farther to the west than the original position of the Fifth Corps.

One brigade of Couch's Second Corps was held in reserve on Howard's left rear, just in case. The contracted line was a strong one for defense, both ends anchored on the river, but the concept of fighting with one's back to a river is not regarded by the military experts as a particularly healthy exercise; especially when the defender has lost the initiative and reminds one of a spiritless boxer shielding his head with both arms against the rights and lefts of his lighter but more aggressive opponent, while waiting hopefully for the bell to mark the end of the round.

To the south of the V were the other three corps of the army, the Second, Twelfth and Third, forming an awkward salient which jutted out in a semicircle from the apex of the second line of defense, and interposed between the two wings of Lee's army. Slocum's Twelfth and Couch's Second Corps formed the U around Chancellorsville and Fairview, with Sickles' Third Corps way out on the tip of the salient at Hazel Grove.

Salients are traditionally vulnerable pieces of real estate, but this one would not have the opportunity of either proving or disproving the doctrine, because Hooker docilely yielded Hazel Grove without a fight on Sunday morning. Probably it was just as well that he did, considering his mental state, because the Third Corps could not have held the position against strong pressure from two sides unless ordered support from other corps should aid in leveling out the salient by means of a forward movement on one or both flanks.

Hazel Grove was a position worth a fight to retain and the risk of the salient was justified as a temporary expedient. But it was an unsafe position unless the army commander was determined to make a positive effort to reduce its vulnerability by exploiting its inherent and acquired advantages.

Shortly before daylight on Sunday morning, May 3, Hooker rode out to see Sickles at Hazel Grove. That high ground, in conjunction with Fairview, if productively utilized was the key to dominance of the battlefield. Guns posted at the Grove could make Fairview untenable; if in Confederate hands they would be able to enfilade both the western and southern exposure of Slocum's Twelfth Corps, which presently held a lease on Fairview.

Not since the arrival of his right wing on April 30 had Hooker made any serious offensive gestures in the direction of the enemy. All he had done was to pull in additional corps from Fredericksburg, one after the other, until he had six of his seven corps at Chancellorsville, with an initial strength of about 90,000 men. Surely with such preponderance the army had a right to expect at least a modicum of initiative from its commander after more than two days in the Chancellorsville area.

LEE DECIDES TO PRESS THE ATTACK

Jackson's Corps under Jeb Stuart's command passed the night of May 2 in the area initially occupied by Howard's Federal Eleventh Corps, in a position of readiness from which it could attack in any one of three directions: to the northeast toward United States Mine Ford and Hooker's communications; directly east, down the Turnpike to Chancellorsville; or in a southeasterly direction against Hazel Grove to connect with the divisions of McLaws and Anderson, which under Lee's immediate command were disposed from the unfinished railroad and Catharine Furnace, across the Plank Road and the Turnpike, to a point on Mott Run about a mile east of the Chancellorsville crossroad.

Lee was snatching a few hours of sleep in a pine grove along the Furnace Road when he was awakened shortly before 2:30 A.M. by the arrival of a member of Jackson's staff, come to report to the Commanding General on affairs on Jackson's front. It was the first eyewitness account of the stirring events of the preceding evening, and Lee was eager for the details. He was told of the wounds suffered by Jackson and A. P. Hill and Stuart's succession to command and, in a general way, the present dispositions in the area of Dowdall's Tavern.

Lee was at once alert, particularly when the officer told him that Jackson's intent had been to cut Hooker off from United States Mine Ford. In Lee's view, however, the important thing was first to effect a junction of the two separated wings. A message to that effect was soon on its way to Stuart:

> *It is necessary that the glorious victory thus far achieved be prosecuted with the utmost vigor, and the enemy given no time to rally. As soon, therefore, as it is possible, they must be pressed, so that we may unite the two wings of the army. Endeavor, therefore, to dispossess them of Chancellorsville, which will permit the union of the whole army.*
>
> *I shall proceed myself to join you as soon as I can make arrangements on this side, but let nothing delay the completion of the plan of drawing the enemy from his rear and from his positions. I shall give orders that every effort be made on this side at daybreak to aid in the junction.*

Hooker's pre-dawn visit to Sickles' position at Hazel Grove conceivably was seized upon by the Third Corps Commander as an opportunity to present the case for a buildup of strength in that area, to justify an offensive move by the Federals. That would be in the Sickles' character; his two divisions had staked out a claim to that valuable position and had successfully contested an effort by Rodes' Confederates to dispossess them the preceding evening. Sickles could see no valid reason for cravenly pulling out, feeling confident that he could hold the Grove if given effective support, a commendable attitude that should have made sense to a superior with a semblance of fighting spirit.

Whatever passed between the two generals is not known, but it is obvious that Hooker had but one thought, to concentrate his divisions behind the fortified lines that he had decreed as the new and shortened defensive position to the north. Lee was prepared to take losses in order to capture the important key to the battlefield, a major obstacle to a junction of his two wings, but Hooker generously and gratuitously volunteered to save him the trouble. Sickles was forthwith directed to withdraw from Hazel Grove at daylight and take position at Fairview, perpendicular to and astride the Turnpike, to reinforce the line held by the Twelfth Corps and Berry's division of his own Third Corps.

Sickles promptly complied and in short order had marched his troops out of the salient, barely ahead of Jeb Stuart, who had already mounted a dawn attack in that direction. Stuart's purpose was to adjust his line, but the order was misunderstood, and the engagement became general. The Confederate blow found its target on the move and managed to mess up Sickles' rear elements sufficiently to capture several guns, but that was all. Stuart lost no time in putting Archer's Brigade on the vacated position, at the same time running up thirty guns whose gunners found themselves in the happy position of being able to enfilade the Federal position at Fairview, together with one of Slocum's divisions in trenched to the southeast of Fairview.

In conformity with his conviction that Sickles' corps at Hazel Grove should not be left out on a limb, but before actually directing its withdrawal, Hooker had ordered Pleasonton's cavalry on the night of May 2 to pull out and go into camp on the north side of the Rappahannock. Pleasonton initiated the retrograde movement at 4 o'clock on Sunday morning, but in the course of the march the morning battle of May 3 erupted. The cavalry was temporarily sidetracked by an unusual assignment which required it to form a buffer line across Fairview, under orders to stop and turn back escapees from the front line. If the curious mission emanated from Hooker, as it probably did, the order was in keeping with the current attitude of mind of the commanding general. In any event, no further combat seems to have been required of Pleasonton's force, which could and should have been used as dismounted cavalry where it would have done the most good.

Furthermore, Averell's cavalry division had now moved up to United States Mine Ford, with nothing to do. In combination, then, Hooker had over 5,000 able-bodied cavalrymen to utilize as reserve in addition to the 30,000 men of the First and Fifth Infantry Corps, but there was no spirit left in the army commander.

The collateral advantage handed to the Confederates without a struggle was the removal of the Hazel Grove roadblock to an easy junction of the forces under Stuart and Lee. The early morning withdrawal by Sickles consequently got the Confederates off to a favorable start and they lost no time in exploiting their improved fortunes with murderous artillery fire effect.

Stuart's eagerness to launch his attack as early as possible after sunrise, and his relative unfamiliarity with the capabilities of his newly acquired infantry, taken together resulted in a somewhat uncoordinated initial effort by the Confederates of the left wing. The first advance by the several brigades of the leading attack echelon was consequently disjointed and ineffectual. The Federal position at Fairview had been strongly fortified by log emplacements as much as three feet in height in some places. On the front manned by the divisions of Berry and Williams, facing west, the woods had been cleared to a considerable width to provide an effective field of fire that materially strengthened the defense.

From the artillery standpoint, possession of Hazel Grove gave Stuart a decided advantage over the Federal guns at Fairview. If nothing but an artillery duel should develop, the contestants would exchange compliments on fairly even terms, so far as position was concerned. But for punishment to the infantry, the Federals, closely massed, would be likely to suffer more than the Confederates, who were disposed for the attack in three successive waves, with a distance of some three hundred yards between lines. Stuart had improved his time by moving to the front during the night all the guns he possibly could. The result was that after the Confederates occupied Hazel Grove they had fifty guns in position there and on the Turnpike near Melzi Chancellor's (Dowdall's), capable of directing a powerful converging fire on the Federals at Fairview, their only remaining bulwark in front of Chancellorsville, and on Hooker's headquarters, the Chancellor House, as well.

The Hooker-imposed absence of Artillery General Hunt at Banks' Ford was now to be keenly felt. From time to time Hooker had been shifting guns away from the front line into his secondary defense in rear of Bullock's, and even as far back as United States Mine Ford, until forty guns remained at Fairview, giving the Confederates a 5-4 advantage. The disparity was further emphasized by the fact that the Federal artillery at Fairview could not place its shells directly in front of its own infantry, but only on the enemy at a distance, which imposed on the foot soldiers almost the full responsibility of repelling attacks, without benefit of artillery support.

The heavily wooded character of the terrain and the aggressive attitude of the Confederates led to piecemeal attacks, lacking central direction and with varying success. Liaison between organizations was poor and units repeatedly advanced without support on either flank, frequently without even the knowledge that the troops to their right or left were in motion or even present.

THE FIGHTING BECOMES GENERAL

By 7 A.M. the fighting along the Turnpike had become general and everybody in the vicinity began to get in the act. Two Confederate brigades, concentrating on the Federal center near the pike, hit a regiment composed almost wholly of recruits, on the extreme right of Slocum's line, and broke through with a whoop and a rush, driving the bewildered and inexperienced outfit to the rear. This first break in the line caused a gap that exposed the flank of Berry's division. One brigade of that division quickly lost an entire regiment, which retreated beyond Chancellorsville, and when stopped could only muster 100 men. The pressure on Berry became so heavy that he dispatched a staff officer to Hooker's headquarters to inquire whether he should try to hold. Berry then crossed the Turnpike to confer with his brigade commander in that sector. Recrossing to his division command post, he was killed on the road by a Confederate sharpshooter posted in a nearby tree, the first division commander of either army to lose his life in this battle.

During the early morning hours the infighting waxed fast and furious on the mile or so of front covered by the advanced portion of the Federal line. The determined Confederates under Stuart's urging attacked repeatedly, with varying success. Much of the fighting was at close quarters. Berry's troops, taking the brunt of it, after a time began to yield ground.

As the Confederate pressure directed on Berry's division mounted in fury, portions of the line commenced to crumble. The disintegration was hastened by the somewhat less than courageous action of Brig. General Joseph W. Revere, a descendant of the Revolutionary hero, who commanded the Second Brigade of Berry's division. When Berry was killed, Revere mistakenly assumed that he was the senior brigadier and therefore in command of his sector.

Taking advantage of what he considered his prerogative, and concluding that it was too hot a spot for the comfort of his brigade of all New York regiments, Revere led the entire outfit to the rear with disastrous effect on the brigades which remained. This embarrassed the fighting men of the Excelsior Brigade, formerly commanded by Sickles, who were justly proud of their reputation, and wholly unaccustomed to what they rightly regarded as action approaching cowardice on the part of their brigade commander. Sickles was on another part of the field when this occurred, but when he learned of it, he flew into a towering rage at the subordinate who had acted contrary to his own orders, summarily removed Revere from command, and relegated him to the limbo of temporarily inactive generals.

If Hooker's mind had not been so preoccupied with defensive considerations, he might have given thought to the actual situation that existed at daylight, May 3. The fact was that Stuart's wing was in an extremely ticklish position. His front and right flank were in danger of attack from 25,000 men of Sickles' and Slocum's corps but his left flank was potentially even more vulnerable. The 30,000 men comprising the two corps of Meade and Reynolds, in effect a reserve line but available for an attack, could easily have been moved a short distance to the right and thrown powerfully against Stuart's left flank while he was engaged with Sickles and Slocum's troops at Hazel Grove and Fairview.

It cannot be doubted that Stuart could have been overrun and possibly decimated in a two-pronged attack, unleashed by the simple expedient of an encouraging and eagerly awaited order to the disappointed Federal corps commanders: "Gentlemen, you may attack." Instead of which, the veteran troops of the First and Fifth Corps, all hardy fighters, remained virtually idle in a position of readiness, while Sickles and Slocum and Hancock's division of Couch's corps were allowed to fight the battle with the immediate odds in favor of the Confederates, who profited by the virtual guarantee of noninterference from Hooker's strong and unused reserve.

While the battle raged on the Federal right, Anderson's Confederate Division was assaulting the Federal center and McLaws its left, where Hancock's division of the Second Corps and part of Slocum's Twelfth were covering the two parallel roads leading east toward Fredericksburg. Soon Stuart's continuous hammering and the defection of several Federal regiments on the right of Berry's division, which peeled off, one after the other, as their respective flanks were turned, endangered the entire Federal right.

Fortunately French's division of the Second Corps was thrown in at the psychological moment to save Hooker's right from caving in. French drove the Confederates back, only to be in turn outflanked on his right. Further support from other troops, however, redressed the balance and the danger to the all-important Bullock's Farm strongpoint was temporarily averted.

The Chancellor House had already taken considerable punishment from the tireless Confederate artillery, the continual roar of guns and rattle of musketry making it impossible to carry out any kind of staff operations at army headquarters. Hooker himself doesn't seem to have made the slightest effort to direct the actions of his various corps or even to coordinate their actions. There is no evidence that he issued any combat orders beyond answering inquires with the inadequate reply that the units in question were to "retire when out of ammunition." There was no attempt to replenish ammunition, at least so far as Hooker personally was concerned, and seemingly no real interest in the subject. Nor is there any evidence that the army commander made any move to visit any part of the convulsive battlefield during the desperate fighting on the right flank. Had General Hunt been on hand, it is safe to say that the resupply of the guns would have been given intelligent direction, but as it was, the corps of both Sickles and Slocum soon exhausted their ammunition and had no choice but to displace to the rear behind the support line, giving up Fairview in the process.

At 9 o'clock Hooker stood on the porch of the Chancellor House, with worried face, leaning against a pillar and with ears cocked in the hope of hearing Sedgwick's guns from the direction of Fredericksburg. He had ordered Sedgwick the evening before to come in on Lee's rear at Chancellorsville, the instructions being to arrive at daylight. There was of course no sign of Sedgwick, and it was now more than three hours past the deadline, which in itself should have been enough to convince Hooker that Sedgwick was confronted with something more than an easy march, and that all of Lee's troops consequently were not facing Hooker. That should have been the signal for Hooker to snap out of his lethargy, go over to the offensive, and turn the tables on Lee.

While in this brown study, wondering what to do, a solid shot from a Confederate battery on the Plank Road struck the pillar against which Hooker was leaning, throwing him heavily to the ground. For a few moments he was stunned and unable to move; then he recovered, rose to his feet, and mounted his horse. By that time Sickles' divisions and a part of Slocum's corps had been forced to withdraw, all requests for support having been refused, leaving only Geary's division of the Twelfth Corps, Hancock's reduced division of the Second Corps, and a battery of guns between the semi-disabled Hooker and Lee's army. Geary's division was slowly being turned and disaster loomed.

When Hooker was knocked senseless for a few moments, his second-in-command, General Couch, whose Second Corps was nearby, was told that Hooker had been killed, which if true would automatically place him in command of the army. Dismounting quickly, Couch rushed to the Chancellor House, saw the shattered pillar, but couldn't find Hooker. Speculating on what steps he would take to restore the morale of the army and the fortunes of the battle, he suddenly came upon Hooker and members of his staff, all mounted and apparently in good shape. But that was the last Couch saw of the commanding general anywhere near the front. Although Hooker moved to the rear to relax in a more secure climate, he neglected to communicate with Couch or offer any advice on the further movements or actions of the divisions still under fire and in contact with the enemy. Couch was left to his own devices to salvage what he could at this critical stage, just as Sickles was abandoned to his fate at Hazel Grove the evening before.

Like Sickles, Couch was a fighting general. He addressed himself courageously to the task of preventing a complete disaster to the Federal forces. Even at that eleventh hour, he felt that the day could be saved. Several dozen guns, rushed into position to the right of the Chancellor House, now burning furiously from the fire caused by Confederate shells, could in his opinion drive from their lodgment the Confederates pressing Geary's flank and then neutralize the thirty deadly guns that were pounding the Federal line from Fairview, not 600 yards away. Couch had already had one horse killed under him as he moved from point to point in his strenuous efforts to keep intact the hard-pressed troops of Geary and Hancock and to bring additional guns and men to their support. It was love's labor lost, however, because Hooker had made up his mind to abandon the field, according to Couch, or he would not willingly have permitted Sickles' corps and most of Slocum's to withdraw from contact.

While engaged in this task, a staff officer summoned Couch to army headquarters. Hancock was left in command of the field, as Couch followed the messenger, to find Hooker half a mile in rear of Chancellorsville, lying on a cot in a tent at the far side of an open field. Other officers were present, including General Meade, who was still hoping that his corps would be allowed to take part in the battle. As Couch entered the tent, Hooker raised on his side with the remark: "Couch, I turn the command of the army over to you. You will withdraw it and place it in the position designated on this map," pointing to a field sketch.

There was nothing for Couch to do but follow instructions, no matter how strongly he felt about Hooker's lack of courage, for the latter was still the senior. His relinquishment of command was conditional and oral, and could have been countermanded just as easily if Couch had shown the nerve to take matters into his own hands. Hooker was still acting somewhat dazed from the severe bruising he had received, but he appeared to be in full possession of his mental faculties, which was most unfortunate for the army. It would be interesting although futile to speculate on how the Battle of Chancellorsville might have turned out if Couch, Meade, Reynolds, Slocum, Sickles, and some of the division commanders had at this point put their heads together, called in a senior surgeon with guts, and declared Hooker physically incapable of retaining control of the army. That's the way it would probably have turned out in a dramatized version, but as it was, Couch hastened to obey the order, which was to further contract the V-shaped inner line and remain strictly on the defensive. It is, nevertheless, a striking commentary as to the effect of Hooker's intransigence on the strong mind of a superior type of general officer, that after Chancellorsville had passed into history Couch refused to serve further "under such an officer."

HANCOCK AND GEARY

There was little opportunity during the Chancellorsville campaign for Union generals to distinguish themselves by acts of heroism or tactical feats, chiefly because the battle was a Hooker-imposed static one for the Army of the Potomac after gaining contact with Lee's army that is, all except for Sedgwick's corps. And in that case it is not surprising that Sedgwick failed to achieve success in the face of Hooker's confusing orders and less than bold attitude in withholding from one-fifth of his army even a semblance of cooperation from the remaining four-fifths. Hooker had in his army any number of capable generals both as corps and division commanders-Couch, Meade, Slocum, Reynolds, Berry, Hancock, Sykes, Geary, Williams, and others. Virtually all were forced by the army commander's lack of enterprise to do little else than ward off Confederate attacks in a defensive posture after they had reached the end of the line in the wilderness at Chancellorsville.

Winfield Scott Hancock was an outstanding example of a promising combat leader who was allowed no scope to demonstrate his capabilities. Hancock was every inch a soldier—it was in his blood and he loved everything about soldiering, even paperwork. He had an aggressive, enthusiastic, martial temperament; the danger and excitement of battle stirred every fiber of his being. Hancock represented the highest standards of the professional soldier and exemplified the type of general who, if given half a chance by the vainglorious Hooker, could in company with other capable generals have provided for the Army of the Potomac the opportunity that was denied it of fulfilling its destiny on the field of Chancellorsville.

Less than two divisions, commanded by Hancock and Geary, now remained in position to face the concentrated fury of Lee's entire force, which had been united automatically by the successive withdrawals of the Federal corps from Hazel Grove and Fairview. Two of Hancock's brigades had previously been detached, Caldwell's to United States Mine Ford and Meagher's Irish Brigade from the time the army first crossed the Rappahannock. Geary's flank had already been turned, but he still fought tenaciously against heavy odds, although the inevitable result could be foreseen.

Hancock's depleted division fought manfully along Mott's Run, but his fate too was a foregone conclusion. The only uncertainty was how long it would take to finish him off. With the increasingly rapid pace of the Federal disintegration process, Hancock soon found his division virtually the only cohesive Federal unit still fighting. His position quickly became critical. A full Confederate division was centering its attention on Hancock, whose line was under the direct charge of the same Colonel Miles who had earned the admiring comments of his superiors in the fighting of May 2. Assailed from two directions, and to protect the flank of Geary's line which faced south and crossed the Plank Road, Hancock was forced to face the eleven regiments of his division both east and west, with the result that his troops were now fighting back to back, only a few hundred yards separating the two parallel lines.

The conditions were far from healthy. Hancock's horse went down with a bullet in its brain. Couch was slightly wounded, but stayed on the field. Miles was seriously wounded. The Chancellor plain became a veritable inferno of screaming shells and zipping bullets. Geary's division was overrun and forced to retire as best it could to Bullock's. But Hancock's depleted division hung on, buying time at a heavy cost and fighting alone where a few hours earlier three army corps, seven divisions, had fought. Finally the word came down that the First Division could withdraw, and it was none too soon, if there was to remain any semblance of an organization to be withdrawn.

By 10 o'clock the field surrounding the Chancellor House had been vacated by the Federals, all of whom had retired in fairly good order to the north and in rear of the newly constructed entrenchments centering on Bullock's. The dazed and bone-weary but exultant Confederates moved in and took possession, but they were so nearly exhausted by their efforts of the past few days that little or no attempt was made to effect the capture of enemy guns or men.

Perhaps the victors suspected a trap, for the Federal units had retired in what appeared to be a well-disciplined movement on the whole, even if it was in successive fragments; or else the Confederates were too tired to care.

But when General Lee, sometime after ten, rode up to the ruined and still fiercely burning house that had been Hooker's headquarters, his weary, powder-blackened men suddenly awoke to a realization of the magnitude of their triumph and began to cheer their commanding general with unrestrained enthusiasm.

Gradually the firing died down and a weird sort of spontaneous armed truce took the place of the bitter fighting that had marked the early hours of what under more peaceful conditions would have been a beautiful May Sunday morning. The human body can take a lot of punishment, but there comes a time when nervous energy has been sapped and a period of recuperation is necessary. That stage had been reached and passed by both armies, save for the 30,000 men of the fresh First and Fifth Federal Corps, whose hands were tied by a nonfunctioning army commander who simply let nature take its course without lifting a finger to help shape the course, and without delegating his responsibility to others who were both competent and willing.

Cessation of the actual fighting was followed by an uneasy and, of course, unacknowledged truce, during which both armies turned their attention to straightening out their lines, reassembling units within their own divisions, attending to such wounded as could be reached, and generally restoring internal order of a sort. Roaring flames were now threatening large numbers of men who had become lost in the forest or wounded in the fierce ebb and flow of the action below Chancellorsville.

The heavy shelling of the morning had set fire to many wooded areas where the dry leaves, abatis, and dead wood of the forest provided ideal fuel for the licking flames. Many of the wounded, who would otherwise have been saved either by friendly troops or as prisoners, could not be reached and were left to be consumed alive by the flames. By common consent of those who went over the battlefield after the carnage was ended, the charred bodies—many of which were found clinging close to what they evidently hoped would be sheltering trees, others with supplicating hands outstretched until a merciful death came to their relief—bore mute witness to the frightful fate which overtook literally hundreds of the wounded.

THE SCENE SHIFTS TO FREDERICKSBURG

It will be recalled that Hooker's Saturday evening order to Sedgwick, in command of his own Sixth Corps and Gibbon's division of the Second Corps at Fredericksburg, caused Sedgwick to believe that Lee was retreating on Gordonsville, with Sickles harrying' his trains, and that all Sedgwick had to do was to march the intervening ten miles to Chancellorsville, brushing Early aside in passing.

Lowe's balloons had reported withdrawals by the Confederates manning the heights west of Fredericksburg. The prospective mission appeared to be a relatively easy one, at least in its initial stages. What would happen when Sedgwick had completed his march was left up in the air. Without being too specific, Hooker had given Sedgwick the impression that at daybreak, May 3, he was expected to attack Lee's rear while Hooker assaulted him in front.

The Sixth Corps, already across the river before receipt of Hooker's order, moved north at midnight toward Fredericksburg, while Gibbon's division awaited the laying of his bridge before crossing at Falmouth. Early's skirmishers held up the advance with fire, and it was daylight before Sedgwick could occupy Fredericksburg and prepare to attack Marye's Heights, where Early's reinforced division was strongly intrenched, although spread thinly along the row of hills to the Howison House, where his right was anchored.

Once again Hooker's plan had miscarried, due mostly to his own shortsightedness, lack of imagination and tactical ingenuity, and almost complete absence of logistical foresight. It was nothing short of stupid to predicate the action of his main army on such a thin reed of probability as Sedgwick's arrival at Chancellorsville by daylight, and it was almost criminal for Hooker to hold 86,000 men idle in a defensive posture while expecting 23,000 to carry the major burden of the attack.

Events on the Chancellorsville front on Sunday morning apparently had no effect in causing Hooker to make the slightest revision in his estimate of the situation, or his appraisal of the relative combat capabilities of the two forces at either end of the corridor. His sole thought, if indeed he did any thinking after being stunned by the concussion, seemed to be to pull into an even smaller shell and wait supinely for help to come to him from down Fredericksburg way.

CHAPTER 26

Chancellorsville III: Fredericksburg and Salem Church

MAJOR General John Sedgwick, "Uncle John" to the men of the Sixth Corps, Army of the Potomac, with which his name is indelibly linked, was a favorite in the army. Idolized by his own command, despite the rigid discipline which he enforced, he had a jovial smile and was looked upon as a father always zealous in the interest of his children. He was not a brilliant leader, being somewhat slow on the uptake, but his common sense was proverbial, and, although modest and unobtrusive, he possessed an iron will and soldierly courage; when committed to battle he always seemed to grow in stature and mental capacity.

The Sixth Corps was the largest in the army by several thousand men, numbering 23,667 "present for duty equipped," of which 5 percent were officers, according to the official strength returns for April 30, 1863. Hooker had 404 guns in the Chancellorsville campaign, 54 of them assigned to Sedgwick. According to Livermore, 93 percent of the men reported as present were, for the army as a whole, considered as battle effectives, which would give the Sixth Corps in round figures 22,000 men. Including Gibbon's division of approximately 4,500, Sedgwick commanded a force of over 26,000 men to which were opposed the 10,000 of classmate Early's reinforced division on the heights west of Fredericksburg.

Although the topography of the area in the immediate vicinity of Fredericksburg was new to Sedgwick, it was familiar ground to the three divisions of the Sixth Corps, still under the command of Brigadier Generals W. T. H. Brooks, Albion P. Howe, and Major General John Newton, and to Colonel Hiram Burnham, now commanding the Light

Division, which had recently been detached from its partly divisional status and given an independent role as a separate division of the corps.

At the first Battle of Fredericksburg, December 13, 1862, the Sixth Corps, under the command of Major General William F. Smith as part of Franklin's Left Grand Division, crossed the Rappahannock below Fredericksburg and deployed on the plain in company with Franklin's other corps. But Burnside's incompetence and Franklin's inability to use his own discretion resulted in almost complete inactivity by the Sixth Corps, disposed along the Richmond road, while Reynold's First Corps did all the fighting on that portion of the battlefield.

When the Chancellorsville Campaign opened in late April, the Sixth, First, and Third Corps, under Sedgwick (as both corps and wing commander), Reynolds, and Sickles respectively, were secretly moved from their camps above Falmouth to crossing positions in rear of Stafford Heights, below the town of Fredericksburg. Sickles, held in reserve, was soon ordered to Chancellorsville, where Hooker was massing the main body of the army after the successful flank march of the Fifth, Eleventh, and Twelfth Corps.

Shortly before daylight on Tuesday, April 28, Brooks' division at Deep Run and Wadsworth's (of Reynolds' corps) a mile below at Pollock's Mill, crossed the Rappahannock in boats and established bridgeheads, while the remaining divisions of the two corps were held in readiness to cross to the other side the following day. Some skirmishing occurred during the morning as five bridges were laid, three at Franklin's Crossing and two below, but the better part of the time of the Confederates was devoted to entrenching, with an occasional burst of artillery fire thrown in Reynolds' direction at the southern end of the plain.

Barksdale's Brigade of McLaws' Division, later supported by Hay's Brigade with the rest of Early's Division in reserve, held the Confederate line from the Rappahannock, across from Falmouth, to the Howison House, a distance of about two miles, on the morning of Saturday, May 2. By that time Lee's army, less Early and Barksdale, had left for Chancellorsville, the intervening days being spent by Sedgwick in making demonstrations and crossing the rest of his two corps, reduced to one corps when Hooker pulled Reynolds out during the night of May 1–2.

BUTTERFIELD'S ROLE

The understanding sympathy of those who have served as chiefs of staff goes out to Major General Dan Butterfield, Hooker's chief, who was forced to spend almost his entire time during the campaign at Falmouth in charge of what in later wars would be called the rear echelon of the army command post. Hooker's judgment may be open to question in relegating the general who occupied the exalted position of army chief of staff to a spot where his chief task was to coordinate the operations of the widely separated wings of the army. Not that the function was not a vital one, but in this case Hooker was holding all the strings of planning and execution tightly in his own hands. For such a restricted role, without discretionary authority, an intelligent, experienced staff officer of lesser rank could have done all that Butterfield was permitted to do. The chief of staff could have rendered more effective service, even though limited to coordination, at Chancellorsville, where in effect after May 1, when the battle was joined, Hooker's army functioned virtually without a real head.

One has only to read in the Official Records the contents of the vast number of telegraphic messages sent every few minutes by Butterfield to Hooker throughout Sunday, May 3, to be convinced that the chief of staff was making every effort to keep the commanding general informed. His reports were so complete and clearly expressed that developments that day on the Fredericksburg-Salem Church front are portrayed like an unrolled, continuous panorama. Butterfield painted the picture in so businesslike a manner that Hooker's failure to carry out his announced purpose of attacking Lee from Chancellorsville in support of Sedgwick's advance cannot be attributed to lack of intelligence; on the contrary, it only serves to compound the failure in the eyes of history.

More perceptive than his commander in his awareness that President Lincoln would be anxiously awaiting word of what was transpiring along the Rappahannock, Butterfield took it upon himself to send Lincoln a telegram at 8:50 A.M. Sunday morning, couched in diplomatic language that must have started the President burning with impatient curiosity. It was the first word Lincoln had received. The message read: "Though not directed or specially authorized to do so by General Hooker, I think it not improper that I should advise you that a battle is in progress."

In striking contrast, a telegram from Hooker's headquarters to Butterfield four hours later, at 12:45 P.M., told of Hooker's reluctance to even intimate the dire straits of the army to the President:

I think we have had the most terrible battle ever witnessed on earth. I think our victory will be certain, but the General told me he would say nothing just yet to Washington, except that he is doing well. In an hour or two the matter will be a fixed fact. I believe the enemy is in flight now, but we are not sure.

A fair comment on that message—considering what had happened Saturday night and Sunday morning at Chancellorsville-Jackson's flank attack, the Federal withdrawal from Hazel Grove and Fairview, the disabling of Hooker, the contraction of the army's defense line, and the occupation of the Chancellor clearing by Lee's forces—would be: who is kidding whom? The only element of consistency in the message was Hooker's patent attempt to keep alive in Sedgwick's mind the fiction that he was going to attack simultaneously with Sedgwick, to pin Lee between them. To give any other impression to Sedgwick might be to cool his enthusiasm for the prescribed offensive.

Butterfield's anxiety to see some of the action away from his desk was revealed in the telegram he sent Hooker expressing regret that the general was "even slightly wounded" and inquiring somewhat pathetically if he could not be permitted to join Sedgwick, since it was now impossible for him to join Hooker even had the authority been granted. The message closed with the almost despairing cry: "while I do not know who would replace me here, I am heartsick at not being permitted to be on the actual field, to share the fate and fortunes of this army and my general."

Still thinking of Lincoln and determined that he would do his best to make up for Hooker's taciturnity, Butterfield again wired the President at 1:30 P.M.:

From all reports yet collected, the battle has been most fierce and terrible. Loss heavy on both sides. General Hooker slightly, but not severely, wounded. He has preferred thus far that nothing should be reported, and does not know of this, but I cannot refrain from saying this much to you. You may expect his dispatch in a few hours, which will give the result.

In the meantime, Hooker apparently reached the belated conclusion that it might be advisable to let the President in on the progress of the battle, so he drafted a telegram and sent it by orderly to United States Mine Ford, where it was put on the wire and reached Lincoln at 4 P.M.

We have had a desperate fight yesterday and today, which has resulted in no success to us, having lost a position of two lines which had been selected for our defense. We may have another turn at it this P.M. I do not despair of success. If Sedgwick could have gotten up, there could have been but one result.

As it is impossible for me to know the exact position of Sedgwick as regards his ability to advance and take part in the engagement, I cannot tell when it will end. We will endeavor to do our best. My troops are in good spirits. We have fought desperately today.

No general ever commanded a more devoted army.

Inferentially at least it was all Sedgwick's fault, and the remark does Hooker no credit. Indeed it suggests the small boy out walking with his parents who runs ahead half a block in play, stumbles, falls, and calls back to mother and father in a shrill, reproachful voice: "Now see what you made me do!"

By 4:30 P.M. Lincoln's impatience for further news overcame his desire not to burden field headquarters in the midst of the battle as he telegraphed Butterfield: "Where is General Hooker? Where is Sedgwick? Where is Stoneman?"

CONFUSING ORDERS FROM HOOKER

Hooker's mental gyrations and strategic ineffectiveness, from the time Lee seized the initiative and commenced to outmaneuver and outfight him, are clearly portrayed in his series of telegraphic orders to Sedgwick from morning to night on Saturday, May 2. The instructions to his corps on the field at Chancellorsville were in many cases oral and fragmentary, and therefore lacking substance for a study in continuity, but those to Sedgwick, ten miles away, were perforce reduced to writing.

Because Lee had been so aggressive and had pressed his attacks on Hooker from three sides with such marked success, the latter felt sure that practically the entire Confederate army was in contact with him. Therefore, he assumed Sedgwick must be faced at Fredericksburg with merely nominal opposition, which seemed to present him with a favorable opportunity to deliver a strong blow against Lee's rear and thus achieve one of the original objectives of the pincers movement, even though belated.

Acting upon that strategic conception, Hooker had dispatched the first of his series of messages to Sedgwick, through Chief of Staff Butterfield, at 9:30 A.M., Saturday, May 2. The gist of the order was for the Sixth Corps "to attack the enemy on his front if an opportunity presents itself with a reasonable expectation of success." At that time, of course, Jackson was engaged in marching around Hooker's flank and the wishful thinking Federal commander cherished the illusion that Lee was retreating.

Hooker probably received a message shortly thereafter which advised that the enemy remained strong on Sedgwick's front, for at 9:45 A.M. he sent word to Sedgwick: "You are all right. You have but Ewell's (Early's) Division in your front; balance all up here (Chancellorsville)." By afternoon the bemused Hooker had fully convinced himself that his earlier estimate as to Lee's withdrawal was correct, so he sent off a priceless message to Sedgwick (just one hour before Jackson charged into his own right flank):

4:10 P.M. May 2: You will cross the river as soon as indications will permit; capture Fredericksburg with everything in it, and vigorously pursue the enemy. We know that the enemy is fleeing, trying to save his trains. Two of Sickles' divisions are among them.

Shortly after that message sped over the wires to Sedgwick the sky fell in on Hooker, who for several hours had no time to think about his left wing. At 7:05 P.M., however, Sedgwick was puzzled to receive the next message: "The Major General commanding directs you to pursue the enemy on the Bowling Green road." What Hooker was thinking about when he dictated that order is anybody's guess. Presumably he pictured Sedgwick as having already completed his 4:10 P.M. mission, but Hooker was certainly shooting arrows into the air and developing fantasies of his own, because Sedgwick would naturally have to pursue his enemy in the direction the Confederates would choose to withdraw, if any, and it didn't have to be in a southerly direction by the Bowling Green Road.

However, Sedgwick tried to follow instructions, as the following message which he sent to Hooker via Butterfield at 8 P.M. indicated:

General Brooks has taken the. Bowling Green road, in front of him; is still skirmishing, and will advance as long as he can see, and will then take position for the night. Newton is moving in the direction of Hamilton's Crossing, and at daylight the entire corps will be in motion.

Sedgwick was still trying to make sense of Hooker's wishes insofar as they could be interpreted from his disjointed and peremptory combat orders when the crowning message, dispatched at 9 P.M. from Hooker's headquarters reached him at 11 P.M. below Fredericksburg:

The major-general commanding directs that General Sedgwick cross the Rappahannock at Fredericksburg on receipt of this order, and at once take up his line of march on the Chancellorsville road until you [sic] connect with us, and he will attack and destroy any force he may fall in with on the road. He will leave all his trains behind, except the pack-train of small ammunition, and march to be in our vicinity at daylight. He will probably fall on the rear of the forces commanded by General Lee, and between us we will use him up. Send word to General Gibbon to take possession of Fredericksburg. Be sure not to fail.

Sedgwick was of course already across the Rappahannock with his whole corps and engaged in developing the Confederate position, when the last message was received. But it was now clear that, traveling light, Hooker wanted him to take Fredericksburg, brush aside any Confederates in his path, and proceed with all dispatch to Chancellorsville by the most direct route, which was certainly not the Bowling Green Road leading to Richmond. "Uncle John" therefore made plans accordingly, which of course took some time in the darkness, involving as it did the issuance of new orders to his three division commanders and the commanding officer of the Light Division.

THE SECOND BATTLE OF FREDERICKSBURG

Taking his cue from Hooker, Butterfield kept needling Sedgwick to lose not a minute's time in getting the show on the road, the final attempt being made exactly at midnight in a message delivered to Sedgwick in person by one of Hooker's aides who had come down to Fredericksburg from United States Mine Ford to give Butterfield a more complete fill-in on the Chancellorsville situation than was possible by telegraph.

From the statement brought by General Hooker's aide, it seems to be of vital importance that you should fall upon Lee's rear with crushing force. He will explain all to you. Give your advance to one who will do all that the urgency of the case requires.

Both Hooker and Butterfield were under the misapprehension that Early's Confederate Division had been greatly reduced, a presumption that was undoubtedly built up by the frequent messages, from the signal stations and Professor Lowe's balloons opposite Fredericksburg and at Banks' Ford, reporting the observed movements of Confederate units and trains in rear of their position on the heights west of Fredericksburg. Present day veterans of recent wars will recall similar fallacies put out as facts by higher head-quarters whose personnel, going by the book or in pursuance of a purpose unknown to the troops on the field, were prone to announce solemnly that the enemy had withdrawn, when in fact nothing of the sort had happened, as the troops being shot at by the ephemeral enemy knew only too well.

BUTTERFIELD KEEPS HOOKER INFORMED

At army headquarters in Falmouth Butterfield kept watch on Sedgwick's Sunday morning movements across the river in order to keep his boss at Chancellorsville informed of the progress of the left wing. Acutely conscious of the fact that Hooker at the other end of the battlefield was figuratively biting his finger nails (but doing little else as he awaited the Sixth Corps' anticipated approach to attack Lee's rear), Butterfield started sending dispatches even before daylight, as the reports came in from Sedgwick.

Between 5:30 and 9 A.M., Sunday, May 3, the following messages, sent off to Hooker, gave him a progressive bird's eye view of the fighting in and west of Fredericksburg:

5:45 A.M.: Heavy cannonading in Sedgwick's front for the last twenty minutes, apparently in front of Fredericksburg.

6:08 A.M.: Balloon reports enemy reappearing on heights in front of Sedgwick's crossing. Sedgwick, judging from the sound, is meeting with strong resistance.

6:20 A.M.: Sedgwick reports himself at Sumner's old battleground at 5:30 A.M., hotly engaged, and not sanguine of the result.

6:45 A.M.: Sedgwick's prospects here look unfavorable, from reports. He is not out of Fredericksburg.

7:05 A.M.: Sedgwick still in front of Fredericksburg, as far as I can judge. Trains were running up all night to vicinity of Hamilton's Crossing. It may be that the enemy were reenforced.

8:30 A.M.: Our skirmishers just occupied rebel rifle-pits on Hazel Run. Gibbon moving to right, with prospects of flanking the enemy. Enemy resist desperately.

8:45 A.M.: Sedgwick at 7:40 o'clock reports about making combined assault on their works; Gibbon on right; Newton center; Howe on left. If he fails, will try again.

Impatient at the delay, and apparently feeling that Sedgwick was dragging his heels against unimportant opposition, Hooker at 9:15 A.M. sent him the following message: "You will hurry up your column. The enemy's right flank now rests near the Plank Road at Chancellorsville, all exposed. You will -attack at once." Sedgwick's thoughts have not been recorded, but he doubtless knew that Hooker had at Chancellorsville over twice as many men as Lee could muster, had committed only about half of them in action, and yet persisted in hounding Sedgwick to carry the major burden for the entire army.

Early had shifted his weight to the right when the bulk of Sedgwick's corps had crossed and driven the Confederate skirmishers back into the woods from the Bowling Green Road (Old Richmond Stage Road). Most of his own division was on the ridge below Fredericksburg, with the brigades of Barksdale and Hays holding the two-mile line from Taylor's Hill, at the river, through Marye's Heights, to the Howison House. Marye's Hill, the key position with the stone wall and sunken road at its base, which had proven to be Burnside's nemesis in December, was occupied by only two regiments supported by eight guns, from the Plank Road to Hazel Run.

Jubal Early with one division and a couple of brigades was making a noble effort to outsmart his West Point classmate, John Sedgwick, and succeeding rather well in upsetting the time schedule of still another classmate, Joe Hooker. It would not be surprising if General Lee, with his vast stored-up knowledge of the characters of so many of the prewar West Pointers, had personally advised Stonewall Jackson to leave Early at Fredericksburg on the ground that he probably knew Sedgwick best and could deal with him more effectively for that reason.

Sedgwick's movement by the flank in the direction of Fredericksburg was started soon after midnight May 2–3, Newton's division in the lead, followed by the Light Division arid then Howe's division. Brook's division remained for the time being to protect the bridges at Deep Run and below. The Confederates contested the advance as they slowly fell back, but Sedgwick's column kept advancing and reached Fredericksburg at daylight. With the completion of a bridge opposite the Lacy House, Gibbon's division crossed over and took position on Sedgwick's right about 7 o'clock Sunday morning.

Using the town as a base, Sedgwick launched repeated attacks on the Confederate position to the west. Between 8 and 10 A.M. Newton made the first attempt along Hazel Run and was repulsed. A second assault against Marye's Hill was also stopped cold. Gibbon's division then tried to get around Taylor's Hill to turn the Confederate left, but the heavy artillery fire that played on the canal prevented him from bridging it, and he too had to admit failure.

Then Howe's division tried to turn the hill south of Hazel Run but met with no success. It was becoming rather plain that the Confederates were in strength and determined to keep the heights for themselves, concurrently making something of super-optimists out of both Butterfield and Hooker.

As Lee was to do at Gettysburg eight weeks later, Sedgwick had tried the enemy right and left and found them invulnerable. He now decided to make a direct frontal assault, putting out of his mind no doubt the terrible disaster to Burnside's divisions which resulted from the identical attempt over the same ground at the first Battle of Fredericksburg.

Sedgwick was a cautious and deliberate general both in planning and execution. He had missed the first battle of Fredericksburg in December while convalescing from the serious wounds received at Antietam, but he knew all about what Burnside had done and failed to do, particularly in front of the stone wall at the foot of Marye's Hill. Sedgwick reasoned it all out. He was not going to be rushed into a premature attack, regardless of the continuous pressure from Hooker and Butterfield, until his plan had been perfected and fully explained to his officers and men. His efforts to flank the Confederate position at either end of the line had fizzled, due partly to the fact that Gibbon's attempt to move around Taylor's Hill near the Rappahannock had been slow in getting underway.

This had given the Confederates time to bring up enough guns on that flank to interdict the crossings over the canal, with such effect that Gibbon didn't even try to repair the bridges. A half hour earlier he could have achieved his purpose against negligible opposition, and Sedgwick's later frontal attack might conceivably have been avoided.

Sedgwick's deliberations, which led to the head-on charge against the stone wall and the heights above it, considered three major premises: Hooker's insistence that the Sixth Corps hasten to Chancellorsville by the most direct route; the failure of the attempts to outflank the ridge on right and left, which left only the alternatives of a frontal assault or nothing; and Burnside's ill-fated venture over the same ground in December, which had led to bloody failure and 6,300 casualties. Sedgwick's decision was a bold, calculated risk that laid his reputation as a field general on the line.

Recalling that every one of the six charges made in December had demonstrated the sacrificial courage of the men of Sumner's Right Grand Division, Sedgwick was confident that what they had done his soldiers of the Sixth Corps could certainly do. He reasoned that all previous attempts had failed because the attacking lines had halted and thrown themselves on the ground to load and fire as well as to escape the hail of bullets that hit them from the sunken road. The result, in Sedgwick's thinking, had been to cool their ardor and subject them to far greater punishment than they would have suffered had they kept moving. This time there would be no stopping to fire and reload; but to make doubly certain he issued orders that the assault echelon should advance over the open field at the double with unloaded rifles, bayonets fixed, to give the enemy cold steel. And it worked!

Advancing in two columns, with the strength of a reinforced division, under Newton's command, and with Colonel Burnham of the Light Division in charge of the assault echelon, the Federals advanced with fixed bayonets on and alongside the Plank Road without stopping to load and fire their pieces. As in December, they were assailed by heavy artillery fire of grape and canister, which failed to stop them, and when within twenty-five yards of the stone wall, history repeated itself as a sheet of flame from the sunken road blasted their faces in a murderous fire of musketry. This time, however, the momentum of the Federals was so great that they swept over the wall, engaged the surprised Confederates in violent but short-lived hand-to-hand combat, and, still without stopping to load and fire, rushed up Marye's Hill and captured the crest.

It was all over in fifteen minutes from the time the charge started. The routed Confederates took to their heels in panic, throwing away guns, pistols, knapsacks—anything that might impede their flight. As the victorious Federals reached the top of Marye's Hill, it was a mighty pleasant sight, although one to which they were unaccustomed, to look across the broad plateau to the west and feast their eyes on the large number of fleeing Confederates, riderless horses, and artillery and wagon trains careening at a mad gallop across the fields to safety.

While Newton was capturing Marye's Hill, Howe's division carried the heights below the town, putting the entire ridge in Federal hands, and driving Early's troops in a rapid retreat by the Telegraph Road to the south. The cost to Sedgwick's men was a heavy one, but the price was ridiculously cheap when compared with the previous fruitless attempt over the same ground in December.

Then Burnside lost 6,300 men and accomplished nothing. This time Sedgwick, with a loss of only 1,500 killed and wounded, had broken the enemy resistance, captured a thousand prisoners, a handful of battle flags, and fifteen pieces of artillery (six of which were recovered when Early returned to Fredericksburg), and cleared the way for his advance on Chancellorsville. The defending Confederates had been split right down the middle, so that the divided segments were forced to escape in two directions. The opportunity for use of a cavalry regiment or two, to exploit the success, was one that the horse cavalry used to dream about, but there was no Federal cavalry at hand to make history.

THE SIGNIFICANCE OF BANKS' FORD

Banks' Ford on the Rappahannock River, about halfway between Falmouth and United States Mine Ford, the latter Hooker's lifeline for the movement of his army in both directions, was a valuable pawn in the hands of either Lee or Hooker. Both realized its importance and both utilized its facilities during the campaign.

Hooker's strategy had contemplated the uncovering of United States Mine Ford and Banks' Ford in succession, as his right wing swung around Lee's left on April 28–30 and came up on his rear at Chancellorsville. The first phase concluded, Meade's Fifth Corps was proceeding along the River Road to seal off Banks' Ford, the occupation of which would have immeasurably shortened the communications between Hooker's two wings, when Hooker inexplicably pulled the advancing divisions back in a foolish and unnecessary shift from the offensive to the defensive, even though there was at that time no enemy to defend against except Anderson's Division and a handful of Stuart's cavalrymen.

The following day, May 1, Hooker had sent his Chief of Artillery, General Hunt, to take charge of the approaches to Banks' Ford on the left or north bank, to prevent the Confederates from crossing at that point in case they should take it into their heads to do so. Hunt reported that

Engineer General Benham's 600 men were insufficient for the purpose, and requested that a full division be sent. The result was that twenty-two guns of the horse artillery and two batteries of Napoleons were ordered up from Sedgwick's wing, while Gibbon was concurrently instructed to detach one of his brigades from Falmouth to reenforce Benham.

Anderson's Confederate Division, after withdrawing from Chancellorsville on the approach of Hooker's three corps on April 30, had fallen back to the junction of Mine Road and Plank Road, where it spent the rest of the day digging entrenchments to strengthen the line from Banks' Ford on the right to the Plank Road. But when Jackson came up from Fredericksburg on the morning of May 1, he pulled Anderson off that job in order to advance with Jackson's Corps and McLaws' Division against Hooker's Chancellorsville hideout in the Wilderness. Upon Lee's arrival from Fredericksburg later in the day, however, he wisely disapproved of Jackson's decision to give up the position at Banks' Ford and directed Wilcox's Brigade of Anderson's Division to return and reoccupy the rifle pits covering the ford on the south side of the river. Whether Lee was then aware of the fact that Reynolds' corps was marching up from Fredericksburg is not known. If so it undoubtedly influenced his decision. The Federals thought that was the reason when Hunt reported the reoccupation at 6:45 P.M. Whether Lee was smart or just lucky in acting when he did, the fact is that Reynolds would have crossed at Banks' Ford if the bridge had been laid and interesting tactical developments would certainly have followed.

Two pontoon bridges had been delivered at Banks' Ford by Benham's engineers May 1, but not laid. It was not until the afternoon of Sunday, May 3 that one of them was put down, between three and 4 o'clock, after Wilcox had left the position to reenforce Early's troops against Sedgwick's advance from Fredericksburg. It was also about that time that Hooker ordered the second bridge to be transferred to United States Mine Ford, providing three bridges at that place. Hooker was taking no chances on his own security and evidently getting ready, even then, to retreat from Chancellorsville. Apparently he was willing to weaken Sedgwick's auxiliary equipment even further than he had already, but Benham used his head, having already calculated the width of the river at both fords, and only sent half the second bridge to Hooker. It was a good thing that he did, as will be seen later.

LEE MAKES ANOTHER BOLD DECISION

Shortly after 12 noon General Lee, resting in the vicinity of the Chancellor House as his hard-fighting Confederates reshuffled themselves after the tough but successful battle which gave them possession of all the important terrain features of the battlefield, was handed a bit of bad news. Hooker's left wing had captured Fredericksburg and driven Early's Confederates from their position on the heights where Longstreet's Corps had brought Burnside to disaster in December!

There was no time to savor the fruits of victory. Lee must immediately turn to meet the new threat from the east. But by this time he had taken the full measure of Joe Hooker and found him sadly wanting in enterprise. Lee did not hesitate. He would again take a calculated risk, divide his force once more in the face of the enemy, leave a holding force to occupy Hooker's attention and move with McLaws' Division and one of Anderson's brigades to oppose Sedgwick. Jackson's Corps, under Stuart, would remain in contact at Chancellorsville, while Lee in person would march with McLaws, back over the ground they had covered in their advance May 1, to engage Sedgwick as soon as the two forces should meet. Instead of attacking Lee's rear, as Hooker had planned, Sedgwick would be confronted, in a meeting engagement on even terms, by the confident general who had just proven his superiority over Hooker's much larger force, and in the process taken all the fight out of its commander.

Jackson's Corps, which had been fighting ever since five-thirty the previous evening, after its twelve-mile march through the Wilderness, and had enjoyed very little rest during the night, was much reduced in strength by casualties and close to exhaustion by fatigue, hunger, and thirst. Withal it was preparing to renew the battle by moving on Hooker's last defense line with the object of forcing it back across the river.

General Colston, commanding one of Jackson's divisions, was designated to lead the attack. At 1 o'clock he was summoned to report to Lee who was standing in a small tent beside the road. In Colston's words:

In low, quiet tones he said to me: General, I wish you to advance with your division on the United States Ford road. I expect you will meet with resistance before you come to the bend of the road. I do not want you to attack the enemy's positions, but only to feel them. Send your engineer officer with skirmishers to the front to reconnoitre and report. Don't engage seriously, but keep the enemy in check and prevent him from advancing. Move at once.

Colston adds that at the time he was not a little puzzled and wondered why the army was not to continue the advance and hurl Hooker into the river. He learned the reason later in the day, when the sounds of battle were heard from the direction of Fredericksburg, and it is quite likely that he reflected as well on the ability of his commanding general to keep his own counsel.

Although not exactly planned that way, the Battle of Salem Church was fought on terrain that was made to order for the Confederates, a wooded ridge line running north and south where the Orange Turnpike comes closer to the Rappahannock than at any other point between Chancellorsville and Fredericksburg. Anchored firmly at the river on the left and the Turnpike on the right, the position was a difficult one to overrun frontally, a necessity if Sedgwick were to make any speed in his march on Chancellorsville.

Much of the landscape east of the ridge was open, to afford the defenders a decidedly advantageous field of fire through which the Federals would have to advance on their march from Fredericksburg. It was fine maneuver country, and a pleasant change from the dense wilderness in the Chancellorsville area.

McLaws' Confederates had the longer distance to travel, approximately five miles from their position southeast of Chancellorsville to Salem Church, but with no opposition to slow them down they reached their objective by 3 o'clock. Sedgwick on the other hand, moving against Wilcox's Confederate Brigade which fought the delaying action, necessarily made slower progress from the Fredericksburg heights, which his corps had captured at mid-day Sunday, May 3, to Salem Church, three to four miles distant.

SEDGWICK ADVANCES

After the fighting of Sunday morning, which resulted in the complete evacuation of Marye's Heights, Sedgwick pulled his divisions together and prepared for the march to Chancellorsville. Gibbon was directed to remain with his reduced division in Fredericksburg to prevent stray Confederate units from crossing to the north bank. Brooks' division, which had not moved from its crossing position at Deep Run, was placed at the head of the column, in extended order by column of brigades, with skirmishers to the front and flank and artillery on the road. Newton's division followed that of Brooks, marching in column along the Orange Plank Road. Howe's division and the Light Division brought up the rear.

Wilcox's Confederate Brigade, which had hastened from Banks' Ford to Early's support at Fredericksburg in the morning, provided the sole resistance as he withdrew slowly before Sedgwick's advancing troops. A section of horse artillery to the right of the Federals greatly hampered their advance by occupying each successive crest, firing as long as possible, and then displacing to the next crest.

Early's Confederate Division, after its defeat on the heights, withdrew along the Telegraph Road to the southwest, but on finding that it was not being pursued, halted after covering about two miles. Remaining in the vicinity until Sedgwick had passed, Early returned on Monday morning, May 4, reoccupied his former position on the heights, and prepared to cut off Sedgwick's possible retreat to Fredericksburg.

By this maneuver the Confederates had again turned the tables on the Federals. Once more Hooker's plan had backfired; instead of pocketing Lee between wings of the Union army, Sedgwick now found himself in a comparable position, with Confederate troops on his front and rear.

THE MEETING ENGAGEMENT

When Sedgwick's leading elements arrived within a mile of Salem Church, about 4 P.M., they were met by a handful of cavalry skirmishers and greeted with solid shot from two rifled guns posted near the church. The open space between was crossed by a small stream where hostile guns, firing steadily as long as their ammunition held out, definitely checked the Federal advance.

Brooks' division, already deployed, pressed forward as soon as the Confederate guns had retired, and after an extended period of brisk fighting drove McLaws' defenders off the ridge. Newton's division, advancing in column on Brooks' right rear, was unable to develop battle formation promptly, whereupon Wilcox's Brigade, counterattacking, came in on Brooks' flank to force him in turn off the crest.

Federal artillery, ably supporting the infantry, checked the counterattack, affording Newton the opportunity to move up to reinforce Brooks. A second time the Federals attacked and again the Confederates were driven back in confusion. By that time the sun had set and darkness put an end to the seesaw battle for the day. The troops on both sides, remaining under arms, thereupon settled down until morning.

Critics of Sedgwick have charged that he was unconscionably and unnecessarily show in all his movements on May 2 and 3 and hence contributed substantially to the loss of the Chancellorsville campaign by the Union army. This amateur analyst doesn't subscribe to that theory in light of the facts. On the contrary, Sedgwick's tactics, considered in context with Hooker's lack of initiative and disjointed orders to him from the other side of the battlefield, were based on sound thinking and careful evaluation of all the factors present. Hooker's demands were unrealistic and can even be called hypocritical, for he assured Sedgwick that he would attack Lee in front as Sedgwick came up on his rear, when in fact he had no intention of doing so. If he had, Lee could not successfully have detached. the divisions of McLaws and Anderson; Sedgwick would have marched on to Chancellorsville unopposed except by Wilcox's retiring Brigade, and Lee would have been caught in a vise between Hooker and Sedgwick, from which even that redoubtable leader could have extricated himself only by superhuman efforts.

As it was, with Hooker content to allow Lee complete freedom of action at both ends of the field, Sedgwick, with a 2 to 1 advantage over Early, accomplished the first half of his mission almost as soon as it was possible, even though hours later than Hooker's logistical, impracticable table of time-and-space factors had stipulated. By midafternoon, however, when he reached Salem Church, the situation was entirely different than he had been led by Hooker to believe.

Lee was there, halfway between Chancellorsville and Fredericksburg, facing him with perhaps 6,000 men, increased to 10,000 a few hours later when Anderson came up; and Early stood at his rear with another 8,000 to 9,000, his original strength less losses incurred in the Sunday morning battle at Fredericksburg. The opposing forces at Salem Church could therefore be considered approximately equal, but with the odds in Lee's favor because Sedgwick was now faced with a fight in two directions.

Given the advance knowledge that Hooker intended that Sedgwick should be left to fight Lee without help from the main army, and that McLaws was marching east to meet him, there is little doubt that Sedgwick would have adopted for the march a formation of two divisions abreast and one in reserve, even though that would probably have lost another hour. Nevertheless, he could then have developed in sufficient strength to launch a coordinated assault against McLaws with a 2 to 1 superiority, with every chance of success. Instead of which his three divisions, strung out in column, were perforce thrown into the attack piecemeal and inconclusively.

It was no wonder the greatly disturbed Sedgwick slept fitfully the night of May 3. With little knowledge of what Hooker had been doing or intended, he knew he was behind schedule, that the Confederates had blocked him, and, it was rumored, had even reoccupied the heights at his rear. It has been said that every so often during the night he threw off his blanket, rose from the damp grass, walked a few paces and listened carefully; then returned, threw himself on the ground and tried vainly to sleep. On the other hand General Lee, who believed that Sedgwick still had two corps at his disposal instead of only one, may safely be said to have slept soundly, as was his custom, to awake refreshed, alert, and ready to finish the task of driving Sedgwick into the river regardless of numbers.

In the course of the afternoon, the Confederates who had remained to guard Banks' Ford were pulled away to join the battle over by the Turnpike, whereupon General Benham quickly laid his bridge. Early the next morning, May 4, the report reached Sedgwick that 15,000 of the enemy, moving from the direction of Richmond, had occupied the heights at Fredericksburg and cut his communications with the town and Gibbon's division. That would be Jubal Early, retracing his steps and resuming his former position, his strength exaggerated approximately 100 percent.

SEDGWICK BOXED IN

Sedgwick's official report indicates that he anticipated some such eventuality, and in order to protect his rear and prevent the Confederates from cutting him off from Banks' Ford as well, Howe's division, in the rear, early in the morning was formed in line of battle facing east, extended to the left to rest his flank on the river and secure the ford. Thus Sedgwick repeated Hancock's tactics of the previous day at Chancellorsville and had his divisions facing in two directions against the aggressive Confederate brigades, a type of maneuver that is not considered in the best military families to be overly conducive to high morale on the part of the participants. Nevertheless, General Howe's men performed their task in splendid fashion, repelling an effort by the Confederates to achieve the very result that Sedgwick was guarding against, and in their success taking 200 prisoners and a battle flag.

During the night, General Gouverneur G. Warren, of Hooker's staff, who had joined Sedgwick at Fredericksburg to observe his advance and guide the column, returned to army headquarters by way of Banks' Ford and United States Mine Ford and reported the day's action in person to the army commander. Shortly after midnight he was directed to send a dispatch to Sedgwick, the significance of which has to be read in context to be appreciated:

> *I find everything snug here. We contracted the line a little, and repulsed the last assault with ease. General Hooker wishes them to attack him tomorrow, if they will. He does not desire you to attack again in force unless he attacks him at the same time. He says you are too far away for him to direct. Look well to the safety of your corps, and keep up communication with General Benham, at Banks' Ford and Fredericksburg. You can go to either place, if you think best.*
>
> *To cross at Banks' Ford would bring you in supporting distance of the main body, and would be better than falling back to Fredericksburg.*

The above message, delayed in transmission, did not reach Sedgwick till late in the forenoon of May 4, by which time he was boxed in, could not have reached Fredericksburg if he had wanted to, and was in no shape to retire safely by Banks' Ford, either. His east flank rested on the river about halfway between Banks' Ford and Fredericksburg; the line extended south across the Turnpike, then west at right angles for two miles, where it again turned north across the road and anchored part way to the river. Hence his west flank rested on no natural obstacle. The three-sided line, covering a distance of at least five miles, could not readily be contracted without inviting attack while moving into a new position.

Sedgwick's decision was to stand fast and await attack, possibly from three directions; then, after dark, to fall back on Banks' Ford. In view of Hooker's above quoted order he had little choice, and by this time had no doubt come to the same conclusion as the corps commanders with Hooker, that the general was a defeated man, devoid of initiative, incapable of attacking, and thinking only of safety and any excuse to get his army away from it all at the earliest opportunity. Hooker's unwarranted superiority complex was likewise revealed in that sentence which implied that because Sedgwick was too far away for Hooker to lead him by the hand and personally guide his actions, the only course open to Sedgwick was to retreat. A strange man, Joe Hooker, who seemingly had no confidence in the abilities of anyone but himself, and even that satisfaction had been denied him as a result of his disgraceful timidity in this campaign.

Lee's discovery that the Union army had materially strengthened its fortifications on the new defense line convinced him that it would be folly to attack Hooker at Chancellorsville with only a part of his force, while engaged with the remainder at Salem Church. His revised strategy was to detach Anderson's three remaining brigades from Stuart, leaving only Jackson's three reduced divisions to contain Hooker; bring Anderson to strengthen McLaws and Early on the perimeter of Sedgwick's position; and drive the latter out.

Lee was satisfied by this time that Hooker had no intention of coming to Sedgwick's aid by moving troops over the River Road and thence down the Mine Road to connect up with Sedgwick between the river and the Turnpike.

That possibility had been on his mind the preceding afternoon when he had sent McLaws from Chancellorsville to Salem Church and shifted Anderson, less the brigade with McLaws, to take position astride the River Road opposite Hooker's left flank, for the dual purpose of frightening his opponent with the possibility that his communications across the Rappahannock were being threatened, and concurrently to guard against a surprise Federal attack on McLaws' left rear.

Lee's Converging Attack

Lee's plan of action for the afternoon of May 4 was for Anderson to move around Sedgwick's left, join Early west of the Fredericksburg heights, form a continuous line and, with McLaws forming the pivot opposite Sedgwick's center, launch a converging attack calculated to drive the Federals into the river.

Although Anderson reached the field about noon, much time was lost in disposing the troops for the attack. It was 6 o'clock before the combined forces of Anderson and Early were ready to push off. The first part of the plan worked beautifully; Sedgwick's troops were forced back across the Turnpike in the direction of the river, but it was growing dark and McLaws failed to see what was transpiring on the right until it was too late to make his contribution to speed the Federal withdrawal.

Howe's division, facing Fredericksburg, with the Light Division on his left, again bore the brunt of the Confederate attack. Strong artillery support enabled the Federals to contest the enemy advance, which came to a halt when a dense river fog settled over the field, making it difficult to distinguish friend from foe. The Confederates had to pay for their impetuous attack, however, losing heavily in killed, wounded, and captured. Among the several hundred Confederates taken prisoner were a number of officers, including one general (allegedly), but the attack served its purpose, for as soon as it was dark the divisions of Newton and Brooks, with the Light Division, were directed to retire rapidly to the river. There they took position in a contracted, protective semicircle on the heights near Banks' Ford and in the rifle pits that had been constructed by the Confederates, while Howe's division was left as rear guard until the others had completed the movement, when it too pulled back and formed on Newton's right.

Never before had Lee ordered a night attack, but this time he did so in the fear that otherwise Sedgwick would construct a new line of fortifications and force the Confederates to fight the battle all over again the next day. It was to Lee imperative that the Federals be driven into or over the river that night, so that he could return to Chancellorsville to continue his interrupted attack to put the final quietus on Hooker. All available artillery was moved forward rapidly with orders to shell Bank's Ford and make it as unhealthy as possible.

Sedgwick during the evening received a telegram from Hooker directing him to hold his position on the south bank till morning. But the order-changing department at army headquarters soon justified its existence, for another telegram arrived, at 2 A.M., telling Sedgwick instead to cross the river during the night, take up the bridge, and cover the ford.

THE SIXTH CORPS WITHDRAWS

Old soldier that he was, Sedgwick stood not on the order of his going, lest "the old man" change his mind again. Benham's headwork now paid off. During the afternoon of May 4 he had thrown the second bridge at Scott's Ford, part of the time under long-range Confederate shelling, whereupon the troops moved with alacrity to put the river between them and the enemy. Within an hour, between 2 and 3 A.M., May 5, Sedgwick's entire corps, including his trains and 55 guns, crossed on the two bridges (probably at the double); after which the bridges were taken up and the battle of Salem Church passed into history.

That is, all but the anticlimax. For as the rear element of the Sixth Corps was on the bridge, still another dispatch was received from Hooker countermanding the order to withdraw. This was "change-order No. 4," which Sedgwick properly and understandably ignored, going instead into bivouac and sending a detachment to cover the ford.

News of Sedgwick's recrossing having been sent to Gibbon, who still held Fredericksburg, orders were at once issued to Hall's brigade to relinquish its hold on the town, retire to the north bank and take up the bridge, all of which was accomplished under cover of darkness and with only mild interference from the Confederates.

Sedgwick's casualties at the battle of Salem Church amounted to almost 3,000 of a total of 4,600 for the Sixth Corps during the entire campaign. Confederate casualty records are less dependable than the Federal, but it would seem reasonable to conclude that Lee took at least equal losses, in percentage of troops engaged, at Salem Church, where together with the Marye's Hill engagement the Sixth Corps captured 15 guns, 5 battle flags, and 1,400 prisoners.

On the morning of the 5th, having effectively disposed of the threat to his rear, but conscious of the fact that Sedgwick was quite capable of recrossing at Banks' Ford, Lee ordered Early and Barksdale to return and resume their watch on the Fredericksburg heights, while McLaws and Anderson once again retraced their steps to Chancellorsville.

The returning divisions of McLaws and Anderson reached their old positions at Chancellorsville during the afternoon of Tuesday, May 5, in the midst of a violent storm which practically guaranteed that there would be no active fighting until morning. Now that Sedgwick had been disposed of and Lee's separated forces were again united General Lee felt confident that one more blow would be sufficient to drive Hooker back across the Rappahannock.

HOOKER'S COUNCIL OF WAR

The decision "to cross or not to cross" the Rappahannock at Banks' Ford had not yet been resolved for Sedgwick when Hooker decided to call a council of war at midnight, May 4–5. This was the army commander's first and only full-fledged council of the campaign, for which a number of possible reasons suggest themselves. It must be remembered that not only was Hooker supremely confident, in the early stages, in his self-assurance that his plans were perfect, but he then disdained advice or counsel from his subordinates and members of his official and personal staff, who were not even informed as to his intentions.

Now however he had been so badly shown up by his own deficiencies and the superior performance of General Lee that his own confidence in Joe Hooker had evaporated. This self-assurance was to be replaced, temporarily at least, by sufficient humility to prompt him to consult his corps commanders in what appeared on the face of it to promise an open discussion as to what the next move should be.

The suspicion cannot be ruled out, however, that the retreat of the Army of the Potomac across the Rappahannock, opposed by less than half as many men in Lee's Army of Northern Virginia, was already a fait accompli in Hooker's mind; had been in fact, if only subconsciously, for two days. If true, the council would be a mere rubber stamp. Whatever censure should descend on Hooker from the Administration and the public would then be shared by his corps commanders, fellow architects of the withdrawal blueprint.

Shortly after midnight the generals arrived at Hooker's tent; corps commanders Couch (second in command), Meade, Sickles, Howard, and Reynolds. Chief of Staff Butterfield and Chief Engineer Warren were also present. Sedgwick had other things on his mind at Banks' Ford, and Stoneman was miles away in the direction of Richmond. Slocum, the only other corps commander on the field, had some distance to travel. He only arrived after the conference had broken up.

Hooker opened the meeting with a few remarks to set the tone, emphasizing that his instructions compelled him to cover Washington, and conveying by implication the thought that that was the most important thing, to which the mere defeat or even the destruction of Lee's army was secondary. He then added a gratuitous and uncalled for insult to the soldierly character of the men of his army who, with the exception of elements of the Eleventh Corps and several renegade regimental and brigade commanders in the fighting of May 3, had demonstrated the greatest courage and fighting ability throughout. Contrary to the evidence, Hooker expressed apprehension of what he termed the want of steadiness in some of the troops, as exemplified by unnecessary firing along some parts of the line, as though the act of showing an interest in offensive measures deserved condemnation. In any event, he presented that weak argument to the council as one basis for determining the question of advancing or retiring. After further pointing out the obvious fact that if his own army were destroyed it could not protect Washington, a form of logical but specious reasoning that was nothing but camouflage in support of his own thesis, Hooker with Butterfield left the generals to consult among themselves.

Just as at courts-martial, where opinions are expressed by the individual members of the court, commencing with the junior and running up the scale to the ranking senior, so it was at councils of war. Dan Sickles took the lead in speaking his piece, which was in favor of withdrawing the army. This was patently in support of what were obviously Hooker's sentiments. Butterfield and Sickles were two of Hooker's intimate cronies, in spite of which Sickles ventured to criticize his superior for seeming to place on the corps commanders the responsibility for deciding to fight or quit, and also for his negligence in not insisting that their opinions be reduced to writing. On that score he need not have worried, for as a meeting to guide the army commander the council was to prove a sheer waste of time.

Sickles, a politician, admitted that he knew more about that subject than the other generals, while conceding with a rare show of modesty that his colleagues of the professional army were probably more expert in matters of military strategy. He then went on to comment on the gains made by the Northern Peace Party in the recent election, pointing out the dire political results that could stem from a clear cut defeat of the Union army. On that premise he primarily rested his argument in favor of retiring.

Meade, Reynolds, and Howard were more brief in their remarks, all voting to stay and fight it out. There was, however, a subsequent difference of opinion between Hooker and Meade as to what position Meade had taken at the council. The argument became so heated that Meade exchanged letters on the subject with Reynolds, Sickles, Howard, and Warren several weeks after the battle. All four generals confirmed the fact that Meade wanted Hooker to attack, but Sickles' letter added that at the close of the discussion, when Hooker announced his decision to recross the river, Meade's "original preferences appeared to have been surrendered to the clear conviction of the commanding general of the necessity which dictated his return to the north bank of the Rappahannock, and his unhesitating confidence in the practicability of withdrawing his army, without loss of men or material."

Couch was a bit reticent when it came his turn to speak, possibly because he was thoroughly disgusted with Hooker and his bungling, and feared he might say things that would be harmful to the cause of the army by airing dirty linen. His vote was in favor of retirement, which he afterwards explained simply gave expression to his conviction that the Army of the Potomac did not deserve to be further sacrificed under Hooker's incompetent leadership. But in his written account after the war, Couch says that he expressed a doubt similar to Meade's whether the army could successfully get their guns safely away, and stated that he would favor an advance if he were permitted to designate the point of attack.

With the majority three to two in favor of going over to the offensive, Hooker and his Chief of Staff returned to the tent and called on each of the five corps commanders to indicate plainly whether or not they recommended an advance. Meade, Reynolds, and Howard categorically voted in favor, Couch and Sickles just as categorically against. Whereupon Hooker, in spite of the majority vote, announced that he would take upon himself the responsibility of ordering the retirement.

After Hooker had left, Reynolds followed Couch out of the tent with the remark, clearly echoing the sentiments of the group: "What was the use of calling us together at this time of night when he intended to retreat anyhow?"

There would be another, later, council of war in a small white farmhouse just over the crest of Cemetery Ridge, Gettysburg, on the night of July 2, 1863, after two days of bitter fighting between these same two armies. There would be a striking similarity between the two councils, except that at the second council Meade would be sitting in the place of Hooker as the army commander.

At Gettysburg the same question would be voted on and the result of the ballot would again be to stay and fight it out. It is a certainty that memories of Chancellorsville would be in Meade's mind; for at Gettysburg he would accept the recommendation of the corps commanders, stand fast on the famous ridge, and watch Lee lose his first great battle as Pickett's charge shattered itself against the rock of Union determination.

FINAL ACT OF THE DRAMA

During what remained of the rest of that night and through Tuesday morning, May 5, the troops of each corps labored to cut new roads, several as long as three miles, from their positions to United States Mine Ford, where three bridges awaited the retrograde movement. The idea was that Lee was not to be afforded the opportunity of interfering with the withdrawal, which he might very well do if the entire army were to converge on the single road that provided the only avenue of approach to the ford after the last road junction had been passed.

In the afternoon a heavy rainstorm churned the newly cut roads into mud, as the Rappahannock rose rapidly until it lapped at the bridges, still usable but in danger of being washed away if the waters should rise much further.

Sometime during the day Hooker in person crossed the river, leaving orders that indicated the hour at which each corps should move during the night. The corps commanders were not advised that the commanding general had left the field, which in effect was an act of abdication, however unofficial.

About midnight General Couch received a note from Meade advising that Hooker had in fact crossed, that the river was now over the bridges, communication had been severed with the north shore, and that General Hunt had expressed his fear that the bridges would be lost. Couch immediately rode over to army headquarters and conferred with Meade, who agreed that the former was now in command of the army. Couch thereupon announced that the crossing orders were suspended and the army would stay where it was and fight it out.

Nature had come to the welcome aid of the Army of the Potomac by a pretty slim margin, but apparently in time to restore the self-respect of the tens of thousands who made up its ranks. Then by a quirk of fate the river crested and started to recede, uncovering the bridges, and restoring communication. Couch received a sharp message from Hooker 9 A.M. directing him to execute the original evacuation order and by nine o'clock in the morning all troops and trains had safely effected the crossing, Meade's corps acting as rear guard. The bridges were quickly taken up and the entire operation completed in a matter of hours without the Confederates making the slightest move to interfere.

For that last phase of the campaign it was First Fredericksburg all over again. In each instance the stormy weather was officially blamed for the failure of Lee's army to discover that the Union army was withdrawing under cover of darkness. General Lee made no effort to hide his disappointment on the two occasions, December 15, 1862, and May 5, 1863, when Burnside and Hooker respectively, without punishment, extricated the powerful Army of the Potomac from the much smaller but tenacious Confederate bulldog.

To cross a river in a retrograde movement on a limited number of pontoon bridges is an extremely vulnerable operation for a retreating army. Lee knew this full well. But he also understood human nature; his divisions had fought magnificently against odds both at Fredericksburg and Chancellorsville, and had to rest sometimes. Just the same, it was a bitter experience, after defeating Hooker at Chancellorsville and Sedgwick at Salem Church, for Lee to return to Chancellorsville only to find, on the morning of May 6, that the large bird had duplicated the action of the smaller at Banks' Ford and flown across the Rappahannock at United States Mine Ford; but it was even more disappointing that not a single Confederate of Stuart's three divisions had discovered that 75,000 Blue infantry, with their artillery, were moving in a steady procession across a swollen river in their very presence.

It was young Dorsey Pender, brigade commander in A. P. Hill's Light Division, who at an early hour galloped up to Lee's tent to bring him the news. Pender's skirmishers had moved forward to gain contact with the Federals behind their strong entrenchments, preparatory to the launching of the planned general attack, only to find the lines empty, with no sign of a single Union soldier anywhere. "Why, General Pender!" remarked Lee in a surprised tone. "That is the way you young men always do. You allow those people to get away. I tell you what to do, but you don't do it. Go after them, and damage them all you can."

LINCOLN RECEIVES THE NEWS

At 11 A.M., May 5, by Hooker's direction, Butterfield had wired the President the bad news, the gist of which was as follows: The cavalry have failed in executing their orders. Averell's Division returned; nothing done; loss of 2 or 3 men. Buford's regulars not heard from. General Sedgwick failed in the execution of his orders, and was compelled to retire, and crossed the river at Bank's Ford last night; his losses not known.

The First, Third, Fifth, Eleventh, Twelfth, and two divisions of Second Corps are now on south bank of Rappahannock, intrenched between Hunting Run and Scott's Dam, Trains and Artillery Reserves on north bank of Rappahannock. Position is strong, but circumstances, which in time will be fully explained, make it expedient, in the general's judgment, that he should retire from this position to the north bank of the Rappahannock for his defensible position. Among these is danger to his communication by possibility of enemy crossing river on our right flank and imperiling this army, with present departure of two-years and three-months' (nine-months') troops constantly weakening him. The nature of the country in which we are prevents moving in such a way as to find or judge position or movements of enemy. He may cross tonight, but hopes to be attacked in his position.

At 1 P.M., May 6, Butterfield advised Lincoln that the army had recrossed and been given orders to return to camp. At 4:30 P.M., same day, Hooker wired the President that he had withdrawn because the army had none of its trains of supplies with it and he saw no prospect of success from a general battle with the enemy in that area. Moreover, that no more than three of his corps had been engaged and he thought there was a better place nearer at hand to fight the whole army.

Lincoln was sunk! Overcome with shocked disappointment, all he could say to his intimates was "My God! What will the country say? What will the country say?"

HOOKER'S FATE IS DECIDED

Impatient to learn firsthand what had happened and to size up once more what manner of general he had placed in command of the army, the President set out at once for Falmouth in company with General Halleck. Lincoln remained with Hooker for a short time only, but left Halleck with instructions to "remain till he knew everything."

Halleck was a keen lawyer, who knew how to cross-examine witnesses. He had no love for Hooker, who had ignored him and reported direct to the President ever since his appointment. Smarting under such a humiliating situation, Halleck could be counted on to get the full story and report to Lincoln everything that he could extract from the corps commanders, however reluctant they might be to volunteer information that would reflect unfavorably on the reputation of their army commander.

While no record is available to give a blow-by-blow account of Halleck's unofficial "court of inquiry," on his return to Washington the President, Secretary of War Stanton, and the General-in-Chief went into a huddle, from which emerged the unanimous conclusion that both the defeat at Chancellorsville and the retreat were inexcusable and it would be unsafe to entrust to General Hooker the conduct of another battle. Hooker had told Halleck at the conference that he could resign the command without embarrassment, since he had never sought it in the first place (tongue-in-cheek, no doubt), and that he would be happy to do so if he could be restored to the command of his old division.

The Treasury faction headed by Secretary Chase had become a political force to be reckoned with. That group still backed Hooker, otherwise he would almost certainly have been removed from command right after Chancellorsville. Politics or no politics, however, the die had been cast and Hooker as army commander was on the skids. Nevertheless it took Lee's invasion of Maryland and Pennsylvania, a few weeks later, to provide the necessary grease.

The administration was able to just barely needle Hooker into resigning in the nick of time, and to supplant him with General Meade less than three days before the Battle of Gettysburg.

A STRIKING CONTRAST

The fighting over, it was expected of army commanders that they issue a communique to their officers and men, expressing satisfaction with their efforts, pin-pointing their accomplishments, and in a general way commenting on the results achieved.

Lee's task was the easier of the two. He had fought the greatest battle of his career, had worsted his opponent in every phase, and finally forced him, with twice his own strength, to retreat ignominiously across the river, swallowing his own flamboyant boasts as he left the field ahead of his own troops.

Lee's modest character, self-effacement, typical readiness to give credit to his subordinates, and thanks to the Almighty for his victories, are revealed in the general order which he published after the battle.

With heartfelt gratification the general commanding expresses to the army his sense of the heroic conduct displayed by officers and men during the arduous operations in which they have just been engaged. Under trying vicissitudes of heat and storm, you attacked the enemy, strongly intrenched in the depths of a tangled wilderness, and again on the hills of Fredericksburg, 15 miles distant, and by the valor that has triumphed on so many fields, forced him once more to seek safety beyond the Rappahannock. While this glorious victory entitles you to the praise and gratitude of the nation, we are especially called upon to return our grateful thanks to the only Giver of victory for the signal deliverance He has wrought. It is, therefore, earnestly recommended that the troops unite on Sunday next in ascribing to the Lord of Hosts the glory due unto His name.

Let us not forget in our rejoicing the brave soldiers who have fallen in defense of their country; and, while we mourn their loss, let us resolve to emulate their noble example.

The army and the country alike lament the absence for a time of one to whose bravery, energy, and skill they are so much indebted for success.

Hooker's general order similarly mirrors the character of the man, but the contrast is a striking one. In his distorted statements, Hooker seems to be whistling in the dark, trying almost pathetically to convince his men that they had done a noble thing by choosing not to fight what he euphemistically termed a "general engagement." It is doubtful that General Orders No. 49, published only six days after General Orders No. 47, fooled anybody but Joe Hooker; but let the order speak for itself.

The major general commanding tenders to this army his congratulations on its achievements of the last seven days. If it has not accomplished all that was expected, the reasons are well known to the army. It is sufficient to say they were of a character not to be foreseen or prevented by human sagacity or resource.

In withdrawing from the south bank of the Rappahannock before delivering a general battle to our adversaries, the army has given renewed evidence of its confidence in itself, and its fidelity to the principles it represents. In fighting at a disadvantage, we would have been recreant to our trust, to ourselves, our cause, and our country.

Profoundly loyal, and conscious of its strength, the Army of the Potomac will give or decline battle whenever its interest or honor may demand. It will also be the guardian of its own history and its own fame. By our celerity and secrecy of movement, our advance and passage of the rivers were undisputed, and on our withdrawal not a rebel ventured to follow.

The events of the last week may swell with pride the heart of every officer and soldier of this army. We have added new luster to its former renown. We have made long marches, crossed rivers, surprised the enemy in his intrenchments, and whenever we have fought we have inflicted heavier blows than we have received.

We have taken from the enemy 5,000 prisoners; captured and brought off seven pieces of artillery, fifteen colors; placed hors de combat 18,000 of his chosen troops; destroyed his depots filled with vast amounts of stores; deranged his communications; captured prisoners within the fortifications of his capital and filled his country with fear and consternation.

We have no other regret than that caused by the loss of our brave companions, and in this we are consoled by the conviction that they have fallen in the holiest cause ever submitted to the arbitrament of battle.

CHAPTER 27

Lee Invades Pennsylvania

THE STORY of the Battle of Gettysburg actually begins in Virginia, after Lee's defeat of Hooker at Chancellorsville, when the hopes of the Confederacy were high and the morale of the North correspondingly low.

The brief interval between the battles of Chancellorsville and Gettysburg was destined for the Confederacy to be in retrospect the brightest period of the war. Victory after victory had been won in the first two years, with Chancellorsville the crowning touch, and with such regularity that the Southern troops had come to hold the Federals in utter contempt.

As of early June 1863 the Confederate rank and file had reached the zenith of military self-assurance. This in turn led quite naturally to a state of overconfidence, despite Lee's own appraisal of Chancellorsville as a battle in which his army lost thirteen thousand men, failed to gain any ground, and was unable to pursue the enemy. Just the same, the South was riding the crest, while Lincoln was still hopefully changing generals in the search for one who could and would "go forward and give us victories"; but the future of the Union was indeed dark.

STRATEGIC BACKGROUND OF THE CAMPAIGN

In Lee's opinion the time was opportune for a bold stroke which might win the war for the South in a few short weeks. The general, an engineer and skilled tactician but an indifferent quartermaster, was painfully aware of the logistical shortcomings and the shrinking man power of the Confederacy. The distinguished British General Fuller has called him one of the worst quartermasters in history, and it is an historical fact that the Confederate troops were notoriously badly served logistically. Food and clothing were always in short supply and it was common saying among the soldiers that "one of the principal objects in killing a Yankee was to get his boots."

There was a dearth of cavalry and artillery horse replacements; other requirements were difficult to fulfill because the Southern railroads were neither efficient nor strategically located; the Southern economy was wavering; and Confederate affairs in the west were in serious shape, with Grant besieging Pemberton in Vicksburg and Bragg in trouble keeping Rosecrans from advancing further in eastern Tennessee.

The campaigns of the first two years in the east had been fought mostly on Virginia soil and the strain was beginning to tell. But recognition by England and France was still a definite possibility, with all the advantages such backing would entail.

All these factors pointed to the advisability of carrying the fight to the North with the added advantage of relieving the pressure on Richmond and imposing it on Washington, Baltimore, and Philadelphia. The Army of the Potomac had understandingly become somewhat demoralized after Fredericksburg and Chancellorsville. It was no, secret that there was a growing division of Northern sentiment with respect to the conduct and continuance of the war.

Collaterally, and not the least of the advantages to be gained by a successful invasion of Maryland and Pennsylvania was the serious threat to Washington, about which the Lincoln Administration was perennially jittery. Such a campaign could well have the effect of recalling not only the Army of the Potomac from Virginia soil, but also some of the troops from the west, with resultant lifting of the pressure on Vicksburg and Chattanooga.

Everything added up to the desirability of taking the calculated risk of a full-scale invasion. And so it was decided. Plans were laid, directives issued, and the Army reorganized from two to three corps, following Stonewall Jackson's accidental wounding and subsequent death at the hands of a reconnaissance party of his own troops as he was returning in the darkness to his own lines west of Chancellorsville. The Southern papers rejoiced audibly over the coming shift to the offensive. No apparent effort was made to keep the campaign a secret, possibly because the high command was so supremely confident of success. In any event, the Richmond and other newspapers advertised the forthcoming invasion weeks in advance, boasting of the manner in which they would fatten on the spoils to be taken from the prosperous farmers and full storehouses of the North.

Stuart's cavalry corps was accordingly assembled in the Culpeper-Brandy Station area to cover the shift of Lee's main body from Fredericksburg to Culpeper in preparation for the invasion of Maryland and Pennsylvania. The infantry movement had begun June 3, when two divisions of Longstreet's corps, McLaws' at Fredericksburg and Hood's on the Rapidan, pulled out from their respective positions and headed for Culpeper Court House. The following day Ewell's corps started for the concentration area, while the corps of A. P. Hill, in conformity with Lee's plan, remained at Fredericksburg to keep Hooker occupied and the Army of the Potomac under observation while the other two corps advanced into Pennsylvania.

JEB STUART STAGES A REVIEW

Confident in its proven superiority over the heretofore indifferently led and unaggressive Federal cavalry, the Confederate cavalry corps, ten thousand strong, was bivouacked in early June, 1863 between Culpeper, Virginia and the Rappahannock. The camps were in the vicinity of Brandy Station, a whistle-stop which lies five miles west of the river that runs through historic Fredericksburg and across which George Washington is reputed to have shied his silver dollar.

In command was General E. B. Stuart, the *beau sabreur* of Southern chivalry, whose exploits had become legend and whose appearance in a cavalry fight was synonymous with victory. Not one to hide his light under a bushel, or to disappoint the Southern belles, Stuart decided that a massive review of his mounted legions, to be followed by a gay dance for the officers, would be an appropriate prelude to the forthcoming long march through Maryland into Pennsylvania.

The rolling meadows of lovely Virginia furnished the perfect stage for the magnificent spectacle. The Confederate squadrons swept by at the walk, trot, and gallop, while Southern feminine hearts swelled with pride. General Stuart himself was a bit unhappy because General Lee had failed to show up as promised to take the review. Several days later, however, on June 8, the Commanding General did appear and the ceremony was repeated, to the annoyance of the rank and file. This time the troops passed in review only at the walk, since Lee prohibited the faster gaits in order to conserve horse flesh for the coming invasion.

FEDERAL CAVALRY SPRINGS A SURPRISE

Stuart had planned to move on June 9, the day following Lee's review of his troops. On that day his brigades were somewhat scattered, although within supporting distance of one another, and he had patrols on the Rappahannock at Beverly Ford and Kelly's Ford, separated by about six miles.

General Pleasonton had now superseded Stoneman in command of the Federal cavalry corps. He had been a West Point classmate of General Stuart; the double promise of crossing sabers with an old friend and affording his troops the opportunity of demonstrating their newly-developed combat efficiency in a test of strength presented an exciting prospect.

On Hookers' orders, and with a combined force of about ten thousand mounted and dismounted men—three divisions and one brigade of, cavalry, five batteries of horse artillery, and two brigades of infantry. Pleasonton crossed the Rappahannock at the two fords before daylight June 9, drove in the Confederate pickets, completely surprised Stuart, and gave him the hardest cavalry battle he had yet fought.

At Brandy Station the Federal cavalry had the gratifying experience of assuming the offensive. Stuart was caught in a pincers movement, suffered over five hundred casualties, and was fortunate to come off without a severe defeat. With a little luck, and somewhat better coordination, Pleasonton could have won a resounding victory. One of Stuart's subordinates, who was captured, had in his possession papers which included Lee's order for an immediate advance into Pennsylvania. Which was solid confirmation with a vengeance.

After the fight at Brandy Station numerous skirmishes occurred between the opposing cavalry, in which the Con federates were invariably driven back by the Union horse men of Pleasanton, Gregg, and Buford.

The northern cavalry had at last come into its own! Brandy Station was no accident. The day of easy Confederate triumphs was gone, never to return.

The long-range results of the cavalry fight at Brandy Station had favorable implications for the Federals in neutralizing the superiority of the Southern cavalry and in toning down the hell-for-leather cockiness and dash of Stuart's cavaliers. But it failed to deter or even delay the execution of Lee's plans for the invasion of the North, which started on schedule as Pleasonton re-crossed the Rappahannock after completing his reconnaissance in force.

LEE INVADES PENNSYLVANIA

There is no evidence to indicate that the Federal cavalry surprise at Brandy Station made any particular impression on Lee's mind. It was indeed too early to evaluate the effects of the battle and even though Lee may have taken the time to study the reports, he would in all probability have rated it a stand-off and put it out of his thoughts so far as having any strategic significance was concerned. It was the first time in two years that the Northern horsemen had demonstrated large-scale cavalry combat capabilities; and understandably Lee might have considered the affair to be merely an exception to the established rule of Confederate supremacy in the saddle.

Furthermore, his thoughts were centered on the invasion of Northern territory, his plans had matured, and his corps commanders had their orders.

LEE'S DIRECTIVE TO HIS CORPS

Lee's broad directive to his corps commanders for the invasion was essentially as follows:

> *The Second Corps under Ewell, with Jenkins' cavalry brigade attached, would lead the advance through the Shenandoah Valley, crossing the Potomac in three columns along routes touching Hagerstown, Greencastle, Chambersburg, Shippensburg, and Carlisle on the west; and Frederick, Emmitsburg, Gettysburg, and York on the east. The*

troops were ordered to collect horses, cattle, and flour. The First Corps, under Longstreet, was directed to follow Ewell's troops, but east of the Blue Ridge, and to cross at Williamsport, Maryland. The Third Corps, under A. P. Hill, was told to watch the Army of the Potomac on the Rappahannock and to keep it occupied while the other two corps advanced into Pennsylvania; if Hooker should pull out, Hill was to cross the Potomac at Shepherdstown and follow the western line of advance through Greencastle and Chambersburg.

General Stuart, on whom Lee had come to rely as "the eyes of the Army," was given the important dual mission of right flank guard of the Army on its march into Pennsylvania and constant reconnaissance to keep Lee informed of the movements of the Army of the Potomac.

In issuing his march orders to Ewell, Lee commented: "Your progress and direction will of course depend upon the development of circumstances. If Harrisburg comes within your means, capture it." The suggestion that he might be able to capture Harrisburg became in Ewell's mind virtual orders to do so, in the opinion of the late Douglas Southall Freeman. Ewell was instructed to keep 6ne division east of the mountains to deter the Federal Army, if it should cross the Potomac, from moving west ward before Lee could concentrate. And it was decided, probably by Ewell, that it would be appropriate to destroy the bridge across the Susquehanna at Wrightsville, a short distance northeast of York, in Pennsylvania.

Ewell's Rapid Advance Stirs the South

Covered by Jenkins' cavalry brigade, Ewell set out from the Culpeper concentration area on June 10 for the Cumberland Valley, with orders to clear the Valley in Virginia of Federal troops, some thirteen thousand of whom were stationed at Berryville, Winchester, Martinsburg, and Harper's Ferry; then cross the Potomac, move through Maryland, and carry the war into Pennsylvania.

General Ewell, successor to Stonewall Jackson, emulated that fast-moving soldier by executing so rapid and effective an advance, in his first big opportunity as a corps commander, that in less than three weeks his force had travelled over two hundred miles, driven the Federals out of Virginia, spread confusion and alarm throughout the north, and was knocking at the front door of Harrisburg, Pennsylvania's capital on the Susquehanna River.

With some 23,000 officers and men in his three-division corps, plus Jenkins' cavalry, "Baldy" Ewell, wooden leg and all, snaked rapidly north, reached Winchester, Virginia on the third day, June 13; crossed the Potomac and seized Hagerstown and Sharpsburg in Maryland; and two days later, on June 15, his cavalry were collecting horses and cattle in Chambersburg, Pennsylvania.

THE WINCHESTER SIDESHOW

The opposition of the Federal General Milroy, in command at Winchester, was rather sketchy in the face of the aggressive attack of the Confederates. At Cedarville on the evening of June 12 Ewell had detached Jenkins' cavalry and Rodes' infantry division to seize McReynolds' Federal brigade at Berryville, but the latter withdrew to Winchester, in time to be routed with Milroy's main body. Unobserved by the Federal commander, Early's divisions were disposed during the 14th on three sides of the town and at 6 P.M., in a sudden attack from the west, Early seized the outworks and drove the garrisons into the main fort, leading Milroy to decide on an immediate retreat to the north. A few miles above Winchester Milroy ran into a skilfully placed brigade of Johnson's division. Following a sharp engagement the Federals, who had lost heavily, scattered and continued the retreat in the darkness.

In the Winchester affair the Confederates took 3,300 prisoners and pursued the remainder of Milroy's force in the direction of Harper's Ferry until the Southerners tired of the foot race. Meantime Jenkins' troopers, about 1,500 strong, chased Milroy's wagon train all the way to Chambersburg and, after successfully appropriating all available livestock in the vicinity, returned to Hagerstown to await the arrival of the supporting infantry.

On June 17 the Federal garrison at Harper's Ferry was removed to Maryland Heights across the river, completely clearing the Valley of the Shenandoah of Union troops. The unhappy Milroy kept right on going until he reached Baltimore, where he faded into a more or less painless anonymity for the rest of the war.

EWELL ADVANCES ON HARRISBURG AND YORK

Continuing the march, Ewell sent one of his divisions under Early to take the easterly road by way of Chambers burg and Cashtown to Gettysburg en route to York. Near Greenwood the Confederates destroyed Thaddeus Stevens' iron works at Caledonia, but the Southerners probably paid heavily for this act when Stevens rode herd on them during reconstruction days.

General Ewell, a graduate of West Point, had been a civil engineer on the Columbia Railroad in Pennsylvania. At one time he was stationed at Carlisle in charge of the United States Barracks. He lost his leg in the second Battle of Bull Run, and when he rode on horseback, which he seldom did except in battle, he was invariably strapped to his horse. It is likely that he was placed in the advance be cause of his familiarity with the country, especially about York, Columbia, and Harrisburg, where important events were expected to take place.

When Ewell took possession of Chambersburg on the 24th, and set up headquarters in the court-house, he issued three separate requisitions demanding "5,000 suits of clothing, including hats, boots and shoes; 5,000 bushels of grain (corn or oats), 10,000 pounds of sole leather and an equal quantity of horseshoes, 6,000 pounds of lead, 10,000 pounds of harness leather, 400 pistols, 'all the caps and powder in town, also all the Neat's Foot Oil', 50,000 pounds of bread, 500 barrels of flour, 11,000 pounds of coffee, 100,000 pounds of hard bread, 25 barrels of vinegar, 25 barrels of sour kraut," and a scattering of other supplies. Judge Kimmell, appointed as a general superintendent of affairs during the war for the Chambersburg area, is reported to have replied to the demands: "Why, gentlemen, you must sup pose that we are made of these things—10,000 pounds of sole leather, 10,000 pounds of harness leather, 100,000 pounds of bread, 25 barrels of sour kraut—it is utterly out of our power to fur- nish these things, and now, if you are going to burn us out, you will only have to do it. That's all I have to say about it." As a result of this inter change, the people of Chambersburg furnished what they could, but the results fell far short of Ewell's expectations. General Early, one of

Ewell's division commanders, reached Gettysburg June 26, on his way east. Overnight he demanded of the Gettysburg citizens certain specified supplies, including ten barrels of whiskey, the value of the total requisition being set at $6,000 in goods, or $5,000 in cash. The citizens, however, professed poverty, having taken time by the forelock and shipped most of their valuable property to several spots in Philadelphia and elsewhere. Early made no effort to enforce his demands.

On June 27 York surrendered to Early and, unlike Gettysburg, paid him $28,000. Early then moved on toward the Wrightsville bridge, with the full intention of crossing the Susquehanna to cut the Pennsylvania Central Railroad and to attack Harrisburg from the rear. Before he could carry out his plan the local troops burned the bridge and narrowly escaped destroying the town along with it.

While Early was striking for Harrisburg by way of Wrightsville, Ewell entered Carlisle and sent the Cavalry General Jenkins and his Corps Engineer to reconnoiter the defenses of the capital, at the same time raising the Confederate flag over the famous Carlisle Barracks, later burned by Stuart.

STATE CAPITAL IS THREATENED

At 9 o'clock on Sunday morning, June 28, the advance guard of Jenkins' cavalry reached Mechanicsburg, eight miles southwest of Harrisburg. Shortly thereafter Jenkins' entire Confederate force of cavalry and mounted infantry, with four pieces of field artillery, passed through the town and encamped about a mile outside, while Jenkins himself returned to take up his headquarters at the Ashland House. The next day, Monday, Jenkins moved on toward Shiremanstown and a village called Bridgeport, on the bank of the Susquehanna by the Harrisburg Pike (now Lemoyne). At Oyster's Point, on the turnpike about an equal distance between Mechanicsburg and Bridgeport, the Confederate cavalry ran into a force of Blue infantry sent forward by General Couch. A brief skirmish ended in an artillery duel between the Union guns planted at Oyster's Point and Jenkins' guns at the Stone Church about a half-mile north of Shiremanstown. There were no casualties on either side in this exchange of pleasantries at the northernmost point reached by any *major* Confederate force during the Civil War.

When Jenkins reported back, on June 29, Lee ordered Hill and Longstreet to join Ewell at Harrisburg, believing that Hooker was still south of the Potomac. Thus Harrisburg became the objective of the entire Army of Northern Virginia. The movement was well under way in the early afternoon hours of June 29, just two days before the initial clash of the two forces at Gettysburg.

There is little doubt that Harrisburg could easily have been taken on Sunday, June 28, when elements of Ewell's corps reached the heights overlooking the city on the west bank of the mile-wide Susquehanna. The South having fully advertised its forthcoming punch, the North was alerted. On June 12 Pennsylvania's war Governor Curtin had issued a proclamation calling on the people of Pennsylvania to hasten to the defense of the State. This proclamation had little effect in strengthening the State's posture of defense.

President Lincoln on June 15 specifically called upon Pennsylvania and contiguous States to raise a total of 120,000 new troops, the response to which was relatively sketchy. Possibly 50,000 militia in all responded to the call, but New York was the only State which sent a number of uniformed regiments from New York City to Harrisburg. Those which reported were organized into two divisions. A few rifle pits were dug and breastworks thrown up here and there on both sides of the Susquehanna, but no plans seem to have been made to destroy the river bridges or set up effective blockades.

Major General Darius N. Couch, who had led the Second Corps at Chancellorsville and was senior corps commander of the Army of the Potomac, had completely lost confidence in General Hooker, in common with practically all the other general officers, but he was the only one who felt strongly enough about the matter to refuse to serve further under him. He had therefore asked to be relieved after Chancellorsville and in early June was assigned by the War Department to the Department of the Susquehanna, with headquarters at Harrisburg. Without any regular troops to form the core of an adequate defense, there was little Couch could do but make plans on paper. Fortunately for Harrisburg any further advance was halted when Lee recalled his army to Cashtown.

LEE REVERSES DIRECTION

Rodes' infantry led the march and the column was on the way to the Pennsylvania capital when the news reached Lee that Hooker's army had crossed the Potomac and was at that moment concentrated in the vicinity of Frederick, Maryland. Lee reacted quickly, sending word to Ewell to reverse his direction of march, move south, and join the other corps west of the mountains, at Chambersburg. However, those orders were quickly superseded by new instructions to the Corps Commanders to concentrate in the area of Cashtown, a few miles west of Gettysburg at the eastern exit from the South Mountains.

The information that Hooker had crossed the Potomac several days before, many hours before Stuart's cavalry had crossed, failed to reach Lee until late on June 28 or early the following morning, and the news did not come from Stuart. The longheaded Longstreet had engaged a spy by the name of Harrison, without Lee's knowledge, but with instructions to pass through the Federal army and pick up all the information possible. Harrison travelled to Washington, thence north through Maryland and Pennsylvania, gathering valuable information. On June 28 he reported to Longstreet's headquarters that at least two Federal corps had reached Frederick and that General Meade had succeeded Hooker. Although Lee was startled at the news and a bit dubious as to its accuracy, he immediately recalled Ewell from the Susquehanna and directed Hill and Longstreet, in that order, to move east of the mountain, leaving Pickett's division as train guard at Chambersburg.

Ewell's trip through Pennsylvania had been a rewarding one. Between June 10 and 29 his corps had captured 28 guns, almost 4,000 prisoners, 5,000 barrels of flour, 3,000 head of cattle, and a trainload of ordnance and medical stores at Chambersburg, in addition to food, horses, and quartermaster supplies which were seized and issued to his own men. One of Lee's objectives, the procurement of much needed supplies, was thus achieved, at least in part. All this with losses on his part of only three hundred men. Ewell's star was riding high and the South figured that a second Stonewall Jackson had emerged.

Ewell was moving rapidly through Maryland and Pennsylvania in the two-week period between June 10 and 29, without opposition worthy of the name except the natural hostility that could be expected from the townspeople and farmers who were forced to exchange their goods for worthless Confederate money or the equally doubtful I.O. Us of the Confederate government. Meantime what was the Army of the Potomac doing down in Virginia?

It will be recalled that Hooker sent Pleasonton June 9 on a reconnaissance in force to tangle with the Confederate cavalry south of the Rappahannock in the Culpeper area and to bring back information of the whereabouts and, if possible, the probable intentions of the Army of Northern Virginia.

Pleasanton executed his mission admirably. Hooker therefore knew by June 10, at the latest, that Lee was on the move for Pennsylvania. But it was not until June 25, more than two weeks later, that the head of Hooker's Army crossed the Potomac at Edward's Ferry, by which time Lincoln had made up his mind that Hooker must never be permitted to fight another battle as army commander.

HOOKER'S REMOVAL FORESHADOWED

Hooker started on the night of June 13 toward Manassas Junction, expecting to cross the Potomac near Leesburg. But he did not attempt to move across until June 25–26. During this long-time lapse Hooker was apparently trying to make up his mind. Unbelievable as it may sound, on June 13 Lee's army was stretched out for a length of at least seventy-five miles, with the head at Martinsburg and the tail at Chancellorsville, yet Hooker did little but write letters to Lincoln. He made no effort to seize the passes over the Blue Ridge, or to comply with Lincoln's frantic urging that he grasp the golden opportunity to break Lee's back at any one of a number of places. Instead Hooker actually ordered four infantry corps and his cavalry to fall back on Manassas Junction from Thoroughfare Gap and Leesburg, while three other corps were instructed to withdraw to Dumfries and await orders.

On June 22 Hooker sent Lincoln his opinion "that Ewell had moved up country for purposes of plunder, and if the enemy should conclude not to throw new additional force over the river, I desire to make Washington secure and, with all the force I can muster, strike for his line of retreat in the direction of Richmond."

These were hardly the words of a general anxious to come to grips with an enemy who had invaded his own territory. In any event his proposed action would hardly have brought Lee back, since Lee had voluntarily left Virginia soil and taken the calculated risk of leaving the way to Richmond open for Hooker. Lee, shrewd at estimating situations, doubtless was satisfied in his own mind that Lincoln would never permit Washington to be exposed in the manner suggested by Hooker.

At last, however, on June 26, after repeated urgings, Hooker put his army into motion. Once started he advanced rapidly by hard marches on Frederick, so maneuvering his columns as to keep between Lee and Washington and Baltimore, and to that extent frustrating one of Lee's major objectives. One report credits Hooker's march from Fairfax to Frederick as one of the most rapid of the war, the Eleventh Corps having covered fifty-four miles in two days.

According to General Henry J. Hunt, Chief of Artillery of the Army of the Potomac, Hooker ordered the Twelfth Corps to march on June 28 to Harper's Ferry, cut Lee's communications and, in conjunction with Reynolds who was occupying Middletown and the South Mountain passes with three corps, to operate on Lee's rear. Washington through General Halleck countermanded Hooker's order, whereupon the latter sought permission to abandon Harper's Ferry. This too was refused, at which Hooker huffily asked to be relieved of command. Apparently Washington was just waiting for this opportunity. The request was granted so promptly that it must have made Hooker's head swim.

HOOKER IS REPLACED BY MEADE

There is no doubt that the Army of the Potomac, officers and men alike, in company with Secretary Stanton and President Lincoln, had utterly lost confidence in Joe Hooker. The President's patience was exhausted.

On June 28, one day after York had surrendered to Early; when Gordon was approaching the Wrightsville bridge; Ewell had entered Carlisle; Jenkins' cavalry was reconnoitering the defenses of Harrisburg; and Jeb Stuart was far away to the south at Rockville, frittering away valuable time while these interesting events were transpiring, Lincoln appointed George Gordon Meade as Commander of the Army of the Potomac.

The transfer of command, with the invading enemy roaming at will and now deep in Union territory, was risky business in spite of its dramatic aspect. The Chief of Staff to Secretary Stanton, General Hardie, a friend of both Meade and Hooker, was entrusted by Lincoln with the mission of delivering the Presidential order to both commanders and making it effective. Hardie changed to civilian clothes to afford him a better chance of evading Stuart's troopers. He then made his way to Frederick and about 4 o'clock on the morning of June 28 located Meade's headquarters tent, several miles outside the town, after being repeatedly accosted and delayed en route by drunken Federal soldiers making the most of the Maryland whiskey.

Awakened from a sound sleep, Meade's first groggy reaction was that he was under arrest; the Federal high commanders must have been a bit on the nervous side about that time. When Hardie broke the news, Meade protested that the army expected Reynolds to succeed to the command, and offered all the arguments he could think of in opposition to the order. But Hardie had been well briefed, so finally off the two generals went on horseback to see Hooker and effect the transfer of command. Shortly thereafter Hooker and Hardie departed for Baltimore and Washington respectively, while Meade walked alone into the army commander's tent to face his destiny.

Meade's promotion from command of the Fifth Corps to army commander was a surprise, and not too welcome a one at that. His son and aide has written that Hooker had made no future plans whatsoever with respect to the army. General Meade was therefore forced to start from scratch, not only to ascertain the whereabouts of Lee, but to learn just how the other corps of the Army of the Potomac were disposed. Under the circumstances one cannot envy General Meade the timing of his assignment to command.

It is a popular belief that General J. E. B. Stuart disregarded Lee's orders for the invasion of Pennsylvania and, instead of paralleling Ewell's route and protecting his right, rode around the Army of the Potomac, engaged in fruitless side-enterprises, and ended up by failing to rejoin his own army until the last stage of the Battle of Gettysburg. In the meantime Lee knew nothing of Stuart's whereabouts, received no information of Hooker's movements, and presumably was obliged to carry out his risky major foray deep in enemy country without benefit of cavalry reconnaissance or flank security.

The controversy has never been satisfactorily resolved. One widely accepted version, that Gettysburg might have resulted in a Confederate victory and thus altered the course of history, had Lee's cavalry functioned as he intended it should, and had Stuart suppressed his undoubted flair for glamorous exploits, fails to take into account a number of factors which had a decided influence on the event and which place a goodly portion of the responsibility on General Lee himself.

LEE'S INSTRUCTIONS TO STUART

There was no misunderstanding as to what Stuart was to do, only how he should do it. The instructions given him were twofold: first, to screen the advance of the two corps, A. P. Hill's and Longstreet's, as they followed Ewell across the Potomac and into Maryland; for the second phase, to cross the Potomac with his own cavalry brigades, serve as right flank guard of the army as it moved north into Pennsylvania, and at the same time keep Lee informed of the movements and actions of the Army of the Potomac.

By June 22 the Federal cavalry had withdrawn to the north, although Lee didn't know it. That evening Stuart received written instructions from Lee, which read in part as follows:

> *If you find that he (Hooker) is moving northward, and that two Brigades can guard the Blue Ridge and take care of your rear, you can move with the other three into Maryland, and take positions on General Ewell's right, place yourself in communication with Hill: guard his flank and keep him informed of the enemy's movements, and*

collect all the supplies you can for the use of the Army. You will, of course, take charge of Jenkins' brigade and give him necessary instructions.

The letter then went on to give information on Ewell's line of advance and explicit orders against plundering in the enemy's country.

On the night of June 23, at Stuart's headquarters near Middleburg, Virginia, another dispatch from Lee came in:

If General Hooker's Army remains inactive, you can leave two Brigades to watch him, and withdraw with the three others, but should he not appear to be moving northward, I think you had better withdraw this (west) side of the mountains tomorrow night, cross at Shepherdstown next day, and move over to Frederick town. You will, however, be able to judge whether you can pass around their Army without hindrance, doing them all the damage you can, and cross the river east of the mountains. In either case, after crossing the river, you must move on and feel the right of Ewell's troops, collecting information, provisions, etc. Give instructions to the commander of the brigades left behind to watch the flank and rear of the army and (in event of the enemy leaving their front) retire from the mountains west of the Shenandoah, leaving sufficient pickets to guard the passes, and bringing everything clean along the valley, closing upon the rear of the army. I think the sooner you cross into Maryland, after tomorrow, the better.

Lee's orders of June 22 and 23, while anything but concise, were clear enough when read together. If the Federal army stayed on the Rappahannock, Stuart was to keep it under observation with a part of his force. The instructions were concise with respect to Robertson's cavalry, which was to move from the mountains west of the Shenandoah, then north to close upon the rear of the army, and protect Lee's line of communication. If and when Hooker moved, Stuart was to move north to the east of Blue Ridge Mountains, cross the Potomac at Shepherdstown and continue on to Fredericktown, covering the flank of Lee's army in close contact with Ewell, the advance corps. Thus Lee believed he would be adequately served by his cavalry, as he should have been.

Stuart Uses His Own Discretion

In studying those instructions it is clear that Lee allowed Stuart too much discretion and that the latter interpreted his orders as sanction for another grandiose raid such as he had staged in 1862. It is equally clear that if explicitly followed the orders would have robbed Stuart of the chance for the independent adventure that his spirit seemed to ·crave. For him the choice was easy. In his own words he decided "to move entirely in the enemy's rear, intercepting his communications with his base (Washington) and, inflicting damage upon his rear, to rejoin the army in Pennsylvania in time to participate in its actual conflicts."

Lee Had Plenty of Cavalry

Stuart had the choice of two possible routes: the one through the Shenandoah Valley; the other to sweep around the rear of Hooker's army, pass between him and Washington, cut communications, do all the damage possible, and then join Ewell in Pennsylvania. Like Custer the dashing Stuart selected the dramatic and exciting alternative, leaving two of his brigades, about 3,000 men, to hold the Blue Ridge passes in Virginia until the army had cleared and then to revert to General Lee for such further missions as the latter might assign.

It is generally believed that because Stuart was in the wrong place at the wrong time, and Lee was therefore deprived of vital information at a critical period, the Army of Northern Virginia had no cavalry operating directly with it as it advanced into Pennsylvania. That was not true. Even before June 10 Lee had detached Imboden's cavalry brigade of 2,000 men from the cavalry corps and had sent them into Maryland to destroy the railway from Cumberland to Martinsburg, and the Chesapeake and Ohio canal. Imboden certainly must have been included in Lee's plans for further cavalry missions after completing the task of destruction. There was also Jenkins' cavalry brigade of 3,800 officers and men, likewise detached from Stuart's command after the review on June 5. A brigade of that size, preceding 'the army in its northward trek, was certainly adequate, coupled with Imboden's brigade, the aggregate exceeding 5,000 soldiers, for rather widespread reconnaissance in addition to its covering mission.

Stuart took with him on his historic ride around Hooker the three brigades of Wade Hampton, Fitzhugh Lee, and W. H. F. Lee. This force totaled fewer than 5,000 troopers, but they were a compact, experienced body of hard riding cavalrymen under commanders in whom Stuart had full confidence, and with whom he had worked closely in many previous battles. Therefore there appears to have remained available to Lee, and under his direct command, a cavalry force of some 8,000, viz: Jenkins' brigade (with Ewell), Imboden's brigade, and the brigades of Robertson and Jones, under the command of Robertson.

Colonel John S. Mosby, after scouting Hooker's positions on the Rappahannock with his rangers, had informed Stuart that the Army of the Potomac was widely scattered and that Stuart, if he moved promptly, should have little difficulty in passing through or around them. We shall see, however, that Stuart missed that opportunity when he moved out with his three brigades on June 24. On the 25th he found that all the roads he had planned to use were occupied by the Army of the Potomac moving north, so that he was forced to take a long detour to the southeast, which in fact did put him in Hooker's rear and within a few miles of Washington.

Stuart had left General Robertson with his two brigades of cavalry and two batteries of field artillery in the vicinity of Middleburg to cover Ashby's and Snicker's Gaps, watch the enemy, and harass his rear if he should withdraw. In the latter event (as actually happened), Robertson was instructed by Stuart to withdraw to the west side of the Shenandoah, cross the Potomac, and follow the Army of Virginia, keeping on its right and rear. He was further directed to report "anything of importance" to General Longstreet, by communicating with him "by relays through Charlestown."

Mosby was not backward in criticizing Robertson for being dilatory, to say the least, in following his instructions. He has written that instead of keeping on the right of the army and in close contact with the enemy Robertson dallied in the mountain gaps June 26 to 29, when he received orders from Lee to rejoin the army. He states that the rear guard of the Federal army crossed the Potomac on June 26, east of the Blue Ridge, while Robertson crossed at Williamsport, about twenty-five miles west of the Blue Ridge, five days later, on July 1, the day the fighting began at Gettysburg.

Be that as it may, Robertson's 3,000 troopers were of no perceptible use to Lee during the invasion, any more than were Stuart's 5,000. On the other hand there is no evidence that Lee himself or his staff made any subsequent effort to recover these two powerful reconnaissance tools when it became evident that his basic plan for their utilization had gone awry.

Major Henry B. McClellan, Chief of Staff of the Cavalry Corps, Army of Northern Virginia, in his *Life of Stuart* says: "It was not the want of cavalry that General Lee bewailed, for he had enough of it had it been properly used. It was the absence of Stuart himself that he felt so keenly; for on him he had learned to rely to such an extent that it seemed as if his cavalry were concentrated in his person, and from him alone could information be expected."

STUART RIDES OFF INTO THE BLUE

Stuart of course knew perfectly well that he was not to delay in joining Ewell, already well on his way. But he was still smarting over Brandy Station and the resulting public indignation which the leading Southern newspapers took no pains to conceal. Like Custer at the Little Big Horn thirteen years later, Stuart needed renewed public acclaim to replace him on his pedestal. It was high time to get going.

Lee's orders had been to cross the Potomac as soon after June 24 as practicable. The cavalry assembly point was fixed at Salem, on the Manassas Gap railroad eight miles west of Thoroughfare Gap. The columns were directed by Stuart to move shortly after midnight, June 24. The march was planned through Glasscock's Gap of Bull Run Mountain (about seven miles northeast of Warrenton), thence to Haymarket and turn northward, the shortest road to Ewell's flank in Pennsylvania.

However on the Warrenton-Centreville Turnpike Stuart encountered Hancock's Federal Second Corps moving north toward. Gum Spring and Edward's Ferry—most the same route Stuart had intended to follow. So he changed course to the southeastward on June 26, from Buckland to Bristoe Station (close to Manassas Junction), to Brentsville, thence north to a bivouac near Wolf Run Shoals on Occoquan Creek. Here he paused to rest and graze his horses, some of which were worn out by hard campaigning earlier in the month.

It was now the morning of June 27. Stuart had been on the march for fifty hours, yet had covered only thirty-four miles and was still twenty-five miles from the nearest fords of the Potomac, which he was to cross "as soon after June 24 as practicable." Rather a dismal showing for the supposedly mobile cavalry. Without further contact with Federal troops the column crossed the Occoquan at Wolf Run Shoals and moved northward through Fairfax Station to Fairfax Court House, where a halt of several hours was called. While there Stuart received a message that the Army of the Potomac was converging on Leesburg. This information decided his further course, so on he moved to the Leesburg-Alexandria Turnpike, turned west and then north through Dranesville to the Potomac, which was reached at 3 A.M., June 28. During the night all troopers and guns crossed without mishap at the deep but passable Rowser's Ford.

Stuart was now across the Potomac. He had been on the road seventy-two hours, yet had reached only the southern fringe of Maryland soil, within twenty miles of Washington, and had no idea where Lee might be at the moment. His orders required him to join Ewell and cover his right, but his horses were tired, his men and animals were living off the country (he had left his own trains in Virginia in order not to slow him down), and he wasn't sure just where Ewell was to be found. According to the local residents, the Army of the Potomac was en route to Frederick and only the day before Hooker had been at Poolesville, to the west. Well, at least he had circled the enemy's rear as planned!

Should he take the road through Frederick, which was probably in the hands of the Federals, or the one through Hanover, keeping to the east of Hooker's army, and heading towards York or Carlisle? Naturally the road to Hanover was selected; by noon of Sunday, the 28th, the column reached Rockville, 12 miles from Washington, where Fortune either smiled or frowned on Jeb Stuart, depending on the point of view.

Stuart Captures a Wagontrain

Rockville was on the direct supply line between Washington and Hooker's army. While Stuart paused there, word came in that a Federal wagontrain was approaching. Soon the mounted Federal guards moved into the town, entirely unaware of the presence of the enemy. Suddenly they spotted the gray-clad horsemen and turned to spread the alarm to the one hundred and fifty wagons stretched out on the highway. Brand new, with shining harness, fat mules, and loaded with oats, corn, bacon, sugar, hams, and considerable bottled whiskey, the prize was too rich a one for Stuart's men to lose.

It was a mad chase, down the road toward the Capital. as the wagons turned and started back at a fast trot. But it was a hopeless attempt, 125 of them being captured. Stuart couldn't bear to give them up. Valuable time was lost writing out paroles for the 400 prisoners who had been taken and, since the vehicles couldn't be paroled along with the men, they were taken along. A worse millstone could hardly be imagined.

Early in the morning of June 29, after a night march of about twenty miles through Maryland, the advance guard ran into a small Federal command at Cooksville, took prisoners, and moved on to Hood's Mill where more delay was caused in tearing up the track of the B & O Railroad.

After noon the march was resumed to Westminster where a small body of Union cavalry charged them bravely but ineffectually. There forage was found for the horses—the distribution and feeding depriving the troops of rest or sleep for most of the night.

Affair at Hanover

Groggily the column moved on toward Hanover on June 30. Reaching the high ground overlooking the town from the south, Stuart, riding up front, spotted an advancing squadron of blue cavalry, a part of Jud Kilpatrick's cavalry division. A swift Confederate charge drove the Federals back into Hanover, but they were promptly reorganized and launched a countercharge during which Stuart came very close to being captured. With an aide at his side, the general left the road in a wild gallop through tall timothy grass, culminating in a magnificent leap across a wide and deep gully, to clear which his thoroughbred must have covered a distance of not less than twenty-five feet in the air. At that point the pursuing cavalry lost interest in the chase.

The 6th Michigan and 1st West Virginia Cavalry regiments, of Custer's and Farnsworth's brigades respectively, are known to have been recently armed with the Spencer repeater, and both were engaged with Stuart's troopers in the Hanover skirmish. Whether they used their Spencers effectively from horseback is questionable, but the fact remains that Kilpatrick definitely blocked Stuart from the two roads leading north from Hanover to Carlisle. The Southerners were forced to bypass Hanover and take the round-about route through Jefferson to Dover, a few miles northwest of York, which they reached on the morning of July 1, after marching all night. In Stuart's official report he admits that his captured train was a serious embarrassment and that he thought he might save it by the detour to the east. It is a certainty he would have lost the train had he tried to force his way through Kilpatrick's division, but conversely he might have rewritten the Battle of Gettysburg.

So Near, Yet So Far

The Hanover affair occurred June 30 just fourteen miles east of Gettysburg, where on the following morning other Federal cavalry was destined to open the Battle of Gettysburg. Although Stuart didn't know it, he was but a short march away from a junction with Lee's main body, if only he could have turned west and shaken off Kilpatrick.

Meade himself was at Taneytown that day, where he had set up army headquarters. On all the roads west of Stuart's chosen line of march the blue hosts were marching northward, while the cavalry divisions of Kilpatrick and Gregg, two-thirds of Pleasonton's Federal corps, had fanned out to the east to screen the Army of the Potomac and intercept Stuart, whose general whereabouts were no longer a secret.

The Confederates had picked up several hundred prisoners on the 29th and 30th, which added that much more weight to the pace-slowing impedimenta that had already put Stuart at least two days behind even his retarded march schedule. Had he known what was transpiring a few miles away in the direction of Gettysburg there is no doubt that he would have jettisoned his captured wagons, paroled his prisoners, and taken off at a smart clip across country, despite the jaded condition of his men and horses. As a possible result the Battle of Gettysburg might not have been fought at that place.

After another night march from Hanover, Stuart reached Dover on the morning of July I but found no Confederates there. After a few hours' rest he started for Carlisle via Dillsburg, reaching the former town in the late afternoon. All rations had been consumed, the men and horses were practically exhausted, and the troops were beginning to wonder how they might escape from their predicament. Brig. Gen. W. F. "Baldy" Smith was in command at Carlisle, but Stuart didn't know that and, thinking the garrison was made up of home-guard troops, sent in a flag of truce calling for surrender on pain of having the town put to the torch.

About this time one of Stuart's messengers returned with the news that he had found the army and that Lee wished him to move to Gettysburg. Before leaving, Stuart directed that the cavalry barracks at Carlisle be burned, but nothing else was disturbed.

It was the afternoon of July 2, the second day of the Gettysburg battle, before Stuart, riding ahead of his men, joined Lee on Seminary Ridge. Tradition has it that Lee's only comment was: "Well, General Stuart, you are here at last." Whether true or not, Lee's written reactions are officially recorded in his report on the battle, in which he confined himself to the mild statement that "the movements of the army preceding the Battle of Gettysburg had been much embarrassed by the absence of the Cavalry."

CHAPTER 28

Confederate Strategy in June 1863

MILITARY strategy, inadequately defined in most dictionaries, is generally regarded among professional army officers as the science of implementing national war plans by disposing major forces of all arms and services in such a way as to impose one's own will upon the enemy. The manner in which the troops are employed, after contact is established between the opposing forces, brings into play what is called military tactics.

Applied to the Battle of Gettysburg, Lee's strategy was conceived along the Rappahannock in late May of 1863, activated in the invasion of Pennsylvania, dissolved into the tactical slugging match of July 1–3, and reached its anticlimactic conclusion with the virtually unhindered recrossing of the Potomac into Virginia on the night of July 13.

LEE'S FLEXIBLE PLANS
Simply stated, Lee figured that he had everything to gain and little to lose by going over to the strategic offensive, shifting the theater of operations to northern soil for a welcome change, improving the faltering source of food and supply for his army, and collaterally keeping the Federals off balance and the Lincoln administration mortal terror of losing Washington or at least Baltimore or Philadelphia.

There is no evidence that Lee's invasion timetable was anything but a flexible one. He knew exactly what he wanted to accomplish, but not precisely how. And that was typical of Lee, whose confidence in his heretofore victorious troops was unlimited; who invariably outlined military objectives and then left it to his corps commanders to achieve those objectives in their own way; and who was quite willing to "play by ear" within reasonable limits. Depending on how the situation should develop, he might shoot for Washington, Baltimore, Philadelphia, Harrisburg, or with luck even New York.

Although scarcely conclusive, a letter from Colonel W. H. Swallow, General Rodes' Adjutant General, to author Hoke in 1886, stated that "General Ewell and Colonel Turner, of his staff, both told me in confidence at Berryville, before crossing the Potomac, that York, Pennsylvania or that vicinity was to be the ground where General Lee expected to concentrate his army. I believed that if Longstreet had not tarried so long at Chambers burg, York would have been the point of concentration on the 30th instead of Gettysburg."

Lee Misses Jackson

Although neither Lee nor anyone else could have fore seen the effect, the death of Stonewall Jackson at Chancellorsville created a void which was never filled, either by Longstreet, upon whom Lee subsequently relied as his "old war horse," or by Ewell, who for a few short weeks gave a flashy but unsustained preview of a worthy successor to Jackson.

Longstreet was an extremely able general and a courageous leader in the field. But he proved himself to be the tortoise to the Jackson hare when it came time to duplicate the fantastic bursts of speed which characterized Jackson's "foot cavalry" under the rapid-fire movements which the latter was wont to execute with such startling success on so many fields. Whether Lee was justified in expecting Longstreet or Ewell to emulate the Jackson techniques or not, Gettysburg proved that if Lee had counted on another Jackson in the execution of his plans, he was sadly disillusioned.

Longstreet Is Obstinate

The conclusion is likewise inescapable that Longstreet suffered from delusions of grandeur in the belief that his strategic sense was so highly developed as to qualify him to offer advice to Lee with confidence that it would be accepted per se. In expounding his theories, before the march into Pennsylvania, to the patient, gentlemanly Lee, Longstreet opposed the invasion on the premise that the Army of Northern Virginia should take strong defensive positions and force the enemy to attack.

His self-assurance as to the soundness of his own strategic thinking, and because he evidently mistook Lee's courteous attention for acquiescence, resulted at Gettysburg in effectively disrupting Lee's attack plans and in allowing the Federals sufficient time to stabilize their position on Cemetery Ridge.

After the war Longstreet admitted that he had failed to win Lee over to his own conception of the strategic defensive, but maintained doggedly that in then pressing his case for the tactical defensive, in conjunction with Lee's preference for the strategic offensive, the latter had tacitly concurred. This was obviously not the case, in view of Lee's directives and orders on every one of the three days at Gettysburg.

Interestingly enough it turned out to be Meade, not Lee, who embraced the Longstreet theory, seized and held a strong position on Cemetery Ridge, and permitted Lee to shatter his forces against the Federal position. Thus it might be argued that events at Gettysburg vindicated Longstreet's theory, were it not for the fact that his execution of Lee's orders on the battlefield left much to be desired. In dragging his heels on July 2 and 3, Longstreet demonstrated fairly conclusively, in retrospect at least, that Stonewall Jackson's loss to the Confederacy had been, from Lee's standpoint, an irreparable one.

LACK OF ENEMY INFORMATION

Lee's strategic plans for the invasion of Maryland and Pennsylvania were militarily well conceived and sound in principle. The disposition and movements of his three infantry corps were executed in conformity with the overall plan to march into Pennsylvania through the Shenandoah and Cumberland Valleys under the protection of the high mountain range to the south. The mission of the three brigades of cavalry under the immediate command of General J. E. B. Stuart was to parallel, east of the Blue Ridge Mountains, the northerly march of the infantry in combined screening and reconnaissance operations. Stuart's slowness in getting under way and his failure to regain touch with Ewell or to send any information whatsoever to Lee on the location and movements of the Army of the Potomac kept Lee in the dark as to Hooker's and later Meade's whereabouts or intentions. As the situation developed, this failure played a large part in causing the inevitable meeting of the two armies to take place at Gettysburg rather than in the York area, at Chambersburg, Emmitsburg, or elsewhere.

Lee was handicapped not only by the loss of Jackson but also by the fact that he had just reorganized his two corps into three, of which only one, Longstreet's, was under the command of an experienced corps commander. Ewell and A. P. Hill, newly promoted from command of divisions, both showed promise based on experience, but were untried in the employment of larger bodies of troops. Longstreet, who was born in South Carolina and spent his early life in Georgia, concurred in the choice of Ewell for one of the corps on the basis of lineal rank, ability, and services, but felt that D. H. Hill, of North Carolina, who he maintained was A. P. Hill's superior in rank, skill, judgment, and distinguished services, should have been appointed. Next in rank was Lafayette McLaws, of Georgia, one of Longstreet's own division commanders. McLaws had a distinguished battle record, but he was not in the best of health, nor was he a Virginian. Longstreet implied that the latter was a strong influence against Lee's selection of D. H. Hill or McLaws for corps leadership, and in failing to select either one Lee had impaired some what the morale of his troops. Granting Lee's right to make his own selection, the probability exists that cooperation between the corps commanders at Gettysburg would have been more effective if Longstreet's recommendations had been accepted. A study of the history of the battle discloses much evidence of a lack of harmony and necessary team spirit between Longstreet, Ewell, and A. P. Hill.

LEE'S ARMY IS OVEREXTENDED

The Army of Northern Virginia flowed northward in the latter days of June, strung out along the Cumberland Valley and spreading ever more widely into the triangular area Chambersburg-Harrisburg-York, with Ewell pointed for Harrisburg via Carlisle from the west and Columbia from the south. These scattered forces, infantry and cavalry alike, offered a rare opportunity for an enterprising opponent, offensively minded and with his army well concentrated, to break up the invasion and inflict severe punishment if not destruction on the invaders. By direct routes Harrisburg and York are each more than fifty miles distant from Chambersburg, Lee's command post for almost a week. But that didn't worry Lee, who as late as June 28 thought the Army of the Potomac was still in Virginia, with Hooker still in command.

Lee had every reason to feel that his line of communications and supply all the way back to Virginia by way of the Cumberland and Shenandoah Valleys was reason ably secure. All Federal forces had been forced to evacuate the valley of Virginia by Ewell's advance corps. Two divisions of cavalry left behind by Stuart were presumably protecting his rear and the important passes through the mountains to the east; and Stuart himself with three divisions of cavalry had been told to operate on Ewell's right, east of the mountains and paralleling the latter's march into Pennsylvania.

From the start of the invasion, it will be noted, Lee himself rode with Longstreet's corps, which he apparently regarded as the temporary army reserve and his major reliance in case of unexpected developments requiring speedy action. Or, as believed by some, he may have ridden there to keep Longstreet on his toes. In, effect, then, it was chiefly Ewell's corps which had fanned out widely, with A. P. Hill close enough to give Lee on short notice at least two-thirds of his main army for the initial stages of a general engagement.

CHAPTER 29

Meade Takes Command

THERE does not appear to have been any strategic planning worthy of the name to meet Lee's threat, so far as the employment of the Army of the Potomac was concerned. Washington was concerned primarily with its own security, although Lincoln saw clearly the importance of going after Lee. Even after the President had pushed Hooker into moving, and the Army of the Potomac had reached the Frederick area, Lincoln had no intention of permitting Hooker to fight another battle. He waited only for a valid excuse to remove him. It seems clear that Hooker, forced to move in a direction at variance with his own undigested plans, was thinking only from hour to hour. And Meade, when he took over at Frederick, failed to find any estimates of the situation, possible plans, contingent orders, or anything else that he could put into operation, modify, or improve upon. He did not know the exact location and disposition of the elements of Hooker's army other than his own corps, and he was forced by necessity, with the Confederates ranging widely to the north, to take prompt and effective action with inadequate information to guide him. Necessarily then his first day of command was spent in familiarizing himself with the strength and dispositions of his army and in considering possible plans.

MEADE'S TIMID ATTITUDE
The extent to which Halleck's directive influenced Meade's subsequent actions can only be imagined. Like many of the Federal generals, Meade was apparently obsessed with the myth of Lee's invincibility, because he greatly overestimated the Confederate invasion strength and from the time he took command of the army seemed strangely timid about crossing swords with Lee. It had not been noticeable in his previous service as

brigade and division commander, but his actions from Frederick on reveal a defensive psychology, as will presently appear. From time to time Lincoln almost despaired of him as he had of previous army commanders; first when Meade mentioned that he had forced Lee "to fall back from the Susquehanna"; and again when, after the Battle of Gettysburg, Meade congratulated his army on "freeing Northern soil of the invader," as though that were all that was expected.

At the time he took command, Meade's army was concentrated in the Frederick area, while the Confederates were scattered all over the landscape to the north. This would seem to have offered a splendid opportunity for Meade, keeping his army together, to defeat Lee's separate corps by installments. However, his telegram to Halleck, dispatched within a few hours of the time when he was officially notified of his appointment, could not at such an early stage represent the result of any considered strategic planning.

Recalling Hooker's plan to have Slocum's Twelfth Corps move from the Frederick area toward Harper's Ferry and, reinforced by the large garrison at that important crossing of the Potomac, to operate on Lee's line of communication and supply down the valley, it would be interesting to speculate on subsequent developments had Meade adopted Hooker's plan. Washington didn't like the idea, however, and when Halleck refused to permit the Harper's Ferry garrison to come under Hooker's control, Slocum was recalled and Hooker submitted his resignation. Whereupon, with Meade in command, Halleck immediately reversed himself and assigned the Harper's Ferry garrison to him, thus tacitly agreeing to the Hooker project under his successor.

A heavily reinforced army corps on Lee's tail, with a moderate sized cavalry contingent as covering force (which was entirely practicable), was an intriguing possibility. If, keeping his main body intact, Meade had moved energetically northward, it is conceivable that he might have bottled Lee in the mountains west of Cashtown with a pivot of maneuver and overwhelmed Ewell's divisions piecemeal as they came hurrying back, under Lee's concentration orders, from the, York and Carlisle area.

Such an exciting prospect was apparently not within the scope of Meade's imaginative processes. He seems merely to have offered lip service to the very practicable idea of moving rapidly north to attack and defeat Lee's forces in detail. So Slocum's Twelfth Corps retraced its steps from South Mountain and joined the main body in its measured and cautious march in the general direction of the Confederate army and the Susquehanna River.

Meade evidently reasoned that Lee must scatter in order to subsist and, while he talked about possibly defeating his enemy in detail, his orders for the advance of his army on June 28 and 29 were not such as to realize that prospect. A study of the map, the road net, and the terrain indicates that Meade's logistics were based primarily on a program: first, to cover Baltimore and Washington; second, to indicate a defensive line, in keeping with the security of the Capital, upon which to meet Lee's attack, if made; and third, to attack Lee if, after finding him, he could do so with impunity. The important supply point and communication center at Frederick was taken care of by Meade's order to General French to move the 7,000 men of the Harper's Ferry garrison to Frederick, which nicely covered Meade's rear in the direction of the Potomac.

MEADE PLAYS IT SAFE

It is not surprising under the circumstances that Meade played it safe in deciding to adhere strictly to Halleck's admonition so to maneuver as to assure the security of Baltimore and Washington. The Army of the Potomac had been under a cloud for a long time, and the impression prevailed strongly among some of its high ranking officers that to put it mildly it was not exactly in favor at the War Department. Major General Henry J. Hunt wrote bitterly that "rarely, if ever, had it heard a word of official commendation after a success, or of sympathy or encouragement after a defeat." At the very least the frequent changes in army commanders presupposed a lack of confidence on the part of the administration in the ability of the generals commanding, which seems to have been warranted by the facts. There was certainly no indication, however, that Washington had lost confidence in the army itself.

One can imagine the overwhelming procession of thoughts that must have crowded Meade's mind as the appointed army commander walked alone into his tent on the outskirts of Frederick after bidding Generals

Hooker and Hardie goodbye on the afternoon of June 28. All he had to do was to halt Lee's march on Harrisburg, bring him to battle, preferably on a field that offered superior advantages to his own army, be certain that in so doing he would protect the Capital, and then defeat Lee and wind up the business by sending him on his way back to Virginia!

But first Meade must find out what he had to fight with and just where the troops were.

THE PIPE CREEK PLAN

The "Pipe Creek circular," written late on the night of June 30 and based on the report of his engineers, directed that, if and when the circular was made effective, the Army would form line of battle along the general line of the creek with the left at Middleburg and the right at Manchester. The map shows that this position would cover the main routes to Baltimore and Washington, and the important railroads running to the same cities, with the added advantage that Parr's Ridge-Dug Hill Ridge would furnish an excellent reserve line to fall back on in case of need.

Meade was strongly criticized for the Pipe Creek circular, although the circular itself explained what he had in mind, in the following words:

> *This order is communicated that a general plan, perfectly understood by all, may be had for receiving attack, as made in strong force upon any portion of our present position. Developments may cause the Commanding General to assume the offensive from his present positions.*

At the same time Meade made it plain to his corps commanders that he had no intention of assuming the offensive "until Lee's movements or positions should render such an operation certain of success." He even went so far as to inform them that, if the enemy should attack, he would hold them in check long enough to remove his trains and baggage and then withdraw to the defensive position generally along Pipe Creek.

The famous Pipe Creek order has been the subject of endless controversy. Writers favorable to Meade defend the order as a legitimate document which any thoughtful army commander would distribute to his high ranking subordinates as precautionary instructions in the event of a contingency requiring a retrograde movement. His detractors, on the other hand, maintain that the Pipe Creek order was simply further evidence of Meade's defensive psychology and unwillingness to take the risk of attacking Lee, no matter how favorable the situation.

Another factor that should not be overlooked was that Meade could not be sure, at that stage, that Lee would come through the Cashtown Pass. Lee could perfectly well have moved south under cover of the Blue Ridge and turned east on the Waynesboro-Westminster road, in an effort to turn Meade's left flank and interpose himself between the Army of the Potomac and Washington. This was the possibility which Halleck feared when he implied that Meade was moving too far east, uncovering Frederick and the area immediately east of the Blue Ridge. Seen in this light, the Pipe Creek circular was about as good a hedge as could be devised at the moment, pending more detailed information on Lee's position and movements.

In any event, there can be no blinking the fact that the initiative was left largely to Lee. Meade's every thought seemed to be based on the desire to get Lee back to Virginia, without a fight if possible, and this theme continued to dominate as Lee retreated southward after the battle, Meade's slowness in pursuit furnishing the final evidence.

On the night of June 28, Meade's first day of command, his army had reached the line Emmitsburg New Windsor, on a front of over twenty miles, with Buford's cavalry covering the left at Fairfield, Gregg's the right at Westminster, and Kilpatrick's in front near Hanover. On that day Ewell was at Carlisle and York, Longstreet at Chambersburg, and Hill between Fayetteville and Cash town.

Meade's selection of the small village of Taneytown for his headquarters during the advance was a logical one, be cause it was the ideal point from which to keep in touch with the chessboard movements of his seven corps. Conversely, incoming mounted couriers and foot messengers would have no difficulty in locating the command post. Situated on the Frederick branch of the Northern Central Railroad, the town was an important crossroad on high ground which commanded an exceptionally good view of the countryside in all directions. Taneytown in 1863 had attained the ripe age of 109 years, but according to local historians the story that it was named after Chief Justice Taney of the U.S. Supreme Court is incorrect, since that distinguished gentleman happened to have been born in 1777. The town is a part of Carroll County, Maryland, reputed to be the fourth richest agricultural county in the United States.

The advance for June 30 was in reality a continuation of the previous day's march. It will be noted that three corps are pointed toward Gettysburg; on June 30 Meade formed these three, the First, Third and Eleventh, into a provisional left wing, in view of probable early contact with the enemy, and placed General Reynolds in command.

General Buford, whose cavalry division was now operating in the vicinity of Gettysburg, kept sending back in formation of the enemy from that vicinity. On June 30 Meade issued the following precautionary and informative circulars:

Circular #1:

The Commanding General has received information that the enemy are advancing, probably in strong force, on Gettysburg. It is the intention to hold this army pretty nearly in the position it now occupies, until the plans of the enemy have been more fully developed.

Three corps, 1st, 3rd and 11th, are under the command of Major General Reynolds, in the vicinity of Emmettsburg, the 3rd Corps being ordered up to that point. The 12th Corps is at Littlestown. Gregg's division of cavalry is believed to be now engaged with the cavalry of the enemy, near Hanover Junction.

Corps commanders will hold their commands in readiness at a moment's notice, and upon receiving orders, to march against the enemy. Their trains (ammunition trains excepted) must be parked in the rear of the place of concentration. Ammunition wagons and ambulances will alone be permitted to accompany the troops. The men must be provided with three days' rations in haversacks, and with sixty rounds of ammunition in the boxes and upon the person.

Corps commanders will avail themselves of all the time at their disposal to familiarize themselves with the roads communicating with the different corps.

Circular #2:

The Commanding General requests that, previous to the engagement soon expected with the enemy, corps and all other commanding officers address their troops, explaining to them briefly the immense issues involved in the struggle. The enemy are on our soil; the whole country now looks anxiously to this army to deliver it from the presence of the foe. Our failure to do so will leave us no such welcome as the swelling of millions of hearts with pride and joy, as our success would give to every soldier of this army. Homes, firesides and domestic altars are involved. The army has fought well heretofore; it is believed that it will fight more desperately and bravely than ever, if it is addressed in fitting terms.

Corps and other commanders are authorized to order the instant death of any soldier who fails in his duty at this hour.

These circulars were followed shortly thereafter by orders for the march of July 1, which were directed to be executed immediately upon their receipt. Since the battle was joined on the morning of July 1, the order for the final march is of sufficient interest to be reprinted in full:

1st Corps to Gettysburg

2nd Corps to Taneytown

3rd Corps to Emmitsburg

5th Corps to Hanover

11th Corps to Gettysburg (or supporting distance)

12th Corps to Two Taverns

Cavalry to front and flanks, well out in all directions, giving timely notice of operations and movements of the enemy. All empty wagons, surplus bag gage, useless animals, and impedimenta of every sort, to Union Bridge, three miles from Middleburg; a proper officer from each corps with them; supplies will be brought up there as soon as practicable.

The General relies upon every commander to put his column in the lightest possible order. The Telegraph Corps to work east from Hanover, repairing the line, and all commanders to work repairing the line in their vicinity between Gettysburg and Hanover. Staff officers to report daily from each corps, and with orderlies to leave for orders. Prompt information to be sent into headquarters at all times. All ready to move to the attack at any moment.

The Commanding General desires you to be in formed that, from present information, Longstreet and Hill are at Chambersburg, partly toward Gettysburg; Ewell, at Carlisle and York; movements indicate a disposition to advance from Chambersburg to Gettysburg. General Couch telegraphs, 29th, his opinion that enemy's operations on Susquehanna are more to prevent cooperation with this army than offensive.

The General believes he has relieved Harrisburg and Philadelphia, and now desires to look to his own army and assume position for offensive or defensive, as occasion requires, or rest to the troops. It is not his desire to wear the troops out by excessive fatigue and marches, and thus unfit them for the work they will be called upon to perform.

Vigilance, energy, and prompt response to the orders from headquarters are necessary, and the personal attention of corps commanders must be given to reduction of impedimenta. The orders and movements from these headquarters must be carefully and confidentially preserved, that they do not fall into the enemy's hands.

It is pertinent to note that, in Meade's orders for June 29 and 30, the army was disposed in two north–south columns within supporting distance of one another. The order for July 1, after later information had been received as to Lee's movements, had four of the seven corps con verging on Gettysburg, while the Second, Fifth, and Sixth Corps were moved to within a short distance of the possible defense line of Big Pipe Creek. Sedgwick's Sixth Corps of over 15,000 men was in army reserve at Manchester, on the direct road to Baltimore, but over thirty-five miles distant from Gettysburg.

LEE REACTS PROMPTLY TO MEADE'S THREAT
Meade's threat to Lee's flank and rear confronted the latter with an entirely new problem requiring prompt decision and action, as the Army of the Potomac fanned out from Frederick along the roads to the north.

On arrival of the main body of his army in the Chambersburg area on Friday, June 26, Lee had established his head quarters in a grove which at that time stood along the pike leading to Gettysburg, near the eastern edge of Chambers burg. It was once known as Shetter's Woods, later as Messersmith's Woods, and was for years a popular place for local picnics and celebrations. Lee remained there until Tuesday morning June 30, received reports from his troops, held councils of war, planned the attack on Harrisburg, and finally issued the orders to cross South Mountain to seek out the Union army.

It was on the night of June 28 that Longstreet's scout had brought the first news of the presence of Meade's army and it was there, at Shetter's Woods, that Lee learned his old opponent, the Army of the Potomac, was not only un expectedly alive and kicking under a more worthy com- mander, but was actually moving rapidly forward in such a way as to constitute an acute danger to the widely dispersed Army of Northern Virginia.

Lee was quick to react. The first and most important job was to effect a rapid concentration of his army, preferably east of the Blue Ridge where he would have room for maneuver and could deny the vital pass at Cashtown to the Federals. The showdown battle was near at hand. He must have his troops assembled where he could employ them to advan- tage in whatever manner the next few days might indicate.

Stuart was still far to the south, with the Federals crowding the roads between Lee and himself. Although little has been written on the subject, the Confederate cavalry brigades under Lee's immediate command were all seemingly too far north or too far in Lee's rear in the valley to perform the reconnaissance missions necessary to determine the dispositions and movements of the Union forces, which were then only a few miles away on the other side of the mountains.

On the 29th Ewell was recalled from the Susquehanna and told to rejoin the other corps at Chambersburg. Then, on second thought, Lee directed all three of his corps to concentrate in the Cashtown area, east of the mountains. These orders of course took some time to reach Ewell, but he was no laggard when explicit instructions were given. His retrograde movement was initiated and executed with commendable dispatch.

SITUATION ON THE EVE OF BATTLE

On the night of Tuesday, June 30–July 1, the eve of the battle, this was the situation: more than 70,000 troops were in camp within a few miles of Gettysburg—27,000 Union infantry and cavalry and about 43,000 Confederate infantry, with a small scattering of cavalry.

On the Union side, Reynold's First and Howard's Eleventh Corps, totaling over 22,000 men, were bivouacked four to eight miles southwest of Gettysburg along Marsh Creek, with two-thirds of Buford's overstrength cavalry division, some 4,000 men, on the Chambersburg turnpike about a mile and a half northwest of Gettysburg.

With the exception of the aforementioned units, the Army of the Potomac was poised at varying distances south and southeast of Gettysburg: Sickles' corps a few miles east of Emmitsburg, eight miles south; Slocum's at Littles town, and Sykes' at Union Mills, both within fifteen miles of Gettysburg on the Gettysburg-Westminster road; Han cock's Second Corps at Uniontown, about twenty-four road miles from Gettysburg; while Sedgwick was out of immediate circulation at Manchester, on the direct road between Baltimore and Hanover. The Federal cavalry was tactically well disposed and active to the front and flanks, serving Meade far more effectively than was the case with Stuart and his detached brigades.

On the Confederate side, A. P. Hill's corps of 23,000 and Longstreet's 14,000 (excluding Pickett's division of 5,000 which was left to protect the rear and the trains at Chambersburg), an aggregate of approximately 37,000 men, were stretched out on the road between Chambers burg and Gettysburg or in bivouac on both sides of that pike. Hill's Corps was in the lead, with Heth's division east of South Mountain, having cleared the Cashtown pass. The other two divisions of Hill's corps, Pender's and Anderson's, joined Heth at Cashtown overnight, with Anderson going into bivouac at Cashtown and Pender joining Heth a few miles further east along Marsh Creek, about four miles from Gettysburg.

Ewell's corps of 23,000 was moving in from the north, with advance elements of Rodes' division bivouacking near Heidlersburg on the Harrisburg road, less, than ten miles from Gettysburg, while Ewell's other divisions were on the march to Cashtown by all available roads from Harrisburg, Carlisle, and York. Johnson's division of this corps spent the night at Greenwood, coming by way of Shippensburg, through Scotland.

The Confederate cavalry was still widely scattered, Stuart near Hanover and Jenkins covering Ewell's flank and rear to the north. Imboden's cavalry, twenty miles southwest of Chambersburg in the valley, was keeping the way open for the troopers of the two cavalry brigades commanded by Generals Jones and Robertson, who were coming up from the Potomac with instructions to protect the rear of Ewell's trains on arrival and then to follow the army towards Gettysburg.

It is a truism that the influence of terrain features and characteristics on military operations is all important; and the fact is confirmed by the frequency with which battles are identified as a result of the decisive part played by rivers, mountains, hills, roads, and towns in the drama of warfare.

GETTYSBURG AMPHITHEATER A TACTICAL PARADISE

Gettysburg was no exception. On the contrary, it is one of the foremost examples in American military history of the extent to which the topographical features of the countryside mark the course of battles. The Blue Ridge Mountains, the Cashtown pass, Oak Ridge, Seminary Ridge, Cemetery Ridge, the Emmitsburg road, Culp's Hill, the Round Tops, Willoughby Run, Marsh Creek, Devil's Den—all afford eloquent testimony of the impelling significance of terrain features in determining the what, where, why, and how of a battle which has few counterparts in American history from the viewpoint of tactical possibilities.

The town of Gettysburg nestles in a small valley surrounded by low ridges and hills, with the South Mountain range looming on the horizon ten miles to the west. About a half mile west of the town square is a moderate elevation called Seminary Ridge, running north and south, named from the Lutheran Theological Seminary that stands on its crest, midway between the Cashtown and Fairfield roads and about 300 yards from each. The ridge is covered throughout its entire length with open woods. The ground slopes away to the west and then rises to form McPherson's Ridge about 500 yards from the first. Both ridges start at Oak Hill, 1,200 yards north of the Chambersburg pike.

Willoughby Run crosses the Chambersburg pike in a north–south direction between McPherson's and still a third short, unnamed ridge to the west, and empties into Marsh Creek a few miles southwest of Gettysburg. Still further west is the last of the four parallel ridges, known as Herr Ridge, each of them several hundred yards apart and all forming natural successive positions, plentifully covered with open woods. These ridges, small valleys, and streams, coupled with an unfinished railway, just north of and paralleling the Cashtown pike, which crossed them all through cuts and fills, formed the stage upon which occurred the first skirmishes of the battle of Gettysburg. While Seminary Ridge and its angled prolongation through Gettysburg itself subsequently constituted the main Confederate position, an even more important key position was Cemetery Ridge, extending more than two miles directly south from the town. The ridge is flanked at its northern end by Cemetery Hill at the southeastern fringe of Gettysburg, and at its southern extremity by Big Round Top which is connected by a saddle to Little Round Top, several hundred yards to its north. Cemetery Ridge generally parallels the Emmitsburg road, with Big Round Top, the highest point' in the area, towering perhaps a hundred feet above Little Round Top. Both hills are boulder-studded-glacial deposits-terminating at the western base in a skirmisher's nightmare called Devil's Den.

East and southeast of Cemetery Hill rises wooded Culp's Hill, of almost equal importance with Round Top, since possession of Culp's Hill was vital to the troops occupying Cemetery Hill and Ridge, for flank protection and to preclude the devastating enfilade artillery fire of an opponent who could otherwise make Cemetery Hill untenable. The troops who control the Round Tops, Cemetery Ridge, Cemetery Hill, and Culp's Hill come pretty close to dominating the battlefield for defensive operations.

When the concentration of the opposing armies was complete, they faced one another on parallel ridges separated by approximately 1,200 yards of apple orchards and cultivated fields of wheat and grass, with the Emmitsburg Road bisecting them down a shallow valley, the whole adding up to a unique amphitheater upon which the major scenes of the drama were destined to be played out.

It may be interesting to note that in and around the town of Gettysburg is the greatest concentration of trap ridges in the southern part of Pennsylvania. Originally identified as such by Pennsylvania's first geologist, and shown on a geological map published in 1858, the possibility exists that General Meade and the geologist, Henry D. Rodgers, were acquainted before the war. Both were residents of Philadelphia, and it is an intriguing speculation that Meade may have been subconsciously aware of the solid strength of the Gettysburg hills.

LEE IN THE SADDLE EARLY; MEADE STAYS AT COMMAND POST

General Lee was in the saddle early on July 1, accompanying the rather slow movement of Longstreet's corps, which had been held up to allow one of Ewell's divisions, returning by the Carlisle-Chambersburg road, to pass through Longstreet's column. Having already issued the necessary orders for the concentration, Lee left the details of execution to his corps commanders, as was his custom, and consequently was free to devote his attention to consideration of possible plans for the inevitable battle, wherever it might occur.

General Meade, still playing a conservative game of chess, remained at his command post in Taneytown, estimating the situation, receiving a succession of reports from his cavalry, and conferring with his staff and the general officers whom he most trusted.

The march orders which he had sent out the night of June 30 for the next day directed Reynolds, now in command of the three-corps left wing (First, Third, and Eleventh Corps), to move his own First Corps to Gettysburg early next morning, followed by Howard's Eleventh, with Sickles' Third to inch westward a few miles from Bridgeport to Emmitsburg, eight miles south of Gettysburg. Reynolds was given authority to order Sickles farther forward if needed, but Meade was still apparently concerned about the mountain pass west of Emmitsburg and wanted to be sure that Lee should not catch him napping. Slocum's corps at Littlestown was to advance to Two Taverns, four miles closer and just halfway between Littlestown and Gettysburg on the Baltimore road.

Meade remained uncertain of Lee's intentions and was reluctant to pass up his Pipe Creek line of defense. So he compromised by advancing what might be called his first line of four corps to Gettysburg and vicinity, while retaining Hancock's, Sykes', and Sedgwick's corps on the arc Taneytown-Hanover-Manchester, within short marching distance of Big Pipe Creek, ready to jump either way. Sykes' projected move from Union Mills to Hanover, while the long way about to Gettysburg, had the merit of closing that very vital road net at Hanover, fourteen miles east of Gettysburg, in case Stuart's cavalry should become too aggressive, or Early's corps, known to have been at York, should decide to come down that way.

CHAPTER 30

Gettysburg I: July 1, 1863

WEST POINTER John Buford, a major in the Inspector General's Department, was a man of ideas with a capacity to make them work. It was in 1862 that General Pope, then commanding the Army of Virginia, accepted as sound Buford's lack of confidence in the effectiveness of the current cavalry techniques practiced in the Army. Pope promoted him rapidly from major to brigadier general and placed him in command of the largest of the three cavalry brigades in the service, so that he might try out what was then a somewhat revolutionary concept.

Stuart's Southern horse outfits had set the pattern of mass charges with the saber, which was in character be cause the Confederate cavalry was largely made up of men who had lived their lives in the saddle, mostly owned their own mounts, and for whom mounted maneuvers and skirmishes represented more fun than work.

BUFORD'S NEW TACTICS

For his part Buford considered the saber to be of little practical value. He thought of the horse as a means of transportation, useful chiefly because of the greatly increased mobility which it gave to the mounted troops. He treated cavalry as mounted infantry, and instilled that belief in his brigade and later his division, until it became practically instinctive. The procedure was to move rapidly to a critical position and dismount the troops to quickly form an infantry skirmish line, while one out of every four men became horseholder for the group, under cover to the immediate rear, ready at all times for the set of fours to re mount in an instant and gallop off to a new position. Buford knew that the inexperienced Union cavalry could never meet the Confederate cavalry on equal terms in mounted combat, so he made a winning virtue out of stark necessity.

An outstanding example of his methods had occurred just before second Manassas. Buford's brigade was at Thoroughfare Gap when Longstreet came through at the head of Lee's columns. Buford dismounted his cavalry and with 3,000 troopers held up 27,000 Confederates for six hours. Although Pope failed to support Buford, and Longstreet finally broke through to bring on the second Battle of Manassas, Buford had so dramatically demonstrated the effectiveness of the new technique that it be came virtually standing operating procedure from then on.

Buford's rise to fame as a cavalry leader stemmed logically from his success in proving the efficacy of his new methods. It was he who fought Stuart to a standstill at Aldie and Middleburg, as Lee's invasion was getting under way. So effective was the work of the Federal cavalry in Virginia during June that Stuart never did learn the significance of Hooker's movements. He was delayed to such an extent in his own time-table that he was forced to make a wide sweep around Hooker's rear by way of Rockville, a dozen miles north of Washington, with results disastrous to Lee's invasion program.

FEDERAL CAVALRY ADVANCES TO GETTYSBURG

On June 29 Buford's cavalry division was covering the Eleventh Corps west of Emmitsburg. Buford learned that Hill and Longstreet were in the direction of Chambers burg and Ewell in the Carlisle-York area. He saw the importance of occupying Gettysburg, so he marched there on June 30. He arrived just in time to make contact with the leading scouts of Pettigrew's brigade of Heth's Confederate division. Heth had sent Pettigrew to capture some stocks of shoes thought to be at Gettysburg. Pettigrew withdrew to Cashtown, while Buford outposted the high ground west of Gettysburg.

In anticipation of the enemy's return, Buford on the night of June 30 had divided the area west and north of Gettysburg into two parts. He assigned Gamble's brigade to the western sector and Devin's to the northern, and designated the Chambersburg pike as the dividing line, with pickets extending from beyond the Fairfield road on the south-west to a hillock near Rock Creek on the north east. Buford was spread rather thin, if indeed he had any serious idea that he could for long hold an outpost line extending for some five miles in the above described arc against Heth's division of 7,500 men and five artillery batteries. But it was a bold calculated risk and when the payoff came between 8:00 and 10:00 o'clock the next morning he had his dismounted squadrons in position to stage a typically Bufordian delaying action.

THE FIRST CLASH

The gray light of dawn was beginning to outline the trees, buildings, and other objects for the four-man Federal picket posted on the Chambersburg turnpike near Willoughby Run about a mile and a half west of Gettysburg. It was 5:20 on the morning of Wednesday, July 1. The night had proven uneventful for the lonely cavalry groups strung across country in a huge semicircle along Willoughby Run, from southwest to northeast cutting across the several roads that reached out from the town, where the pickets had been placed by Buford's cavalry commanders the preceding afternoon after driving out a scouting party of Confederates, who fled toward Cash town.

Corporal Alphonse Hodges, Company F, 9th New York Cavalry, Buford's Division, had very much on his mind the division commander's warning to his troopers that Confederate troops were on the move and they must be even more alert than usual. There had been no sign of the enemy, expected from the direction of Cashtown. The corporal's relief would soon take over and permit him to get back to a welcome breakfast of hard tack and bacon, with a scalding tin-cup full of fragrant coffee to wash it down.

As the darkness faded and visibility improved, the corporal observed shadowy figures moving down the road toward him, half a mile away. Sending his men to notify the pickets to right and left and the support in rear, Hodges advanced down the road for a closer look. Just then the enemy fired on him. Jumping for cover, he sent several shots in their direction and then judiciously doubled back to McPherson's Ridge where he joined the organized skirmish line that his regimental commander, as soon as he heard the shots, had promptly built up from the pickets on duty north and south of the pike.

The Battle of Gettysburg had opened.

In a few moments the advance guard of Pettigrew's Confederate brigade, heretofore unaware of the existence of more than a reconnaissance detachment of the enemy in Gettysburg, appeared in force, deployed to right and left of the road, and pushed forward their skirmish lines. Buford immediately dispatched couriers to Meade, Reynolds, and his own corps commander, General Pleasonton.

MORE UNITS DRAWN INTO THE FIGHT

During that hectic two-hour period on the morning of July 1, what started out as a dignified frontal meeting engagement with advance elements of both forces astride the Chambersburg pike soon developed into a snarling dog fight. Heth's Confederate division moved into position with two brigades in line and two in support, confronting two Federal cavalry brigades. The Federals had dismounted and consequently were able to use only 75 percent of their strength for fighting; the horse holders—one for every four men—had their hands full keeping the animals quiet in rear of the fighting line. It is likely that Buford had considerably less than 3,000 rifles on the line against Heth's strength of more than twice that number. Buford was further handicapped by a shortage of artillery. Calef's Battery A, Second U.S. Artillery alone supported the Federal cavalry with six guns. Several times, unaided by rifle fire, it disrupted violent enemy infantry rushes.

Both sides suffered heavy casualties in the early stages, particularly in and near the railroad cuts which parallel the Chambersburg Pike north of the Seminary and near McPherson's farmhouse. The cut near McPherson's was especially critical. Initially Gamble's brigade of Buford's division took position with its right resting on the cut and extending south across the road. When Wadsworth's division (First Corps) arrived and relieved the cavalry about 10 A.M. Calef withdrew, being replaced by Hall's 2nd Maine Battery which in turn supported Wadsworth.

Buford had personally taken advantage of the Lutheran Seminary on the ridge and was putting it to effective use as an observation post. His message to General Reynolds reached the latter as he was leading his First Corps up from its overnight bivouac on Marsh Creek. Hearing the sounds of battle, Reynolds quickly diverted the column across country and galloped to the Seminary, from which he and Buford rode on to the front on the last personal reconnaissance that Reynolds was ever to make.

The battle-experienced Reynolds lost no time in estimating the situation. He sent word back to Howard to rush the Eleventh Corps forward, and directed the divisions of Wadsworth and Robinson, now within a short distance of the field, to assume the burden of the fight by passing through and relieving the weakened lines of the hard-fighting dismounted cavalry.

McPherson's Woods

In the course of the melee, as the lines surged back and forth on and between the ridges, Davis' Confederate brigade drove Cutler's Federal brigade back to Seminary Ridge and was in turn decimated and driven from the field by the Fourteenth New York Infantry and the Sixth Wisconsin in combination. On another part of the battle field Archer's Confederate brigade seized McPherson's Woods where it was in turn attacked by the famous "Iron Brigade," composed of troops from Wisconsin, Michigan, and Indiana. Archer's brigade was outflanked, and captured almost to a man, including General Archer himself.

McPherson's Woods will be remembered for two other reasons, for it was there that a sharpshooter's bullet killed John F. Reynolds, and the Confederates belatedly learned that they had tangled with a tougher foe than the local troops that had been encountered in their virtually unopposed advance through northern territory. Catching sight of the black-hatted members of the Iron Brigade, an excited Confederate soldier was heard to shout: "Hell, that aint no milishy—that's the Army of the Potomac!"

Lee's Divisions Converge on Gettysburg

Meantime, Buford had side-slipped Devin's cavalry brigade to the vicinity of Oak Hill, northwest of the town, to dispute the advance of Ewell's troops who were approaching Gettysburg from the north by the Carlisle and Harrisburg roads. There the hard-fighting cavalrymen duplicated their stellar performance on *the* Chambersburg road, forced Rodes'

Confederate division to deploy and slow down, and made it extremely difficult for Ewell and A. P. Hill to coordinate the advance of their respective corps from the north and west. After which, sometime in the early afternoon, the exhausted troopers of both cavalry brigades were pulled out and reassembled in the shallow valley south of Gettysburg along the Emmitsburg Road. There they caught their second wind, and under took the mission of protecting the army's left flank in the general area south of the town.

By 11 A.M. Reynold's entire First Corps was suitably deployed on both sides of the Cashtown Pike and hotly engaged, while Devin's cavalry brigade was covering the right flank east of the Mummasburg Road in the Oak Hill area and disputing the right of way of advance elements of Ewell's threat from the north. For the time being, despite the vastly superior Confederate forces at the point of con tact, the Federals had the advantage of position, the confidence that went with it, and the morale-inducing satisfaction that they had stopped Lee in his tracks for the moment at least.

Heavy fighting swirled in and about the railroad cut, occupied by Federal infantry who inflicted severe casualties on Confederates advancing from the northwest. When the Federals withdrew from the cut it was quickly occupied by a Mississippi regiment, most of whom were in turn promptly captured as the result of a sudden Union countercharge. The railroad bed came under enfilade fire from Confederate artillery, which gave Hall's Battery a bad time as it withdrew in successive stages to the east under orders from General Wadsworth, who feared the complete loss of his major artillery support.

Human flesh and blood simply cannot sustain that kind of toe-to-toe slugging without occasionally stopping for breath and realignment. By noon both contestants found it necessary to take time out to reestablish their lines and prepare for the next round. This was not long in coming.

BUFORD'S CONTRIBUTION

The significant contribution which Buford's cavalry made to the final checkmate of the Confederates at Getty burg has never received adequate recognition. It covered the left front and effectively screened Meade's army from observation as it advanced to meet Lee. Buford, with only two of his three brigades (Merritt's had been left at Mechanicstown to guard the trains), was first on the scene at Gettysburg's critical crossroads at the right time. Then with not over 4,000 cavalrymen he delayed the advance of Hill's corps from Cashtown and Ewell's corps from Heidlersburg, causing the leading divisions of both to effect premature deployments. At the same time he gave the Union Army the necessary breather for Reynold's First Corps and Howard's Eleventh to reach the scene, engage the Confederates in a desperate struggle and then, falling back, to solidly occupy Cemetery Ridge, which turned out to be the keystone of the Federal defense.

To sum up Buford's accomplishments in the face of overwhelming Confederate superiority; although he was finally engulfed by main force, his troops had held for over two hours and by their dogged delaying tactics had gained time for the First Corps to come up and further delay Lee's concentration, and for Meade to speed the development of the rest of his army in the direction of Gettysburg. It is not too much to say that Buford's cavalry was the major instrument that caused the battle to be fought at Gettysburg rather than elsewhere. They were successful in preventing coordinated action in the approach march by Hill and Ewell. That in turn delayed Long street's corps, which failed to reach the battlefield in time to exploit Hill's afternoon success in driving the First and Eleventh Federal Corps back to Cemetery Ridge. The successive chain of events contributed much to Ewell's failure to attack and seize Culp's Hill until it was too late.

> "*I AM satisfied that Longstreet and Hill have made a junction. A tremendous battle has been raging since nine and one-half A.M. with varying success. At the present moment the battle is raging on the road to Cashtown, and in short cannon range of this town (Gettysburg); the enemy's line is a semi-circle on the height from north to west. General Reynolds was killed early this morning. In my opinion there seems to be no directing person–we need help now.*"

Buford's well-known dispatch to cavalry commander Pleasanton, who was at Meade's headquarters in Taney town, early on the afternoon of July 1, told the story up to then in a few brief, pithy sentences.

Howard's three-division Eleventh Corps had bivouacked the night of June 30 about eight miles south of Gettysburg along Marsh Creek, but for some unexplained reason failed to emulate the rapid movement of the First Corps to the battlefield to support Buford, and it was not until 1 P.M. that the leading elements of Howard's corps came up the Emmitsburg road. By that time Buford had in formed Howard of Ewell's advance from Heidlersburg, whereupon Howard promptly sent word to Sickles at Emmitsburg and Slocum at Two Taverns to send up reinforcements at once.

SEVEN SUCCESSIVE COMMANDERS
During the early hours of the developing battle, that portion of the Union army reaching the field was successively commanded by four general officers, Brig. Gen. John Buford, and Major Generals John F. Reynolds, Abner Doubleday, and Oliver O. Howard. Doubleday commanded the Third Division of Reynolds' corps, and assumed overall command when he reached the field and was informed of Reynolds' death. Howard, commanding the Eleventh Corps, reached the field in person shortly before noon. As senior in command he took over from Doubleday, but his chief contribution was to place the troops of the First and Eleventh Corps as they streamed back to Cemetery Ridge in the afternoon. Two more corps commanders, Major Generals Hancock and Slocum, also became acting army commanders during the course of the day, for it was not until midnight of the first day that General Meade himself arrived on the field to personally take charge of the campaign. Rarely if ever has history recorded a single battle in which the supreme command on the field was vested in seven different generals in a period of less than sixteen hours. The confusion among the lower echelons, caused by the rapid change in command, will be readily understood by those who have had battlefield responsibility.

On taking over army command from Doubleday, Howard assigned one of his division commanders, General Schurz, temporarily to command the Eleventh Corps, instructing him to extend Doubleday's (First Corps) defensive line in the direction of Barlow Knoll. Schurz placed Schimmelfennig's and Barlow's divisions with three batteries in support, as directed, holding Steinwehr's division and two batteries in reserve on Cemetery Hill, an extremely wise decision as it turned out.

Schurz disposed his 6,000 men in the open about 800 yards north of Gettysburg, astride the Harrisburg, Carlisle, and Mummasburg Roads, but the line was terribly thin to cover such a wide frontage and failed by a considerable margin to connect with Doubleday's First Corps to the west of town.

By the middle of the afternoon two of Ewell's divisions, Rodes' and Early's, and two of Hill's, Heth's and Pender's, were linked up in a wide semicircle north and west of Gettysburg. The Federals were now threatened on two fronts by the combined Confederate corps, which initiated a formal, coordinated attack on the Union First and Eleventh Corps. There was severe fighting for over an hour, during which Devin's dismounted Federal cavalrymen were driven from their position on Rock Creek. Barlow's division of the Eleventh Corps suffered the same fate after restoring the line given up by the cavalry under overwhelming pressure. By 4 P.M. the Confederates out numbered the Federals so heavily, both west and north of Gettysburg, that a withdrawal to Cemetery Hill was ordered by Howard.

The Federals Break for Cemetery Ridge

Fighting a desperate rear guard action, and struggling to prevent outflanking maneuvers by the Confederates on both the left and right of the overextended Federal line, the First and Eleventh Federal Corps were pressed relentlessly back on Gettysburg. Doubleday's corps withdrew through the southern edge of town and across Seminary Ridge and the Emmitsburg Road south of Gettysburg, while the Eleventh Corps was forced to pass directly through the heart of the town. Buford's cavalry, after being relieved, had reassembled in the open area south of Gettysburg between Seminary and Cemetery Ridges, covering the left flank. During the withdrawal of the First Corps, the cavalrymen again went into effective action and prevented Hill from interfering with the retrograde movement of the infantry by coming around on the latter's left rear.

The retreat of the Eleventh Corps, first to break, uncovered the right flank and rear of the First Corps, which might otherwise have held for a longer period. The latter well-disciplined organization, however, effected its withdrawal in reasonably good order and what remained of it was placed on the left of Steinwehr's reserve brigade, which had been posted on its arrival on the crest of Cemetery Hill and from which it was not moved during the first day's fighting.

Steinwehr, a professional soldier who had served in the German Army, with methodical Teuton thoroughness had immediately put the men of his brigade to work digging gun emplacements and rifle pits among the tombstones of the cemetery. This salutary move served the dual purpose of strengthening the position for defense and giving a much-needed lift to the morale of the surviving portions of the First and Eleventh Corps.

The retreat of the two divisions of the Eleventh Corps, in contradistinction to the action of the First Corps, unfortunately developed into what may fairly be called a rout. The men got themselves thoroughly entangled in the streets of Gettysburg, were overrun by the pursuing Confederates, and lost several thousand effectives as prisoners. The rout would have been even worse had not Steinwehr sent forward one of his two brigades to the north side of Gettysburg to serve as a rear guard in covering the panicky withdrawal of the other two divisions of the corps.

HANCOCK RESTORES ORDER

As the retiring Federals streamed back from two directions toward Cemetery Hill, the presence of General Hancock on the eminence, and his calmness in the face of the disorganized retreat had a magic effect in restoring shattered morale and in bringing some order out of chaos. The losses of the First and Eleventh Corps on the first day had exceeded 10,000 men in killed, wounded, captured, and missing, leaving less than half of their original strength for the heavy work ahead. Despite their losses, it was no time to stand on ceremony or to sympathize with their predicament. General Hancock was a determined character. He had galloped up from army headquarters at Taneytown under orders from Meade to take charge of operations, and to advise the commanding general if the Gettysburg area was the place to stand and fight. The vital importance of his recommendation, for or against, placed a heavy responsibility on Hancock, but he was equal to it. Observing Culp's Hill a few hundred yards to the east of Cemetery Hill, and immediately recognizing its tactical significance, Hancock ordered Doubleday, just arriving with the depleted First Corps, to send a division to occupy it. Doubleday was understandably upset, protesting that he had no men to spare and that they were not in condition to make any further effort right then. Hancock refused to accept his protestations, despite the circumstances, and exerting his authority as acting army commander, summarily ordered him to send Wadsworth's division to Culp's Hill. This was done, but the state of mind and strength of the occupying division was such that the Confederates could probably have pushed them over with a feather had they made the effort at any time during the afternoon.

Howard's official report, summing up with fair accuracy, as far as it went, the events of the first day, during most of which he had acted as the overall field commander, stated that "The First and Eleventh Corps, numbering less than 18,000 men, nobly aided by Buford's Division of cavalry, had engaged and held in check nearly double their numbers from 10:00 o'clock in the morning until 7:00 in the evening."

To the objective reader, who recalls that Howard's Eleventh Corps had been in disrepute ever since Stonewall Jackson surprised and routed them on the Union right flank at Chancellorsville, Major Halstead's account may sound slightly prejudiced. The Eleventh Corps contained many regiments composed largely of men of foreign lineage, especially Germans. A rallying cry attributed to the soldiers of the corps had been: "I fights mit Sigel," the name of the illustrious German who first led them. After a change of commanders and the disaster at Chancellorsville, some of the other corps had added the rather unkind legend: "I runs mit Howard."

Hancock's diplomatic attitude undoubtedly prevented what could easily have been a bitter difference of opinion, with resultant conflicting actions, further loss of confidence, and the probable loss of Cemetery Hill, Cemetery Ridge, and the Battle of Gettysburg.

THE CONFEDERATES MISS AN OPPORTUNITY

The Confederates had lost a rare opportunity to win the battle before dark the first day, and the blame must fairly be divided between Lee and Ewell. As Lee, from his position on Seminary Ridge in the early afternoon, through his field glasses watched the Federals streaming back through Gettysburg and across the fields to the protection of Cemetery Hill, he felt instinctively that victory was in his grasp. He immediately dispatched his Adjutant General, Colonel W. H. Taylor, to tell General Ewell that he, Lee, could see the enemy retreating over the hills in confusion and apparently greatly disorganized. Colonel Taylor's account quotes Lee as using these words: "It was only necessary to press 'those people' in order to secure possession of the heights; and, if possible, he wished General Ewell to do this." Taylor writes that he immediately galloped over to General Ewell and delivered Lee's order and that Ewell did not indicate any objection but left the impression on Taylor's mind that the order would be executed.

Lee's message to Ewell reached the latter early in the afternoon, before Hancock had come up to Cemetery Hill and was bringing order into the Union ranks. Ewell's corps had suffered heavily in the day's fighting up to that time and both he and Hill had earlier received specific orders from Lee not to bring on a general engagement, but to wait until the army was assembled. Johnson's division of Ewell's corps had not yet arrived, so in the exercise of the discretion which Lee invariably permitted to his corps commanders, and also having in mind Lee's earlier admonition, Ewell vacillated. Finally, despite vehement urging from at least two of his general officers, he put off the pursuit until evening. By this time Union reinforcements had arrived and it was too late for Ewell to make the attack with reasonable assurance of success.

General Johnson, whose division had been on the way from the Chambersburg area since early morning, was under orders on arrival to extend the Confederate line from Rock Creek to the east. But his division did not arrive until after sunset, and in the meantime the Federals occupied Culp's Hill and profitably thickened their defensive line on Cemetery Hill and the Ridge.

EWELL FAILS TO MEASURE UP
Ewell's reputation suffered badly as a result of his indecision. The hopes of the Confederacy that they had found a worthy successor to Stonewall

Jackson were rudely shattered. Undoubtedly Lee, after the great promise which Ewell had shown in his rapid and aggressive march through Pennsylvania, expected him to do as Jackson would have done. But Ewell was cast in a different mold and had not yet learned to successfully interpret Lee's discretionary orders in the Jacksonian manner. Ewell was accustomed to positive and precise instructions from Jackson, his former corps commander. He lacked the self-assurance and initiative, possibly even the character necessary to exercise corps command in a decisive way.

The Confederate Colonel Swallow, who was present and witnessed all that transpired, has said that he personally pointed out the opportunity to Generals Early and Hays of Ewell's corps, convinced Early that Culp's Hill could be seized, with its strategic command of the Baltimore road, and that the two generals then prepared to launch the attack on Culp's Hill as soon as they could secure positive orders from Ewell. But in that they were unsuccessful.

So depressed were Ewell's subordinates, knowing how Jackson would have acted under similar circumstances, that one of them, General Trimble, is reported to have thrown his sword aside with the statement that he would refuse further to serve under such a general. Ewell's failure to differentiate between bringing on a general engagement and aggressively exploiting such an opportunity as was presented to him to completely disrupt Meade's buildup, simply means that Ewell, in refusing to take a calculated risk, failed to demonstrate the qualities of a great general.

Even after Johnson's division arrived and took position on the left of the Confederate line, and before it had advanced any great distance, Johnson received orders to halt. Colonel Taylor has quoted Johnson as telling him after the war that no reason was given for him to halt. But considering the timing of the message, early evening of July I, it is apparent that Ewell was tired, confused, and unable to think constructively, hence took the easy course and marked time. By that time, however, the golden opportunity had passed. It was perhaps just as well that Ewell did not send Johnson forward.

In Ewell's official report he gave as his reasons for not ordering the attack the fact that he could not bring artillery to bear on Cemetery Hill; that all his troops on the field were worn out by twelve hours of marching and fighting; that Cemetery Hill was not assailable from the town; that when Johnson's division arrived it was his intention to take possession of Culp's Hill, which in turn would command Cemetery Hill. Before Johnson's arrival, Federals had been reported moving in the direction of Ewell's left flank and by the time their movement had been reconnoitered and Johnson had arrived, "the night was far advanced," in Ewell's words.

The road from Chambersburg to Gettysburg must have been a frustrating stretch of real estate during June 30 and July 1, not only to Generals Lee and Long street, but also to the many thousands of junior officers and men who were being urged forward uphill along the long, hot, dusty, and congested pike on which infantry, artillery, and wagon trains vied for the right of way.

CONFEDERATE TRAFFIC JAM

That single road approach through Cashtown pass to the Gettysburg battlefield had a significant effect on Con federate fortunes. Just one conveniently located parallel highway would have been worth a couple of divisions to General Lee. As it was, he waited too long to start his army forward. The fortunes of war paved the way for the Union army, close to defeat on the afternoon of the first day, to dig its claws into Cemetery Ridge and hang on until nightfall, when the corps of Sickles and Slocum arrived on the field to help redress the numerical balance of power.

General Lee, mounted on Traveller, had left Chambersburg in company with Longstreet on June 30. He bivouacked that night at Greenwood, ten miles east of Chambersburg and about half way between that town and Cashtown. He was still anxiously waiting for some word from Stuart, but was by that time fully convinced that he had to get his army east of the Blue Ridge to meet Meade, of whose strength and detailed dispositions he was still unaware.

Early on the morning of July 1 the last division of Hill's corps, Anderson's, filed past Greenwood. Soon thereafter Lee mounted and rode along with Longstreet at the head of the latter's corps, which had been ordered to follow Anderson's division to Cashtown. Coming to a road junction a short distance ahead, they ran into Johnson's division of Ewell's corps which was cutting into the main pike from another dirt road that angled in from the northwest. This division, responding to Lee's first order of June 29 to return to Chambersburg, had come down the Carlisle Pike toward Chambersburg. On the road Johnson received Lee's message shifting the objective to Cashtown, whereupon he changed direction at Green Village, a few miles below Shippensburg, passed through Scotland and cut into the Chambersburg-Gettysburg Road near Greenwood. So there he was, blocking the only road to Cash town. On Lee's order Longstreet halted his own corps to give Johnson the right of way, not knowing that behind that division were trailing the complete wagon trains of both Johnson and, Rodes. Including Johnson's infantry and artillery, the column covered a good fifteen miles, so Longstreet's corps settled down for a wait that must have consumed at least six hours.

LEE RIDES TO THE SOUND OF GUNS

Impatient to get forward and learn what was happening east of the mountain, Lee and Longstreet, with their respective staffs, rode on past Johnson's marching men. As their horses climbed the western slope of the Blue Ridge, they met the occasional rumble of artillery fire and, after crossing the crest, the unmistakable sound of heavier firing. Leaving Longstreet to "hasten" the march of his corps, Lee spurred forward alone and after a fast ride met A. P. Hill at Cashtown. The latter, a sick man, knew little except that Heth's division had advanced on Gettysburg. Anderson was then sent for but he knew no more than Hill, so Lee galloped on again toward the front, never before having been so completely blanketed, in the presence of the enemy, by the traditional fog of war.

As a direct result of the aforementioned road pm, McLaws' division of Longstreet's corps failed to reach Marsh Creek, four miles west of Gettysburg, until a little after dark on July 1, while Hood's division, following McLaws, arrived in the same area about midnight. Longstreet's third division, commanded by General Pickett, remained at Chambersburg to guard the army trains.

Longstreet has written that his artillery was not able to hit the road from Greenwood until 2 A.M. on July 2, but there is some question as to the exactness of his memory on that point.

Imboden's cavalry, having covered the arrival of the cavalry brigades of Jones and Robertson from the Shenandoah Valley, was ordered to move from Mercersburg to Chambersburg to relieve Pickett's understrength division. The latter was then to proceed to Gettysburg. As it turned out, Imboden's brigade entered Chambersburg on Wednesday afternoon, July 1, and was thus available for a more active cavalry mission had Lee chosen to assign one.

MEADE FINALLY TAKES CONTROL

It was almost noon of July 1 before Meade received the first news of the opening engagement west of Gettysburg. One of Reynolds' aides had been sent post-haste with the news when Reynolds and Buford first met about 10 o'clock at the Lutheran Seminary, about the time the First Corps was rushing in to relieve Buford's dismounted cavalry. The essence of Reynolds' message was that the enemy was advancing in strong force and might well seize the Gettysburg heights before Reynolds could do so, but that he would contest the advance "inch by inch" and "if driven into the town, I will barricade the streets and hold them back as long as possible."

Shortly after the Reynolds' message was received Meade had the Buford dispatch to Pleasonton (quoted in full on page 135) and about 1 o'clock received further news of Reynolds' death. The logical man to succeed Reynolds, General Hancock, was close at hand. Within a few minutes he was given written orders from Meade to turn over the command of his Second Corps to Gibbon, proceed to Gettysburg, take over the First, Eleventh, and Third Corps and "if you think the ground and position there a better one to fight a battle under existing circumstances, you will so advise the General and he will order all his troops up."

During the next few hours, as other news filtered back from the front, Meade became convinced that Lee was concentrating his entire army at Gettysburg. Having reached that accurate conclusion, and without waiting for a positive recommendation from Hancock, Meade mentally discarded the Pipe Creek directive and at 4:30 P.M. sent word to Sykes' Fifth and Slocum's Twelfth Corps, at Hanover and Littlestown respectively, to move to Gettysburg, at the same time notifying Sedgwick to move his Sixth Corps from Manchester to Taneytown.

By 6 P.M. Meade had finally begun to cerebrate, sending a message to Hancock that Gettysburg seemed to be the inevitable battlefield, and that "if we can get up our people and attack with our whole force tomorrow, we ought to defeat the force the enemy has." At 7 P.M. further orders were sent to Sykes' Fifth Corps to speed up its march; to the Second Corps to move up from Taneytown; and to the Sixth Corps to proceed directly by forced marches to Gettysburg, thirty-five miles distant, with the significant comment that "we shall be largely outnumbered with out your presence." That statement was in fact a substantial exaggeration, since Meade credited Lee with some 20,000 men in excess of his actual strength. But it had become traditional for Federal army commanders, for reasons best known to themselves, to overestimate the Con federate strength.

About 10 P.M., accompanied by his artillery chief, General Hunt, and the rest of his staff, Meade started on horseback for the front. It was pitch dark, and the road was crowded with foot soldiers and artillery. One stop only did he make, to confer with General Gibbon, commanding the Second Corps, which by that time had arrived within a few miles of Gettysburg. It was after midnight when Meade rode up to Cemetery Hill and took over command from Slocum, who then rejoined his own corps.

Once on the ground, Meade took hold vigorously, made a personal reconnaissance of the Ridge position, conferred with his several corps commanders on the ground, and ordered certain readjustments in the line. By 9 A.M., July 2 he had six of his seven infantry corps (Sedgwick being still on the road) skillfully disposed for defense along the "fish hook."

BATTLEFIELD CONTROL

Disturbing lack of positive information had plagued both Lee and Meade during the early hours of July 1. As the concentration of the two armies progressed with the successive arrival on the held of new divisions from all points of the compass, however, the picture began to become clearer to both commanders. By early afternoon Lee was on Seminary Ridge in person, in time to see his troops drive the Federals back to Cemetery Hill. On the other side, Meade was still operating by remote control from his command post at Taneytown, thirteen miles from the battlefield, from which point he did not stir until two hours before midnight.

In contrast to present day techniques, and in retrospect, Civil War battles seem almost primitive insofar as communications, firepower, and battlefield control are concerned. The principles of war, however, were the same in 1863, when the exercise of troop leadership, skill in maneuver, logistical know-how, maintenance of morale among the men in the ranks, and all the other imponderables of warfare were just as important and, when effectively utilized by experienced and capable generals, just as rewarding as in today's atomic age.

The manner in which an army commander employs the means at his command, before, during, and after a battle, affords the measure of his generalship. The Confederate army was led by one of the finest gentlemen and ablest generals that this or any other country has ever produced. The Union army was commanded by a comparative newcomer who, it is true, had proven himself as a division commander and briefly as a corps commander, but who had yet to demonstrate his capacity to handle a large army with a sizable cavalry contingent attached. He was of course relatively unfamiliar with this army, the control of which was thrown into his lap while on the march, virtually in the face of a confident, invading enemy of supposedly equal strength.

Lee had at Gettysburg only four corps commanders to deal with Longstreet, Ewell, A. P. Hill, and J. E. B. Stuart; since Stuart was elsewhere, really only three, two of whom, Ewell and Hill, were new and as yet not blooded in corps command.

Meade had eight corps commanders in his army, Reynolds, Hancock, Sickles, Sykes, Sedgwick, Howard, Slocum, and Pleasonton. He would probably have been better off with half that number if someone had had the foresight to have reorganized the Army of the Potomac into a more compact, more easily controlled type of fighting machine. Not the "Grand Divisions" of earlier, unhappy days, but something akin to them, such as the temporary three-corps wing that Reynolds commanded until his death in the early hours of the battle.

Meade's precautionary Pipe Creek retirement order, which, incidentally, never reached General Reynolds, had caused some misunderstanding, and in fact was almost disastrously interpreted by General Slocum, commanding Twelfth Corps. Slocum's reluctance to assume the responsibility of commanding the fight on the afternoon of July 1, at Gettysburg, despite the fact that he was senior corps commander after Reynolds' death, is somewhat difficult to understand. General Howard stated in his official report that on three separate occasions during the afternoon he had sent messages to Slocum at Two Taverns, less than five miles from Gettysburg, appealing for support. The third messenger reached Slocum about 4:30 P.M. on the Baltimore pike, about one mile from Gettysburg, at which time Slocum sent back a message that he had already sent a division to the right and would send another to the left as requested but "that he did not wish to come up in person to the front and take the responsibility of the fight." Slocum afterward stated that "it was against the wish of the commanding general to bring on a general engagement at that point" (apparently referring to the alternative position selected in the Pipe Creek order).

Despite his reluctance, when Slocum reached Cemetery Hill about 7 P.M. and discovered the true situation, he accepted the command that Hancock turned over to him. Hancock then rode back to Taneytown to confer with General Meade.

TROOP DISPOSITIONS AT CLOSE OF FIRST DAY

By midnight of the first day, with the two armies partially concentrated, the buildup had developed in such a way that the Confederate line occupied the terrain on and in prolongation of Seminary Ridge to the west, bending around through the town of Gettysburg and on to the east across Rock Creek in the direction of Culp's Hill. Thus it formed a curving line initially over three and ultimately about five miles in length, with sufficient cover in the woods and the town to prevent detailed observation of their movements from the Union side.

The Union line, in the form of the historic "fish hook," was initially somewhat shorter and practically ideal for defense, due to the character of the wood-covered ridge, the open fields toward the enemy main line, the rocky hills, and the useful road net leading south and east from the fish hook; and also because it gave Meade the advantage of interior lines that immeasurably simplified his problem of shifting reserves on short order to meet enemy thrusts against any part of the line.

With the Federal bow-shaped line presenting its convex side to the Confederates, its chord, when the entire length of the position was finally occupied, was not more than three miles as the crow flies from Meade's extreme right flank to his left; while Lee, the concave face of whose line was toward the Union position, had about nine miles to cover in the transmission of messages from the extreme of one flank to the other.

COMPARATIVE STRENGTHS

At the close of the first day, with darkness covering the field of battle, Lee still held the advantage of numbers, but his superiority was diminishing and during the night disappeared entirely. By 6 A.M. on the second day, the Army of the Potomac had been reinforced by over 25,000 fighting men, giving Meade a decided edge in numerical strength, in addition to which the flexibility of control afforded by his position magnified the effect of his numerical superiority.

Hancock's Second Corps and Sykes' Fifth Corps were now up, together with the reserve artillery. The only absentees were Sedgwick's Sixth Corps and the two cavalry divisions of Gregg and Kilpatrick. The Sixth Corps, more than 15,000 men, making a forced march from Manchester, thirty-five miles distant, trudged the roads all that night. With a short rest the following morning this corps reached Gettysburg about mid-afternoon July 2, when it became the army reserve east and in rear of the Round Tops.

Pickett's division of Longstreet's corps remained at Chambersburg awaiting relief by Imboden's cavalry; Law's brigade of Hood's division had not yet reached the field, and Stuart's cavalry was still absent. Otherwise the Army of Northern Virginia was now fully assembled and in the positions ordered, the cavalry brigades of Jones and Robertson having reached the Chambersburg area.

LONGSTREET FAVORS THE DEFENSIVE

General Lee and his chief lieutenant, Lieutenant General James Longstreet, were far apart in their military thinking—both strategic and

tactical—prior to and during the course of the invasion and the culminating Battle of Gettysburg. At no time during those historically decisive
days of June and July, 18631, was there anything but a superficial meeting
of minds between the two, concerning lines of action to be pursued.

Longstreet was opposed to the invasion in the first place, believing
that the cause of the Confederacy would be better served by reinforcing
the western armies, under the direct command of Lee, with the object
of defeating Grant and relieving Vicksburg. When those views were
rejected, he had urged Lee to adhere to the strategic defensive in the
course of his march into Pennsylvania, and, recalling Fredericksburg, to
lure the Army of the Potomac into another attack against a position of
Lee's own choosing, and thus to allow Hooker, then in command of the
Union army, to shatter it in a repeat performance.

Lee was more offensive-minded. While he had listened politely to his
"old war-horse," he was not impressed with Longstreet's theory. The latter
was fully assured in his own mind, however, that Lee, while refusing to
adopt the plan for a *strategic* defensive, had in fact accepted Longstreet's
conception of the *tactical* defensive. He held to that assurance all through
the battles at Gettysburg, with complete and almost casual disregard of
Lee's actions and direct orders to the contrary.

Such misunderstanding, if it can be called only that, was more than
an imponderable; it became a concrete and quite possibly *the* decisive
factor in the outcome of the battle. The Gettysburg story is not complete without recording the historic exchange of views between Lee and
Longstreet on the afternoon of the first day, and the certain impact, on
the tactical developments of July 2 and 3, of the diametrically opposed
thinking of the two generals. As Longstreet with his staff rode along
the Chambers burg Pike through Cashtown toward the sound of firing,
his trained eye had appraised the tactical possibilities of the terrain
west of Gettysburg. He reconstructed the broad outlines, based on the
positions of the large number of dead and wounded soldiers of both
armies, of the clash that morning between Heth's infantry and Buford's
cavalry.

It was late afternoon of July 1 when he crossed the last low ridge,
saw the houses of Gettysburg off to the east, and joined Lee on Seminary

Ridge. From this slight eminence Lee had for some time been observing the Federals retreating across the shallow valley to Cemetery Hill.

The exact words used by Lee and Longstreet at this initial meeting on the battlefield have been variously 'reported by historians, who agree generally to their substance. Lee remarked that they seemed to have run into Meade's main body, that something must have happened to Stuart, and that he had sent word to Ewell "to seize that hill south of town (Cemetery Hill) if practicable." He added further that he had not intended to fight at Gettysburg, but could not withdraw without impairing the morale of his men, and that "if Meade is there tomorrow I will attack him."

Longstreet's opinion as to the wisdom of adhering to the tactical defensive had not changed, and Lee's comments seemed to fall on deaf ears. Whether or not Ewell should succeed in driving the Federals off the hill, Long street pressed his argument that the thing to do was to move around Meade's left flank, place Lee's army between Meade and Washington, and duplicate Fredericksburg by forcing Meade to attack. Lee reacted impatiently to what he must have regarded as Longstreet's obstinacy, and repeated that if Ewell didn't move "those people" tonight, he would attack them next day.

Thus perversely does the fate of battles hinge on a turn of the wheel. Here was Longstreet, Lee's most experienced corps commander, proposing in effect that Lee move into the very position for defense (the Big Pipe Creek area), the occupancy of which had so obsessed Meade's mind until a few hours before; while Meade, himself planning a defensive battle, had preempted the Longstreet thesis and was getting set to do a Fredericksburg in reverse by encouraging the Confederates to pound themselves to death against the hard anvil of Cemetery Ridge and the Round Tops.

Considering what actually happened on the last two days of the battle, Longstreet's plan, had Lee adopted it, might have resulted in a Confederate victory. But at the time neither Lee nor Longstreet could possibly know, in Stuart's absence, the extent of the Federal concentration, nor the exact location of those elements of Meade's army which had not yet arrived on the field. An interesting war game could be developed by simulating Longstreet's proposed flank march at daybreak of July 2.

There would have been meeting engagements all over the place, south east of Gettysburg. No one can say with any assurance who would have come out on top.

A pertinent commentary may be found in a conversation between Ewell and Meade several years after the war. Meade, in answer to Ewell's question, stated flatly that if Ewell had pushed his advantage and attacked Cemetery Hill during the afternoon of the first day (as Lee had directed him to do, "if practicable") he would unquestionably have driven the disorganized Federals off the hill, which in turn would have uncovered the rest of Cemetery Ridge and changed the entire complexion of the Federal buildup. While Meade did not actually say so, the implication was plain that the Pipe Creek order would have immediately been invoked and Meade's army put into reverse under extremely adverse circumstances.

Lee, however, was giving the orders and his corps commanders were expected to carry them out loyally and to the best of their ability. How these subordinate commanders responded left much to be desired, although there is something to be said on both sides. In retrospect, it is clear that at Gettysburg Lee fought his worst battle. He failed to outline a comprehensive or concise plan of action, issued his orders in oral and fragmentary form, and made no visible effort to coordinate the operations of the three corps. As read, the orders sound more like conversational suggestions, leaving to Ewell and Longstreet, particularly, an excess of discretionary authority, in the exercise of which Lee's hastily conceived and inadequately transmitted battle plans lost whatever cohesiveness they may have had in his own mind.

THE SITUATION ON THE NIGHT OF JULY 1

At the end of the first day the Federals had lost the town of Gettysburg—while Lee had firm possession of the Chambersburg and Hagerstown roads to the west, thus securing his line of communications and supply through the South Mountain passes and the Cumberland Valley. The Chambersburg Pike was the corps dividing line, with A. P. Hill to the south and Ewell to the north and east. The Confederates occupied a horseshoe position with the open end facing south, which controlled all the road spokes of the wheel of which Gettysburg was the hub, except the Emmitsburg, Taneytown, and Baltimore Pikes. Seminary Ridge was manned by Hill's men southwardly to a point opposite Cemetery Hill, and "no man's land" was therefore only a few hundred acres of open ground south of Gettysburg and between the two ridges, although of course the opposing armies were likewise in contact east of the town in the area of Culp's Hill.

LEE DECIDES TO ATTACK EARLY ON JULY 2

Lee's own determination to follow up the advantage which the Confederates had gained on the first day was never in question. Aggressive action to keep the Federals off balance, and then defeat them in detail before Meade's concentration could be fully achieved, was for Lee the approved solution to a logical military estimate of the situation. Everything he said and did on the eve of and during the morning of the second day confirmed his intention to launch an attack as early as practicable on the morning of July 2. He planned to make the main effort with Ewell's corps against the Union right flank.

And it was certainly possible to have done so at least four hours before Longstreet finally gave his corps the signal to advance, late in the afternoon. The trouble lay in the fact that Longstreet and Ewell each interpreted the Lee plan in a different manner than intended by Lee. For that the blame must rest chiefly on the latter, because of his failure to convert his decision into either clean-cut missions to the several corps or definite attack orders. There is no record of Lee having summoned his three corps commanders to receive definite orders simultaneously at his headquarters on the Chambersburg Road, near Seminary Ridge, a central point that was within a few minutes hand-gallop of all three corps commanders. On the contrary, Lee spent the morning of July 2 thinking over the implementing details of his attack plan, waiting impatiently for word from Stuart and for the arrival of the last of his infantry divisions, and in successive but separate conversations with Longstreet and Ewell at various points of the compass. In retrospect the Confederates would have profited greatly by a Command conference between Lee, Longstreet, Ewell, and Hill.

EWELL OPERATES IN A MENTAL VACUUM

On the evening of the first day's battle, after Ewell had failed to exploit the early Confederate success by seizing Culp's Hill and making Cemetery Hill, the northern anchor of the Federal position, untenable, Lee rode over to Ewell's headquarters on the northern edge of Gettysburg to discuss the plans for the next day.

The power of decision seemed utterly to have left that corps commander. Johnson's division had lately arrived and all elements of the corps were on hand. Nevertheless Early and Rodes took the lead away from Ewell in arguing against a renewal of the principal effort from that direction, on the ground that the Federals had been greatly reinforced, had made their position too strong to take, and that losses from the July 1 fighting and the exhausted condition of their own troops made such an attack a hazardous gamble. Ewell himself had little to say except to concur in the views of his division commanders. Lee, whose own feelings of frustrated disappointment can easily be imagined, reluctantly proceeded to revamp his own plan by informing Ewell that the attack would instead be made by Longstreet against Meade's left or southern flank, with Ewell launching a concurrent attack from the north when he should hear Longstreet's guns open.

LONGSTREET'S STALLING TACTICS

Ex post facto writers of the anti-Longstreet faith have condemned that general unmercifully on the premise that he nullified all chance for a Confederate victory by willful disobedience of specific orders from Lee "to attack with his corps at daylight on July 2." Direct evidence is lacking to support that view, and it does Longstreet an injustice in the face of Lee's own vacillation in reaching a decision on the form and character of the attack. Whether Longstreet, in the exercise of the discretion invariably allowed by Lee, made victory impossible by his slowness in launching his attack is another matter. His own version, written after the war, stated:

> On the night of the 1st I left General Lee without any orders. On the morning of the 2nd, I went to his headquarters at daylight and renewed my views against making an attack. He seemed resolved,

however, and we discussed the probable results. About sunrise General Lee sent Colonel Venable of his staff to General Ewell's headquarters, ordering him to make a reconnaissance of the ground in his front, with a view to making the main attack on his left. A short time afterward he followed Colonel Venable in person. He returned about 9:00 o'clock and informed me that it would not do to have Ewell open the attack. He finally determined that I should make the main attack on the extreme right. It was fully 11: 00 o'clock when General Lee arrived at this conclusion and ordered the movement.

But Longstreet does not explain why it took him fully five hours *after* 11:00 A.M., or until 4:00 P.M. to move the two divisions of his corps the few miles intervening from their bivouac west of Seminary Ridge to the jump-off position assigned them on the Emmitsburg road.

All evidence shows clearly that Longstreet was strongly opposed to the attack as planned and ordered by Lee, and that he made every effort to change the latter's mind by argument, by delay in insisting on waiting for the arrival of Law's brigade of Hood's division, and by childish excuses of one sort or another. His preoccupation with his own proposed plan of action to outflank Meade by moving to the south of Round Top and setting up a defensive line there was such that he seemed blind to the fact that Lee's mind had been made up to attack up the Emmitsburg Road with the object of rolling up the Federal line from south to north. Longstreet was in that frame of mind that led him to be hypercritical of everything Lee said or did with respect to the projected attack, including the early staff reconnaissance that Lee had initiated to ascertain the Federal strength and dispositions along the Ridge; the character and direction of the approach march to get his troops into position for the attack; the development for the attack; and even the direction of the attack itself.

It does appear that Longstreet had some justification for his dissatisfaction with the way the situation was developing, in that Lee, at variance with his usual custom, pretty much took out of Longstreet's hands the preparatory moves leading up to the actual attack, even to the extent of ignoring the customary command channels by himself tracing on

McLaw's map the exact position astride the Emmitsburg road where Lee wished him to place his division for the attack.

It was unheard of to bypass a corps commander and give instructions directly to a division commander, and it added fuel to the flames of discontent that were already consuming the usually placid Longstreet. First the repudiation of his own cherished plan; then a reconnaissance by one of Lee's staff officers that proved to be completely inadequate but upon the accuracy of which Lee based his tactical decisions for Longstreet's corps; next Lee's designation of that same staff officer, a mere captain, to lead Long street's troops into position; and finally the crowning humiliation of ignoring Longstreet's presence and giving direct attack orders to one of his subordinates. All this was too much for Longstreet, who sulked like a spoiled child, revealing by his actions and side remarks his inner most thoughts which in modern terms might be paraphrased as "O.K., you old so-and-so; it's your baby and if that's the way you insist on playing it, go to it, but I'm against the whole business and I won't lift a finger to make your plan work the way you think it should."

Right or wrong, it *was* Lee's baby and there are some who think Longstreet should have been summarily relieved from command, as a result of his attitude, then and there. The patient Lee was sorely tried, but kept his temper hour after hour while Longstreet temporized. Finally that patience was used up and Lee gave Longstreet peremptory and unequivocal oral orders to launch the attack without further delay.

CHAPTER 31

Gettysburg II: July 2, 1863

As THE rapidly marching Federal corps reached the battlefield during the night of July 1 and the morning of July 2, they were successively assigned positions along the "fish hook" in prolongation, to right and left, of the initial positions taken by the First and Eleventh Corps following their retreat on the afternoon of July 1.

MEADE EXTENDS THE DEFENSIVE POSITION

The Twelfth Corps was assigned a sector on the right of First Corps to include Culp's Hill. However, the first division of that corps to arrive, Geary's, had reached the battle held at 4:30 P.M., on the 1st. Hancock, who was then acting for Meade on the ground, directed Geary to extend the line to the left of the First Corps along Cemetery Ridge and to occupy Little Round Top which Hancock saw dominated the ridge and the roads on both sides of it. When A. S. Williams, with the other division of the Twelfth Corps arrived, he was placed on the north as in tended; but this resulted in the corps being split. Meade planned to move Geary over to the right to occupy Culp's Hill on July 2, as soon as Geary could be relieved on Little Round Top by Sickles' troops. Geary actually made this move, as will be related later, but in so doing left Little Round Top unguarded.

Hancock's Second Corps, which came up shortly after daylight on July 2, was placed on the ridge to the left of the First Corps. On the left of Hancock was placed Sickles' Third Corps (less French's division, at Harper's Ferry), as far as Round Top. The Fifth Corps was in reserve, with its trains near Granite Schoolhouse Lane which connects the Baltimore Pike with the Taneytown Road. The Sixth Corps did not arrive from Manchester until the afternoon of July 2. Buford's cavalry division was guarding the left flank near Round Top, with Kilpatrick and Gregg maneuvering their respective divisions well out on the right flank toward Hanover and Westminster.

Having failed to take advantage of his golden opportunity to seize Culp's Hill on the afternoon of July 1, Ewell toyed with the idea of attacking that eminence on July 2. About daylight his reconnaissance parties (from Johnson's division) advanced on Culp's Hill but found the Federals in possession. Ewell decided to wait a bit longer and let Longstreet carry the burden.

Meade, seeing that Ewell did not follow up his reconnaissance or "demonstration," directed Slocum to prepare to attack Ewell with the Fifth and Twelfth Corps as soon as the Sixth Corps should arrive. Both Slocum and Warren advised strongly against the projected attack because of the unfavorable character of the ground, so Meade dropped the idea and reverted to his previous plan of waiting for Lee to further reveal his intentions.

LULL BEFORE THE STORM

The morning of July 2 was spent by both armies in improving their positions, fitting newly arrived units into their allotted slots, making small but unimportant passes at one another, bringing up artillery ammunition, and attending to the dead and wounded.

The rank and file of course did only what they were required to do, performing the multitude of housekeeping chores which from time immemorial have occupied soldiers when not actually engaged in battle. Thursday, July 2, was sultry and cloudy with occasional drizzles of rain after a clear moonlit night. As many men as could passed the time stretched out on the ground or propped against convenient trees.

They knew that the fighting of the first day would be resumed sooner or later. Many improved the time by writing letters to loved ones, quietly discussing the impending battle, or exchanging stories on their individual and unit experiences of the day before. The old-timers naturally spent their leisure time in catching naps or resting, having learned from other campaigns that stored up energy can be money in the bank on occasions when war ignores the fact that nights were made for rest and sleep.

Skirmishers were moderately active off and on during the morning, with short but spirited exchanges of rifle fire between opposing pickets. The Confederates were observed from the Federal position to be extending their right on Seminary Ridge, a mile away, and it was chiefly the activity of their scouts which provoked the rifle fire that occasionally broke the stillness of the morning. The men in gray had been instructed to feel out the enemy to determine the length and compactness of his line and the location of his left flank, especially the latter.

Both armies were fully assembled by midmorning except for the Federal Sixth Corps, Pickett's Confederate division, Law's brigade of Longstreet's corps, and of course the peripatetic Jeb Stuart. Meade's strength now exceeded Lee's by a small, infantry-artillery margin. But the initiative remained with Lee, who was prepared to exercise it. Meade, having made up his mind to fight a defensive battle, applied himself to the task of making his position as strong as possible.

MEADE'S ORDERS TO SICKLES

On the evening of July 1 Meade had ordered Sickles to relieve Geary's division on Little Round Top by occupying that position so that Geary might rejoin his own Twelfth Corps. The orders were oral and not nearly as explicit as they should have been. Meade neglected to make a personal reconnaissance on the left at daylight the next morning, possibly because his mind was centered on the north end of the line where he anticipated a repetition of the pressure of the first day against Cemetery Hill and Culp's Hill. In this thinking he accurately estimated Lee's intentions, which in due course were thwarted by Ewell's unwillingness to undertake the job.

However, when the Second Corps came up shortly after daylight on July 2, and was placed to the left of the First Corps, Meade personally repeated his instructions to Sickles to extend his command "from the left of the Second Corps over the ground held by Geary." Geary knew that he was to be relieved by Sickles in order to rejoin Slocum, and Sickles had precise orders to relieve Geary, but as so often happens when adequate staff work is lacking, the plans and orders of the commanding general were not carried out as intended.

It seemed to be the custom in 1863 to leave the order writing to the top echelon of command. But from regimental up to and including corps commanders, oral and in most cases extremely fragmentary orders were the rule. Hence majors and captains on staff duty could and did foul up many a situation for an entire division by transmitting—perhaps inexactly—a hurriedly phrased remark of a corps commander such as "Tell Smith to come up immediately," or "Put your brigade on the left and guide on Jones."

Be that as it may, Sickles didn't think much of the position assigned his corps, because it was on low ground. He greatly preferred a line about a half mile to the west, on higher ground along the Emmitsburg Road, with the left at Sherfy's Peach Orchard.

MEADE'S SUPERIOR BATTLE HEADQUARTERS

Meantime Meade had moved his headquarters up from Taneytown to a small, whitewashed, unpretentious farm house just off the Taneytown Road. It stood in a defiladed area almost due east and but a few hundred yards in rear of what is now called the "high water mark" or "bloody angle" on Cemetery Ridge, where Hancock's Second Corps was posted. The term defiladed area is used here in a relative sense only, because the building, with its stone-floored, grape-arbored patio on the south side, was protected only from direct observation by Cemetery Hill and Ridge. Spent rifle balls and unspent artillery missiles could and did strike the house, forcing Meade on the third day to transfer his headquarters to a quieter spot further east on a small hill which Slocum had selected for his corps command post.

This was an ideal spot for quick and easy contact with all parts of the Federal line and the reserve elements. Messengers to and from the ammunition and supply trains had relatively safe and easy access to their destinations; and Meade was able to direct personally, or at least under his own eyes, the rapid shift of brigades and divisions, both infantry and artillery, in the giant game of chess in which on July 2 and 3 he maneuvered his troops so successfully.

Sickles, riding over there to see Meade, requested permission to move his corps forward, urging the general to come and see for himself. Instead

Meade told General Hunt, his Chief of Artillery, to return with Sickles and look over the terrain. But Hunt gave Sickles neither a yes nor a no decision. He agreed that the desired position had a better field of fire, and if strongly occupied was generally more desirable from the standpoint of the Third Corps. Despite Sickles' urging, Hunt refused to authorize him to occupy the new position without Meade's specific approval.

Hunt estimated that Meade could only thus extend his line by using the Fifth Corps, which was in reserve pending the arrival of the Sixth. This was a calculated risk that Meade was not prepared to take, although as it turned out, Longstreet's delay until 4 P.M. in attacking the Federal left made it in retrospect perfectly feasible, had the advanced line been occupied in the morning. Not being psychic, Meade could hardly have been expected to read Longstreet's mind and therefore cannot be blamed for withholding approval of Sickles' request.

Geary's division of Slocum's corps, as previously noted, held the left to and including Little Round Top during the night of July 1. Slocum's orders to Geary to move to Culp's Hill may or may not have specified that the move was to follow relief by Sickles' corps. Sickles was purposely slow in assigning his troops to the position. Geary, becoming impatient at the delay, on his own responsibility withdrew his division from the ridge and rejoined Slocum. He explained later in extenuation that he had sent a staff officer to Sickles to guide his troops but found Sickles apparently undecided or at least vague as to just when he would effect the relief. Thus the Round Tops were left unoccupied, except for a small signal detachment until as will be described later—General Warren discovered the absence of troops on that key position.

SICKLES' CORPS ADVANCES TO EMMITSBURG ROAD

About noon the cavalry and the signal station on Little Round Top began to send in reports that the Confederates were massing in large force opposite Round Top and the left of the Third Corps. Sickles thereupon sent Colonel Berdan with two regiments on reconnaissance to ascertain the Confederate strength in the woods west of the Emmitsburg Road. Berdan found out right quickly that the Southerners were there in large numbers that were rapidly growing larger. Soon thereafter Sickles took the bull by the horns, and without authority moved his entire corps forward to the new line.

Shortly after 1 P.M. the movement commenced, practically in parade formation and with colors flying. The officers of Hancock's corps on Sickles' right stared in mystification and concern, first because they thought the entire line of the army must have been ordered forward and the orders had failed to reach the Second Corps, and secondly because Sickles' move meant that their own left flank was thus left nakedly exposed.

The departure of Buford's Cavalry was one of the unexplained occurrences of the second day. While it is true that his men were tired after their strenuous work of July first, cavalry on the flank south of Gettysburg was absolutely indispensable—a gold mine for Meade in the absence of Stuart on the Confederate side. It is quite likely that Meade had given Pleasanton, his cavalry commander, general instructions which covered the contingency of a reversal and withdrawal of the army to the south. Pleasanton has stated that on the afternoon of July 2, "General Meade gave me the order to get what cavalry and artillery I could as soon as possible and take up a position in the rear to cover the retreat of the army from Gettysburg." It would be helpful in solving the riddle if it were known whether orders had been sent to Merritt at Mechanicstown (Thurmont) to relieve Buford, or if the instructions were garbled and Pleasanton pulled Buford out prematurely without providing a replacement. Whatever happened, Sickles' forward move uncovered the left flank of the Army of the Potomac and there was no cavalry there to provide the necessary protection. It is of course always easy to criticize after the event, and the paucity of written orders, even scribbled instructions on field message blanks or the back of an old envelope, affords a wonderful opportunity for ex post facto explanations.

MEADE'S COUNCIL OF WAR

Meantime, what was General Meade doing? He was holding a council of war.

Meade had a liking for councils of war, at least in the early days following his sudden elevation to army command, possibly because he had been catapulted into the top echelon at a time when he personally felt that either Reynolds or Hancock had stronger claims to the promotion. He may have reasoned that, at that stage, it was diplomatically wise to consult his corps commanders and invite their best judgment on the course to be pursued, or it could have been that he needed and wanted reassurance that he was following the right course. Councils of war had never been militarily fashionable, or even sound-at least under that name-but they were considered by some commanders the thing to do during the Civil War, particularly by those generals who weren't too confident of their own judgment.

About 3 P.M. Meade had summoned his corps commanders to the Leister House, his small, frame command post on the Taneytown Road, for a council of war. Sickles asked to be excused for the reason that his corps was in direct contact with the enemy and he was greatly concerned about his left flank. The request was disapproved, but by the time Sickles reached Meade's command post, rifle and artillery fire could be heard to the west. Meade met Sickles at the door, told him to return at once to his front, broke up the council, and followed Sickles.

MEADE AGAIN TAKES CONTROL

In the few minutes that elapsed before Sickles and Meade successively reached the new Third Corps position along the Emmitsburg Road, Confederate artillery fire had increased in volume and enemy infantry was observed moving out from the woods of Seminary Ridge to the south. Sickles' offer to return his line to Cemetery Ridge was countered by Meade's comment that it was too late, he must fight it out where he was, and he, Meade, would move troops at once to support him. All credit to Meade for a prompt and soldierly decision to make the best of a bad bargain. And Meade was as good as his word. Watching the battle closely, he saw immediately that Sickles must be withdrawn or supported. The former was too risky, so Meade promptly ordered Sykes' Fifth Corps, in reserve where Rock Creek crosses the Baltimore Pike, into line on Hancock's left to restore the original continuity of the defensive position on Cemetery Ridge.

Nor did Meade stop there. He also sent for Caldwell's division of Hancock's Second Corps, a division from Slocum's Twelfth Corps in the vicinity of Culp's Hill, and later for additional troops from Sedgwick's Sixth Corps, recently arrived from Manchester as the newly designated Army Reserve.

Viewed objectively, Meade deserved to win the game July 2. Thrown off balance initially by Sickles' action, and despite his own failure to make certain that the cavalry was still protecting the army left flank (which it was not), he reacted constructively and decisively to correct the errors insofar as it was within his power, even though in so doing he weakened his right wing and com mitted a portion of his newly constituted Army Reserve. It was sound procedure, despite the risk that Ewell might exploit the opportunity thus offered him on Meade's right (which Ewell again failed to do), and it paid off by giving the Federals numerical superiority at the point of impact. Without Meade's prompt action in shifting his troops there might well not have been a "third day."

THE CONFEDERATE ATTACK

As described in the previous chapter, General Lee had planned to attack the left of the Federal army on July 2. The attack, first ordered for daylight, was postponed until 11 A.M. But as the hours passed and Longstreet's attack failed to materialize, Lee became increasingly impatient. The orders had been clear enough, they just weren't being executed.

Lee's plan of attack, simply expressed in his report of the battle, was this:

> It was determined to make the principal attack upon the enemy's left, and endeavor to gain a position from which it was thought that our artillery could be brought to bear with effect. Longstreet was directed to place the divisions of McLaws and Hood on the right of Hill, partially enveloping the enemy's left, which he was to drive in.
>
> General Hill was ordered to threaten the enemy's center to prevent reinforcements being drawn to either wing, and cooperate with his right division in Longstreet's attack.
>
> General Ewell was instructed to make a simultaneous demonstration upon the enemy's right, to be converted into a real attack should opportunity offer.

With Pickett still on the road from Chambersburg, Law's brigade having finally arrived from New Guilford, Longstreet had only two of his three divisions available. Since he objected to "fighting with one boot off," he kept whittling and taking catnaps and generally stalling in the hope that Pickett would reach the field before Lee should force the issue and demand action forthwith.

Tacitly accepting Longstreet's delaying tactics, Lee reluctantly permitted him to wait for Law. Later, to replace Pickett, he attached Anderson's division of Hill's corps to Longstreet's command, with instructions to make a frontal attack in cooperation with the First Corps envelopment of the Federal left. The remainder of Hill's corps was to keep on its toes to exploit any advantage that might accrue to the Confederates from the planned joint attack by Longstreet and Ewell against the enemy left and right flanks.

Lee knew about Sickles' occupation of the Peach Orchard and Emmitsburg Road, because he pointed out to Longstreet personally the tactical importance of the Peach Orchard, suggesting that there was the major target against which the attack should be directed. But he was clearly uninformed of the fact that the Federal line extended to the south, in a salient to Devil's Den, or he would not have kept insisting that the Peach Orchard marked the left of the Federal line, or that Longstreet's attack "must be up the Emmitsburg Road" to roll up the Union line from south to north. Lee evidently believed Sickles' line to be a portion of the main Federal position, and apparently it didn't occur to Longstreet or anyone else on the Confederate side to send out recon naissance parties during the early part of the afternoon to learn first-hand the outline and strength of the position. The divisions of Hood and McLaws, which were shifted from the Seminary Ridge position to the south to make the major effort, were not in position for the jump-off until 4 P.M. In order to avoid observation from Round Top they had been exhaustingly marched by a circuitous route in the stifling heat, but finally reached their designated position astride the Emmitsburg Road south of a line drawn through the Peach Orchard. They found themselves moving north against an enemy in position and directly in front of them, whereas they had been led to believe that the hostile line faced to the west.

As soon as he discovered the true situation General Hood sent repeated messages and staff officers to Longstreet urging that he permitted to extend further to the east and to circle Round Top in order to outflank Meade's line on the left rear. But Longstreet was obdurate and replied to each request simply that General Lee had said to attack up the Emmitsburg Road.

As the massive Confederate artillery of sixty batteries concentrated their fire on the key Federal hinge at the Peach Orchard, and the infantry moved to close in for the assault, Longstreet himself caught fire. He put aside his personal pique over Lee's uncompromising attitude, and jumped into the fight with the vigor and decisiveness which always characterized him when the heat of battle took hold of his soldierly mind and heart.

The afternoon was far gone, however—it was well after 4 o'clock—his two divisions had been committed, and it was too late for him to effectively coordinate their confused reactions. He did the best he could, but it was not good enough. His earlier stalling now came back to plague him, when, instead of attacking as a team, Hood and McLaws entered the fray disjointedly and successively, with the result that neither was able to attain other than local and inconclusive successes.

THE ROUND TOPS ARE REOCCUPIED

It was nip and tuck, considering the time and space factors, whether Hood's Texans would grab and hold the unoccupied Round Tops. These were the key to assured victory, though neither Meade nor Lee seem to have been aware of that fact, certainly not Lee.

It was at this stage that General Warren, Meade's Chief Engineer, established his secure niche in the hall of fame of American arms. After leaving Meade and Sickles on the latter's front, Warren rode over to Little Round Top to have a look. To his amazement he found it empty except for a handful of signal personnel who for some reason were packing up to pull out. Maybe they were just lonely. In any case Warren persuaded them to stay and continue to wave their flags as evidence to the enemy that the hill was occupied.

Warren's appreciation of topography and its tactical significance was of a high order. He realized at once the crisis that Confederate possession of Little Round Top would cause for Meade and the Army of the Potomac. From the commanding elevation that overlooks much of the battlefield he could see the Confederates like waves overlapping the Federals as Hood's men spread ever farther to the east toward the high ground on which he stood.

Warren lost no time in plugging the gap. By extreme good fortune Barnes' division of the Fifth Corps was seen advancing rapidly along the western base of Little Round Top to counterattack and neutralize the early Confederate success in breaking Sickles' line and forcing the Third Corps back. In the name of the Commanding General, Warren detached Vincent's brigade and directed it to the crest of Little Round Top just in time to meet and repulse with the bayonet the extreme right regiment of Hood's division, which had already crossed the shoulder of Big Round Top and was moving rapidly to take Little Round Top and consolidate its gains.

In a letter written in 1872 General Warren adds color to his dramatic action in saving Little Round Top by stating that, when he arrived there and noted that it was the key to the whole position, and that the Confederates could assemble unseen in the woods west of the Emmitsburg Road, he directed a nearby battery commander to fire a single shot into the enemy woods. This was done and, according to Warren, the Confederate infantry naturally turned their heads in the direction of the shot. In so doing, their infantry gun barrels and bayonets reflected the sunlight, revealing that they were in line and already greatly outflanking the Federal position. Whereupon Warren immediately sent word to General Meade that Little Round Top was in danger, to send him a division at once. It was at that point that Meade summoned help from the Fifth Corps.

PEACH ORCHARD AND THE WHEATFIELD

Sickles' new line as formed made a perfect V, with the point at the Peach Orchard. Humphrey's division was on the right, extended some distance up the Emmitsburg Road. Birney's division was on the left, partly on the Emmitsburg Road and then refused along a lane in a south easterly direction extending for nearly a mile from the Peach Orchard to Devil's Den along the edge of the now famous Wheatfield. The strength of the Third Corps was about 12,000 men.

The Peach Orchard position—the forward point of Sickles' salient—was an arrowhead pointed straight toward and almost touching the heart of the Confederate line on Seminary Ridge and about two-thirds of the distance across country from Cemetery Ridge. The Orchard was on the high point of the shallow valley between the two armies, the angle of that point being formed by the intersection of the two ridges, one along the Emmitsburg Road, the other leading east to Devil's Den. The country south of a line drawn through Round Top, Devil's Den, the Wheatfield, and Peach Orchard, was open, rolling, and broken into numerous fields surrounded by stone and rail fences.

The Confederate attack, as previously noted, was disjointed and largely uncontrolled. But the Southerners were fiery and aggressive and the conflagration spread rapidly from right to left as McLaw's brigades took up the fight after Hood became engaged. Successively the brigades of Wright, Perry, and Wilcox, of Anderson's division, initiated their frontal attack against Humphrey's position on the north end of the field.

Longstreet himself concentrated on the reduction of the Peach Orchard, which was the keystone of the advanced Federal line and the specific objective which Lee had directed to his attention and desired that he capture. The fighting in and around Sherfy's Peach Orchard was terrific and the losses on both sides correspondingly great. In spite of this, at the very heart of the position, right on the crest of the ridge, an 87-year old farmer, John Wentz, remained unharmed in the cellar of his small cottage all during the battle, while from the front yard a son whom he had not seen for twenty-four years served his gun of the Washington Battery of New Orleans when Longstreet finally broke the Union line and forced the Federals to fall back on Cemetery Ridge.

For almost four hours the battle raged at close range, up and down the line, over the Wheatfield, amid the rocks of Devil's Den, on the slopes of Little Round Top, and across the Emmitsburg Road between Seminary and Cemetery Ridges. The concurrent attack against the Federal right by Anderson's brigades was as lacking in coordination as was Longstreet's against the left, consequently was equally unproductive insofar as Lee's plans were concerned.

When the Peach Orchard was taken the center of gravity of the battle shifted to the Wheatfield. In this small cockpit many regiments from five different corps slugged it out, hour after hour, until the earth oozed blood and the brooks ran in crimson streams. In six successive attempts the Confederates captured the field and six times were driven back by vicious counterattacks. In this limited area the field was covered with dead and wounded of both armies—five hundred Confederate dead were found in the Wheatfield alone. It is doubtful if at any time or at any place in America has so much human blood been spilled in a comparable battle area, except possibly at Antietam. The Wheatfield has been aptly called the "whirlpool" of the battle, because of the manner in which regiments on both sides were seemingly sucked into its vortex. But it could with equal justification have been termed a quicksand, from the way in which it swallowed up regiment after regiment of Blue and Gray.

Seldom in the history of warfare have two forces engaged in a battle of such fluidity as characterized the fighting over the Wheatfield. Time after time one of the contestants would gain a tactical success only to find a fresh opponent springing up on flank or rear. Thus the success would be quickly wiped out only to find the new winner confronted with a similar embarrassment from still another direction.

The supporting frontal attack by Anderson's division, directed at Humphrey's segment of Sickles' line along the Emmitsburg Road from the Peach Orchard to a point near the Codori House, might have paid off had there been a more competent directing head. Only three of Anderson's five brigades became fully engaged. Although uncoordinated, those three brigades made a valiant effort. Wright succeeded in effecting a lodgment on Cemetery Ridge. Posey's brigade, slated to follow Wright on the left, failed to reach even the Emmitsburg Road, while Mahone's brigade did not move at all. Wright's was the only one which penetrated the Federal line on Cemetery Ridge, but he was unsupported, left high and dry. Of course he was soon ejected, as one might remove a thorn imbedded in his arm.

CONFEDERATE COMMAND INEFFECTIVE

A. P. Hill does not seem to have been very active as a corps commander during the second day of the Battle of Gettysburg. Lee's own movements and actions in the late afternoon have not been recorded. Longstreet was busy from 4 o'clock on, But in retrospect Lee, Hill, and Ewell might just as well have been playing pinochle at Cashtown so far as any direct action on their part to influence the battle of the late afternoon was concerned.

Pickett's division of Longstreet's corps arrived from Chambersburg about the middle of the afternoon, but was not employed. Neither were two of Hill's divisions, which sat it out in the center of the Confederate line without lifting a finger to intervene.

What was Lee doing? Why didn't he throw one or more of the divisions under Pickett, Pender, and Heth into the battle? Meade was certainly moving his knights and bishops with considerable skill, checking Longstreet's aggressive maneuvers with effective countermeasures. But Lee, having laid down the overall plan, followed his usual procedure and left the details of the action to his corps commanders. It would therefore seem that Meade's leadership in contrast to Lee's clearly entitled the former to a victory on points so far as the second round was concerned.

THE FINAL PHASE

The final phase of the day's operations proved to be an anticlimax, despite some tough fighting and a fair number of casualties. When he heard Longstreet's artillery open up about 4 o'clock, Ewell also commenced firing an artillery bombardment against Culp's Hill, preparatory to the planned infantry attack. To this the Federal artillery replied from Cemetery Hill with devastating effect. Several hours passed before Johnson's division advanced and seized, the positions on Culp's Hill which had been vacated by The Twelfth Corps divisions of Geary and Ruger, sent to the aid of the Third Corps at the Peach Orchard. The remaining brigade of the Twelfth Corps, Greene's, fighting a magnificent defensive action, managed to hold out until reinforced by elements of the First and Eleventh Corps. The Confederate Johnson succeeded in reaching almost to the Baltimore Pike, but in the darkness of early evening failed to realize and exploit the advantage which he had gained. When daylight came, the Federal Twelfth Corps had been reconstituted and it was then too late.

When Johnson attacked Culp's Hill, Early drove for Cemetery Hill. Rodes was supposed to assist, but failed to make it, and this attack likewise miscarried. And thus ended the second day.

LOSSES

Both armies suffered heavily in killed and wounded. Meade's horse was shot out from under him, Sickles was wounded and lost a leg, and Warren was slightly wounded. Among the brigade commanders killed were Weed, Willard, Zook, and Vincent of the Union Army, and Barksdale and Semmes of the Confederates. Division commander Pender was wounded and died a few days later. General Hood was severely wounded. Meade's official report stated that 65 percent of the Union casualties in the three-day battle occurred on the second day.

THE SICKLES CONTROVERSY

The Sickles controversy became a cause celebré after the war, and a resume of the pros and cons is given here.

Major General Daniel E. Sickles, the only one of Meade's corps commanders who was not a professional soldier, had formerly been a Congressman representing New York State. He did not always think along the same well-charted military lines as those of his colleagues in the Army of the Potomac who had been trained and indoctrinated at West Point. There could be no doubt that he was a rugged individualist, and it is equally certain that he not only had plenty of self-confidence, but believed strongly in taking the law into his own hands on occasion, if in the opinion of Dan Sickles the situation demanded action. The historic example is the time when he shot and killed Philip Barton Key, the son of Francis Scott Key, author of *The Star Spangled Banner*, for allegedly toying with the affections and honor of Sickles' wife, and was acquitted with the help of defense counsel Stanton, later the Secretary of War.

There is good reason to believe that Sickles lacked Meade's confidence, which is understandable in view of the miserable showing almost universally made in their military roles, in the early years of the war, by the ambitious politicians whom Lincoln was persuaded to clothe with the stars and authority of general officers. General Humphreys, a Regular commanding one of the divisions in Sickles' corps, was a favorite of Meade's and the man upon whom he relied to keep the Third Corps on an even keel.

On that background must be partly viewed the unilateral action which Sickles took on the early afternoon of the second day when, clearly in disobedience of orders, he vitiated Meade's tactical plan of passive defense along Cemetery Ridge, unhinged the Federal line on the left, exposed the vital anchor of the Round Tops to possible capture by the enemy, and created a wide gap on his own right and on the left of Hancock's Second Corps. To which Meade added the compounding error of shipping Buford's cavalry division off to Westminster without making certain of an immediate replacement from Kilpatrick's division. The result was that the Third Corps found itself lined up close to the enemy, parallel to but from half to three-quarters of a mile west of the main Federal line, with both flanks high in the air and correspondingly vulnerable.

In support of his action Sickles later pointed to Meade's vague and discretionary instructions on the posting of the Third Corps when they arrived from Emmitsburg; to Geary's departure, without waiting to be relieved, from Little Round Top, which had been occupied by two of Geary's regiments the night of July 1–2; and to his, Sickles, repeated urgings that Meade personally examine the "more desirable" position that Sickles was so determined to occupy. He further recounted General Hunt's concurrence in Sickles' recommendation, without mentioning Hunt's stated reservation, however, that the new line would be too long for the Third Corps to hold effectively by itself. Finally he used in self-justification Lincoln's oblique approval of his actions when Sickles subsequently applied for a Court of Inquiry and was dissuaded by the President in these words:

> *Sickles, they say you pushed your men out too near the enemy, and began the fight just as that council (Meade's afternoon council of war) was about to meet, at three o'clock in the afternoon of the battle. I am afraid what they say is true, and God bless you for it. Don't ask us to order an inquest to relieve you from bringing on the battle of Gettysburg. History will set you all right and give everybody his just place, and there is glory enough to go all round.*

Lincoln's appraisal of Sickles' action; written long after the battle, when there had been plenty of time to fit all the pieces of the picture together, reflected his dissatisfaction with Meade's cautious procedures, in contrast to which the Sickles move was on the bold, offensive side, and that was of course the prescription which the President had for a long time been urging on his generals.

Furthermore, on the asset side of Sickles' ledger, his action that day did in fact set in motion events which importantly affected the course of the three-day battle. His corps took the heaviest punishment from Longstreet's at tack, being so badly shattered that it was never again reconstituted as a fighting team under the Third Corps, designation. On the other hand the two Confederate divisions of Hood and McLaws, which Longstreet employed against Sickles that afternoon, likewise suffered heavy losses. They failed to achieve their objective of rolling up Meade's line, and found themselves at the end of the day locked in a position in the Devil's Den area from which Longstreet virtually refused to withdraw them July 3 for Lee's planned frontal attack on Meade's center.

It can therefore be argued, with considerable plausibility, that Sickles' action strongly influenced the course and possibly the final outcome of the battle. Technically he was entirely out of order in taking it upon himself to change position without Meade's express approval. In so doing he jeopardized both the commanding general's plan of defense and the security of the Cemetery Ridge position. But he did succeed in blunting much of Lee's offensive strength. He so immobilized two-thirds of Long street's corps that the latter were relegated to a minor role for the remainder of the battle; while Lee was forced to draw additional divisions from A. P. Hill's corps to strengthen Pickett for the final suicidal charge on the afternoon of July 3.

THE OPPOSING COMMANDERS REVIEW THE SITUATION

At the conclusion of the second day's battle, this was the situation. The Union army held its original defense position almost intact along the fish hook from Culp's Hill to Round Top inclusive, the exception being that Johnson occupied a portion of the Federal position on the east slope of Culp's Hill. The Confederate army had fought its way across the open fields between Seminary and Cemetery Ridges, was in possession of much of the Emmitsburg Road, the Peach Orchard position, part of Devil's Den, and held a precarious grip on the woods and rocks at the base of Big Round Top. On the other flank, Johnson had a toehold in rear of the Federal line; but there is no evidence to show that Ewell or anyone else was aware of the great opportunity thus offered to exploit what was actually a potentially critical breach of the Federal position.

It is reasonable to believe that Lee could have defeated Meade and driven him from the field of Gettysburg at any time of his own choosing during the twenty-four hour period between 3 P.M., July 1 and 3 P.M., July 2, had Longstreet, Ewell, and Hill reacted individually and unitedly as a team in response to Lee's wishes and in accordance with his plans. But Meade was given all the time he needed to bring up and dispose his forces. Despite the Sickles' episode, when Longstreet at long last launched his attack, about P.M., the last of Meade's corps, Sedgwick's 15,000 men, had arrived and the cards were fully stacked against Lee.

However he may have estimated the tactical situation, Lee decided to attack Meade's center the third day, confident that it was his weakest point and could be pierced. Now that Jeb Stuart had arrived with his cavalry, Lee was eager to wind up the business by a frontal attack that would split Meade asunder. Meantime the cavalry, circling to the north and east would get in Meade's rear, complete his discomfiture, and then gather up the pieces.

There occurred that evening an incident which again in retrospect-was an omen of what was to transpire on the third and final day. Contrary to his usual custom, Longstreet neglected to ride over to Lee's headquarters to report and talk over plans, sending a written message instead. He remained overnight where he was, among his troops on the field west of Round Top, apparently still smarting over Lee's refusal to accept his cherished tactical plan of operations, while Lee in return contented himself with sending word to Longstreet that he must be prepared to resume the attack in the morning.

The fates had been kind to Meade, who at this point was thinking pretty straight. He divined Lee's plans for the third day and was so confident of what would happen that he told General Gibbon, commanding one of Hancock's divisions at the center of the line on Cemetery Ridge, that if Lee should attack next day it would be on his, Gibbon's, front. And to make certain that the Confederates would be given a hot reception he directed his Chief of Artillery to reshuffle his guns and mass them to bear heavily on the front of that portion of the line. The Army of the Potomac had fought well and its morale was up. The Northerners had gotten the breaks the second day and were confident in the security of their strong defensive position. They had stopped Lee almost in his tracks and were now ready for the best he might offer on his third try

The Army of the Potomac used the night of July 2 to good advantage in strengthening its defenses. The Round Tops were made virtually impregnable, and artillery was wheeled up to provide powerful bands of cross fire from Little Round Top and Cemetery Hill across the open space between the contestants west of Cemetery Ridge.

CULP'S HILL REMAINS CRITICAL

The dangerous crack in the Federal line on the eastern and southeastern slopes of Culp's Hill, which reached almost to the Baltimore Pike, was marked down to receive the Twelfth Corps' attention as soon as daylight should permit a resumption of the fighting. All of Slocum's regiments which had been shifted to the support of the Third Corps on the afternoon of July 2 had now been returned to him, with the addition of Shaler's brigade of the Sixth Corps, and Lockwood's Independent Brigade, attached to assure ample strength for Slocum to dislodge the enemy. Johnson's Confederate division was equally determined to exploit its advantageous position, widen the entering wedge and place itself squarely on the rear of the Federal right center. If this attempt should prove successful it would pave the effect of clamping a neck hold, on the Federal body. But because of the difficult character of the ground, Johnson had been unable to bring his artillery with him and was thus at a marked disadvantage compared to Slocum.

Slocum's men had been thoroughly disgusted when they returned from the left. They were tired, hungry, and ready to move back into their intrenchments on Culp's Hill for a good rest and some hot food only to find their snug breastworks swarming with enemy troops. They were forced to bide their time until morning, and to catch such sleep as they might on the open ground along the Baltimore Road and in the adjacent meadows. Some were not too annoyed, however, to mingle pleasantly with the interlopers at nearby Spangler's Spring, within a few yards of the Union right flank in one direction and the Confederate left flank in the other. Naturally enough the spring was the object of visits by thirsty soldiers from both lines during the night.

SLOCUM RESTORES CULP'S HILL

With Johnson and Slocum poised for action as soon as it should become light enough to see clearly, the battle on the right was promptly joined. Stonewall Jackson's old brigade led off the attack, meeting Geary's division head-on. Almost immediately the fighting spread all along Slocum's front. Time and again the Confederates hurled themselves against the determined Federals. The fight raged for hours until about 10 o'clock, when a counter charge by the Federals slowly forced Johnson's men out of the breastworks they had seized in the previous day's fighting.

As the Confederates stubbornly withdrew and came under the fire of the Federal batteries they were assailed by repeated charges of grape and canister and mercilessly cut down until the dead covered their path of retreat in the front of Geary's division.

It was in this engagement that Maryland opposed Maryland, with one regiment in Johnson's Confederate division pitted against three from Slocum's corps. In the early days of the war each had been recruited from the same part of the border State and by a quirk of fate they met on Culp's Hill to fight grimly in mortal combat, brother against brother, and neighbor, against neighbor.

The name of Culp was a common one in the Gettysburg of 1863. Young Wesley Culp was born there, but had gone south as a youth, only to return as a member of Virginia's "Stonewall Brigade." On July 2, with the Confederates occupying the town, Culp seized the opportunity to visit his two sisters and promised them he would be back again. But he never returned, because Wesley Culp the next day became one of the "unknown soldiers" on Culp's Hill.

For seven hours, from 4 to 11 in the morning, the fierce fighting continued, with what must have been a tremendous expenditure of ammunition, because it ruined one of the finest oak forests in that area. For decades this forest had been Gettysburg's favorite picnic grounds, but it was shot to death that morning, some trees having close to two hundred musket balls imbedded in their trunks. After the battle, those trees that were not cut down for transfer, in sections, to various historical societies of the New England states, crumbled into dust in a few years and for half a century at least that particular "plateau of death" remained a hillside of desolation.

Meade's council of war the night of July 2 had confirmed his defensive plan, so all the Federals had to do was sit tight, keep on the alert, and wait for the inevitable Confederate attack which Meade anticipated would be launched against his center, and in preparation for which he moved up all available artillery from General Hunt's Reserve.

CHAPTER 32

Gettysburg III: July 3, 1863

LEE AND LONGSTREET STILL AT CROSS PURPOSES

ACROSS the way, on Seminary Ridge, Lee figured that Meade had weakened his line at the center, in order to hold Ewell back on the Federal right and to pin Longstreet down on his left, after the latter had pushed virtually into the vestibule of the Round Tops and was keeping one large boot in the door overnight.

Furthermore Lee reasoned that he now had Pickett's division and Stuart's cavalry; scarcely more than half of his infantry had done any serious fighting on the second day; while the penetration of Cemetery Ridge by Wright's brigade, which failed to split the Federal line only because it had been unsupported by the rest of Anderson's division, had convinced him of the practicability of a frontal attack. The attack which he planned for July 3 was to drive in Meade's center with Longstreet's corps, while Ewell would continue his efforts to take over Culp's Hill, and the cavalry was to circle around Gettysburg to the north, place itself squarely on the Federal rear, and turn the anticipated Confederate breach of the Federal line into a rout.

Full of fight and confidence, Lee rode out early to Longstreet's field headquarters southwest of Round Top to discuss the details and to give him final instructions for the attack. Still at cross purposes with his commanding general, Longstreet hastened to tell Lee that his scouts had been out all night and "you still have an excellent opportunity to move around to the right of Meade's army and maneuver him to attack us." Pointing to Cemetery Ridge Lee replied, "The enemy is there and I am going to strike him." Still Longstreet persisted, unwilling to yield to Lee's judgment, even going to the extent of stating that it couldn't be done. His exact words, as he reported them himself after the war were: "General, I have been a soldier all my life. I have been with soldiers in couples, by squads, companies, regiments, divisions and armies, and should know as well as anyone what soldiers can do. It is my opinion that no fifteen thousand men ever arrayed for battle can take that position."

General Lee quickly brought the discussion to an end by inviting Longstreet to ride around with him while he explained the attack plan in detail. General Alexander, Longstreet's Chief of Corps Artillery, was to mass his guns to concentrate their fire on Cemetery Hill with a view to putting the enemy guns out of action, to demoralize the infantry, and pave the way for Longstreet, with Pickett's division as the spearhead, to crash through the center and roll up the Federal line in both directions.

It seemed to Lee to be a good plan, but he neglected to inquire as to the amount of artillery ammunition available. Neither Longstreet nor himself had checked that important detail or, if Longstreet had done so he failed to mention it to Lee. As it developed later, the oversight was a serious one and had a notable effect on the outcome of the fight.

Battery after battery was wheeled into position, from the Peach Orchard northward along the Emmitsburg Road as far as the Codori House; along Seminary Ridge, partly concealed by the woods along the crest; and around the ridge to the Harrisburg Road—possibly one hundred and twenty guns all together.

In a final effort to change Lee's mind, Longstreet in formed him that he could not expect the divisions of Hood and McLaws to participate in the attack because they were in close contact with superior Federal forces, and if they should be pulled out and shifted to a new line of departure for the attack against Meade's center, the Federals would naturally move out to occupy the vacated position and thus be on Longstreet's flank and rear.

LEE COMPROMISES

Confronted with Longstreet's continued unwillingness to carry out the attack as conceived, what Lee should have done was to replace him then and there. Instead he once more compromised what he regarded as the better plan and allowed Longstreet to keep Hood and McLaws where they were. In their place he assigned Heth's division and two brigades of Pender's, both from A. P. Hill's corps, thus giving Longstreet about the same number of men he would have had were he to employ only the First Corps.

As this change necessitated some troop reshuffling, Lee sent word to Ewell that Longstreet's attack would be delayed until 10 A.M. Meantime, although Lee did not know it, Johnson was already being mauled on the north flank and was in no shape to disengage even if the word had reached him that Longstreet would not attack as early as planned. Once more, as on the first and second days, the carefully conceived plans of General Lee were to be thwarted by an almost complete lack of coordination by his three corps commanders on the several areas of the battlefield. Once again, through his own failure to issue clean-cut, succinct battle orders to his army, through the three key men who must perforce execute them, and for the success of which it was essential that they work together as a team, Lee for the third successive day contributed to the justly earned historic appraisal of Gettysburg as his worst-fought battle.

Even after his last-minute agreement to change the composition of the attacking force and to bring two-thirds of Hill's corps into the planned assault under Longstreet's command, Lee labored under the mistaken notion that the attack would be launched at 10 A.M. He may have thought that his separate orders to Longstreet, Hill, Ewell, and Stuart were adequate to effect a synchronized effort between them. But in the later execution of the plan it became crystal clear that, if indeed the battle plans had been carefully explained, somewhere down the line through corps, divisions, and brigades, the picture of what was specifically expected of the lower echelons was some what fuzzy. Nor could it be expected that elements of two different corps, hastily merged into a single attack echelon just before the jumpoff, would function as smoothly as an already integrated group of divisions that had fought together as a team and knew each other's capabilities and limitations. And finally, in command of the attack was a general, Longstreet, who was opposed to the plan, reluctant to carry it out, and convinced that it was doomed in advance to fail. Certainly the fates were less than kind to General Lee that day.

CONFEDERATE PLAN OF ATTACK

The Confederate battle plan was simple in conception. Eleven brigades, about fifteen thousand men, under Long· street, would attack frontally. the Union center, while the remainder of Hill's corps would support the left and the divisions of Hood and McLaws would keep the Federals occupied on the right. Ewell was to threaten the Federal right rear and Stuart would exploit the breakthrough.

Pickett's division of three brigades, Beth's division of four brigades under Pettigrew, two of Pender's brigades under Trimble, and Wilcox's and Perry's brigades made up the assault echelon. They would advance in two echelons, the leading wave of six brigades covering about a mile of front, from Peach Orchard on: the right to the hollow road just south of Gettysburg on the left. The second wave, two hundred yards in rear of the first, in eluded four brigades, while Wilcox's was echeloned to the right rear of the second line to protect the flank against a possible oblique counterattack during the advance.

Lee indicated the objective as a clump of trees on the crest of Cemetery Ridge several hundred yards northeast of the Codori House, located on the Emmitsburg Road. From this it followed that the attack must be a converging one that would require the infantry on the flanks of the long line to make a change of direction as they neared the enemy ridge.

ASSAULT TROOPS PREPARE TO JUMP OFF

The assault troops were placed under cover of the woods on Seminary Ridge and only their officers were permitted to move up to the crest to examine the terrain over which they would soon lead their men. Most of the officers could see clearly the strong post-and-plank fences which lined the Emmitsburg Road on both sides, and could also note other fences that crisscrossed the fields over which they would advance. The sharp-eyed among them, looking further eastward to the Federal defense line on the military crest of Cemetery Ridge, observed a post-and-rail fence which ran north and south and behind which it was possible to catch glimpses of a stone wall, two and one-half to three feet high, that had been built up from loose boulders that were readily at hand to the industrious boys in blue.

Fifty Confederate regiments lay waiting in the stifling heat of midday for the signal to form up for the attack. Nineteen of them were Virginians, fifteen were from North Carolina, seven from Alabama, and three each from Mississippi, Florida, and Tennessee. While they waited, and the artillery gunners stood poised to fire their cannon, General Longstreet paced up and down in an agony of conflicting emotions, knowing in his heart that the die was cast but hoping desperately that some miracle might occur to lift from his shoulders the heavy responsibility of sending those fifteen thousand men into what was certain death or dismemberment for a large proportion of them.

The signal was to be the firing of two guns, one after the other, from their position at the Peach Orchard, upon hearing which all the Confederate batteries would open fire simultaneously, concentrating on the Federal batteries in the area of the objective, and continuing the bombardment until the enemy guns were silenced and unable to inflict serious punishment on the advancing infantry. The latter were not to move until the artillery fire had done its work. Longstreet was assigned the responsibility of determining when that moment should arrive, at which time General Pickett, in command of the assault troops, would ride out to lead the charge.

Longstreet Unhappily Seeks to Pass the Buck

Everything was set. It was now past noon, and still Longstreet temporized. Unworthily, he wrote a note to his artillery commander, Colonel Alexander: "If the artillery fire does not have the effect to drive off the enemy or greatly demoralize him, so as to make our effort pretty certain, I would prefer that you should not advise Pickett to make the charge. I shall rely a great deal upon your judgment to determine the matter and shall expect you to let General Pickett know when the moment offers."

It is an old army saying that "the buck is never passed upward," but Alexander deserved better of his corps commander than to have such a momentous "buck" as that one passed down to him. Alexander diplomatically responded by informing the General that he could scarcely be expected to accurately appraise the results of his artillery fire, since the enemy infantry was pretty well concealed; and if there was any alternative to the planned infantry charge, it had better be determined beforehand, and not after the artillery bombardment opened. Furthermore, Alexander stated, there was only enough artillery ammunition for this one effort, and if that didn't work there would be none left for a second try.

Concluding the exchange of written notes, Longstreet repeated his earlier message to Alexander in a slightly modified form, which in effect instructed him to advise Pickett when he, Alexander, thought the infantry attack would be warranted.

Generals Hancock and Gibbon were seated under a group of trees with members of their staffs enjoying an unusual repast of stewed chicken, which Gibbon's devoted colored servant had somehow managed to promote, when General Meade rode up, was invited to share the ancient fowl, and promptly accepted. A handy cracker box was pressed into service for a seat, and the meal was well underway when two additional generals, Newton and Pleasanton, attracted no doubt by the pleasant aroma, sauntered up and were offered a fallen log as their place at the table.

About 12:30 the group finished their meal, wiped their several mouths with the backs of their hands, lit cigars and were, for a few precious moments at least, at such peace with the world as only a field soldier can experience after a satisfying replenishment of the inner man.

Meade soon hastened back to headquarters, Hancock started to dictate some routine orders to a field clerk, and the rest wandered off or lolled on the ground while the fateful minutes ticked on.

Suddenly the world blew up in their faces!

The Artillery Duel

At 1 p.m. or a few minutes after, the two signal guns at the Peach Orchard signaled the opening of the Confederate bombardment. All along the two-mile line upon which were ranked more than 120 pieces the guns belched forth twenty-four, twenty, twelve-, and ten-pound projectiles of solid shot and shells of various shapes.

Almost immediately over eighty Federal guns, from all along Cemetery Ridge, replied to the challenge with twenty- and ten-pound Parrotts, ten-pound rifle ordnance, and twelve-pound Napoleons. Together the combined and incessant roar of more than 200 guns was the greatest ever heard on the American continent, before or since.

Quickly the battlefield was covered with a pall of smoke through which the booming crash of the guns and the bursting shells afforded a scene that would have tested the powers of a John Milton to describe. Lieutenant Haskell, Gibbon's aide, compared the cannonading to second Bull Run, Antietam, and Fredericksburg, remarking that "at the early battles we thought that we had heard heavy cannonading; they were but holiday salutes compared to this. Besides the great ceaseless roar of the guns, which was but the background of the others, a million various minor sounds engaged the ear. The projectiles shriek long and sharp. They hiss, they scream, they growl, they sputter, all sounds of life and rage; and each has its different note, and all are discordant."

The two divisions of Hancock's Second Corps, the Second and Third, which occupied the right center of the Federal line with some 6,000 men, held a defensive front of about 1,000 yards, including the clump of trees which Lee had indicated as the target for Pickett's charge. When the barrage opened, the Union infantry at once seized their arms and leaped to their assigned positions under cover behind the stone wall and in thickets, hugging the ground as closely as possible. As a result, and be cause the Confederate artillery had been advised that the reverse slope of Cemetery Ridge was the place to drop their shells, on the premise that the Federal infantry would naturally take shelter on the slope away from the enemy, the Blue infantry suffered little damage from the terrific bombardment. Far greater hurt was done to the supports, the medical services, the supply and ammunition dumps, and the artillery; horses, mules, and every other living thing which happened to be in the impact area were the victims which bore the brunt of the Confederate artillery fire.

For two solid hours, until 3 P.M., the heavy artillery duel continued, with scarcely a pause. Batteries destroyed or out of ammunition in the Federal lines were quickly replaced, but the artillery losses on both sides, guns, men, and animals, were severe. Meade's artillery commander, General Hunt, handled his guns with considerably greater skill and efficiency than did his opposite number, Confederate General Pendleton. Without waiting for orders from General Meade, Hunt foresaw that a massive infantry attack was scheduled to follow the artillery preparation, and wisely ordered his guns to cease firing some ten or fifteen minutes ahead of the Confederate cease-fire. This action was misinterpreted by the Confederates to mean that they had been successful in silencing the

Federal batteries, which was of course their main purpose. Shortly before Hunt ordered the Federal batteries to suspend firing, Alexander had sent a written message to General Pickett: "If you are coming at all, come at once, or I can not give you proper support; the enemy's fire has not slackened at all; at least eighteen guns are still firing from the Cemetery district."

Several minutes later the Federal artillery did slacken off and the Confederates observed a number of guns in the Cemetery moving out. Alexander thought this was the psychological moment and dashed off the final historic message: "For God's sake come quick; eighteen guns are gone; unless you advance quick, my ammunition won't let me support you properly."

"GENERAL, SHALL I ADVANCE?"

Pickett with the curly locks rode jauntily up to Longstreet, saluted, and said: "General, shall I advance?" Unable or unwilling to speak, Longstreet slightly inclined his head, whereupon Pickett wheeled his horse, galloped to the center of the line, and the Confederate mass started to move.

The battlefield was now strangely silent. As the long gray infantry lines emerged from the center of the woods on Seminary Ridge, every eye focused on the amazing picture. Some units marched with their rifles at the right shoulder; others carried them at the trail or in the position of a hunting piece. The lines marched as on parade, with colors flying, fifteen thousand men, and those in both armies who were temporary observers never forgot the sight.

On horseback, on the crest of Cemetery Ridge, General Gibbon, commanding the Second Division of the Second Corps, watched the impressive spectacle with his aide, as the Confederates corrected their alignment and moved eastward across the shallow valley.

UNION GUNS DECIMATE PICKETT'S TROOPS

Responsive to General Hunt's strict instructions to his batteries, the Federal guns remained silent for a short space of time, while the gray masses moved steadily forward over half the distance to the Federal lines.

About the time the forward line was approaching the Emmitsburg Road, Hunt's guns reopened. As the advance continued, and Pickett's men came closer and closer, the gunners changed from shell to shrapnel and then to canister, wreaking terrific havoc among the unwavering Confederate lines, which grimly closed ranks each time a shell found its mark. Federal artillery from Little Round Top, reinforcing the indirect frontal fire of the batteries along the Ridge, created a devastating effect in enfilading Pickett's advancing lines, while the Confederate guns remained silent, through fear of hitting their own men or because they were out of ammunition.

HANCOCK SPOTS AN OPENING; BREAKS PICKETT'S RIGHT

General Hancock, quick to spot the opening, took immediate steps to exploit the opportunity by throwing the three Vermont regiments of Stannard's brigade into the gap. Although Hancock was wounded in this effort, the "Green Mountain" boys, nine months' men who had never before been under fire, dashed into the breach and poured a murderous flanking fire first northward into Kemper's brigade, and shortly afterward in the opposite direction against Perry and Wilcox.

It was too much for Wilcox and Perry, first demoralized by artillery and now, completely blocked off from their comrades, being shot to pieces by the Vermonters. Wavering momentarily, the two Southern brigades, or rather what remained of them, were soon thoroughly bewildered, commenced to wander back toward their lines, and were no longer a factor in the battle.

THE CONFEDERATES KEEP MOVING

Now the leading Confederate wave has broken down the fences, crossed the Emmitsburg Road, and moved steadily closer to the watching and waiting men of Gibbon's division. These latter, under brigade commanders Harrow, Webb, and Hall, represent six States—four Pennsylvania regiments, three each from New York and Massachusetts, and one each from Minnesota, Michigan, and Maine. Confidently and with commendable discipline they withheld their fire as instructed, although the temptation to open up must have been almost irresistible.

General Pickett, on his coal-black horse, followed closely behind his advancing lines and took position in the orchard of the Codori house, within musket range of the Federal position on the ridge. At that point he was posted to exercise whatever control might remain to the commander of an attacking column under such conditions.

PETTIGREW'S DIVISION IS CHOPPED UP

Pettigrew's division, advancing on the left toward Han cock's right at Ziegler's Grove, was in trouble. A Federal regiment, which had been stationed in extended order west of the Emmitsburg Road, was wheeled at a right angle as the Confederates moved toward the ridge, to be greeted by a deadly flanking fire that badly shook Pettigrew's brigades. On they came, however, until every weapon of the Federal arsenal on that part of the front opened on them simultaneously. Human flesh and nerves simply couldn't stand such punishment. The Southern lines broke, the men ran for cover, and the dead and wounded covered the field.

Pickett's right had been broken and repulsed. Now the left had suffered a similar fate. Everything depended on the regiments in the center, and the support which Ander son's division' in reserve was waiting to furnish.

It is the moment for the final charge and, despite al ready heavy losses, the Confederates are ready. They have passed over the level ground and are slowly dogtrotting uphill on the western slope of Cemetery Ridge, within a hundred yards or less of the stone wall, when Gibbon's officers give the word to the trigger—impatient men of the Second division. A blaze of rifle fire in the faces of the advancing Confederates crumples many of them, with but little seeming effect. Pausing only to lower their own muskets to return the fire, the momentum of their drive carries them up to the wall.

The destiny of the world may well have hung in the balance during the next five minutes, minutes in which the preservation of the Union, the downfall of the Confederacy, and the death of slavery were finally decided.

THE HIGH WATER MARK

One hundred and fifty yelling men in gray pour over the wall, with General Armistead at the center, sword still raised with his hat on the point.

The Federal guns at the "Angle" have fallen silent because those who had served them up to the last were now either dead or wounded. Webb's Union brigade panics and breaks for the rear: It is a tense moment. In short order the retreating Federals are stopped, turned back, and recover their nerve. Fresh batteries are rushed forward, unlimber and open fire within half a dozen yards of Armistead and his men, while the recovered infantrymen pour fire from all sides into the little island of Confederates. Armistead puts his hand on a captured Federal gun and is shot to death.

Wilcox, meanwhile, had not advanced, and, Petti grew being routed, Pickett's division was left alone, but undaunted. Their fierce onset struck first upon Webb's brigade, which, posted behind a low stone wall, occupied Gibbon's front line. They broke this, and charged right among the batteries, where a fierce hand-to-hand struggle took place . . . Gibbon, as it chanced, was a little to the right, urging the regiments there to follow Pettigrew's routed troops, and was struck down. Webb's brigade fell back from the stone wall over which the assailants were surging, but only to the second line behind the crest. Gibbon had a little before sent Lieutenant Haskell to Meade with tidings that the enemy were upon him. He was returning, and had just reached the brow of the hill, when he met Webb's brigade falling back.

Discouraged and bewildered, exhausted from their strenuous approach march and hand-to-hand fighting, and with out visible support from their comrades on the other side of the wall, the temporarily victorious Confederates turn wearily to the west, back over the wall and down the hill. Armistead's little band of doughty fighters had been alone in their penetration of Meade's defense. "The line to the right and left, as far as I could observe, seemed to melt away until there was little of it left," was the way in which Colonel Shepard of Tennessee, one of Trimble's brigade commanders, put it in his report. Longstreet had been right—Lee had asked the impossible of the men whom he thought to be invincible—the battle of Gettysburg was over.

A Cheer of Victory from the Union Lines

As the broken gray lines staggered back to Seminary Ridge, leaving over 7,000 of the attacking: force dead or wounded, and many hundreds more as prisoners in the hands of the Federals, 40,000 men in blue stood massed along the crest of Cemetery Ridge from the cemetery to Round Top, while cheer after cheer of victory rang out all along the line. These men were not to be denied, and understandably so. The cheers were not of exultation over a brave but fallen foe, but of elation over the first clean-cut victory, even though a defensive one, that the Army of the Potomac had won since the beginning of the war. That long-suffering, badly generalled army had finally been given competent, intelligent leadership and it fought at Gettysburg that day better than it had ever fought be fore.

Monuments on Cemetery and Seminary Ridges now mark the positions from which the two army commanders observed the climactic clash of July 3. Lee watched from Seminary Ridge the advance and repulse from the very be ginning, when Pickett's consolidated brigades first formed up under cover for the assault. Meade, who had been forced by the galling Confederate artillery fire to move his command post to Power's Hill during the bombardment, rode up to the crest of Cemetery Ridge just in time to see his troops recover their equilibrium, counter-attack Armistead's penetration, and drive the unwelcome invaders from the Federal lines.

Longstreet was calm and collected as he watched the rise and fall of the Confederate fortunes. It was still his battle, and he moved promptly to rally the defeated foot soldiers and to reshuffle the artillery in preparation for the Federal counterattack which he was sure would follow hard on the heels of Meade's successful defense.

The divisions of Hood and McLaws, which had been firmly locked in position and kept busy by the Federal Fifth Corps on their front at Devil's Den and the Round Tops during Pickett's assault, were ordered to withdraw to the positions they had held before the fight on the second day, while Longstreet busied himself with such other details as were found necessary in tidying up the unfortunate reverse and to be ready for whatever the god of war might be preparing to dish out to his depleted corps.

"THIS WAS ALL MY FAULT!"

On another part of the field, Lee moved among the men and officers who had survived the attack, as they dragged weary bodies back to the relative security of Seminary Ridge. Riding up to where Pickett was reporting to Longstreet, Lee remarked: "This was all my fault, General Pickett. This has been my fight and the blame is mine. Your men did all men can do. The fault is entirely my own."

Fifteen thousand soldiers had headed east only a short hour before, full of fight and confident of victory. Scarcely more than half of them returned, sullen, and exhausted, but they returned at a walk, acting not in the least like men who had been defeated. This had been a new and unpleasant experience for them and they didn't like it. The spirit of the Army of Northern Virginia was anything but quenched and these men would have asked for nothing better than to have their old enemy try to come across and take *their* line.

THE BATTLE ENDS WITH A CAVALRY FIGHT

Kilpatrick's cavalry division of two brigades had been operating on Meade's right flank, in the direction of Hanover, on July 2, when new orders were received from Pleasanton to detach Custer's brigade for duty with Gregg. The remaining brigade under Kilpatrick's direction was to cover the army left in the vicinity of Round Top. The mixup that sent Buford's cavalry back to Westminster on the morning of the second day had finally been discovered at Meade's headquarters and the orders to Kilpatrick, belated as they were, meant that the Union army would again have a force of cavalry to protect its flank and give Longstreet's divisions a few extra headaches.

The two brigades which were to execute this mission were commanded respectively by Brig. Gen. Wesley Merritt and Brig. Gen. Elon J. Farnsworth. The latter, until a few days before Gettysburg a captain-aide on Pleasonton's staff, had, in company with Custer and Merritt, been jumped four grades for gallantry in the field and given his star in the latter days of June; but his formal commission had not yet been issued. Merritt's brigade, a part of Buford's division, had been on a special mission in the vicinity of Thurmont, Maryland, and only reached Gettysburg on July third.

FEDERAL CAVALRY ON THE SOUTH FLANK

About noon of July 3 the two brigades took position near the Confederate artillery at the southern end of Seminary Ridge. When the artillery cannonade which preceded Pickett's charge had been underway for some time, the Federal cavalry engaged the Confederate regiments on their front. For a time there was lively but inconclusive fighting between gray infantry and blue horsemen in the rear of Law's Confederate division, which was still in contact with the left of Meade's main line on the slopes of Round Top and in the Devil's Den area.

Kilpatrick's orders from Pleasanton were to press the Confederate right and to attack at the first opportunity. The young general, who had supreme confidence in the ability of his troopers to fight successfully over any kind of terrain, was eager to get into the battle.

At 5 o'clock in the afternoon, sometime after Pickett had been repulsed and returned to the Confederate lines on Seminary Ridge, Kilpatrick, who was under the impression or at least chose to believe that Meade was about to launch a major counterattack, ordered Farnsworth to send the first West Virginia regiment of his brigade to attack a Texas regiment on its front. Twice the West Virginians charged and twice were driven back with severe losses. Dissatisfied with the meager results, Kilpatrick directed General Farnsworth personally to lead a final charge in the hope of breaking the Confederate line.

With three hundred men in the attacking echelon Farnsworth gallantly led a hell-for-leather mounted attack which one of the Charge of the Light Brigade at Balaklava in the Crimean War. As in the case of that suicidal charge of the British against the Russians, Farnsworth's attack was equally fruitless. The Federals galloped impetuously through the Confederate infantry, over rocks and fences, some half mile or more deep into hostile territory, circled around, and galloped back, gathering in about one hundred prisoners but suffering over sixty casualties, including General Farnsworth, who was killed on the return journey. It was a brief and thrilling performance, but in reality proved nothing. The participants always stoutly maintained, however, that it was a worthwhile effort that would have had an important effect on Union fortunes had Meade ordered the counterattack along the army front which Hancock had urged as he was borne from the field on a stretcher earlier in the afternoon.

MEADE DECIDES NOT TO COUNTERATTACK

Confident that the Confederate attack would not be repeated, Meade rode over to Round Top and from Sykes' corps on the left ordered out skirmish parties to test the strength and further intentions of the enemy on that front. It soon appeared that Lee's artillery was still very much in control of the situation on Seminary Ridge, decisively commanding the ground in the direction of the Federal line. Longstreet's divisions had been ordered back and were moving calmly to the west toward the Peach Orchard, as several Union brigades eased their way forward across the Wheatfield and through the woods on its fringe.

A. P. Hill's line was still virtually intact to the north and it became apparent that the Confederates had the strength and will to give Meade a hot reception should he choose to follow up the repulse of Lee's forces with a serious counter attack.

Armies of the size that fought at Gettysburg do not switch over from the defensive to the offensive at the drop of a hat. Time is necessary to re-group, estimate the situation, make the major decisions, and issue the necessary orders, which must then percolate through the intermediate echelons of command and be absorbed and understood down the line if the component parts of the machine are to operate smoothly and effectively.

Meade had in reserve Sedgwick's large corps and a part of Sykes', the troops of which had done little fighting during the battle and could have been employed as a counter striking force. There were plenty of critics of Meade's timidity in failing to throw this available force at Lee's discomfited divisions in order to turn their repulse into a retreat. After-the-event strategists can always present evidence to support their contentions. It is true nevertheless that another, more audacious commander such as the late General Patton probably would not have "taken counsel of his fears," but would instead have promptly sent Sedgwick's corps tearing around Lee's right, and Patton-like have gotten away with it. There is no doubt that Meade had discussed the possibility with Hancock and perhaps others, but without formulating a definite plan or issuing precautionary oral orders, which suggests that he wasn't too sold on the idea himself.

But it was George Gordon Meade and not George S. Patton who was Army Commander that day. Meade, thinking and acting defensively for three solid days, was not quick enough on the mental trigger to exploit his success. Nor can it be forgotten that he had left the initiative to Lee from the very beginning. Some generals, like leopards, cannot change their spots on the spur of the moment. At least four of Meade's corps commanders, Hancock, Doubleday, Howard, and Pleasonton, subsequently put themselves on record as having supported the idea of an immediate counterattack, but it remained for cavalryman Pleasonton to record the most positive, and it must be ad mitted, somewhat flamboyant account of his views. General Pleasonton wrote:

> *From the suddenness of the repulse of the last charge on July 3rd, it became necessary for General Meade to decide at once what to do. I rode up to him, and, after congratulating him on the splendid conduct of the army, I said: "General, I will give you half an hour to show yourself a great general. Order the army to advance, while I will take the cavalry and get in Lee's rear, and we will finish the campaign in a week." He replied: "How do you know Lee will not attack me again; we have done well enough." I replied that Lee had exhausted all his available men; that the cannonade of the last two days had exhausted his ammunition; he was far from his base of supplies; and by compelling him to keep his army together, they must soon surrender, for he was living on the country. To this the general did not reply, but asked me to ride up to Round Top with him; and, as we rode along the ridge for nearly a mile, the troops cheered him in a manner that plainly showed they expected the advance.*

Meade's late afternoon reconnaissance to Round Top developed into quite a dramatic episode. Accompanied by General Pleasonton, his son,

Major Meade, and several members of his staff, Meade rode out to the front of Cemetery Ridge. With his little cavalcade he galloped rapidly along the ridge to Little Round Top, accompanied by resounding cheers from the delighted Federals all along the way.

ANTICLIMACTIC CAVALRY FIGHT

As the climax to the Gettysburg campaign was being reached between the ridges south of the town on the after noon of the third day, a collateral phase of Lee's final attack plans was being played out about 2.5 miles east of Gettysburg between the York and Hanover roads.

So much has been written about Pickett's charge and its dramatic role in featuring the high watermark of the rebellion that the cavalry fight behind the Federal line, which occurred about the same time as Pickett's charge was being driven home, was not only dwarfed by comparison, but has been correspondingly neglected by historians. Yet that spirited clash between four Confederate brigades under command of Major General J. E. B. Stuart and three Union brigades commanded by Brig. Gen. David Mc M. Gregg could have played an extremely significant part in the third day's activities.

As it happened, only two of the three brigades of Gregg's cavalry division were on hand to deter Stuart. While Kilpatrick's cavalry division had met the Confederate horse men at Hanover several days before and hastened their northward trek toward York, Gregg's division had been following Stuart's march, nipping at his heels. The men and horses had had little rest.

General Lee's overall plan for the operations of the third day contemplated the penetration of the Federal center on Cemetery Ridge from the converging attack of the fifteen thousand men under Pickett. In order to exploit the anticipated breakthrough, Stuart's cavalry was assigned the mission of circling the Confederate left to the north around Gettysburg, coming in on Meade's rear at the psychological moment, and giving the Army of the Potomac the coup de grace.

Stuart's force consisted of the three brigades under Wade Hampton, Fitz Lee, and Chambliss, which had been proceeding north to the east of Meade's army, and Jenkins' brigade of mounted infantry, plus four batteries of artillery, a total of something over 6,000 men. Stuart had finally rejoined Lee at Gettysburg on the afternoon of July 2, with men and horses just about worn out, and it isn't likely that one night's rest had restored either to a fine edge for combat.

Moving to the north of Gettysburg and passing around Ewell's left to a point two miles east of Culp's Hill, Stuart's horsemen, about 2:30 P.M. and without opposition, took position along the elevated wooded region known locally as Cress Ridge, which runs north–south and from which they could command all the roads in the rear of Meade's line.

Half a mile to the east of Cress. Ridge was another low ridge which was occupied by McIntosh's Federal brigade, and it was in the open fields between the two tree-covered ridges that the picturebook cavalry drama was enacted.

About the time Stuart showed up, McIntosh's Federal brigade was the only one nearby. Irvin Gregg's brigade was a short distance to the south, but was hastily brought up when a fight became imminent. George A. Custer's brigade, a part of Judson Kilpatrick's division, was on a temporary detached mission in the area but had received orders from Kilpatrick to rejoin him southwest of Round Top. Custer had started out in accordance with these orders when Gregg, seeing that a lively fight was in prospect, hastily pressed Custer's brigade into service. Always ready at the drop of a hat for anything that promised a fight, Custer was only too happy to oblige. With this addition to his depleted division, Gregg now had about 5,000 sabers and several artillery batteries to engage Stuart's somewhat superior strength, although Jenkins' mounted infantry through some mistake had only ten rounds of ammunition per man, a rather sketchy supply for a knock down fight.

The engagement between the two cavalry forces started when dismounted skirmishers opened fire on one another in the vicinity of the Rummel House, which soon led to a buildup of larger bodies of dismounted men who joined the fire fight, while the field artillery contributed its share of destruction. This was not quite the conventional procedure for the Confederate cavalry, however, and it wasn't long before the horse squadrons were massed in preparation for the typical mounted charge so dear to southern hearts.

The combined brigades of Wade Hampton and Fitz Lee, formed in close columns of squadrons, sabers flashing in the sun, advanced in beautiful alignment. They were met by heavy artillery and rifle fire which caused great gaps in their line. On they came, despite losses, and it was at that stage that Custer, the "boy general," rode to the fame that was to end so disastrously not many years later on the Little Big Horn. Custer's brigade, drawn up in close mounted column, was promptly ordered by Gregg to charge the oncoming Confederates. Placing himself at the head of his squadrons. Custer led them out to meet Hampton and Lee. As the two forces approached one another, each increased the gait to the trot and then to the gallop. Meeting head-on, the clash was so violent that many of the horses were turned end over end, carrying their riders to the ground with a crashing impact. From then on the fight became something of a Donnybrook Fair, with charges and countercharges all over the field, creating enough excitement to satisfy the most ardent proponent of the cavalry charge as a method of gaining a decision.

Other elements of Gregg's division executed effective flank attacks against the gray squadrons, during one of which the Confederate General Hampton was seriously slashed by a Federal saber. The surprising resistance of the Federal cavalry seemed to demoralize the Confederates. After a bit the two forces separated as though by tacit agreement and reestablished their lines with Stuart's men on the ridge from which they had started, while Gregg remained in possession of the battlefield. When darkness fell, Custer's brigade marched away in belated obedience to Kilpatrick's earlier order. Stuart's Confederates with drew to the north and returned to Lee's Army west of Seminary Ridge. And thus ended the third and last day of the Battle of Gettysburg.

Epilogue

GETTYSBURG marked the climax of the Confederacy's supreme effort of the war. The Fourth of July 1863 in retrospect was an Independence Day of vast historic significance, coupling as it did the capitulation of Vicksburg and the failure of Lee's invasion of the North, with all that those two important events were destined to mean for the preservation of the Union.

Viewed strictly as a military operation the battle could be termed a draw in that neither contestant was destroyed, there was no question of a surrender, and the casualties were comparable. Furthermore the ostensible winner, Meade, was sufficiently in shock, mentally if not physically, that he made no effort for at least forty-eight hours after the fighting was over to again risk tangling with his opponent, although the latter remained within sight and hearing until Sunday, July 5, and practically invited him to resume the battle.

From the strategic viewpoint, however, it was a stunning setback for the Confederacy. Gettysburg and Vicksburg together revived the Northern morale, drove the antiwar element underground, assured nonintervention on behalf of the Confederacy at the hands of England and France, and correspondingly brought home to the South the virtual hopelessness of winning.

The Confederate losses had been crippling but not mortal, and to that dubious extent Gettysburg was a Northern success. Meade himself never claimed it as a military victory, and the attitude of the Confederate rank and file, as they trudged wearily back to the Potomac and then to Virginia, was certainly not that of a defeated army.

The tactical fruits of the Gettysburg battle should however have fallen into the Federal lap, had Meade displayed the qualities of generalship to pluck them. Lincoln saw that clearly and was sorely disappointed at Meade's post battle sluggishness. The opportunity to end the war in short order had been a golden one, in the President's view, but now it would have to run its course for two more long, weary, bloody years.

Lee and many of his generals were realistic enough to realize that their bold gamble had failed and that it was only a question of time until the doom of the Confederacy would be sealed. The Army of the Potomac had fought magnificently and, for a change, been led with professional competence, which was something new and foreboding.

The Almighty must have taken a direct hand in shaping the events which culminated in Gettysburg, either because He just couldn't trust the North to win the war by themselves or else on the premise that He had universal plans for later centuries which called for a United America, and developments by 1863 had failed to conform to His long-range program.

It has been said, more or less jocularly, that the Lord is on the side of the general with the most battalions, yet it doesn't always work out that way. Both Lee and Meade were God-fearing men, and the latter had more battalions. But Gettysburg was the first major battle that Lee lost in more than two years of war; it was historically his worst fought battle, and on the record the Lord of Hosts seems to have shaped affairs so that the hopes of the Confederacy should be dashed at that small crossroads community.

Certainly the battles at Gettysburg were not planned for that exact spot by either the North or the South. Lee's objective had been the York-Harrisburg area, where he would be in position to turn to his own advantage what ever strategic opportunity might present itsel—a thrust at Baltimore, Washington, Philadelphia, or even New York. The stakes were high, and a mighty clash of arms somewhere, to determine who would sweep the chips from the table, was inevitable.

The defensive-minded Meade had his thoughts centered on a line along Big Pipe Creek, about sixteen miles southeast of Gettysburg. Here he believed he could best protect Baltimore and Washington, in accordance with Stanton's directive of June 28, against an anticipated attack by Lee, when Lee should turn back from his advance toward the Susquehanna.

When the battle was joined by the armed clash a mile and a half west of Gettysburg on the morning of July 1, neither commander was ready for it nor desired to engage in a decisive test of arms on that day. Neither army had been concentrated—Lee was in the process of effecting his concentration, but Meade was still in a state of uncertainty as to where he would finally assemble his forces. As the picture unfolded, it became obvious that Gettysburg was the logical spot, forced by logistic circumstances. But ex post facto convictions that the convenient road net, of which the town was the center, or the parallel ridges which later gained such fame, were major tactical considerations that led either or both of the army commanders to select Gettysburg for the battle, are mere second sight. Once committed, the three days of battle witnessed a massive slugging match between heavyweights. After the respective approach marches, which converged on Gettysburg from all points of the compass, there was a minimum of footwork and feinting, even by the cavalry. On the first day the contestants felt each other out without using their full strength; on the second, the aggressor sparred for openings, while the defender awkwardly but successively parried each blow; and on the third the challenger, boring in for the knockout blow, was thrown back with bloodied nose. At the end of the third round, both fighters were figuratively leaning on the ropes in their respective corners. While neither could claim a clean-cut victory, and the decision was awarded to the defender on points, that decision proved to be an inconclusive one because the challenger, although injured, was given a respite to recover and to take on his opponent again and again.

Why did Lee fail at Gettysburg? There can be no categorical answer, because a host of factors contributed to the final result and the weight given to each depends in turn upon other imponderables, ad infinitum. And there in may lie the principal reason why the battle of Gettysburg offers such a fascinating subject for study, for conversation, for far-ranging speculation and for delightful, friendly argument.

Historians even now do not fully agree on specifics. One will say that Meade won a tactical victory but threw away the strategic fruits by letting Lee escape with most of his booty, wounded, and prisoners, with all 241 guns, and with seven of Meade's own field pieces. Another will say that Meade won because he had more luck and made fewer mistakes than Lee. Still another may point out that Lee may have been the loser because, in the only Civil War battle fought on Pennsylvania soil, the Army of the Potomac was commanded by a Pennsylvanian; two of the corps commanders who played a prominent part in shaping the destiny of the battle, Reynolds and Hancock, were Pennsylvanians; and many of the units which fought in the forefront during critical phases of the battle were Pennsylvania regiments, which displayed fanatic zeal in defending their home folks and native soil and thus swung the balance in favor of the Union forces. And so on.

There will always be honest differences of opinion regarding Lee's failure to win at Gettysburg. The answers to the what, when, where, and how of the battle can all be found in recorded facts. But the persistent search for the answer to the why is buried in a confusing combination of factors, no one of which can fairly be considered decisive in itself, although each was a constituent element in the end result. The various elements are presented herewith:

Lee's selection of Ewell and A. P. Hill, inexperienced and untried as leaders of large bodies of troops, for two of his three principal commanders, when he reorganized' his army after the battle of Chancellorsville.

Hooker's reorganization of the Federal cavalry and its long overdue restoration to a combat role, with the result that the cavalry of the opposing armies were placed on a more equal footing.

Lee's discretionary orders to Stuart at the start of the invasion, under which Stuart guessed wrong, turned right instead of left when he bumped into Hancock's corps north of the Rappahannock, and from then on until the end of the second day of the battle of Gettysburg was out of touch with Lee's army, with all the disadvantage to the latter thus implied.

Lee's compounding failure to use the cavalry that was still available to him, despite the absence of Stuart and his three brigades.

Lee's overconfident belief that his men were invincible, plus his failure to coordinate the functioning of his three army corps on the field at Gettysburg, and the absence of clear-cut attack orders to the several elements of his command.

Ewell's failure to cerebrate under discretionary authority, which in turn caused him to forfeit the opportunity to take Cemetery Hill the afternoon of the first day and virtually to mark time for the remaining two days.

Longstreet's recalcitrant dragging of his feet all through the campaign.

Harmonious cooperation missing between the three corps commanders, Longstreet, Ewell and Hill, and a fateful lack of decision in the use of supporting troops during the battle.

Overextension of the Confederate line, resulting in in sufficient depth for maximum offensive results, and loss of time in the transmission of messages and orders from one flank to the other.

The absence of Stonewall Jackson.

The Confederate errors of omission and commission were in certain instances caused or at least affected by positive or negative action on the part of the Federals, for better or worse. But since Lee did not achieve a victory as he so confidently expected, a more searching analysis to determine the reasons for his failure is naturally beamed in his direction. Conversely, since the shortcomings and errors on the Federal side, and there were plenty, did not lead to a defeat, nor even to prevent a quasi-victory, the impact of such errors as did occur was of temporary duration.

Certain it is that the Battle of Gettysburg has earned the reputation of being the best known battle of the Civil War. For many years military students assigned to general staff duty of foreign armies have crossed the oceans for a detailed study of all aspects of that campaign, as a part of their professional education. It may even be that Gettysburg deserves to join the ranks of Creasy's Fifteen Decisive Battles of the World; indeed it is already so classified by some military historians.

The phenomenal resurgence of interest shown in recent years by the people of the United States in all phases of the War between the States testifies to the enduring value of the stirring events of those historic days nearly 100 years ago.

Could it be that later wars, in which the grandsons and great-grandsons of the boys in Blue and Gray gave their lives for their united country, have played a significant part in fulfilling the immortal words of Abraham Lincoln, on the field at Gettysburg:

> *We here highly resolve that these dead shall not have died in vain— that this Nation, under God, shall have a new birth of freedom—and that government of the people, by the people, for the people, shall not perish from the earth.*

BIBLIOGRAPHY

Alexander, Gen. E. P. *The Battle of Fredericksburg.* Southern Historical Society Papers, Vol. X, Richmond, VA., 1882.

Andrews, J. Cutler. *The North Reports the Civil War.* Pittsburgh: University of Pittsburgh Press, 1955.

Bates, Samuel P. *The Battle of Chancellorsville.* Meadville: Pennsylvania, 1882.

Battles and Leaders of the Civil War, Vol. III. Contributions by Union and Confederate Officers. New York: The Century Company, 1884.

Bigelow, John. *The Campaign of Chancellorsville.* New Haven and London: Yale University Press, 1910.

Carter, Capt. R. G., U.S.A. *Four Brothers in Blue, From Bull Run to Appomattox.* Washington: 1913.

Catton, Bruce. *Glory Road.* Garden City: Doubleday & Co., 1952.

Catton, Bruce. *Mr. Lincoln's Army.* New York: Doubleday & Co., 1951.

Coco, Gregory A., ed. *Through Blood and Fire: The Civil War Letters of Major Charles J. Mills.* Privately Printed, 1982.

Comte de Paris. *History of the Civil War in America,* Vol. II. Philadelphia: The John C. Winston Co., 1907.

Cox, Maj. Gen. Jacob D. *Military Reminiscences of the Civil War,* 2 volumes. Charles Scribner's Sons, 1900.

Cullum, Bvt. Maj. Gen. George W. *Register of the Officers and Graduates of the U.S. Military Academy,* 3 volumes. Houghton-Mifflin and Company, 1891.

Doubleday, Abner. *Chancellorsville and Gettysburg.* New York: C. Scribner's Sons, 1882.

Early, J.B. *Autobiography of Lt. Gen. Jubal A. Early C.S.A.* Philadelphia: J.B. Lippincott, 1912.

Freeman, Douglas S. *Lee's Lieutenants: A Study in Command.* 3 vols. New York: Scribner's, 1942–44.

Freeman, Douglas Southall. *R. E. Lee, Vol.* New York: Charles Scribner's Sons, 1935.

Fremantle, Lt. Col. Arthur J. L., H. M. Coldstream Guards. *The Fremantle Diary.* Edited by Walter Lord. Boston: Little, Brown and Co., 1954.

Haskell, Frank Aretas. *The Battle of Gettysburg.* New York: P. F. Collier & Son, 1910.

Henderson, Colonel G. F. R. *Stonewall Jackson and the American Civil War,* Vol. II. New York: Longmans, Green and Co., 1927.

Hoke, Jacob. *Gettysburg, The Great Invasion of 1863.* Dayton, Ohio: 1887.

Johnson , Robert U. and Clarence C. Buel, eds. *Battles and Leaders of the Civil War.* 4 vols. New York: Century, 1887–88.

Krick, Robert K. *Stonewall Jackson at Cedar Mountain.* Chapel Hill and London: University of North Carolina Press, 1990.

Lord, Edward O. *History of the Ninth New Hampshire Volunteers.* Concord, 1895.

Luvaas, Jay, ed. *The Civil War: A Soldier's View.* Chicago: University of Chicago Press, 1958.

McClellan, George B. *McClellan's Own Story*. New York: Charles L. Webster & Co., 1887.

Miers, Earl S., and Richard Brown. *Gettysburg*. New Brunswick: Rutgers University Press, 1948.

Pratt, Fletcher. *Eleven Generals*. New York: Wm. Sloane Associates, 1949.

Quaife, Milo, ed. *From the Cannon's Mouth: The Civil War Letters of General Alpheus S. Williams*. Detroit: Wayne State University Press, 1959.

Redway, Maj. G. W. *Fredericksburg*. London: Swan, Sonnenschein and Co., 1906.

Report of the Joint Committee on the Conduct of the War. 3 vols. Washington, D.C.: Government Printing Office, 1863.

Schenck, Martin. *Civil War History*. Iowa City: State University of Iowa, December 1956. Article entitled "Burnside'sBridge."

Sears, Stephen W. *The Civil War Papers of George B. McClellan*. New Haven and New York: Ticknor & Fields, 1989.

Sears, Stephen W. *George B. McClellan: The Young Napoleon*. New Haven and New York: Ticknor & Fields, 1988.

Sears, Stephen W. *Landscape Turned Red: The Battle of Antietam*. New Haven and New York: Ticknor & Fields, 1983.

Steele, Matthew Forney. *American Campaigns*, 2 volumes. Washington: War Department Document No. 324.

Styple, William P., ed. *Letters from the Peninsula: The Civil War Letters of General Philip Kearny*. Kearny, N.J.: Belle Grove Publishing, 1988.

U.S. War Department, *The War of the Rebellion: Official Records of the Union and Confederate Armies*. Washington D.C.: Government Printing Office, 1880–1901.

Walker , Francis A. *History of the Second Army Corps*. New York: Scribner's, 1986.

West Point Alumni Foundation, The. *1954 Register of Graduates of the United States Military Academy*, 1802–1954.

Williams, Kenneth P. *Lincoln Finds a General*, Vol. II. New York: The MacMillan Company, 1949.

Williams, T. Harry. *Lincoln and His Generals*. New York: Alfred A. Knopf, 1952.

Wilson, James H. *Under the Old Flag*. 2 vols. New York: D. Appleton, 1912.

Index

A

Alexandria, 11, 56, 62, 125
  McClellan rode out from, 151
  Pope's army to, 148
  telegrams to Halleck from, 117
  War Department from, 150
Alexandria Railroad, 395, 50, 56,
  60, 273, 383, 386, 409
Anderson, G. B., 181
Anderson, R. H., 77, 115, 133,
  174, 231, 292, 395, 396
anticlimactic cavalry fight, 628–30
Antietam Creek, 202–4, 210, 212,
  234, 253, 271, 364
Antietam, Union army at, 240–1
Aquia Creek, 11, 13, 25, 69,
  273, 290
army
  Army of Northern Virginia, 46,
    57, 140, 154, 199, 230, 262,
    351, 437, 538, 624
  Army of the Potomac, 149,
    171, 193, 206–9, 239, 241,
    262, 273–4, 279, 337, 351,
    456, 489, 552, 583
  Army of Virginia, 50, 53, 62,
    65, 91, 110, 138, 149–50, 166
  moves into position, 385–6
  orders, 325–6
artillery duel, 617–19
Artillery Reserve, 320
assault troops prepare, 615–16

attack
  Confederate, 598–600
  Confederate plan of, 614–15
  Hooker's attacking force, 218
  Jackson counterattack, 226–9
  Meade's division
    spearheads, 332–5
  Red Man's method of, 188
  See also federal attack
attitude, Meade's timid, 550–2
Augur, C. C., 31, 37
Averell, William W., 355,
  467, 478

B

Banks' corps, 45, 55, 99
  8,800 against 20,000, 42–3
  federal divisions of, 33
Banks' Ford, 357, 396, 512
  on Rappahannock River, 501
  significance of, 501–2
Banks, Nathaniel P., 11
  army, 73
  blocks Jackson's advance, 31–3
  federals, 44
  guesses wrong, 34–5
  infantry, 38
  judgment, 37
  two- division corps, 44
Barksdale's Mississippi
  Brigade, 297–8
Barnett's Ford on August 8, 31

battlefield, 112
  character of, 292–4
  control, 580–2
Battle of Antietam, 229–30,
  249–50, 256, 369, 430
Battle of Cedar Mountain, 45
Battle of Chancellorsville, 369,
  383, 384
Battle of Fredericksburg, 289,
  354, 428, 490
Battle of Gettysburg, 545
Battle of Salem Church, 504
Battle of Second Manassas, 94
battle plan, McClellan, 210–12
Bayard, George D., 20
  cavalry, 33, 38
  federal cavalry, 31
  union cavalry, 49
Benedict Arnold, 80
Beverly Ford Stuart, 54
Blackford, W. W., 51, 52, 87
Bloss, John M., 171
Blue Ridge
  and Lincoln, 267
  Mountains, 155, 189
boats, volunteers cross in, 306–7
Booth, John Wilkes, 291
Borcke, Von, 314
Boteler's Ford, 260
Brandy Station, 49
breath-taking military
  pageant, 331–2
bridge
  as laid under enemy fire, 304–5
  laying by federal
    engineers, 389–90

Bristoe Station, 59–61
Bristol Firearms Company,
  270
Broad River, 69
Buford, John, 20, 564
  brigade, 134
  cavalry, 42, 565, 596
  contribution, 569–71
  new tactics, 564–5
Bull Run Mountains, 71, 77,
  98, 110
Burnside, Ambrose E., 7, 151,
  175, 268
  artillery, 311
  background, 269–70
  battle orders vague and
    indecisive, 301–3
  bridge, 203, 234, 244–5
  corps, 244
  corps alert, 237–9
  creates three grand
    divisions, 279–80
  disintegration of, 361–2
  as dissuaded from suicidal
    assault, 350–3
  dubious performance, 243–4
  flank, careless reconnaissance,
    234–5
  forces, 319
  lack of confidence in, 300–1
  loses another battle, 360–3
  marks time, 288–9
  McClellan and, 207–8,
    239–40
  Ninth Corps, 211, 214, 235,
    244, 248, 250

slowness, 314–15
takes charge, 181–2
telegraphic report to
    Halleck, 354
temporizes as generals mark
    time, 322–5
tentative plan, 294–6
as troop leader, 271–2
vacillation, 299
weight begins to tell, 182–4
Butterfield, Daniel, 130, 364
anxiety, 492
Fifth Corps, 342
keeps Hooker
    informed, 496–501
role, 491–3

C

campaign
Chancellorsville, 440
Fredericksburg, 274
Lee plan of, 160–2
Maryland, 247
Peninsular, 5
Pope Northern Virginia, 366
strategic background of,
    522–4
captured diary, 398–400
careless reconnaissance, on
    Burnside's Flank, 234–5
Catoctin Mountain, 170
cavalry combat, 134–5
cavalry fight
anticlimactic, 628–30
battle ends with, 624
cavalry skirmishes, 166–8

Cedar Mountain
fight at, 83
Pope corps at, 44
Cemetery Ridge, 249,
    623, 628
federals break for, 572–3
center grand division, 280–1, 295,
    300, 366
Chancellorsville
campaign, 440
confederates at, 472
federal concentration at,
    387–9
Chancellorsville-Jackson's flank
    attack, 492
Chantilly
affair at, 146
fight at, 147
Chilton, R. H., 163
Clark's Mountain, 47
Cochrane, John, 356
Colonel Miles, 198
Colquitt, A. H., 177, 181
Colston, R. E., 392
combat imminent, 25–8
commanders
review the situation, 607–9
seven successive, 571–2
Confederate
arms, 423
army, 74, 105, 178, 194, 251,
    278, 377
artillery officers, 345
attack, 598–600
battle plan, 614
brigade, 346, 479

cavalry, 391, 449, 560, 564
at Chancellorsville, 472
command ineffective, 603–4
countermeasures, 406–8
defenders, 347
defense, 219, 247, 253–4
flank, 318
force, 2, 65, 174, 213
gun, 242, 339, 345
keep moving, 620–1
miss an opportunity, 574–5
move forward, 416–17
movements, 70, 253
pin down, 245–6
plan of attack, 614–15
position, 204–5, 292, 293
reports, 186
repulse at Malvern Hill, 5
Second Corps, 283
skirmishers, 463
traffic jam, 577–8
troop, 287, 522
troop, dispositions, 291–2
venture, 110–12
victory at Bull Run, 145–6
confusing orders, from
    Hooker, 493–6
confusion, at Orange Court
    House, 28–30
control
battlefield, 580–2
Meade again takes, 597–8
Meade takes, 579–80
Couch, Darius N., 340, 531
corps leads off, 337–8

Second Corps, 307, 319, 376,
    386, 445, 474
counterattack
Jackson, 226–9
Longstreet, 134
Meade decides not to, 626–8
Cox, Jacob D., 124, 147–8, 179,
    211, 235–6, 253
attack, 254
Kanawha troops, 66
Crampton's Gap, 181
action at, 173–5
Crawford, 38
federal brigade, 41
Cress Ridge, 629
Crimean War, 625
Crook, George, 179
Culpeper, 30
Culp's Hill, 609–10
Slocum restores, 610–11
Curtin, Andrew G., 176
Custer, George A., 629

D

Davis, Benjamin F., 116, 155,
    196, 380
Davis, Hasbrouck, 384
depressing aftermath of
    battle, 347–8
Dilger, Hubert, 460
Doubleday, Abner, 86
Douglas, Henry Kyd, 198
driving corps commander, 31
Dunker Church, 204,
    215–17, 225

E

Early, Jubal, 25

Elements of Military Art and Science, 6

Emmitsburg road, Sickles' corps advances to, 595–6

enemy fire, bridges as laid under, 304–5

enemy information, lack of, 547–8

Engineer Corps, 279–80

enthusiasm, 401

Eve of Battle, situation on, 559–60

Ewell, 85–8, 97, 548

    advances on Harrisburg and York, 529–30

    corps, 524, 559

    fails to measure up, 575–7

    operates in mental vacuum, 588

    rapid advance stirs the south, 527–8

F

Farnsworth, John, 167

federal advance, 205–7

federal army, 262, 297

federal artillery, 227, 506

    at Hazel Grove, 459–63

    skillfully handled, 320–2

federal attack, 109, 347

    lacked power and depth, 335–6

    on McLaw, 510

federal brigade, 253

federal camp, 51

federal cavalry, 262, 265, 383, 384, 457–9, 525–6, 559

    advances to Gettysburg, 565–6

    runs gauntlet, 196–7

    on south flank, 625–6

federal command

    confusion, 235–7

federal commander, 64, 71, 78, 208

federal communications, 61

federal concentration, at Chancellorsville, 387–9

federal confusion, 90–3

federal corps, 114, 130, 199–200, 226, 391, 406, 417

    Federal Eleventh Corps, 449

    Federal Signal Corps, 411

    Federal Twelfth Corps, 162, 222

federal dispositions, 426–8

federal engineers, bridge laying by, 389–90

federal force, 184, 455

federal garrison, 189

federal gun, 198, 231

federal infantry corps, 391

federal reconnaissance, 410

federal skirmishers, 185

federal soldiers, 155

federal troops, 18, 37, 76, 107, 175, 394

federal withdrawal, 42

Ferrero's brigade, 246

Ferry, Edward, 153
fight
  becomes general, 479–84
  more units drawn into, 567–8
first clash, 566
Fitzhugh, William, 311
Flank, Lee concentrates on
    right, 309–11
Franklin, William B., 172,
    279–81, 303, 323–4, 363
  corps, 139, 216
  corps to Pope, 123
  disposal, 331
  gets unexpected orders, 330–1
  left grand division, 300
  official report, 139
  Sixth Corps, 173, 214, 227,
    228, 308
Frederick city changes, 168–9
Fredericksburg
  campaign, 274
  crossing below, 307–9
  developments at, 446–9
  scene shifts to, 487–8
Fredericksburg-Salem
    Church, 491
Freeman, Douglas Southall, 115
Fremont, John, 10, 22

G
Garland's brigade, 181
Garnett, 36, 37
gauntlet, federal cavalry
    runs, 196–7
general- in-chief, 5–9

General Orders No. 8, 360,
    362, 363
General Orders No. 11, 19
General War Order, 1
Gettysburg
  amphitheater a tactical
    paradise, 560–2
  Federal Cavalry advances
    to, 565–6
  Lee divisions converge
    on, 568–9
Gibbon, John, 86–9
  federal brigade, 218
Gillette, Lieutenant, 152
Gordon's brigade, 38
grand division, 366
  center, 280–1, 295, 300
  left, 281, 300, 322, 330, 331
  right, 280, 300
  Sumner, 284, 321–2
Gregg's brigade, 121
Griffin's brigade, 127
grim reaper, 339–40
Grover's brigade, 107

H
Halleck, Henry W., 6–10, 12–14,
    25, 47, 113, 317, 321
  Burnside telegraphic report
    to, 354
  disagrees, 275–6
  frantic order to Haupt, 63–4
  General-in-Chief, 16
  judgment, 45
  letters and telegrams, 16